A NEW HISTORY OF IRELAND

UNDER THE AUSPICES OF THE
ROYAL IRISH ACADEMY

VIII
A CHRONOLOGY OF IRISH HISTORY
TO 1976

A NEW HISTORY OF IRELAND

UNDER THE AUSPICES OF THE ROYAL IRISH ACADEMY

A NEW HISTORY OF

IRELAND

EDITED BY

T. W. MOODY F. X. MARTIN
F. J. BYRNE

VIII

A CHRONOLOGY OF
IRISH HISTORY TO 1976

A COMPANION TO
IRISH HISTORY
PART I

OXFORD
AT THE CLARENDON PRESS
1982

Oxford University Press, Walton Street, Oxford OX2 6DP

London Glasgow New York Toronto
Delhi Bombay Calcutta Madras Karachi
Kuala Lumpur Singapore Hong Kong Tokyo
Nairobi Dar es Salaam Cape Town
Melbourne Auckland

and associates in
Beirut Berlin Ibadan Mexico City Nicosia

Published in the United States
by Oxford University Press, New York

British Library Cataloguing in Publication Data
A new history of Ireland
Vol. 8: A chronology of Irish history to 1976
1. Ireland – History
I. Moody, Theodore William   II. Martin, Francis Xavier
III. Byrne, Francis John
951.5   DA910   78-41122
ISBN   0-19-821744-7

Printed in Great Britain
at the University Press, Oxford
by Eric Buckley
Printer to the University

PREFACE

THIS volume of the *New history of Ireland*, the second to appear, comprises the chronology that was intended as one of several components of the volume as originally planned. The other components now make up volume IX, which will appear about the same time as this volume. What had been contemplated as volume IX will appear as volume X. Volumes VIII, IX, and X will together constitute a three-part 'Companion to Irish history'.

In preparing and organising the material for volumes VIII and IX we found that our task increased not only in bulk but also in complexity. The two volumes have required far more time and effort on the part both of the compilers and of the editors than had been estimated, and this explains why these volumes are so much behind schedule. But we have felt it necessary to give the highest priority to the foundation work that they represent.

The chronology is intended to be used in conjunction with the maps, genealogies, and lists in volume IX, and *vice versa*. We have endeavoured to ensure complete concordance of related material in the two volumes (for example between the chronology and the succession lists), but we are aware that discrepancies may have escaped our vigilance, and we should be glad to be notified of any that users of the volumes may observe.

The index to the present volume amounts to a reorganisation on an alphabetical plan of as much of the material in the chronology as can usefully be arranged under persons, places, and topics. Dates are given instead of page references, and this should make the index doubly serviceable.

We take this opportunity of recording our indebtedness to a special friend of the *New history of Ireland*. Dan Davin, who retired from the arduous responsibility of Publisher to the Academic Division of the Oxford University Press in September 1978, showed a strong and positive interest in the project since it was first mooted in 1962–3, and his constant understanding and support have been indispensable in bringing it out of the region of speculation into that of realisation. To this large-minded and stout-hearted Irish New Zealander, distinguished both as writer and publisher, we tender our warm gratitude, and to him and his wife our hearty good wishes for his retirement.

With deep sorrow we record the death of John Gerald Simms on 9 April 1979. A gifted historian and noble personality, endeared to a wide circle, he was one of our most valued contributors. He carried the central narrative of the history from 1660 to 1691 in volume III, compiled the bibliography to that volume, and helped the editors in a variety of ways. He wrote the first chapter of volume IV (1691–1714), began the bibliography for that volume, and contributed largely to the present volume and to volume ix. We honour his dedication to historical scholarship, we miss him sorely, and we cherish his memory.

We have pleasure in acknowledging help and facilities received from the National Library of Ireland and the libraries of Trinity College, Dublin, and the Royal Irish Academy. Acknowledgements for help received in the compiling of particular sections of this chronology are made in the several introductions. Finally we record our best thanks for the devoted work of our secretary, Richard Hawkins, and of our typist, Peggy Morgan.

A great part of the content of this volume could not have been provided without the munificent donations of Dr John A. Mulcahy of New York and the American Irish Foundation, which enabled us to employ young scholars to carry out research that would not otherwise have been available. We have pleasure in acknowledging our indebtedness to the directors of the American Irish Foundation and to Dr Mulcahy, whose donation is associated with the names of his parents, the late Patrick and Agnes Mulcahy of Dungarvan.

T. W. MOODY
F. X. MARTIN
F. J. BYRNE

Royal Irish Academy
January 1980

CONTENTS

CONTRIBUTORS

Francis John Byrne   M.A. (N.U.I.); M.R.I.A.; professor of early and medieval Irish history, University College, Dublin

Charles Doherty   M.A. (N.U.I.); assistant lecturer in early Irish history, University College, Dublin

Darach Mac Fhionnbhairr B.A., Ph.D. (N.U.I.); third secretary, Irish embassy, Vienna

Francis Xavier Martin M.A., Ph.D. (Cantab.); M.R.I.A.; professor of medieval history, University College, Dublin

Theodore William Moody B.A. (Q.U.B.), M.A. (Dubl.), Ph.D. (Lond.), Hon. D.Lit. (Q.U.B.), Hon. D.Litt. (N.U.I.); F.R. Hist. Soc.; M.R.I.A.; Corr. F.B.A.; fellow emeritus, Trinity College, Dublin

Michael Joseph O'Kelly M.A., D.Litt. (N.U.I.); F.S.A.; M.R.I.A.; professor of archaeology, University College, Cork

John Gerald Simms M.A. (Oxon., Dubl.), Ph.D. (Dubl.); M.R.I.A.; late fellow emeritus, Trinity College, Dublin (died 9 Apr. 1979)

Christopher John Woods M.A. (Cantab.), Ph.D. (Nottingham); part-time lecturer in modern history, St Patrick's College, Maynooth

ABBREVIATIONS AND CONVENTIONS

Abbreviations and symbols used in this volume are listed below. They consist of (a) the relevant items from the list in *Irish Historical Studies*, supplement 1 (Jan. 1968) and (b) abbreviations, on the same model, not included in the *Irish Historical Studies* list.

a.	*ante* (before)
A.F.M.	*Annala rioghachta Eireann: Annals of the kingdom of Ireland by the Four Masters from the earliest period to the year 1616*, ed. and trans. John O'Donovan (7 vols, Dublin, 1851; reprint New York, 1966)
A.O.H.	Ancient Order of Hibernians
A.U.	*Annála Uladh, Annals of Ulster; otherwise Annála Senait, Annals of Senat; a chronicle of Irish affairs, 431-1131, 1155-1541*, ed. W. M. Hennessy and B. MacCarthy (4 vols, Dublin, 1887-1901)
abd	abdicated
abp	archbishop
Ann. Camb.	'Annales Cambriae', ed. E. Phillimore, in *Y Cymmrodor*, ix (1888)
Ann. Inisf.	*The Annals of Inisfallen (MS Rawlinson B503)*, ed. and trans. Seán Mac Airt (Dublin Institute for Advanced Studies, 1951)
Ann. Tig.	'The Annals of Tigernach', ed. Whitley Stokes, in *Revue Celtique*, xvi–xviii (1895-7)
anon.	published anonymously
app.	appointed
b.	born
bar.	barony
Bk Leinster	*The Book of Leinster, formerly Lebar na Núachongbála*, ed. R. I. Best, Osborn Bergin and M. A. O'Brien (5 vols, Dublin Institute for Advanced Studies, 1954-67)
bp	bishop
c.	*circa* (about)
c.c.	catholic curate
C.S.	chief secretary

Can. Reg.	Canons regular of St Augustine
Chron. Scot.	*Chronicum Scotorum: a chronicle of Irish affairs ... to 1135, and supplement ... 1141–1150,* ed. W. M. Hennessy (London, 1866)
commn	commission
commr	commissioner
con.	conservative party
cons.	consecrated
cr.	created
cttee	committee
d.	died
D.M.P.	Dublin Metropolitan Police
D.U.P.	Democratic Unionist Party
D.I.A.S.	Dublin Institute for Advanced Studies
dep.	deposed
E.E.C.	European Economic Community
ed.	edited by, edition, editor or editors
Éire	26-county area, 1937–49
fl.	*floruit* (flourished)
G.A.A.	Gaelic Athletic Association
G.B.	Great Britain
H.C.	house of commons
H.L.	house of lords
I.F.S.	Irish Free State (1922–37)
I.R.A.	Irish Republican Army
I.R.B.	Irish Republican Brotherhood
I.R.S.P.	Irish Republican Socialist Party
I.T.G.W.U.	Irish Transport and General Workers' Union
ind.	independent
Ire.	Ireland
jcr	justiciar
kg	king
L.C.	lord chancellor
L.C.J.	lord chief justice
L.D.	lord deputy
L.J.	lord justice
L.L.	lord lieutenant
lab.	labour party
lib.	liberal party

N.D.	no date of publication given, and date not ascertained
N.I.	Northern Ireland
N.I.C.R.A.	Northern Ireland Civil Rights Association
N.I.L.P.	Northern Ireland Labour Party
N.P.	no place of publication given, and place not ascertained
N.U.I.	National University of Ireland
nat.	nationalist party
O.E.C.D.	Organisation for Economic Cooperation and Development
O.E.E.C.	Organisation for European Economic Co-operation
O.Cist.	Order of Cîteaux (Cistercian monks)
O.F.M.	Order of Friars Minor (Franciscan friars)
O.P.	Order of Preachers (Dominican friars)
O.S.A.	Order of St Augustine (Augustinian friars)
O.S.B.	Order of St Benedict (Benedictine monks)
Officials	Official I.R.A.
p.	*post* (after)
P.D.	People's Democracy
P.M.	prime minister
Provos	Provisional I.R.A.
R.I.	Republic of Ireland (from 1949)
R.I.A. Proc.	*Proceedings of the Royal Irish Academy*
R.I.C.	Royal Irish Constabulary
R.T.E.	Radio Telefís Éireann
R.U.C.	Royal Ulster Constabulary
reapp.	reappointed
s.a.	*sub anno* (under year)
S.D.L.P.	Social Democratic and Labour Party
succ.	succeeded
T.C.D.	Trinity College, Dublin
U.C.C.	University College, Cork
U.C.D.	University College, Dublin
U.C.G.	University College, Galway
U.D.A.	Ulster Defence Association
U.F.F.	Ulster Freedom Fighters
U.K.	United Kingdom

U.P.N.I.	Unionist Party of Northern Ireland
U.U.U.C.	United Ulster Unionist Council
U.V.F.	Ulster Volunteer Force
un.	unionist party
V.U.P.P.	Vanguard Unionist Progressive Party

The en rule (–), solidus (/), and saltire (×) are used in dates, as in the following examples:

678–80   denotes a process extending from the first to the second date.

678/80   denotes alternative dates for a specific event.

678 × 680 denotes the period within which a specific event, which cannot be more precisely dated, occurred.

Between 1582 and 1752 the solidus is also used where events are dated both in the Old Style and New Style (see below, pp 2–3): e.g. 19/29 July 1693.

The form of entries in the chronology up to 1169 differs from that in later sections, as in many cases only a single entry appears under a given year, and comparatively few events can be dated to the day and month. In that section, consequently, where a precise date is available it is given in parenthesis at the end of the entry; and where two or more entries appear under a given year, the second and any subsequent entries are inset 3 mm.

From 1169, entries that cannot be dated precisely within a year have, as a rule, been placed after the dated entries for that year, unless the evidence is sufficient to warrant placing them earlier. All such entries are set full out to the margin.

Where two or more successive entries bear the same date, the date is not repeated; instead, the second and any subsequent entries are inset 3 mm. For example:

1695

Sept. 7 Act (7 Will. III, c. 4) forbids catholics to send their children abroad for education or to 'teach school' in Ire.

Act (7 Will. III, c. 5) forbids catholics to keep arms, or horses valued at £5 or more

GENERAL INTRODUCTION

WE have here attempted to provide what has hitherto been almost entirely lacking, a chart of events in the history of Ireland from the earliest times to the end of 1976. Like the text of the New History itself, this chronology aims at covering a wide spectrum of social living. But politics occupy a major place, partly because political events can be more precisely identified and dated than events in other fields, and partly because political history has been so much more thoroughly investigated than other fields. As with the text of the New History, the chronology takes account of the wider context (the British Isles, the Continent, America, and the world) of Irish life by including a substantial number of external events that either have had a direct bearing on, or have been indirectly of some importance for, Irish history.

A chronology presents problems of selection no less formidable than the writing of history itself. Partly the compilers have been guided by the text of the New History and by suggestions from the contributors. It is intended that all datable events to which importance is attached in the text should appear in the chronology. But the chronology also supplements the text in that events mentioned there without being precisely dated, or mentioned only by implication, are included; and many events that do not appear in the text because of the scale or nature of the treatment are recorded in the chronology. Thus, though closely linked with the text, the chronology is a work of independent research by the editors and a number of associated scholars.

The chronology is organised in periods, corresponding with the primary divisions of the New History, each section (or sub-section) being compiled by two or more scholars. Every entry is based either on primary sources or on reliable secondary works, and for every entry there is a corresponding index card, containing full references to sources and authorities, in the office of the New History. The scale of treatment in any given period is determined partly by the historical character of the period, partly by the evidence available, and partly by the state of research on the period. Till the end of the sixteenth century we are faced with a continuing dilemma: on the one hand, a dearth of information on many topics, particularly social and economic history, and in cultural history a lack of chronological exactitude; on the other, a plethora of information from annals and genealogies concerning political and ecclesiastical personages and events of both national and local importance. In the first case we are tempted to include every item to which a precise date can be attached, regardless of whether it was of great significance in itself; in the second, research in medieval Irish history has not yet digested enough of the raw material to enable us to distinguish the significant from the trivial. The compilers have, in general, necessarily depended for their selection on the few standard works available on early, medieval, and early modern Irish history, including, of course, volumes i–iii of the New History itself.

The contributors to the text of the New History are in general committed to a harvesting of existing knowledge, accepting the imperfections and lacunae thus involved. But this limitation has had to be frequently set aside and new research specially undertaken by contributors in the course of fulfilling their assignments. Similarly the compilers of the chronology in all its periods have had to undertake detailed research on innumerable special topics, involving much time-consuming effort. While we have aimed at pin-pointing all well-known events of major importance, we have also sought to establish and to clarify other significant events that have hitherto been neglected or only vaguely stated by historians. And in all cases we have tried to attain a maximum of accuracy and precision both of dating and of information. Until the twelfth century it is rarely possible to date events except by the year; from 1169 it becomes increasingly possible to add the month and the day; and from the early sixteenth century most events can be dated by year, month, and day. Publication dates are generally given in years, but often (for example throughout the period covered by Edward Arber (ed.), *The term catalogues, 1668–1709* A.D. (3 vols, London, 1903–6)), a greater degree of precision has been attained.

During the period 1582–1752 there was a discrepancy between the calendar used in Ireland and England and that used over a large area of continental Europe. The calendar universally used in Europe down to 1582, that introduced by Julius Caesar in 45 B.C., which provided that every fourth year should be a leap year of 366 days, was based on a calculation of the solar year at $365\frac{1}{4}$ days. This was a slight overestimate, and as a result the calendar year had by the sixteenth century come to diverge by ten days from the solar year. A new calendar was, therefore, established by Pope Gregory XIII in his bull of 24 February 1582, which corrected the overestimate by providing that the last year of a century should not be a leap year unless the number was divisible by 400. Thus 1600 would be a leap year, but 1700 would not. The bull prescribed that the day following 4 October 1582 should be 15 October, and also that the year should begin on 1 January instead of on Lady Day, 25 March. Most catholic states adopted the Gregorian or New Style calendar in the sixteenth century, most protestant states in the eighteenth century, and Russia and the Balkan states not till the twentieth century. The Julian or Old Style calendar used in Ireland was ten days behind the New Style calendar from 5 October 1582 to 28 February 1700 (Old Style) and eleven days behind from 29 February

1700 to 2 September 1752. The Gregorian calendar was adopted in the dominions of the British crown by an act of 1751 (24 Geo. III, c. 23), which prescribed that 2 September 1752 should be followed by 14 September, and that the official beginning of the year should be 1 January in and after 1752. In this chronology events in Ireland and Great Britain of the period 1582–1752 have been dated according to Old Style for the day and the month, but according to New Style for the year. Where events in continental history are mentioned both styles of dating are shown, in the form:

1584

June 30/July 10 Assassination of William the Silent, prince of Orange

The style of this chronology is necessarily telegraphic, but within that constraint the aim has been to convey as much information as clearly, correctly, and readably as possible. Abbreviations, of which a complete list appears at the beginning of this volume, are freely used for such words as 'appointed' (app.), 'bishop' (bp), 'lord chancellor' (L.C.), 'Ireland' (Ire.), 'Irish Republican Brotherhood' (I.R.B.), 'lord lieutenant' (L.L.). Published books are cited by short titles and in the form:

1685

May Roderick O'Flaherty's *Ogygia* (London)

The titles of published articles and unpublished books, of plays, and of operas and other musical compositions are given between single quotation marks. It is difficult in a chronology so extensive as this to do justice to the arts and sciences and to religious and intellectual achievement, and especially so for the recent past. In this connection we have frequently used the expedient of recording only the date of death of a writer or composer or painter, because this serves as a signpost to contemporary reviews and estimates of his work. And while we have aimed at including individual writings of special importance, however recent, we have made an exception of historical works published in and after 1938, believing that the task of selection was too invidious for us and recognising that such historical works have found, or will find, their place in abundance in the bibliographies of this history.

Events connected with, but subsequent to, the subject of an entry are sometimes added within parentheses, for example:

1580

Aug. 4 Sir James of Desmond captured (executed, 3 Oct.)

Related events are often linked by cross-references, in the form:

1763

Sept. 10 First number of *Freeman's Journal* (see 19 Dec. 1924)

1924

Dec. 19   Last number of *Freeman's Journal* (see 10 Sept. 1763)

Acts of parliament from the sixteenth century onwards are entered according to the date on which they received the royal, or the presidential, assent, and are cited (within brackets) as chapter numbers of regnal years or calendar years. Before 1801 acts of the English or of the British parliament are either so described or have '[Eng.]' or '[G.B.]' added to the official citation. From 1922 onwards, when three parliaments are involved, acts of the Oireachtas are distinguished by the addition of '[I.F.S.]' from 1922 to 1937, '[Éire]' from 1937 to 1949, and '[R.I.]' from 18 April 1949, to the official citation; acts of the Northern Ireland parliament are all described as such in their official titles; and acts of the Westminster parliament are distinguished by the addition of '[U.K.]' to the official citation.

For Irish proper names, an Old Irish standard has been adopted up to A.D. 900, no attempt being made to restore older archaic or proto-Irish forms, and a Middle Irish standard for 901-1333. The year 1333 has been selected as a demarcation point, on the ground that the death of the Brown Earl of Ulster in this year can be taken as marking the start of the Gaelic resurgence; Modern Irish orthography does not commonly occur in manuscripts until the end of the fourteenth century. Classical Modern Irish forms are used for 1334-1534, after which English forms are used except for individuals who are best known under the Irish form of their name. Certain well-established hybrid forms, such as Turlough Luineach O'Neill, have also been employed. Place-names have been given in their current English form (as used by the Ordnance Survey), except where obscure or unidentifiable. Welsh proper names are normally given in the Modern Welsh form (e.g. Rhigyfarch rather than Ricemarch).

Surnames in Mac and in Ua (spelt Ó from 1216—see Mac Airt, *Ann. Inisf.*, p. li) come into general use in the eleventh century, though where genealogical data are absent it is sometimes difficult to distinguish these from the use of 'mac' (son) and 'ua' (grandson) in their literal sense, for the scholarly convention of signalling the surname by the use of capitals is modern. Similarly, Irish sources, medieval and modern, are necessarily ambiguous in the use of 'Uí' (descendants), which may signify either (a) from the fifth century onwards, a dynastic group, and often, secondarily, the territory they occupy or rule, or (b) from the eleventh century onwards, the plural of Ua as a component of a surname. Thus Uí Néill can mean either (a) the dynasties which claimed descent from Niall Noígiallach or (b) the members of the Ua Néill family (coincidentally themselves a subdivision of the Uí Néill), which took its name from Niall Glúndub (d. 919). The high-king Domnall ua Néill (956-80) was actually the grandson of Niall Glúndub, but his son Áed Ua Néill (d. 1004) was the first O'Neill; so too Toirrdelbach ua Briain (d. 1086) was the grandson of Brian Bóruma, while his son Muirchertach Ua Briain (d. 1119) was the first O'Brien. Irish also uses such terms as Clann Néill, Clann Bhriain (children of Niall or Brian) to denote the holders of a surname, usage which has helped to perpetuate mistaken notions about the 'clan system' in Gaelic Ireland (Irish rarely uses the word *clann* as a common noun to mean a sept or kindred group). We have accordingly used the anglicised plural 'the O'Neills', 'the O'Briens', or circumlocutions such as 'the Mac Fir Bhisigh family', in preference to Irish plurals or collectives.

Our spelling of Norse names is pragmatic. We have usually accepted well-established anglicisations rather than attempted an Old Norse standard (which would in fact be more correctly described as a thirteenth-century Classical Icelandic standard, at several removes geographically and chrono-logically from the Hiberno-Norse and Anglo-Danish areas of activity). Thus we have preferred Olaf to Old Norse Óláfr (or its dialect variant Áleifr) as well as to Old Irish Amlaíb and Anglo-Saxon Anlaf (both Irish and Anglo-Saxon have preserved the archaic Old Norse nasal which had been lost by the Classical Old Norse period); similarly we have used Sitric rather than Sigtryggr, Sitriuc, or Sihtric. Sometimes, however, we have retained the Irish form, as in the case of Ragnall, which could represent either of two distinct Old Norse names, Ragnarr and Rögnvaldr. This and other hibernicised forms (e.g. Gofraid, Ímar, Somarlaide) become com-moner in the eleventh and twelfth centuries with the assimilation of the Norse, and are naturally always used for Norse names borrowed by the Irish.

'Derry' is used consistently throughout the chronology to denote the town (from 1604 the city) at the mouth of the river Foyle, though its official name was altered to Londonderry on 29 March 1613. The older name is still used by most people locally and throughout Ireland. We have retained it, partly on this ground, partly for its brevity, and partly because of its convenience in distinguishing the city from the county associated with it. County Londonderry was an artificial entity when it was established in 1613, and the territories comprising it had never been known as Derry or by any one Irish name before the city of London's connection with it.

Acknowledgements for help received by the compilers are made in the introduction to the individual sections of this chronology. But it is appro-priate here to thank Professor Brian Ó Cuív for his help and advice through-out the chronology on writings in Irish and on the history of the Irish language, and to Professor Brian Boydell and Professor Anne Crookshank on the history of music and the visual arts. We are grateful to Dr Christopher Woods for his practical interest in the period 1534-1603 in addition to his share in the whole chronology from 1603, and to Dr Elizabeth Malcolm for the many entries she supplied on the production, consumption and control of alcoholic drink from 1635 onwards. To the many others, too numerous to mention by name, who have helped us on particular points we gratefully acknowledge our indebtedness.

We are deeply conscious that, in such a pioneer work as this, the likelihood of errors is as great as the certainty of omissions. We have done our utmost to minimise both, within the time at our disposal, already much extended, and we have not felt justified in extending it further. The present volume of the New History is the first of three volumes of reference material. In the third we intend to include, among other elements, corrigenda and addenda to this chronology. We should be grateful if, with this in view, users of it would inform us of any errors they may observe in it or of omissions that they think ought to be repaired.

PREHISTORIC AND EARLY IRELAND

INTRODUCTION

IN the earliest section, in addition to scientific dating on archaeological evidence, we have inserted a few pseudo-historical dates to illustrate the view medieval Irishmen had of their own prehistory and for purposes of comparing this with information obtained by modern methods: see, for instance, the entries at 465 B.C. and 450 B.C. relating to Emain Machae (Navan fort, Co. Armagh). Entries have also been made which relate to the history of chronology itself (e.g. A.D. 1), showing the difficulties that confronted medieval scholars in achieving absolute dating. Such problems have recently been well discussed by Kenneth Harrison, *The framework of Anglo-Saxon history to A.D. 900* (Cambridge, 1976).

Our primary sources are the Irish annals, a voluminous record of events both important and trivial, supplemented by the genealogical tracts, the bulk of which are as yet unpublished. The genealogies do not give any absolute chronological data, but, when combined with the annals and the few other records, such as charters in Irish and Latin from the eleventh and twelfth centuries, enable us to obtain a relative chronology for certain personages and events unrecorded in the annals (e.g. the estimate of the probable floruit of Niall Noígiallach, *c.* 445–53). But prior to the twelfth century our presentation of political events has been highly selective, outlining the broad course of development (e.g. the entry for 782–815), rather than reproducing the annalists' year-by-year record of battles and assassinations. Since the annals are interested in obituary notices and unusual or catastrophic events, they may, like newspaper headlines, give an impression of excessive gloom. So long as the Óenach Tailten (Fair of Teltown, Co. Meath) was celebrated annually it only attracted attention when disturbed or suspended, whereas notices of its later revivals are themselves evidence for the artificial character of these occasions (see 716, 772, 774, 811, 873, 876, 878, 888, 889, 916–19, 1007, 1120, 1167/8); the multiplicity of petty kingdoms and the nature of dynastic feuding have ensured a high incidence of regal obits, and our selection has itself exaggerated the proportion of violent deaths so recorded. Constructive achievement is less newsworthy, at least until the era of the self-conscious reformers and royal propagandists of the twelfth century, and in the realm of the arts and literature too often anonymous; we have tried to redress the balance by including every work which can be assigned to a specific or approximate date. But we have also

included all annalistic records of famine and pestilence, together with the
weather conditions which often precipitated them, since their effect on
social conditions was more devastating and widely spread than that of local
warfare or viking raids. In this field we have been guided by Sir William P.
MacArthur, 'The identification of some pestilences recorded in the Irish
annals' in *I.H.S.*, vi, no. 23 (Mar. 1949), pp 169–88, and 'The pestilence
called "scamach" ' in *I.H.S.*, vii, no. 27 (Mar. 1951), pp 199–200. Regional
bias is also apparent, reflecting the centres of annalistic activity: until the
mid eighth century the north and the midlands receive much fuller treatment than Connacht or Leinster, while Munster affairs are not adequately
recorded until the tenth century.

   The origin of the Irish annals is still a matter of scholarly debate, as is
the date at which they become a contemporary record: see A. P. Smyth,
'The earliest Irish annals: their first contemporary entries and the earliest
centres of recording' in *R.I.A. Proc.*, lxxii, sect. C (1972), pp 1–48; Kathleen
Hughes, *Early Christian Ireland: introduction to the sources* (London, 1972),
pp 97–159; M. O. Anderson, *Kings and kingship in early Scotland* (Edinburgh and London, 1973), pp 1–42, 103–18, 205–11; Gearóid Mac Niocaill,
The medieval Irish annals (Dublin, 1975). We incline to the view that
chronological notices—not necessarily full-fledged annals—were being
made as early as the 590s, and that some at least of the entries for the earlier
part of the sixth century were based on reasonably accurate computation.
The authenticity of the entries for the fifth and sixth centuries, is, however,
highly controversial: we have included those which seemed to reflect
genuine tradition, though their chronology may be inexact, e.g. 446 (second
entry), 485, 495, 516, 552/3, and most of the ecclesiastical obits (the martyro-
logies, the most reliable source of hagiographical tradition, here supply us
with day and month); other entries are included as essential points of
reference in any discussion of the early annals, but the more blatant examples
of political and ecclesiastical forgery have been omitted.

   We have gone to some pains to ascertain the precise year intended by the
annalists. Unlike many medieval chronologists, they consistently begin the
year on 1 January and indicate the day of the week (feria) and the age of
the moon (epact) on this date. However, the systematic employment of these
criteria seems to have been adopted only in the second half of the tenth
century, whereas A.D. dating was perhaps introduced as late as *c.* 1100.
Retrospective application of these data to earlier annals led often to accumu-
lation of error, most clearly seen in *A.F.M.* and *Chron. Scot.* P. Walsh,
'The dating of the Irish annals' in *I.H.S.*, ii, no. 8 (Sept. 1941), pp 355–75,
demonstrated that this confusion is secondary. In the best MS of A.U.
(T.C.D., H.1.8), the A.D. dating is in the primary hand, a blank being left
for insertion of the feria and epact, which was done by a second hand. The
A.D. dates are behind those implied by the feria and epact from 482 to 1013,

and we have followed the now generally accepted convention of adding one year throughout this period (thus *A.U.* 664 means *A.U. s.a.* 663 [= 664]). M. O. Anderson has pointed out (op. cit., pp 24-30) that this 'correction' does not always give the true historical date for entries in the sixth and seventh centuries (see our entries for 597, 684, 685, 704). We have worked from photostats of H.1.8. for A.U. and of Bodleian Rawlinson B 488 for Ann. Tig. (the chronology intended by the latter, however, awaits elucidation by a critical editor). We have given all duplicate entries made by the primary hand of A.U. (as at 457/61, 562/3) but have ignored the numerous interpolations by later hands; we have also indicated the variant dates implicit in *Ann. Inisf.* as supplied in Mac Airt's edition (e.g. 447/8, 516/20), and also, where relevant, from the Welsh *Ann. Camb.* Significant variations cease after the seventh century. To illustrate the accuracy of such absolute dating we have included all annalistic references to eclipses before 1000; see F. J. O'Connor, 'Solar eclipses visible in Ireland between A.D. 400 and A.D. 1000' in *R.I.A. Proc.* lvi, sect. A, no. 4 (1952), pp 61-72. The first native Irish observation of an eclipse seems to be that of 594.

Where the true date of an event is known from sources other than the Irish annals, or can be internally corroborated by mention of the day of the week as well as of the month, this has been indicated, together with any annalistic variation. But since many entries probably started life as marginalia, which were not always assigned to the correct year by later copyists, it cannot be assumed that the proven accuracy or otherwise of any one entry holds good for all the others in a given year, and long after the annals have become a contemporary record one must still reckon with the fact that many entries were made retrospectively.

We have included a relatively large proportion of entries relating to foreign events that were of direct or indirect relevance to the Irish at home or abroad; many of these are indeed noted by the Irish annals, and occasionally we have used their own words (in quotation marks). Continental annals and other records, such as works of hagiography and monastic library catalogues and necrologies, are of great importance for the history of the Irish abroad, the more so because news of their activities rarely reached the Irish annalists at home. Occasionally a continental charter enables us to give a greater degree of precision (see the second entry for 946). We were particularly fortunate, through the kindness of Professor Ludwig Hammermayer of Munich, to have had access to the typescript of his article 'Die irischen Benediktiner-"Schottenklöster" in Deutschland und ihr institutioneller Zusammenschluss vom 12. bis 16. Jahrhundert' (now published in *Studien und Mitteilungen zur Geschichte des Benediktiner-Ordens und seiner Zweige*, Band 87, Heft iii-iv [1976], pp 249-337), which clarifies many points of chronology in the foundation of the Irish Schotten-klöster in Germany in the eleventh, twelfth, and thirteenth centuries.

Our thanks are due to Mrs Helen Littleton, research assistant to the New History of Ireland, for her work in the early stages of this compilation; and to Mr Denis Bethell, to the late Dr Kathleen Hughes, to Dr Michael Herity, Professor Etienne Rynne, and Dr Roger Stalley for many helpful comments, suggestions, and corrections.

GLOSSARY

Ailech. The prehistoric stone fort north-west of Derry in Inishowen, Co. Donegal, which was the titular capital of the Cenél nEógain dynasty; after the latter established their overlordship of the Northern Uí Néill, *c.* 734, the title 'king of Ailech' was equivalent to 'king of the North' (In Fochlae, In Tuaiscert).

airchinnech. Used in the same sense as Latin *princeps* to denote an abbot or other head of a church; often an official or administrator in charge of a subordinate church or institution within a monastic town, or the abbot of a subordinate monastery within a monastic *paruchia.*

Airgialla. A loose conglomeration of kingdoms, including the Airthir, Uí Chremthainn, Uí Macc Uais, and Uí Thuirtri, occupying the central lands of the ancient province of Ulster and owing allegiance to the Uí Néill; from 827 they fell under the over-lordship of the Cenél nEógain, who continuously encroached upon their territory; in the early twelfth century the Airgialla kingdom of Fernmag (Farney) conquered all of Co. Louth. See vol. ix, maps 18 and 30.

Brega. An over-kingdom of the Southern Uí Néill comprising Co. Meath together with south Co. Louth and north Co. Dublin.

Bréifne. A kingdom established in Co. Leitrim by a branch of the dominant Uí Briúin dynasty of Connacht in the eighth century; by the twelfth century the Ua Ruairc kings of Bréifne (the later diocese of Kilmore) and of Conmaicne (a vassal state comprising the diocese of Ardagh) were extending their dominion deep into Co. Meath.

comarbae. 'Coarb'; literally 'heir'; in ecclesiastical usage the 'heir' of a founder saint was the abbot of the principal church of a monastic confederation or *paruchia.*

Connachta. Originally a collective term for the dynasties claiming descent from the legendary Conn Cétchathach, including the Uí Néill; from the seventh century restricted to those dynasties ruling west of the Shannon, hence the province of Connacht.

Cruthin. A people dominant in Ulster but distinct from the Ulaid; from the eighth century they formed two kingdoms, Dál nAraidi in Co. Antrim and Uí Echach Cobo in west Co. Down; until 972 many of their kings were also kings of Ulster. The name Cruthin was also used in Irish to denote the Picts of Scotland.

Dál Cais. Ruling dynasty of the Déis Tuaiscirt in east Co. Clare, which in the tenth century established the kingdom of Thomond (Tuadmumu, i.e. north Munster).

Dál Riatai. Dynasty of a kingdom in north-east Co. Antrim which in the fifth century established its rule over Irish colonists (*Scotti*) in Argyll and the Isles.

Feis Temro. 'Feast of Tara'; pagan inauguration ceremony of the kings of Tara.

fer léigind. 'Lector'; head of a monastic school.

Laigin. The dominant peoples of Leinster.

Leinster. The province of the Laigin in the early and medieval period comprised only the south-east of Ireland south of Dublin, though by the twelfth century it also included Osraige (Ossory) and Fine Gall (in north Co. Dublin), being coterminous with the ecclesiastical province of Dublin.

Leth Cuinn. 'Conn's half'; the northern half of Ireland dominated by the Uí Néill and Connachta, but not including Ulster (see below).

Leth Moga. 'Mug's half'; named after Mug Nuadat, legendary ancestor of the Eóganacht dynasties of Munster; theoretically included Leinster and Munster.

Mide. An over-kingdom of the Southern Uí Néill originally comprising Co. Westmeath and west Co. Offaly; ruled by the Clann Cholmáin dynasty who established their supremacy over all the midlands from the mid eighth century; by the eleventh century the name Mide is applied to this wider area, including Brega and Tethbae, and the term Iarthar Mide (western Mide) comes into use for the original territory.

mormáer. A term of Pictish origin variously rendered 'great steward' or 'earl'; in Scotland, at least, it denoted a great nobleman who also acted as a senior royal official or deputy.

Munster. Irish *Mumu*; provincial over-kingdom ruled by the king of Cashel and co-terminous with the ecclesiastical province of Cashel; from the early twelfth century divided between the Ua Briain (Dál Cais) kingdom of Thomond or Limerick and the Mac Carthaig (Eóganacht) kingdom of Desmond (Desmumu, i.e. South Munster) or Cork.

Norse. Here used to denote the Scandinavian colonists in Scotland, Ireland, and Man, who were mainly of Norwegian origin.

Óenach Carmain. 'Fair of Carman'; site uncertain but probably near Carlow; the pro-vincial assembly of the Laigin, presided over by the king of Leinster.

Óenach Tailten. 'Fair of Teltown'; the annual assembly of the Uí Néill, presided over by the high-king of Tara.

ollam. 'Ollave'; the highest rank in one of the learned professions.

Osraige. A large over-kingdom coterminous with the diocese of Ossory; until the ninth century a border state of Munster but thenceforth increasingly orientated towards Leinster, of which it formed a constituent kingdom in the twelfth century.

rígdomnae. 'King-material'; a prince eligible for succession to the kingship.

St. 'Saint'; applied throughout this section of the chronology to all those who achieved recognition in the calendars or in popular cult. Official canonisation by Rome was a later development; for an early example see 1051. Not only the monastic founders but all prominent churchmen of the fifth, sixth, and seventh centuries were commemorated in the Irish calendars.

Tethbae. Originally a territory comprising Co. Longford and containing two kingdoms of the Southern Uí Néill, Cairpre (at Granard) and Maine (at Ardagh); from the end of the eleventh century, however, the name is applied to the western part of Co. Westmeath and adjoining portions of Co. Offaly, where the Maine dynasty had moved under pressure from the Conmaicne (see Bréifne).

tuath. 'People'; 'tribe'; 'tribal kingdom'; 'territory'; also used to denote the laity, lay property, secular society, or the 'state' as opposed to the church; 'tribal' is here used to denote a state of political and social development reflected in the Old Irish law tracts in which the petty king of a *tuath* was the king *par excellence*, regardless of his political power; more debatably, such a king was leader of a population-group or community, and only secondarily ruler of a specific territory. With the increasing territorialisation of power by over-kings from the eighth century the political importance of the *tuath* declined, and by the eleventh century the *tuath* had no political significance, but was a small district within a *trícha cét* or petty kingdom, and was represented, not by a king, but by a *toísech* (originally a military term meaning 'leader').

Uí Maine. A large over-kingdom in south-east Connacht, represented in the twelfth century by the diocese of Clonfert, but earlier extending well into Co. Roscommon; its ruling dynasty was not genealogically related to the Connachta proper.

Uí Néill. A widespread confederation of dynastic kingdoms under the titular high-kings of Tara, who from the seventh century claimed to be kings of all Ireland. Most prominent of the Northern Uí Néill were the dynasties of Cenél Conaill (diocese of Raphoe) and

Cenél nEógain (diocese of Derry, but from the ninth century expanding into Co. Tyrone); and of the Southern Uí Néill the Clann Cholmáin of Mide and the Síl nÁedo Sláine of Brega.

Ulaid. The dominant people in Ulster.

Ulster. In prehistoric times a provincial kingdom covering the whole north of Ireland and centred at Emain Machae (Navan Fort, near Armagh); from the fifth century reduced to the territory east of the Bann, comprising Co. Down, Co. Antrim, and north Co. Louth. In early medieval times the name Ulster is never used (except in clearly antiquarian contexts) to denote the Uí Néill kingdom of the North or their vassal states of Airgialla.

vikings. Here used to denote the Scandinavian sea-raiders not permanently based in Ireland (see Norse).

CHRONOLOGY, TO 1169

(A) TO 431

F. J. BYRNE, CHARLES DOHERTY, AND M. J. O'KELLY

2,000,000–30,000 B.C. Pleistocene period: intense cold of great ice age
Topography of Ire. much as today; sea-level fluctuating
Gortian warm stage in mid-Pleistocene: climate warmer than today; plants not now native to Ire. but to North America, European mainland, and Asia, flourish
Later interglacial warm stage around 100,000 B.C.: no record of man or animals

30,000 B.C. Wooly mammoth (*elephas primigenius*), bear, reindeer, and hyena recorded

11,500–8500 B.C. Climate again genial; gentians and mountain avens growing in open spaces; copses of birch
Reindeer and giant Irish deer (so-called Irish elk) in south; also wolf, lynx, bear, fox, and Irish hare

8500–8000 B.C. Final spell of severe cold

8000 B.C. Post-glacial time begins; woodlands spread

6500 B.C. Rising sea-level cuts Ire. off from Britain
Earliest evidence for presence of man in Ire. at Mount Sandel near Coleraine (Co. Londonderry)

5730 B.C. Radiocarbon dating of deposits at Toome Bay (Co. Londonderry)

3800 B.C. Radiocarbon dating of forest clearance at Ballynagilly (Co. Tyrone): possible evidence for pastoral economy and domestic cattle

3000 B.C. After various fluctuations, sea-level stabilised
Forest clearance continues; cereal crops grown; pottery vessels and polished stone axes in use
Axe factory at Tievebulliagh (Co. Armagh) distributing products widely in Ire. and Britain
Building of megalithic tombs begins

a. **2500** B.C.   Neolithic settlement at Lough Gur (Co. Limerick)
Wheat cultivated on site of Newgrange (Co. Meath)

2500 B.C.   Radiocarbon dating for building of passage-grave at Newgrange (Co. Meath)

2000 B.C.   Radiocarbon dating for Beaker culture at Newgrange (Co. Meath) and Ballynagilly (Co. Tyrone): introduction of copper metallurgy; flat axes cast in open moulds
Forest clearance continues

1800 B.C.   Collective burial practice of preceding millenium superseded by single-grave burials
Food vessel and urn-type pottery used for funerary purposes
Tin (probably from Cornwall) alloyed with copper to make bronze
Gold worked: lunulae, sun-disks, etc.

1500 B.C.   Flat axe developed into palstave form; long slender rapiers and kite-shaped or shouldered spearheads made
Radiocarbon dating for copper-mining at Mount Gabriel (Co. Cork)

1200 B.C.   Later phase of bronze age: gold ornaments very numerous; many new types of object, including weapons and ornaments, made under influences emanating from northern Europe: socketed axes, gouges, hammers, razors, etc.

800 B.C.   Sheet-bronze buckets and cauldrons; bronze horns numerous; gold gorgets; wooden vessels

753 B.C.   Varronian date for foundation of Rome (21 Apr.): beginning of era *ab urbe condita*

680 B.C.   Radiocarbon dating for first circular inhabitation enclosure at Emain Machae (Navan fort near Armagh)

c. **600–500** B.C.   'Periplous' of Himilco, the Carthaginian: earliest documentary reference to Ire.

c. **540–475** B.C.   Hecataeus of Miletus *fl.*; first writer to mention Celts

c. **500** B.C.   Iron metallurgy in Ire., though bronze-age economy still in evidence (see 200 B.C.)

465 B.C.   Radiocarbon dating for destruction by fire of later structure at Emain Machae

450 B.C.   Pseudo-historical date for foundation of Emain Machae as capital of Ulster kingdom (according to 12th-century text of 'Lebor Gabála')

c. **390** B.C.   Gauls occupy Rome

c. **330–300** B.C.   Pytheas's 'Concerning the ocean'; earliest reference to British Isles (*Pretanikai nesoi*)

323 B.C.   Death of Alexander the Great (13 June)

312 B.C. Beginning of Seleucid era (so-called 'era of Alexander' or 'kingdom of the Greeks') (Sept./Oct.)

307 B.C. Pseudo-annalistic date for foundation of Emain Machae (according to 8th-century Irish World Chronicle)
  Pseudo-historical date for destruction of Dind Ríg and foundation of kingdom of Leinster (according to Lebor Gabála; dated to 300 B.C. by Orthanach ua Cáelláma Cuirrig (d. 840))

c. **300** B.C. Earliest La Tène influences reach Ire. through trade with (and possibly migration from) Continent

279-275 B.C. Gauls ravage Thrace, Greece, and Asia Minor: kingdom of Galatia founded

200 B.C. Bronze and iron finds from crannog at Rathtinaun, Lough Gara (Co. Sligo)
  Sculpture in stone and wood; Turoe stone

135-51 B.C. Poseidonius of Apamea *fl.*; detailed 'Celtic ethnography' included in his 'Histories'

c. **100** B.C.–A.D. **500** Proto-Irish linguistic period: language of ogham inscriptions

55 B.C. Julius Caesar invades Britain

52-51 B.C. Caesar's 'De bello Gallico'; first appearance of name *Hibernia*

38 B.C. Beginning of Spanish era (used in Spain and Portugal from 5th to 15th century)

22 B.C. Date of Incarnation according to Marianus Scottus (d. 1082)

8×4 B.C. Birth of Christ

1 B.C. Birth of Christ (25 Dec.) according to Dionysius Exiguus (see A.D. 525)

A.D. **1** Era of Incarnation (Dionysian era): Anno Mundi 5199 according to Eusebius (d. 338) and St Jerome (d. 420); 3952 according to Bede (d. 735)

1-500 Building of crannogs, hill-forts, and ring-forts continues; earliest examples of La Tène-influenced art-styles in Ire.

c. **17-23** Strabo's 'Geography'; includes description of Ire. (*Ierne*) and Irish, perhaps derived from Poseidonius (see 135-51 B.C.)

20 Pseudo-annalistic obit of Conchobar mac Nessae, kg of Ulster at Emain Machae (Irish World Chronicle; A.D. 58 according to Book of Cuanu, cited *A.U.* 482)

28 Date of crucifixion of Christ according to Victorius of Aquitaine (see 457): era of Passion

30 Probable date of crucifixion (7 Apr.)

c. **43** Pomponius Mela's 'De situ orbis'; includes description of Ire. (*Iuverna*)

43 Emperor Claudius conquers Britain

61 Rebellion of Iceni under Boudicca

78-84 Agricola, Roman governor in Britain; projects invasion of Ire. (83); defeats Caledones under Calgacus at Mons Graupius

97-8 'De vita C. Iulii Agricolae', by Cornelius Tacitus, Agricola's son-in-law

c. **122-33** Hadrian's wall built

c. **130-80** Ptolemy's 'Geography'; includes detailed map of Ire. with identifiable names of rivers, towns, and tribes; first contemporary documentary evidence for Érainn (*Iverni*), Ulaid (*Voluntii*), and Emain Machae (*Isamnion*)

c. **143** Antonine wall built

196 Clodius Albinus, governor of Britain, proclaims himself emperor and leads army to Gaul

197 Hadrian's wall breached by Maeatae

208-11 Emperor Septimius Severus campaigns in northern Britain against Maeatae and Caledones; dies at York (211)

c. **253-68** Solinus's 'Collectanea rerum memorabilium'; includes description of Ire. and Irish

284 Diocletian divides Roman empire into east and west for administrative purposes

c. **290** Radiocarbon dating for fort on Cathedral Hill, Armagh

296 Hadrian's wall breached a second time; restored by Constantius Chlorus

297 First mention of Picts: attack Roman Britain in conjunction with Irish (*Hiberni*)

297-*c.* 450 Irish raids on Roman Britain

c. **305-20** St Anthony and St Pachomius: beginnings of monasticism in Egypt

324/7 Pseudo-annalistic date for fall of Emain Machae according to Irish World Chronicle (327 according to Gilla Cáemáin (*fl.* 1072); *A.F.M.* 331)

330 Emperor Constantine I establishes Constantinople (formerly Byzantium) as eastern capital of Roman empire (see 29 May 1453)

338 Death of ecclesiastical historian and chronologist, Eusebius of Caesarea

c. **360** St Basil establishes cenobitic monasticism in Asia Minor

366 Pseudo-annalistic obit of Cormac mac Airt, kg of Tara and ancestor of Uí Néill, according to Book of Cuanu (cited *A.U.* 482)

367-70 Assault on Britain by Picts, Irish (*Scotti*), and Saxons; Hadrian's wall breached for third time; restored by Theodosius

c. **371-97** St Martin, bp of Tours, encourages monasticism in Gaul

380–91   Ammianus Marcellinus's 'Rerum gestarum libri': first mention of *Scotti* and *Atecotti*

383   Magnus Maximus withdraws legions from Britain in attempt to seize western empire; invades Italy (387); defeated and killed by Emperor Theodosius (July 388)

c. **393**   St Jerome's 'Adversus Jovinianum'; alleges Irish cannibalism

395–9   Stilicho defends British coasts

c. **400**   St Ninian founds monastery of Candida Casa (Whithorne) in Galloway

405   Pseudo-annalistic date for death of Niall Noígiallach (Niall of the Nine Hostages; see *c.* 445–53) according to Gilla Cáemáin (see 324/7) and *A.F.M.*

406   German tribes breach Rhine frontier

410   Sack of Rome by Alaric the Visigoth
Emperor Honorius instructs British *civitates* to arrange their own defences

411–18   British heretic Pelagius *fl.*; alleged by St Jerome to be Irish

c. **418**   Orosius's 'Historiae adversum paganos'; contains description of Ire.

420   Death of St Jerome

c. **420**   Death of Sulpicius Severus, author of hagiographical works about St Martin of Tours

422–32   Celestine I pope

428   'Notitia dignitatum': last official record of civil and military establishment in Roman Britain

c. **429/30**   Death of Bp Honoratus of Arles, founder of monastery of Lérins

429   St Germanus of Auxerre visits Britain

430   Death of St Augustine, bp of Hippo

430/35   Death of John Cassian of Marseilles, monastic founder and teacher

431   Palladius sent as first bp to Irish Christians by Pope Celestine
'Annals of Ulster' begin

(B) 432–1169

F. J. BYRNE AND CHARLES DOHERTY

432   Traditional date of St Patrick's mission

433/4   Prosper of Aquitaine's 'Contra Collatorem' attacks semi-Pelagian teaching of John Cassian and attributes conversion of Ire. to Pope Celestine

435/6   Death of Bressal Bélach, kg of Leinster

438 Codex Theodosianus; legal separation of eastern and western empire

440-61 St Leo I, the Great, pope

444 Traditional date of foundation of Armagh
Pope Leo writes to Cyril of Alexandria concerning date of Easter
Welsh 'Annales Cambriae' begin

c. **445-53** Probable floruit of Niall Noígiallach (see 405), founder of Uí Néill dynasty

445 Death of Nath Í mac Fiachrach

446 British appeal in vain to Aetius for Roman protection
Battle of Femen (in Brega): Mac Caírthinn mac Cóelboth, kg of Leinster, killed

447 St Germanus visits Britain again (see 429)

447/8 Death of St Secundinus (Sechnall), missionary bp in Ire. (27 Nov.); founder of Dunshaughlin (Co. Meath)

449 Traditional date for Anglo-Saxon invasion of Britain

c. **450** Probable date of fall of Ulster over-kingdom (Emain Machae), according to 'Lebor Gabála' (see 680 B.C., 465 B.C., 307 B.C., A.D. *c.* 290, 324-7)

454 Pope Leo I formally accepts Alexandrian date for Easter 455 (24 Apr.)

454/6 Lóeguire mac Néill celebrates Feis Temro (Feast of Tara), pagan inauguration rite

456 Suggested date (5 Apr.) for arrival of St Patrick (James Carney, *The problem of St Patrick* (Dublin, 1961), pp 21-30)

457 Victorius of Aquitaine draws up new paschal cycle

457/61 Death of St Patrick (17 Mar.) (early dating; see 493)

459/60 Death of Auxilius, missionary bp in Ire.; founder of Killashee (Co. Kildare)

461/3 Death of Lóeguire mac Néill, kg of Tara

465/8 Death of St Iserninus, missionary bp in Ire. (*Epscop Fith*), founder of Kilcullen (Co. Kildare) and Aghade (Co. Carlow)

467/8 Death of St Benignus, bp of Armagh

467/9 Ailill Molt mac Nath Í celebrates Feis Temro

468 Emperor Anthemius hires British auxiliary troops under Riothamus on Loire against Euric the Visigoth; beginnings of Breton settlement of Armorica

476 Deposition of Romulus Augustulus, last Roman emperor of west (cf. 29 May 1453)

481 Death of St Iarlaithe mac Treno, 'third bp of Armagh'

482   Battle of Ochae (in Meath or Leinster): Ailill Molt mac Nath Í killed; Uí Néill monopolise Tara kingship

483   Assassination of Cremthann mac Éndai Chennselaig, kg of Leinster

485   Battle of Granard: Coirpre mac Néill, kg of Tara, defeats and kills Findchad mac Garrchon, kg of Leinster

486   Clovis the Frank conquers north Gaul

487   Death of Bp Mel of Ardagh (6 Feb.)

489/91   Death of St Cianán of Duleek (24 Nov.)

a. c. **490**   St Éndae founds earliest Irish monastery at Aran

c. **490**   Dál Riatai establish kingdom in Scotland

490/92   Death of St Mac Caille, bp of Cruachu Bríg Éle (Croghan, Co. Offaly) (25 Apr.)

c. **490/92**   Death of Óengus mac Nad Froích, kg of Cashel

493   Traditional date for death of St Patrick (Wed., 17 Mar.) (also entered in *A.U.* 492)

495   Second battle of Granard: Echu mac Coirpri defeats and kills Fróech mac Findchado, kg of Leinster

496   Death of St Mac Cuilinn, bp of Lusk (6 Sept.)
Baptism of Clovis

497   Death of Cormac, bp of Armagh, *heres Patricii* (heir of Patrick)

497/8   Death of St Mo Choí of Nendrum (23 June)

499/500/01   Death of Bp Ibar of Begerin, Wexford Harbour (23 Apr.)

c. **500**   Composition of archaic Leinster genealogical poems by Laidcenn mac Bairchedo and others

c. **500–700**   Archaic Old Irish linguistic period

506   Death of St Mac Caírthinn, bp of Clogher (23 Mar.)

507/9   Death of St Mac Nisi, bp of Connor (3 Sept.)

511 × 520   Gaulish bps rebuke Breton priests Lovocatus and Catihernus for unorthodox practices

512/13   Death of St Erc, bp of Slane (2 Nov.)

516   Battle of Druim Derge (Co. Westmeath or Offaly?): Laigin finally lose midlands to Uí Néill

c. **516/17**   Battle of Mons Badonicus: Britons stem Saxon advance (*Ann. Camb.* 516)

516/17   Death of St Moninne (Darercae) of Killeevy (6 July)

516/20 Death of St Conláed, bp of Kildare (3 May)

c. **520** St Benedict of Nursia composes his rule
Floruit of St Illtud, founder of Welsh monasticism

520-*c.* 620 Efflorescence of early Irish monasticism

521 Death of St Búite of Monasterboice (7 Dec.) on birthday of St Colum Cille
(*A.U.* 519; *Ann. Inisf., Ann. Camb.* 521)

523 Boethius's 'De consolatione philosophiae'

524/6 Death of St Brigit of Kildare (1 Feb.) (*Ann. Camb.* 521)

525 Dionysius Exiguus composes his paschal cycle

527-65 Reign of Emperor Justinian

527/8/534/42 Death of St Ailbe of Emly (12 Sept. or 30 Dec.)[1]

534/6 Death of Muirchertach Mac Ercae, kg of Tara

535 First year after consulate of Paulinus (last Roman consul in west)

535-53 Justinian reconquers Italy from Ostrogoths

535 Death of St Mochtae of Louth (20 Aug.), disciple of St Patrick

536 Famine

537 Battle of Camlann in Britain; Arthur killed by Medrawd; plague in Britain
and Ire. (*Ann. Camb.*)

c. **540** Cassiodorus establishes monastic library of Vivarium (Squillace)
Beginnings of paschal controversy in Ire.

542 First year after consulate of Basilios (last Roman consul in east)

542-3 'Justinian's plague' reaches Gaul from Egypt

544 Tuathal Máelgarb, kg of Tara, assassinated

544/5 First plague, called *blefed* (bubonic plague): death of St Mo Bí Clárainech
of Glasnevin (12 Oct.)

546 Derry founded by St Colum Cille (Columba)

547 Maelgwn Gwynedd, kg of North Wales, dies of plague

547/8 Clonmacnoise founded by St Ciarán

548/9 Death of St Tigernach, bp of Clones (4 Apr.)
Death of St Ciarán of Clonmacnoise (9 Sept.) (*Ann. Camb.* 544)

549 Recurrence of plague: deaths of St Mac Táil of Kilcullen (11 June); St
Sinchell of Killeigh (25 June); St Finnian of Clonard (12 Dec.; *Ann. Inisf.*
552); and St Colum of Terryglass (13 Dec.; *Ann. Inisf.* 552)

[1] Possibly two or three different saints; *Ann. Inisf.* 528 and *A.U.* 534 specifically say Ailbe of Imlech
Iubair.

c. **550**   Beginnings of monastic Hiberno–Latin writing: hymns and penitentials

c. **550**–*c.* **600**   Earliest Irish law texts committed to writing

551/6   Second plague, called *buide conaill* (relapsing fever)

552/3   Uí Fidgeinti defeat Corco Óchae (Co. Limerick)

554   Distemper called *samthrosc* (smallpox)

558   Clonfert founded by St Brendan

558/60   Feis Temro celebrated for last time, by Diarmait mac Cerbaill
Bruide mac Máelchon, kg of Picts, defeats Dál Riatai

555/8/9   Bangor founded by St Comgall

c. **559**   Composition of 'Liber Anatoli', Irish paschal forgery

560/61   Battle of Cúl Dreimne (near Drumcliff, Co. Sligo): Diarmait mac
Cerbaill, kg of Tara, defeated by Northern Uí Néill

561   Exile of St Colum Cille (Columba) (*Ann. Camb.* 562)

562/3   Battle of Móin Dairi Lothair (Co. Londonderry): Ulster Cruthin defeated
by Northern Uí Néill: beginning of Northern Uí Néill expansion

563   Iona founded by St Colum Cille (Pentecost Sunday, 13 May)

564   Great wind
Death of St Mo Laisse (Laisrén) of Devenish (18 Sept.)

564/5   Diarmait mac Cerbaill killed by Áed Dub mac Suibni, Cruthin kg of
Ulster

565   Death of St Brendan of Birr (29 Nov.) (*Ann. Camb.* 574, *Ann. Inisf.* 573)

c. **565**   Death of St Samson, bp of Dol in Brittany

567/8   Colmán Bec, son of Diarmait mac Cerbaill, invades Hebrides with Conall
mac Comgaill, kg of Dál Riatai

567/70   Death of Gildas

568   Lombards invade Italy

570   Death of St Íte of Cluain Credail (Killeedy, Co. Limerick) (15 Jan.)

572–81   Báetán mac Cairill kg of Ulster and 'high-king'

c. **572–92**   Urien, British kg of Rheged, campaigns against Angles of Northumbria; floruit of his court poet Taliesin; earliest Old Welsh poetry (see
c. 590)

c. **574**   Áedán mac Gabráin consecrated kg of Dál Riatai by St Colum Cille; first
recorded ecclesiastical sacring of kg in Britain or Ire.

575   Convention of Druim Cett (Co. Londonderry): St Colum Cille negotiates
alliance between Áedán mac Gabráin and Áed mac Ainmerech, kg of
Northern Uí Néill

576   Abundant nut crop

576/7   *Scintilla leprae* (?smallpox; ?skin disease)

c. **577**   West Saxons capture Bath, Gloucester, and Cirencester

577   Ulaid invade Isle of Man (*Ann. Inisf.* 579)
Breton leader Waroc captures Vannes

578   Ulaid expelled from Isle of Man

577/8   Death of St Brendan of Clonfert (16 May)

579/80   Death of St Finnian of Moville (10 Sept.)

580/81   Áedán mac Gabráin invades Orkneys

c. **580**   Floruit of Luccreth moccu Chérai, west Munster poet: earliest reference
to Ulster sagas

c. **580**-*c.* **650**   Floruit of poet Senchán Torpéist, author of lost genealogical work,
'Cocangab Már'

c. **580**-*c.* **680**   Latin literature flourishes in Ire.: works of Latin grammar and
biblical exegesis

582/3   Áedán mac Gabráin wins battle in Isle of Man (*Ann. Camb.* 584)

584/6   Death of Bruide mac Máelchon, kg of Picts

588   Great snow

588-626   Fiachnae mac Báetáin, Cruthin kg of Ulster and 'high-king'

589   Hot summer
Spanish Visigoths converted to catholicism
Death of St David of Menevia (1 Mar.) (*Ann. Camb.* 601)

590-604   St Gregory the Great, pope

c. **590**   St Columbanus begins Irish mission on Continent: founds Annegray,
Luxeuil, and Fontaines
Northumbrian victory over northern British (Gododdin) at Catraeth (Catterick,
Yorkshire): elegy by Aneirin, 'Canu Aneirin'

594   Eclipse of sun (23 July) (*A.U.* 591; *Ann. Inisf.* 594)[1]
Death of Gregory of Tours

a. **597**   The Cathach psalter: earliest Irish MS, allegedly written by St Colum
Cille

597   St Augustine's mission to Kent
Death of St Colum Cille (Sun., 9 June) (*A.U.* 595; *Ann. Camb.* 595; *Ann.
Inisf.* 597): Dallán Forgaill composes archaic Old Irish elegy, 'Amra Coluim
Chille'

---

[1] *A.U.* notes two eclipses in 591 and 592 which might be those of 4 Oct. 590 (magnitude 0·65) and
of 19 Mar. 592 (0·58), but it is more likely that both entries are duplicates for the total eclipse (1·00)
of 594.

598 Battle of Dún Bolg (near Baltinglass, Co. Wicklow): Áed mac Ainmerech, Uí Néill high-king, killed by Brandub mac Echach, kg of Leinster

c. **600** St Columbanus writes to Pope Gregory the Great on paschal controversy

601 Earthquake in Bairrche (Mourne mountains)

601 or 602/5 Death of St Comgall of Bangor (10 May)

603 Council of Châlons: St Columbanus refuses to attend
Battle of Degsastan: Angles of Northumbria under Aethelfrith defeat Scots under Áedán mac Gabráin (*A.U.* 600)

604 Assassination of joint high-kings of Tara, Colmán Rímid and Áed Sláine, and of Áed Róin, kg of Uí Failgi

605/8 Brandub mac Echach, kg of Leinster, killed

605 × 617 Letter of Laurentius of Canterbury to Irish clergy concerning Irish and British nonconformity in dating of Easter

606 Death of St Colmán mac Lénéni, poet and founder of Cloyne
Composition of 'Epistola Cyrilli', British or Irish paschal forgery

608/9 Death of Áedán mac Gabráin, kg of Dál Riatai (17 Apr.) (*A.U.* 606; *Ann. Camb.* 607)

609/12/15 Death of St Mo Lua (Lugaid moccu Óchae) of Clonfertmulloe (4 Aug.); founder of Druim Snechtai (Dromsnat, Co. Monaghan)

610 St Columbanus expelled from Burgundy by Kg Theuderic II; welcomed in Neustria by Kg Clothair II

c. **610 × 615** 'Vita Samsonis', earliest Latin life of St Samson of Dol

611 Death of Colmán moccu Beógnae, author of 'Aipgitir Crábaid' (earliest example of Old Irish prose)

612 St Columbanus leaves St Gall in Bregenz; departs for Lombardy (autumn); welcomed by Kg Agilulf

c. **612** Death of Rhydderch Hael, kg of Ail Cluaid (British kingdom of Strathclyde at Dumbarton)
Death of St Kentigern (Caíntigern), bp of Glasgow

c. **613 × 614** St Columbanus writes to Pope Boniface IV about 'Three Chapters' schism

615 Death of St Columbanus at Bobbio (Sun., 23 Nov.)

616 Battle of Chester: Aethelfrith of Northumbria defeats Selyf ap Cynan, kg of Gwynedd; Northumbrian power reaches Irish sea (*A.U.* 613; *Ann. Inisf.* 614; *Ann. Camb.* 613)

617 Aethelfrith defeated and killed by Raedwald, kg of East Anglia; Edwin of Deira becomes kg of Northumbria

617-33 Bernician princes in exile in Dál Ríatai

p. **617** Edwin of Northumbria conquers British kingdom of Elmet in south Yorkshire

617/19 Martyrdom of St Donnán of Eigg and 150 companions by pirates (17 Apr.); Tory Island plundered

622-33 Isidore of Seville's 'Etymologiae'

622 Death of St Cóemgen (Kevin) of Glendalough (3 June)

623-39 Reign of Dagobert I, kg of the Franks; obtains submission of Breton Judicaël, kg of Dumnonia

624/5 Eclipse of sun (21 June 624 or 10 June 625) (*Ann. Inisf.* 626, *A.U.* 625, *Ann. Camb.* 624)[1]

625 Mongán, son of Fiachnae mac Báetáin, kg of Ulster, killed by Britons of Strathclyde

625-33 St Paulinus's mission to Northumbria: conversion of Edwin

c. **625** Death of St Máedóc of Ferns (31 Jan.)

626 Rhun, son of Urien of Rheged, baptises Edwin, kg of Northumbria (*Ann. Camb.*)

627/9 Battle of Carn Feradaig (Cahernarry, Co. Limerick); Fáilbe Fland, kg of Cashel, defeats Guaire Aidni of Connacht

628/9 Letter of Pope Honorius to Irish clergy concerning paschal controversy

c. **630**-*c.* **650** Composition of 'De duodecim abusivis saeculi', Irish homiletic tract Cogitosus's 'Vita Brigitae': beginnings of Irish hagiography

c. **630** Edwin of Northumbria invades Anglesey and Man
St Fursu leaves Ire. for East Anglia; founds Cnobesburh

630 Synod of Mag Léne: southern Irish conform to Roman Easter

631 Irish embassy to Rome on Easter question

632 Death of Muhammad
Cadwallon of Gwynedd flees to Ire.
Cummian's paschal letter: urges Ségéne of Iona to accept Roman Easter; refers to St Patrick as *papa noster*

632/3 Battle of Hatfield Chase: Cadwallon and Penda of Mercia kill Edwin, kg of Northumbria (*Ann. Camb.* 630)

635-51 St Aidan's mission from Iona to Northumbria: founds Lindisfarne

636/8 Expulsion of St Carthach (Mo Chutu) from Rahan: foundation of Lismore

---

[1] The eclipse of 624 was of magnitude 0·47, and that of 625 of magnitude 0·25. The annalist's phrase 'annus tenebrosus' may refer to the two eclipses within 12 months.

636   Death of St Isidore, bp of Seville

637/9   Battle of Mag Roth (Moira, Co. Down): high-king (Domnall mac Áedo) defeats Ulaid and Dál Riatai; Congal Clóe, kg of Ulster and claimant to kingship of Tara, killed
Death of Mo Chutu of Lismore (14 May)

638   Caliph Omar takes Jerusalem

639   Death of Áed Dub, abbot and bp of Kildare, brother of Fáelán mac Colmáin, kg of Leinster (since 633) and ancestor of Uí Dúnlainge dynasty

639/41   Death of St Mo Laisse (Laisrén) of Leighlin (18 Apr.)

640   Embassy from northern Irish to Rome (*a.* 2 Aug.)
Letter of pope-elect (John IV) to Tómméne, bp of Armagh, and other northern Irish church leaders, urging conformity to Roman Easter (2 Aug. × 25 Oct.)

p. **640**   Ita (d. 652) and Gertrude, widow and daughter of Pepin the Elder, found double monastery on Irish model at Nivelles

640 × 644   St Fursu leaves East Anglia for France: founds Lagny

642/3   Death of Domnall mac Áedo, 'king of Ireland' (late Jan.)
Domnall Brecc, kg of Dál Riatai, killed by Britons of Strathclyde (Dec.)

649   Battle of Carn Conaill (near Gort, Co. Galway): Guaire Aidni, kg of Connacht, defeated by Diarmait mac Áedo Sláine

649/50   Death of St Fursu in France (16 Jan.); buried at Péronne (Peronna Scottorum, Picardy) by founder, Erchinoald, mayor of the palace in Neustria

c. **650**   Penda of Mercia attacks East Anglia; destroys Cnobesburh: St Foillan, brother of St Fursu, flees with community to Péronne
Book of Durrow, earliest of great Hiberno-Saxon illuminated manuscripts

c. **650?-***c.* **685**   Northumbrians extend dominion over north-west England, absorbing British kingdom of Rheged (?including Galloway)

c. **650-750**   High achievement in Irish metal-working; stone sculpture: Ossory group of high crosses
Classical period of Old Irish laws

a. **652**   St Foillan, with patronage of Ita of Nivelles and her brother Grimoald, mayor of the palace in Austrasia, founds Fosses

652   Death of scholar Manchianus (Manchéne, abbot of Min Droichet): last year of 11th 532-year Paschal cycle according to 'Munich computus' (*Ann. Inisf.* 649)
Fínán's church at Lindisfarne built

652/4   Death of St Caimmín of Iniscaltra

655   St Foillan murdered by robbers near Nivelles (31 Oct.)

c. **655**   Composition of 'De mirabilibus sacrae scripturae', Irish exegetical tract

655/7   Death of St Ultán moccu Chonchobair, bp of Ardbraccan and hagiographer (4 Sept.)

656   Death of Sigibert III of Austrasia; Grimoald enthrones his own son as Childebert III; Dagobert II, son of Sigibert, sent to Ire. by Bp Desiderius of Poitiers

656/8-665/6   Joint reign of Diarmait and Blathmac, sons of Áed Sláine, as kgs of Tara

657   Chlothar III succeeds in Neustria and Burgundy ('Fludubuir rex Francorum', *A.U.* 656)

659   Death of St Gertrude, abbess of Nivelles (17 Mar.)

660   Death of Fínán mac Rímedo, bp of Lindisfarne

661   Death of Laidcenn mac Baíth Bannaig, scholar

661/2   Death of Cummíne Foto, abbot of Clonfert (12 Nov.)

663   Death of Guaire Aidni, kg of Connacht

664   Synod of Whitby: Roman Easter accepted in Northumbria; Colmán, bp of Lindisfarne, and his adherents retire to Ire.; found Inishbofin (668); Mayo 'of the Saxons' (?founded by St Garalt (d. 732))
Eclipse of sun (1 May) (*A.U.* 664)
Bubonic plague reaches Ire. (1 Aug.)

664-8   Great plague

665/6   Death of Ailerán Sapiens
Death of St Feichín of Fore (20 Jan.)

c. **668-730**   Gradual transition from tribalism to dynastic polity in Ire.

669-90   Theodore abp of Canterbury

669   Death of Cummíne Find (Commeneus Albus), abbot of Iona, author of 'Liber de virtutibus Columbae'
St Chad app. bp of Mercians

670   Great snow; famine

670-*c.* 690   Armagh seeks to establish its primacy; Muirchú and Tírechán write hagiographical works on St Patrick

c. **670**   Irish monk at Nivelles writes Life of St Gertrude (see 659)

672   Synod of Hertford: Abp Theodore legislates against irregular practices characteristic of Scoto-Irish clerics in England

673   Máel Rubai of Bangor founds monastery of Applecross in Scotland

674   Benedict Biscop founds Wearmouth

675-95   Reign of Fínsnechtae Fledach; composition of 'Baile Chuind', earliest regnal list of kings of Tara

676 Wilfred, bp of York, secures return of Dagobert, son of Sigibert, from Ire. (see 656): enthroned as Dagobert II of Austrasia (killed 679)
Comet in September and October (*A.U.* 677; *Ann. Camb.* 676; Bede, Aug. 678)

678 × 683 Composition of law-text, 'Cáin Fuithirbe', by poet Aimirgein mac Amalgado of the Déisi Muman

678/9 Death of Cenn Fáelad, scholar

679-704 St Adomnán abbot of Iona

c. **680** Bp Áed of Sletty (Co. Laois) recognises primacy of Armagh

c. **680 × 691** Antiphonary of Bangor written

681/2 Benedict Biscop founds Jarrow

682 British invaders defeat Irish Cruthin of Dál nAraidi at Ráith Mór Maige Line (Rathmore, east of Antrim)
British prince Merfyn killed in Isle of Man

683 Recurrence of plague (*mortalitas puerorum*) (Oct.); continues till 685

684 Northumbrian invasion of Brega (June) (*A.U.* 685)

685 Battle of Nechtansmere (Dunnichen, near Forfar): Brude, son of Bile, kg of the Picts, defeats and kills Ecgfrith, kg of Northumbria (Sat., 20 May) (*A.U.* 686)
Great wind; earthquake in Isle of Man (*Ann. Camb.* 684)

685/6 First visit of Adomnán to Aldfrith, kg of Northumbria

686 Death of Banbán, scholar of Kildare

686/7 Adomnán's embassy to Aldfrith: ransoms Irish captives (see above, 684); Adomnán dedicates his 'De locis sanctis' to Aldfrith

687 Battle of Tertry: Pepin of Austrasia mayor of the palace of all Francia

688 Partial eclipse of sun (3 July) (*A.U.* 689)

689 Martyrdom of St Kilian at Würzburg (8 July)

691 Great storm: 16 monks of Iona drowned (16 Sept.)

c. **692 × 697** Adomnán's 'Vita Columbae'

696 Death of St Mo Ling of St Mullin's (17 June)

696/7 Adomnán visits Ire.: synod of Birr; promulgation of Law of Adomnán (Cáin Adomnáin), protecting non-belligerents; general acceptance of Roman Easter in Ire.
Britons and Ulaid devastate Mag Muirthemne (north Co. Louth)

c. **698** Echternach Gospels written and illuminated for monastery founded by St Willibrord

698-700 Three years of famine and pestilence; cannibalism rumoured

698 Battle of Telach Garraisc in Fernmag (Co. Monaghan), due to dynastic strife in Airgialla; Conchobar Machae, kg of Airthir, and Áed Airdd, kg of Dál nAraidi, killed

699 Cattle plague in England

700 Cattle plague reported in Ire. at Mag Trego in Tethbae (1 Feb.)

c. **700-750** Moylough belt shrine; Tara brooch; Ardagh chalice

c. **700-*c.* 900** Classical Old Irish linguistic period

702 Írgalach ua Conaing, kg of Brega, killed at Ireland's Eye by British raiders

703 Ulaid defeat British raiders in Ards peninsula
Bede, in 'De temporibus', places Incarnation in Anno Mundi 3952 (see A:D. 1)

704 Loingsech mac Óengusso, 'king of Ireland', killed invading Connacht (Sat., 12 July) (*A.U.* 703)
Death of St Adomnán (23 Sept.)

706 Death of Cellán, abbot of Péronne (Picardy)

707 Two earthquakes in north of Ire. (Dec.)

709 Cellach Cualann, kg of Leinster, defeated, together with British mercenaries, by Uí Chennselaig
Plague, called *baccach* (poliomyelitis?) with dysentery
Death of Aldhelm, abbot of Malmesbury (and bp of Sherborne since 705)

c. **710** Nechtan, kg of Picts, accepts Roman Easter

710 Ine, kg of Wessex, defeats Geraint, kg of Dumnonia; English conquest of Devon

710 × 725 Compilation of Irish canon law ('Collectio Hibernensis') by Cú Chuimne of Iona and Rubin mac Connad of Dairinis (Molana Island, near Youghal)

710-22 Reign of High-king Fergal mac Máele Dúin: Cenél nEógain become dominant sept in North

711 Moslem conquest of Visigothic Spain
Britons defeated by Dál Riatai at Loch Arklet near Loch Lomond

713 Dorbbéne, scribe of Schaffhausen MS of Adomnán's 'Vita Columbae', dies after occupying abbatial chair of Iona for 5 months (Sat., 28 Oct.)

715 Death of Pepin of Heristal, mayor of the palace in Austrasia (*Ann. Camb.* 714)
Death of Cellach Cualann, kg of Leinster: Uí Dúnlainge und Uí Chennselaig contest Leinster kingship

716 Iona accepts Roman Easter

717 Nechtan expels Columban communities from Pictland
Óenach Tailten (Fair of Teltown) disturbed by Fogartach mac Néill, kg of Brega

719-41 Charles Martel mayor of the palace of Francia

720 Tidal wave (Oct.)
Othmar founds monastery of St Gallen, Switzerland

721 Earthquake (Oct.)
Cleric Inmesach attempts to establish law of 'Peace of Christ' throughout Ire.
Cathal mac Finguine, kg of Cashel, challenges Uí Néill; devastates Brega in alliance with Murchad mac Brain, kg of Leinster
Writing and illumination of Book of Lindisfarne by Eadfrith left unfinished by his death

722 Battle of Almu (Allen, Co. Kildare): High-king Fergal mac Máele Dúin killed by Laigin (Fri., 11 Dec.)

723 St Boniface consecrated bp for German mission

725 Bede in 'De temporum ratione' initiates use of Incarnation era (see A.D. 1, 703)

727 Relics of St Adomnán brought to Ire.: renewal of Law of Adomnán

729 Death of Ecgberht of Iona (Easter Sunday, 24 Apr.)

730 Earthquake (Wed., 8 Feb.)
Relics of Adomnán returned to Iona (Oct.)

730-c. 750 Consolidation of major provincial dynasties throughout Ire.

731 Bede's 'Historia ecclesiastica gentis Anglorum'

732 Charles Martel defeats Moslems at Tours

733 Cathal mac Finguine invades midlands as far as Tailtiu (Teltown, Co. Meath)
Eclipse of moon (22 Jan.)

734 Armagh relics of SS Peter, Paul, and Patrick on circuit to establish primacy of Armagh (Lex Patricii, Cáin Phátraic)
Flaithbertach mac Loingsig, last high-king from Cenél Conaill, aided by fleet from Dál Riatai, defeated and deposed by Áed Allán mac Fergaile of Cenél nEógain

734-41 Óengus mac Forgusso, kg of Picts, reduces Dál Riatai

734-43 Reign of High-king Áed Allán mac Fergaile

735 Battle of Fochairt (Faughart, Co. Louth): High-king Áed Allán defeats Ulaid
Battle of Belach Éile (unidentified pass in northern Éile: bar. Ballybritt and Clonlisk, Co. Offaly): Cathal mac Finguine defeated by Laigin
Death of St Bede the Venerable (26 May)

736 Death of Colmán mac Murchon, abbot of Mag mBili (Moville, Co. Down),
     author of Latin hymn to St Michael

737 Áed Allán and Cathal mac Finguine meet at Terryglass; primacy of Armagh
     recognised throughout Ire. (Lex Patricii)

738 Battle of Uchbad (Ballyshannon, Co. Kildare): Áed Allán defeats Laigin;
     Áed mac Colggen, kg of Leinster, and many sub-kgs killed (Tu., 19 Aug.)

739 Death of St Samthann of Cluain Brónaig (Clonbroney, Co. Longford) (19
     Dec.)
     Death of Cuanu ua Béssáin, scribe of Trevet (Co. Meath)

739-1042 Uí Dúnlainge monopolise kingship of Leinster

740 Earthquake in Islay (12 Apr.)

c. 740 Compilation of 'Senchas Már', Irish legal corpus
     Ending of Iona chronicle: compilation of annals continued in Ire.
     Earliest genealogical corpus for whole of Ire. compiled

742 Death of Cathal mac Finguine, kg of Cashel

742-3 Outbreak of bolgach (smallpox)

742-5 Councils for reform of Frankish church

742-8 St Boniface clashes with St Vergilius and other Irish missionaries in
     Germany

743 Battle of Seredmag (near Kells, Co. Meath): Áed Allán killed by Domnall
     Midi of Clann Cholmáin

743-63 Reign of High-king Domnall Midi; beginning of alternate succession of
     Cenél nEógain and Clann Cholmáin to high-kingship (until 1002)

744 Forggus mac Cellaig, kg of Connacht, proclaims Laws of Cíarán of Clon-
     macnoise and Brendan of Clonfert

746 Death of Óengus mac Tipraiti, abbot of Cluain Fota Báetáin (Clonfad, Co.
     Westmeath), author of Latin hymn to St Martin

747 Death of Cú Chuimne of Iona, canon lawyer and author of Latin hymn to
     Virgin Mary (see 710 × 725)
     Death of Rumann mac Colmáin, poet
     St Chrodegang of Metz initiates reforms among canons regular in Frankish
     church

748 Law of Uí Suanaig of Rahan proclaimed in Leth Cuinn

c. 750-800 St Gall Gospels and Book of Kells illuminated

750-c. 850 Flowering of Old Irish literature: sagas and lyric poetry

750 Death of Congus, bp of Armagh: succ. as comarbae Pátraic (heir of Patrick)
     by Abbot Céle Petair (d. 758); abbatial rule displaces episcopal jurisdiction in
     Armagh until 1105

750–89 Fiachnae mac Áedo Róin, kg of Ulster, restores fortunes of Dál Fiatach dynasty

c. **750–75** Composition of Irish World Chronicle at Bangor

751 Pepin anointed kg of the Franks

752–67 Slébéne abbot of Iona: visits Ripon in Northumbria to ascertain date of Anglo-Saxon invasion of Britain

753 Eclipse of sun (9 Jan.) (*A.U.* 753)
High-king Domnall Midi proclaims Law of Colum Cille

754 St Boniface martyred in Frisia
Slébéne, abbot of Iona, visits Ire.

c. **754** Death of St Pirmin, founder of Reichenau

757 Battle of Cenn Febrat (south-east Limerick) between Munstermen: Bodbgal, abbot of Mungret, killed
Slébéne proclaims Law of Colum Cille

757–96 Offa kg of Mercia

759 Airechtach, priest of Armagh, unsuccessfully opposes succession to abbacy of Fer dá Chrích, son of Bp Suibne (d. 730); battle of Emain Machae: Fiachnae mac Áedo Róin, kg of Ulster, kills Dúngal, kg of Brega, and Donn Bó (prince of Airgialla and brother of poet Blathmac mac Con Brettan)

760 Great snow (2 Feb.)
Battle between monasteries of Clonmacnoise and Birr
Monastery of St Gallen (see 729) adopts Benedictine rule

761 Death of Óengus mac Forgusso, kg of Picts

762 Great snow and eclipse of moon

763 Death of high-king Domnall Midi mac Murchado (20 Nov.)

763–70 Reign of High-king Niall Frossach

764 Great snow for nearly 3 months
Battle between monasteries of Clonmacnoise and Durrow
Eclipse of sun (4 June) (*A.U.* 763)
Great drought and dysentery

765 Slébéne visits Ire. again (see 754)
Death of former high-king, Flaithbertach mac Loingsig (deposed 734), in religious retirement

767 Death of Slébéne of Iona
Law of Patrick proclaimed

768–814 Charlemagne kg of the Franks

768 Welsh church adopts Roman Easter at instance of Elfoddw (Elbodug), bp of Gwynedd (d. 809) *c.* **770**-*c.* **840**   Céle Dé (Culdee) reform movement within Irish church

770   Higĥ-king Niall Frossach goes into religious retirement
Dynastic strife in Leinster: new high-king (Donnchad Midi) invades; defeated
at Sciath Nechtain (near Castledermot) but camps at Ailenn (Knockaulin)
and devastates Leinster
Ciannachta Breg defeat Uí Théig at Áth Cliath (Dublin), but are drowned by
high tide while recrossing River Liffey

770-97   Reign of High-king Donnchad Midi

772   Thunderstorms at Óenach Tailten (1 Aug. and 29 Sept.) cause widespread
panic
Law of Commán and Áedán of Roscommon proclaimed throughout Connacht

772-86   Period of recurrent famine and plague

773   Bloody flux
Drought and famine followed by abundant acorn crop
Eclipse of moon (Dec.)

774   High-king Donnchad Midi disturbs Óenach Tailten
Bloody flux

775   High-king devastates Munster border
High-king clashes with community of Clonard
Flaithrí mac Domnaill, kg of Connacht, defeats Uí Maini; Law of Ciarán pro-
claimed in Connacht

776   Durrow supplies troops in high-king's invasion of Munster
Dynastic strife in Dál nAraidi; Uí Thuirtri of Airgialla begin to infiltrate east
of Bann
Translation of relics of St Erc of Slane and St Finnian of Clonard
Outbreak of rabies

777   Disturbance at Óenach Tailten: Donnchad Midi, high-king, defeats
Ciannachta
Bad summer: wind and rain
Bloody flux and other epidemics
Cattle murrain

778   High-king and Bressal, abbot of Iona, proclaim Law of Colum Cille
Death of Niall Frossach at Iona (see 770)
Bloody flux and cattle murrain
Battle of Roncesvalles: Roland, Carolingian prefect of Breton march, killed by
Basques

779   Death of Móenán mac Cormaic, abbot of Péronne
Cattle murrain continues; famine and disease
Smallpox
Great wind (Oct.)

c. **780**   St Benedict founds monastery of Aniane
Uí Briúin establish dynasty in Bréifne (Co. Leitrim)

780 Great snow (Apr.)
High-king defeats Laigin at Kilcock; devastates churches in Leinster
Synod of Tara: Dublittir, abbot of Finglas, presides at meeting of Uí Néill
and Laigin
Law of Commán and Áedán renewed

781 Disturbances at Armagh on Quinquagesima Sunday (25 Feb.): Condálach
mac Ailello killed

782 Alcuin of York joins court of Charlemagne

782-815 Tipraite mac Taidg (d. 786), kg of Connacht, and Muirgius mac
Tommaltaig (786-815), establish Uí Briúin hegemony in Connacht

783 Battle among Uí Chennselaig for control of Ferns
Tipraite mac Taidg and Dub dá Leithe I mac Sínaig, abbot of Armagh, pro-
claim Law of Patrick at Cruachu
Death of Dub dá Thuath mac Stéléni, poet
Great thunderstorm (2 Aug.); Clonbroney monastery destroyed by wind
Scamach (influenzal pneumonia)

784 Law of Ailbe of Emly proclaimed in Munster
Death of St Vergilius of Salzburg
Abortive summit meeting between high-king and Fiachnae mac Áedo Róin, kg
of Ulster, at Inis na Ríg (island off Skerries, Co. Dublin) off coast of Brega
Relics of 'son of Erc' (?St Erc of Slane) brought to Tailtiu (Teltown, Co.
Meath)

785 Great storm (Jan.); Dairinis (Molana island, near Youghal) flooded
Scamach (see 783)

787 Dub dá Bairenn, abbot of Clonard, makes visitation of his Munster *paruchia*
Tassilo III, duke of Bavaria since 740, deposed by Charlemagne; Bavaria
incorporated into Empire

788 Disturbance at Armagh: man killed in doorway of stone oratory ('in hostio
oratorii lapidei'—first annalistic reference to church of stone)[1]
Law of Ciarán proclaimed in Connacht

790 Death of Siadal, abbot of Dublin

791 High-king Donnchad Midi drives Áed 'Ingor' mac Néill, kg of Ailech,
from Tailtiu to Carn Maic Caírthinn (unidentified), killing Cathal mac
Echdach, kg of Uí Chremthainn, and other Airgialla princes

792 Death of St Máel Ruain of Tallaght

793 Death of Dub dá Leithe I, abbot of Armagh; disputed succession till 807
Vikings raid Lindisfarne
Muirgius mac Tommaltaig and Aildobur, abbot of Roscommon, proclaim Law
of Commán in Connacht
Law of Ailbe proclaimed in Munster; Artrí mac Cathail 'ordained' kg of Cashel

[1] The church itself, of course, could have been standing for many years. The church of Duleek, Co.
Meath (Damliacc Cianáin 'the stone house of Cianán') is so called from its foundation (see 489/91), and
is specifically mentioned as a stone church by Tírechán (see 670-*c.* 690).

794 Vikings raid islands off British coast
High-king aids Laigin against Munster

795 First viking raids on Ire.

795-837 Period of isolated viking raids on Irish coast: many monasteries sacked

796 Death of Dublittir of Finglas (15 May)
Death of Offa, kg of Mercia (July)

797-819 Reign of High-king Áed 'Ingor' Oirdnide

799 Thunderstorm on 29 Sept. causes panic
Gormgal, abbot of Armagh, proclaims Law of Patrick in Connacht

c. **800** 'Félire Óengusso', martyrology in Old Irish verse, by Óengus mac
Óengobann 'the Culdee'
Stowe Missal written

800 Charlemagne crowned emperor of the west by Pope Leo III (25 Dec.)

801 Relics of St Rónán of Dromiskin enshrined in silver and gold

802 Iona raided by vikings

804 Death of Alcuin
Great storm (17 Mar.); coast of Co. Clare eroded; Mutton Island divided into
three, with reputed loss of 1,010 lives
Assembly of Dún Cuair (Rathcore, Co. Meath): Áed Oirdnide prepares to
invade Leinster; clergy freed from military hostings at instance of Fothad
na Canóine of Fahan Mura

804-5 High-king reduces Leinster

806 Fínsnechtae Cetharderc, deposed kg of Leinster, regains kingdom
Iona raided by vikings: chief relics removed to Kells
High-king proclaims Law of Patrick
Plague

807 Columban church at Kells built on site donated by Armagh
Battle between monasteries of Cork and Clonfert
Death of Élarius, anchorite and scribe of Loch Cré

807-8 Ferdomnach writes Book of Armagh

807-13 Vikings raid western seaboard

808 Death of Torbach, scribe, *fer léigind*, and abbot of Armagh
Death of Fínsnechtae Cetharderc at Kildare: dynastic strife in Leinster; high-
king invades (808 and 809)

810 Promulgation of law against maiming cattle by Dáire and by Aduar mac
Echín in Munster

811 Ulaid defeat vikings
Community of Tallaght impose boycott on celebration of Óenach Tailten
against high-king
Visitation of Connacht by Nuadu, abbot of Armagh, with Law of Patrick

812   Law of Dáire proclaimed in Connacht

813   Law of Dáire proclaimed among the Uí Néill
Council of Chalon legislates against Irish *episcopi vagantes*

814   Death of Charlemagne (28 Jan.) (*A.U.* 813)
Church at Kells completed

814-40   Louis I the Pious emperor of the west

815   Egbert, kg of Wessex, conquers Cornwall

815×831   Clemens Scottus teaches at palace school of Louis the Pious

816   Council of Chelsea legislates against wandering Irish clerics
Death of Cynan, son of Rhodrí, kg of the Britons (Welsh)

816-37   Gosbert, abbot of St Gallen, begins collection of manuscripts for library

817   Louis the Pious and St Benedict of Aniane enforce Rule of St Benedict of
Nursia for Frankish monasteries and that of St Chrodegang for canons
Battle between monasteries of Taghmon and Ferns
Columban community solemnly curse high-king at Tara, for death of Máel
Dúin, abbot of Raphoe

818   High-king attempts partition of Leinster
Diarmait, abbot of Iona, goes to Scotland with shrine of Colum Cille
Artrí mac Conchobair, bp of Armagh, with shrine of Patrick, on visitation in
Connacht
Cuanu, abbot of Louth, takes shrine of St Mochtae to Lismore, in flight from
high-king

819   High-king ravages Leinster as far as Glendalough; dies at Áth dá Ferta in
Mag Conaille (Co. Louth)
Disturbance at Armagh prevents celebration of Pentecost; son of Eochaid mac
Fiachnai (kg of Ulster, 790-810) killed

819-33   Reign of High-king Conchobar mac Donnchado

820   Fedelmid mac Crimthainn becomes kg of Cashel
Death of Constantín, son of Fergus, kg of Fortriu (Constantine, kg of Picts
and Scots: founder of Dunkeld)

821   Death of Cenwulf, kg of Mercia

822   Death of St Benedict of Aniane
Death of Mac Riagoil ua Magléni, bp and abbot of Birr, scribe of Book of Mac
Regol

823   Fedelmid mac Crimthainn and Artrí mac Conchobair promulgate Law of
Patrick in Munster
Bangor raided by vikings: bps and scholars killed; shrine of St Comgall
destroyed

824   Monastic community of Kildare attack Tallaght
Bangor raided again by vikings; Skellig raided by vikings: hermit Étgal captured and dies

825 Ulaid defeat vikings
Vikings defeat Osraige
Death of Colmán mac Ailello, abbot of Slane 'and of other churches in France and Ireland'
Death of Cuanu of Louth, scholar and bp
Death of Diarmait, grandson of Áed Rón (kg of Ulster, 708–35), anchorite and scholar, founder of Castledermot
Dícuil's geography, 'De mensura orbis terrarum', written at Frankish court
Dúngal teaches at Pavia
Plague and famine
Artrí mac Conchobair proclaims Law of Patrick in Connacht

826 Law of Dáire renewed in Connacht
Fedelmid mac Crimthainn raids Clonmacnoise

826–35 Struggle over abbacy in Armagh between Bp Artrí mac Conchobair, supported by Cummascach, kg of Airgialla, and Eógan Mainistrech, abbot of Clonard, supported by Niall Caille, kg of Cenél nEógain

827 Battle of Leth Caim (in Kilmore, east of Armagh city): Niall Caille defeats Uí Chremthainn and Muiredach mac Echdach, kg of Ulster; Cenél nEógain establish dominion over Airgialla
Disturbance at Óenach Tailten: High-king Conchobar slaughters Gailenga
Meeting between High-king Conchobar and Fedelmid mac Crimthainn at Birr

828 Monastic community of Cork attack Múscraige

829 Diarmait, abbot of Iona, goes to Scotland with shrine of Colum Cille

831 Diarmait returns to Ire. with shrine of Colum Cille
Battle of Carlingford Lough: vikings defeat monastic force from Armagh

832 Armagh raided by vikings
Fedelmid mac Crimthainn raids Clonmacnoise

833–46 Reign of High-king Niall Caille

833 Niall Caille and Northern Uí Néill defeat vikings at Derry
Fedelmid mac Crimthainn sacks Clonmacnoise and Durrow

834 Beginning of continuous viking attacks on Frankish empire
Death of Óengus, son of Fergus, kg of Fortriu (Angus, kg of Picts and Scots)

835 High-king 'ordains' Bran mac Fáeláin kg over Leinster

835–52 Diarmait ua Tigernáin and Forindán mac Muirgile contest abbacy of Armagh

836 Diarmait of Armagh on visitation of Connacht with Law of Patrick and insignia of office
Fedelmid mac Crimthainn takes abbacy of Cork; raids Kildare and captures Forindán of Armagh
Viking base at Arklow: Kildare raided

837–76 Intense viking activity in Ire.: semi-permanent bases established

837   Large viking fleets on Boyne and Liffey: vikings ravage all Ire.

837-45   Widespread viking raids over whole country

838   Meeting between high-king and Fedelmid mac Crimthainn at Cluain Conaire (Cloncurry, Co. Kildare)
Vikings defeat Connachta in battle

839   Treaty between Rus and Byzantine empire
Viking fleet on Lough Neagh
Vikings defeat men of Fortriu in Pictland

840   Death of Louis I the Pious (20 June) (*A.U.* 840)
Death of Einhard, biographer of Charlemagne
Death of Orthanach ua Cáelláma Cuirrig, bp of Kildare and historian
Fedelmid mac Crimthainn claims high-kingship at Tara
Vikings raid Armagh

841   High-king repels Fedelmid's invasion of Leinster
Permanent Norse encampments at Linn Duachaill (Annagassan, Co. Louth) and Dublin: extensive raids inland
Death of Máel Díthruib of Terryglass

841-72   Grimald, abbot of St Gallen, develops monastic library; persuades Irish bp Marcus and his nephew Móengal, returning from pilgrimage to Rome, to remain (*a.* 853)

842   Law of Patrick proclaimed in Munster by Forindán and by Diarmait, rival abbots of Armagh
Clonmacnoise raided by vikings from Annagassan; Birr and Seirkieran raided from Dublin
Viking fleets on Boyne and at Ards peninsula in Ulster

843   Treaty of Verdun: division of Frankish empire
Death of Donnacán mac Máele Tuili, scribe and anchorite, in Italy

c. **844**   Union of Picts and Scots under Cináed mac Ailpín of Dál Riatai: formation of kingdom of Alba (Scotland)

844   Death of Merfyn Vrych, kg of Gwynedd (north Wales)
Vikings on Lough Ree raid Clonfert

845-82   Hincmar abp of Rheims

845   Viking leader Turgéis drowned by Máel Sechnaill mac Máele Ruanaid, kg of Mide
Johannes Scottus Eriugena joins royal school at Laon

846-62   Reign of High-king Máel Sechnaill I mac Máele Ruanaid

846   Death of Ferdomnach, scribe of Book of Armagh
Charles the Bald confirms canon of council of Meaux (845) re-establishing hospices for Irish pilgrims

847   Death of Fedelmid mac Crimthainn, scribe, anchorite, and kg of Cashel (18 Aug.)

High-king Máel Sechnaill destroys pirate base of Luigni and Gailenga on Lough Ramor

848 Irish victories over Norse in midlands, Leinster, and Munster: High-king Máel Sechnaill in Mide, Tigernach in Brega, Ólchobar mac Cináeda, abbot of Emly and kg of Cashel, with Laigin at Sciath Nechtain (near Castledermot), Eóganacht Caisil at Dún Máele Tuili
Norse occupy Cork: besieged by Ólchobar, kg of Cashel
Irish embassy to Charles the Bald requests passage for 'king of the Irish' to Rome

848–58 Sedulius Scottus at Liège

849 Máel Sechnaill I plunders Dublin
Struggle for power among Norse: naval expedition by 'king of the Gaill' seeking to establish domination over Irish vikings
Indrechtach, abbot of Iona, comes to Ire. with relics of Colum Cille

c. **849/50** Cináed mac Ailpín, kg of Alba, moves relics of Colum Cille to Dunkeld

850 Cináed mac Conaing, kg of North Brega, allies with Norse against high-king: destroys Lagore and burns wooden church at Trevet with 260 people in it

851 'De praedestinatione', by Johannes Scottus Eriugena, against doctrines of Gottschalk
Dub-Gaill (Danes?) attack Finn-Gaill (Norse?) of Dublin
Máel Sechnaill executes Cináed mac Conaing, kg of North Brega, by drowning
Meeting between Ulaid and Uí Néill at Armagh: Matudán mac Muiredaig, kg of Ulster, recognises Máel Sechnaill as high-king in presence of Abbot Diarmait, Féthgno, bp of Armagh, and Suairlech, abbot of Clonard

852 Norse raid Armagh
War between Dub-Gaill and Finn-Gaill: Dub-Gaill defeated at Carlingford
Deaths of Forindán and Diarmait, rival abbots of Armagh

c. **852** St Fintan, returning from pilgrimage to Rome, joins monastery at Rheinau

853 Olaf (Amlaíb) 'son of king of Laithlind' assumes sovereignty over Norse kingdom of Dublin

853–60 Móengal (Marcellus) active as teacher at St Gallen

854–8 High-king reduces Munster to submission

854 Dub-Gaill raid Anglesey
Indrechtach ua Fínnachta, abbot of Iona, killed in England on his way to Rome (12 Mar.)

855–6 Ethelwulf, kg of Wessex, spends year on pilgrimage in Rome

856 Death of Hrabanus Maurus, abp of Mainz
Horm, leader of Dub-Gaill, killed by Rhodri Mawr, kg of Gwynedd (north Wales)

857–9 Rise of Cerball mac Dúnlainge, kg of Osraige

857-74 Solomon establishes independent kingdom of Brittany

858 Death of Cináed mac Ailpín, kg of Picts and Scots
Death of Ethelwulf (kg of Wessex, 839-55) (13 Jan.)
High-king (Máel Sechnaill) invades Munster and takes hostages

859 Assembly of Ráith Áedo maic Bricc (Rahugh, Co. Westmeath) in presence
of Féthgno, abbot of Armagh, and Suairlech, abbot of Clonard: Máel
Gualae, kg of Cashel, cedes Osraige to Leth Cuinn; Máel Sechnaill I recognised as high-king of all Ire.

c. **860** First Norse discovery of Iceland

861-2 Áed Findliath, kg of Ailech, allies with Dublin Norse against high-king

862 Death of Domnall mac Ailpín, kg of Picts and Scots
Death of Máel Sechnaill I (Fri., 27 Nov.)[1]

862-79 Reign of High-king Áed Findliath

863 Dublin Norse plunder Boyne tumuli of Knowth, Dowth, and Newgrange

865 Total eclipse of sun (1 Jan.); eclipse of moon later in month
Death of Tuathal mac Artgusso, chief bp of Fortriu (southern Pictland) and
abbot of Dunkeld
Death of Cellach mac Ailello, abbot of Kildare and Iona, in Pictland

866 High-king destroys viking encampments in north of Ire.
Dublin Norse ravage Pictland

867 Johannes Scottus's 'De divisione naturae' ('Periphyseon')
Danes under Ivar and Halfdan capture York (1 Nov.)

868 High-king victorious over Brega, Leinster, and Norse at battle of Cell ua
nDaigri (Killineery, near Drogheda)

869 Olaf of Dublin raids Armagh: burns churches; 1,000 killed or captured

870 Mention of high-king's house at Armagh: man killed before its door
Dublin Norse under Olaf and Ivar capture rock of Dumbarton, capital of
Strathclyde Britons
Cenél nEógain and Norse allies take Dunseverick by storm

871-99 Alfred the Great kg of Wessex

872 Ardgal, kg of Strathclyde Britons, killed at instigation of Constantine, son
of Cináed, kg of Alba

873 First failure to hold Óenach Tailten
Death of Ivar, 'king of Norse of all Ireland and Britain', at Dublin

874 Iceland colonised from Norway
Death of Féthgno mac Nechtain, abbot of Armagh (6 Oct.)

---

[1] Or Tu., 30 Nov. 863 (*A.F.M.*, *Chron. Scot.*); *A.U.* gives the date as 'ii Kal. Dec., iii feria' (= Tu.,
30 Nov.), which could be an error for 'v Kal. Dec., vi feria'.

875 Death of Martin, Irish teacher of Greek at Laon
Halfdan attempts to unite kingdoms of Dublin and York; kills Eystein, son of Olaf

876 Second failure to hold Óenach Tailten
Death of Donatus, Irish bp of Fiesole
Death of Constantine I, son of Cináed, kg of Alba

876-916 'Forty years peace': relative respite from viking attacks on Ire.

877 Rhodri Mawr, kg of North Wales, defeated by Danes in Anglesey and flees to Ire.
Halfdan killed by Finn-Gaill in battle at Strangford Lough

878 Great wind, lightning, and 'rain of blood'
Third failure to hold Óenach Tailten
Rhodri Mawr killed by English
Áed, son of Cináed, kg of Alba, killed
Shrine of St Colum Cille brought from Iona to Ire.
Lunar eclipse (Wed., 15 Oct.); solar eclipse (Wed., 29 Oct.)
Death of St Fintan of Rheinau (15 Nov.), after 22 years as *inclusus* (see *c*. 852)

879 Death of Áed Findliath at Dromiskin, Co. Louth
Máel Cobo mac Crunnmáil, abbot of Armagh, and *fer léigind* Mochtae, captured by vikings of Strangford Lough

879-916 Reign of High-king Flann Sinna

880 Péronne destroyed by Norse

885? Battle of Hafrsfjord: Harald Fairhair kg of Norway

885 Eclipse of sun (16 June)

885-7 Northmen besiege Paris

887 Death of Máel Muru of Othan (Fahan Mura, Inishowen, Co. Donegal), historian and poet

c. **888** Danes commence minting coins in England

888 Death of Cerball mac Dúnlainge, kg of Osraige
Óenach Tailten not held

888-907 Alan I the Great kg of Brittany

889 Óenach Tailten not held

c. **891** Compilation of Anglo-Saxon Chronicle begins

892 Great wind destroys forests and lifts wooden churches and houses from foundations (11 Nov.)

893 Asser (Welsh monk of St Davids and bp of Sherborne, d. 909), writes 'De rebus gestis Aelfridi'
Clash between Cenél nEógain and Ulaid during celebration of Pentecost at Armagh: many killed; Aitíth mac Laigni, kg of Ulster, pays compensation to Abbot Máel Brigte; 4 Ulaid hanged

895 Magyars migrate to Hungary

896 Poet Flann mac Lonáin killed at Waterford
Flannacán mac Cellaig, kg of Brega and poet, killed by Norse

899 Death of Alfred the Great, kg of Wessex (26 Oct.)

899-925 Edward the Elder kg of Wessex

900 Magyar raids on western Europe begin
Death of Domnall, son of Constantine, kg of Alba (Donald II)

c. **900** Cathal mac Conchobair, kg of Connacht, submits to High-king Flann
Sinna
English coins begin to circulate in Ire.

900-*c.* 911 Hiberno-Norse infiltration of Cumberland, Lancashire, and Cheshire

900-*c.* 1050 Early Middle Irish linguistic period
Decline of Latin learning; elaboration of Irish native traditions; *dindshenchas*
poetry
Secularisation of monastic schools

901-8 Cormac mac Cuilennáin, kg and bp of Cashel, challenges Uí Néill high-
kingship (author of 'Cormac's glossary')

902 Norse evacuate Dublin

c. **902** Ingimund's invasion of Wirral district (Cheshire)

905 Magyar invasion of Italy noticed in Annals of Innisfallen

907 Rus attack Constantinople
Cormac mac Cuilennáin with fleet on Shannon against midlands and Connacht
(25 Dec.-1 Jan.)

908 Battle of Belach Mugna (in bar. Idrone, Co. Carlow): Flann Sinna defeats
and kills Cormac mac Cuilennáin

909 High-king Flann Sinna and Abbot Colmán mac Ailella build stone oratory
at Clonmacnoise
Death of Cadell, kg of Deheubarth (south Wales), son of Rhodri, kg of Gwynedd
(north Wales)

c. **909 × 916** Flann's cross (Cross of Scriptures) erected at Clonmacnoise

909/10 Foundation of abbey of Cluny

911-25 Reconquest of Danelaw by Edward the Elder

911 Treaty of St Clair-sur-Epte; Rollo, duke of Normandy

911-33 Brittany devastated by vikings of Loire and Normandy: large-scale
exodus of monks and nobles to England and France

912 Eclipse of sun (17 June); rainy year; comet

913 Death of Eadwulf, high reeve of Bamburgh in Northumbria (called 'king
of northern English' by Irish annalists)
Vikings defeat Ulster fleet off English coast

914 Large viking fleet at Waterford

a. **916** High-king Flann Sinna has Book of Durrow enshrined in metal *cumtach*

916 Death of high-king, Flann Sinna mac Máelsechnaill (25 May)
New high-king, Niall Glúndub mac Áeda, revives Óenach Tailten
Death of Anarawd, son of Rhodri, kg of Gwynedd

916-19 Reign of High-king Niall Glúndub

916-37 Renewed viking activity in Ire.

917 High-king marches against Ragnall (Ragnvald), grandson of Ivar; besieges
Waterford (22 Aug.-*c.* 11 Sept.)
Comet
Battle of Cenn Fuait (Glynn, near St Mullins, Co. Wexford); Sitric (Sigtrygg
Gale), grandson of Ivar, prevents Laigin from joining forces with high-king;
Augaire mac Ailella, kg of Leinster, Máel Máedóc mac Diarmata, abbot of
Killeshin, scholar and 'bishop of Leinster' and 600 others killed
Sitric occupies Dublin

918 Death of Aethelflaed, 'Lady of the Mercians', sister of Edward the Elder,
kg of Wessex
Ragnall, grandson of Ivar, with Waterford Norse, defeats Scots on banks of
Tyne

918-21 Ragnall, grandson of Ivar, kg of Waterford, reigns in York

919 Easter falls on 25 Apr.
Battle of Islandbridge (Cell Mo Shámóc) (Wed., 15 Sept.): Sitric, grandson of
Ivar, defeats and kills high-king, Niall Glúndub, Áed mac Eochocáin, kg of
Ulster, Máel Mithig mac Flannacáin, kg of Brega, and Máel Cráebe mac Duib
Sínaig, kg of Airgialla

919-36 Henry I (the Fowler) of Saxony kg of Germany

919-44 Reign of High-king Donnchad Donn

920 High-king, Donnchad Donn, defeats Dublin Norse
Cormac mac Mothla, bp and vice-abbot of Lismore, abbot of Cell Mo Laise
(Kilmolash, Co. Waterford), and kg of Déise Muman, killed by Uí Fothaid
Aiched (of baronies of Iffa and Offa, Co. Tipperary)

920-52 Dublin kings strike coins at York

921 Viking fleets on Lough Foyle and Mulroy Bay (Co. Donegal)
Godfrid, grandson of Ivar, raids Armagh (Sat., 10 Nov.) but spares churches
and hospitals
Eclipse of moon (Tu., 19 Dec.)

921-33 Muirchertach, son of Niall Glúndub, campaigns against Norse in north
of Ire.

921-6/7 Sitric, grandson of Ivar, kg of Dublin, reigns in York

921-7 Godfrid, grandson of Ivar, rules in Dublin

922   Foundation of Norse town of Limerick

922-37   Renewed Norse raids throughout Ire.: semi-permanent Norse settlements on Lough Neagh and Strangford Lough

924   Death of Muiredach mac Domnaill, abbot of Monasterboice (Muiredach's Cross) (27 Nov.)

924-37   Hostilities between Dublin-Waterford and Limerick Norse

925-39   Athelstan kg of England

926   Fleet from Strangford Lough under Halfdan, son of Godfrid, establishes base at Annagassan, Co. Louth (4 Sept.); Halfdan defeated and killed by Muirchertach mac Néill (Th., 28 Dec.); Norse besieged at Áth Cruithne (Greenmount, Co. Louth) until relieved by Godfrid from Dublin
Death of Colmán mac Ailella, abbot of Clonard (888-) and Clonmacnoise (904-), scribe and bp: builder of stone church of Clonmacnoise

927   Death of Máel Brigte mac Tornáin, abbot of Armagh and Iona: donor of Book of Mac Durnan to Kg Athelstan
Death of Sitric 'king of Dub-Gaill and Finn-Gaill'; Godfrid unsuccessfully claims kingdom of York with help of Dublin and Annagassan fleets; returns to Dublin within 6 months
'Dub-Óenach nDonnchada': last regular celebration of Óenach Tailten by High-king Donnchad disturbed by Muirchertach mac Néill

928   Céle Dabaill mac Scannail, bp, scribe, and abbot of Bangor, sets out on pilgrimage to Rome

929   Death of Céle Dabaill in Rome (14 Sept.)
Death of Fergil, abbot of Terryglass, on pilgrimage in Rome

930   *Althing* established in Iceland: Ulfljót appointed *lögsögumadr* (law speaker)

933?   Death of Harald Fairhair, kg of Norway

934   Death of Godfrid, grandson of Ivar; succ. by his son Olaf (Olaf Godfridsson) as kg of Dublin
Death of poetess Uallach, daughter of Muinechán
Eric Bloodaxe, son of Harald Fairhair, kg of Norway, expelled in favour of his brother, Haakon the Good

935   Conchobar mac Domnaill, *rígdamna* of Ailech, buried in royal cemetery at Armagh ('in cimeterio regum')

936   Otto I, the Great, crowned kg at Aachen
Joseph, abbot of Armagh, bp, scribe, anchorite, and scholar dies; succ. by Máel Pátraic mac Máel Tuile, who dies 5 months later

937   Battle of Brunanburh: Athelstan defeats Constantine, kg of Scots, and Olaf, son of Godfrid
Alan II Barbetorte, with help of English fleet, defeats vikings, retakes Nantes, and restores Breton kingdom

938 High-king and Muirchertach mac Néill lay siege to Dublin

939 High-king Donnchad has Book of Armagh enshrined
Death of Athelstan (27 Oct.)

940 Edmund, kg of England, grants Danish Mercia to Olaf, son of Godfrid
St Dunstan abbot of Glastonbury

941 Lakes and rivers frozen
Death of Olaf, son of Godfrid
Muirchertach mac Néill ('of the leather cloaks') campaigns in Munster and captures Cellachán, kg of Cashel, who submits to high-king, Donnchad Donn

942 Hywel Dda becomes kg of all Wales except Gwent and Morgannwg (in south-east)

943 Olaf Cuarán, son of Sitric (Olaf Sigtryggsson), driven out of York; replaced by his cousin Ragnall, son of Godfrid
Muirchertach mac Néill killed by Dublin Norse under Blacair, son of Godfrid, at Ardee (Sun., 26 Feb.)
Death of Áed mac Scannláin, kg of Irluachair (Eóganacht Locha Léin, around Killarney), 'a scholar learned in Latin and Irish'

c. **943** Constantine II, kg of Scotland, abdicates

944 Edmund expels Olaf Cuarán and Ragnall, son of Godfrid, from Northumbria
Cellachán of Cashel defeats Cennétig mac Lorcáin, kg of Dál Cais, in Thomond
Death of Donnchad Donn mac Flainn, kg of Tara
Congalach mac Máel Mithig, kg of Brega, and Bróen mac Máel Mórda, kg of Leinster, plunder Dublin

944-56 Reign of Congalach Cnogba (mac Máel Mithig) of Knowth dynasty of North Brega as high-king (with opposition from Ruaidrí ua Canannáin, kg of Cenél Conaill, until 950)

945 Edmund of England cedes Cumbria to Malcolm I of Scotland in return for assistance on land and sea
Olaf Cuarán takes kingship of Dublin from Blacair, son of Godfrid

946 Edmund, kg of England, killed (26 May); succ. by his brother Edred
Emperor Otto I grants charter to Irish monastery of Waulsort in the Ardennes (19 Sept.), founded by Count Eilbert (Máel Callainn, first abbot)

947 Ruaidrí ua Canannáin defeats Congalach Cnogba and Olaf Cuarán at Slane
Eric Bloodaxe accepted as kg in Northumbria

948 High-king defeats and kills Blacair, son of Godfrid, pretender to Dublin kingship; Colmán mac Máel Pátraic, abbot of Slane, captured and killed
Edred harries Northumbria and burns Ripon: Northumbrians abandon Eric Bloodaxe
Death of Cormacán mac Máel Brigte, 'chief poet and companion of Niall Glúndub'

949 Olaf Cuarán returns to Northumbria in attempt to take kingship of York

949/50 Death of Hywel Dda

950 Ruaidrí ua Canannáin, kg of Cenél Conaill and pretender to high-kingship, campaigns against high-king for 6 months in Mide and Brega; defeats Dublin Norse under Godfrid, son of Sitric, with slaughter of 2,000 but is himself killed (30 Nov.); high-king, Congalach Cnogba, victorious; Dublin Norse burn Cáenechair, *fer léigind* of Slane, in bell-tower (first documentary reference to round towers; see 966)

950-1 High-king Congalach Cnogba campaigns against Dál Cais in Thomond

951 Outbreak of smallpox (*clamthruscad*) and bloody flux among Dublin Norse: death of Godfrid, son of Sitric
High-king, Congalach Cnogba, frees Clonard from royal exactions

952 Death of Custantín, son of Áed, kg of Alba (Constantine II), in religious retirement at St Andrew's
'Gaill defeat Scots, Britons and English in battle' (*A.U.*); Eric Bloodaxe expels Olaf Cuarán from Northumbria

953 Bp Adalbero I of Metz summons St Catroe, 2nd abbot of Waulsort, to rule monastery of St Clement
Death of Dub Innse, bp and scholar of Bangor

954 Compilation of Annales Cambriae and earliest Welsh genealogical collection
Death of Cellachán Caisil, kg of Munster
Máel Coluim, son of Domnall, kg of Alba, killed (Malcolm I)
Eric Bloodaxe expelled from Northumbria and killed; Edred assumes kingship

954-86 Owain, son of Hywel Dda, kg of all Deheubarth (south Wales)

955 Domnall ua Néill, kg of Ailech, brings fleet from mouth of Bann through Lough Neagh and River Blackwater to Lough Erne and Lough Owel: Fergal ua Ruairc, kg of Bréifne, submits
Otto the Great overthrows Magyars on Lechfeld (10 Aug.) and ends their raids into central Europe
Death of Edred, kg of England (23 Nov.): succ. by his nephew Edwy, son of Edmund

956 High-king Congalach mac Máel Mithig ambushed and killed in Leinster by Dublin Norse

956-80 Reign of Domnall (son of Muirchertach) ua Néill

957 Mercia and Northumbria renounce allegiance to Edwy in favour of his brother Edgar

959 Death of Edwy, kg of England (1 Oct.): succ. by his brother Edgar

960-88 St Dunstan abp of Canterbury

961-92 St Oswald bp of Worcester; abp of York, 972-92

962 Death of Illulb (Indulf), kg of Alba
Otto the Great crowned emperor of west (2 Feb.)

963-84 St Ethelwold bp of Winchester

963 High-king, Domnall ua Néill, brings fleet from Blackwater across Sliab
Fuait (Fews mountains, Co. Armagh) to Lough Ennell
Fergal ua Ruairc, kg of Connacht, attacks Munster and ravages Dál Cais
Rise of Dál Cais: Mathgamain mac Cennétig seizes kingship of Cashel

965 Famine
Death of Áed, brother of last high-king Congalach Cnogba, at St Andrews
Dub dá Leithe II mac Cellaig, displaces Muiredach mac Fergussa (d.
966) as abbot of Armagh: Uí Sínaig monopolise abbacy (to 1105)

966 Death of Fergal ua Ruairc, kg of Connacht (956–   )
Death of Cormac ua Cillín, abbot of Clonmacnoise, Roscommon, and Tomgraney (Tuaim Gréine); builder of great church of Tomgraney and its bell-
tower; scholar and bp
Dub, son of Malcolm I, killed by Scots

967 Mathgamain mac Cennétig defeats Norse at battle of Sulchoít (Sologhead,
Co. Tipperary); captures Limerick

c. **970 × 980** St Catroe of Armagh founds monastery at Metz

970 Battle of Cell Móna (Kilmona, near Rahugh, Co. Westmeath): high-king,
Domnall ua Néill, defeated by Domnall mac Congalaig, kg of Brega, and
Olaf Cuarán; Ardgar mac Matudáin, kg of Ulster, killed
Murchad, kg of Ailech, and Domnall ua Néill burn Louth, Dromiskin, Monaster-
boice, and Dunleer, where 350 men and women are burned in refectory

971 High-king, Domnall ua Néill, expelled from Mide by Clann Cholmáin;
returns with northern army and builds fortress in every *tuath* in Mide
Culén, son of Indulf, kg of Scots, killed by Welsh of Cumbria

971 × 975 Edgar cedes Lothian to Cináed II mac Máel Coluim (Kenneth II),
kg of Scots

972 Death of Áed mac Loingsig, last Cruthin kg of Ulster: Dál Fiatach monopolise
kingship

973 Coronation of Edgar, kg of all England, at Bath (Pentecost, 11 May);
receives homage of Welsh, Scottish, and Norse kgs
Dub dá Leithe II, abbot of Armagh, clashes with abbot of Emly on visitation
of Munster; Mathgamain mac Cennétig imposes settlement in favour of
Armagh

975 Death of Cináed ua hArtacáin, 'chief poet of Ireland'
Death of Edgar, son of Edmund, kg of England
Death on pilgrimage of 'Domnall son of Eógan, king of the Welsh' (Dyfnwal,
son of Owain, of Cumbria)
Monastery of St Martin's at Cologne assigned to Irish monks

976 Mathgamain mac Cennétig killed by Máel Muad mac Brain of Uí Echach
Muman
Gilla Coluim ua Cannannáin, kg of Cenél Conaill, campaigns in Uí Failge with
help of Scots

978   Battle of Belach Lechta (in Ballyhoura mountains, north Co. Cork): Brian Bóruma mac Cennétig defeats and kills Máel Muad mac Brain and becomes kg of Munster
Death of St Catroe (see 953)

978–82   St Forannán 3rd abbot of Waulsort: Thierry, bp of Metz, grants house of Hastiens to that monastery

c. **980**   'Peace of God' movement begins in France and Burgundy

980   Máel Sechnaill II mac Domnaill, kg of Mide, defeats Olaf Cuarán, kg of Dublin, and Hebridean Norse, at battle of Tara and succeeds to high-kingship on death of Domnall ua Néill at Armagh
Renewed Danish attacks on England

980–1002; 1014–22   Reign of Máel Sechnaill II mac Domnaill

981   Máel Sechnaill II captures Dublin[1]
Death of Olaf Cuarán at Iona[1]

982   Hostilities between high-king and Brian Bóruma

983   Brian Bóruma obtains submission of Leinster

987   Hugh Capet, *dux Francorum* ('duke of the French'), crowned kg of France (3 July)

988   Death of St Dunstan

988/9   Death at Armagh of Dúnchad Ua Bráein, abbot of Clonmacnoise, scribe, scholar, and anchorite (16/19 Jan.)

989   Máel Sechnaill II captures Dublin again: imposes tax of ounce of gold on every garth in city

990   Airbertach mac Coisse Dobráin, *fer léigind*, captured by vikings at Ros Ailithir (Roscarbery); later ransomed by Brian at Inis Cathaig (Scattery Island)
Death of Airard mac Coisse, chief poet of Ire. (obit falsely given in *A.F.M.* 1023)

990–93   Hostilities between high-king and Brian Bóruma

991–4   Olaf Tryggvason leads viking raids on England

991   Battle of Maldon: Bryhtnoth of Essex killed by vikings
Death of Dublittir ua Bruatair, lector of Leighlin

992   Emperor Otto II grants charter to monastery of St Symphorian at Metz (25 Jan.); rebuilt by St Fíngen, abbot of St Clement's, at request of Bp Adalbero II, for Irish pilgrims

993   Muirecán mac Ciaracáin, acting abbot of Armagh, makes circuit of Tír nEógain and 'ordains' Áed Ua Néill[2] as kg

---

[1] Both these entries are recorded in 980 by *Ann. Tig.* and *Chron. Scot.*, but in 981 by *A.F.M.* 979.
[2] This is the first occurrence of the surname Ó Néill (O'Neill), denoting descent from Niall Glúndub (see 919), as distinct from the sept-name Uí Néill, which denotes all descendants of Niall Noígiallach (see *c.* 445–53).

994 Death of Gerard, bp of Toul, patron of Irish monks (23 Apr.)
Sitric Silkbeard expelled from kingship of Dublin

c. **995** Norse establish mint at Dublin

995 Máel Sechnaill II captures Dublin for third time: seizes ring of Thor and sword of Carlus
'Cináed, son of Máel Coluim, king of Alba' (Kenneth II, son of Malcolm I), killed

995-1000 Olaf Tryggvason kg of Norway

997 Ire. partitioned between Máel Sechnaill II and Brian Bóruma
Battle among the Scots: Constantin, son of Culén, kg of Alba (Constantine III), and others killed
Death of Máel Coluim, son of Domnall, kg of North Britain (Cumbria)

998 Death of Dub dá Leithe II mac Cellaig, *comarba* of Patrick and Colum Cille (June)

999 Máel Sechnaill destroys Lia Ailbe (sacred standing stone of Brega at Clonalvey, Co. Meath)
Battle of Glenn Máma (near Saggart, Co. Dublin): Brian Bóruma defeats Máel Mórda, kg of Leinster, and Sitric Silkbeard (Sigtryggr Silkiskeggi), kg of Dublin (30 Dec.)[1]

1000 Brian Bóruma captures Dublin (Jan.) and burns Wood of Thor: Sitric Silkbeard submits

c. **1000** Conversion of Iceland to Christianity
Gero, abp of Cologne, brings Irish monks to St Pantaleon's

1001 Muirecán mac Ciaracáin (d. 1005) expelled from abbacy of Armagh by Máel Muire mac Eochocáin

1002 Máel Sechnaill II acknowledges Brian Bóruma as high-king

1002-14 Reign of Brian Bóruma mac Cennétig

1002-23 Wulfstan abp of York

1004 Death of Eochaid ua Flannacáin, *airchinnech* of Lis Oíged (guest-house of Armagh) and Cluain Fiachna (Clonfeakle, Co. Tyrone), 'a distinguished professor of poetry and history', brother of Abbot Dub dá Leithe II (d. 998) (obit *s.a.* 1005 in *Ann. Inisf.*)
Battle of Cráeb Tulcha (Crew Hill, Co. Antrim) (Th., 14 Sept.): Áed Ua Néill, kg of Ailech, defeats and kills Eochaid mac Ardgail, kg of Ulster, but is himself killed; great slaughter of Ulster dynasts

1005 'Ulaid abandon their land because of scarcity, and scatter throughout Ireland' (*Ann. Inisf.*)
Brian Bóruma visits Armagh: leaves 20 ounces of gold on altar and confirms primacy of Armagh (entry by his secretary Máel Suthain in Book of Armagh)
Kenneth III, kg of Scots, killed by his successor, Malcolm II
Death of St Fíngen of Metz (see 992), abbot of St Vannes, at Verdun

---

[1] A marginal note in *A.U.* says the battle was fought on Th., 30 Dec., which date is incorrect for 999.

1005-8   Dynastic anarchy in Ulster

1006   Brian Bóruma claims hostages from north: undisputed high-king of Ire.

1007   Óenach Tailten revived by Máel Sechnaill (see 927)
Book of Kells stolen; recovered without its shrine almost 3 months later

1009   Oratory at Armagh roofed with lead

1010   Death of Máel Suthain Ua Cerbaill, kg of Eóganacht Locha Léin and scholar, at Aghadoe

1013   Numerous fortresses constructed by Brian Bóruma
Leinster and Dublin revolt against Brian; Jarl Sigurd of Orkney invited to aid them
Svein (Swegn) Forkbeard, kg of Denmark, conquers England

1014   Battle of Clontarf (23 Apr., Good Friday): Munster forces under Brian Bóruma defeat and kill Máel Mórda, kg of Leinster, and Jarl Sigurd of Orkney, with much slaughter on both sides: Brian killed (buried at Armagh)
Máel Sechnaill II resumes high-kingship

1014-42   Decline of Uí Dúnlainge dynasty in Leinster

1015   Plague and disease among Norse and Leinstermen

1016-35   Canute the Great kg of England and Denmark

1016-63   Niall mac Eochada kg of Ulster

c. **1016**   St Colomann, Irish pilgrim to Jerusalem, martyred at Stockerau near Vienna

1016   Death of Mac Liac, 'chief poet of Ireland'
Death of Airbertach mac Coisse Dobráin of Ros Ailithir, biblical scholar and geographer (see 990)

1018   Battle of Carham: Scots under Malcolm II confirm hold on land between Forth and Tweed: Owain, son of Dyfnwal, killed on Scottish side (last British kg of Cumbria)

1020   Death of Findláech mac Ruaidrí, 'king of Alba' (*mormáer* of Moray)

1022   Niall mac Eochada, kg of Ulster, defeats Dublin Norse in sea battle
Death of Máel Sechnaill II (2 Sept.)
Llywelyn ap Seisyll, kg of Deheubarth (south Wales), defeats and kills Irish pretender Rhain

1022-72   High-kingship in abeyance
Age of scholarly activity; synthetic historians; compilation of 'Lebor Gabála'; translations of Latin epics into Irish; devotional literature

1023   Eclipse of sun (10 Jan.)
Eclipse of moon (24 Jan.)
Tadg mac Brian Bóruma killed; Donnchad mac Briain undisputed kg of Munster
Death of Llywelyn ap Seisyll

1024 'Oenreicc, king of the world, dies; Cuanu succeeds to the kingship of the world' (*A.U.* 1023): Emperor Henry II (d. 13 July) succ. by Conrad II

Death of Fachtna while on pilgrimage in Rome, *fer léigind* and priest of Clonmacnoise

Cuán Ua Lothcháin, chief poet of Ire. and historian, murdered by men of Tethba

1025 Cellach Ua Selbaig, abbot of Cork, goes on pilgrimage to Rome

1027 Máel Ruanaid Ua Máel Doraid, kg of Cénel Conaill, goes on pilgrimage to Rome

Death of Donnchad mac Gilla Mo Chonna, abbot of Dunshaughlin, 'the wisest of the Irish', in Cologne

Death of Richard, 'king of the French' (*Ann. Tig.*), i.e. Richard II, duke of Normandy

Canute goes to Rome for coronation of Emperor Conrad II

1028 Sitric Silkbeard, kg of Dublin, and Flannacán, kg of Brega, go on pilgrimage to Rome

c. **1028 × 1036** Christchurch cathedral founded by Sitric and Dúnán, first bp of Dublin

1029 Death of Máel Coluim mac Máel Brigte meic Ruaidrí, 'king of Alba' (*mormáer* of Moray)

1030 Eclipse of sun (31 Aug.)

Flaithbertach Ua Néill, kg of Ailech, goes on pilgrimage to Rome

Death of Tadg in Eich Gil Ua Conchobair, kg of Connacht

Death of Gormlaith, daughter of Murchad mac Finn, mother of Sitric Silkbeard and of Donnchad mac Briain, kg of Munster

1030–72 Conchobar Ua Máel Sechlainn kg of Meath

1033 Donnchad mac Gilla Pátraic, kg of Osraige (Ossory), celebrates Óenach Carmain, claiming kingship of Leinster

1034 Macnia Ua hUchtáin, *fer léigind* of Kells, and 30 companions drowned coming from Scotland with the *culebad* (flabellum) of Colum Cille and 3 relics of St Patrick

Death of Malcolm II: succ. by his grandson Donnchad mac Crínáin (Duncan I), first kg to rule over territory approximating to modern Scotland

Amlaíb (Olaf), son of Sitric Silkbeard, killed in England on route to Rome

1035 Death of Canute, kg of England and Denmark

1036 Death of Cellach Ua Selbaig, abbot of Cork

Death of Flaithbertach Ua Néill

Sitric Silkbeard deposed from kingship of Dublin by Echmarcach, son of Ragnall

1036–61 Niall mac Máel Sechnaill kg of Ailech

1038   Death at Rome of Cairbre ua Coímgelláin, abbot of Aghaboe
Echmarcach deposed from kingship of Dublin by Ivar Haraldsson
'Battle between Cuanu *rí Allsaxan* and Otta *rí Frangcc*, in which 1000 were killed around Otta' (*A.U.*)[1]

1039   'Truce of God' begins to be added to 'Peace of God'
Eclipse of sun (*Ann. Inisf.*)
Death of Iago, kg of Gwynedd; Gruffydd ap Llywelyn becomes kg of Gwynedd and Powys
Death of Donnchad mac Gilla Pátraic, kg of Osraige and Leinster

1040   Donnchad mac Briain promulgates *Cáin Domnaig* (law on Sabbath observance)
Death of Harold I Harefoot, kg of England
Donnchad mac Crínáin (Duncan I), kg of Scotland, killed by Mac Bethad mac Findlaích (Macbeth), *mormáer* of Moray, who succeeds to kingdom

1040–50   Donnchad mac Briain attempts to claim high-kingship

1042   Death of Ailill of Mucknoe, head of Irish community in Cologne
Grandson of Domnall mac Duib dá Boirenn, kg of Uí Echach Muman, goes on pilgrimage to Rome
Death of Sitric Silkbeard

1042–66   Edward the Confessor kg of England

1042–72   Diarmait mac Máel na mBó kg of Leinster; establishes dominance of Uí Chennselaig dynasty

1045   'Famine in France, and Cologne and Rome were laid waste' (*Ann. Tig.*)
Death of Crínán, abbot of Dunkeld (father of late kg, Duncan I), in 'a battle amongst the Scots themselves'

1046   Synods of Sutri and Rome; Emperor Henry III has 3 rival popes deposed; is crowned emperor (25 Dec.) by Clement II
Death of Art Uallach Ua Ruairc, kg of Connacht
Dubliners expel Ivar Haraldsson (d. 1054) and restore Echmarcach to kingship

1046–67   Áed in Gaí Bernaig kg of Connacht: Ua Conchobair family establish dominance in central Connacht and expel Ua Flaithbertaig family of Uí Briúin Seóla into Iar-Chonnacht

1047   'Great famine among Ulaid, so that they left Ulster and went into Leinster' (*A.F.M.*)

1048   Seljuk Turks reach frontier of eastern empire
'The pope and twelve of [his] *áes gráda* [retinue] were poisoned by the previous pope' (*A.U.*; possibly referring to the death of Clement II in 1047, attributed by rumour to Benedict IX)

1049   Irish monk Aaron of Cologne consecrated abp of Cracow (d. 1060)

---

[1] Probably refers to the battle of Bar-le-Duc, 15 Nov. 1037, in which Odo II, count of Champagne, was defeated and killed by Count Gezelo of Upper Lorraine; Odo had been defeated by the emperor Conrad II (Cuanu) in 1034.

1049-54 Leo IX pope

1049-64 Dub dá Leithe III abbot of Armagh; compiler of Book of Dub dá Leithe (*fer léigind* since 1046)

c. **1050** Stowe Missal enshrined by Donnchad mac Briain, 'king of Ireland'

c. **1050-*c.* 1200** Late Middle Irish linguistic period: reworking of traditional sagas; elaboration of pseudo-historical tracts; new recensions of genealogical tracts

1050 Assembly of clergy and laity at Killaloe presided over by Donnchad mac Briain: passes laws to curb disturbances caused by inclement weather and poor harvest
Macbeth, kg of Scotland, goes to Rome on pilgrimage

1051-4 Toirrdelbach (mac Taidg) ua Briain revolts against his uncle Donnchad mac Briain

1051 Fall of Earl Godwin of Wessex: his sons Harold and Leofwine flee to Ire.
Death of kg and queen of Gailenga on return from pilgrimage to Rome
Sacred tree of Mag mAdair (inauguration site of Dál Cais, Co. Clare) thrown down by Áed Ua Conchobair
Pope Leo IX in Regensburg (early Oct.) canonises 'Irish' bp Erhard (d. *a.* 700)

1052 Marianus Scottus I (Máel Brigte) enters monastery of Moville (Co. Down)
Echmarcach deposed from kingship of Dublin; Diarmait mac Máel na mBó asserts his sovereignty
Expedition of Donnchad mac Briain against Dublin and Leinster
Death at Cologne of Bráen mac Máel Mórda, ex-kg of Leinster
Godwin and Harold restored to favour

1054 'A battle between the men of Alba and the Saxons, in which fell 3000 of the Scots and 1500 of the Saxons around Dolfinn mac Finntuir' (*A.U.*): Macbeth defeated by Siward, earl of Northumbria

1054/5 Birth of Gruffydd ap Cynan of Gwynedd in Dublin

1055 Gruffydd ap Llywelyn kg of all Wales
Aelfgar of East Anglia banished to Ire.: aids Gruffydd against Earl Harold with Irish mercenaries

1056 Marianus Scottus I leaves Moville for Cologne
Death of Flann Mainistrech, *fer léigind* of Monasterboice and historian
Death of Áed ua Forréid, bp (since 1032) and *fer léigind* of Armagh

1057 Macbeth, kg of Scotland, killed in battle by Máel Coluim, son of Duncan (15 Aug.)

1058 Marianus Scottus I moves to Fulda
Toirrdelbach ua Briain and Diarmait mac Máel na mBó attack Limerick
Dublin fleet participates in attack on England by Gruffydd ap Llywelyn and Magnus, son of Harald Hardrada, kg of Norway, to restore Aelfgar to earldom of Mercia
Lulach, stepson and successor of Macbeth, killed by Máel Coluim (Malcolm III Canmore)

1059   Donnchad mac Briain submits to Áed Ua Conchobair, kg of Connacht
Marianus Scottus I ordained priest at Würzburg and becomes *inclusus* at Fulda

1060   Conflict in Armagh over abbacy: Cummascach Ua hErodáin (d. 1074)
attempts to oust Dub dá Leithe III

1061-4   Ardgar Mac Lochlainn kg of Ailech

1061   Great diseases in Leinster—'the *bolgach* [smallpox] and the *tregait* [colic]'

c. **1063**   First appearance of Rule of St Augustine for canons

1063   Abdication of Donnchad mac Briain; Toirrdelbach ua Briain kg of
Munster
Colic in Leinster; spreads throughout country
Harold Godwinson subdues Gwynedd
Gruffydd ap Llwelyn killed (5 Aug.) (*A.U.* 1064)
Death of Niall mac Eochada, kg of Ulster (Th., 13 Nov.)

1064   Death of the blind Ua Lonáin, chief poet of Munster
Death of Ardgar Mac Lochlainn, kg of Ailech, at Telach Óc (Tullaghogue, Co.
Tyrone): buried in royal mausoleum at Armagh ('in mausolio regum')
Death of Donnchad mac Briain in Rome
Echmarcach, son of Ragnall, kg of Man and Galloway, goes on pilgrimage to
Rome (d. 1065)
Death of Dub dá Leithe III mac Máel Muire, abbot of Armagh (1 Sept.)

1065-91   Dynastic confusion in Ulster

1066   Irish missionary bp Johannes martyred in Mecklenburg
Battle of Stamford Bridge (25 Sept.): Harald Hardrada, kg of Norway, defeated
and killed by Harold Godwinson
Battle of Hastings (14 Oct.): Harold Godwinson defeated and killed by William,
duke of Normandy

1067   Marianus Scottus II of Donegal (Muiredach mac Robartaig) sets out on
pilgrimage to Rome
Áed in Gaí Bernaig Ua Conchobair killed at Oranmore by Toirrdelbach ua
Briain and Áed Ua Ruairc

1067-87   Áed Ua Ruairc kg of Connacht

1068   Law enacted by Toirrdelbach ua Briain, 'so that neither cow nor horse
was housed at night'
Toirrdelbach ua Briain brings standard of kg of England from Leinster
Sons of Harold Godwinson attack Bristol with Irish fleet

1068-83   Áed mac Néill kg of Ailech

1070   Marianus Scottus II settles at Regensburg
Death of Murchad mac Diarmata meic Máel na mBó, kg of Dublin (21 Nov.)

1070-89   Lanfranc abp of Canterbury

1071 Alp Arslan defeats eastern emperor, Romanus Diogenes, at Manzikert: downfall of Byzantine power in Asia Minor; Seljuks occupy Jerusalem; Robert Guiscard takes Bari, and expels Byzantines from Italy

1072 Diarmait mac Máel na mBó, kg of Leinster, killed at battle of Odba (near Navan), by Conchobar Ua Máel Sechlainn, kg of Mide (7 Feb.)
Normans invade Scotland 'and take the son of the king of Scotland hostage' (*A.U.*)
Gilla Cáemáin mac Gilla Samthainne, poet and historian, *fl.*

1072-86 Toirrdelbach ua Briain high-king with opposition

1073 Conchobar Ua Máel Sechlainn assassinated; decline of Southern Uí Néill

1073-8, 1080-85 Sulien bp of St David's

1073-85 Gregory VII (Hildebrand) pope

1074 Death of Dúnán, first bp of Dublin (6 May); his successor Patricius (Gilla Pátraic) consecrated by Lanfranc; Lanfranc's letters to Toirrdelbach ua Briain and Gofraid, kg of Dublin, urging ecclesiastical reforms
Toirrdelbach ua Briain expels Gofraid (d. 1075) and instals his own son Muirchertach as kg of Dublin (*Ann. Inisf.* 1075), but fails to subdue the North

1075 Church of St Peter at Regensburg granted to Marianus Scottus II and Irish pilgrims
Gregory VII's 'Dictatus papae'
First investiture decree
Gruffydd ap Cynan invades Gwynedd with Dublin fleet

1075/9 Gofraid Méránach (Godred Crovan) conquers Isle of Man

1076/83 Pope Gregory VII writes to Toirrdelbach ua Briain (25 Feb. 1076/ 24 Feb. 1083)

1078 Donn Sléibe mac Eochada, kg of Ulster, offers allegiance to Toirrdelbach ua Briain
Sulien resigns bishopric of St David's in favour of Abraham

1079 Conchobar Ua Conchobair celebrates Óenach Carmain and claims kingship of Leinster
Death of Cellach Ua Ruanada, poet and '*ollam* of Ireland'
'Five Jews came over the sea with gifts to Toirrdelbach ua Briain, and they were sent back again over sea' (*Ann. Inisf.*)

c. **1080-***c.* **1130** General establishment of communes in north Italian cities

1080 Ua Cinn Fáelad, kg of Déise, goes on pilgrimage to Jerusalem
Áed Ua Flaithbertaig, kg of west Connacht, killed by Ruaidrí Ua Conchobair
Sulien resumes bishopric of St David's on death of Abraham

1082 Death of Marianus Scottus I (Máel Brigte) at Mainz
Death of Conchobar Ua hUathgaile, *fer léigind* of Glenn Uissen (Killeshin)

1083 Death of Muirchertach Ua Cairill of Downpatrick, 'doctor of jurisprudence and history'

1083-1121   Domnall Mac Lochlainn kg of Ailech

1084   Death of Niall Ua Sesnáin, 'learned senior of Munster'
Donn Sléibe mac Eochada allies with Donnchad Ua Ruairc; Ua Ruairc killed by
   Toirrdelbach ua Briain at battle of Móin Cruinneóice (near Leixlip)
'Great sickness'
Patricius, bp of Dublin, drowned in Irish Sea (10 Oct.)

1085   Illness of Toirrdelbach ua Briain
'Death of Domnall son of Máel Coluim, king of Alba' (Donald, son of Mal-
   colm III and Ingibjorg)
'Máel Snechtai, son of Lulach, king of Moray' (*mormáer*, son of Lulach, kg
   1057–8)
Bp Sulien of St David's resigns a second time; succ. by Wilfred

1086   Death at Lismore of Máel Ísu Ua Brolcháin, religious poet of Armagh
   (16 Jan.)
Domesday survey in England
Death of Toirrdelbach ua Briain (Tu., 14 July)
Donnchad mac Domnaill Remair, kg of Leinster and Dublin, defeats Brega
   forces near Clonliffe; grants Clonkeen (Co. Dublin) to Christchurch

1086-93   Diarmait, son of Toirrdelbach, disputes kingship of Munster with his
   brother Muirchertach Ua Briain

1087   Death of William the Conqueror (9 Sept.)
Ruaidrí Ua Conchobair becomes kg of Connacht

1087-1100   William II (Rufus) kg of England

1088   Death of Tigernach Ua Bráein, abbot of Clonmacnoise
Death of Marianus Scottus II (Muiredach mac Robartaig) at Regensburg
Muirchertach Ua Briain sends William Rufus timber to roof Westminster Hall
Rhys ap Tewdwr expelled from Deheubarth by sons of Bleddyn of Powys:
   recovers his kingdom with aid of Dublin fleet

1089   Emperor Henry IV takes Irish monks of Weih-Sankt-Peter at Regensburg
   under his protection
Muirchertach Ua Briain invades Connacht; cuts down the Ruadbethech (sacred
   tree at Roveagh, near Clarinbridge, Co. Galway) and camps at Lough Hacket
Death of Lanfranc, abp of Canterbury (24 May) (see vacant until 1093)
Muirchertach Ua Briain kills Donnchad mac Domnaill Remair and seizes
   kingship of Dublin and Leinster

c. **1090-1130**   Flowering of Irish romanesque metalwork

1090   Irish monks of St Jakob at Regensburg request free passage to Poland from
   Kg Vratislav of Bohemia
Muirchertach Ua Briain submits to Domnall Mac Lochlainn; Mac Lochlainn
   fails to maintain high-kingship
Death of Sulien, bp of St David's (31 Dec.)

1091 × 1105   Bell of St Patrick's Testament enshrined at Armagh *a.* **1091**   Gofraid Méránach, kg of Man, takes kingship of Dublin

1091   Death of Máel Ísu mac Amalgada, abbot of Armagh (18 Dec.): immediate succession of his brother Domnall

1092   Ruaidrí Ua Conchobair, kg of Connacht, blinded by Flaithbertach Ua Flaithbertaig
Manuscript of 'Annals of Inisfallen' written: continued by various hands until 14th century
Death of Máel Ísu Ua hÁrrachtáin, abbot of Emly

1093   Diarmait Ua Briain submits and is reconciled to his brother Muirchertach, who instals him (*a.* 1096) as *dux* in Waterford
Domnall Ua Máel Sechlainn, kg of Mide, submits to Muirchertach Ua Briain at Limerick
Ua Briain imprisons Áed Ua Conchobair of Connacht at Limerick and gives Síl Muiredaig (patrimony of O'Connors and related kindreds in Co. Roscommon) to Gilla na Náem Ua hEidin
Áed Ua Conchobair murdered by Ua Flaithbertaig: Ua Briain exacts vengeance and crushes revolt in Connacht
Domnall Mac Lochlainn, kg of Ailech, makes peace with Donnchad mac Duinn Sléibe Ua hEochada, kg of Ulster
Fever
St Anselm, abp of Canterbury, writes to Bp Domnall Ua hÉnna and other Irish bps
Rhys ap Tewdwr, kg of South Wales, and Turcaill (Thorkil) mac Eóla of Dublin killed by Normans (Easter week)
Malcolm III and his son Edward killed near Alnwick while invading Northumberland (13 Nov.); succ. by his brother Donaldbane (Domnall Bán dep. 1094); death of Malcolm's queen St Margaret

1093-1109   St Anselm abp of Canterbury

1093-1114   Muirchertach Ua Briain 'high-king with opposition'

1094   Muirchertach Ua Briain expels Gofraid Méránach from Dublin, imprisons Conchobar Ua Conchobair Failge, and kills Domnall Ua Máel Sechlainn, kg of Mide
Stalemate between Ua Briain and Mac Lochlainn
Donnchad, son of Máel Coluim (Duncan II), killed by Donaldbane, who resumes kingship of Scotland
Muirchertach Ua Briain campaigns in Mide; partitions kingdom between Donnchad and Conchobar Ua Máel Sechlainn
'Great severity of weather throughout Ireland causing dearth' (*A.U.*)
Welsh revolt against Normans

1095   Great snow (3 Jan.)
Muirchertach Ua Briain campaigns in Connacht (21 June to 29 Sept.): expels Síl Muiredaig into Bréifne and gives kingship of Connacht to Domnall Ua Ruairc
Pope Urban II proclaims first crusade at council of Clermont; 'Scotti come in crowds from the land of mist' to join

Great plague

Death of Gofraid Méránach (Godred Crovan), kg of Man and the Isles, in Islay

Birth of St Malachy (Máel Máedóc Ua Morgair)[1]

William Rufus campaigns unsuccessfully in Gwynedd

Death of Eógan, head of Irish community in Rome

Death of Donngus Ua hAingliu, bp of Dublin (22 Nov.)

1095/6   Foundation of see of Waterford

1096   Great plague continues: laws of abstinence and almsgiving promulgated by clergy and princes

Máel Ísu Ua hAinmere consecrated bp of Waterford by St Anselm (27 Dec.); Anselm's first letter to Muirchertach Ua Briain

1097   Round tower of Monasterboice burned and library destroyed

Donaldbane blinded by Edgar, who succeeds to kingdom of Scotland with Anglo-Norman aid

Abp Anselm leaves for Rome without royal licence (Nov.) (absent from England until 23 Sept. 1100)

c. **1097 × 1102**   Bp Samuel of Dublin claims metropolitan jurisdiction in defiance of Canterbury

1098   Foundation of Cîteaux

Death of reforming bp of Munster, Domnall Ua hÉnna

Magnus Barefoot, kg of Norway, secures Norse possession of the Isles by treaty with Edgar, kg of Scots; attacks Anglesey and kills Hugh, earl of Shrewsbury

1099   Battle of Cráeb Tulcha (see 1004): Ulaid defeated by Domnall Mac Lochlainn of Cenél nEógain, kg of the North (Ailech)

Great famine

Death of Rhigyfarch the Wise, son of Bp Sulien, author of 'Vita Davidis' and writer of Ricemarch's Psalter

1100   William II, Rufus, kg of England, killed (2 Aug.)

Domnall Mac Lochlainn ravages Fine Gall (north Co. Dublin)

Muirchertach Ua Briain marches to Assaroe; Dublin fleet destroyed off Inishowen

1100–35   Henry I kg of England

c. **1100**   Gerald of Windsor, castellan of Pembroke, marries Nest, daughter of Rhys ap Tewdwr

1101   Domnall Mac Lochlainn expels Ua Canannáin and instals his own son Niall as kg of Cenél Conaill

First synod of Cashel: Muirchertach Ua Briain grants Cashel to church; Máel Ísu Ua hAinmere bp of Cashel (and papal legate?)

Ua Briain marches through Connacht and the North, and destroys Ailech

Domnall Mac Lochlainn releases Donnchad Ua hEochada, kg of Ulster, from captivity in return for hostages (22 Dec.)

---

[1] Contemporary sources also give the name as 'Ua Mongair'.

1102 Robert de Bellême, earl of Shrewsbury, and his brother Arnulf of Montgomery, earl of Pembroke, revolt against Henry I

Death of Mugrón Ua Morgair, 'archlector of Armagh and of all the west of Europe', father of St Malachy, at Mungret

Muirchertach Ua Briain marries his daughters to Sigurd, kg of Man, son of Magnus Bareleg, kg of Norway, and to Arnulf of Montgomery, who sends Gerald of Windsor as his envoy

Henry crushes revolt of Robert and Arnulf; imposes embargo on trade with Ire.

Death of Domnall Ua Ruairc, kg of Connacht and Bréifne

Abp Anselm writes to Muirchertach Ua Briain urging ecclesiastical reforms; restores good relations between him and Henry I

1103 Abp Anselm leaves for Rome (Easter) (remains abroad until 1107)

Muirchertach Ua Briain marches to Armagh to ally with Ulaid against Domnall Mac Lochlainn (30 July)

Battle of Mag Coba (near Dromore, Co. Down): Muirchertach Ua Briain's Leinster and Dublin forces defeated by Domnall Mac Lochlainn with heavy losses (Wed., 5 Aug.)

Magnus Bareleg, kg of Norway, killed by Ulaid in skirmish on coast of Co. Down (Aug.)

1103 × 1114 Dublittir Ua hUathgaile, *fer léigind* of Killeshin, witnesses Irish charter in 'Book of Durrow' granting Int Ednén (Inan, near Clonard, Co. Meath), to Durrow

1105 Domnall mac Amalgada, abbot of Armagh, falls ill at Dublin on peace mission: dies at Duleek (buried at Armagh, Sat., 12 Aug.); succeeded by his great-nephew, Cellach mac Áeda, who is consecrated bp (23 Sept.)

Edgar, kg of Scotland, sends camel as gift to Muirchertach Ua Briain

Muirchertach Ua Briain banishes Donnchad Ua Máel Sechlainn from kingship of western Mide

Henry I gives custody of Pembroke to Gerald of Windsor

c. **1105** Foundation of Savigny

1106 See of Limerick founded: Gilla Espuic (Gilbert) bp

Cellach of Armagh makes visitation of Cenél nEógain and Munster: acknowledged as abp and primate

Death of Tuathal Ua Cathail, abbot of Glendalough (Pentecost)

'School-book of Glendalough' written

Toirrdelbach Ua Conchobair becomes kg of Connacht: inaugurated at Áth in Termainn (?Athenry)

Máel Muire mac Célechair meic Cuinn na mBocht, scribe of Lebor na hUidre (Book of the Dun Cow), killed in stone church of Clonmacnoise by marauders

Muirchertach Ua Máel Sechlainn deposed in favour of Murchad mac Flainn Ua Máel Sechlainn

c. **1107** Gilla Espuic's correspondence with St Anselm; composes 'De statu ecclesiae'

1107 Death of Edgar, kg of Scotland (7 Jan.)

End of investiture dispute in England; Anselm's return from exile

Many cattle die in severe snow (Wed., 13 Mar.)

1108   Flemish colonisation of Dyfed (Pembroke)

1109   Death of St Anselm, abp of Canterbury (21 Apr.) (see vacant until 1114)
Easter falls on 25 Apr.
Abduction of Nest, wife of Gerald of Windsor, by Owain ap Cadwgan of Powys

1110   David Scottus, head of cathedral school at Würzburg, accompanies
Emperor Henry V's expedition to Italy and writes pro-imperial account

1111   Bp Hartwig of Regensburg consecrates abbey of Irish monks at St Jakob
(St James)
Muirchertach Ua Briain raids Clonmacnoise
Expedition by Ulaid to Telach Óc (Tullaghogue, Co. Tyrone): they cut down
sacred tree of Cenél nEógain
Synod of Ráith Bressail: diocesan organisation of Irish church planned
Synod of Uisnech: Clonmacnoise claims diocese of western Mide
Domnall mac Taidg Ua Briain seizes kingship of the Isles
Muirchertach spends three months in Dublin (29 Sept.–25 Dec.)

1112   Domnall Mac Lochlainn ravages Fine Gall as far as Droichet Dubgaill
(first mention of bridge at Dublin)

1112 × 1114   Pope Paschal II writes to Scots laity and clergy and to Turgot, bp
of St Andrews

1113   Death of Niall ua hÁeducáin, bp of Lismore, for whom Lismore crosier
was made
Domnall Mac Lochlainn deposes Donnchad mac Duinn Sléibe Ua hEochada
and divides Ulster between Eochaid Ua Mathgamna and sons of Donn
Sléibe; Muirchertach marches to Mag Coba; Cellach, abp of Armagh,
arranges truce; Donnchad Ua hEochada blinded by Ua Mathgamna

1114   Henry I campaigns in Wales against Gruffydd ap Cynan: Owain ap
Cadwgan submits
Illness of Muirchertach Ua Briain
Toirrdelbach Ua Conchobair, kg of Connacht, submits to Domnall Mac
Lochlainn, kg of Ailech; they invade Thomond; Ua Conchobair makes
secret peace with Ua Briain
Muirchertach Ua Briain deposed by his brother Diarmait

1114–22   Ralph abp of Canterbury

1115   Bernard elected bp of St David's on nomination of Henry I (18 Sept.)
Death of Turgot, bp of St Andrews, at Durham
Toirrdelbach Ua Conchobair fortifies Buinne in Beithe (Illanavecha on Shannon
in Co. Offaly): partitions Mide; makes gifts to Clonmacnoise
Restoration of Muirchertach
Domnall mac Taidg Ua Briain killed in Connacht
Mide divided between 2 sons of Domnall Ua Máel Sechlainn
Domnall mac Muirchertaig Ua Briain and Dublin Norse kill Donnchad mac
Murchada, kg of Leinster

1115-53 St Bernard first abbot of Clairvaux

1116 Owain ap Cadwgan killed by Gerald of Windsor
Great famine in spring; affects Leinster and Munster
Muirchertach Ua Briain retires to Lismore: Diarmait assumes kingship
'Ladmunn, son of Domnall, grandson of kg of Alba, killed by men of Moray'
(Lodmund, son of Donald, son of Malcolm III)

1117 Death of Diarmait mac Énna Mac Murchada, kg of Leinster, at Dublin
Áed Ua Ruairc, kg of Bréifne, attacks Kells, killing abbot, Máel Brigte mac
Rónáin, and many of community (Fri., 27 July)
Death of Bp Máel Muire Ua Dúnáin at Clonard (24 Dec.)

1118 'A wondrous story is told by pilgrims: an earthquake in the Alps, with
great destruction of towns and people' (*A.U.*; probably occurred 3 Jan. 1118)
Death of Pope Paschal II (21 Jan.)
Death of Matilda, wife of Henry I of England and daughter of Malcolm III
(1 May)
Death of Diarmait Ua Briain at Cork
Toirrdelbach Ua Conchobair invades Munster and partitions it between
Conchobar and Toirrdelbach, sons of Diarmait Ua Briain of Thomond, and
Tadg Mac Carthaig of Desmond; marches to Dublin; expels Domnall, son
of Muirchertach Ua Briain, and obtains submission of Énna Mac Murchada,
kg of Leinster

1118/19 Toirrdelbach Ua Conchobair attacks Killaloe and destroys Kincora
(Dec.-Jan.)

1119 Death of Muirchertach Ua Briain at Killaloe (Thurs., 13 Mar.)
Toirrdelbach Ua Conchobair occupies Killaloe
Niall mac Domnaill Mac Lochlainn (see 1101) killed by Cenél Moén (branch
of Cenél nEógain near Lifford) (Mon., 15 Dec.)

c. **1120×1134** Christianus Mac Carthaig, abbot of St Jakob at Regensburg,
founds Benedictine priory at Cashel

1120 Foundation of Premonstratensian order
Óenach Tailten revived by Toirrdelbach Ua Conchobair
Domnall Mac Lochlainn marches to Athlone; Ua Conchobair buys peace
David Scottus elected bp of Bangor; makes profession to Abp Ralph of Canter-
bury (4 Apr.)

a. **1121** Shrine of St Laichtíne's Arm made for Tadg and Cormac Mac Carthaig
and Máel Sechnaill Ua Cellacháin, kg of Uí Echach Muman

1121 Death of Domnall Mac Lochlainn at Derry (Wed., 9 Feb.)
Toirrdelbach Ua Conchobair in Munster; plunders from Cashel to Tralee;
plunders Lismore; divides Munster between Mac Carthys and O'Briens
(camps at Birr from 1 Nov. to 1 Feb. 1122)
Death of Samuel, bp of Dublin; dispute between Cellach of Armagh and
Gregorius (Gréne), bp-elect, who is consecrated by Ralph, abp of Canterbury

1122-56 Toirrdelbach Ua Conchobair 'high-king with opposition'

1122   Áed Ua Ruairc, kg of Bréifne, killed in raid on Mide

Toirrdelbach Ua Conchobair in Mide: Murchad Ua Máel Sechlainn and Énna Mac Murchada, kg of Leinster, submit; Ua Conchobair campaigns with fleet and land forces throughout Munster

Concordat of Worms (23 Sept.): end of investiture controversy

Discovery of shrine of St Colmán at Lynn (Co. Westmeath): composition of 'Betha Colmáin meic Luacháin'

c. **1122-4**   St Malachy studies with Bp Máel Ísu Ua hAinmere at Lismore

1122 × 1148   Land-grant by Tigernán Ua Ruairc, kg of Bréifne, to Kells guaranteed by Máel Brigte Ua Fairchellaig, abbot of Drumlane, in presence of the Brecc Máedóic (shrine of St Máedóc)

1123   First Lateran Council held by Calixtus II

A fragment of the True Cross comes to Ire., and is enshrined in the Cross of Cong by Toirrdelbach Ua Conchobair at Roscommon

1123-4   Toirrdelbach Ua Conchobair campaigns in Munster; defeats Desmond fleet; encamps at Thomond Bridge (until Easter 1124)

1123-36   William of Corbeil abp of Canterbury

1124   Round tower at Clonmacnoise finished by Gilla Críst Ua Máel Eóin and Toirrdelbach Ua Conchobair

Toirrdelbach Ua Conchobair builds castles at Galway, Collooney, and Ballinasloe (first mention of castles in Ire.)

Death of Tadg Mac Carthaig at Cashel

Death of Alaxandair mac Máel Coluim, kg of Alba (Alexander I)

Foundation of first English Savigniac house at Tulketh in Lancashire (July; moved to Furness, July 1127)

Ua Conchobair defeats revolt of Mide and Bréifne near Granard; kills son of Cormac Mac Carthaig and other hostages of Desmond at Athlone: collapse of Mac Carthaig's campaign in Mide

1124-7   St Malachy bp of Down and Connor and abbot of Bangor

1125   William of Malmesbury's 'Acta regum'

Stone church of Armagh reroofed after 130 years

Toirrdelbach Ua Conchobair marches to Aghaboe and obtains submission of Osraige

Tigernán Ua Ruairc, kg of Bréifne, submits to Ua Conchobair

Ua Conchobair banishes Murchad Ua Máel Sechlainn and divides Mide between Ua Ruairc and 3 Ua Máel Sechlainn princes; gives kingship of Dublin to Énna Mac Murchada, kg of Leinster

1126   King David I of Scotland demands metropolitan status for St Andrew's

Cellach spends 13 months away from Armagh, trying to make peace

Consecration of church of SS Paul and Peter at Armagh (21 Oct.)

Death of Énna Mac Murchada, kg of Leinster

Toirrdelbach Ua Conchobair encamps in Ormond (1 Aug.-1 Feb. 1127): defeats Cormac Mac Carthaig and instals his own son Conchobar as kg of Dublin and Leinster

1127   Death of Gilla Críst Ua hÉicnig, kg of Airgialla and Fir Manach, at Clogher

Toirrdelbach Ua Conchobair invades Munster by land and sea as far as Cork: deposes Cormac Mac Carthaig and divides Munster between Cormac's brother Donnchad and Conchobar Ua Briain; Cormac goes into religious retirement at Lismore

Dynastic strife in Ulster: Conchobar Mac Lochlainn invades and takes hostages

St Malachy retires to Lismore

Toirrdelbach and Conchobar Ua Briain restore Cormac Mac Carthaig to kingship of Desmond

Conchobar Ua Conchobair expelled from Dublin

Toirrdelbach Ua Conchobair invades Munster with fleet of 190 ships: defeats Munster fleet

Gilla Comgaill Ua Tuathail, abbot of Glendalough (grandfather of St Laurence O'Toole), killed by Fortuatha Laigen (subject peoples of Wicklow area)

Cerball Mac Fáeláin, kg of Uí Fáeláin, killed at Kildare by Donnchad Ua Conchobair Failge, while defending abbacy for his daughter

Foundation from Furness of Savigniac house at Erenagh (Co. Down) (8 Sept.) by kg of Ulster (Niall Mac Duinn Sléibe, d. 1127, or Ragnall Ua hEochada, d. 1131)

Toirrdelbach Ua Conchobair grants land at Tuam to clerics of Síl Muiredaig (see 1093)

1127-34   Building of Cormac's chapel at Cashel

1127-1226   Irish romanesque architecture and sculpture flourishes

1127×1138   Cormac Mac Carthaig builds 12 churches at Lismore

1128   Gilla Pátraic, son of Tuathal Ua Cathail, abbot of Glendalough, killed by Uí Muiredaig

Marriage of Empress Matilda and Geoffrey, count of Anjou (Henry II, their son, born 1133)

Tigernán Ua Ruairc, kg of Bréifne, plunders Louth and ambushes Cellach, abp of Armagh, killing some of his retinue

Toirrdelbach Ua Conchobair ravages Leinster from Wexford to Dublin at instigation of Tigernán Ua Ruairc

Tigernán Ua Ruairc defeated by Conchobar Mac Lochlainn at Oldbridge and again by Magnus Mac Lochlainn at Ardee

Conchobar Mac Lochlainn with Airgialla and Ulaid invades Brega and burns Trim

1128/9   Magnus Mac Lochlainn displaces his nephew Conchobar as kg of Ailech but is killed within three months by Cenél Conaill and Ua Gairmledaig of Cenél Moén[1]

Cellach, abp of Armagh, makes peace for year between Connacht and Munster

1129   Ulaid revolt against Conchobar Mac Lochlainn

Death of Cellach of Armagh at Ardpatrick on visitation in Munster (Mon., 1 Apr.): buried at Lismore (4 Apr.); Uí Sínaig instal Muirchertach mac Domnaill as abbot of Armagh (5 Apr.) in opposition to St Malachy

Drought in summer: Toirrdelbach Ua Conchobair builds castle and bridge at Athlone

---

[1] *A.U., Ann. Tig.* 1128; *Ann. Inisf.* 1129; *A.F.M.* 1128 and 1129.

c. **1130**   Compilation of Leinster codex Rawlinson B 502: earliest Irish genealogical manuscript

1130   David I defeats and kills Óengus, son of daughter of Lulach, *mormáer* of Moray: 4,000 killed; compilation of Gaelic *notitiae* in 'Book of Deer'
Toirrdelbach Ua Conchobair's fleets plunder Tory Island (Co. Donegal), Valentia Island (Co. Kerry), and Cork harbour
Conchobar Mac Lochlainn defeats Ulaid: peace made at Armagh
Tigernán Ua Ruairc defeats and kills Diarmait Ua Máel Sechlainn, kg of Mide

1130–43   Innocent II pope (unable to enter Rome until end of schism, 1138)

c. **1130–*c.* 1180**   Rise of European universities: Salerno, Bologna, Paris, Oxford

1131   Toirrdelbach Ua Conchobair's fleet ravages Desmond
Great alliance against Ua Conchobair: Conchobar Ua Briain gains submission of Leinster and invades Mide; defeated by Connnacht forces; Conchobar Mac Lochlainn invades Connacht; defeated at Curlew mountains; Ragnall Ua hEochada, kg of Ulster, defeated and killed near Ardee by Tigernán Ua Ruairc while returning from Connacht expedition

1132   Toirrdelbach Ua Conchobair invades Munster; gives kingdom of Mide to Muirchertach Ua Máel Sechlainn
Foundation of Cistercian abbeys at Rievaulx and Fountains
Diarmait Mac Murchada, kg of Leinster, has abbess of Kildare violated and deposed
Tigernán Ua Ruairc submits to Conchobar Mac Lochlainn at Ardee
Conchobar Ua Briain attacks Athlone in alliance with Murchad Ua Máel Sechlainn and Tigernán Ua Ruairc
Munster fleet under Flaithbertach Ua Flaithbertaig destroys Galway castle
St Malachy consecrated abp of Armagh

1133   Cormac Mac Carthaig invades Connacht and destroys Dún Mugdorn (Doon Castle, near Westport, Co. Mayo) and Dunmore (Co. Galway)
Eclipse of sun
Murchad Ua Máel Sechlainn and Tigernán Ua Ruairc destroy castle and bridge at Athlone
Disease of cattle and pigs

1134   Muiredach Ua Dubthaig, bp of Tuam, and Áed Ua hOissín, abbot, make peace between Connacht and Munster
Consecration of Cormac's chapel at Cashel: Connacht clergy withdraw in displeasure
Diarmait Mac Murchada and Dubliners attack Osraige, Waterford, and Conchobar Ua Briain; Desmond forces ravage Dál Cais
Death of Ímar Ua hÁedacáin of Armagh in Rome
Death of Muirchertach mac Domnaill, abbot of Armagh (17 Sept.): succ. by Niall mac Áeda, last Uí Sínaig abbot, in opposition to St Malachy
St Malachy installed as abp of Armagh against opposition of Cenél nEógain of Tulach Óc (Tullaghogue, near Dungannon)
St Malachy makes visitation of Munster
Olaf, kg of Man, and Ivo, abbot of Furness, found Rushen abbey

1134/9 Christianus Mac Carthaig, abbot of St Jakob at Regensburg, founds Schottenkloster at Würzburg

1135 Death of Máel Ísu Ua hAinmere, bp of Waterford and Lismore
St Malachy purchases the Bachall Ísu (crosier of St Patrick) (7 July)
Death of Henry I, kg of England; succession of Stephen of Blois (22 Dec.)

c. **1135** Geoffrey of Monmouth's 'Historia regum Britanniae'
Dublin mint ceases to operate

c. **1136** Foundation of Schottenkloster of St Jakob at Erfurt

1136 Dynastic strife in Connacht: Toirrdelbach Ua Conchobair imprisons his son Ruaidrí
Toirrdelbach Ua Conchobair falls ill; his castle at Loch Cairrcín (Ardakillen Lough near Roscommon) destroyed by raiding party from Tethba
Conchobar Mac Lochlainn, kg of Ailech, killed by Fir Maige Ítha (branch of Cenél nEógain) (25 May)
St Malachy makes second visitation of Munster; ousted from Armagh by Abbot Niall mac Áeda; resigns archbishopric and retires to bishopric of Down

1137 Niall mac Áeda resigns abbacy of Armagh: Gilla Meic Liac (Gelasius), abbot of Derry, consecrated abp of Armagh
'Colic disease'
Great wind
Connacht devastated in warfare between Toirrdelbach Ua Conchobair and Tigernán Ua Ruairc
Death of Gruffydd ap Cynan, kg of Gwynedd
Conchobar Ua Briain and Diarmait Mac Murchada with 200 ships from Dublin and Wexford lay siege to Waterford; Ua Briain submits to Mac Murchada in return for overlordship of Desmond

1137–70 Reign of Owain Gwynedd, kg of North Wales

1138 Toirrdelbach Ua Conchobair, Tigernán Ua Ruairc, and Donnchad Ua Cerbaill, kg of Airgialla, campaign against Diarmait Mac Murchada and Murchad Ua Máel Sechlainn in Mide
Cormac Mac Carthaig, kg of Desmond, assassinated by Diarmait Súgach, son of Mathgamain Ua Conchobair Ciarraige, at Mag Tamnach (Mahoonagh, Co. Limerick), at instigation of Toirrdelbach Ua Briain
Gospels of Máel Brigte written at Armagh
Death at Cong of Amlaíb Mór Mac Fir Bisig, '*ollam* of all Uí Fiachrach in learning and poetry'

1139 Foundation of Savigniac Abbey of St Mary's at Dublin
Death of Cú Chonnacht Ua Dálaig of Mide, 'chief poet of Ireland'
Second Lateran Council (Apr.); Theobald, abp of Canterbury, present; Innocent II captured by Roger of Sicily (22 July); released shortly afterwards
St Malachy visits Rome to ask Innocent II for 2 pallia; meets St Bernard at Clairvaux
Toirrdelbach Ua Conchobair diverts course of River Suck

1139-45   Civil war in England between Stephen and Matilda

1139-61   Theobald abp of Canterbury

c. **1140×1149**   Christianus Mac Carthaig founds Benedictine house at Roscarbery

1140   St Malachy builds wooden oratory at Bangor
Theobald, abp of Canterbury, consecrates Patricius, bp of Limerick
Christianus Mac Carthaig, abbot of St Jakob at Regensburg, founds Schottenkloster at Nuremberg
Gilla Meic Liac, abp of Armagh, makes visitation of Connacht
Dubliners defeat Waterford Norse
Toirrdelbach Ua Conchobair builds two bridges at Athlone and banishes Murchad Ua Máel Sechlainn into Munster
Death of Niall mac Áeda, ex-abbot of Armagh

1140-4   Building of new choir of St Denis: birth of Gothic architecture in France

1141   Conchobar Ua Briain assumes kingship of Dublin
Diarmait Mac Murchada kills Domnall Mac Fáeláin, king of Uí Fáeláin, and Murchad Ua Tuathail, kg of Uí Muiredaig, and blinds Muirchertach Mac Gilla Mo Cholmóc, kg of Fir Chualann, together with 14 other north Leinster dynasts

c. **1142**   Christianus Mac Carthaig founds Schottenkloster of Jakob. at Constance

1142   Ottar, grandson of Ottar, from Hebrides, takes kingship of Dublin
Foundation of first Irish Cistercian house at Mellifont
Death of Conchobar Ua Briain at Killaloe

1143-8   Gilla Mo Dutu Ua Casaide, poet and historian, *fl.*

1143   Toirrdelbach Ua Briain invades Connacht: cuts down Ruadbethach (see 1089)
Muirchertach Mac Lochlainn deposed from kingship of Cenél nEógain by Domnall Ua Gairmledaig
Toirrdelbach Ua Conchobair banishes Murchad Ua Máel Sechlainn into Munster and imposes his own son, Conchobar, as kg of all Mide

1144   Conchobar Ua Conchobair killed by Ua Dubláich of Fir Tulach as 'stranger in sovereignty' (*rí echtar-cheneóil, A.F.M.*): Toirrdelbach exacts vengeance and divides eastern Mide between Tigernán Ua Ruairc and Diarmait Mac Murchada, and western Mide between Murchad and Donnchad Ua Máel Sechlainn
Toirrdelbach Ua Conchobair releases his son Ruaidrí and other prisoners at request of bps and clergy
Meeting of clergy and laity at Terryglass: peace made between Ua Conchobair and Toirrdelbach Ua Briain

1144/5   Epidemic disease in Connacht and Munster

1145 Gilla Meic Liac, abp of Armagh, builds lime-kiln at Emain Macha
Muirchertach Mac Lochlainn restored to kingship with help of Cenél Conaill
and Donnchad Ua Cerbaill, kg of Airgialla
'Great war this year, so that Ireland was a trembling sod' (*A.F.M.*)

1145-6 Internal dissension in Connacht; widespread but indecisive warfare
between Toirrdelbach Ua Conchobair and forces of Munster and Bréifne

1145-55 Gothic west portal of Chartres cathedral built

1145 × 1151 St Bernard of Clairvaux writes to Diarmait Mac Murchada 'king
of Ireland' admitting him to membership of Cistercian confraternity

1146 Ragnall, son of Turcaill, *mormáer* of Dublin, killed by forces of South
Brega

1147 Muirchertach Mac Lochlainn and Donnchad Ua Cerbaill invade Ulster
and ravage Leth Cathail (Lecale, south Co. Down)
Start of second crusade

1147-8 Savigniac monasteries join Cistercian order

c. **1148** Diarmait Mac Murchada founds Cistercian abbey at Baltinglass

1148 Synod of Inis Pátraic (St Patrick's Isle, off north Dublin coast): St Malachy
given authority to seek pallia from pope
Church of Arroasian canons at Knock near Louth completed by Donnchad Ua
Cerbaill and Bp Áed Ua Cáellaide and consecrated by St Malachy
Muirchertach Mac Lochlainn divides Ulster between 4 sub-kings; deposes
Cú Ulad Mac Duinn Sléibe; Donnchad Ua Cerbaill and Tigernán Ua
Ruairc attempt to restore Cú Ulad; peace made at Armagh between Mac
Lochlainn, Ua Cerbaill, and Ulaid
Ottar, grandson of Ottar, kg of Dublin, killed by sons of Turcaill
Death of St Malachy at Clairvaux on his journey to Pope Eugenius III (2 Nov.)
Irish monk Marcus of Regensburg writes 'Visio Tundali'

1149 Cú Ulad Mac Duinn Sléibe recovers kingdom of Ulster; Muirchertach
Mac Lochlainn invades but recognises Cú Ulad as kg on intercession of
Donnchad Ua Cerbaill
Mac Lochlainn makes royal progress to Louth; Tigernán Ua Ruairc submits
Mac Lochlainn and Ua Cerbaill proceed to Dublin; Diarmait Mac Murchada
submits
Toirrdelbach Ua Briain invades Connacht and destroys fortress of Galway

1150 Cardinal Paparo detained by Kg Stephen on his way to Ire.
Death of Muiredach Ua Dubthaig, bp of Tuam, at Cong (15 May)
Muirchertach Mac Lochlainn marches to Inis Mochta (Inishmot, Co. Meath,
on Louth border); obtains submission of Tigernán Ua Ruairc and Donnchad
Ua Cerbaill; Toirrdelbach Ua Conchobair sends hostages; Mac Lochlainn
divides Mide between Ua Conchobair, Ua Ruairc, and Ua Cerbaill
Toirrdelbach Ua Briain marches north; gains allegiance of Dubliners, who
arrange a year's truce between him and Mac Lochlainn

1151   Battle of Móin Mór (in north Co. Cork): Toirrdelbach Ua Briain, kg of Munster, defeated by Toirrdelbach Ua Conchobair and Diarmait Mac Murchada: 7,000 Munstermen killed

Muirchertach Mac Lochlainn marches to Curlew mountains: obtains hostages of Connacht and Leinster from Ua Conchobair

Abp Gilla Meic Liac makes second visitation of Connacht

Stone church of Cluain Coirpthe (Kilbarry, Co. Roscommon) built by Cú Chaille Ua Scolaige and Gilla in Choimded Ua hAinglide

Cardinal Paparo arrives in Ire.; stays fortnight at Armagh

1152   Cardinal Nicholas Breakspear, papal legate to Norway, brings pallium to Trondheim

Synod of Kells convened (6 Mar.); later transferred to Mellifont: Cardinal Paparo brings four pallia and completes diocesan organisation of Irish church; departs (24 Mar.)

Áed Ua Crimthainn, *fer léigind* of Diarmait Mac Murchada, becomes abbot of Terryglass: commences compilation of 'Book of Leinster' (Lebor na hUath-chongbála) in collaboration with Bp Finn of Kildare

Donnchad Ua Cerbaill attacks and wounds Gilla Meic Liac, abp of Armagh: deposed from kingship of Airgialla by Muirchertach Mac Lochlainn

Mac Lochlainn makes treaty with Toirrdelbach Ua Conchobair

Ua Conchobair divides Munster between Tadg and Toirrdelbach Ua Briain and Diarmait Mac Carthaig

Mac Lochlainn marches to Rathkenny (Co. Meath); joined by Ua Conchobair and Diarmait Mac Murchada; Mide divided between Murchad Ua Máel Sechlainn and his son Máel Sechlainn; Tigernán Ua Ruairc defeated and deposed in favour of Áed mac Gilla Braite Ua Ruairc; Diarmait Mac Muchada abducts Derbforgaill, daughter of Ua Máel Sechlainn and wife of Tigernán Ua Ruairc

Death of Henry, earl of Northumberland and Huntingdon, son of David I of Scotland (12 June)

1152–90   Frederick Barbarossa emperor of Germany

c. **1153**   Death of Christianus Mac Carthaig, abbot of St Jakob at Regensburg, at Cashel

1153   Death of Murchad Ua Máel Sechlainn at Durrow

Lorcán Ua Tuathail (St Laurence O'Toole) becomes abbot of Glendalough

Death of David I, son of Máel Coluim, 'king of Scotland and England' (*Ann. Tig.*) (24 May)

Death of Pope Eugenius III (18 July)

Death of St Bernard of Clairvaux (21 Aug.)

Muirchertach Mac Lochlainn campaigns successfully in Mide against Toirrdelbach and Ruaidrí Ua Conchobair on behalf of Toirrdelbach Ua Briain; grants all Mide together with Uí Failge and Uí Fáeláin to Máel Sechlainn Ua Máel Sechlainn; grants Bréifne and Conmaicne to Tigernán Ua Ruairc

Toirrdelbach Ua Conchobair brings back Derbforgaill from Diarmait Mac Murchada; Tigernán Ua Ruairc submits

Ua Conchobair banishes Toirrdelbach Ua Briain and divides Munster between Tadg Ua Briain and Diarmait Mac Carthaig

Tadg Ua Briain blinded by Diarmait Finn; Toirrdelbach restored to kingship of Thomond by Muirchertach Mac Lochlainn

Máel Sechlainn Ua Máel Sechlainn destroys bridge and fortress of Athlone; Toirrdelbach Ua Conchobair builds bridge at Áth Liac (Ballyleague, near Lanesborough, Co. Roscommon)

1154 Muirchertach Ua Tuathail, kg of Uí Muiredaig, kills Mac Cuirr na Colpthach Ua Fiachrach, kg of Uí Enechglaiss (Arklow district)

Connacht fleet under In Cosnamach Ua Dubda defeats Hebridean fleet under Mac Scelling, hired by Muirchertach Mac Lochlainn, off Inishowen

Mac Lochlainn invades Connacht and Bréifne; marches to Dublin and obtains submission

1154-9 Adrian IV (Nicholas Breakspear) pope

1154-89 Henry II kg of England

c. **1155 × 1161** Foundation of Schottenkloster of St Mary's at Vienna

1155 Rhys ap Gruffydd becomes ruler of part of Deheubarth (South Wales)

Death by poison of Máel Sechlainn Ua Máel Sechlainn, kg of Mide, at Durrow (31 Jan.)

Tigernán Ua Ruairc captures Donnchad Ua Cerbaill at Kells; imprisons him on Lough Sheelin: released after 6 weeks by Gofraid Ua Ragallaig

Cattle plague

Adrian IV crowns Frederick Barbarossa emperor (18 June)

Flaithbertach Ua Brolcháin, abbot of Derry, constructs new doorway for church of Derry

Proposal for invasion of Ire. by Henry II discussed at Council of Winchester but rejected (29 Sept.)

1155-6 John of Salisbury visits Pope Adrian IV at Rome (Nov.–July); obtains papal privilege (bull *Laudabiliter?*) approving projected conquest of Ire. by Henry II

1156 Defeat of Godred, kg of Western Isles and Man, by Somarlaide, kg of Argyll (6 Jan.); kingdom of the Isles divided

Toirrdelbach Ua Conchobair brings fleet to Lough Derg; obtains submission of Toirrdelbach Ua Briain

Death of Toirrdelbach Ua Conchobair, kg of Connacht (20 May); buried at Clonmacnoise

Muirchertach Mac Lochlainn receives submission of Ulaid and Osraige and confirms Diarmait Mac Murchada as kg of Leinster

1156-66 Muirchertach Mac Lochlainn 'high-king with opposition'

1156/7 Great frost, lakes frozen

St Mary's Abbey (O.Cist.), Dublin, affiliated to Buildwas (Shropshire)

1157 Donnchad Ua Máel Sechlainn, kg of Mide, treacherously kills Cú Ulad Ua Caindelbáin, kg of Lóegaire

Muirchertach Mac Lochlainn 'king of all Ireland' grants Latin charter to Cistercian abbey at Newry

Consecration of Mellifont in presence of High-king Muirchertach Mac Loch-lainn, Donnchad Ua Cerbaill, Tigernán Ua Ruairc, papal legate (Gilla Críst Ua Connairche) and abps of Dublin and Tuam: Donnchad Ua Máel Sech-lainn, kg of Mide, excommunicated: replaced as kg by his brother Diarmait

Muirchertach Mac Lochlainn marches to Limerick; destroys Roscrea; divides Munster between Diarmait Mac Carthaig and Conchobar Ua Briain; banishes Toirrdelbach Ua Briain

Henry II campaigns against Owain Gwynedd and receives his submission

Death of Cú Ulad Mac Duinn Sléibe, kg of Ulster

c. **1158 × 1166**   Foundation of Schottenkloster of Heiligenkreuz at Eichstätt

1158   Toirrdelbach Ua Briain blinds Conchobar Ua Briain and his son

Great church of Aghadoe completed by Amlaíb, son of Óengus Ua Donnchada

Synod of Brí mac Taidg (Breemount, near Laracor, Co. Meath): 25 bps assembled under papal legate, Gilla Críst Ua Connairche; Flaithbertach Ua Brolcháin given status of mitred abbot and jurisdiction over all Columban churches; Connacht bps forcibly prevented from attending by Diarmait Ua Máel Sechlainn, kg of Mide

Áed Mac Duinn Sléibe, kg of Ulster, killed on expedition with Muirchertach Mac Lochlainn in Tír Conaill

1159   John of Salisbury's 'Policraticus' and 'Metalogicon'

Battle of Áth na Caisberna (near Ardee, Co. Louth): Muirchertach Mac Loch-lainn defeats Ruaidrí Ua Conchobair and Tigernán Ua Ruairc

Muirchertach Mac Lochlainn ravages Connacht

1159–81   Alexander III pope: resides at Sens in France until 1165

1160   Muirchertach Mac Lochlainn crushes revolt in Cenél nEógain led by Domnall Ua Gairmledaig and Muirchertach Ua Néill

Brótur son of Turcaill, kg of Dublin, killed by Máel Crón Mac Gilla Sechnaill, kg of South Brega

Death of Gilla na Náem Ua Duinn, *fer léigind* of Inis Clothrann, historian and poet (17 Dec.)

1160 × 1162   Diarmait Mac Murchada grants Latin charter to Augustinian priory at Ferns

1160/61   Death at Würzburg of Gilla na Náem Laignech, bp of Glendalough (7 Apr.)

1161   Death of Ragnall Ua Dálaig, '*ollam* of Desmumu in poetry'

Muirchertach Mac Lochlainn invades Bréifne and secures submission of Ruaidrí Ua Conchobair; divides Mide between Ua Conchobair and Diarmait Mac Murchada

Domnall Cáemánach, son of Diarmait Mac Murchada, attacks Wexford

Assembly of laymen and clerics at Áth na Dairbrige (near Kells, on Meath–Cavan border); Muirchertach Mac Lochlainn receives general submission; confirms jurisdiction over Columban churches in Mide and Leinster to Flaithbertach Ua Brolcháin; Ardbraccan freed from billeting troops of kg of Lóegaire

Death of Áed Ua hOissín, abp of Tuam

1161/2 Death of Meurug, bp of Bangor: Owain Gwynedd secures election of Arthur of Bardsey, whom he sends to be consecrated in Ire. (*c.* 1165)

1162 Flaithbertach Ua Brolcháin clears 80 houses at Derry to build monastic enclosure

Synod of Clane, in presence of Diarmait Mac Murchada and Gilla Meic Liac: primacy of Armagh reaffirmed; ordinance that only alumni of Armagh should be recognised as *fir léigind* (lectors) in Irish churches

Death of Gregorius (Gréne), abp of Dublin, 'distinguished for his wisdom and knowledge of various languages' (8 Oct.)

Lorcán Ua Tuathail consecrated abp of Dublin by Gilla Meic Liac, abp of Armagh

Muirchertach Mac Lochlainn raids Fine Gall

Diarmait Mac Murchada gains complete control over Dublin

c. **1162** Diarmait Mac Murchada grants Baldoyle by charter to Augustinian priory of All Hallows, Dublin

1162 × 1165 Jerpoint (O.Cist.) founded by Domnall Mac Gilla Pátraic, kg of Osraige

c. **1162 × 1165** Diarmait Mac Murchada, confirms by charter grant of Diarmait Ua Riáin, kg of Uí Dróna, to monks of Killenny

1163 Council of Tours attended by Irish and Scottish prelates

Flaithbertach Ua Brolcháin builds lime-kiln at Derry

Mention of bridge at Cork: Muirchertach mac Domnaill Ua Máel Sechlainn drowned in River Lee after falling from it while drunk

Diarmait Ua Máel Sechlainn deposed by men of Mide

1163 × 1165 Pope Alexander writes to unnamed Irish kg (Muirchertach Mac Lochlainn or Donnchad Ua Cerbaill)

1164 Ruaidrí Ua Conchobair builds castle at Tuam

Death of Máel Cóemgin Ua Gormáin, magister of Louth, 'chief doctor of Ireland and abbot of the monastery of the canons of Termonn Feichín [Termonfeckin] for a time' (*A.U.*)

Muirchertach Mac Lochlainn and Gilla Meic Liac, abp of Armagh, forbid Flaithbertach Ua Brolcháin, abbot of Derry, to accept invitation of Somarlaide, kg of Argyll and the Isles, to take abbacy of Iona

Stone church of Derry completed by Flaithbertach Ua Brolcháin and Muirchertach Mac Lochlainn

Malcolm IV, kg of Scotland, defeats and kills Somarlaide, helped by Dublin fleet, near Renfrew

Death of Muirchertach Ua Tuathail, kg of Uí Muiredaig, father of St Laurence O'Toole

Council of Northampton (Oct.): Abp Becket leaves England (remains in exile until 1 Dec. 1170)

1165 War between Muirchertach Mac Lochlainn and Ulaid: Mac Lochlainn restores Eochaid Mac Duinn Sléibe as kg of Ulster on intercession of Donnchad Ua Cerbaill

Muirchertach Ua Briain expels his father, Toirrdelbach, and takes kingship of Munster

Gilla na Trínóite Ua Dálaig, *ollam* of Desmond, killed

Henry II campaigns unsuccessfully in Wales; hires Dublin fleet for 6 months

Ruaidrí Ua Conchobair invades Desmond

Rhys ap Gruffydd, lord of Deheubarth, captures Robert fitz Stephen, constable of Cardigan (Nov.)

'Death of Máel Coluim Cennmór, son of Éanric, high-king of Alba: the best Christian that was of the Gael by the sea on the east for almsdeeds, hospitality and piety' (*A.U.*) (Malcolm IV; 9 Dec.)

1166   Assembly of clerics of Leth Moga in Lismore: 12 bps consecrate new cathedral

Muirchertach Mac Lochlainn treacherously seizes and blinds Eochaid Mac Duinn Sléibe, kg of Ulster (Easter)

Ruaidrí Ua Conchobair invades Mide: receives submission of Dublin, Leinster, and Airgialla

Muirchertach mac Néill Mac Lochlainn, high-king of Ire., killed by Donnchad Ua Cerbaill and Tigernán Ua Ruairc

Tigernán Ua Ruairc marches to Ferns: destroys castle of Diarmait Mac Murchada; Ruaidrí Ua Conchobair banishes Mac Murchada from Ire. (1 Aug.); Mac Murchada flees to Bristol

Ruaidrí Ua Conchobair makes circuit of Ire. and is acknowledged as high-king by general assembly at Athlone

1166–83   Ruaidrí Ua Conchobair 'high-king with opposition'

1167   Diarmait Mac Murchada in Aquitaine: offers fealty to Henry II and receives permission to recruit help in Wales

Completion of Nuns' Church at Clonmacnoise by Conchobar Ua Cellaig, kg of Uí Maine, to replace wooden oratory

Diarmait Mac Murchada returns from Wales with small force of Flemings under Richard fitz Godebert of Rhos; recovers kingdom of Uí Chennselaig (Aug.)

Death of Toirrdelbach mac Diarmata Ua Briain, kg of Thomond

Ruaidrí Ua Conchobair presides over assembly of laity and clergy of Leth Cuinn at Áth Buide Tlachtga (Athboy, Co. Meath)

Ua Conchobair marches to Armagh: divides Tír Eógain between Niall Mac Lochlainn and Áed (in Macáem Tóinlesc) Ua Néill

Antipope Paschal II crowns Frederick Barbarossa a second time

c. **1167/8**   Foundation of Schottenkloster of St Nicholas at Memmingen

1167/8   Óenach Tailten held by Ruaidrí Ua Conchobair, 'king of Ireland' (*Ann. Tig.* 1167; *A.F.M.* 1168)

c. **1168 × 1179**   Domnall Mór Ua Briain, kg of Thomond, grants Latin charter to Holycross abbey

1168   Muirchertach, son of Toirrdelbach Ua Briain, killed by Conchobar, grandson of Conchobar Ua Briain

Owain Gwynedd captures Rhuddlan; offers alliance against Henry II to Louis VII of France

Ruaidrí Ua Conchobair divides Munster between sons of Cormac Mac Carthaig and Domnall Mór, son of Toirrdelbach Ua Briain

Donnchad Ua Cerbaill, kg of Airgialla, killed by servant

Death of Amlaíb Mac Innaigneorach, 'chief *ollam* of Ireland in harp-playing'

Death of Flannacán Ua Dubthaig, bp of Elphin, historian and genealogist, at Cong

1169 Ruaidrí Ua Conchobair establishes annual grant to school of Armagh for students from Ire. and Scotland

Diarmait Ua Máel Sechlainn, kg of Mide, killed by his nephew, Domnall Bregach: Ua Conchobair expels Domnall and divides Mide between himself and Tigernán Ua Ruairc

MEDIEVAL IRELAND, 1169–1534

INTRODUCTION

THE eleventh and twelfth centuries witnessed a revolution in historical documentation throughout Europe. For chronological purposes annals and chronicles, biography and hagiography take second place henceforth to record material in governmental and private archives. Foremost in the development of centralised bureaucracy were the papal chancery and the Norman and Plantagenet kings of England in the twelfth century. By the end of that century Ireland had fallen within the administrative orbit of both these powers. The change in the nature of our documentation is all the more striking because of the relative lack of governmental institutions and administrative records in pre-Norman Ireland, though there is evidence that some Irish kings had an embryonic chancery in the decade before the Anglo-Norman invasion, when they issued Latin charters to the new religious houses of Cistercian monks and Augustinian canons (see 1157, 1160×1162). The dating of charters, Irish and Norman, and indeed of royal and papal letters, does not become precise until the thirteenth century, but the increase in the quantity of such documents, and of the circumstantial evidence that allows most of them to be dated fairly closely, makes possible a much more detailed chronology. In this section we have been able to introduce day and month, as well as year, as the norm rather than the exception.

The quality and quantity of records multiply with the formal introduction of English administrative practice into Ireland. The regular production and preservation of governmental records probably began in 1204, when King John had a castle built at Dublin to house the treasury, and this development was strengthened by the establishment of an Irish chancery in 1232. Indeed, it was only in the first year of John's reign, 1199, that the enrolment of chancery records (i.e. the filing of copies of all documents issued) began in England, and in the Roman chancery only a small proportion of papal letters were similarly registered even in the thirteenth century. But the destruction of the Irish Public Record Office at the Four Courts, Dublin, in 1922, has, in the words of Professor Otway-Ruthven, 'deprived us of a governmental archive which would have been the envy of almost any state in the world; incomparably richer than, for instance, that of Scotland or even France'.[1] The disaster is mitigated by the fact that much

---

[1] In T. W. Moody (ed.), *Irish historiography, 1936–70* (Dublin, 1971), p. 17.

administrative business had to be referred to the royal government in England and has consequently left its mark in documents preserved in the English Public Record Office, London, which remains a rich source of material for the historian of medieval Ireland.[1]

Nevertheless, although exchequer records begin as early as the reign of Henry I, for the beginning of our period the historian of England, and of English involvement in Ireland, must still depend largely on narrative sources such as the 'Gesta regis Henrici secundi' and the chronicles of Roger of Howden and William of Newburgh. A new age of historiography seems to dawn with the 'Expugnatio Hibernica' of Giraldus Cambrensis and the French rhymed chronicle known as the 'Song of Dermot and the earl', which in their very different ways aimed to be works of literature as well as history. To these accounts of the Anglo-Norman invasion we owe a wealth of historical detail as well as romantic colour, together with some precise dates (although Giraldus's sense of chronology is notoriously weak).[2] But these authors found no successors among the Anglo-Irish of the later middle ages in Latin, French, or English. In fact, what narrative history there is comes from the Gaelic revival of the fourteenth and fifteenth centuries, in the 'Caithréim Thoirdhealbhaigh', a lively but chronologically unreliable account of the wars in Thomond from c. 1276 to 1318, and in the chronicle of thirteenth-century Connacht that has been disguised by its incorporation into the text of the Annals of Loch Cé and Annals of Connacht. The historical tradition of the Anglo-Irish, as Campion found cause to complain in the sixteenth century, remained weak, in spite of their strong sense of identity. It is represented by a series of jejune annals, of which the best known are those of the fourteenth-century Kilkenny Franciscan, Friar Clyn. Clyn takes care to give precise dates in terms of ecclesiastical feasts and saints' days, but he normally begins the year on 25 March. Gaelic Irish annalistic writing continued to flourish and became more detailed, although chronological precision within a given year remained unusual, and the form rarely developed into a chronicle or narrative. There is also a geographical imbalance in favour of the north-west of Ireland, as the main centres of compilation lay in northern Connacht and, later, in Fermanagh; in Munster the annalistic tradition had been of late growth and petered out early in the fourteenth century.

The increasing precision in dating afforded by English, Anglo-Irish, and continental record-material carries with it complications familiar to medieval historians but unknown to the Irish annalists: variations in style between

---

[1] See Eric St John Brooks, 'The sources for medieval Anglo-Irish history' in T. D. Williams (ed.), *Historical Studies*, i (London, 1958), pp 86–92, together with Aubrey Gwynn, 'Bibliographical note on medieval Anglo-Irish history', ibid., pp 93–9.

[2] We have, however, after some hesitation, followed Giraldus as against the 'Song' in placing Asculv's attempt on Dublin in 1171 before Ua Conchobair's siege of the same year; see J. F. O'Doherty, 'Historical criticism of the Song of Dermot and the earl' in *I.H.S.* i, no. 1 (Mar. 1938), pp 4–19.

the various chanceries (and even between different international religious orders) for the beginning of the year (25 Dec., 1 Jan., 25 Mar., and other dates), the use of regnal years in both royal and papal documents (presuming knowledge of the relevant date of accession or coronation), and the additional complication of the English exchequer year, which began at Michaelmas (29 Sept.).

We wish to acknowledge the help we have received in this section of the chronology from Professor Alan Bliss, Professor James Carney, Dr Art Cosgrove, Professor Michael Dolley, Miss Marie-Thérèse Flanagan, Dr Robin Glasscock, Dr Françoise Henry, Dr Joseph Long, Professor J. F. Lydon, Mr K. W. Nicholls, Dr Seymour Phillips, Professor D. B. Quinn, Professor Edwin Rae, and Professor J. A. Watt.

GLOSSARY

Angaile, Anghaile. 'Annaly', the ancient Tethbae, Ó Fearghail's lordship in Co. Longford; this southern portion of Conmhaicne was now independent of its former overlord, Ó Ruairc of Bréifne.

cantred. An Anglo-Welsh term (Welsh *cantref*) denoting a territorial lordship and applied by the Anglo-Normans to the area of the Irish *trícha cét* or petty kingdom (see *tuath*, in the glossary to the previous section). In the regions of early Anglo-Norman settlement the cantred is fairly faithfully reflected in the modern barony; the corresponding term commote (Welsh *cwmwd*) is sometimes used for the smaller subdivision, the Irish *tuath*, for which the medieval Latin *theodum* is also found.

Clann Rickard Burkes. Here used to denote the lordship of Mac Uilliam Uachtar (Upper MacWilliam) in Co. Galway, which derived its name Clann Riocaird from Richard de Burgh (d. 1343), or perhaps from his grandfather Richard 'the Younger'; the name is attested as early as 1343 in the annals.

'custos'. 'Keeper'; in the early days of the Anglo-Norman invasion, a royal deputy charged with the government of a royal town or demesne, or of the whole lordship of Ireland; in the later middle ages, a temporary deputy for an absent justiciar or lieutenant.

feudal 'aid'. Originally a payment due from a vassal to his lord on certain specified occasions: for his ransom, for the knighting of his son, for the marriage of his daughter; hence due to the crown from the tenants-in-chief. Extraordinary aids might, however, be levied by consent of the royal council, and were extended to all classes of society as a tax on chattels; the crown might also request a 'courteous aid' or voluntary contribution for special royal needs.

feudal service. The *servitium debitum* or duty of attending for military service with the required number of knights, the essential service by which a tenant-in-chief held his fief from the crown; in Ireland a 'royal service' of 40 shillings was the equivalent of the English scutage, the monetary commutation of this service.

gallóclaig, gallóglaigh. 'Galloglass'; Scots and Hebridean mercenary forces hired by Gaelic Irish lords from the mid-thirteenth century and endowed with lands held by military tenure (*óglóchas*); 'galloglass' is an English plural from 'gallogla', 'foreign warriors', as distinct from *óglaigh dúthaigh* or native gentry who held by military tenure.

Loch Cé. Here used for the house of Premonstratensian canons on Holy Trinity Island, Lough Key, Co. Roscommon, and the annals compiled there; 'Lough Key' is used where a purely topographical location is intended.

Mac Uí Néill Buidhe. The style used by the O'Neill lords of Clandeboye (Clann Aodha Buidhe), descended from Áed Buide Ó Néill, king of Tír Eógain (1260-83); in the mid-fourteenth century this branch of the O'Neills, excluded from the kingship, established an autonomous lordship east of the Bann in lands won from the defunct earldom of Ulster.

Mac William Burkes. Here used to denote the lordship of Mac Uilliam Íochtar (Lower MacWilliam) in Co. Mayo; this branch descended from Sir William Liath de Burgh (d. 1324), but, as the lord of Clann Riocaird was also styled Mac Uilliam (Uachtar), the surname must derive from the common ancestor William (d. 1205).

Meath. The Anglo-Norman lordship was theoretically coextensive with the twelfth-century Ua Máel Sechlainn kingdom of Mide and thus with the thirteenth-century dioceses of Meath and Clonmacnoise; Westmeath was not separately shired until 1542, and until the end of the sixteenth century Meath in the larger sense (to which some would add Longford and Cavan) was reckoned as a fifth province alongside Ulster, Munster, Leinster, and Connacht.

Ó Conchobhair Sligigh. Although the style 'O'Connor Sligo' was first adopted by Tadhg Óg Ó Conchobhair in 1536, we use it by anticipation to denote the ruler of the autonomous lordship of Cairbre (Carbury, Co. Sligo) which was established by the Clann Bhriain Luighnigh sept of the O'Connors in the fourteenth century, and who was variously styled Mac Domhnaill Mhéig Mhuircheartaigh and lord of Carbury, Sligo, or Íochtar (Lower) Connacht; the masculine genitive 'Sligigh' appears to have displaced the older feminine genitive 'Sligighe' of the name Sligeach.

tallage. Originally an arbitrary tax levied by the crown on all royal demesne lands, including towns and royal boroughs; hence a municipal rate due to the crown. With the rise in social status of burgesses in fourteenth-century England their tallage became confounded with the theoretically voluntary feudal 'aid'.

tánaiste. 'Tanist', literally 'second'; the heir-designate to a Gaelic Irish lordship; in sixteenth-century English usage 'tanistry' became a blanket term to cover all aspects of brehon law custom concerning inheritance of land as well as of lordship.

Trian Conghail. A pseudo-antiquarian term invented in the fourteenth century to denote Ulster east of the Bann, the area over which Mac Uí Néill Buidhe claimed overlordship.

Ulster. The medieval earldom of Ulster was coterminous with the twelfth-century Irish over-kingdom of that name (Ulaid), but extended its authority by conquest over the coasts of Co. Londonderry and Inishowen. With the political extinction of the native Ulster royal dynasty of Mac Duinn Sléibe in the 1280s, the O'Neills of Tír Eógain began to style themselves 'kings of Ulster' and revive the ancient connotation of the name to cover the whole of the north of Ireland. The collapse of the earldom after 1333 and the spread of Ó Néill hegemony made this a reality; until the end of the sixteenth century the province of Ulster was held to include Co. Louth, but not Co. Cavan, which as East Bréifne historically belonged to Connacht. However Ó Néill claimed hegemony over Ó Raghallaigh of Cavan.

Uriel, Oriel. Irish Oirghialla (earlier Airgialla); in practice restricted to the Mac Mathghamhna (earlier Ua Cerbaill) lordship of Monaghan and Co. Louth (English Uriel) which they lost to the Anglo-Normans in 1189, although the Mág Uidhir lordship of Fermanagh and the residual area of Oirthir (Orior, east Co. Armagh) under Ó hAnluain were equally Airgiallan.

CHRONOLOGY, 1169-1534

F. J. BYRNE, DARACH MAC FHIONNBHAIRR, AND F. X. MARTIN

1169

May Robert fitz Stephen, Hervey de Montmorency, and Maurice de Prendergast land at Bannow Bay (Co. Wexford)

Wexford captured by Diarmait Mac Murchada, assisted by Normans; custody given to Robert fitz Stephen

Mac Murchada invades Ossory, Uí Fáeláin, and Uí Muiredaig (Co. Kildare)

Ua Conchobair and Tigernán Ua Ruairc invade Uí Chennselaig; Mac Murchada submits and delivers his son Conchobar as hostage

Maurice fitz Gerald arrives at Wexford

1170

Ua Conchobair campaigns against Domnall Mór Ua Briain in north Munster; Robert fitz Stephen in retinue of Ua Briain

Apr. 4 Conchobar Mac Lochlainn, kg of Cenél nEógain, killed; succ. by his brother Niall mac Muirchertaig

c. **May** Raymond (le Gros) fitz William lands at Baginbun (Co. Wexford)

Aug. 23 Richard de Clare (Strongbow), earl of Pembroke, lands near Waterford

Aug. 25 Waterford captured by Strongbow and Raymond le Gros; Strongbow marries Aífe, daughter of Mac Murchada

Diarmait Mac Carthaig fails to capture Waterford

Sept. 21 Dublin captured by Mac Murchada and Norman allies; custody given to Miles de Cogan (1 Oct.)

Mac Murchada invades Uí Fáeláin, Ossory, and Mide; Domnall Ua Máel Sechlainn submits

Conchobar, son of Mac Murchada, executed by Ruaidrí Ua Conchobair

Henry II places embargo on shipping to Ire.

Ailech raided from Orkneys

Nov. 23 Death of Owain Gwynedd, kg of north Wales

Dec. Magnus Mac Duinn Sléibe, kg of Ulster (Ulaid), and Amlaím, son of abbot of Moville, ex-abbot of Mellifont, expel Augustinian canons regular from Saul (Co. Down)

Dec. 29 Thomas Becket murdered at Canterbury

1171

c. **May 1** Diarmait Mac Murchada, kg of Leinster, dies at Ferns; succ. by his son-in-law Strongbow

Magnus Mac Duinn Sléibe, kg of Ulster, killed by his brother Donn Sléibe, who
  succeeds to kingship

Domnall Mór Ua Briain submits to Ruaidrí Ua Conchobair

c. **May 16**   Askulv (Hasculf), deposed kg of Dublin, defeated and killed while
  attacking city with assistance of fleet from the Orkneys and Man under John
  the Wode

June-Aug.   Dublin besieged by Ua Conchobair, Ua Ruairc, Ua Máel Sechlainn,
  and Ua Cerbaill

Aug.   Robert fitz Stephen imprisoned by Irish at Wexford

Oct. 17   Áed, son of Tigernán Ua Ruairc, killed by Norman sortie from Dublin
  Henry II lands at Crook (near Waterford)

Oct.   Submission of Diarmait Mac Carthaig (at Waterford) and Domnall Mór
  Ua Briain (near Cashel) to Henry II
  Irish hierarchy in session at Waterford

Nov. 6   Henry II issues summons for synod at Cashel

Nov. 11   Henry II at Dublin; submission of kgs of north Leinster, Bréifne,
  Airgialla, and Ulster
  Henry II grants charter to city of Dublin

1171-2

winter   Second synod of Cashel in session (see 1101)

Provincial synod at Tuam

1172

c. **Apr. 1**   Meath (Ua Máel Sechlainn kingdom of Mide) granted to Hugh de Lacy
  by Henry II; custody of towns of Waterford and Wexford given to Robert fitz
  Bernard

Apr. 17   Henry II sails from Wexford for Milford Haven; de Lacy app. jcr,
  and 'custos' of Dublin

May   Henry II receives absolution for death of Becket from papal legates at
  Avranches

De Lacy campaigns in Meath, supported by Domnall, son of Annad Ua Ruairc;
  Tigernán Ua Ruairc killed at Tlachtga (Hill of Ward, Co. Meath)

Sept. 20   Pope Alexander III writes to the Irish kgs advocating fealty to
  Henry II

c. 1172

Introduction of Knights Hospitallers to Ire. at Wexford

1172-3

Merchants of Lucca and Flanders trade with Cork city

1172/3

Donn Sléibe Mac Duinn Sléibe, kg of Ulster, killed by his nobles: succ. by his
  brother Ruaidrí[1]

---

[1] *Ann. Tig.* 1172 and 1173; *A.F.M.* 1172.

1173

Strongbow and de Lacy with Henry II in Normandy; William fitz Audelin app. 'custos' of Ireland

Aug.   Strongbow app. 'custos' of Ireland

Domnall Bregach Ua Máel Sechlainn killed by Art Ua Máel Sechlainn at Durrow

Normans invade Uí Failge, Uí Chennselaig (Strongbow repulsed), Ormond (fort built at Kilkenny), and the Decies (Lismore plundered)

Naval engagement at 'Port of Lismore' (?Youghal): Cork fleet defeated by Adam de Hereford; Raymond le Gros drives Diarmait Mac Carthaig from Lismore

1173 × 1177

Diarmait Mac Carthaig, 'king of Munster', grants charter to Gill Abbey, Cork

1174

Mar. 20   Death of Flann Ua Gormáin, 'arch-lector of Armagh and of all Ireland' (since 1154; had studied in France and England for 21 years)

Mar. 27   Death of Gelasius (Gilla Meic Liac), abp of Armagh

Ruaidrí Ua Conchobair campaigns in Meath; destroys Norman forts at Trim and Duleek

Normans defeated at Thurles by Domnall Mór Ua Briain and Conchobar Máen-maige Ua Conchobair; Strongbow retreats to Waterford

Synod of Birr: diocese of Iarthar Mide (west Meath) assigned to Clonmacnoise

c. **1174**

Henry II grants charter to Dublin, conceding free trading rights throughout his dominions

Priory of Knights Hospitallers established at Kilmainham

1175

Domnall Cáemánach Mac Murchada killed by O'Nolans (of Forth, Co. Carlow)

Diarmait, son of Tadg Ua Briain, and Mathgamain Ua Briain blinded by Domnall Mór Ua Briain at Castleconnell

Diarmait Mac Carthaig, kg of Desmond, deposed by his son Cormac Liathánach

Normans campaign in Meath: Magnus Ua Máel Sechlainn, kg of Iarthar Mide, hanged at Trim

Death of Flaithbertach Ua Brolcháin, abbot of Derry

Death of Conchobar mac Meic Con Chaille, abp of Armagh, at Chambéry, Savoy, while returning from visit to pope

Oct. 6   Treaty of Windsor between Henry II and Catholicus O'Duffy (Cadla Ua Dubthaig), abp of Tuam, on behalf of Ua Conchobair, witnessed by Laurence O'Toole (Lorcan Ua Tuathail), abp of Dublin

1175-6

Ruaidrí Ua Conchobair and Normans campaign together in Ormond and Thomond; Limerick city captured

1176

Diarmait Mac Carthaig restored to kingship of Desmond with support of Raymond le Gros; Cormac Liathánach Mac Carthaig killed

Niall Mac Lochlainn, kg of Cenél nEógain, killed; succession contested between Áed Ua Néill ('In Macáem Tóinlesc') and Máel Sechlainn Mac Lochlainn

Apr.   Domnall Mór Ua Briain unsuccessfully besieges Limerick

Apr. 20   Richard de Clare (Strongbow), dies; succ. by Gilbert, a minor (d. *c.* 1185)

William fitz Audelin and John de Courcy arrive in Ire.; fitz Audelin app. 'procurator' of Ire.

Death of David Fitz Gerald, bp of St Davids: his nephew Giraldus Cambrensis, elected by chapter but fails to secure royal confirmation

Norman fort at Slane destroyed by Máel Sechlainn Mac Lochlainn; forts at Galtrim, Kells, and Derrypatrick abandoned

Normans campaign in Meath and Airgialla; restore castles at Kells and Slane

Custody of Limerick given to Domnall Mór Ua Briain, who burns city; Raymond le Gros relieves Norman garrison and abandons Limerick; peace established between Ua Briain and Ruaidrí Ua Conchobair

Oct.   Frederick Barbarossa makes peace with Alexander III at Anagni (at Venice, with Lombard league and Sicily, 23 July 1177)

Dec. 25   Rhys ap Gruffydd, lord of Deheubarth (south Wales), holds poetical and musical competition at Cardigan; attended by contestants from England, Scotland, and Ire. (first recorded eisteddfod)

1177

c. **Jan. 6**   Cardinal Vivian, papal legate to Ire. and Scotland, lands at Downpatrick, after regularising marriage of Godred, kg of Man, to Finnguala, daughter of Niall Mac Lochlainn

c. **Feb. 1**   John de Courcy invades Ulster and captures Downpatrick; builds castle

Synod at Dublin presided over by Cardinal Vivian

May   Council of Oxford: Dafydd ap Owain of Gwynedd and Rhys ap Gruffydd of Deheubarth recognised as vassal kings under Henry II; John, 10-year-old son of Henry II, designated 'Lord of Ire.'; Hugh de Lacy app. 'procurator' of Ire.; Leinster divided into 3 'custodies' under de Lacy at Dublin, William fitz Audelin at Wexford, and Robert le Poer at Waterford; Desmond granted to Robert fitz Stephen and Miles de Cogan; grant of Meath to de Lacy confirmed; speculative grant of Thomond renounced by original grantees (later in year taken up by Philip de Braose)

June 24 Battle of Downpatrick: De Courcy defeats Ruaidrí Mac Duinn Sléibe, kg of Ulster, and allied army of Cenél nEógain and Airgialla

Domnall Mór Ua Briain campaigns in Desmond against Diarmait Mór Mac Carthaig

Ruaidrí Ua Conchobair defeats his son Muirchertach and Miles de Cogan in Connacht

Áed Ua Néill killed by Máel Sechlainn Mac Lochlainn

De Courcy invades Dál nAraide, Uí Thuirtre, and Fir Lí (Co. Antrim); burns Coleraine

De Braose, fitz Stephen and de Cogan invade Thomond; de Braose abandons attempt to capture Limerick

Fitz Stephen and de Cogan invade Desmond

Priory of St Thomas Martyr (Victorines) founded at Dublin

1177 × 1181

Diarmait Ua Dimmusaig, kg of Uí Failge, grants charter to Cistercian monastery at Monasterevin (Co. Kildare)

1178

Dúnlang Ua Tuathail, kg of Uí Muiredaig and brother of Abp Laurence O'Toole, killed by Robert le Poer and Wexford garrison; le Poer killed by Irish

Clonmacnoise plundered by de Lacy

Art Ua Máel Sechlainn recovers kingship of Mide with aid from Normans and Uí Failge

Domnall Óc Ua Gairmledaig, kg of Cenél Moen (between Tír Eógain and Tír Conaill), killed by Ruaidrí Ua Flaithbertaig, who succeeds to kingship

John de Courcy defeated by Murchad Ua Cerbaill and Ruaidrí Mac Duinn Sléibe in Machaire Conaille (north Co. Louth)

John de Courcy defeated in Dál nAraide by Cú Mide Ua Floinn, kg of Uí Thuirtre and Fir Lí

Ruaidrí Mac Duinn Sléibe, kg of Ulster, expelled into Tír Eógain by de Courcy

c. 1179

Knights Templar found preceptories at Clontarf (Co. Dublin) and Crooke, Kilbarry, and Rincrew (Co. Waterford)

1179

Dynastic warfare and famine in Tír Eógain

Third Lateran council: Laurence O'Toole app. papal legate in Ire.

Synod at Clonfert presided over by Laurence O'Toole

p. **1179**

Irish monks of Schottenkloster at Vienna take control of German monastery at Kiev

1179–1202

William the Lion, kg of Scotland, attempts to assert sovereignty over Norse areas in his kingdom

c. **1180**

John de Courcy marries Affreca, daughter of Godred, kg of Man

Hugh de Lacy marries daughter of Ruaidrí Ua Conchobair

1180

De Courcy evacuates Downpatrick; retreats to Áth Glaise (unidentified)

a. **Feb.**   Tommaltach, nephew of Ruaidrí Ua Conchobair, elected abp of Armagh (takes possession of see, 1181)

Sept. 18   Louis VII of France dies; succ. by Philip II Augustus

Nov. 14   Death of Laurence O'Toole (Lorcán Ua Tuathail), abp of Dublin, at Eu in Normandy

1180 × 1190

Christchurch cathedral, Dublin, rebuilt in transitional style

Carrickfergus castle built by de Courcy

1181

Ruaidrí Mac Duinn Sléibe returns to Ulster; he and Cú Mide Ua Floinn, kg of Uí Thuirtre and Fir Lí, defeated by Domnall Mac Lochlainn

John de Lacy and Richard of the Peak app. joint keepers of Ire. (arrive, May)

May 23   'Cath na rígdamna': Brian Luignech and Áed, sons of Toirrdelbach Ua Conchobair, defeated and killed by Flaithbertach Ua Máel Doraid, kg of Cenél Conaill, ally of Donnchad, son of Domnall Midech Ua Conchobair

Sept. 6   John Cumin elected to see of Dublin

Hugh de Lacy app. 'custos' of Ire.

Máel Sechlainn Mac Lochlainn and Echmarcach Ua Catháin invade Uí Thuirtre and Fir Lí

Miles de Cogan, Raymond le Gros and sons of fitz Stephen killed by Mac Tíre, lord of Uí Maic Caille (Imokilly, east Co. Cork), at Lismore

1182

Domnall, son of Áed Mac Lochlainn, defeated by Normans at Dunbo (Co. Antrim)

Ruaidrí Ua Conchobair and his son Conchobar Máenmaige defeat Flaithbertach Ua Máel Doraid and Donnchad, son of Domnall Midech Ua Conchobair

1183

Abdication of Ruaidrí Ua Conchobair, kg of Connacht; succ. by his son Conchobar Máenmaige

1184

Art Ua Máel Sechlainn, kg of Mide, killed by Diarmait, son of Toirrdelbach Ua Briain; succ. by Máel Sechlainn Bec

Mar.-   De Lacy campaigns with Ua Cerbaill in Airgialla; captures Armagh

Tommaltach Ua Conchobair, abp of Armagh, resigns temporarily in favour of Máel Ísu Ua Cerbaill, bp of Clogher

Sept. 1   Philip of Worcester app. 'procurator' of Ire.

Romanesque rebuilding of Tuam cathedral

1184-6

Hostilities between Conchobar Máenmaige and his father, Ruaidrí Ua Conchobair, who is supported by Domnall Mór Ua Briain

c. 1185

Priory of Crutched Friars (Fratres Cruciferi) established at Dublin

1185

Pope Lucius III orders annual convocation of abbots of Schottenklöster (Irish Benedictine monasteries in Germany) to be held at Regensburg

Máel Sechlainn Mac Lochlainn, kg of Cenél nEógain, killed while invading Meath by William le Petit; succession contested between Domnall, son of Áed Mac Lochlainn, and Ruaidrí Ua Flaithbertaig

c. Mar.   Armagh occupied by Philip of Worcester

Apr. 25   Prince John, lord of Ireland, lands at Waterford; grants charter for union of sees of Dublin and Glendalough; makes speculative grants in Ormond to William de Burgh and Theobald Walter (le Botiller); builds castles at Tibberaghny (Co. Kilkenny), Ardfinnan (Co. Tipperary), and Lismore

p. Apr. 25   Diarmait Mac Carthaig, kg of Desmond, killed by Theobald Walter; succ. by his son Domnall Mór

June 24   Domnall Mór Ua Briain defeats garrison of Tibberaghny: Prince John's foster-brother, son of Ranulf de Glanville, killed

Dec. 17   John departs for England; John de Courcy app. jcr

Domnall Mór Ua Briain grants church of Mungret (Co. Limerick) by charter to Brictius, bp of Limerick

1186

July 25   Hugh de Lacy killed at Durrow

1187

Ruaidrí Ua Flaithbertaig, contestant for kingship of Cenél nEógain, killed by Flaithbertach Ua Máel Doraid, kg of Cenél Conaill

Áed Ua Ruairc killed in Conmaicne (Co. Longford) after having pillaged Drumcliffe with Normans from Meath

Godred, kg. of Man and the Isles, dies (10 Nov.); succ. by his illegitimate son Ragnall (Reginald)

Giraldus Cambrensis's 'Topographia Hiberniae'

c. 1188

Giraldus Cambrensis's 'Expugnatio Hibernica'

1188

Ruaidrí Ua Canannáin, ex-kg of Cenél Conaill, killed by Flaithbertach Ua Máel Doraid at Sligo

Normans from Dromore invade Tír Eógain: Domnall Mac Lochlainn, kg of Cenél nEógain, killed; succ. by his cousin Muirchertach

De Courcy campaigns in Connacht and Tír Conaill with Conchobar 'Ua nDiarmata', son of Ruaidrí Ua Conchobair

1189

Conchobar Máenmaige Ua Conchobair, kg of Connacht, killed by his own retainers; succession contested between his son Cathal Carrach, and Cathal Crobderg, son of Toirrdelbach Mór

Death of Murchad Ua Cerbaill, kg of Airgialla, in religious retirement at Mellifont

'Mac na hAidche' Ua Máel Ruanaid, exiled kg of Fir Manach, and Ua Cerbaill (successor of Murchad), kg of Airgialla, defeated and killed by Normans

Armagh raided by de Courcy

July 6   Henry II, kg of England, dies; succ. by his son Richard I

William Marshal marries Isabella de Clare (heiress of Strongbow)

1189 × 1199

Prince John grants charter to Cork city

c. 1190

Prince John makes speculative grants to Bertram de Verdun and Roger Pipard in Airgialla

1190

Domnall Mór Mac Carthaig defeats Norman raiders at Durrus (west Co. Cork)

June 10   Emperor Frederick I (Barbarossa) drowned in Cilicia; succ. by his son Henry VI

July 6   Canonisation of Malachy (Máel Máedóc Ua Morgair) (d. 1148)

c. 1190-1200
Romanesque doorway built at Killaloe cathedral

1192
Synod at Dublin presided over by Muirges Ua hÉnna, abp of Cashel and papal legate

Piers Pipard and William le Petit app. jcrs

May 15   Prince John grants charter to Dublin, recognising city guilds

Fíngen, son of Diarmait, son of Cormac Mac Carthaig, abandons his monastic profession

Normans build castles at Ardnurcher and Kilbixy (Co. Westmeath)

Normans campaign in Ormond and Thomond; defeated at Thurles by Domnall Mór Ua Briain; build castles at Kilfeakle, Knockgraffon, and Bruis (Co. Tipperary) (1193)

Dec. 11   Richard I captured at Vienna by duke of Austria (released, 3 Feb. 1194)

Simon Rochfort elected to see of Clonard

1192 × 1201
Cathal Crobderg Ua Conchobair, kg of Connacht, grants charter to Cistercian monastery at Knockmoy (Co. Galway)

1193
Jan. 25   Prince John grants 3 cantreds in Fermanagh to Piers Pippard

Death of Muirchertach Mac Murchada, kg of Uí Chennselaig

Death of Derbforgaill (Dervorgilla), widow of Tigernán Ua Ruairc, at Mellifont

1193–
Gilbert de Nangle campaigns in Connacht: raids Iniscloghran on Lough Ree

1194
Domnall Mór Ua Briain, kg of Thomond dies; succ. by his son Muirchertach Finn

Fíngen Mac Carthaig imprisoned by his kinsmen

Apr.   Walter de Lacy and John de Courcy app. jcrs; Meath granted to de Lacy

July 5   De Lacy grants charter to Drogheda (south town)

1195
Ten cantreds in Connacht granted by William de Burgh to Hugh de Lacy

Jcrs (de Courcy and de Lacy) on circuit in Leinster and Munster

Cathal Crobderg Ua Conchobair campaigns with O'Briens and MacCarthys against Normans in Munster

De Courcy and Ua Conchobair parley at Athlone

Hamo de Valognes app. jcr

1196

Muirchertach Mac Lochlainn, kg of Cenél nEógain, killed by Mac Blosgaid Ua Catháin; succ. by Áed Méith, son of Áed Ua Néill; O'Neills begin to replace MacLoughlins as dominant dynasty in Tír Eógain

Domnall Mór Mac Carthaig attacks Norman settlements in Imokilly; raids Kilfeakle, Co. Limerick

Normans campaign in Munster; peace made with Domnall Mór Mac Carthaig

Ruaidrí Mac Duinn Sléibe leads combined Norman and Connacht army against Cenél nEógain and Airthir of Armagh and is defeated

1197

Normans invade Thomond in support of Conchobar Ruad Ua Briain against his brother Donnchad Cairprech

De Courcy campaigns in Airgialla, Ciannachta, and as far as Derry; builds castle at Mount Sandel (near Coleraine)

Hamo de Valognes excommunicated by John Cumin, abp of Dublin; Dublin city under interdict

Death of Flaithbertach Ua Máel Doraid, kg of Cenél Conaill; succ. by Echmarcach Ua Dochartaig

Feb. 16-23 De Courcy invades Tír Eógain, Derry, and Inishowen; defeats and kills Ua Dochartaig

Apr. 28 Death of Rhys ap Gruffydd, lord of Deheubarth

Dec. 18 Prince John grants charter to city of Limerick

1198

Jan. 8 Election of Pope Innocent III

Meiler fitz Henry app. jcr

Muirchertach Finn Ua Briain, kg of Thomond, deposed by his brother Conchobar Ruad

Áed, son of Brian Bréifnech Ua Conchobair, killed by Cathal Carrach Ua Conchobair

Dec. 2 Death of Ruaidrí Ua Conchobair, ex-kg of Connacht and former high-king

1199

Death of Richard de Carew, lord of Cork

De Courcy campaigns in Tír Eógain and Inishowen; raids Ardstraw and Raphoe; captures Derry; Áed Ua Néill leads retaliatory naval attack on Larne (Co. Antrim)

Apr. 6 Richard I, kg of England dies; succ. by his brother John

Muirchertach Finn Ua Briain imprisoned by Normans at Limerick

Normans build castles at Askeaton (Co. Limerick) and Granard (Co. Longford)

1199/1200

Norman invasion of Tír Eógain defeated at Donaghmore by Áed Ua Néill

Armagh raided by Ruaidrí Mac Duinn Sléibe and Normans from Ardee

1200

Cathal Crobderg Ua Conchobair invades Meath

Feb.-Apr. Cathal Carrach Ua Conchobair, William de Burgh, and Muirchertach and Conchobar Ruad Ua Briain encamp at Áth Liac (? Athleague, Co.
Roscommon, or Ballyleague, near Lanesborough, Co. Longford), and
devastate all Connacht

Cathal Carrach, son of Conchobar Máenmaige Ua Conchobair, installed as kg of
Connacht by William de Burgh; Cathal Crobderg seeks refuge with Áed Ua
Néill in Tír Eógain and de Courcy in Ulster

Death of Roland, son of Uhtred, lord of Galloway

Nov. 6 John grants 2 cantreds adjoining Athlone in Connacht to Geoffrey de
Costentin

c. **1200**

Standardisation of classical Modern Irish grammar and of poetic diction and
metre by bardic schools

c. **1200-*c.* 1650**

Classical Modern Irish linguistic period

1200 × 1201

22 Feb. 1200 × 21 Feb. 1201 Innocent III writes to 'king of Connacht' answer-
ing his queries concerning right of asylum in churches

1200 × 1225

'Song of Dermot and the earl' composed in Norman-French

1201

Death of Catholicus O'Duffy (Cadla Ua Dubthaig), abp of Tuam

c. **Jan. 12** Grant to William de Braose of lands in Thomond granted to his uncle
Philip in 1177

Death of Tommaltach Ua Conchobair, abp of Armagh; succession contested
between Echdonn Mac Gilla Uidir and Humphrey de Tikehull, kg's nominee

Ruaidrí Mac Duinn Sléibe, kg of Ulster, killed by followers of John de Courcy

William de Burgh invades Múscraige and Cairpre (west Co. Cork) with Muirchertach Ua Briain and his brothers

Áed Ua Néill and Ua hÉicnig, kg of Fir Manach, invade Connacht in support of
Cathal Crobderg Ua Conchobair; Ua hÉicnig killed

De Courcy and Hugh de Lacy invade Connacht in support of Cathal Crobderg Ua Conchobair; defeated by Cathal Carrach Ua Conchobair near Kilmac-duagh (Co. Galway)

Hugh de Lacy captures Cathal Crobderg and de Courcy in Meath

Conchobar Bec Mac Lochlainn killed by Éicnechán Ua Domnaill

c. 1202

Episcopal seat of Meath removed from Clonard to Trim by Bp Simon Rochfort

1202

Jan. 24 Felix Ua Duib Sláine, O. Cist., bp of Ossory, dies; succ. by Hugo de Rous, Can. Reg.

Disputed election to see of Armagh; Echdonn Mac Gilla Uidir (Eugenius) elected abp

William de Burgh invades Connacht in support of Cathal Crobderg Ua Concho-bair; Cathal Carrach Ua Conchobair killed near Boyle; Cathal Crobderg restored as kg of Connacht

Synods at Athlone and Dublin under Johannes de Monte Celano (John of Salerno), papal legate

Felix Ua Ruanada, prior of Saul (Co. Down), installed as abp of Tuam by papal legate against opposition of Ua Dubthaig family (election confirmed by Innocent III, 20 Feb. 1203)

1203

William de Burgh campaigns in Connacht; builds castle at Meelick

Conchobar Ruad Ua Briain, kg of Thomond, killed by his brother Muirchertach Finn, who recovers the kingship

Jcr (Meiler fitz Henry) on circuit in Thomond; submission of de Burgh, Ua Conchobair, and Ua Briain at Limerick

Domnall Carrach Ua Máel Doraid killed in an attempt to win the kingship of Cenél Conaill with support of Meiler, son of Meiler fitz Henry, and the de Nangles

Hugh de Lacy defeats de Courcy at Downpatrick; de Courcy retreats to Tír Eógain

July 8 Custody of Limerick granted to William de Braose

1204

Northern Irish clergy intrude Amalgaid Ua Fergail, abbot of *recles* at Derry, as abbot of Iona in protest against establishment there of Benedictine monastery by Celestine (Cellach)

Six cantreds in Connacht granted to Hugh de Lacy in semi-confirmation of earlier grant of ten cantreds (see 1195)

Domnall Mór Mac Carthaig defeats Normans at Redchair (north Co. Cork)

Feb. Walter de Lacy commissioned to raise a feudal 'aid' in Ire.

Apr. 29 Commn to examine charges against William de Burgh (26 Mar.) super-seded; restoration of his lands, excepting those in Connacht

June 24 Philip II Augustus enters Rouen; English crown loses duchy of Normandy

c. **Aug.** Order for building of castle at Dublin to house treasury

Aug. 31 Walter de Lacy and Meiler, son of Meiler fitz Henry, ordered to summon de Courcy

c. **Sept.** Hugh de Lacy defeats and captures de Courcy, but releases him on safe-conduct

Nov. 2 Writs of *mort d'ancestor* and *novel disseisin* applied to Ire.

John orders Walter de Lacy (bailiff for William de Braose) to deliver Limerick to jcr (Meiler fitz Henry)

1205

May 29 Hugh de Lacy created earl of Ulster

July 1 Papal commn to examine contention between de Courcy and de Lacy

July 2 John grants charter to Waterford

De Courcy makes unsuccessful expedition from the Isles to Ulster

Death of William de Burgh; lands resumed by crown during minority of heir, Richard

Dec. 20 John recognises Cathal Crobderg Ua Conchobair as tributary kg of Connacht, holding one-third of province as feudal barony from crown

1206

Apr. 3 John fails to have Ailbe Ua Máel Muaid, bp of Ferns, elected abp of Cashel

Normans build castle at Cork

Lands of Theobald Walter (le Botiller) (d. 1205) resumed by crown during minority of heir, Theobald

Dec. 1 Domnall Mór Mac Carthaig, kg of Desmond, dies; succ. by his brother, Fíngen, son of Diarmait, with opposition from Diarmait, son of Domnall Mór

1206-7

winter Limerick captured by Meiler, son of Meiler fitz Henry, from Walter de Lacy

1207

Normans build castle at Dunloe (Co. Kerry)

Muirchertach Ua Briain campaigns in Ormond; destroys castles at Birr and Ballyroan (Co. Leix)

Jcr (Meiler fitz Henry) forced to cede Ardnurcher to Hugh and Walter de Lacy

c. **Feb. 1** Fíngen Mac Carthaig, kg of Desmond, deposed by his nephew Diarmait 'Dúna Droignéin'

Feb. 21 Feudal 'aid' levied on Leinster and Meath

John summons Walter de Lacy (14 Apr.), William Marshal, and Meiler fitz Henry (Oct.) to England

Nov. 9 Trial of crown pleas in private courts prohibited

Speculative grants in Connacht to John, nephew of William Marshal and to Gilbert de Nangle

Éicnechán Ua Domnaill, kg of Cenél Conaill, killed while invading Fir Manach; succ. by his son Domnall Mór

1207-8
William Marshal in Ire.

1208
Geoffrey de Marisco defeats Meiler fitz Henry at Thurles

Mar. 20 Commn to examine administration of Meiler fitz Henry

Mar. 23 Order for trial of Irish felons by English law in cases affecting settlers

Mar. 28 New grant of Leinster to William Marshal

Apr. 18 New grant of Meath to Walter de Lacy

June John de Grey, bp of Norwich, app. jcr: Meiler fitz Henry forced to cede castle of Dunamase to William Marshal

Muirchertach Finn Ua Briain imprisoned in Limerick at instigation of his brother Donnchad Cairprech

William de Braose flees to Ire.; received by his son-in-law Walter de Lacy, and by William Marshal

1208-13
England under papal interdict

1209
David the Welshman, bp of Waterford, killed by Ua Fáeláin, kg of the Déise (Decies, Co. Waterford)

Fíngen Mac Carthaig, ex-kg of Desmond, killed by the O'Sullivans

Ualgarg Ua Ruairc, kg of Bréifne, deposed in favour of Art, son of Domnall Ua Ruairc (killed by Cormac Ua Máel Sechlainn, 1210)

c. 1210
Royal grants in north-east Ulster to Alan of Galloway, Thomas, his brother, earl of Atholl, and Duncan of Carrick

c. 1210/11 Robert, bp of Waterford, attacks and imprisons Malachy, bp of Lismore

1210
William de Braose flees to Wales

June Feudal 'aid' levied for John's expedition to Ire.

June 20 John lands at Waterford; charter granted to Donnchad Cairprech Ua Briain for kingdom of Thomond; Muirchertach Finn Ua Briain set free

July 2   Trim captured by John

July 4   Cathal Crobderg Ua Conchobair submits to John at Ardbraccan (Co. Meath): accompanies him as far as Carrickfergus

July 9   Carlingford captured by John

July 28   Carrickfergus captured by John; the de Lacys flee; Maud de Braose and her son William captured by Duncan of Carrick

Aug. 11   Fore castle (Co. Westmeath) captured by John

Aug. 14   John seizes hostages from Cathal Crobderg at Rathwire (released, 1211)

Aug. 24/5   John leaves for England

Jcr (de Grey) builds bridge and castle at Athlone; makes 'peace of Athlone' with Cathal Crobderg Ua Conchobair (confirmed by charter, 1215)

1210/11

June   Convocation at Tuam for the annexation of coarbial lands to their respective dioceses

1211

William le Petit app. jcr

Death of William de Braose in exile in France

Diarmait Mac Carthaig imprisoned in Cork; his cousin Cormac Óc Liathánach Mac Carthaig assumes control of Desmond

De Grey and Philip de Nangle build castle at Cáeluisce (Belleek)

Áed Ua Néill, with Cenél nEógain, Cenél Conaill and Airgialla, defeats Normans at Cáeluisce

1212

Diarmait Mac Carthaig released; supported in Desmond by Normans of Cork

De Grey builds castle at Clones; invades Tír Eógain; defeated by Áed Ua Néill

c. **Nov.**   Death of John Cumin, abp of Dublin

Thomas fitz Roland ('Mac Uchtraig'),[1] earl of Atholl, and sons of Ragnall Mac Sumarlaide of the Isles bring fleet to Derry and, in conjunction with Cenél Conaill, devastate town and Inishowen

1213

John de Grey, Henry of London, and William Marshal in France

Gilbert de Lacy restored to favour

Clones castle destroyed by Áed Ua Néill

Cáeluisce castle burned by Ua hÉicnig

Cormac, son of Art Ua Máel Sechlainn, defeats de Grey and Donnchad Ua Briain at Kilnagrann in Fir Chell (Co. Offaly)

Philip II Augustus prepares to invade England; William Marshal leads 500 Irish barons to England at summons of John

---

[1] Son of Roland (d. 1200), son of Uhtred.

May 15 John reconciled with pope

July 6 Papal confirmation of annual tax of 300 marks for Ire.

July 23 Henry of London, abp of Dublin, app. jcr

July 28 John grants charter to Drogheda (north town)

July 30 John grants bishopric and abbey of Glendalough to Henry of London, abp of Dublin (confirmed by Pope Honorius III, 1216)

Oct. 3 John surrenders kingship of England to holy see

Felix Ua Ruanada, abp of Tuam, seeks refuge in Dublin

c. 1213 × 1240

Muiredach Albanach Ua Dálaig, poet, *fl.*

1214

Thomas fitz Roland, earl of Atholl, builds castle at Coleraine

Normans build castles at Roscrea, Clonmacnoise, and Durrow; expel Cormac Ua Máel Sechlainn from Delbna (bar. of Garrycastle, Co. Offaly)

Thomas fitz Roland and Ruaidrí, son of Ragnall (of the Isles), plunder Derry

Cormac Ua Máel Sechlainn campaigns in Delbna against Máel Sechlainn Bec Ua Máel Sechlainn; defeats Normans at Clonmacnoise; destroys castle at Birr

Ualgarg Ua Ruairc campaigns against Philip de Nangle in Cairpre (?Carbury, north Co. Sligo, or north Co. Longford)

Donnchad Cairprech Ua Briain invades Desmond in support of Cormac Óc Liathánach Mac Carthaig

Entire family of Domnall Mór Ua Súilliubáin massacred by Diarmait Mac Carthaig

July 11 Livery granted to Richard de Burgh

July 27 Battle of Bouvines: Philip II Augustus defeats Emperor Otto IV and his English allies

1215

June 24 Proclamation of Magna Carta

June 27 Further grants in north-east Ulster to Thomas fitz Roland, earl of Atholl

July 3 John grants charter to Dungarvan
Custody of counties of Waterford and Desmond and vill of Dungarvan granted to Thomas fitz Anthony

July 5 Walter de Lacy restored to his lands in Meath
Trí Tuatha (east Co. Roscommon) granted to Geoffrey de Costentin in exchange for lands near Athlone
John grants Dublin right to hold in fee farm (exemption from sheriff's jurisdiction and right to assess own taxes)
John grants charter to Waterford

July 6 Geoffrey de Marisco app. jcr

Sept. 13   John grants charter for Connacht to Cathal Crobderg Ua Conchobair; Richard de Burgh granted livery of his father's lands in Connacht

Nov. 11   Fourth Lateran council opened by Innocent III; about 20 Irish prelates attend: Schottenklöster formally organised as 'national' order under abbot of St Jakob at Regensburg (see 1185)

1216

Jcr (de Marisco) builds castle at Killaloe

Abbots of Mellifont and Jerpoint deposed by Cistercian general chapter

p. **Aug. 11**   Death of Echdonn Mac Gilla Uidir (Eugenius), abp of Armagh, at Rome; succ. by Luke Netterville (elected *a.* Aug. 1217)

Oct. 18/19   John, kg of England, dies; succ. by his son Henry III (minority until 1227)

Nov. 12   Magna Carta issued for Ireland (transmitted, Feb. 1217)

Trad Ó Máel Fábaill of Cenél Fergusa (Inishowen) killed with his brothers by Muiredach, son of *mormáer* of Lennox

Sees of Mayo and Glendalough suppressed by Innocent III

1216/17

Felix Ó Ruanada, abp of Tuam, imprisoned by Máel Ísu, son of Toirrdelbach Ó Conchobair, abbot of Roscommon

Hostilities near Armagh between Normans and O'Neills and MacMahons

1217

Jan. 14   Royal mandate against promotion of Irishmen to cathedral benefices

Feb. 28   Papal tax levied for 5th crusade

Hugh de Lacy in France; granted safe conduct by Henry III to travel to English court

June 23   Reginald de Braose granted livery of his father's lands in Munster, including custody of Limerick city

Nov. 2   Office of treasurer created in Irish exchequer

Nov. 10   Feudal 'aid' levied

c. 1218-19

Foundation of house of Premonstratensian canons at Trinity Island, Lough Key, by Clarus Mac Máilín, archdeacon of Elphin

1219

Muirchertach Ó Floinn, lord of Uí Thuirtre, and Congalach Ó Cuinn, lord of Mag Lugad and Síl Cathusaig (Co. Antrim), killed by Normans

Collegiate church of St Patrick, Dublin, raised to cathedral status

Death of John de Courcy

Apr. 23   Papal recognition of rights of crown in Irish episcopal elections

May 14   William Marshal dies; succ. by his son William

Normans begin invasion of Tír Briúin na Sinna (east Co. Roscommon) in association with Murchad Carrach Ó Fergail

c. **1219**

Gilla Brigte Albanach and Muiredach Albanach Ó Dálaig, poets, take part in 5th crusade

1220

c. **Aug.**   Walter de Lacy returns to Ire.; campaigns against Ó Ragallaig

Aug. 11   De Marisco continued as jcr; feudal 'aid' levied

1220–21

Jcr (de Marisco) campaigns in Desmond; builds castle at Mag Rátha (Carbery, west Co. Cork)

Cistercian general chapter orders visitation of Irish Cistercian houses

24 July 1220 × 23 July 1221   Cathal Crobderg Ó Conchobair and his son Áed, with the kingdom of Connacht, taken under papal protection by Honorius III

1221

Cathal Crobderg Ó Conchobair invades Calad na hAngaile (in bar. Rathcline, Co. Longford); Walter de Lacy abandons construction of castle at Áth Liac (Ballyleague; see 1200)

Diarmait, son of Ruaidrí Ó Conchobair, contender for kingship of Connacht, killed by Thomas fitz Roland, earl of Atholl, while returning from the Isles with fleet

Walter de Lacy grants lands of Ualgarg Ua Ruairc in west Bréifne to Philip de Nangle

July 3   Henry of London, abp of Dublin, app. jcr (acting, 4 Oct.)

1222

autumn   Jcr (Henry of London) campaigns against Hugh de Lacy; peace arranged at Dundalk

Dublin imposes tax on wines

Dec. 27   Grant to Hugh de Lacy of those lands given him by his brother Walter, as well as those in right of his wife Lesceline de Verdon

1223

William de Lacy campaigns in Meath

June 3   Custody of Cork, Desmond, and Decies granted to John Marshal; seneschalship of Munster, with custody of Limerick castle, granted to Richard de Burgh (5 June)

summer   Instructions to fortify royal castles against Hugh de Lacy; papal letters of excommunication against expected invaders *c.* 1223

Death of Giraldus Cambrensis

William Marshal the Younger grants charter to Carlow

1223-4

Hugh de Lacy campaigns with Áed Ó Néill in Ulster, Meath, and Leinster; besieges Carrickfergus

1224

First Irish Dominican foundations, at Dublin and Drogheda

Cathal Ó Ragallaig recovers his stronghold on Loch Uachtair (Co. Cavan) from de Lacys

Feb. Ó Conchobair opens negotiations with English court for succession of his son Áed as kg of Connacht

May 2   William Marshal the Younger app. jcr (acting, 24 June)

May 28   Cathal Crobderg Ó Conchobair, kg of Connacht, dies; succ. by his son Áed

Charters to Cîteaux from Áed Ó Conchobair, Donnchad Cairprech Ó Briain, kg of Thomond, and nobles of Thomond

June 14   Uí Briúin, Conmaicne, and Calad (territories in Cos Leitrim and Longford), held by William de Lacy, granted to Áed Ó Conchobair

summer   Coleraine castle destroyed by Hugh de Lacy and Áed Ó Néill

Aug. 11   Trim surrenders to jcr

c. **Sept.**   Hugh de Lacy still in alliance with Ó Néill

c. **Oct.**   Hugh de Lacy surrenders to jcr at Dundalk; sent to kg

Nov. 8   Geoffrey de Marisco app. to act in place of jcr (absent in England)

c. 1224-30

First Irish Franciscan foundations, at Youghal and Cork

1225

Toirrdelbach, son of Ruaidrí Ó Conchobair, installed as kg of Connacht by Áed Ó Néill

Toirrdelbach Ó Conchobair expelled by Áed Ó Conchobair, assisted by de Marisco and Donnchad Cairprech Ó Briain

May 12   Walter de Lacy granted his brother Hugh's lands and castles in Ire.

Dec. 11   St Laurence O'Toole canonised by Honorius III

1226

Abbot of Clairvaux app. by general chapter to reform Irish Cistercian houses

Áed, son of Domnall Ó Ruairc, killed by Cathal Ó Ragallaig

Kilmore castle (Co. Cavan) destroyed by Cathal Ó Ragallaig

Jan. 29 Clerical subsidy levied

May 12 Lands and castles of Hugh de Lacy in Ire. committed to custody of Walter de Lacy

June 25 Geoffrey de Marisco reapp. jcr (acting, *c.* July)

June 30 Mandate for summons of Áed Ó Conchobair to surrender Connacht, and delivery of custody of his kingdom to Richard de Burgh

July 10 William Marshal the Younger ordered to surrender castles of Carmarthen and Cardigan before going to Ire.; unrest among his retainers in Ire.

Dec. 18 Lands held in custody by Thomas fitz Anthony granted to Richard de Burgh

1227

Opposition to Cistercian visitors by Mellifont and 5 daughter houses; their abbots deposed; filiation of Mellifont broken up

Apr. 20 Hugh de Lacy restored to his lands

Áed Ó Conchobair refuses to attend tribunal at Dublin; meeting arranged with de Marisco at Athlone; Ó Conchobair's men attack de Marisco and burn town; forfeiture of Áed Ó Conchobair

May 21 All Connacht granted as fief to Richard de Burgh

Áed Ó Conchobair flees to Tír Conaill; Áed, son of Ruaidrí Ó Conchobair, installed as kg of Connacht by Richard de Burgh

Jcr (de Marisco) campaigns in Connacht in support of Toirrdelbach, son of Ruaidrí Ó Conchobair; builds castles at Rindown and Athleague

Sept. 3 Port of Ross restricted to ships of lordship of Leinster

1228

Áed Ó Conchobair, kg of Connacht, murdered; succ. by Áed, son of Ruaidrí Ó Conchobair, with opposition from his brother Toirrdelbach

Feb. 13 Richard de Burgh app. jcr

May 8 Mandate for summons of hierarchy and magnates in Ire. to be sworn to observance of laws granted by Kg John

May–Sept. Stephen of Lexington, Cistercian visitor, in Ire.; decrees refiliation of Irish houses; enters Mellifont (27 July)

July 16 Henry III grants union of sees of Lismore and Waterford (not effected until 1363)

a. **Nov. 12** Death of Henry of London, abp of Dublin; succ. by Luke (elected *a.* 13 Dec.)

Drogheda imposes tax on wines

Coleraine castle rebuilt

Writing of Cistercian Annals of Boyle transferred to Premonstratensian house at Trinity Island, Lough Key

1229

Death of Diarmait Mac Carthaig, claimant to kingship of Desmond, at Dún Droignén (Castlemore, bar. Muskerry E., Co. Cork); Cormac Óc Liathánach unopposed as kg

Fedlimid, son of Cathal Crobderg Ó Conchobair, campaigns against sons of Ruaidrí Ó Conchobair; plunders Rindown

Feb. 14   Reginald, kg of Man, killed by his brother Olaf

June 18   Henry III grants charter for lands occupied by Robert de Mandeville in Ulster during reign of John

Henry III grants charter to Dublin, giving power to elect mayor

July 25   Lands 'nearer to the Irish' in Connacht granted to Geoffrey de Costentin in exchange for the Trí Tuatha (see 1215)

Sept. 20   Henry III grants charter to Drogheda (north town), recognising guilds

c. **1229**

Alan of Galloway visits Ire.; marries daughter of Hugh de Lacy

1230

Áed Méith Ó Neill, kg of Tír Eógain, dies; succ. by his son Domnall Óc

Fedlimid Ó Conchobair installed as kg of Connacht by Richard de Burgh, Donnchad Cairprech Ó Briain and Cormac Mac Carthaig

Apr. 27   Requisition of all Irish exchequer moneys by Henry III

1231

Death of Ualgarg Ó Ruairc, kg of Bréifne (*a.* 1196–), on pilgrimage to Holy Land

Fedlimid Ó Conchobair captured by Richard de Burgh at Meelick; Áed Ó Conchobair restored as kg of Connacht

Apr. 6   William Marshal the Younger dies; succ. by his brother Richard (homage, *c.* 8 Aug.)

July 27   Requisition of all Irish exchequer moneys for the Welsh campaign of Henry III

Cormac mac Tommaltaig Mac Diarmata, kg of Mag Luirg, builds market town at Port na Cairrge (Rockingham, Lough Key)

a. **1232**

Kerry shired as separate county

1232

Domnall Got Cairprech, son of Domnall Mór Mac Carthaig, invades Ó Mathgamna's territory of Carbery

Hostilities between Domnall Mór Ó Domnaill and Domnall Mac Lochlainn

June 16   Henry III confirms charter to Waterford city (see 1215)

Hubert de Burgh, jcr of England, app. jcr of Ire. for life; dismissed shortly after 29 July

July 28   Separate chancery created for Ire.; Ralph de Neville, bp of Chichester and chancellor of England, first chancellor; Geoffrey de Tourville his deputy

c. **Aug.**   Fedlimid Ó Conchobair freed by order of Henry III

Aug. 25   Hubert de Burgh banished from England

Sept. 2   Maurice FitzGerald app. jcr

Castle begun at Galway by Richard de Burgh, and at Dunamon by Adam de Staunton

1233

Richard de Burgh refuses to surrender Meelick castle

Áed Ó Conchobair, kg of Connacht, defeated and killed by Fedlimid Ó Conchobair, who recovers kingship

Fedlimid Ó Conchobair destroys Anglo-Irish castles of Galway, Hen's Castle, Hag's Castle, and Dunamon

Feb. 4   Commn to audit accounts of Richard de Burgh, jcr 1228-32

May 4   Connacht resumed by crown

Aug.   Richard Marshal flees to Wales

Aug. 28   Henry III abandons preparations for Irish expedition

1233/4

Death of William de Lacy while on expedition to recover lands from Ó Ragallaig

1234

Óengus Mac Gilla Finnén, kg of Fir Manach, killed by Domnall Mór Ó Domnall

Donnchad Cairprech Ó Briain attacks Limerick

Fedlimid Ó Conchobair campaigns in Meath; burns Ballylochloe and Ardnurcher

Diarmait, son of Cormac Óc Liathánach Mac Carthaig, defeated and killed by Anglo-Irish

Domnall Óc Ó Néill, kg of Tír Eógain, defeated and killed by Domnall Mac Lochlainn, who assumes kingship

c. **Feb. 2**   Death of Alan, earl of Galloway; Hugh de Lacy intervenes in succession dispute on behalf of Thomas, son of Alan

Richard Marshal returns from Wales

Apr. 1   Jcr (Maurice FitzGerald), Richard de Burgh, and the de Lacys attack Richard Marshal and Geoffrey de Marisco: Marshal wounded; de Marisco captured

Apr. 16   Richard Marshal dies; succ. by his brother Gilbert (livery, 25 May)

Apr. 28   Peter de Rievaulx, treasurer, dismissed; de Tourville given custody of treasury (25 Aug.)

May 25   Hubert de Burgh and Henry III reconciled

Sept. 27   Connacht restored to Richard de Burgh

1235

Jan. 4   Papal commn of inquiry into alleged abuses in Ire.

Mar. 23   Felix Ó Ruanada resigns see of Tuam (dies at Dublin, 1238)

June 2   Papal release of Gilbert, Walter, and Anselm Marshal from oath taken to Henry III; they and their lands in Wales and Ire. taken under papal protection (18 June)

c. **June 1**   Jcr (Maurice FitzGerald), Richard de Burgh, and Hugh de Lacy campaign in Connacht and Munster; Donnchad Cairprech Ó Briain submits; Fedlimid Ó Conchobair flees to Tír Conaill

Jcr campaigns against Ó Flaithbertaig and Ó Máille

Jcr captures Mac Diarmata's stronghold at Rock of Lough Key with siege engines

Ó Conchobair submits to jcr

Aug. 3   Geoffrey de Marisco and Henry III reconciled

Anglo-Irish garrison abandons Rock of Lough Key; Cormac Mac Diarmata destroys it

Meelick castle destroyed by Ó Conchobair

1236

Death of Áed Ó Flaithbertaig, kg of Iar-Chonnacht

Alexander II of Scotland defeats Hugh de Lacy: Alan of Galloway's daughters confirmed in their inheritance

summer   Jcr (Maurice FitzGerald) campaigns in Connacht; installs Brian, son of Toirrdelbach Ó Conchobair, kg; builds castle at Onagh (bar. Athlone)

late in year   Richard de Burgh campaigns in Connacht; builds castle at Loughrea

Jcr builds castle near Armagh

1237

Revolt of O'Briens

Fedlimid Ó Conchobair defeats Brian, son of Toirrdelbach Ó Conchobair, at Drumrat; attacks Rindown

Limerick imposes tax on wines

The 5 'king's cantreds' restored to Fedlimid Ó Conchobair

May 21   Olaf, son of Godred, kg of Man, dies

Oct. 5   Clerical subsidy levied

a. **Oct. 17**   Death of Donnchad (Donatus) Ó Fidabra, abp of Armagh

Cathal Ó Ragallaig grants Trinity Island, Lough Oughter, to Clarus Mac Maílín, archdeacon of Elphin, for foundation of Premonstratensian canons (see 1250)

1237-8

Encastellation of Connacht by Anglo-Irish

1238

Jcr (Maurice FitzGerald) and Hugh de Lacy campaign in Tír Eógain; depose
Domnall Mac Lochlainn, kg of Tír Eógain, in favour of Brian, son of Niall
Ó Néill

Mar. 23 Requisition of all Irish exchequer moneys by Henry III

c. **1238**

Speculative grant to Maurice FitzGerald in Tír Conaill by Hugh de Lacy

1239

Battle of Carn Siadail (Carnteel, bar. Dungannon, Co. Tyrone): Domnall Mac
Lochlainn regains kingship of Cenél nEógain

Death of Ruaidrí, son of Toirrdelbach Ó Conchobair

Fergal, son of Cú Chonnacht Ó Ragallaig, killed by Conchobar, son of Cormac
Mac Diarmata; retaliatory raids on Mac Diarmata (1240) by Cú Chonnacht
Ó Ragallaig

a. **Mar. 4** Albrecht Suerbeer of Cologne provided to see of Armagh

c. **1239**

Thomas Aquinas pupil of Peter of Ireland, professor of philosophy at University
of Naples

1239-41

Jcr (Maurice FitzGerald) campaigns in Cairpre Dromma Cliab and Luigne
(baronies of Carbury and Leyney, Co. Sligo)

1240

Kiev destroyed by Mongols (see *p.* 1179)

Fedlimid Ó Conchobair at English court

Apr. 11 Death of Llywelyn Fawr, prince of north Wales, at Aberconway

c. **July** Henry III announces his intention of making expedition to Ireland in
1241

Nov. 15 Papal commn to examine proposed union of Clogher and Armagh
dioceses

c. **1240**

Ardstraw incorporated into diocese of Cenél nEógain (Derry/Ráith Lúraig) at
expense of Clogher

1241

Death of Muirchertach Finn Ó Briain, ex-kg of Thomond

Death of Walter de Lacy

Jcr (Maurice FitzGerald) campaigns in Connacht against Mac Diarmata and
Ó Floinn

June 16 Henry de Bath and William le Brun commissioned to view state of Ire., to extend and settle waste land in Connacht, and to recover alienated crown rights

June 27 Gilbert Marshal dies; succ. by his brother Walter

autumn Domnall Mór Ó Domnall, kg of Tír Conaill, dies; succ. by his son Máel Sechlainn

Battle of Caiméirge (? near Maghera): Domnall Mac Lochlainn defeated and killed by Brian Ó Néill and Máel Sechlainn Ó Domnall; eclipse of Mac Lochlainn dynasty

1242

Donnchad Cairprech Ó Briain, kg of Thomond, dies; succ. by his son Conchobar

Jcr (Maurice FitzGerald) and Fedlimid Ó Conchobair campaign in Lower Connacht and Tír Conaill against Tadg, son of Áed, son of Cathal Crobderg Ó Conchobair; Tadg captured by Cú Chonnacht Ó Ragallaig

Sons of Áed Ó Conchobair destroy de Nangle's castle in Bréifne

Walter and John Bisset expelled from Scotland for their part in murder of Patrick, son of Thomas, earl of Galloway; they occupy Galloway lands in north-east Ulster

Jan. 2 Henry III grants Cork city right to hold in fee farm (see 1215) and recognises guilds

Mar. 23 Feudal 'aid' levied

May 4 Requisition of all Irish exchequer moneys by Henry III

William, son of Geoffrey de Marisco, executed as pirate

1243

Death of Hugh de Lacy; earldom of Ulster reverts to crown (see 1263)

Apr. 19 Requisition of all Irish exchequer moneys by Henry III

Apr. 24 Order for construction of large assembly hall in Dublin castle

summer Death of Richard de Burgh in retinue of Henry III in Poitou

1244

Cormac Óc Liathánach Mac Carthaig, kg of Desmond, dies; his son Domnall Ruad killed by John fitz Thomas, having been handed over by Domnall Gall, his brother; succ. by Cormac Finn, son of Domnall Mór

Fedlimid Ó Conchobair campaigns against Ó Ragallaig to revenge castration of Tadg Ó Conchobair (c. 11 Feb.)

Feb. 13 Papal commn to examine Armagh primacy

May 14 John de Verdon restored to his lands in Meath, part of inheritance of his wife Margery, granddaughter of Walter de Lacy

June 11 Feudal service exacted for Scottish war

July 7 Irish kings and lords summoned to join Henry III in an expedition to Scotland

July 13   Requisition of all Irish exchequer moneys by Henry III for Scottish wars

Donnchad Mór Ó Dálaig, poet, dies

a. 1245

Lighthouse built at Hook Head, Co. Wexford (still in use, 1980)

1245

Jan. 10   Feudal 'aid' levied for Welsh expedition of Henry III

Fedlimid Ó Conchobair and Maurice FitzGerald with Henry III in Wales

Aug. 18   Pope Innocent IV nominates abp of Dublin, bps of Ossory and Kildare as conservators of rights of Franciscan friars

Nov. 4   John fitz Geoffrey app. jcr (acting, c. Aug. 1246)

Death of Walter Marshal (24 Nov.) and his brother Anselm (22-4 Dec.)

Castles built at Sligo by Maurice FitzGerald, and at Áth in Chip (near Carrick-on-Shannon) by Miles de Nangle

Geoffrey de Marisco dies in exile

1246

June 18   William de Cheney, seneschal of Leinster, ordered to allow chancery writs there

Nov. 1   Máel Sechlainn Ó Domnaill unsuccessfully besieges Sligo castle

c. 1246-c. 1280

Gilla Brigte Mac Con Mide, poet, *fl.*

a. 1247

Connacht shired

1247

Cormac Finn Mac Carthaig, kg of Desmond, dies; succ. by his brother Domnall Got Cairprech

Toirrdelbach Ó Conchobair and Donnchad Mac Gilla Pátraic campaign against d'Exeters, de Stauntons, and other Anglo-Irish in Connacht

Máel Sechlainn Ó Domnaill, kg of Tír Conaill, defeated and killed by Maurice FitzGerald and Cormac of Clann Ruaidrí Uí Chonchobair at Ballyshannon (Mac Sumarlaide, *gallóglach* captain, also killed); succ. by Ruaidrí Ó Canannáin

Feb. 22   Richard, son of Richard de Burgh (d. 1243), granted livery of his father's lands

Mar. 20   Requisition of Irish exchequer moneys by Henry III

May 3   Marshal inheritance divided among 5 co-heiresses

May 18   Miles de Nangle expelled from Bréifne by Cathal Mac Ragnaill and Toirdelbach, son of Áed, son of Cathal Crobderg Ó Conchobair

June 16   Henry III grants charter to Drogheda (north town), recognising guilds

June 24   Innocent IV sanctions transfer of see of Cenél nEógain from Ráith Lúraig (Maghera) to Derry

Roscommon and Ardcarne burned by Anglo-Irish

1248

Tradry (Co. Clare) granted to Robert de Muscegros, who builds castles at Bunratty and Clarecastle

Geoffrey de Cogan killed by Fíngen, son of Diarmait Mac Carthaig

Ruaidrí Ó Canannáin, kg of Tír Conaill, defeated and killed by Gofraid, son of Domnall Mór Ó Domnaill, who succeeds to kingship

Anglo-Irish raids on Umall (the Owles, Co. Mayo) and Iar-Chonnacht

Jcr (John fitz Geoffrey) campaigns in Tír Eógain; builds bridge across Bann at Coleraine

1249

Mar. 16   Cardinal John de Froisinone app. papal legate in Ire.

Fíngen, son of Diarmait Mac Carthaig, killed by the de Cogans and his uncle Domnall Cairprech Mac Carthaig

Jcr (John fitz Geoffrey) campaigns in Leinster and Desmond

Áed, son of Fedlimid Ó Conchobair, attacks Anglo-Irish of Tireragh (Co. Sligo); defeats Piers de Bermingham

Jcr campaigns in Connacht; Toirrdelbach, son of Áed, son of Cathal Crobderg Ó Conchobair, installed as kg in opposition to Fedlimid Ó Conchobair, who flees to Tír Eógain

Sept. 8   Jordan d'Exeter defeats Áed and Toirrdelbach, sons of Áed, son of Cathal Crobderg Ó Conchobair, at Athenry; Áed killed

Donnchad Mac Gilla Pátraic killed by Anglo-Irish

1250

Premonstratensian canons from Loch Cé brought to Trinity Island, Lough Oughter (see 1237) by Clarus Mac Maílín (d. 1251)

Toirrdelbach Ó Conchobair expelled from Connacht by Fedlimid Ó Conchobair with assistance from Tír Eógain

Maurice FitzGerald campaigns in Tír Eógain with Cú Chonnacht Ó Ragallaig

May 29   Conchobar Ó Briain confirmed in tenure of Thomond for a fine

June 16   Crusade to Holy Land to be preached in Ire., with authority of Pope Innocent IV and permission of Henry III

Sept. 24   Pope revokes ordinance of certain Irish prelates excluding Englishmen from Irish canonries

1251

Oct.   Mint opened at Dublin (over £43,000 coined before closure, 1254)

1251 × 1254

Conchobar Ó Briain grants charter in favour of Cîteaux

1252

Dublin city adopts uniform standard of weights and measures

Feudal 'aid' levied on clergy

'Irish riot' at Oxford university; written agreement of peace (see 1267)

Jcr (John fitz Geoffrey) campaigns in Tír Eógain; Brian Ó Néill submits; his son Ruaidrí taken as hostage; castles begun at Cáeluisce (Belleek) and Mag Coba (Dromore)

Aug. 29   Domnall Got Cairprech Mac Carthaig, kg of Desmond, killed by John fitz Thomas FitzGerald and his son Maurice at Baile Uí Dúnadaig (east Co. Cork); succ. by his son Fíngen

Dec. 20   Henry III grants charter to Drogheda (north town), giving power to elect a mayor

c. 1252

Carthusian monastery at Kinalehin (Co. Galway) founded by John de Cogan

1252-3

Florence (Flann) Mac Floinn, abp of Tuam, negotiates with Henry III for union of sees of Annaghdown and Tuam

1253

Séfraid Ó Donnchada and others of his family killed by Fíngen Mac Carthaig

Castle of Mag Coba destroyed by Brian Ó Néill

Áed, son of Fedlimid Ó Ragallaig, campaigns against Cathal Ó Ragallaig and Cathal Ó Conchobair (expelled from Connacht by Fedlimid Ó Conchobair, 1250)

Mar. 13   Clerical tenth levied

July 2   Leasing of king's demesne lands by royal officials prohibited

July 5   Lands in Uí Maine granted to Richard de la Rochelle and Jordan d'Exeter (7 July)

July 10   Provisional grant of Connacht to Stephen Longespée, cousin of Henry III

July 21   Royal mandate to jcr for colonisation of all waste lands in Ire.

July 23   Liberty rights in Meath granted to Geoffrey and Matilda de Geneville

Carrickfergus, Tír Eógain, Uí Echach (Iveagh), and Uí Thuirtre assigned in dower to Eleanor, consort of Henry III

July 30   Royal mandate to jcr against official interference with Conchobar Ó Briain

Aug. 11   Requisition of Irish exchequer moneys for war in Gascony

a. **1254**

Limerick and Tipperary shired as separate counties

1254

Dedication of St Patrick's cathedral, Dublin

Feudal 'aid' levied for marriage of Catherine, daughter of Henry III, and for defence of Gascony

Jan. 8   Royal order for closure of Irish mint (see Oct. 1251)

Feb. 11   Grants in Connacht and Thomond to Geoffrey de Lusignan, half-brother of Henry III

Feb. 14   Edward, son and heir of Henry III, designated 'lord of Ireland'

July 21   Feudal 'aid' levied for knighting of Edward

Aug. 4   Clerical tenth levied

c. **Nov.**   Richard de la Rochelle app. jcr

1255

Áed, son of Fedlimid Ó Conchobair, goes to Tír Eógain to make peace between his father and northern kings and brings back Connacht exiles

Brian Ó Néill campaigns against Cú Chonnacht Ó Ragallaig

Jan. 2   Requisition of all Irish exchequer moneys for war in Gascony

June 22   Two Connacht cantreds, held in fee farm (see 1215) by Fedlimid Ó Conchobair, granted by Henry III to Geoffrey de Lusignan

Aug. 17   Lord Edward commanded to go to Ire.

Oct. 14   Pope Alexander IV confirms and defines primatial rights of Armagh

Dec. 12   Death of Luke, abp of Dublin

1256

Jan. 26   Pope condemns English attitudes to Irish laws of inheritance

Walter de Burgh campaigns in Lower Connacht with Ó Ragallaig

Mar. 21   Pope authorises Máel Pátraic Ó Scannail, bp of Raphoe, to excommunicate 'idolators' in his diocese

c. **May 3**   Battle of Mag Slécht (south of Ballymagauran, Co. Leitrim): Cathal Ó Ragallaig, kg of Muintir Máelmórda (east Bréifne) (*c.* 1220-   ), and his brother Cú Chonnacht defeated and killed by Áed Ó Conchobair and Conchobar, son of Tigernán Ó Ruairc, kg of Bréifne

c. **May 16**   Ó Ruairc makes further inroads on the O'Reillys, who appeal to de Burgh and de Nangle for assistance

Alan de la Zouche app. jcr by Lord Edward

July 27   Fulk de Sandford provided to see of Dublin; election of Ralph de Norwich, chancellor, annulled

Jcr (de la Zouche) and Áed Ó Conchobair parley at Rindown

De Burgh campaigns against Ruaidrí Ó Flaithbertaig; occupies Lough Corrib

Grant of lands in Uriel and England to Geoffrey de Lusignan in lieu of earlier Connacht grants

1256-7

Áed Ó Conchobair campaigns against Conchobar Ó Ruairc; supports sons of Ualgarg Ó Ruairc

1257

Tadg, son of Conchobar Ó Briain, implicates his father in rebellion

Death of John Bisset

Cathal, son of Áed, son of Cathal Crobderg Ó Conchobair, blinded by Fedlimid Ó Conchobair

Ó Conchobair, Walter de Burgh, and jcr (de la Zouche) parley at Athlone

Battle of Credran Cille (north Co. Sligo): FitzGerald advance northwards halted; Cáeluisce castle destroyed by Gofraid Ó Domnaill; Sligo burned

Anglo-Irish raids into Thomond against Conchobar Ó Briain

Conchobar Ó Ruairc, kg of Bréifne (a. 1250-   ), killed by the O'Reillys; succ. by Amlaíb, son of Art Ó Ruairc (d. 1258)

Apr. 3   William de Bagepuz app. escheator

c. **May 27**   Death of Maurice FitzGerald

May 29   Walter de Salerno, dean of St Paul's, provided to see of Tuam (d. 1258)

1258

Llywelyn ap Gruffydd proclaimed Prince of Wales

Gofraid Ó Domnaill, kg of Tír Conaill, dies; succ. by his brother Domnall Óc

Domnall, son of Conchobar Ó Ruairc, made kg of Bréifne by Fedlimid Ó Conchobair; deposed by Art, son of Cathal Riabach Ó Ruairc, later this year

Jordan d'Exeter killed intercepting Dubgall Mac Sumarlaide's naval raid on Connacht

Tadg Ó Briain, Fedlimid Ó Conchobair, and Brian Ó Néill parley at Cáeluisce; high-kingship conceded to Ó Néill

Anglo-Irish attack Conchobar Ó Briain: burn Ardrahan and Kilcolgan (south Co. Galway)

p. **July 17**   Bp Tommaltach Ó Conchobair of Elphin el. abp of Tuam

Stephen Longespée app. jcr (acting *c.* Mar. 1259)

1259

Conchobar Ó Briain destroys FitzGerald manors in Co. Galway

Art, son of Cathal Riabach Ó Ruairc, imprisoned by Áed Ó Conchobair

Áed Ó Conchobair marries daughter of Dubgall Mac Sumarlaide, who brings dowry of 160 *gallóclaig*

Gilbert de Nangle captured by Áed Ó Conchobair; released on sureties

Death of Tadg, son of Conchobar Ó Briain

Further meeting of Brian Ó Néill and Fedlimid Ó Conchobair, at Devenish: Domnall Ó Ruairc restored as kg of Bréifne

Nov. 7   John fitz Thomas FitzGerald granted lands formerly held by Thomas fitz Anthony in Decies and Desmond, and custody of Dungarvan

1260

Walter de Burgh campaigns in Connacht against Fedlimid Ó Conchobair

Fíngen Mac Carthaig campaigns in Ciarraige Luachra (north Kerry)

Conchobar Ó Briain defeats Maurice fitz Maurice FitzGerald at Kilbarron (Co. Clare)

Domnall Ó Ruairc, kg of Bréifne, killed by Mac Tigernáin of Tellach Dúnchada (bar. Tullyhunco, Co. Cavan)

Domnall Óc Ó Domnaill drives Maurice fitz Maurice FitzGerald from Tír Conaill; raids Cairpre (north Co. Sligo)

Mar.   Death of Stephen Longespée; William of Dene app. jcr

Apr. 29   Royal order against Scots migration into Ire.

May 16   Battle of Downpatrick: jcr defeats Áed Ó Conchobair and Brian Ó Néill, kg of Tír Eógain; Ó Néill killed; succ. by Áed Buide Ó Néill

1261

John de Verdon in Ire.; builds castle at Moydow (Co. Longford)

c. **Mar.**   Bp Máel Pátraic Ó Scannail, O.P., of Raphoe, el. abp of Armagh

Castleconnell destroyed by Ó Briain

Battle of Callan (near Kenmare): Fíngen Mac Carthaig defeats jcr (William of Dene), Richard de Burgh, and John fitz Thomas FitzGerald; fitz Thomas and his son Maurice killed; numerous castles destroyed

Áed Buide Ó Néill, kg of Tír Eógain, deposed by his brother Niall Cúlánach

Conchobar Ó Briain reconciled with Dublin government

Art, son of Cathal Riabach Ó Ruairc, escapes from confinement (see 1259): installed as kg of Bréifne; makes peace with Áed Ó Conchobair

c. **July**   Death of William of Dene; Richard de la Rochelle app. jcr (*c.* Oct.)

Sept. 29   Fíngen Mac Carthaig, kg of Desmond, killed by Miles de Courcy while attacking Ringrone; succ. by his brother Cormac

1262

Jcr (de la Rochelle), Walter de Burgh, and John de Verdon campaign in Connacht against Fedlimid Ó Conchobair and his son Áed; build castle at Roscommon; make peace with Ó Conchobair at Derryquirk (near Tulsk, Co. Roscommon)

Walter de Burgh campaigns in Desmond; Cormac Mac Carthaig defeated and killed at Mangerton: succ. by his cousin Domnall Ruad

1262-3

Irish kings offer high-kingship to Haakon IV, kg of Norway, for support in expelling English from Ire.

1263

Áed Buide Ó Néill recovers kingship of Tír Eógain from Niall Cúlanach Ó Néill

July 15 Walter de Burgh created 2nd earl of Ulster (see 1243)

Sept. 31-Oct. 1 Battle of Largs: Alexander III, kg of Scotland, defeats Norwegians (Hebrides ceded to Scotland, 1266)

Dec. 15 Death of Haakon IV, kg of Norway, in Orkneys

De Burgh campaigns in Connacht: builds castle at Áth in Gaill (Ballymote, Co. Sligo)

Bp Hugh of Taghmon resists Armagh jurisdiction in diocese of Meath

1264

Art Ó Máel Sechlainn campaigns in Delbna, Bregmaine, and Calraige (western Westmeath and Offaly)

Walter de Burgh captures FitzGerald castles of Ardrahan and Lough Mask

Fedlimid and Áed Ó Conchobair make peace at Athlone with jcr (de la Rochelle), de Burgh, and Maurice fitz Maurice FitzGerald

May 14 Battle of Lewes: Simon de Montfort defeats and captures Henry III

June 18 Parliament at Castledermot

Sept. 24 Gilbert de Clare, earl of Gloucester, granted livery of his Irish lands

Dec. 6 Maurice fitz Maurice FitzGerald captures jcr, Theobald Butler, and John de Cogan at Castledermot, and imprisons them at Lea castle; Geoffrey de Geneville app. 'custos'

Abp Máel Pátraic Ó Scannail brings Franciscan friars to Armagh

1265

Fedlimid Ó Conchobair, kg of Connacht, dies; succ. by his son Áed

Áed Buide O'Neill and Walter de Burgh campaign in Tír Conaill

Áed Ó Conchobair and Domnall Óc Ó Domnaill destroy castles of Sligo, Banada, and Ardcree

Apr. 19 Assembly at Dublin convened by 'custos' (de Geneville) to establish concord between the magnates

May 6 Henry III summons de la Rochelle, de Geneville, de Burgh, and Maurice fitz Maurice FitzGerald; Roger Waspayl app. 'custos'

June 10 Hugh of Taghmon, bp of Meath, app. jcr by de Montfort

Aug. 4 Battle of Evesham: Simon de Montfort defeated and killed by Henry III and Edward

Norman-French poem composed on building of defences at New Ross

1266

Death of Toirrdelbach Ó Conchobair, ex-kg of Connacht, in religious retirement at Knockmoy

Abp Máel Pátraic Ó Scannail, O.P., begins new cathedral at Armagh

Papal grant of clerical tenth for 3 years to Henry III

Widespread activity against Anglo-Irish of Connacht; castles destroyed at Ardnaree (by Ó hEgra), Castletogher (by Ó Floinn), and elsewhere in Tireragh and Iar-Chonnacht

Art Ó Ruairc, kg of Bréifne (1258–   ), deposed by Áed Ó Conchobair in favour of Conchobar Buide, son of Amlaíb (d. 1258), son of Art

c. Michaelmas   David de Barry app. jcr

Nov. 24   Magnus son of Olaf, last kg of Man, dies; Alexander III of Scotland assumes sovereignty of Man

c. Dec.   Giovanni de Alatre provided to see of Clonfert

1267

Murchad Mac Suibne captured by Domnall, son of Magnus Ó Conchobair, in Umall (the Owles, Co. Mayo); dies in custody of Walter de Burgh, earl of Ulster

Anglo-Irish retaliate in Cairpre (north Co. Sligo; see 1266); Ballysadare burned; 'Mac Uilliam' de Burgh campaigns in Tír Maine (south Co. Roscommon)

Sept. 29   Henry III at Montgomery confirms terms of treaty of Pipton made by Simon de Montfort with Llywelyn ap Gruffydd (1265)

'Irish riot' at Oxford; written agreement of peace (see 1252)

1268

Friars of the Sack (Saccati) established at Dublin

Dubgall, son of Ruaidrí Mac Sumarlaide, dies

Áed Ó Conchobair defeats Anglo-Irish in Tír Maine

May 22   Conchobar Ó Briain, kg of Thomond, killed by Diarmait, son of Muirchertach Ó Briain; succ. by his son Brian Ruad

July 12   Henry III intervenes against alienation of lands in Ire. by his son Edward

c. July 25   Maurice fitz Gerald FitzGerald, baron of Offaly, dies

Aug. 1   Naval engagement between sons of Domnall Gall Mac Carthaig and O'Driscolls

Robert d'Ufford app. jcr (acting, *c*. Nov.)

1269

Jcr (d'Ufford) campaigns in Connacht: fortifies Roscommon castle; rebuilds Sligo castle

1270

Máel Pátraic Ó Scannail, O.P., abp of Armagh, dies

Sligo castle again destroyed by Domnall Óc Ó Domnaill (see 1265)

Richard d'Exeter app. deputy jcr

Battle of Áth in Chip (near Carrick-on-Shannon): Walter de Burgh defeated by Áed Ó Conchobair; his brother William Óc killed

Battle of Áth Malais (Ballymalis, Co. Kerry): Domnall Ruad Mac Carthaig defeated by Maurice fitz Thomas FitzGerald (unidentifiable) and Clann Chormaic Liathánaig (sept of MacCarthys)

Áed Ó Conchobair destroys castles of Roscommon, Rindown, Onagh, Kilcolman, Castlemore-Costello, and Ballymote

Clarecastle captured by Brian Ruad Ó Briain

on or *a*. Michaelmas James de Audley app. jcr

Feudal levy summoned to Athlone; jcr campaigns in Connacht

c. **1270**

First Carmelite friary established, at Leighlinbridge

'Liber exemplorum' (manual for preaching) compiled by Franciscan friar, based on practice in Ire. *c.* 1250–*c.* 1270

1271

May 4 Fulk de Sandford, abp of Dublin, dies

July 28 Walter de Burgh, 2nd earl of Ulster and 1st lord of Connacht, dies, succ. by his son Richard (the 'Red Earl'), a minor

Thomas fitz Maurice FitzGerald dies

Nicholas de Verdon killed by O'Farrells in Angaile (Annaly, Co. Longford)

Áed Ó Conchobair destroys more Anglo-Irish castles, including Sligo, Temple-house, and Athleague

Jcr (de Audley) leads expedition to Desmond and Thomond; Brian Ruad Ó Briain submits

Bad weather, famine, and disease

1272

David Mac Cerbaill (Mac Carwill), abp of Cashel, founds Cistercian monastery at Cashel

Henry Butler of Umall killed by Clann Muirchertaig Muimnig (sept of O'Connors)

Áed Ó Conchobair invades west Meath as far as Granard; destroys bridge and castle of Athlone, and castles of Rindown and Roscommon

June 11 Death of James de Audley on campaign in Thomond; Maurice fitz Maurice FitzGerald app. jcr; campaigns in Offaly

July 1 John de Muscegros, sheriff of Limerick, commissioned to treat for peace with Irish kings

Nov. 16   Henry III, kg of England, dies; succ. by his son Edward I

Dec. 7   William fitz Warin appointed seneschal of Ulster; opposed by Henry de Mandeville, bailiff of Tuaiscert (north Co. Antrim)

1273

Jcr (Maurice FitzGerald) leads expedition to Thomond; Brian Ruad Ó Briain submits

Michaelmas   Geoffrey de Geneville app. jcr

Clann Muirchertaig Muimnig and O'Flahertys expelled from Umall and Iar-Chonnacht by Anglo-Irish

Irish wool taxed at Bruges

1274

General chapter of Cistercian order restores filiation of Mellifont (see 1227)

Jcr (de Geneville) campaigns in Leinster mountains; defeated at Glenmalure

May 3   Death of Áed Ó Conchobair, kg of Connacht

c. **Aug.**   Succession of Tadg Ruad, son of Toirrdelbach, son of Áed, son of Cathal Crobderg, to kingship of Connacht

Nov. 7   Theobald de Verdon granted livery of his lands

Nov. 13   Franciscans in Ire. exhorted by papal letters of Gregory X to preach crusade

Thomas de Clare, brother of earl of Gloucester, marries daughter of Maurice fitz Maurice FitzGerald

Irish students agitate at Oxford; written agreement of peace (see 1252, 1267)

1275

Anglo-Irish of Louth campaign against Ó hAnluain

May 25   Custom levied on wool, woolfells, and hides

Edward I issues writs in favour of merchants of Lucca, appointed with merchants of Florence to receive customs of Ire.

a. **1276**

Henry de Mandeville murdered; fitz Warin indicted but acquitted

1276

Jcr (de Geneville), Thomas de Clare, and Maurice fitz Maurice FitzGerald campaign in Leinster; defeated again at Glenmalure

Domnall Óc Ó Domnaill supports Áed Muimnech, son of Fedlimid Ó Conchobair, returned from Munster to contest kingship of Connacht

Jan. 26   Thomond granted in fee tail to Thomas de Clare

June 17   Robert d'Ufford reapp. jcr

Sept. 26–Feb. 22   Stephen de Fulbourn, treasurer and bp of Waterford, campaigns in Ulster

1276-7

Parliaments at Kildare and Kilkenny

David Mac Cerbaill (Mac Carwill), abp of Cashel, petitions kg for grant of English
law to Irish

First Welsh war of Edward I

1277

May 11 Toirrdelbach, son of Tadg Ó Briain of Cáeluisce, defeats Thomas de
Clare and Brian Ruad Ó Briain, kg of Thomond; Brian murdered by de Clare
at Bunratty; succ. by Toirrdelbach, with opposition from Donnchad, son of
Brian

May 22 Edward I requisitions all income from earldom of Ulster for Welsh war

a. **Michaelmas** Jcr (d'Ufford) campaigns successfully in Glenmalure; fortifies
Castlekevin

Roscommon castle destroyed again by Áed Muimnech Ó Conchobair and
Domnall Óc Ó Domnaill

Nov. 9 Treaty of Aberconway: Llywelyn ap Gruffydd submits to Edward I

c. **1277-80**

Eclipse of Mac Duinn Sléibe dynasty in Ulster

1278

Tadg Ruad Ó Conchobair, kg of Connacht, killed by sons of Cathal Mac Diarmata;
succ. by Áed Muimnech, son of Fedlimid Ó Conchobair

Toirrdelbach Ó Briain defeats Donnchad, son of Brian Ruad Ó Briain, and Thomas
de Clare at Quin

Dingle (Co. Kerry) raises £121 on import tax on wine

Easter (?) Parliament (location unknown)

Nov. 13 Liberty of Kildare restored to Agnes de Vesci

1279

Feb. 8 John of Darlington provided to see of Dublin

June 16 Death of Tommaltach Ó Conchobair, abp of Tuam; succession contested

Sept. 22 Parliament at Dublin

Thomas de Clare begins castle at Quin

1280

Grants by Domnall Ruad Mac Carthaig to Domnall Máel Cairprech, son of
Domnall Got Cairprech, in Desmond south of River Lee, and to Fedlimid

Mac Carthaig in Múscraige, Uí Chonaill, and Eóganacht Uí Donnchada (south Co. Kerry); Killorglin and Dunloe castles burned by the Mac Carthys

Áed Muimnech Ó Conchobair, kg of Connacht, killed by Clann Muirchertaig Muimnig; succ. by Cathal Ruad, son of Conchobar, of that sept

Stephen de Fulbourn, bp of Waterford, app. deputy jcr

Jan. 5   Richard, 3rd earl of Ulster, granted livery of his father's lands

June 10   Order for resumption of liberty rights in de Verdon lands in Meath; shired as part of Co. Dublin

Anglo-Irish magnates directed to assemble for purposes of examining Irish petition for English law

Dec. 12   Christina de Marisco surrenders her Irish lands in exchange for others in England

1281

Mints reopened at Dublin and Waterford (see 8 Jan. 1254; Waterford mint closes 1282, Dublin 1283)

Thomond divided between Toirrdelbach and Donnchad Ó Briain, who accept Thomas de Clare's overlordship, through arbitration of Domnall Ruad Mac Carthaig, supported by government

Battle of Dísert dá Chrích (Desertcreaght, bar. Dungannon, Co. Tyrone): Domnall Óc Ó Domnaill, kg of Tír Conaill, defeated and killed by Áed Buide Ó Néill and Thomas de Mandeville; succ. by his son Áed

p. **Easter**   Parliament at Dublin

c. **Apr.-Aug.**   Jcr (d'Ufford) campaigns in Thomond

Nov. 21   Stephen de Fulbourn app. jcr

a. 1282

Priory of Augustinian friars established at Dublin

1282

Mar. 21   Outbreak of last Welsh war of independence

July 21   Muirchertach Mac Murchada, kg of Leinster, and his brother Art killed at Arklow

Customs profits of Ross granted to Donati firm of Florence

Oct. 2   Feudal 'aid' levied

Dec. 11   Llywelyn ap Gruffydd, last native prince of Wales, killed by English forces at Irfon Bridge

c. 1282

Accession of Donn Carrach Mág Uidir, first of his name to hold kingship of Fir Manach

1282-3

Kilkenny imports wine, pepper, saffron, ginger, almonds, cummin, figs, and raisins

1283

Áed Buide Ó Néill, kg of Tír Eógain, defeated and killed by Brian Mac Math-gamna, kg of Airgialla, and Gilla Ísu Ó Ragallaig, kg of east Bréifne; succ. by Domnall, son of Brian Ó Néill

Domnall Ruad Mac Carthaig, with Anglo-Irish support, campaigns against Domnall Máel Mac Carthaig of Uí Chairpre

a. **Mar. 14** Attempted revival of diocese of Annaghdown with election of John d'Ufford to see (never consecrated)

June David, brother of Llywelyn, captured; executed at Shrewsbury

Nov. Loan for Welsh war

1283-4

Jcr (de Fulbourn) campaigns against Leinster Irish; Lea castle in Offaly[1] burned by Irish of Leinster and Meath

1283 × 1290

Nicholas de Cusack, O.F.M., bp of Kildare, writes warning Edward I of seditious teachings of Irish friars

1283-95

Encastellation of north Wales by Edward I

1284

Donnchad, son of Brian Ruad Ó Briain, killed by Toirrdelbach Ó Briain

Mar. 3 Statute of Rhuddlan establishes direct royal administration over principality of Wales

Apr. William fitz Roger, prior of Kilmainham, app. deputy jcr

May 5 Thomas fitz Maurice FitzGerald granted livery of his lands

July 24-Aug. 27 Jcr (de Fulbourn) campaigns in Connacht

1285

Cairpre Ó Máel Sechlainn, kg of Mide, campaigns in support of Irish of Offaly

Hostilities between Magnus Ó Conchobair of Clann Muirchertaig Muimnig and the Cusacks and Costelloes

June 5 Requisition of all moneys arising out of Irish issues for war in Wales

Dominican and Franciscan friars in Ire. denounced for 'making much of the Irish tongue'

c. 1285

De Fulbourn's administration of exchequer condemned; addition of second baron to Irish exchequer and audit removed to Westminster

---

[1] Now in Co. Leix.

1286

Narragh and Ardscull (Co. Kildare) burned by Leinster Irish; In Calbach, brother of Ó Conchobair Failge (O'Connor Faly), captured at Kildare and imprisoned in Dublin castle

Richard de Burgh campaigns in Connacht and Ulster; Domnall Ó Néill, kg of Tír Eógain, deposed in favour of Niall Cúlánach, son of Domnall Óc Ó Néill

July 12 Bp Stephen de Fulbourn, jcr, translated from Waterford to Tuam

Oct. 1 Death of Maurice fitz Maurice FitzGerald

1287

Aug. 29 Death of Thomas de Clare

Jcr (de Fulbourn) campaigns in Thomond

Death of Gerald fitz Maurice FitzGerald

1288

Cathal Ruad Ó Conchobair, kg of Connacht, captured and deposed by his brother Magnus

July 3 Death of Stephen de Fulbourn, abp of Tuam and jcr; John de Sandford, abp of Dublin, app. jcr (7 July)

Jcr campaigns in Connacht (July), Leinster, and Desmond (Sept.)

autumn William de Bermingham elected to see of Tuam

Sept. 9 Jcr summons royal service to Kildare against Irish of Offaly and Leix

1289

Magnus Ó Conchobair and jcr (de Sandford) unsuccessfully campaign against Cairpre Ó Máel Sechlainn

Sept. 23-Oct. 5 Jcr campaigns successfully in Leix and Offaly

In Calbach Ó Conchobair Failge defeats Prendergasts and de Berminghams

p. **Michaelmas** Parliament at Dublin

1290

Domnall, son of Brian Ó Néill, recovers kingship of Tír Eógain from Niall Cúlánach Ó Néill

Cairpre Ó Máel Sechlainn, kg of Mide, killed by David Mac Cochláin, lord of Delbna; succ. by his son Murchad (d. 1293)

a. **Jan. 13** Parliament at Dublin

Apr. 3-8 Parliament at Kilkenny

Aug. 6 Custody of Donnchad, son of Toirrdelbach Ó Briain, granted to Richard de Burgh

Sept. 12 William de Vesci, heir of Agnes de Vesci (d. 1290), app. jcr (arrives in Ire., 11 Nov.)

1290-91

Toirrdebach, son of Domnall O Domnaill, kg of Tír Conaill in opposition to his brother Áed

1291

Niall Cúlánach Ó Néill killed in attempt by Richard de Burgh to reinstate him in kingship of Tír Eógain; Domnall Ó Néill deposed in favour of Brian, son of Áed Buide Ó Néill

Hostilities between Magnus and Cathal Ó Conchobair, rival claimants to kingship of Connacht

Mar. 18 Clerical tenth granted for 6 years
Pope Nicholas IV commissions abps of Armagh, Cashel, and Tuam, their suffragans, and Franciscans in Ire., to preach crusade

May 6 Parliament at Dublin

June Irish Franciscan provincial chapter at Cork: dispute between Irish and Anglo-Irish friars; 16 killed, many wounded

Compact of Trim: Nicholas Mac Máel Ísu, abp of Armagh, and suffragans of his province pledge mutual support against secular infringements of ecclesiastical liberties

Crown officials seize money of Italian merchant bankers at Dublin, Ross, Kilkenny, Limerick, Youghal, and Cork

1292

Jan. 28 Council at Dublin: feudal 'aid' of a fifteenth granted for royal wars

Feb. 6 Custody of Decies and Desmond, with castle of Dungarvan, granted to Thomas fitz Maurice FitzGerald

Richard de Burgh campaigns in Connacht; Magnus Ó Conchobair submits at Meelick

1293

Death of Magnus Ó Conchobair, kg of Connacht; succession contested between Áed, son of Eógan, supported by jcr (de Vesci) and Cathal, son of Conchobar Ruad (killed later this year), supported by John fitz Thomas FitzGerald, de Bermingham, and Mac Diarmata

Fergal Ó Ragallaig, kg of east Bréifne, killed; succ. by Gilla Ísu Ruad, son of Domnall

July 1 Jcr summons royal service to Kildare (24 July), ostensibly against Irish of Offaly; summons revoked by Edward I

July 21 Transmiss of statutes from parliament at Canterbury to Ire.

Oct. 13 Fitz Thomas FitzGerald presents complaints against de Vesci in parliament at Westminster

Edward I gives safe conduct to Flanders merchants in Ire.

1294

Mints reopened at Dublin and Waterford (Waterford closed, 1295; Cork mint briefly in operation, 1295-6)

Sligo castle destroyed by Áed Ó Conchobair; John fitz Thomas FitzGerald and de Bermingham campaign against him

Mar. 5   Walter de la Haye app. acting jcr

Apr. 1   Fitz Thomas FitzGerald challenged in council at Dublin to single combat by William de Vesci

Apr. 21   De Vesci and fitz Thomas FitzGerald summoned to appear before parliament at Westminster (14 June)

Edward I at war with France; his invasion of Gascony prevented by Welsh revolt

June 4   William fitz Roger app. 'custos'

July 20   Great storm destroys crops; resultant famine and disease

July 24   Fitz Thomas FitzGerald loses case by failing to appear for combat with de Vesci

Oct. 2   Death of John de Sandford, abp of Dublin

c. **Oct.**   Gilbert de Clare in Ire.

Oct. 18   William de Oddingeseles app. jcr

Dec. 11   Richard de Burgh captured by Fitz Thomas FitzGerald at Lea castle in Offaly (see 1283-4)

1294-5

John fitz Maurice FitzGerald campaigns in Leinster; 'Maurice' Mac Murchada submits (19 July 1295)

1295

Séfraid Ó Fergail destroys castles of Moydow, Newcastle, and Street (Co. Westmeath)

Brian, son of Áed Buide Ó Néill, killed by Domnall Ó Néill, kg of Tír Eógain, who assumes title of kg of Ulster (*rí Ulad* or *rex Ultoniae*)

Mar. 12   John fitz Thomas FitzGerald releases Richard de Burgh and recovers rights of lordship over his Connacht lands (13 Mar.)
Parliament at Kilkenny

Apr. 3   Death of William de Oddingeseles (Thomas fitz Maurice FitzGerald app. 'custos')

July   John Balliol, kg of Scotland, refuses summons of Edward I to attend him abroad (issued 29 June 1294); makes alliance with France (22 Oct. 1295)

Aug. 27   Fitz Thomas FitzGerald submits to arbitration of Edward I in claims against Richard de Burgh, earl of Ulster

Oct. 18   John Wogan app. jcr (acting, 3 Dec.)

Dec. 7   Death of Gilbert de Clare, earl of Gloucester

Dec. 16   Edward I declares war on Scots

1296-1323
Scottish wars of Edward I and Edward II

1296
Death of William de Valence, earl of Pembroke

Jan. 2 Robert, O.S.B., of Canterbury, provided to see of Clonfert

Conchobar Ruad, son of Cathal Ó Conchobair, killed in attempt to depose Áed Ó Conchobair from kingship of Connacht

Jan. 7 Parliament at Kilkenny

Mar. 28 Edward I invades Scotland

Apr. 24 William Hotham, O.P., provided to see of Dublin (d. 27 Aug. 1298)

c. **May 13** Jcr (Wogan), Richard de Burgh, de Geneville, and John fitz Thomas FitzGerald with Edward I in Scotland

July 10 John Balliol, kg of Scotland, surrenders and abdicates at Stracathro

Sept. 3 Pardon granted to Richard de Burgh

Nov. 15 Pardon granted to John fitz Thomas FitzGerald

Dublin, Waterford, Limerick, Ross, and Drogheda export corn to Gascony

1297
Irish war supplies for Edward I reach Gascony

Jan. 13 William de Vesci surrenders Kildare and other Irish possessions; regrant for life (22 June); death of de Vesci (July); Kildare shired

Easter term Parliament at Dublin: ordinance against use of Irish dress by Anglo-Irish; shiring of Meath from de Verdon lands (see 12 June 1280)

May William Wallace leads rising of Scots against English; defeats English at Stirlingbridge (11 Sept.)

autumn Irish contingent led by John fitz Thomas FitzGerald and David Caunton arrives in Flanders for Edward I

Oct. 9 Truce in Flanders between Edward I and Philip the Fair

Oct. 23 Richard de Burgh, John fitz Thomas FitzGerald, and others released from projected service in Flanders on account of their exorbitant demands

Feudal service to Castlecomer; jcr (Wogan) campaigns against Irish of south Leinster

Rathangan burned by Irish of Offaly

1298
Hugh Bisset of Antrim harasses Scots with 4 ships

Bunratty besieged by Toirrdelbach Ó Briain; relieved by jcr (Wogan)

Papal rescript for reception of English prior provincial of Dominicans in Ire.

Jan. 27 Parliament at Dublin

Apr.-May Parliament

June 4   Death of Thomas fitz Maurice FitzGerald

July 22   Battle of Falkirk: Edward I defeats Wallace

c. **Sept.**   William fitz Warin, seneschal of Ulster, captured by Scots

Oct. 22   Richard de Burgh, earl of Ulster, recovers rights of lordship over John fitz Thomas FitzGerald's lands in Connacht

1299

John fitz Thomas FitzGerald and Piers de Bermingham campaign in Offaly

Alexander, son of Áengus Mór Mac Domnaill, killed by Alexander Mac Dubgaill

Jan. 20-27 and May 3   Parliament at Dublin

c. **Sept. 30**   Richard de Burgh app. deputy jcr

1300

Richard de Burgh begins castle at Ballymote

Jcr (Wogan) negotiates subsidies for Scottish war; Irish contingent with Edward I in Galloway

Apr. 24   Parliament at Dublin: subsidy granted

Irish wool taxed at Bruges

Geoffrey of Waterford, O.P., translator of secular Latin works into Norman-French, dies in France

1301

Large Irish army serves with Edward I in Scotland, under command of jcr (Wogan), fitz Thomas FitzGerald, and de Bermingham; William de Ros, prior of Kilmainham, app. deputy jcr (23 Aug.)

1302

Donn Carrach Mac Uidir, kg of Fir Manach, dies; succ. by his son Flaithbertach

Marriage of Elizabeth de Burgh, daughter of Richard de Burgh, earl of Ulster, to Robert Bruce, earl of Carrick

Domnall Ruad Mac Carthaig, kg of Desmond, dies; succ. by his son, Domnall Óc

Jan. 18-Mar. 12   Feudal service to Newcastle Mac Kynegan (Co. Wicklow) commanded by deputy jcr (William de Ros)

Feb. 23   Further appeal for support of Anglo-Irish magnates in Scottish war

Mar. 12   Papal grant of clerical tenth for 3 years to Edward I

May 13-20   Parliament at Dublin

June 30   Maurice de Rochefort appointed deputy jcr; campaigns against O'Nolans in Fotharta (Forth, Co. Carlow)

Oct.-Nov.   Parliament at Dublin

Dec. 3   Parliament at Kilkenny

Dublin mint closed (see 1294)

1302-4

Renewed grant of custom on wool and hides in Ire. to Frescobaldi of Florence

1302-6

Ecclesiastical taxation of Ire.

1303

Peter de Paris, first Irish admiral, transports large Irish army under Richard de Burgh to join Edward I in Scotland

May 10   Death of Nicholas Mac Máel Ísu, abp of Armagh

May 20   Treaty of Paris: peace between England and France; Gascony restored to Edward I

c. **May end**   De Burgh with Edward I in Scotland

Citizens of Drogheda attack de Bermingham's forces

1304

July 20   Stirling castle surrendered to Edward I

Nov. 4   Edmund Butler app. 'custos'

1305

Clann Muirchertaig Muimnig (sept of O'Connors) defeat the O'Reillys

May   William Wallace betrayed and captured; executed at London (23 Aug.)

c. **June 13**   Muirchertach and In Calbach Ó Conchobair Failge murdered by Piers de Bermingham at Carbury castle (Co. Kildare)

Jcr (Wogan) campaigns in Kildare

Richard de Burgh builds Newcastle (Greencastle, Inishowen)

Inquisition to examine de Burgh's claims to Síl Muiredaig (Shilmorthy, Co. Roscommon), forfeited by O'Connors

1306

Ó Máel Sechlainn and Mac Eochacáin campaign against Piers de Bermingham

Mar. 25   Robert Bruce, earl of Carrick, crowned kg of Scotland at Scone

summer   Jcr (Wogan) campaigns in Leinster mountains

June 26   Battle of Methven: Bruce defeated by Edward I; retires to Rathlin Island

Aug.   Toirrdelbach Ó Briain, kg of Thomond, dies; succ. by his son Donnchad; civil dissension among O'Briens

Sept. 24   Domnall Óc Mac Carthaig captured and killed by Domnall Máel, son of Domnall Got Cairprech Mac Carthaig; succ. by his uncle, Donnchad Carrthain

a. **Dec. 6**   Death of Roger Bigod, earl of Norfolk, without heirs; his lordship of Carlow escheated to crown and shired

Roger Mortimer, earl of Wigmore, marries Joan, granddaughter and heiress of Geoffrey de Geneville, lord of Trim (Geoffrey grants seisin of lands to Roger, 1308)

1306-7

Áed Bréifnech Ó Conchobair of Clann Muirchertaig campaigns against Áed Ó Conchobair, kg of Connacht

1307

Amlaíb, son of Art Ó Ruairc, kg of Bréifne, killed; succ. by Domnall Carrach (d. 1311), brother of Conchobar Buide (d. 1273)

Feb.   Robert Bruce returns to Scotland; defeats Edward I at Loudon Hill (May)

Apr. 9   Parliament at Dublin

May 1   Donnchad Ó Cellaig, kg of Uí Maine, defeats Anglo-Irish of Roscommon at Ahascragh

c. **July 3**   Leix castle (besieged by Irish) relieved by John fitz Thomas FitzGerald and Edmund Butler; Geashill castle burned

July 7   Edward I, kg of England, dies; succ. by his son Edward II

Aug. 6   Walter Jorz, O.P., provided to see of Armagh

c. **Oct. 1**   Feudal service to Loughsewdy (Co. Westmeath)

Dec. 20   Templar property sequestrated by Edward II

1307-8

Hugh Bisset campaigns against Robert Bruce in the Isles

1308

May 12   Castlekevin burned by O'Tooles; Anglo-Irish defeated at Glenmalure (6 June); Athy, Dunlavin, and Tobar burned

May-July   William Liath, son of William Óc de Burgh, campaigns in Leinster

June 4   John Wogan reapp. jcr (acting, 16 May 1309)

June 16   Piers de Gaveston app. lieutenant (arrives in Ire., *c*. 25 June)

Oct. 1   William de Burgh app. deputy jcr; campaigns in Leinster (Oct.-Nov.)

1309

Deputy jcr (William de Burgh) campaigns in Leinster

Feudal service of Castlekevin; lieutenant (de Gaveston) campaigns at Glenmalure

Áed, son of Eógan Ó Conchobair, kg of Connacht, killed by Áed Bréifnech, son of Cathal Ruad Ó Conchobair; succ. by Áed Bréifnech

Aug. 16   Connacht granted free of rent to William de Burgh, with custody of Athlone, Roscommon, and Rindown castles

Aug. 21   Richard de Burgh, earl of Ulster, commissioned to treat with his son-in-law Robert Bruce

Maurice de Caunteton raises war in Wexford in alliance with O'Byrnes; jcr campaigns against them (Sept.)

Oct. 15 Roger Mortimer, earl of Wigmore, arrives in Ire. (see 1306)

Oct. Jean, Sire de Joinville, seneschal of Champagne and brother of Geoffrey de Geneville, writes 'Life of St Louis'

1310

Áed Bréifnech Ó Conchobair killed by Seónac Mac Uidilín, officer of his mercenaries, at instigation of William Liath de Burgh: Fedlimid, son of Áed, son of Eógan Ó Conchobair, installed as kg of Connacht by Máelruanaid Mac Diarmata at Carnfree with revival of ancient inauguration ceremonies

Ó Ragallaig and Mac Mathgamna campaign in Airgialla

Jan.-June Trial of Knights Templar in Dublin

Feb. 9 Parliament at Kilkenny: statute against reception of Irishmen as members of Anglo-Irish religious houses

p. **Mar. 24** Parliament at Kildare

Earl of Ulster (Richard de Burgh) builds castle at Sligo

1311

Edward II's government in England taken over by Lords Ordainers

Papal permit for establishment of university (*studium generale*) at Dublin

May 16 John Lech provided to see of Dublin

May 20 Warfare between O'Brien factions; battle near Bunratty; William de Burgh captured by Richard de Clare; Donnchad Ó Briain flees

Donnchad Ó Briain, kg of Thomond, killed near Corcomroe; succ. by Diarmait Cléirech of Clann Briain

June 25 Saggart and Rathcoole burned by O'Byrnes and O'Tooles; jcr (Wogan) summons feudal service against them (autumn)

autumn William de Burgh released; supports Muirchertach, son of Toirrdelbach Ó Briain, in opposition to Diarmait Cléirech Ó Briain, kg of Thomond

Oct. 9 Order for immediate levy of all debts due to crown in Ire.

Nov. 13 Roland Jorz, O.P., provided to see of Armagh

1311-12

Letter from Edward II to sheriffs and seneschals in Ire. commanding that Irish revenues be spent in Ire.

1312

De Verdons revolt in Louth; defeat jcr's force from Ardee

July 8 Parliament at Dublin

Aug. 7 Edmund Butler app. 'custos' and acting jcr

1313

Apr. 30   Theobald de Verdon app. jcr (acting, 19 June 1314)

May 31   Scots land in Ulster

c. **June 1**   Death of Diarmait Cléirech Ó Briain, kg of Thomond; kingship contested between Muirchertach, son of Toirrdelbach of Clann Toirrdelbaig, and Donnchad, son of Domnall of Clann Briain

Aug. 10   Death of John Lech, abp of Dublin; succession contested between Alexander Bicknor and Walter Thornbury

Nov. 28   Temporalities of Templars in Ire. assigned to Hospitallers

Abp of Armagh prevented from carrying his cross in Dublin

1314

William de Burgh supports Muirchertach Ó Briain against Donnchad Ó Briain; de Burgh and Richard de Clare agree to partition Thomond between rival O'Briens

Mar. 22   Edward II requests support of Irish kgs against Scots

Apr. 24   Requisition of all Irish exchequer moneys for Scottish war

June 24   Battle of Bannockburn: Robert Bruce defeats Edward II; Gilbert de Clare, earl of Gloucester and lord of liberty of Kilkenny, killed

Aug. 12   John de Hotham app. to supervise Dublin exchequer

Oct. 21   Geoffrey de Geneville, lord of Trim, dies (see 1306)

Dec. 14   Portion of earl of Gloucester's lands granted to Richard de Clare

1315

Jan. 4   Edmund Butler app. jcr (acting, 28 Feb.)

May 26   Edward Bruce lands at Larne

beginning of June   Parliament at Kilkenny

June 29   Dundalk captured by Bruce

Sept. 1   Jcr ordered to undertake examination of Irish friars and clerics living among Anglo-Irish

Bruce defeats Richard de Burgh, earl of Ulster, at Connor; captures William de Burgh; Carrickfergus besieged by Scots

c. **Sept. 1**   Fedlimid Ó Conchobair, kg of Connacht, deposed by Ruaidrí, son of Cathal Ruad Ó Conchobair of Clann Muirchertaig Muimnig

Oct. 27   Parliament at Dublin

c. **Dec. 6**   Bruce defeats Roger Mortimer, earl of Wigmore, in Meath

1315-17

Famine in western Europe, including Ire.

1316

Jan. 26   Edward Bruce defeats jcr (Butler) at Ardscull; Lea castle burned

mid-Feb.   Scots retreat to Ulster

Feb. 14   Parliament

Feb. 23   Ruaidrí Ó Conchobair, kg of Connacht, defeated and killed at Tóchar Móna Coinneda (Templetogher, Co. Galway), by Fedlimid, who recovers the kingship

Apr. 8   Thomas de Mandeville killed in attempt to relieve Carrickfergus with fleet from Drogheda

c. **May 1**   Edward Bruce crowned kg of Ire. near Dundalk

May 14   John fitz Thomas FitzGerald created 1st earl of Kildare (d. 12 Sept.)

summer   Widespread famine and plague

July 8   Parliament at Kilkenny

c. **July 20**   Stephen d'Exeter and other Anglo-Irish defeated and killed at Ballylahan by Fedlimid Ó Conchobair

July 27   Theobald de Verdon dies without male heir (lands in Meath partitioned among 4 coheiresses, 12 May 1332)

Aug. 7   Election of Pope John XXII

Aug. 8   Jcr commissioned to inquire into grievances contained in Irish petition to kg and council

Aug. 10   Battle of Athenry: Fedlimid Ó Conchobair, kg of Connacht, defeated and killed by William de Burgh and Richard de Bermingham; succ. by his cousin Ruaidrí na Fed

Sept. 5-6   David Ó Tuathail raids up to walls of Dublin

Donnchad Ó Briain, kg of half Thomond, deposed by Muirchertach Ó Briain, who recovers kingship of all Thomond

c. **Sept. 12**   Carrickfergus castle surrendered to Bruce

Nov. 23   Roger Mortimer, earl of Wigmore, app. lieutenant

c. **Nov.-Dec.**   Ruaidrí Ó Conchobair, kg of Connacht, deposed by Mac Diarmata

Dec.   Robert Bruce arrives at Carrickfergus

1316-31

Friar James, O.F.M., of Ire., accompanies Odoric de Pordenone as far as China

1317

Toirrdelbach, son of Áed Ó Conchobair, proclaimed kg of Connacht

Feb.   Scots army moves south from Ulster

c. **Feb. 2**   De Lacys indicted for inviting Edward Bruce to invade Ire.

Feb. 21   Richard de Burgh, earl of Ulster, imprisoned by mayor of Dublin, on suspicion of complicity with Bruce

Feb. 23   Bruces camp at Castleknock

Mar. 28   Concession of crusade tax in England, Wales, and Ire. to Edward II

c. **Apr. 1**   Bruces camp at Castleconnell with Donnchad Ó Briain

Edward II, for security reasons, relocates to Kilmainham parliament due to be held in Dublin

Apr. 7   Lieutenant (Mortimer) lands at Youghal; Bruces retire northwards

Apr. 10   John XXII publishes bull against mendicant friars supporting Bruce invasion

May 8   Earl of Ulster released

c. **May 22**   Robert Bruce returns to Scotland

July 2   Thomas Dun, pirate ally of Bruce, defeated and killed in naval battle by John de Athy

July 5   Aymer de Valence, earl of Pembroke and lord of Wexford, grants charter to Wexford

July   De Lacys outlawed

Aug. 17   Battle of Corcumroe: Donnchad Ó Briain killed by Diarmait, brother of Muirchertach Ó Briain

c. **1317**

Remonstrance addressed to Pope John XXII by Domnall Ó Néill and other Irish leaders

1318

Mar. 8   Toirrdelbach Ó Conchobair receives grant of royal lands of Síl Muiredaig, Feda, and Tír Maine (east and south Co. Roscommon)

Apr.   Berwick captured by Scots

May 6   William FitzJohn, abp of Cashel, app. 'custos' by council

May 10   Battle of Dysert O'Dea: Richard de Clare defeated and killed by Muirchertach Ó Briain

Toirrdelbach Ó Conchobair, kg of Connacht, deposed by Cathal, son of Domnall Ó Conchobair

Aug. 11   Alexander Bicknor, abp of Dublin, app. jcr (acting, 9 Oct.)

Oct. 14   Battle of Faughart: Edward Bruce defeated and killed by John de Bermingham

1318-19

Richard de Mandeville besieges John de Athy in Carrickfergus

1319

Mar. 15   Roger Mortimer, earl of Wigmore, jcr

May 12   John de Bermingham created earl of Louth

May 30   Inquiry instituted into Bruce's adherents in Ire.

June 4   Revaluation of Irish ecclesiastical benefices ordered

June 7   Jcr (Mortimer), earl of Kildare, and earl of Louth empowered to admit Irishmen to English law

Dec. 18   Papal grant of clerical tenth in England, Ire., and Wales for purposes of defence

1319-20

Bridges constructed at Kilcullen (on Liffey) and Leighlin (on Barrow)

1320

Royal declaration clears Edmund Butler of complicity in Scots invasion

Feb. 3   Inquiry into Bruce's adherents in Ire. cancelled

Apr. 27   Parliament at Dublin: approval for foundation of university at Dublin

Michaelmas   Petition for redress from lawless state of Ire. laid before English parliament

Sept. 30   Mortimer returns to England; Thomas fitz John FitzGerald, 2nd earl of Kildare, app. deputy jcr

1320-30

Outbreak of smallpox and other epidemics

1321

Commrs sent from Clairvaux to compel Irish Cistercian houses to receive novices without distinction between Irish and English

Apr. 23   Thomas fitz John FitzGerald, 2nd earl of Kildare, app. jcr (acting, 30 June)

May 1   Death of Thomas, infant heir of Richard de Clare; Maurice fitz Thomas FitzGerald receives custody of de Clare castles and lands

May 16   Armed retainers of Maurice fitz Thomas FitzGerald burn and plunder in west Cork

May 21   John de Bermingham, earl of Louth, app. jcr (acting, 28 Aug.)

autumn   Crop failure and cattle plague

Sept. 13   Death of Edmund Butler

Dec. 8   Jcr commissioned to correct errors in all records and processes of all pleas that were before Roger Mortimer

1322

Rise to prominence of Brian Bán, son of Domnall, son of Brian Ruad Ó Briain, in Thomond

May 22   Thomas, duke of Lancaster, executed

1323

Mar.   Edward II concludes truce with Scots

Mar. 16   Symon Semeonis (Simon FitzSimon) and Hugh le Luminour (the Illuminator), Anglo-Irish Franciscans, leave Ire. on pilgrimage to Holy Land (Symon's 'Itinerarium' (*p.* 1324) contains first datable reference to gipsies in Europe)

July 25   Order for farming out revenue from all lands and wardships, and sale of all marriages, pertaining to crown in Ire.

Aug. 1   Roger Mortimer escapes to France

Nov. 18   John Darcy app. jcr (acting, Feb. 1324)

Nov. 24   Edward II publishes ordinance 'de statu terre Hibernie'

1324

Feb. 12   Death of William Liath de Burgh, cousin of earl of Ulster

Apr. 7   Decree by chapter of Friars Minor at Dublin ordering distribution of Irish friars among Anglo-Irish houses; exclusion of Irishmen from office of guardian

May 13   Parliament at Dublin: magnates ordered to take action against malefactors of their own kindred

July 2   Dame Alice Kyteler convicted of heresy by Richard Ledred (Leatherhead), bp of Ossory

July   Roger Outlaw, son of Alice Kyteler, deputy jcr

Aug. 25   Cathal Ó Conchobair, kg of Connacht, killed by Toirrdelbach Ó Conchobair, who reassumes kingship, with continuing opposition from Mac Diarmata

1324-5

Recurrence of cattle plague

1325

July 8   Parliament at Kilkenny

Domnall Ó Néill, kg of Tír Eógain, dies; succ. by Énrí Ó Néill of Clann Áeda Buide (Clandeboye)

Diarmait Óc Mag Carthaig, kg of Desmond, killed at Tralee by FitzGeralds; succ. by his brother, Cormac

Custody of Cork created by general chapter of Friars Minor at Lyons

Armed retainers of Maurice fitz Thomas FitzGerald seize Bunratty castle and blind constable

c. **1325**

Memorandum on ecclesiastical reform presented at Roman curia by Philip of Slane, bp of Cork

'Book of Kildare' compiled; collection of poems, literary and religious pieces, in Latin, English, and Norman-French

1326

a. **June 24**   Richard de Burgh, 3rd earl of Ulster (the 'Red Earl') dies; succ. by his grandson William (the 'Brown Earl'), a minor

Parliaments at Kilkenny (11 May) and Dublin (*p.* 8 July)

July 31   Union of sees of Cork and Cloyne approved by John XXII

Sept. 24   Mortimer and Queen Isabella land in England

Oct. 29   Custody of lands of late earl of Ulster in Connacht, Tipperary, and Limerick granted to Edmund and Walter, sons of William Liath de Burgh

Traitorous assembly of lords convened by Maurice fitz Thomas FitzGerald in Tipperary

1327

Epidemic of smallpox

Domnall, son of Art Mac Murchada, proclaimed kg by Leinster Irish

Jan. 20   Edward II abdicates in favour of his son Edward III, a minor; rule of Queen Isabella and Roger Mortimer (until 1330)

Feb. 14   Thomas fitz John FitzGerald, 2nd earl of Kildare, app. jcr (letter patent 12 Mar.)

Apr.   Robert Bruce in Ulster

May 10   Parliament at Dublin

July 31   Union of sees of Annaghdown, Achonry, and Kilmacduagh with Tuam, and of Lismore with Waterford, approved by Pope John XXII

Aug. 23   Liberty of Trim restored to Mortimer

Sept. 21   Edward II, ex-kg of England, murdered

p. **Michaelmas**   Outbreak of hostilities between FitzGeralds (with de Berminghams) and de Burghs (with le Poers)

c. **1327/8**

Petition from 'divers men of Ireland' to Edward III that English law be available to Irishmen without special charter

1328

Walter de Burgh and Gilbert Mac Goisdelb (Costello; de Nangle) defeated by Mac Diarmata and Mac Donnchada

c. **Feb.**   Domnall Mac Murchada, kg of Leinster, and David Ó Tuathail captured and imprisoned in Dublin

c. **Feb. 1**   Arnold le Poer leaves for England

Feb. 2   Parliament at Kilkenny

Mar. 17   Treaty of Edinburgh: Edward III makes peace with Scots, recognising kingship of Robert Bruce

Apr. 5   Thomas fitz John FitzGerald, 2nd earl of Kildare, dies; Roger Outlaw, prior of Kilmainham, app. acting jcr (6 Apr.)

Apr. 11   Adam Dub Ó Tuathail burned for heresy at Le Hogges near Dublin

May 4   Treaty of Northampton ratifies treaty of Edinburgh

June 24   Jcr forbids disputing magnates to wage war

summer   Storms ruin crops; scarcity of food and clothing

Epidemic of influenza (*sláetán*)

Aug. 15   Parliament at Dublin

Aug. 22   Royal mandate to jcr to seek opinion of magnates concerning admission of Irish to English law

c. **Sept.**   William de Burgh, earl of Ulster, arrives in Ulster, accompanied by Robert Bruce

Oct. 16 × 31   James Butler created 1st earl of Ormond

Nov. 15   Earl of Ulster given custody of Carrickfergus castle

c. **Nov. 25**   Arnold le Poer and Roger Outlaw indicted for heresy by Richard Ledred (Leatherhead), bp of Ossory˙

1329

Jan. 20   Parliament at Dublin

Feb. 19   John Darcy reapp. jcr (acting, May)

Mar. 14   Death of Arnold le Poer

Apr. 2   Parliament at Dublin: earls of Ulster and Kildare reconciled

c. **June**   Richard Ledred, bp of Ossory, flees from Ire., after being indicted for fomenting discord among magnates

June 7   Robert Bruce, kg of Scotland, dies; succ. by David II, son of Robert Bruce and Elizabeth de Burgh

June 10   John de Bermingham, earl of Louth, and great number of relations and followers (including famous Irish musician, Máelruanaid Mac Cerbaill), killed by Anglo-Irish of Uriel (Co. Louth) at Braganstown

Aug.   Brian Bán Ó Briain invades Ormond; burns Athassel

Aug. 9   Thomas Butler killed by Mac Eochacáin

Aug. mid   Jcr campaigns against O'Byrnes

c. **Aug. 27**   Maurice fitz Thomas FitzGerald created 1st earl of Desmond; receives Kerry as a liberty

Walter de Burgh instigates expulsion of Cathal na Fed Ó Conchobair, brother of Toirrdelbach, kg of Connacht, from Tír Maine (south Co. Roscommon) by the O'Kellys of Uí Maine

1330

Gilla Ísu Ruad Ó Ragallaig, kg of east Bréifne, dies; succ. by his son Risdéard

Toirrdelbach Ó Conchobair in Ulster to procure aid from earl of Ulster against Walter de Burgh

Warfare in Connacht between Ó Conchobair and de Burgh, aided by Mac Donnchada

Earl of Desmond and Brian Bán Ó Briain campaign against O'Dempseys, O'Mores, and O'Nolans

May 31 Roger Outlaw app. deputy jcr (acting, 17 July)

July 8 Parliament at Kilkenny

July Jcr, with earl of Ulster, Muirchertach Ó Briain, and Toirrdelbach Ó Conchobair, campaigns against Brian Bán Ó Briain

Sept. 28 Earl of Desmond and Roger Outlaw summoned to England

Oct. 19 Roger Mortimer (1st earl of March, since 1328), arrested; Edward III assumes personal rule

Nov. 29 Mortimer executed

c. 1330

Manuscript collection of poems and other literary compositions in Hiberno-English, Norman-French, and Latin, compiled (B.M., Harl. MS 913)

1331

Jan. 21 Parliament at Dublin

Feb. 27 Anthony de Lucy app. jcr (acting, 3 June)

Mar. 3 William de Burgh, earl of Ulster, app. lieutenant
Ordinances for conduct of Irish government; include decree that there should be one law (*una et eadem lex*) for Irish and Anglo-Irish, except for betaghs

c. Apr. 25 Irish raid Tallaght

Irish raids in Co. Wexford: capture of Arklow (21 Apr.) and Ferns (Aug.)

July 1 Parliament meets at Dublin (at Kilkenny, 1 Aug.)

Aug. 16 Maurice FitzGerald, earl of Desmond, captured by jcr at Limerick

Edward III plans expedition to Ire. for 1332

Sept. Henry de Mandeville arrested

Walter de Burgh defeats Tommaltach Mac Diarmata in Mag Luirg

Nov. Walter de Burgh arrested by earl of Ulster

1332

Walter de Burgh starved to death while imprisoned by William de Burgh, earl of Ulster, at Greencastle (Co. Donegal)

Jan. 20–May 2 Jcr (de Lucy) campaigns in Munster; captures William and Walter de Bermingham (Feb.)

Apr. 7 Mortimer's outlawry of Hugh de Lacy queried

July Bunratty castle captured by Muirchertach Ó Briain and Mac Con Mara

July 11 William de Bermingham hanged at Dublin

Aug. 4 Jcr ordered to stay execution against magnates imprisoned for felonies; Roger Outlaw commissioned to treat with English and Irish at war with kg

Aug. 12 Battle of Dupplin Moor: earl of Mar, regent of Scotland, defeated and killed by Edward Balliol, with English support

Aug. 17   Parliament at Dublin

Sept. 9-Nov. 15   Jcr leads expedition to Thomond

Sept. 15   Edward III's planned expedition to Ire. abandoned

Sept. 20   Prisage of wine at ports of Dublin, Drogheda, Limerick, and Waterford granted to earl of Ormond

Sept. 24   Edward Balliol crowned kg of Scotland

Sept. 30   John Darcy reapp. jcr (acting, 13 Feb. 1333)

Dec. 3   Thomas de Burgh acting as deputy jcr

Richard FitzRalph of Dundalk app. chancellor of Oxford university (holds post till 1334)

1333

Earl of Desmond released

Áed Ó Domnaill, kg of Tír Conaill, dies; succ. by his son Conchobar

Death of Tommaltach Mac Donnchada, lord of Tír Ailella (Tirerrill, Co. Sligo)

Gilbert Mac Goisdelb (de Nangle) killed by Cathal Mac Diarmata Gall

June 6   William de Burgh, 4th earl of Ulster (the 'Brown Earl'), murdered at instigation of Richard de Mandeville

  Parliament at Dublin

June 29   Thomas de Burgh acting as deputy jcr

July 19   Battle of Hallidon Hill: Edward III defeats Scots

Ó Cellaig at war with Ó Conchobair (until 1339)

1334

Jcr (Darcy) campaigns against Brian Bán Ó Briain and Mac Con Mara; against Domhnall and Diarmaid Óg Mac Carthaigh; and against O'Tooles and O'Byrnes

July 4   David Mág Oireachtaigh provided to see of Armagh

July 16   Thomas de Burgh app. deputy jcr (acting, 19 Oct.)

Sept.   Balliol forced to flee to England

Sept. 5   Custody of Connacht lands of late earl of Ulster granted to his uncle Edmund, son of Richard de Burgh

1335

Parliament (or council): subsidy granted for Scottish war

Aug.   Jcr (Darcy) and earls of Desmond and Ormond with Edward III in Scotland

1336

Castlemore Costello (Co. Mayo) destroyed by Toirdhealbhach Ó Conchobhair

May 3   Ordinances for reform of Irish administration

c. **May 26**   Tomaltach Mac Diarmada, lord of Magh Luirg, dies; succ. by his son Conchobhar

June 22-3   Brian Bán Ó Briain burns Tipperary town; jcr (Darcy) campaigns against him

July 1   Prohibition against holding of lands by officials in areas where they hold office

1337

Peace established between Richard de Burgh and Brian Bán Ó Briain

Ruaidhrí Ó Ceallaigh defeats and captures Toirdhealbhach Ó Conchobhair

Mar. 3   Ordinance by kg and council in parliament at Westminster that land-holders in Ire. should pay subsidy for defence of their marches

Mar. 24   Irishmen enjoying English law granted access to Anglo-Irish religious houses

May 24   Philip IV, kg of France, confiscates Gascony from Edward III: beginning of hundred years war

July 28   John de Charleton de Powys app. jcr (arrives in Ire., 14 Oct.)

c. **Sept.**   Richard de Mandeville raids Isle of Man

1337-44

Richard FitzRalph at papal court, Avignon

1338

Jcr campaigns against Leinster Irish

Edmund de Burgh, son of 3rd earl of Ulster, drowned in Lough Mask by Edmund Albanach de Burgh and his brother Raymond; Toirdhealbhach Ó Conchobhair expels Edmund Albanach to western islands of Connacht

Irish attack Anglo-Irish of Luighne and Corann (Co. Sligo)

Matilda, countess of Ulster, offers to surrender lands in Ulster for others in England

Jan. 14   Parliament (or council) at Dublin: resistance to bearing of abp of Armagh's primatial insignia in city

a. **Feb. 18**   Death of James Butler, 1st earl of Ormond

Mar. 3   Royal order for demise of certain lands in Ulster to Énrí Ó Néill, to be held during minority of Elizabeth, heiress of late earl of Ulster
Ordinance of kg and council that justices of both benches be English by birth
Measures instituted to curtail abuses of alienation and absenteeism among Anglo-Irish

Mar.   Parliament: clerical tenth granted

May 15   Thomas de Charleton, bp of Hereford, app. 'custos' and acting jcr (acting, 19 June)

1339

Marriage of Toirdhealbhach Ó Conchobhair to widow of Edmund de Burgh

Edmund Albanach de Burgh expelled from western islands of Connacht to Ulster

Mint briefly reopened at Dublin (see 1302)

Oct. 29   Ruaidhrí Ó Ceallaigh killed by Cathal, son of Aodh, son of Eóghan Ó Conchobhair

Hostilities between Anglo-Irish and Irish in Kildare, Meath, and Kerry

1340

Tadhg Óg Ó Ceallaigh, nominee of Toirdhealbhach Ó Conchobhair in Uí Mhaine, killed by Uilliam Buidhe, son of Donnchadh Muimhneach Ó Ceallaigh

Aodh, son of Feidhlimidh Ó Conchobhair, protégé of Mac Diarmada, imprisoned by Ó Conchobhair

Cathal Mac Diarmada Gall killed by Donnchadh Riabhach, son of Maolsheachlainn Carrach Mac Diarmada

Conchobhar Ó Domhnaill invades Connacht

Jan. 25   Edward III styles himself 'king of France'

Mar. 3   John Darcy reapp. jcr (for life)

Mar. 14   Edmund Albanach de Burgh and his brother Raymond pardoned for death of Edmund de Burgh, son of 3rd earl of Ulster (see 1338)

Apr. 8   Roger Outlaw acting as deputy jcr

Aug. 4   Mac Murchadha and Ó Nualláin attack Gowran (Co. Kilkenny)

Dec.   Edward III purges his administration in England

Hostilities begin between Ó Ruairc and Clann Mhuircheartaigh Muimhnigh (sept of O'Connors)

1341

Toirdhealbhach Ó Conchobhair captures Roscommon castle

Jan. 23   Ross loses rights as open port

Feb. 13   Death of Roger Outlaw; Alexander Bicknor, abp of Dublin, app. 'custos' and acting jcr (22 Feb.)

Mar. 16   John Morice app. deputy jcr (acting, 16 May)

May 5   Elizabeth, daughter and heiress of William de Burgh, 4th earl of Ulster, betrothed to Edward III's son Lionel (marries Lionel, 9 Sept. 1342)

July 24   General resumption of all grants made since death of Edward I

July 27   Ordinance excluding all but Englishmen beneficed in England from holding office in Ire.

Aug. 2-Oct. 2   Deputy jcr (Morice) campaigns in Leinster against Mac Murchadha

Oct.   Parliament at Dublin, adjourned to Kilkenny (Nov.): petitions critical of administration sent to Edward III

Nov. 25   Order for examination of exchequer and its officials

1342

Conchobhar Ó Domhnaill, kg of Tír Conaill, killed by his brother Niall, who succeeds to kingship

Soldiers from Ire. requisitioned for Brittany

Jan. 16–May 18   Deputy jcr (Morice) campaigns against Irish of Meath

Mar. 31   English expelled from Scotland

Apr. 5   Maurice fitz Thomas FitzGerald, 4th earl of Kildare, granted livery of his lands

p. **July 1**   Toirdhealbhach Ó Conchobhair restores Roscommon castle to royal constable, William de Bermingham

July 16–Sept. 4   Deputy jcr campaigns in Wicklow against O'Byrnes

Nov. 4   Toirdhealbhach Ó Conchobhair, kg of Connacht, deposed by Mac Diarmada and Edmund Albanach de Burgh (Mac William Burke); Aodh, son of Aodh Bréifneach of Clann Mhuircheartaigh, made kg

1343

Muircheartach Ó Briain, kg of Thomond, dies; succ. by his brother Diarmaid, who is expelled by Brian Bán Ó Briain

Toirdhealbhach Ó Conchobhair recovers kingship of Connacht from Aodh, son of Aodh Bréifneach of Clann Mhuircheartaigh; makes peace with Mac Diarmada

Niall Ó Domhnaill, kg of Tír Conaill, deposed by his nephew Aonghus, with aid of Domhnall Dubh Ó Baoighill and Ó Dochartaigh, supported by Aodh Reamhar Ó Néill and MacSweenys

Clann Mhuircheartaigh (sept of O'Connors) expelled from Bréifne by Ualgharg Ó Ruairc, Ó Conchobhair, and Tadhg Mág Raghnaill; take refuge in Tír Aodha (bar. Tirhugh, Co. Donegal) under protection of Aonghus Ó Domhnaill

Clann Rickard Burkes and de Berminghams (Clann Fheórais) invade Uí Mhaine

Maurice FitzGerald, earl of Desmond, occupies Imokilly (east Co. Cork)

May 19   Robert Savage app. seneschal of Ulster

Oct. 26   Conchobhar Mac Diarmada, lord of Magh Luirg, dies; succ. by his brother Fearghal

1344

Feb. 10   Ralph d'Ufford app. jcr (acting, 14 July)

Apr. 20   Custody of lands of late earl of Ormond granted to earl of Desmond

Apr. 24   Sanction for 'bonnaght' in Ulster

June 3   Jcr ordered to resume and regrant all abandoned and waste lands

July 21   Jcr campaigns in south Leinster and Munster

Oct. 11   Pope Clement VI issues dispensation for marriage between Maurice fitz Thomas FitzGerald, earl of Kildare, and Joan, daughter of earl of Desmond

1345

Feb. 22   Assembly at Callan (Co. Kilkenny) under presidency of Maurice FitzGerald, earl of Desmond

Mar.   Énrí Ó Néill of Clann Aodha Buidhe (Clandeboye), kg of Tír Eóghain, deposed by jcr (d'Ufford) in favour of Aodh Reamhar (otherwise Aodh Mór), son of Domhnall Ó Néill

Apr./June   Parliaments at Dublin (24 Apr. and 5 June)

June 26   Earl of Desmond attacks Nenagh

Jcr campaigns against Desmond; captures Askeaton (30 Sept.) and Castleisland (21 Oct.)

Oct. 15   Toirdhealbhach Ó Conchobhair, kg of Connacht, killed by Clann Mhuircheartaigh; succ. by his son Aodh

? autumn   Earl of Kildare arrested and imprisoned in Dublin castle

Dec.   Jct (at Naas) resumes liberty of Kildare into hands of crown

1346

Ualgharg Ó Ruairc, kg of Bréifne (1316-), killed by Ruaidhrí, son of Cathal Ó Conchobhair

Ruaidhrí Ó Conchobhair defeated by Niall Ó Domhnaill, Clann Mhuircheartaigh, and Aodh, son of Feidhlimidh Ó Conchobhair

Apr. 7   John Morice app. jcr (acting 16 May)

Apr. 9   Death of Ralph d'Ufford; Roger Darcy app. jcr by Irish council (10 Apr.) (serves until 15 May)

May 4-5   Ó Conchobhair Failghe and Ó Díomasaigh destroy Lea castle; Mac Giolla Pádraig burns Aghaboe

May 10   Walter de Bermingham app. jcr (acting, 29 June)

May 12   Order to remove exchequer and common bench from Dublin

May 23   Maurice FitzGerald, earl of Kildare, released from Dublin castle

June   Brian Mór Mac Mathghamhna raids Anglo-Irish of Uriel (Co. Louth)

c. **June**   Maurice FitzGerald, earl of Desmond, submits to government

July 31   Richard FitzRalph provided to see of Armagh

Aug./Sept.   Jcr campaigns in Munster

Aug. 17   Papal commission for examination of union of sees of Annaghdown, Achonry, and Kilmacduagh with metropolitan see of Tuam

Aug. 26   Battle of Crécy: English defeat French

Sept.   Irish contingents with Edward III at siege of Calais

Sept. 13   Earl of Desmond leaves to answer charges in England

Oct. 16   Council at Kilkenny: subsidy granted for French and Scottish wars

Oct. 17   David II, kg of Scotland, captured at Neville's Cross, near Durham

Nov.   Jcr and earl of Kildare campaign against O'Mores and O'Dempseys

1347

Tomás Mac Artáin, kg of Uí Eachach Uladh (Iveagh, Co. Down) hanged by Anglo-Irish

Jan. Abp of Cashel and bps of Emly, Limerick, and Lismore oppose collection of subsidy

Feb. 16 James Butler, 2nd earl of Ormond, granted livery of his lands

Apr. 10 Diocese of Ossory exempted from metropolitan jurisdiction of Dublin

c. **May** Earl of Kildare and other Anglo-Irish lords join English army besieging Calais

June 5 Death of Domhnall Mac Murchadha, kg of Leinster; succession of Art Mac Murchadha

Nov. Jcr (de Bermingham) summoned to England; John Larcher app. deputy (28 Nov.)

Dec. 26 Nenagh burned by O'Kennedys

1348

Apr. 5 Edward III confirms primacy of Armagh

Apr. 26-July 27 Jcr (de Bermingham) returns to Ire.; campaigns in Ormond against O'Kennedys, O'Carrolls, and Brian Bán Ó Briain, and in Desmond

May Council at Kilkenny

early Aug. Black Death appears at Howth and Drogheda

? Annalist John Clyn, O.F.M., of Kilkenny, dies

1349

June 18 Statute of labourers passed at Westminster; subsequently applied to Ire.

July 14 Alexander Bicknor, abp of Dublin, dies

July 17 Thomas de Rokeby app. jcr (arrives in Ire., 20 Dec.)

Oct. 3 John de Carew acting as deputy jcr

Nov. Maurice FitzGerald, earl of Desmond, pardoned

1350

Brian Bán Ó Briain, kg of Thomond, killed; restoration of Diarmaid, son of Toirdhealbhach (see 1343)

Aodh, son of Aodh Bréifneach, last of Clann Mhuircheartaigh sept of O'Connors to hold kingship of Connacht (1342–3), killed by Aodh Bán Ó Ruairc

Aodh, son of Toirdhealbhach Ó Conchobhair, kg of Connacht, deposed by Edmund Albanach de Burgh (Mac William Burke) in favour of his cousin Aodh, son of Feidhlimidh Ó Conchobhair

June 25 Great council at Kilkenny

1350 × 1357

Abp FitzRalph of Armagh composes 'De pauperie salvatoris' against mendicant orders

1351

Aodh, son of Toirdhealbhach Ó Conchobhair, recovers kingship of Connacht; expels Aodh, son of Feidhlimidh Ó Conchobhair

Great council at Dublin (17 Oct.) and Kilkenny (31 Oct.): ordinances to curtail hibernicisation of Anglo-Irish; statute of labourers (1351) applied to Ire.

Christmas 'Nodlaig na Garma': convention of poets and men of learning held by Uilliam Buidhe Ó Ceallaigh; Gofraidh Fionn Ó Dálaigh's poem *Filidh Éireann go haointeach*

1352

Aodh Ó Ruairc, kg of Bréifne, killed by Cathal, son of Aodh Bréifneach Ó Conchobhair of Clann Mhuircheartaigh

Aonghus Ó Domhnaill, kg of Tír Conaill, killed by Maghnus Ó Domhnaill; succession contested between his brother Seoán and uncle Feidhlimidh

Ballindoon castle destroyed by Aodh Ó Conchobhair

Mar. 5–June 14 Jcr (de Rokeby) in England; Maurice Rochfort, bp of Limerick, acting as deputy jcr

June 22 Diocese of Ossory restored to metropolitan jurisdiction of Dublin (see 1347)

1353

Two burned at Waterford for heresy

Aodh, son of Toirdhealbhach Ó Conchobhair, kg of Connacht, again briefly deposed in favour of Aodh, son of Feidhlimidh; recovers kingship later this year

Jan.–Feb. Diarmaid Óg Mac Carthaigh expelled from Múscraighe by jcr (de Rokeby) and Cormac Mac Carthaigh, kg of Desmond, who receives extensive grants of crown lands (1 Feb.)

Sept.–Oct. Jcr campaigns against O'Byrnes

Sept. 23 'Statute of the staple'; applies to Ire.

Oct. Parliament at Dublin

1354

Muircheartach Mac Murchadha captured and executed by jcr (de Rokeby)

Aodh Reamhar Ó Néill defeated by Clann Aodha Buidhe (O'Neills of Clandeboye) and citizens of Dundalk

Sept.–Oct. Jcr campaigns against O'Byrnes

1355

Ricard Óg, son of Ulick, son of William Liath de Burgh, defeats forces of Edmund Albanach de Burgh, Síl nAnmchadha, and de Berminghams (Clann Fheórais) of Athenry; burns Tuam

Feb. 5 Death of Pilib, son of Amlaoibh Mág Uidhir, lord of Muintir Pheodhacháin (Co. Fermanagh)

Apr.-May Jcr (de Rokeby) leads general campaign against O'Byrnes and O'Nolans; O'Kennedys harassed from Ormond

May 19 Council at Naas

June 2 Truce between jcr (de Rokeby) and Brian Mór Mac Mathghamhna

July 8 Maurice FitzGerald, earl of Desmond, app. jcr (acting, 17 Aug.)

Aug. 30 Ordinance directing appeal of erroneous judgments from Irish courts to Irish parliament

1356

Diarmaid Óg Mac Carthaigh and his son Donnchadh killed by son of Ó Súilleabháin

Aodh, son of Toirdhealbhach Ó Conchobhair, kg of Connacht, killed by Donnchadh Carrach Ó Ceallaigh; succ. by his cousin Aodh, son of Feidhlimidh

Anglo-Irish continue campaign against O'Byrnes

Jan. 25 Maurice fitz Thomas FitzGerald, 1st earl of Desmond, dies; Maurice FitzGerald, 4th earl of Kildare, app. jcr by council (ratified by kg, 30 Mar.)

Jan. 28 Barons of exchequer reduced from 3 to 2

Apr. 28 Abp FitzRalph of Armagh empowered to treat with Aodh Reamhar Ó Néill, who threatens to invade Louth and attack Dundalk

June Parliament

July 24 Thomas de Rokeby reapp. jcr (acting, 31 Dec.)

Sept. 19 Battle of Poitiers: English defeat French

1357

Peace established between Cathal, son of Aodh Bréifneach of Clann Mhuircheartaigh, and Cathal Óg, son of Cathal of Clann Bhriain Luighnigh (O'Connor Sligo)

Jcr (de Rokeby) campaigns against Leinster Irish

Apr. 23 Thomas de Rokeby dies; John de Boulton app. jcr by council (24 Apr.)

July 14 Amaury de St Amand app. jcr (acting, 27 Nov.)

Aug. 30 Maurice FitzGerald, 4th earl of Kildare, app. deputy jcr (acting, 5 Sept.)

Oct. 3 Treaty of Berwick: David II released; 10-year truce between England and Scotland

Oct. 25 Promulgation of ordinance 'De statu Hibernie' by Edward III

Maurice fitz Maurice FitzGerald, 2nd earl of Desmond, drowned crossing Irish Sea

1358

a. **Apr.** Parliament

Senicín Mac Uidhilín, '*ardchonstábla cúigidh Uladh*' (high-constable of Ulster), dies

Aodh Mór Ó Néill extends power into Oirghialla, Fir Manach and Tír Conaill

Leinster Irish raid marches

Sept. 16   James Butler, 2nd earl of Ormond, app. *custos pacis* for Munster

Nov. 4   Licence for Drogheda to import more freely because of harassment by Irish

Gascon merchants send white wine in quantity to Youghal

1359

Cormac Mac Carthaigh, kg of Desmond, dies; succ. by his son Domhnall Óg

Continuing warfare between jcr (de St Amand) and Leinster Irish

Seoán Ó Domhnaill defeated at Ballyshannon by Cathal Óg Ó Conchobhair Sligigh (O'Connor Sligo), who assumes kingship of Tír Conaill

Jan. 14   Parliament at Kilkenny: subsidy granted

Feb. 16   James Butler, 2nd earl of Ormond, app. jcr (acting, 18 Mar.)

Councils at Dublin (1 Apr. and 5 Aug.) and Waterford (8 Apr.)

July 18–22   Ordinances for administration of Ire.

July 20   Order for exclusion of Irishmen from all secular and ecclesiastical offices within colony
Gerald fitz Maurice FitzGerald granted livery of lands of his late brother Maurice, 2nd earl of Desmond (d. 1357), on account of idiocy of his elder brother, Nicholas

Oct. 28–18 May 1360   Edward III in France; protests (26 Oct.) inability to contribute to Irish expenses

1360

Diarmaid Ó Briain, kg of Thomond, deposed by his nephew Mathghamhain

Art Mág Aonghusa killed by Savages of Lecale

Cathal Óg Ó Conchobhair builds stone bridge at Ballysadare, Co. Sligo

May 8   Peace of Brétigny between Edward III and Philip of France; confirmed by treaty of Calais (24 Oct.)

July 27   Great council at Kilkenny (summoned 8 June): Edward III petitioned to appoint powerful English lord as lieutenant

Oct. 9   Maurice FitzGerald, 4th earl of Kildare, acting as deputy jcr

Nov. 16   Richard FitzRalph, abp of Armagh, dies

Latin hymns of Bp Ledred (Leatherhead) of Ossory entered into Red Book of Ossory

1361

Recurrence of bubonic plague (*cluiche an ríogh* 'the king's game')

Irish exchequer moved from Dublin to Carlow

Mar. 16   Maurice FitzGerald, 4th earl of Kildare, app. jcr (acting, 1 Apr.)

July 1   Lionel, 5th earl of Ulster, third son of Edward III, app. lieutenant (arrives in Ire., 15 Sept.)

Art Mac Murchadha, kg of Leinster, captured by lieutenant; dies in captivity; succession of Diarmaid Láimhdhearg

1362

Aodh Ó Conchobhair and Cathal Óg Ó Conchobhair Sligigh capture Ballintober; invade Meath

Jan. 7 Parliament at Dublin: clerical tenth granted for 2 years

Feb. 10 Reinforcements sent to Ire. for lieutenant (Lionel, earl of Ulster)

Nov. 3 Cathal Óg Ó Conchobhair Sligigh (O'Connor Sligo), kg of Tír Conaill, dies of plague; Seoán Ó Domhnaill recovers kingship

Nov. 13 Lionel, earl of Ulster, created duke of Clarence

1363

June 11 Dioceses of Lismore and Waterford united (see 16 July 1228)

late in year Parliament

1364

Diarmaid Ó Briain, ex-kg of Thomond, dies

Aodh Reamhar Ó Néill, kg of Tír Eóghain, dies; succ. by his son Niall Mór

Apr. 22-Dec. Lieutenant (Lionel, duke of Clarence) in England; James Butler, 2nd earl of Ormond, acts as 'custos' (25 Apr.-25 Jan. 1365)

June 14 'Custos' and chancellor ordered to issue proclamations against dissension arising between English subjects born in England and those born in Ire.

1365

Succession of Pilib Ó Raghallaigh as kg of east Bréifne

Dissension among Clann Bhriain Luighnigh (O'Connors Sligo) between Domhnall, son of Muircheartach, and Tadhg, son of Maghnus

Costelloes invade Luighne (Leyney, north Co. Sligo)

1366

Niall Mór Ó Néill opposed by his brother Domhnall
Tadhg Ó Conchobhair Sligigh defeats Seoán Ó Domhnaill

Prendergasts expelled from Mayo to Clann Rickard by Edmund Albanach de Burgh (Mac William Burke); Clann Rickard Burkes submit to Mac William Burke

Feb. 19 Parliament at Kilkenny: 'statute of Kilkenny' promulgated

May 13 Cathal, son of Aodh Bréifneach Ó Conchobhair of Clann Mhuircheartaigh, killed by Mág Uidhir

Nov. 7 Lionel, duke of Clarence, leaves for England; Thomas de la Dale app. 'custos'

1367

Clann Mhuircheartaigh (sept of O'Connors) migrate into Magh Nise (Mág Raghnaill territory in south Leitrim)

Feb. 20   All Irish debts to Edward III up to 13 Oct. 1362 rescinded

Gerald fitz Maurice FitzGerald, 3rd earl of Desmond (Gearóid Iarla), app. jcr (acting, *c.* 23 Apr.)

June 14   Parliament at Kilkenny

1368

Renewed Anglo-French hostilities

Niall, son of Murchadh Mac Mathgamhna, kg of Oirghialla, protégé of Niall Mór Ó Néill, killed by Brian Mór Mac Mathghamhna, who succeeds to kingship

Tadhg, son of Maghnus Ó Conchobhair Sligigh, deposed and imprisoned by his kinsman, Domhnall, son of Muircheartach, following the division of Cairbre (Carbury, north Co. Sligo) between them

May 1   Parliament at Dublin: Edward III petitioned to order return of absentees

July 28   Ordinance for return of 16 magnates from abroad

autumn   Aodh Ó Conchobhair, kg of Connacht, dies; succ. by his cousin Ruaidhrí, son of Toirdhealbhach

Oct. 17   Lionel, duke of Clarence and earl of Ulster, dies

Nov. 1-24   Jcr (earl of Desmond) campaigns against O'Nolans

1369

Pilib Mág Uidhir and Brian Mór Mág Mathghamhna thwart attempt of Maghnus Ó Raghallaigh to seize kingship of east Bréifne from Pilib Ó Raghallaigh

Mathghamhain Ó Briain, kg of Thomond, dies; succ. by his son Brian Sreamhach

Mar. 3   William of Windsor app. lieutenant (acting, 20 June)

July 30   Parliament at Dublin: subsidy granted

Aug. 24   Edmund and Philippa Mortimer granted livery of Irish lands of Lionel, duke of Clarence

Lieutenant begins campaign in Leinster (continued until summer 1370); captures and executes Diarmaid Láimhdhearg Mac Murchadha, kg of Leinster (succ. by Donnchadh Caomhánach)

1370

Niall Mór Ó Néill recognised as kg of Tír Eóghain by his brother Domhnall

Niall Mór Ó Néill defeats Brian Mór Mac Mathghamhna

Clann Mhuircheartaigh forced by Pilib Ó Raghallaigh to seek refuge with Edmund Albanach de Burgh (Mac William Burke)

Jan. 2   Council at Dublin

Apr. 22   Great council at Dublin: subsidy granted

July 11   Brian Sreamhach Ó Briain defeats and captures earl of Desmond at Monasternenagh; Mac Con Mara captures Limerick

Lieutenant (Windsor) and bp of Meath campaign in Thomond; Mac Con Mara submits (15 Dec.)

1371

Brian Mór Mac Mathghamhna, kg of Oirghialla, dies; succ. by his son Pilib Ruadh

Brian Ó Ceinnéidigh, kg of Ormond, killed by Anglo-Irish

Anglo-Irish settlers expelled from Tír Fhiachrach Muaidhe (barony of Tireragh, Co. Sligo) by Domhnall Ó Dubhda

Jan. 7   Parliament at Kilkenny: subsidy granted

Apr.   Great council at 'Ballydoyle'/Cashel (Co. Tipperary): subsidy granted with opposition

June 8   Parliament at 'Ballydoyle'/Cashel: subsidy granted

Aug. 1-Mar. 13, 1372   Lieutenant (Windsor) campaigns against Ó Mórdha of Laoighis

Sept. 10   Lieutenant ordered to cancel financial demands made on Dublin and Drogheda

Oct. 20   Lieutenant ordered to suspend collection of all taxes granted since 1369

1372

Seoán Mór Ó Dubhagáin, historian of Uí Mhaine, dies in religious retirement at Rindown

De Bermingham captured by Ó Ceallaigh; his heir killed

Jan. 14   Parliament at Kilkenny

Feb. 25   Great council at Dublin

Mar. 6   John of Boothby, chancellor, ordered to withdraw great seal from Windsor's use

c. **Mar. 8**   Robert of Ashton app. jcr (acting, 20 June)

Mar. 21-2   Windsor leaves for England; Maurice fitz Thomas FitzGerald, 4th earl of Kildare, sworn in as 'custos'

Apr.   Earl of Kildare campaigns against Ó Briain, Mac Con Mara, and Clanrickard Burke

June 8   Council at Ballyhea (Co. Cork)

1373

Death of Ádhamh Ó Cianáin, scholar, in religious retirement at Lisgoole

Toirdhealbhach Ruadh Ó Conchobhair prominent in Connacht; defeats de Berminghams

Jan. 7   Parliament at Kilkenny: Edward III petitioned to appoint earl of March as lieutenant, but on no account Windsor

Sept. 20   William of Windsor reapp. governor and 'custos' (acting, 19 Apr. 1374)

Oct.-Nov.   Ralph Cheyne acting as deputy jcr

Nov. 15   John Keppock app. governor and 'custos' by council

Dec. 3   William Tany, prior of Kilmainham, app. jcr by council

Anglo-Irish of Meath attack Ó Fearghail of Anghaile (further raids in 1374 and 1376)

1374

Thomas of Burley, chancellor, campaigns in Meath against Clann Fheórais (de Berminghams)

Mar. 29 Council at Dublin

May 27 Great council at Dublin

Sept. Stephen de Valle, bp of Meath, campaigns in Thomond to support Mac Con Mara against Brian Sreamhach Ó Briain

1374/5

Death of Thomas de Bermingham, lord of Athenry

1375

Toirdhealbhach Ruadh Ó Conchobhair gives Roscommon castle to Ruaidhrí Ó Conchobhair in exchange for Ballintober

Niall Mór Ó Néill defeats Anglo-Irish at Downpatrick; Sir James Talbot de Malahide killed

Toirdhealbhach, son of Muircheartach Ó Briain, attempts to depose Brian Sreamhach Ó Briain with Anglo-Irish assistance

Jan. 20 Parliament at Dublin

June 18 Edward III appoints Nicholas Dagworth to secure increased Anglo-Irish financial support for war in Ire.
Parliament at Kilkenny: subsidy granted

July 26 Donnchadh Caomhánach Mac Murchadha, kg of Leinster, dies; succ. by Art Mór, son of Art

Aug. Lieutenant (Windsor) campaigns in Thomond

Oct. 6 Parliament at Kilkenny: Anglo-Irish representatives summoned to appear before council in England

Nov. 4 Sir Edmund Albanach de Burgh (Mac William Burke) dies; succ. by his son Thomas

1376

Aodh Ó Tuathail, kg of Uí Mháil (Co. Wicklow), dies

Succession of Tighearnán Mór Ó Ruairc as kg of Bréifne

Feb. 16 Maurice FitzGerald, 4th earl of Kildare, app. jcr (acting, 21 June)

July 24 James Butler, 2nd earl of Ormond, app. jcr (acting, c. 1 Oct.)

Jcr campaigns in Leinster against Mac Murchadha, Ó Broin, Ó Mórdha, and Ó Nualláin

Dec. Nicholas Dagworth app. 'surveyor of the state of this land of Ireland'

1377

War between Clann Chuiléin (MacNamaras of Clare) and Clann Rickard Burkes

Ruaidhrí Ó Conchobhair defeats Thomas de Burgh (Mac William Burke) and Maolsheachlainn Ó Ceallaigh at Roscommon

Jan. 8 Parliament at Dublin; Art son of Diarmaid Mac Murchadha pledges support against Irish insurgents in Leinster led by Art Mór, son of Art Mac Murchadha

Apr. Jcr (earl of Ormond) and bp of Meath campaign in Munster
Appeal for measures against prospect of Spanish raids on southern ports

June 21 Edward III, kg of England, dies; succ. by his grandson Richard II (a minor)

1378

Tadhg Mac Con Mara, lord of Clann Chuiléin (?1366–), killed by Aodh Mac Con Mara

Jan. 14 Great council at Castledermot

Mar. 8 Parliament at Castledermot: 100 marks offered to Brian Sreamhach Ó Briain to retire from Leinster

Sept. 20 Robert of Geneva elected pope (Clement VII): beginning of 'great schism'

1378 × 1392/4

'Book of Uí Mhaine' written for Muircheartach Ó Ceallaigh, bp of Clonfert

1379

Apr. 30 Council at Castledermot

May 31 Niall Mór Ó Néill defeats his brother Domhnall and Pilib Mág Uidhir

Jcr (earl of Ormond) campaigns against Mac Murchadha, Ó Broin, Ó Tuathail, and Ó Nualláin; makes peace with Mac Murchadha (10 Oct.)

July 20 King orders Irish officials not to intervene in disputes among friars

Sept. 22 John de Bromych app. jcr (acting, Dec.)

Oct. 22 Edmund Mortimer, 3rd earl of March, 6th earl of Ulster, and lord of Connacht, app. lieutenant

1380

Seoán Ó Domhnaill, kg of Tír Conaill, and his son Maolsheachlainn Dubh killed by Toirdhealbhach 'an Fhíona', son of Niall Ó Domhnaill, and sons of Cathal Óg Ó Conchobhair (d. 1362); Toirdhealbhach succeeds to kingship

Pilib Ó Raghallaigh and Clann Mhuircheartaigh (sept of O'Connors) attack Tighearnán Mór Ó Ruairc

Tadhg, son of Muircheartach Ó Briain, killed by Brian Sreamhach Ó Briain

Thomas de Burgh (Mac William Burke) defeats Richard Óg de Burgh (Clann Rickard Burke) at Áth Leathain (Ballylahan, Co. Mayo)

Apr. 30 Parliament at Castledermot

Lieutenant (Edmund Mortimer) arrives in Ire.

Lieutenant campaigns in Ulster; captures Mág Aonghusa; Niall Mór Ó Néill submits

Aug. 11 Milo Sweetman, abp of Armagh, dies

Nov. 3 Parliament at Dublin: 'statute of Kilkenny' confirmed; subsidy granted

1381

Uilliam Buidhe, son of Donnchadh Muimhneach Ó Ceallaigh, kg of Uí Mhaine, dies; succ. by his son Maolsheachlainn

Niall Mór Ó Néill invades Oirghialla

Dissension between Toirdhealbhach Ruadh Ó Conchobhair (and Clann Aodha mic Feidhlimidh) and Ruaidhrí Ó Conchobhair; Ruaidhrí deprives them of Ballintober (see 1375)

Castle of Ballylahan destroyed by MacDonaghs

Athlone captured by lieutenant (Mortimer)

Antipope Clement VII proposes promotion of Thomas 'O Talman', O.F.M., to see of Armagh

mid-June Peasants' revolt in England

summer Lieutenant (Mortimer) campaigns against Ó Tuathail

Aug. 5 Great council at Clonmel: subsidy granted

Dec. 26/7 Death of Edmund Mortimer

1382

Jan. 9 Council at Cork: John Colton, chancellor, app. jcr (10 Jan.)

Jan. 24 Roger Mortimer, 4th earl of March and 7th earl of Ulster, a minor, app. lieutenant

Mar. 3 Council at Naas: magnates forbidden to leave Ire.; subvention for war against Brian Sreamhach Ó Briain

June 16 Parliament at Dublin

Oct. 4 Feudal service convened at Cashel for expedition against Ó Briain

c. **Nov. 1** James Butler, 2nd earl of Ormond, dies; succ. by his son James (livery, 10 Mar. 1385)

1383

Recurrence of plague

Niall Mór Ó Néill attacks Anglo-Irish of Ulster (further attacks, 1384 and 1385)

Jan. 16 Council at Naas

Jan. 17 Robert Elyot, bp of Killala, suspended by Clement VII, antipope

July 1 Philip de Courtenay app. lieutenant for 10 years (acting, *c.* 11 Sept.)

Lieutenant campaigns against Brian Sreamhach Ó Briain

1384

Pilib Ó Raghallaigh, kg of east Bréifne, dies; succ. by his nephew Tomás

Muircheartach Óg Ó Conchobhair Failghe (O'Connor Faly) dies; succ. by his son Murchadh

Dissension between earls of Ormond and Desmond

Apr. English expedition to Edinburgh

Nov. 25 Ruaidhrí Ó Conchobhair, kg of Connacht, dies; kingdom divided between his nephew Toirdhealbhach Óg Ó Conchobhair Donn (O'Connor Don), son of Aodh, son of Toirdhealbhach, supported by Clann Rickard Burke and Ó Ceallaigh, and Toirdhealbhach Ó Conchobhair Ruadh (O'Connor Roe), son of Aodh, son of Feidhlimidh, supported by Mac Diarmada and Mac William Burke

end of Nov. De Courtenay leaves for England; James Butler, 3rd earl of Ormond, app. acting jcr

late in year Parliament

Dec. 30 Robert Wikeford, abp of Dublin and chancellor, reprimanded for exceeding his brief

1384 × 1406

'Book of Ballymote' compiled for Domhnall Mac Aodhagáin and for Tomaltach Mac Donnchadha (d. 1397) by Solamh Ó Droma, Robert Mac Síthigh, and Maghnus Ó Duibhgeannáin

1385

Modification of privileges and graces of Irish 'limit' of Augustinian friars ordered by general chapter at Gran, Hungary

Spanish and Scottish pirates raid Irish waters

May 6 Lieutenant (de Courtenay) returns to Ire.

summer Lieutenant campaigns against Leinster Irish; Ó Conchobhair Failghe campaigns against Anglo-Irish of Meath; Ó Néill and Mac Mathghamhna threaten Louth

July 17 Council at Kilkenny

July Scots raid Northumberland

Aug. Richard II invades Scotland; sacks Edinburgh

Oct. 23 Great council at Dublin: Richard II petitioned to send his greatest lord to Ire.

Dec. 1 Robert de Vere, earl of Oxford, created marquis of Dublin

Henry Crumpe, O.Cist., monk of Baltinglass, preaches in Oxford and Meath against friars

1386

Domhnall Ó Conchobhair Sligigh raids Barretts' territory in Tír Amhalghaidh (Tirawley, Co. Mayo); Toirdhealbhach Ó Conchobhair Ruadh and Thomas de Burgh (Mac William Burke) make retaliatory raids in Tír Fhiachrach (Tireragh, Co. Sligo)

Art Mór Mac Murchadha defeats Anglo-Irish of Ossory

Beginning of dissension between Clann Seoáin Uí Fhearghail (Ó Fearghail Bán) and Clann Mhurchadha Uí Fhearghail (Ó Fearghail Buidhe)

Ó Conchobhair Ruadh and Mac William Burke raid Clann Rickard

Daltons attack Mág Eochagáin and Ó Fearghail

Mar. 26 Order for arrest of Philip de Courtenay to answer to inquisition of his activities in office

June 8 John Stanley app. lieutenant (arrives in Ire., 30 Aug.)

Oct. Richard II clashes with English parliament; retires to midlands and north of England

Oct. 13 Robert de Vere created duke of Ireland

Nov. 1 Lieutenant renews peace with Art Mór Mac Murchadha

Dec. 1 Action taken against payment of 'smokesilver' in Dublin and Kildare

1387

Ruaidhrí Ó Cianáin, 'chief historian of Oirghialla', dies; scribe of 'Book of Magauran', earliest Irish *duanaire* (poem-book, written for Tomás Mág Shamhradháin, d. 1343)

Gofraidh Fionn Ó Dálaigh, poet, dies

Richard Óg de Burgh (Clann Rickard Burke), dies; succ. by his son William (Uilleag an Fhíona)

Niall Mór Ó Néill entertains 'men of learning' at Eamhain Macha near Armagh

Jan. 2 Order for arrest of Anglo-Irish spies in England

Dec. 17 Robert de Vere defeated at Radcot Bridge, Oxfordshire; flees to France (d. 1392)

1388

Seoán Ruadh Ó Tuathail, lord of Uí Mhuireadhaigh, killed by one of his retainers

Muircheartach, son of Domhnall Ó Conchobair Sligigh, attacks Toirdhealbhach Ó Domhnaill's camp at Assaroe

Feb. 3 'Merciless parliament' in England: attainder of de Vere

Apr. 4 Lieutenant (Stanley) ordered to abolish Robert de Vere's seals

Apr. 26 Alexander de Balscot, bp of Meath, app. jcr

July 6 Great council at Castledermot (adjourned to Clonmel, 20 July): subsidy granted; statute of labourers (1388) adopted

Dec. 8 Thomas de Burgh (Mac William Burke) app. 'custos' of Connacht
Earl of Desmond permitted to give his son in fosterage to Conchobhar Ó Briain

Clann Donnchadha at war with Ó Ruairc (continues, 1389)

c. 1388

Marriage of Robert Savage to daughter of John de Yle, lord of the Isles

1389

William Ó Cormacáin, abp of Tuam, opposed by Gregory Ó Mocháin, incumbent of the see by appointment of Clement VII, antipope (*c.* 1384)

Clann Donnchadha and Domhnall Ó Conchobhair Sligigh make peace with Ó Ruairc and Mac Diarmada (Ó Conchobhair Ruadh alliance)

Niall Óg, son of Niall Mór Ó Néill, captured by Anglo-Irish

Feb. 12 James Butler, 3rd earl of Ormond, app. governor in Kilkenny and Tipperary

May Richard II recovers power in England

Aug. 1 John Stanley app. jcr for 3 years (acting, 25 Oct.)

Aug. 26 Residence in Co. Dublin granted to John Griffin, bp of Leighlin, unable to live within his own diocese because of disturbances

Dec. 3 Parliament at Kilkenny (adjourned to Castledermot 3 Feb.; subsequently to Ballymore and Naas)

1390

Tighearnán Mór Ó Ruairc defeats O'Connor sept of Clann Mhuircheartaigh (who disappear from Bréifne after 1391)

Kilbarron castle (Caisleán Chille Barraine) destroyed by Domhnall Ó Conchobhair Sligigh

Feb. 20 Indenture between jcr (Stanley) and Niall Mór Ó Néill: Niall Óg Ó Néill released

Mar. 12 Parliament at Castledermot

John Colton, abp of Armagh, unable to visit Armagh owing to war between English and Irish; granted exemption by Boniface IX (6 Dec.) from obligation not to revisit part of his diocese before visiting all other parts

1391

Domhnall Óg Mac Carthaigh, kg of Desmond, dies; succ. by his son Tadhg na Mainistreach

All former privileges restored to Irish Augustinian friars by general chapter at Würzburg, Germany

Feb. 20 Royal commn established to examine state of Ire., its causes and remedies

July 16 Irish metropolitans ordered to arrest heretic preachers

Sept. 11 Alexander de Balscot, bp of Meath, reapp. jcr

late in year Council at Castledermot

1392

Yellow Book of Lecan (main section) compiled by Giolla Íosa Mór Mac Fir Bhisigh of Lecan, Co. Sligo

Toirdhealbhach Ó Domhnaill attacks Clann tSeoáin Uí Domhnaill and Clann Énri Uí Néill; captures Domhnall, son of Énri Aimhréidh, son of Niall Mór Ó Néill

Niall Mór Ó Néill leads expedition to Dundalk

Ó Néill and Domhnall Ó Conchobhair Sligigh attack Ó Domhnaill

Jan. 29   Parliament at Trim

c. **May 16**   Énrí Aimhréidh, son of Niall Mór Ó Néill, dies

July 24   James Butler, 3rd earl of Ormond, app. jcr

Oct.   Council at Castledermot

Nov. 29   Custody of Kilkenny lands of Hugh, 2nd earl of Stafford (d. 1386), granted to earl of Ormond

1393

Jan. 13   Parliament at Kilkenny

June 18   Roger Mortimer, 4th earl of March, and his wife Philippa granted livery of their lands in Ire.

Confirmation of 1357 ordinance for government of Ire.

July 6   John, bp of Annaghdown, granted licence to enlist 200 archers in England for recovery of his diocese from Irish control

1394

Jcr (earl of Ormond) campaigns in Munster and Leinster

Mar. 30   Great council at Kilkenny

Oct. 2   Richard II arrives at Waterford

Oct. 28   Battle between Richard II and Leinster Irish; Art Mór Mac Murchadha submits (30 Oct.); Ó Broin, Ó Nualláin, and Ó Mórdha taken to Dublin as hostages

Dec. 1   Parliament at Dublin: ordinance against sale of provisions to Irish outside English jurisdiction

Exchequer and common bench moved from Carlow to Dublin

c. **1394**

Edward, earl of Rutland, created earl of Cork

1395

Death of Cobhlaigh Mhór Inghean Uí Chonchobhair ('Port na Trí Námhad'), successively wife of Ó Domhnaill, Ó Ruairc, and Cathal, son of Aodh Bréifnech Ó Conchobhair

Toirdhealbhach Ó Domhnaill campaigns against Domhnall, son of Énrí Aimhréidh Ó Néill

Jan.-Apr.   Irish kings submit to Richard II: Ó Néill (19-20 Jan., Drogheda), Mac Murchadha (16 Feb. Carlow, to earl of Nottingham), Ó Briain (6 Mar., Dundalk), Niall Óg Ó Néill (*c.* 19 Mar., Dundalk), Mac Carthaigh Mór and Mac Carthaigh Riabhach (6 Apr., Kilkenny), Ó Conchobhair Donn

Muircheartach Ó Ceallaigh, abp of Tuam, active in procuring submissions

Mar. 16   Pilib Mág Uidhir, kg of Fir Manach, dies; succ. by his son Tomás Mór ('An Giolla Dubh')

Apr. 19 Council at Kilkenny

May 1 William (Uilleag) de Burgh of Clann Rickard, Mac Feorais (Walter de Bermingham) of Athenry, and Ó Conchobhair Donn knighted by Richard II at Waterford

May 15 Richard II returns to England

July 6 Issues and profits of great seal in Ire. withdrawn from chancellor and reserved to crown

Dec. 18 Domhnall Ó Conchobhair Sligigh (O'Connor Sligo) dies; succ. by his son Muircheartach Bacach, following intervention of Ó Domhnaill

1396

Lieutenant (Mortimer) campaigns in Anghaile, Bréifne, and Tír Eóghain; burns Armagh

Conchobhar, son of Eóghan Ó Máille, raids Iar-Chonnacht; drowned on return to Aran

Ó Tuathail defeats English and Anglo-Irish force

Mar. 12 Richard II and Charles IV, kg of France, make 20-year truce

Apr. 25 Roger Mortimer, 4th earl of March, app. lieutenant in Ulster, Connacht, and Meath, with William le Scrope as lieutenant in Leinster, Munster, and Louth

summer Parliament at Dublin

1397

Apr. 24 Roger Mortimer, 4th earl of March, reapp. lieutenant for 3 years

Aug. 14 Tomaltach Mac Donnchadha killed by Toirdhealbhach Ó Conchobhair Ruadh and Thomas de Burgh (Mac William Burke)

Sept. 17 Richard II proceeds against Appellants in Westminster parliament

Oct. 8-14 John Colton, abp of Armagh, makes primatial visitation of Derry diocese

Dec. Catalan Raymond, viscount of Perelhos, visits Niall Mór Ó Néill while on pilgrimage to St Patrick's Purgatory

Niall Mór Ó Néill, kg of Tír Eóghain (d. 1398), resigns in favour of his son Niall Óg

1398

Recurrence of plague

Niall Óg Ó Néill and Muircheartach Bacach Ó Conchobhair Sligigh raid Ó Domhnaill's territory of Tír Aodha (Tirhugh, Co. Donegal)

Gerald FitzGerald, 5th earl of Kildare, captured by An Calbhach, son of Murchadh Ó Conchobhair Failghe

Councils at Naas (10 June) and Dunboyne (1 Aug.; adjourned to Naas, 12 Aug.): subsidies granted

July 20 Lieutenant (Roger Mortimer, 4th earl of March and 7th earl of Ulster) defeated and killed by Ó Broin and Ó Tuathail; Lord Grey of Ruthin appointed jcr by council

July 26 Thomas Holland, duke of Surrey, app. lieutenant (sworn in, 7 Oct.)

Sept. 7 Muircheartach Bacach Ó Conchobhair Sligigh defeats Clann Chathail Óig (sept of O'Connors)

? Oct. 12 Gerald FitzGerald, 3rd earl of Desmond (Gearóid Iarla), dies

1399

Domhnall, son of Énrí Aimhréidh Ó Néill, captured by Anglo-Irish near Dundalk and taken to England

June 1–July 27 Richard II in Ireland; campaigns against Art Mór Mac Murchadha in Leinster; forced to return to England by Bolingbroke's landing

Sept. 29 Richard II, kg of England, deposed

Sept. 30 English crown claimed and received by Henry Bolingbroke, earl of Hereford, son of John of Gaunt, duke of Lancaster (Henry IV)

Oct. 11 John fitz Gerald FitzGerald, 4th earl of Desmond, drowned in the Suir at Ardfinnan, returning from expedition against Butlers

Dec. 10 John Stanley app. lieutenant for 3 years (acting, Mar. 1400)

1400

Brian Sreamhach Ó Briain, kg of Thomond, dies; succ. by his brother Conchobhar

Toirdhealbhach, son of Maolmhuire Mac Suibhne, lord of Fánad, dies

Tadhg Ó Cearbhaill, kg of Ely, captured by James, 3rd earl of Ormond

Jan. Alexander de Balscot, bp of Meath, acting as jcr

Stanley campaigns in Meath, Munster, and Leinster; subsidy granted by council at Skreen (*c.* 30 Apr.)

autumn Cú Uladh, son of Niall Mór Ó Néill, dies

Sept. Owain Glyndwr leads rising in north Wales against Henry IV

Sept. 6 Protection granted to Irish pilgrims at St Mary's, Trim

Dec. 14 Henry IV orders assistance from Irish sources for lieutenant

1401

Ruaidhrí, son of Art Mág Aonghusa, lord of Uí Eachach Uladh, killed by sons of Cú Uladh Ó Néill

spring Parliament at Ross: subsidy granted

June 27 Thomas, duke of Lancaster, app. lieutenant for 6 years as from July 18 (arrives in Ire., 13 Nov.)

Aug. 23 Stephen le Scrope, deputy to Lancaster, arrives in Ire.

Sept. 14 Indenture between Ó Conchobhair Failghe and le Scrope

Nov. Owain Glyndwr's letters appealing for Irish alliance intercepted; messengers executed

Nov. 8 Indenture between Ó Broin and le Scrope

Nov. 16 Sir William (Uilleag) de Burgh appointed as one of justices in Connacht

Dec. Parliament at Ross

Dec. 13 Indenture between Eochaidh Mac Mathghamhna and le Scrope: Mac Mathghamhna receives grant for territory of Farney

Dec. 19 Lancaster appoints le Scrope deputy and 'governor of the wars' in his absence

1402

Thomas de Burgh (Mac William) dies; succ. by his son Walter

Maolsheachlainn Ó Ceallaigh, kg of Uí Mhaine, dies; succ. by his son Conchobhar an Abaidh (d. 1403)

Niall Óg Ó Néill submits to Toirdhealbhach Ó Domhnaill

Brian, son of Énrí Aimhréidh Ó Néill, killed by Ó Domhnaill

Clann Chormaic of Duhallow (sept of MacCarthys) attack Barrys

Feb. 4 Indenture between Ó Raghallaigh and le Scrope

Apr. 13 Parliament at Dublin

Sept. Parliament at Dublin

1403

Niall Óg Ó Néill, kg of Tír Eóghain, dies; succ. by his son Brian Óg (d. 1403)

War between earls of Desmond and Ormond

a. **Feb. 24** Parliament at Dublin; adjourned to Waterford (*a.* 24 Feb. and 5 Mar.); adjourned to Kilkenny (18 June)

Mar. 10 All crown revenues in Ire. granted to duke of Lancaster

Mar. 20 Demand for presentation of Irish exchequer accounts in England

July 21 Battle of Shrewsbury: Henry Percy defeated and killed by Henry IV

Nov. 8 Lancaster leaves for England

1404

Scots raid east Ulster

Succession of Domhnall, son of Énrí Aimhréidh Ó Néill, as kg of Tír Eóghain

Feb. 2-Oct. Le Scrope in England

Mar. 3 Council at Castledermot; James, 3rd earl of Ormond, app. jcr

Apr. 28 Parliament at Dublin

summer Ormond campaigns against Ulster Irish

July 14 Owain Glyndwr negotiates treaty with French kg against Henry IV

a. **Aug. 4** Great council at Castledermot: subsidy granted

Aug. 12 Great council at Dublin

1405

Art Mór Mac Murchadha raids in Co. Wexford; attacks Carlow and Castledermot; Ó Broin destroys Newcastle (Co. Wicklow)

Order for redress to Lancaster for moneys left unpaid to him from Irish exchequer

June   Le Scrope leaves for England (absent until autumn 1406); James, earl of Ormond, app. deputy (25 June)

Aug. 1/7   French expedition lands at Milford Haven to aid Owain Glyndwr (leaves in Lent 1406)

Sept. 7   Death of Ormond; Gerald, 5th earl of Kildare, app. jcr by council

Oct. 28   Death of Aughusdín Mág Ráidhín, canon of Saints' Island, Lough Ree, annalist and hagiographer

First reference to whiskey: Risdeárd Mág Raghnaill of Muintir Eólais (south Co. Leitrim) dies after drinking *uisge beathadh* to excess

1406

July 10   Eóghan Ó Conchobhair ('Mac an Abaidh') and Anglo-Irish of Meath defeated by Ó Conchobhair Failghe with assistance from Cathal Dubh and Tadhg, sons of Ó Conchobhair Ruadh; Eóghan slain

Dec. 9   Toirdhealbhach Óg Ó Conchobhair Donn (O'Connor Don) killed by Cathal Dubh, son of Ó Conchobhair Ruadh, and Seaán, son of Hoibert Burke; succ. by his cousin Cathal, son of Ruaidhrí

1407

Aodh Mág Aonghusa, lord of Uí Eachach Uladh, expelled by Clann Chon Uladh (sept of O'Neills)

Tadhg Ó Cearbhaill, kg of Ely, defeated and killed by le Scrope

Jan. 13   Parliament at Dublin (adjourned to Trim)

Aug.   Battle of Cell Achaidh (? Killioghan, Co. Roscommon): Cathal Ó Conchobhair and Uilleag Burke (Clanricard) defeated by Ó Conchobhair Ruadh, Ó Ceallaigh, and Mac Diarmada: Ó Conchobhair captured; his followers besieged in Roscommon castle (siege continues until 1420)

Dec. 8   James, 4th earl of Ormond (the 'White Earl') app. deputy

1408

MacDonaghs build castles at Ballindoon and Collooney

p. **Mar. 25**   Parliament at Dublin

Plague in Meath: death of Sir Stephen le Scrope

Aug. 2   Lieutenant (Lancaster) arrives at Carlingford; arrests earl of Kildare at Dublin (*c.* 9 Aug.)

Aug. 12   Lancaster wounded in Irish attack on Kilmainham

Lancaster campaigns in Meath and Leinster

1408-11

Toirdhealbhach Ó Domhnaill supports Eóghan Ó Ruairc against his father, Tighearnán Mór

Dec. 25 1408-Oct. 31 1411 'Leabhar Breac' written by Murchadh Riabhach Ó Cuindlis in Múscraighe Tíre (north Co. Tipperary)

1409

Jan. 14 Parliament at Kilkenny: grant of tallage

Lancaster returns to England; Thomas Butler, prior of Kilmainham, app. deputy (from 9 Mar.)

Council of Pisa: John Whitehead attends as proctor for Armagh; 2 friars from Ire., Adam Payn, O.S.A., and John Cuock, O.F.M., represent mendicant orders in Ire. and England

Councils at Dublin (22 Apr., 14 Oct.)

summer Ó Conchobhair Ruadh and Ó Ceallaigh defeat Mac Donnchadha and sons of Ó Ruairc and Brian Ó Conchobhair who are besieging Roscommon castle (see 1407 and 1420)

1409-10

League of mendicant friars in Ire. against attacks of John Whitehead (see 1409) at Oxford

1410

May 14 Parliament at Dublin

Oct. 13 Tadhg Ruadh, son of Maolsheachlainn Ó Ceallaigh, kg of Uí Mhaine, dies; succ. by his brother Donnchadh

Nov. 10 Ormond campaigns in Meath against Murchadh Ó Conchobhair Failghe

Domhnall Ó Néill captured and deposed by Eóghan, son of Niall Óg Ó Néill; imprisoned until 1414

1411

Domhnall, son of Conchobhar Ó Briain, *tánaiste* of Thomond, killed by Barry Mór

Thomas, 6th earl of Desmond, deposed by his uncle James FitzGerald; flees to England (returns, 1413/1414)

Sept. Council at Naas

1411-20

Clann Seaáin Uí Eaghra at war with Mac William

1412

Galway town damaged by fire

Aodh, son of Énrí Aimhréidh Ó Néill, escapes from Dublin castle with son of Mág Uidhir

Ormond campaigns in Meath, Louth, and elsewhere

Feb. 4 Council at Drogheda

July   Brian Ó Conchobhair Sligigh makes successful expedition through Lower Connacht, despite general opposition

Aug. 1   Butler summoned to England to answer charges concerning his administration

1413

Pale raided by Mac Murchadha (Wexford), Ó Broin (Dublin), Mac Cába and Ó Raghallaigh (Meath)

Mar. 20   Henry IV, kg of England, dies; succ. by his son Henry V

May 13   Westminster parliament orders expulsion of Irishmen and Irish students from England

June 8   John de Stanley app. lieutenant for 6 years (arrives 23 Sept.)

Aug. 21   Royal order to provide shipping for Thomas FitzGerald, 5th earl of Desmond, and his English recruits (see 1411)

1414

Domhnall Ó Néill recovers kingship of Tír Eóghain

Domhnall Riabhach Mac Carthaigh (MacCarthy Reagh), dies; succ. by his son Domhnall Glas

Pale raided by Mac Murchadha (Wexford) and Ó Conchobhair Failghe, Mág Eochagáin, Ó Mórdha, and Ó Díomusaigh (Meath and Kildare)

Jan. 18   Death of de Stanley (attributed to satire of poet Niall Ó hUiginn); Thomas Cranley, abp of Dublin, app. jcr by council

Feb. 24   Sir John Talbot, Lord Furnival, app. lieutenant for 6 years (arrives in Ire., 10 Nov.)

Feb. 25   Parliament at Dublin

1414-17

Council of Constance: Bp Patrick Foxe of Cork and other Anglo-Irish clergy attend as proctors of dioceses (Geoffrey Schale, O.S.A., of Dublin preaches at council, Jan. 1417)

1415

May 13   Council at Naas

summer   Talbot campaigns against Ó Mórdha, Ó Conchobhair Failghe, Mac Mathghamhna, and Ó hAnluain; northern kgs and lords submit

Sept. 21   Owain Glyndwr goes into hiding (dies within year)

Oct. 25   Battle of Agincourt: English defeat French

1416

Ó Cuirnín's library destroyed by fire in monastery of Inis Mór on Lough Gill

Feb.   Ardghal Mac Mathghamhna, kg of Oirghialla, dies; succ. by his son Brian

Feb. 7-c. June   Talbot in England; Thomas Cranley, abp of Dublin, app. deputy (sworn in, 5 Feb.)

Mar. Parliament at Dublin (adjourned to Trim, 11 May)

June Adam Leyns, O.P., bp of Ardagh, burned to death; Conchobhar Ó Fearghail elected by chapter

Oct. 19 English statute (4 Hen. V, c. 6) prohibits promotion of Irishmen to ecclesiastical dignities in Ire.

Art Mór Mac Murchadha defeats Anglo-Irish of Co. Wexford

Murchadh Ó Conchobhair Failghe defeats Anglo-Irish of Meath; Talbot retaliates, destroying Edenderry castle

Dec. 31/1 Jan. 1417 Art Mór Mac Murchadha, kg of Leinster, dies; succ. by his son Donnchadh

1416-18

Great Book of Lecan compiled by Giolla Íosa Mór Mac Fir Bhisigh with assistance of Murchadh Riabhach Ó Cuíndlis and Ádhamh Ó Cuirnín

1417

Domhnall Ó Néill attacks Neachtan, son of Toirdhealbhach Ó Domhnaill

Jan. 27 Parliament at Dublin

Mar. Henry V orders Irish lieges in England to return to Ire. by end of June

Lieutenant (Talbot) campaigns against Ó Conchobhair Failghe (Croghan destroyed, 9 July) and Ó Fearghail

1418

Risdeárd, son of Tomás Ó Raghallaigh, kg of Muintir Mhaoilmórdha (east Bréifne), drowned in Lough Sheelin; succ. by Eóghan, son of Seaán, son of Pilib Ó Raghallaigh

c. **Feb. 1** Tighearnán Mór Ó Ruairc, kg of Bréifne, dies; succ. by his son Aodh Buidhe

Talbot campaigns against Mac Uí Néill Buidhe (O'Neill of Clandeboye) and Mág Aonghusa

June 26 Gerald, 5th earl of Kildare, Sir Christopher Preston, and Sir John Bellew arrested by Talbot

summer Uilliam Ó Ceallaigh, *tánaiste* of Uí Mhaine, builds Caislén na Mallacht facing Roscommon castle (see 1409)

Thomas Butler (prior of Kilmainham and son of earl of Ormond) departs for service in France (dies in France, 1419)

1419

Domhnall Ó Néill, kg of Tír Eóghain, deposed and expelled to Mac Uidhilín by Eóghan, son of Niall Óg Ó Néill, assisted by Ó Domhnaill, Mac Mathghamhna, and Mág Uidhir

Aodh Buidhe Ó Ruairc dies; succ. by his brother Tadhg, son of Tighearnán Mór, with opposition from Art, son of Tadhg, son of Ualgharg, supported by O'Reillys

Brian Ó Conchobhair Sligigh raids Toirdhealbhach Ó Domhnaill's territory of Tír Aodha

Jan. 9   Council at Trim: Talbot produces documents (including 'Modus tenendi parliamentum') found in Preston's possession

[May]   Council at Naas: subsidy granted

May 4   Donnchadh Mac Murchadha captured by Talbot; Murchadh Ó Conchobhair Failge also captured, but escapes

July 3   Uilliam Ó Ceallaigh defeated and captured by Uilleag Burke (Clanricard) at Áth Lighean (?Ballyleen near Craughwell, or Ballylee near Kiltartan)

July 22?   Talbot leaves for England; his brother Richard Talbot, abp of Dublin, app. deputy

1420

Giolla na Naomh Ó hUidhrín, scholar, dies

Brian Ó Conchobhair Sligigh builds castle at Bundrowes

Dissension between Clann Tomáis Móir and Clann Aodha (septs of Maguires)

Feb. 5   Ordinance against royal officials holding lands, etc. in areas of their jurisdiction (1336) waived

Feb. 10   James, 4th earl of Ormond, app. lieutenant (arrives in Ire., 4 Apr.)

c. **June**   Ormond campaigns against Ó Fearghail (Granard destroyed) and Mág Aonghusa

June 7   Parliament at Dublin; subsidy granted (adjourned to 2 Dec., then to Apr. 1421)

a. **Aug. 10**   Thomas, *de jure* 6th earl of Desmond, dies at Paris

Oct. 31   Donnchadh Ó Ceallaigh released in exchange for Cathal Ó Conchobhair; end of siege of Roscommon (see 1407); death of Uilliam Ó Ceallaigh, *tánaiste* of Uí Mhaine

1421

Murchadh Ó Conchobhair Failghe (O'Connor Faly), dies; succ. by his brother Diarmaid

Eóghan Ó Néill captured by Brian Ballach Mac Uí Néill Buidhe (O'Neill of Clandeboye), while going to meet Ormond at Dundalk; Domhnall Ó Néill recovers kingship

Apr. 28   Parliament at Dublin sends petition against maladministration to Henry V

Pale raided by Ó Mordha (defeats Ormond, 7 May) and Mac Mathghamhna

Aug. 21   Laurence Marbury, chancellor, declared by council to have vacated office (absent since 1 Aug.)

Oct. 10   Great council at Dublin: subsidy granted

1422

Augustinian friars in Ire. organised into 4 regions

Toirdhealbhach 'an Fhíona' Ó Domhnaill, kg of Tír Conaill (d. 1423), resigns in favour of his son Niall Garbh

Ó Domhnaill campaigns with Ó Néill and Mac Uí Néill Buidhe against Ó Conchobhair Sligigh and Ó Ruairc

Jan. 31 Inchiquin, Imokilly, and town of Youghal granted to earl of Desmond by earl of Ormond

Further proclamation for expulsion of Irishmen and Irish students from England

c. **Apr. 10** William fitz Thomas Butler, prior of Kilmainham, app. jcr by council

summer Parliament or council

Aug. 31-Sept. 1 Henry V, kg of England, dies; succ. by his son, Henry VI (minority until 1437)

Oct. 4 Richard Talbot, abp of Dublin, app. jcr

Pale raided by Ó Conchobhair Failghe, Ó Raghallaigh (Meath), Gearalt Caomhánach Mac Murchadha (Co. Wexford), Ó Néill, Ó Domhnaill, Mac Mathghamhna (Louth and Meath), and O'Tooles (Counties Kildare and Dublin)

Complaints against false currency

Pseudo-Aristotle's 'Secreta Secretorum' (translated into French by Geoffrey of Waterford, Irish Dominican, in thirteenth century) translated into English by James Yonge of Dublin for earl of Ormond

1423

Faolán Mac a' Ghabhann na Scéal, scribe of Book of Uí Mhaine, dies

Uilleag an Fhíona (Sir William) Burke (Clanricard), dies; succ. by his brother William

Ó Domhnaill, Ó Néill, Mac Mathghamhna, and Mág Aonghusa campaign into Louth as far as Dundalk; jcr (Talbot) campaigns against them

early Jcr campaigns against Ó Raghallaigh and Ó Tuathail

Feb. 11 Ormond undertakes to refrain from injuring Sir John Talbot

May 9 Edmund Mortimer, 5th earl of March, app. lieutenant

June 10 Order for minting of silver coin

Aug. 4 Edward Dantsey, bp of Meath, app. deputy

autumn Dantsey and Desmond campaign against Ó Conchobhair Failghe, de Bermingham, and Ó Raghallaigh

Aug. 23 James, 7th earl of Desmond, app. 'custos' of Limerick

Nov. 3 Great council: ordinance for standardisation of money weights

Niall Garbh Ó Domhnaill builds castle at Ballyshannon

Observant priory (O.S.A.) established at Banada, Co. Sligo; first house of friars observant movement in Ire.

1424

Mar.   James I of Scotland released from captivity in England (crowned 21 May)

James, 4th earl of Ormond, app. deputy

Ormond campaigns against Mág Aonghusa, Mac Mathghamhna, and Ó Domhnaill in Armagh

autumn   Edmund Mortimer arrives in Ire. with strong force

Mortimer receives submissions of Ó Domhnaill, Ó Néill, Mac Uí Néill Buidhe, and Mac Uidhilín

Oct. 10   Donnchadh Ó Ceallaigh, kg of Uí Mhaine, killed by Mac William Burkes; succ. by his nephew Aodh

1425

Jan. 18   Mortimer dies; Sir John Talbot appointed jcr by council; imprisons Ó Domhnaill, Ó Néill, Mac Uí Néill Buidhe, and Mac Uidhilín

Brian Ballach Mac Uí Néill Buidhe (O'Neill of Clandeboye) killed by people of Carrickfergus; succ. by his son Aodh Buidhe

Mar. 1   James, 4th earl of Ormond, app. lieutenant for 1 year

Ó Conchobhair Failghe (27 Mar.) and Ó Broin (10 Apr.) submit to Talbot

May 26-7   Murdac Stewart, duke of Albany, and his sons Alexander and Walter, executed by James I; James Stewart, surviving son, flees to Ire.

Mac Mathghamhna (12 May), Eóghan Ó Néill (25 July), and Ó Tuathail (8 Aug.) submit to Ormond

Parliament at Kilkenny

1425/6

Toirdhealbhach Ruadh Ó Conchobhair (O'Connor Roe), dies; Cathal, son of Ruaidhri Ó Conchobhair, assumes kingship of all Connacht

1426

Pale raided by An Calbhach Ó Conchobhair Failghe and Gearalt Caomhánach Mac Murchadha

Ó Conchobhair captures Tulsk castle from Cathal Dubh Ó Conchobhair

Eóghan Ó Néill submits to Domhnall Ó Néill

Apr. 13   Conchobar Ó Briain, kg of Thomond, dies; succ. by his nephew Tadhg

Apr. 15   James, 4th earl of Ormond, app. jcr

Nov. 30   Great council at Naas

Portumna becomes first priory of Dominican Observants in Ire.

1427

Niall Garbh Ó Domhnaill campaigns in Trian Conghail (East Ulster) in aid of sons of Mac Uí Néill Buidhe against Domhnall Ó Néill; defeats Mac Uidhilín

Ormond campaigns against Ó Raghallaigh and burns his castle

Mar. 15   John de Grey, lord of Codnor, app. lieutenant for 3 years (arrives in Ire., Aug., accompanied by Donnchadh Mac Murchadha, captured 1419)

Mar. 21   Parliament at Dublin (adjourned to 22 Sept.)

Sept. 16   An Calbhach Ó Conchobhair Failghe burns Mullingar

De Grey campaigns against Mac Murchadha and Ó Conchobhair Failghe; destroys Edenderry castle

Nov. 3   Great council at Dublin

Dec.   De Grey leaves for England; Edward Dantsey, bp of Meath, reappointed deputy

1428

Mar. 23   John Sutton, Lord Dudley, app. lieutenant for 2 years as from 30 Apr.

Aug. 11   Aodh an Einigh, son of Pilib Mág Uidhir, dies at Kinsale, on return from pilgrimage to Santiago; his son Aodh Óg killed by Mac Gíolla Fhinnéin and Clann Donnchaidh Bhallaigh Mhég Shamhradháin; Clann Aodha expelled by Tomás Mór Mág Uidhir

Sutton campaigns against Ó Raghallaigh

Oct. 1-7   Sutton campaigns against Ó Broin

Nov. 5   Parliament at Dublin: articles sent to Henry VI in defence of Ormond interest

Anonymous articles sent to English council to counteract those of Irish parliament

1429

James Stewart dies in Ire. (see 1425)

Eóghan Ó Raghallaigh and Domhnall Ó Néill defeat Tadhg Ó Ruairc and baron of Delvin at Achadh Cille Móir (bar. Clanmahon, Co. Cavan)

May 10   Anne Butler, daughter of earl of Ormond, betrothed to Thomas, son and heir of earl of Desmond, with Inchiquin and Youghal in dower

June 15   Union of sees of Cork and Cloyne (see 1326) effected by provision of Jordan Purcell to both

July 16   Abp Talbot summoned to England to answer concerning Ormond-Talbot feud

p. **July**   Niall Garbh Ó Domhnaill at English court

Oct. 12   Treasurer (Nicholas Plunkett) summoned to present accounts at English exchequer

late   Sutton leaves Ire.; appoints Sir Thomas Strange deputy (*a.* 5 Nov.)

Dec. 9   Great council at Dublin

1430

Scottish forces again in Ulster

Domhnall Ó Néill campaigns in Louth and Meath; submission of Anglo-Irish and Irish lords and of town of Dundalk

Earl of Desmond captures Kilbrittain castle from Mac Carthaigh Riabhach

Jan. 10   Ormond and council send James Cornwalshe to inform English council on state of Ire.

c. **Apr.**   Earl of Ormond leaves for France

Richard Talbot, abp of Dublin, app. jcr by council

May 19   Parliament at Dublin: grant-in-aid for building castles in Counties Dublin, Meath, Kildare, and Louth

Sept. 8   Deputy (Strange) and council grant jcr funds to support force against raids by Ó Raghallaigh, Ó Conchobhair Failghe, and others

Sept. 30   Great council at Dublin

Nov. 13   Tomás Mór Mág Uidhir, kg of Fir Manach, dies; succ. by his son Tomás Óg

Jcr (Talbot) campaigns in Leinster (further campaign, 1431)

1431

Anglo-Irish of Meath attack Clann Chaoich (sept of O'Reillys), Ó Maoilsheachlainn, and Mac Mathghamhna

Mac Uidhilín attacked by Eóghan Ó Néill, Tomás Óg Mág Uidhir, and Eóghan Ó Raghallaigh

Donnchadh Mac Murchadha raids Dublin

Jan. 29   Sir Thomas Stanley app. lieutenant for 6 years as from 12 Apr.

May 25   Parliament at Dublin

July 23   Opening of council of Basle

Nov. 23   Parliament at Dublin

Gearalt Caomhánach Mac Murchadha, *tánaiste* of Leinster, dies

Mac Mathghamhna raids Anglo-Irish of Meath (further raids, 1432)

Polyphonic choir established in St Patrick's cathedral, Dublin

1432

Jan. 1   Domhnall Ó Néill, kg of Tír Eóghain, killed by sons of Diarmaid Ó Catháin; Eóghan, son of Niall Óg Ó Néill, recovers kingship

Ó Néill allies with Eóghan and Toirdhealbhach Carrach, brothers of Brian Ó Conchobhair Sligigh, and with Tomás Óg Mág Uidhir against Niall Garbh Ó Domhnaill, Tadhg Ó Ruairc, and sons of Aodh Mág Uidhir

May 12   Richard, duke of York, nephew and heir of Edmund Mortimer, 5th earl of March (d. 1425), receives livery of his lands

Ó Néill campaigns with Mág Uidhir and Mac Uí Néill Buidhe against Ó Domhnaill in Cenél Moen (bar. Strabane, Co. Tyrone, and Finn valley, Co. Donegal)

Brian Mac Mathghamhna turns against Ó Néill and allies with Anglo-Irish of Meath to raid Armagh

James Butler, 4th earl of Ormond, campaigns against Ó Cearbhaill; destroys castles of Ballybritt (Co. Offaly) and Cluain Uí Chionaith (unidentified)

Stanley in England (late 1432–late 1433); Sir Christopher Plunket app. deputy

1433

spring Parliament

Niall Garbh Ó Domhnaill allies with Mac Uidhilín and Robert Savage against Eóghan Ó Néill; defeated in Dufferin (Co. Down) by Mac Domhnaill of the Isles, who proceeds with his fleet to Inishowen where Neachtan Ó Domhnaill surrenders to Ó Néill; deputy (Plunkett) raids Armagh to aid Ó Domhnaill; Ó Domhnaill marches through Meath and Connacht, but makes peace with Ó Néill at Caoluisge (Belleek); Mac Uidhilín seeks refuge in English Uriel (Co. Louth)

Mar. 26 Poetic convention held by Mairghréag, daughter of Ó Cearbhaill and wife of Ó Conchobhair Failghe, at Killeigh (Co. Offaly); a second (Aug. 15) at Rathangan (Co. Kildare)

Oct. 16 Great council at Dublin

First Franciscan house of Observants in Ire. founded at Quin, Co. Clare, by MacNamaras

1434

Eóghan Ó Néill and Niall Garbh Ó Domhnaill join forces against Neachtan Ó Domhnaill and Brian Ó Conchobhair Sligigh; besiege Castlefinn without success

Ó Néill and Ó Domhnaill campaign in Oirghialla and Meath; Ó Domhnaill captured by Thomas Dillon (30 Sept.)

Nov. 29 Great frost: lakes frozen (lasts until after 15 Feb. 1435)

1434/5

Tadhg Ó Ruairc, kg of Bréifne, dies; succ. by Lochlainn, son of Tadhg na gCaor, with opposition from Clann Tighearnáin

1435

Eóghan Ó Néill campaigns in Rash (Mountjoy Forest, Co. Tyrone) against Neachtan Ó Domhnaill and Brian Óg Ó Néill

Mar. 7 Parliament at Dublin

Apr. 1 Ordinance prohibiting Irish poets and musicians from Anglo-Irish areas

Brian Óg Ó Néill surrenders Ballyshannon castle to Ó Néill, who mutilates him and two of his sons

end of year Stanley takes Niall Garbh Ó Domhnaill prisoner to Isle of Man; Richard Talbot, abp of Dublin, appointed deputy

1436

Jan. 16 Great council at Dublin: petition critical of Stanley's administration sent to Henry VI

An Calbhach Ó Conchobair Failghe raids Meath to avenge Ó Domhnaill; defeated by Anglo-Irish and sons of Domhnall Ó Fearghail (d. 1435)

Nov. 16 Parliament at Dublin

Talbot campaigns in south Leinster (campaign continued, 1437)

c. **1436** 'Libelle of Englyshe polycye' warns English public of strategic importance of Ire.

1437

Cathaoir, brother of Ó Conchobhair Failghe, raids Uí Failghe with Anglo-Irish of Leix

Maghnus Mac Mathghamhna asks Eóghan Ó Néill for aid against his brother Brian

Feb. 21 James I, kg of Scotland, murdered; succ. by his son James II, a minor

Nov. 15 Parliament at Dublin

1438

Tadhg Ó Briain, kg of Thomond, deposed by his brother Mathghamhain Dall

Feb. 12 Lionel, Lord Welles, app. lieutenant (arrives in Ire., Apr.)

Nov. 17 Parliament at Dublin: order for return of all Irish officials to Ire.

1438-42

Tomás Óg Mág Uidhir opposed in Fir Manach by his brother Pilib

1439

William Welles (brother of lieutenant) app. deputy

Niall Garbh Ó Domhnaill dies in Isle of Man; succ. by his brother Neachtan

Mar. 3 English ordinance for return of Irish lieges to Ire., with specified exceptions

Mar. 19 Cathal Ó Conchobhair, kg of Connacht, dies; succession contested between Tadhg, son of Toirdhealbhach Ruadh, and Aodh, son of Toirdhealbhach Óg Ó Conchobhair Donn

spring Plague in Dublin

July 29 Pope Eugene IV provides for union of dioceses of Down and Connor

Bristol city imposes fine of £20 on any mayor admitting man of Irish parentage to council

1440

Brian Ó Conchobhair Sligigh (O'Connor Sligo) dies; succ. by his brother Eóghan

An Calbhach Ó Conchobhair Failghe defeated by Mac Giolla Pádraig and earl of Desmond in Leix

c. **May 19** William Welles captured by Cathaoir, son of Ó Conchobhair Failghe

c. **June** Lieutenant (Lionel, Lord Welles) returns to Ire.

Sept. 7 Walter Burke (Mac William), dies; succ. by his brother Edmund na Féasóige

Nov. 11 Parliament at Drogheda: subsidy granted

1440-48

Philip Norreys (dean of St Patrick's, Dublin, 1457-65) attacks mendicant orders in Ire.

1441

early Lionel, Lord Welles, leaves Ire.; James, 4th earl of Ormond app. deputy

June 23 Great council at Naas

Nov. 17 Parliament at Dublin: petition sent to Henry VI for removal of Ormond from office

1442

Domhnall Glas Mac Carthaigh Riabhach (MacCarthy Reagh) dies; succ. by his brother Donnchadh

Brian Mac Mathghamhna, kg of Oirghialla, dies; succ. by his brother Ruaidhrí

Eóghan Ó Néill supports Mac Uidhilín against Ó Catháin and Mac Uí Néill Buidhe

Neachtan Ó Domhnaill relinquishes jurisdiction over Cenél Moen (see 1432) and Inishowen to Ó Néill

Anglo-Irish attack Ó Tuathail, Ó Broin (Co. Dublin), and Mac Murchadha (Wexford)

Feb. 27 James, 4th earl of Ormond, app. lieutenant

Mar. 20 Aid granted to Waterford for strengthening of city defences

May 20 John Talbot created earl of Shrewsbury

July 6 Great council at Naas; chancellor (Richard Wogan) withdraws to England with great seal (24 July); council adjourns to Dublin (30 July)

Aug. 7 Richard Talbot, abp of Dublin, app. chancellor

Aug. 24 Ormond summoned to English court

Nov. 21 Irish council resumes office of chancellor from Richard Talbot

1443

Pale raided by Ó Conchobhair Failghe and de Berminghams

Attempted displacement of Thomas FitzGerald as prior of Hospitallers in favour of Thomas Talbot

Jan. 25 Parliament at Drogheda

Mar. 4 Richard Wogan reapp. chancellor

July 12 Ormond ordered to restore Michael Griffin as chief baron of exchequer

Oct. 25 Great council at Naas

1444

Eóghan Ó Néill campaigns in Louth as far as Dundalk

John Talbot, son of earl of Shrewsbury, marries Elizabeth, daughter of earl of Ormond

Tadhg Ó Briain, ex-kg of Thomond, dies; Mathghamhain, kg of Thomond, goes blind; succ. by his brother Toirdhealbhach

Eóghan Ó Conchobhair Sligigh (O'Connor Sligo) killed by Clann Chormaic Mheic Donnchadha; succ. by his brother Toirdhealbhach Carrach

Jan. 24 Parliament at Dublin

Mar. 23 Ormond summoned to English court

Mar. 25 Giles Thorndon leaves Ire. to present complaints against Ormond before English council

May Aodh Buidhe Mac Uí Néill Buidhe (O'Neill of Clandeboye) dies; Eóghan Ó Néill attempts to intervene in succession; defeated by Muircheartach Ruadh Ó Néill, Énrí Ó Néill, and Mac Uidhilín; succession of Aodh Buidhe's brother, Muircheartach Ruadh

June 1 Truce between England and France

June 26 Council at Drogheda: complaints against Ormond rejected

Aug. 21 Great council at Drogheda

Aug. 28 Richard Nugent, baron of Delvin, app. deputy

1445

Death of Uilliam, son of Seaán, son of Domhnall Ó Fearghail; Anghaile divided into lordships of Ó Fearghail Buidhe and Ó Fearghail Bán

Neachtan Ó Domhnaill campaigns against Toirdhealbhach Carrach Ó Conchobhair Sligigh

Mairghréag, daughter of Ó Cearbhaill (see 1433), and many Irish lords visit Santiago to gain indulgence

Feb. 5 Parliament at Dublin

Mar. 12 John Talbot, earl of Shrewsbury, app. lieutenant

June 8 Crown lands in Donaghmoyne and Farney granted to Feidhlimidh Mac Mathghamhna for 7 years at £10 a year

Aug. 11 James, 7th earl of Desmond, permitted to attend all further parliaments and councils by proxy

Nov. 18 James, 4th earl of Ormond, acquitted of charges of maladministration during his lieutenancy

Dec. 3 Third baron added to exchequer (see 1356)

Dec. 15 John Cornewalshe app. chief baron of exchequer

Uilliam Ó Raghallaigh becomes first Irish-born provincial of Franciscans in Ire.

1446

Ruaidhrí Mac Mathghamhna, kg of Oirghialla, dies; succ. by his son Aodh Ruadh

Edmund Burke (Mac William) divides lordship of Tír Oilealla (Tirerrill, Co. Sligo) between Seaán, son of Conchobhar Mac Donnchadha, and Tadhg, son of Tomaltach Mór Mac Donnchadha

Neachtan Ó Domhnaill campaigns in Connacht in defence of Clann Tomaltaigh Óig Mheic Donnchadha

Brian, son of Ó Conchobhair Failghe, captured by Anglo-Irish while raiding Meath

War between earls of Desmond and Ormond

Feb. 4   Great council at Dublin

July 17   John Talbot, earl of Shrewsbury and lieutenant, created earl of Waterford

Aug. 12 or 13 or Sept. 2   John Talbot, son of earl of Shrewsbury, app. chancellor

Oct. 18   Royal charter to guild of barbers and surgeons at Dublin

First known use of term 'Pale' to denote area under Dublin control

1447

Jan. 13   Parliament at Trim: ordinance prohibiting officials from holding lands in areas where they hold office (1336) waived once more (see 1420); ordinance against 'O'Reilly's money'

Earl of Shrewsbury leaves for England; Richard Talbot, abp of Dublin, app. deputy

Oct. 20   Great council at Naas

Dec. 9   Richard, duke of York, app. lieutenant

Recurrence of plague (continues, 1448)

1448

Mar. 10   Henry VI grants earl of Shrewsbury half the sum owed to him for costs of Irish government

1449

James, son of earl of Ormond, created 2nd earl of Wiltshire (see 1452)

Eóghan Ó Raghallaigh, kg of east Bréifne, dies; succession contested between his son Seaán, supported by Ó Néill, and Fearghal, son of Tomás Mór (d. 1392), supported by Talbot and Ormond

Feb. 28   Parliament at Dublin

July 6   Richard, duke of York, arrives in Ire.

c. **Aug. 27**   Northern kgs submit to York at Drogheda

autumn   Mág Eochagáin submits to York

Sept.   York on circuit in Munster and Leinster

Oct. 17   Great council at Dublin

Oct. 29   French capture Rouen from English

1450

O'Neills campaign in Trian Conghail (Ulster east of Bann) in aid of Mac Uidhilín against Mac Uí Néill Buidhe

Fearghal Ó Raghallaigh acknowledges Seaán, son of Eóghan, as kg of east Bréifne

Apr. 24   Parliament at Drogheda: act of resumption of grants to increase revenue; subsidy granted

May 2   Duke of Suffolk murdered while going into exile

Tomás Óg Mág Uidhir on pilgrimage to Rome (returns, 1451); Cathal Mág Uidhir, *tánaiste*, killed (*c.* 1 July) by his half-brother Donnchadh Dúnchadh-ach, who is subsequently mutilated by Éamonn, son of Tomás Óg

July   Cade's revolt in England

July 28   Earl of Ormond retained by duke of York for life, at annual fee of 100 marks

Aug. 22   Duke of York leaves Ire.; James, 4th earl of Ormond, app. deputy

Nov. 27   Great council at Drogheda (adjourned to Dublin, 14 Dec.)

1451

Hostilities between Donnchadh Mac Carthaigh Riabhach and Tadhg, son of Cormac Mac Carthaigh of Múscraighe

Opposition to reinstatement of Uilliam Ó Raghallaigh as O.F.M. provincial in Ire.

c. **Feb. 1**   Mairghréag, daughter of Ó Cearbhaill and wife of Ó Conchobhair Failghe, dies (see 1433)

Feb. 11   Duke of York confirmed as lieutenant

Mar. 26   Parliament at Drogheda

1451/2

Parliament at Dublin

1452

Maghnus Ó Duibhgeannáin, scribe of Book of Ballymote, dies

Neachtan Ó Domhnaill, kg of Tír Conaill, killed by his nephews Aodh Ruadh and Domhnall, sons of Niall Garbh; succ. by Ruaidhrí, son of Neachtan, with assistance of Énrí Ó Néill

Eóghan Ó Néill repulsed from Fews by Mac Mathghamhna and Anglo-Irish

Deputy (Ormond) campaigns in Leinster (captures castles of Owney and Lea) and Oirghialla (Ó Raghallaigh and Mac Mathghamhna submit)

Aug. 23   James, 4th earl of Ormond (the 'White Earl'), dies; succ. by his son James, 2nd earl of Wiltshire; Edward FitzEustace app. deputy

1453

Donnchadh Mac Carthaigh Riabhach (MacCarthy Reagh) dies; succ. by his brother Diarmaid an Dúna

Énrí Mac Uí Néill Buidhe defeated and captured by Savages with aid of Dublin fleet

Mar. 31   Aodh Ruadh Mac Mathghamhna, kg of Oirghialla, dies; succ. by his cousin Feidhlimidh, son of Brian

May 12 James, 5th earl of Ormond, app. lieutenant, with John Mey, abp of Armagh, as deputy (on or *a*. 25 June)

May 25 Great council at Dublin

May 29 Constantinople taken by storm by Ottoman Turks under Muhammad II; end of eastern Roman Empire (see 330, 476)

Butlers of Polestown raid into Co. Kildare

1453 × 1455

Forty-two line Bible printed at Mainz by Gutenberg-Fust; probably first book printed from moveable type (see 1551)

1454

Book of Pottlerath (Laud Misc. 610) written for Edmund mac Richard Butler of Polestown

Mar. 27 Richard, duke of York, app. protector of England

Apr. 7 Ruaidhrí Ó Domhnaill, kg of Tír Conaill, killed by his cousin Domhnall, son of Niall Garbh, who succeeds to kingship

July 5 Parliament at Dublin

Oct. 25 Edward FitzEustace dies; Thomas fitz Maurice FitzGerald app. jcr by council

Dec. 1 Duke of York again confirmed as lieutenant

1455

Toirdealbhach Carrach Ó Conchobhair Sligigh (O'Connor Sligo), dies; succ. by his nephew Maghnus, son of Brian

Ó Ceallaigh captures castle of Athlone; Ó Fearghail destroys castle of Street

Feb. 14 Parliament at Dublin

Apr. 18 Great council at Dublin

May 22 Battle of St Albans: Yorkist victory; duke of Somerset killed

c. **July 1** Eóghan Ó Néill, kg of Tír Eóghain, forced to resign by his son Énrí

Oct. 17 Parliament at Dublin

1456

May 28 Domhnall Ó Domhnaill, kg of Tír Conaill, killed by Énrí Ó Néill; succ. by his cousin Toirdhealbhach Cairbreach, son of Neachtan

Nov. 5 Parliament at Naas

1457

Tomás Óg Mág Uidhir attacks sons of Ruaidhrí Mac Mathghamhna; Pilib Mág Uidhir attacks Ó Ruairc

Jan. 28 Parliament at Dublin

Mar. 5 Prior general at Rome grants special and separate vicar to Augustinian friars in Connacht

Mar. 6 Richard, duke of York, reapp. lieutenant (for 10 years as from 8 Dec.)

1458

Énrí Ó Néill and Toirdhealbhach Cairbreach Ó Domhnaill invade north Connacht and Bréifne; Ó Domhnaill obtains hostages from Lower Connacht

Monastery and library of Aghavea (Co. Fermanagh) destroyed by fire

Lochlainn, son of Tadhg Ó Ruairc, joint kg of west Bréifne, dies

Edmund na Féasóige Burke (Mac William) dies; succ. by his brother Tomás Óg

An Calbhach Mór Ó Conchobhair Failghe (O'Connor Faly) dies; succ. by his son Conn

Feb. 3 Parliament at Dublin

1459

Toirdhealbhach Ó Briain, kg of Thomond, dies; succession disputed between his son Tadhg and Donnchadh, son of Mathghamhain (deposed *c.* 1461)

Énrí Ó Néill campaigns against Clann Airt Uí Néill

Earl of Kildare defeats and captures Conn Ó Conchobhair Failghe

Feb. 9 Parliament at Dublin

Oct. 12 Battle of Ludford Bridge: duke of York defeated and escapes to Ire.

Nov. 20 Duke of York attainted by parliament at Coventry

Dec. 4 James, 5th earl of Ormond, app. lieutenant by Henry VI, with Sir Thomas Bathe and John Mey, abp of Armagh, as deputies (12 and 13 Dec.)

1460

Feb. 8 Parliament at Drogheda (adjourned to Dublin, 23 Feb.; several subsequent adjournments): York again confirmed as lieutenant by Anglo-Irish in opposition to Ormond; declaration that only acts of Irish parliament should bind Ire.

Act regulating currency and providing for issue of distinctive Irish coinage: 'Irelands', groats, and 'Patricks'

Conn Ó Conchobhair Failghe defeats Anglo-Irish; baron of Galtrim killed

Tomás Óg Burke (Mac William) dies; succ. by his brother Risdeárd

Mac William Burke founds Franciscan Observantine house at Moyne (Co. Mayo)

Domhnall Riabhach Mac Murchadha founds Franciscan Observantine house at Enniscorthy; and Finghín Mór Ó hEidirsgeóil at Sherkin Island (Co. Cork)

July 10 Battle of Northampton: Henry VI defeated and captured by Yorkists; York leaves for England; Thomas, 7th earl of Kildare, app. deputy

Aug. 3 James II, kg of Scotland, dies; succ. by his son James III, a minor

Sept. 3 Seaán an Einigh Ó Raghallaigh, kg of East Bréifne, defeated and killed by Anglo-Irish; succ. by his brother Cathal

Oct. 31 Henry VI accepts Richard, duke of York, as heir

Dec. 30 Battle of Wakefield: Lancastrian victory; Richard, duke of York, killed; earl of Kildare app. L.J. by council

1461

Mar. 4   English crown assumed by Edward, son of Richard, duke of York, in opposition to Henry VI, who flees to Scotland after defeat at Towton (29 Mar.)

c. **May 1**   James, 5th earl of Ormond and 2nd earl of Wiltshire, executed

May 1   Thomas, 7th earl of Kildare, sworn in as jcr

May 15   Aodh Ó Conchobhair Donn (O'Connor Don), 'kg of Connacht', dies; succ. by Brian, son of Brian Ballach Ó Conchobhair Ruadh, with support of Risdeárd Burke (Mac William)

May 31   Brian Ó Coineóil, bp of Killala, murdered by son of Maghnus Ó Dubhda

June 12   Parliament at Naas

Toirdhealbhach Cairbreach Ó Domhnaill, kg of Tír Conaill, defeated, mutilated, and deposed by his cousin Aodh Ruadh with the help of Maolmhuire Mac Suibhne Fánad

Pale raided by Ó Conchobhair Failghe, Edmund mac Richard Butler, Mág Eochagáin, and sections of MacMahons and O'Ferralls

1462

Jan. 8   Great council at Dublin (adjourned to 8 Mar., then to 3 May)

Feb. 28   George, duke of Clarence (brother of Edward IV), a minor, app. lieutenant; Roland FitzEustace app. deputy (16 May)

John, 6th earl of Ormond, captures Waterford

Battle of Pilltown: Ormond's supporters defeated by earl of Desmond; Edmund mac Richard Butler captured; gives Book of Pottlerath and Book of Carrick as ransom

Aug. 2   Stewardship of Connacht and other appurtenances of earldom of March granted to earl of Desmond

Oct. 15   Parliament at Dublin

Franciscan friary founded at Monaghan by Feidhlimidh Mac Mathghamhna

Énrí Ó Néill attacks Aodh Ruadh Ó Domhnaill and Clann Airt Uí Néill

Brian Ó Conchobhair Ruadh, 'kg of Connacht', defeated and deposed by Tadhg Ó Conchobhair Ruadh

Large numbers of Irish pilgrims visit Santiago da Compostella to gain indulgence

Treaty of Ardtornish: alliance between Yorkists, Eóin Mac Domhnaill, 4th lord of the Isles, and James, exiled 9th earl of Douglas

1463

James, 7th earl of Desmond, dies; succ. by his son Thomas, app. deputy to duke of Clarence (1 Apr.)

Pale invaded by Ó Conchobhair Failghe and O'Byrnes; Ó Broin killed

Nov. 4   Parliament at Wexford (adjourned to Waterford, 14 Nov., to Naas, 20 Feb. 1464, and to Dublin, 27 Feb. 1464)

Edward IV sends presents to Énrí Ó Néill

Tadhg Ó Briain acknowledges Ó Néill's claim to high-kingship

1464

Jan. 31   John Tiptoft, earl of Worcester, app. chancellor

Earl of Desmond and William Sherwood, bp of Meath, at English court

May 8   Conn, son of Niall Garbh Ó Domhnaill, killed by his cousin Éigneachán, son of Neachtan Ó Domhnaill

June 13   Edmund mac Richard Butler of Polestown dies

Aug. 18   Tadhg Ó Conchobhair Ruadh (O'Connor Roe), 'kg of Connacht', dies; disputed succession

Énrí Ó Néill and sons of Neachtan Ó Domhnaill invade Tír Conaill as far as Ballyshannon; Aodh Ruadh Ó Domhnaill supported by Risdeárd Burke (Mac William)

Observant Franciscan friary founded at Adare by earl of Kildare

Aodh Ruadh Ó Domhnaill and Mac William visit Dublin

Struggle for kingship of Uí Mhaine between sons of Donnchadh (d. 1424) and sons of Uilliam Ruadh (d. 1420)

1465

Mar. 30   Cathal Ruadh, son of Tadhg Ó Conchobhair Ruadh, killed by sons of Ó Conchobhair Donn

Aug. 12   Parliament at Trim (adjourned to Dublin, 14 Oct., and to Drogheda, 18 Nov.): act for establishment of university at Drogheda (5 Edw. V, c. xlvi)

Observant Franciscan friary founded at Kilcrea (Co. Cork) by Cormac, son of Tadhg Mac Carthaigh, lord of Múscraighe

Government decree forbidding strangers to fish off Irish coasts without licence

1466

Anglo-Irish attack Oirghialla and Uí Failghe; earl of Desmond and other members of council captured by Ó Conchobhair Failghe

Raids by Tadhg Ó Briain into Desmond and Ormond, by Conn Ó Conchobhair Failghe into Meath, and by Aodh, son of Eóghan Ó Néill, into Oirghialla

Feidhlimidh Fionn Ó Conchobhair Ruadh supported by Risdeárd Burke (Mac William) as Ó Conchobhair Ruadh; they burn Ballintober

Tadhg an Chomaid Ó Briain, kg of Thomond, dies; succ. by his brother Conchobhar Mór (otherwise 'na Srón')

Plague in Meath, Dublin, and Leinster (continues, 1467)

1467

spring   John Tiptoft, earl of Worcester, app. deputy (arrives in Ire., Oct.)

June 15   Philip the Good, duke of Burgundy, dies; succ. by his son Charles the Bold (d. 1477)

Clanricard and O'Briens defeat Mac William and Ó Ceallaigh at Crossmacrin (bar. Kilconnell, Co. Galway); Aodh Ruadh Ó Domhnaill forces Clanricard to make peace

Ó Conchobhair Failghe, Mág Eochagáin, and de Berminghams raid into Meath and Kildare; earl of Desmond campaigns in Kildare (26 June-   )

Dec. 11   Parliament at Dublin (adjourned to Drogheda 4 Feb. 1468; many subsequent adjournments)

Aodh Ó Ceallaigh, kg of Uí Mhaine, dies; succ. by his cousin Aodh na gCailleach, son of Uilliam Ruadh

1468

Torna Mór Ó Maoil Chonaire, historian and poet, dies

Feb. 4   Tiptoft holds parliament at Drogheda: earls of Desmond and Kildare and Edward Plunkett attainted; Desmond executed

Gerald, brother of late earl of Desmond, invades Meath and Leinster

Ó Conchobhair Failghe captured by Anglo-Irish; his brother Tadhg, Mág Eochagáin, and Dalton invade Meath

Anglo-Irish attack Ó Raghallaigh; burn Cavan

Ó Domhnaill fails to install Domhnall, son of Tadhg Ó Ruairc, in opposition to Donnchadh Losc, son of Tighearnán Mór Ó Ruairc

Muircheartach Ruadh Mac Uí Néill Buidhe (Clandeboye) defeated and killed by his nephew Conn, son of Aodh Buidhe Ó Néill, who succeeds to lordship

Cathal Óg, son of Cathal Ruadh Mág Raghnaill, lord of Muintir Eólais (1462-8), dies; succ. by his son Tadhg, with opposition from Uilliam of Clann Mhaoilsheachlainn

1468-9

Ó Domhnaill and Mac William at war with Ó Briain and Clanricard

1469

Jan. 27   Parliament at Drogheda

Feb. 13   Aodh na gCailleach Ó Ceallaigh, kg of Uí Mhaine, killed by sons of Donnchadh; succession contested between Uilliam, son of Aodh, son of Brian, and Tadhg Caoch, son of Uilliam Ruadh

July 28   Edward IV captured by earl of Warwick

Risdeárd (Mac William) resigns in favour of his nephew Ricard Ó Cuairsge, son of Edmund na Féasóige

Pádraig White captures Pádraig Óg Savage and expels him from Lecale with assistance of Énrí Ó Néill and Mac Uidhilín

Domhnall an Dána Mac Carthaigh, kg of Desmond, dies; succ. by his son Tadhg Liath

1470

Mar. 23   Tiptoft app. lieutenant

spring   Tiptoft recalled; Edward Dudley app. deputy

Oct. 3   Henry VI restored by earl of Warwick

a. **Oct. 13**   Dudley leaves for England; Thomas, 7th earl of Kildare, appointed jcr by council

Oct. 18   Tiptoft executed

Nov. 26   Parliament at Dublin

Énrí Ó Néill supports Mac Uidhilín against attacks by Clann Aodha Buidhe and Mág Aonghusa; captures Sketrick Island in Strangford Lough from Clann Aodha Buidhe

Sons of Eóghan Ó Conchobhair Sligigh (d. 1444) installed in Sligo castle by Aodh Ruadh Ó Domhnaill

1471

Feb. 18   George, duke of Clarence, reapp. lieutenant

Apr. 14   Battle of Barnet: earl of Warwick defeated and killed by Edward IV, who regains throne

c. **end Apr.**   Énrí Ó Néill captures Omagh from Clann Airt Uí Néill

May 4   Battle of Tewkesbury; defeat and capture of Henry VI (d. 21 May)

Tomás Óg Mág Uidhir, kg of Fir Manach, resigns in favour of his son Éamonn

Nov. 29   Parliament at Dublin (successive adjournments): coinage revalued; company of archers established for defence of Pale

Conn Mac Uí Néill Buidhe reestablishes his lordship over Trian Conghaill

Tadhg Ó Conchobhair brings Anglo-Irish support against his half-brother Ó Conchobhair Failghe

Earl of Kildare campaigns against Mac Mathghamhna in Farney

Earl of Desmond imprisoned by MacCarthys (until 1472)

Franciscan priory founded at Galbally

Dec.   Earl of Kildare app. deputy

1472

Ó Ceallaigh raids into western Meath; defeated by Anglo-Irish

Énrí Ó Néill defeats Aodh Ruadh Ó Domhnaill at Castlemoyle

Dec. 4   Parliament at Naas (adjourned to Dublin, 11 Mar.): abortive attempt to abolish liberty of Meath (see 1478-9)

1473

July 2   Galway city severely damaged by lightning

Ricard Ó Cuairsge Burke (Mac William) resigns in favour of his cousin Theobald

1474

Mar. 18   Parliament at Dublin: Guild of St George founded

autumn   Conn Ó Conchobhair Failghe (O'Connor Faly) dies; succ. by his son Cathaoir

Aug. 5   Sir Gilbert Debenham app. chancellor; 400 archers assigned to accompany him to Ire.

Feidhlimidh Geangcach, son of Toirdhealbhach Ó Conchobhair Donn (O'Connor Don), last kg of Connacht, killed by Ó Ceallaigh; Tadhg, son of Eóghan Ó Conchobhair, succeeds as 'O'Connor Don'

Observant Franciscan friary founded at Donegal by Aodh Ruadh Ó Domhnaill

1475

a. **Apr. 18**   William Sherwood, bp of Meath, app. deputy

Apr. 18   Further 220 archers sent to Ire. under Thomas Danyell

July 21   Parliament at Dublin (adjourned to Drogheda, 23 Oct.; to Dublin, 5 Feb.); attainder against Sir John of Ormond annulled; coinage revalued again

Aug. 29   Seven-year truce made between England and France

Aodh Ruadh Ó Domhnaill makes expedition through Lower Connacht, Bréifne, Anghaile, Uí Failghe, Meath, Uí Mhaine, and Clanricard

1476

Énrí Ó Néill captures Belfast castle from Mac Uí Néill Buidhe

Domhnall Riabhach Mac Murchadha, kg of Leinster, dies; succ. by Murchadh Ballach

Lower Connacht divided between Aodh Ruadh Ó Domhnaill and Theobald Burke

Dissension between Anglo-Irish of Meath and Leinster

Tadhg Ó Conchobhair Donn (O'Connor Don) killed by his own followers; succ. by Eóghan Caoch, son of Feidhlimidh Ó Conchobhair Donn

Dec. 6   Parliament at Drogheda (adjourned to Dublin, 14 Jan. 1477)

Institution of separate vicar for Irish Augustinian friars

Eóin Mac Domhnaill, lord of the Isles, forfeits earldom of Ross and possessions in Kintyre to James III, kg of Scotland

1477

early   Bp Sherwood in England (see *a.* 18 Apr. 1475)

c. **June**   Further 200 archers sent to Ire. with Bp Sherwood

Énrí Ó Néill invades Tír Aodha in support of Clann Neachtain Uí Dhomhnaill

Gerald, son of James, 9th earl of Desmond, murdered by section of Munster FitzGeralds

John, 6th earl of Ormond, dies; succ. by his brother Thomas (livery, 15 June)

Plague in Tír Conaill

1478

Tadhg Óg Ó hUiginn, poet, dies

Feb. 18   George, duke of Clarence, lieutenant, executed by Edward IV

Mar. 10   John de la Pole, duke of Suffolk, app. lieutenant for 20 years

Mar. 25   Thomas, 7th earl of Kildare, dies; succ. by his son Gerald (Gearóid Mór), who is appointed jcr by council in succession to his father

May 29   Parliament at Naas (adjourned to Dublin, 6 July; to Connell, 14 Sept.); liberty of Meath abolished

c. **July 3**   Octavianus de Palatio provided to see of Armagh

July 6   George, infant son of Edward IV, app. lieutenant, with Henry, Lord Grey, as deputy; dies within year

Aug.   Robert Preston, Lord Gormanston, created viscount

Grey prevented from entering Dublin castle by James Keating, constable

Nov. 6   Parliament at Trim (adjourned to Drogheda, 19 Nov.; to Dublin, 31 May 1479): proceedings of previous parliament annulled; subsidy granted; act of resumption (18 Edw. IV, c. XVI); act to regulate procedure in election of jcr (18 Edw. IV, c. X); liberty of Meath restored

Sligo castle recovered from Ó Domhnaill by Mac William Burke and delivered into hands of Ruaidhrí Ó Conchobhair Sligigh

Cormac Mac Carthaigh Riabhach (MacCarthy Reagh), lord of half Carbery, castrated and deposed by kinsmen; succ. by his cousin Fínghin

Recurrence of plague

1479

early   Grey leaves for England; Robert Preston, viscount Gormanston, app. deputy

May 5   Richard, duke of York (b. 1473), app. lieutenant

c. **Aug.**   Further 300 archers sent to Ire.

a. **Oct. 5**   Gerald, 8th earl of Kildare, app. deputy

Edward IV issues decree condoning earl of Kildare's activities as jcr

Dec. 10   Parliament at Dublin (subsequent adjournments to Dublin and Naas, 1480-81); subsidy granted; liberty of Meath abolished again; poundage restored

Ricard Ó Cuairsge Burke (Mac William, 1469-73) dies

Énrí Ó Néill attacks Clann Airt Uí Néill in Tír Conaill (continues attacks until 1481)

Franciscan friary at Meelick becomes Observant

Guild of English merchants trading in Ire. founded at Dublin

c. **1480**

Conn, son of Énrí Ó Néill, marries Eleanor, sister of earl of Kildare

1480

Tomás Óg Mág Uidhir, ex-kg of Fir Manach, dies

May 12   Richard, duke of Gloucester, brother of Edward IV, app. lieutenant general against James III of Scotland

May 23   Turks begin siege of Rhodes

Énrí Ó Néill, assisted by earl of Kildare, fails to capture Ceann Ard castle (Caledon) from Seaán Mac Uí Néill Buidhe

Éigneachán of Clann Neachtain Uí Domhnaill secures tanistship of Tír Conaill

1481

Oct. 19   Parliament at Dublin (adjourned to 4 Feb.; to 3 June 1482)

Pádraig Óg Savage captured and castrated by Conn Mac Uí Néill Buidhe

Conn Ó Neill captured by Clann Aodha Buidhe

Cathaoir Caomhánach Mac Murchadha killed by Anglo-Irish of Co. Wexford

1482

Art, son of Conn Ó Conchobhair Failghe, invades Meath; captures Oliver Plunkett

Conn Mac Uí Néill Buidhe (O'Neill of Clandeboye) dies; succ. by his son Niall Mór

Brian, son of Feidhlimidh Ó Néill, killed by Eóghan, son of Conn Mac Uí Néill Buidhe

Dec. 3   William Sherwood, bp of Meath, dies

1483

Feb. 7   Parliament at Limerick: act for transfer of unclaimed absentee lands in Carlow and Kildare to earl of Kildare

Apr. 9   Edward IV, kg of England, dies; succ. by his son Edward V (a minor), with his uncle Richard, duke of Gloucester, as protector; Gerald, earl of Kildare, confirmed as deputy

June 25   Edward V, kg of England, deposed by his uncle Richard III

July 19   Edward, son of Richard III, app. lieutenant

Aug. 31   Earl of Kildare confirmed as deputy

Conn Ó Néill ransomed from Clann Aodha Buidhe; Énrí Ó Néill, kg of Tír Eóghain, resigns in his favour

Aodh Ruadh Ó Domhnaill campaigns in Oirghialla; checked by earl of Kildare

Rossa (Roger) Mág Uidhir, bp of Clogher, son of Tomás Óg Mág Uidhir, dies

1484

July-Aug.   Earl of Kildare at English court

Aug. 20   Giolla Pádraig, son of Éamonn Mág Uidhir, *tánaiste* of Fir Manach, killed by his five brothers: dynastic dissension follows

Aug. 21   John de la Pole, earl of Lincoln, app. lieutenant

Sept. 21   Treaty of Nottingham: 3-year truce made between England and Scotland

Sept.   Thomas Barrett, bp of Annaghdown, commissioned to treat with Irish kings and more remote Anglo-Irish lords

Oct. 15   Great council at Naas

Nov.   Réamonn Mac Mathghamhna, kg of Oirghialla, dies in captivity at Drogheda; succ. by his nephew Aodh Óg

Irish province of Dominican order established

1485

Feb. 16   Thomas, earl of Ormond, allowed to be absent from Ire. for 1 year without incurring statutory penalties for absenteeism (permission extended for 3 years, 17 Feb. 1486)

Mar. 18   Parliament at Dublin (adjourned to Trim, 6 June and 8 Aug.; to Dublin, 24 Oct.)

Aug. 22   Battle of Bosworth: Richard III, kg of England, defeated and killed by Henry Tudor, earl of Richmond, who succeeds as Henry VII (Gerald, earl of Kildare, again confirmed as deputy)

Aodh Óg Mac Uí Néill Buidhe killed while raiding Lecale

Aodh Óg, son of Aodh Ruadh Mac Mathghamhna, succeeds as kg of Oirghialla

Eóghan Caoch Ó Conchobhair Donn (O'Connor Don) dies; succ. by his cousin Aodh Óg

Waterford city exempted from rendering account at exchequer

Uilleag Ruadh Burke (Clanricard) dies; succ. by his son Uilleag Fionn

Réamonn, son of Glaisne of Clann Réamoinn Még Mathghamhna, raids into Louth (raids continue, 1486)

1486

Mar. 11   Jasper Tudor, duke of Bedford, uncle of Henry VII, app. lieutenant

June 6   Brian, son of Ruaidhrí Mac Mathghamhna, lord of Dartraighe, killed by Anglo-Irish of Louth

summer   Belfast castle recovered by Clann Aodha Buidhe

July 11   National synod held at Drogheda under Octavian de Palatio, abp of Armagh

July 14   Parliament at Dublin (adjourned to 24 Nov.)

Ruaidhrí, son of Ruaidhrí Mac Diarmada, kg of Magh Luirg, dies; succ. by Conchobhar, son of Cormac of Slíocht Conchobhair

Sept. 5   Aodh Ruadh Ó Domhnaill defeats Mac William Burkes at ford of Ardnaree

Nov. 6   Éamonn Mág Uidhir, kg of Fir Manach, resigns in favour of his cousin Seaán, son of Pilib

Observant Franciscan friary founded at Kilcullen by Roland FitzEustace, lord of Portlester

Conn Ó Néill campaigns in Oirghialla against Clann Réamoinn (sept of Mac-Mahons) (continues campaign, 1487)

1487

Apr. 16 James, son of Edmund mac Richard Butler, dies; Sir James of Ormond (illegitimate son of 6th earl) app. deputy of earl of Ormond in Ire.

May Earl of Lincoln brings 2,000 German mercenaries to Ire.

[May or June] Parliament at Dublin

May 24 Lambert Simnel crowned kg of England at Christ Church, Dublin

June 16 Battle of Stoke: Simnel defeated and captured by Henry VII

Sept. 1 Toirdhealbhach, son of Seaán an Einigh Ó Raghallaigh, kg of Muintir Maoilmhórdha, dies; succ. by his son Seaán

Uilliam Ó Ceallaigh, kg of Uí Mhaine, imprisoned by his kinsmen and dies; succ. by his brother Maolsheachlainn (d. 1488)

Conn Ó Néill fails to capture Ceann Ard castle from Clann Seaáin Buidhe

Dec. 7 James, 9th earl of Desmond, murdered at Rathkeale by his servants; succ. by his brother Maurice

First recorded use of firearms in Ire., by troops of Aodh Ruadh Ó Domhnaill: Brian, son of Cathal Ó Ruairc, killed by shot from Gofraidh Ó Domhnaill at taking of Castlecar (Glencar, Co. Leitrim)

1488

Earl of Kildare acquires 6 hand-guns from Germany for his personal guard

Jan. 11 Parliament at Drogheda

May 25 General pardon to Anglo-Irish supporters of Lambert Simnel

Sir Richard Edgecombe commissioned by Henry VII to take submission of Irish and Anglo-Irish lords

June 11 Battle of Sauchieburn: James III, kg of Scotland, defeated and killed by rebel barons; succ. by his son James IV

July 21 Earl of Kildare submits to Edgecombe; confirmed as chief governor

Kildare campaigns against Mág Eochagáin in Cenél Fhiachach: destroys Balrath castle (bar. Moycashel, Co. Westmeath) with cannon

Desmond defeats Conchobhar Mór Ó Briain

Donnchadh Dubhshúileach Ó Conchobhair Ruadh (O'Connor Roe) dies; succ. by his nephew Feidhlimidh Fionn, supported by Aodh Ruadh Ó Domhnaill

Oct.-Nov. Conn Ó Néill reaches peaceful settlement with Clann Aodha Buidhe and Ó Domhnaill

Maurice O'Fihely, O.F.M. Conv., regent of studies at Milan (at Padua, 1492)

1489

Anglo-Irish nobility submit to Henry VII at Greenwich

Oct. Aodh Ruadh Ó Domhnaill campaigns in Trian Conghail against Mac Uidhilín; captures Belfast castle

Ó Conchobhair Ruadh at war with Ó Conchobhair Donn, Ó Ceallaigh, and Mac Diarmada

Maurice FitzGerald, earl of Desmond, campaigns in midlands and defeats Ó Cearbhaill

1490

Apr. 12 Feidhlimidh Fionn Ó Conchobhair Ruadh (O'Connor Roe) dies; succ. by Ruaidhrí, son of Feidhlimidh Cléireach Ó Conchobhair, supported by Clann Ruaidhrí Meic Diarmada and opposed by Theobald Burke (Mac William) and Sliocht Taidhg Uí Chonchobhair

June Seaán Ó Catháin captured by Scots raiders from Inverary (Argyll)

July 29 Earl of Kildare summoned to English court

Dillons capture Athlone castle

1491

Jan. 14 Parliament at Dublin

Sweating sickness reaches Ire. from England

autumn Conn Ó Néill and Aodh Ruadh Ó Domhnaill fail to reach settlement after arbitration by earl of Kildare

Nov. Perkin Warbeck (claiming to be Richard, son of Edward IV) lands at Cork

a. **Nov. 25** Seaán, son of Toirdhealbhach Ó Raghallaigh, kg of east Bréifne, dies; earl of Kildare campaigns unsuccessfully to secure succession of Seaán's brother, Cathal; succession of Toirdhealbhach's second cousin Seaán

Dec. 6 Charles VIII, kg of France, marries Anne of Brittany

Dec. 7 Sir James of Ormond and Thomas Garth app. captains of army to be sent to Counties Kilkenny and Tipperary; earl of Kildare's authority as deputy superseded

1492

Jan. 13 Parliament at Trim

May 20 Walter FitzSimons, abp of Dublin, app. deputy; James of Ormond app. treasurer, with power to apply all revenues to defence

An Calbhach, son of Ó Conchobhair Failghe, killed by Thomas Garth; earl of Kildare later captures Garth

Recurrence of plague

Ruaidhrí Ó Conchobhair Ruadh (O'Connor Roe) dies; succ. by Aodh, son of Feidhlimidh Fionn

Oct. 12 Columbus makes landfall in New World

1493

Jan. 8 Conn Ó Neill, kg of Tír Eóghain, killed by his brother Énrí Óg, who succeeds to kingship, with opposition from his elder brother Domhnall, supported by Aodh Ó Domhnaill

Mar. Force of 188 archers sent to Ire. under Sir Roger Cotton

Mar. 30 Earl of Kildare pardoned of suspected treason on condition of sending his son to kg within 6 months (earl of Desmond pardoned, 10 Apr.)

June 28   Parliament at Dublin: act of resumption of royal grants to 1422 (8 Hen. VII, c. 20)

Domhnall Ó Néill defeated by Énrí Óg Ó Néill at Glassdrummond (bar. Dungannon, Co. Tyrone)

July 19   Brawl between supporters of Kildare and Ormond at Oxmantown Green

autumn   Ó Domhnaill with Connacht allies campaigns in Trian Conghail; defeats Ó Néill but fails to force submission of Clann Aodha Buidhe, Mág Aonghusa, and Ó hAnluain

a. **Sept. 12**   Robert Preston, Viscount Gormanston, reapp. deputy

Sept. 12   Council at Trim

Oct. 14   Gormanston summoned to English court; his son, William Preston, app. his deputy

Nov.   Earl of Kildare at English court

Conall, son of David Ó Mórdha, kg of Laoighis, killed by Gerald, brother of earl of Kildare; succ. by Niall, son of Domhnall Ó Mordha

Forfeiture of Eóin Mac Domhnaill, last lord of the Isles (d. 1498), by James IV

Cathaoir Ó Conchobhair Failghe defeated by Mág Eochagáin

1493-4

Officials from Counties Kilkenny, Waterford, Carlow, Cork, Limerick, Connacht, Cork and Limerick cities, liberties of Tipperary, Kerry, and Wexford, crosses of Kerry and Wexford, appear in Dublin to acknowledge financial dependence on government

1494

Pale raided by Aodh Óg Mac Mathghamhna and Seaán Ó Raghallaigh

Mar. 14   Domhnall Ó Conchobhair Sligigh (O'Connor Sligo) killed by sons of his cousin, Ruaidhrí Ó Conchobhair, who succeeds him

May 14   Indenture between Henry VII and earl of Kildare

July-Aug.   Aodh Ruadh Ó Domhnaill besieges Sligo castle

Aug. 26   General pardon to Irish supporters of Perkin Warbeck

Sept. 12   Henry, second son of Henry VII, app. lieutenant, with Edward Poynings as deputy (13 Sept.)

Oct. 13   Earl of Kildare and Sir James of Ormond return to Ire. with Poynings

Oct.-Nov.   Poynings campaigns in Ulster

Dec. 1   Parliament at Drogheda; 'Poynings' law'; act of resumption against absentees (10 Hen. VII, cc. 9, 11)

Dec. 12   Richard Hatton commissioned to treat with earl of Desmond

1495

Feb. 27   Earl of Kildare arrested in Dublin and sent to England (5 Mar.)

Mar.   James, brother of earl of Kildare, captures Carlow castle

Apr. 26   William Hattecliffe app. under-treasurer to reform Irish finances; John Pympe app. treasurer of the wars (27 Apr.)

July   Aodh Ruadh Ó Domhnaill visits James IV, kg of Scotland

July 23   Supporters of Perkin Warbeck besiege Waterford city

Nov.   Warbeck at Scottish court

Dec.   Poynings leaves for England; Henry Deane, bp of Bangor, app. jcr (1 Jan. 1496)

Seaán Mág Uidhir submits to Énrí Óg Ó Néill

1496

Fínghín Ó Mathghamhna of Fonn Iartharach, translator of 'Book of Ser Marco Polo' and (in 1475) 'Book of John Maundeville', dies

Mar. 12   Indenture between Henry VII and earl of Desmond

Gerald, 8th earl of Kildare (Gearóid Mór), marries Elizabeth St John

Aug. 6   Earl of Kildare app. deputy (arrives in Ire., 17 Sept.); indenture between Kildare, Ormond, Sir James of Ormond, and Walter FitzSimons, abp of Dublin

Sept. 16   Aodh Óg Mac Mathghamhna, kg of Oirghialla, deposed by his cousin Brian, son of Réamonn Mac Mathghamhna

Oct. 2   Ulster Irish submit to earl of Kildare at Drogheda

Conchobhar Mór (na Srón) Ó Briain, kg of Thomond, dies; succ. by his brother Toirdhealbhach Óg ('An Giolla Dubh')

Dec. 18 or 19   Sir Roland FitzEustace, first Baron Portlester, dies

1497

William Hattecliffe returns control of Irish finances to Kildare's nominees

c. **Mar. 17**   Éigneachán Mór, son of Neachtan Ó Domhnaill, *tánaiste* of Tír Conaill, killed by Conn Mór, son of Aodh Ruadh Ó Domhnaill

Cave of St Patrick's Purgatory on Lough Derg destroyed by papal authority

c. **May 22**   John Cabot on board *Mathew* takes departure on westerly course from Dursey Head, Co. Cork, 51° 33′ N, on his first voyage of discovery (makes landfall in Newfoundland, 24 June)

May 26   Aodh Ruadh Ó Domhnaill resigns in favour of his son Conn (inaugurated, 29 May)

July 17   Sir James of Ormond killed by Piers Ruadh Butler

July 26   Perkin Warbeck lands at Cork

c. **Aug. 1**   Aodh, son of Aodh Ruadh Ó Domhnaill, captured by his brother Conn

Aug. 14   Carrickfergus Franciscan priory becomes Observant: occupied by friars from Donegal

Sept. 7   Warbeck lands in Cornwall with Irish supporters

Sept. 23   Conn Ó Domhnaill defeated by Tadhg Mac Diarmada at Bealach Buidhe (Curlew mountains, Co. Sligo)

Sept. 30   Seven-year truce made between Scotland and England

Oct. 5   Warbeck captured at Taunton

Oct. 19   Conn Ó Domhnaill, kg of Tír Conaill, defeated and killed by Énrí Óg Ó Néill in Fanad; Aodh Ruadh resumes kingship

Nov. 14   Eleanor, daughter of 7th earl of Kildare, wife of Conn Ó Néill, dies

Famine general in Ire.: English troops withdrawn

Brian Mac Mathghamhna, kg of Oirghialla, killed while supporting Whites against MacGuinnesses; succ. by Rossa of Clann Aodha Ruaidh

1498

Mar. 23   Cathal Mac Maghnusa, dean of Lough Erne, a compiler of 'Annals of Ulster', dies

Apr. 7   Charles VIII, kg of France, dies; succ. by Louis XII

July 21   Énrí Óg Ó Néill, kg of Tír Eóghain, murdered by sons of Conn Ó Néill; succ. by his brother Domhnall Clárach

Earl of Kildare, Ó Domhnaill, and Mág Uidhir capture Dungannon from Feidhlimidh, son of Énrí Óg Ó Néill, and leave it in hands of Domhnall Ó Néill

Eóghan Mac Carthaigh, lord of Múscraighe, and Pilib, son of Diarmaid Ó Súilleabháin Béirre, killed by Thomas, brother of earl of Desmond, and Cormac Óg Láidir, son of Eóghan's brother Cormac; succ. by Cormac, son of Eóghan's brother Diarmaid

Toirdhealbhach Óg Ó Briain ('An Giolla Dubh'), kg of Thomond, dies; succ. by his nephew Toirdhealbhach Donn

1499

Toirdhealbhach Donn Ó Briain defeats Piers Ruadh Butler in Co. Limerick

Aodh Ruadh Ó Domhnaill visits Pale; Henry, son of earl of Kildare, given to him in fosterage

Mar. 1   First parliament under Poynings' law, at Dublin (see 26 Aug.)

Tadhg Mac Diarmada, kg of Magh Luirg, dies; succ. by his brother Cormac

Earl of Kildare campaigns in Connacht; captures castles of Athleague, Roscommon, Tulsk, and Castlerea

Aug. 26   Parliament resumed at Castledermot: earl of Ormond exempted from effects of 1494/5 act against absentees

Nov. 23   Perkin Warbeck executed

Nov. 28   Edward, earl of Warwick, executed

Eóin Mór Mac Domhnaill, lord of Isla, and his two sons executed by James IV

1499–1506

Maurice O'Fihely, O.F.M. Conv., edits works of Duns Scotus (printed at Venice)

c. **1500**

Book of Lismore written for Finghín Mac Carthaigh Riabhach

1500

Earl of Kildare captures castle of Ceann Ard (Caledon, Co. Tyrone) from Clann Seaáin Buidhe and entrusts it to Toirdhealbhach, son of Conn Ó Néill

Galway city severely damaged by fire

Aodh Ruadh Ó Domhnaill raids Tír Eóghain; burns castles of Dungannon, Oldcastle, and Loch Laoghaire (Baronscourt)

Pilib, son of Brian Mág Uidhir, builds castle at Lough Ateriff

Feidhlimidh Ó Ruairc, kg of Bréifne, dies; succ. by Eóghan, son of Tighearnán

Charter of Cork city renewed (see 1189 × 1199)

1501

Mar. 17 Scots defeated at Armagh by Sliocht Aodha Uí Néill

Toirdhealbhach, son of Conn Ó Néill, killed while assisting Clann Réamoinn Meic Mathghamhna against Rossa Mac Mathghamhna

Mac Mathghamhna expels Clann Réamoinn Meic Mathghamhna from Lucht Tighe (Loughty)

Toirdhealbhach Donn Ó Briain raids along River Maigue

1502

Jan. 24 Treaty of perpetual peace between England and Scotland; James IV betrothed to Margaret Tudor (marriage, 8 Aug. 1503)

Aodh Ruadh Ó Domhnaill and Seaán Mág Uidhir attack Aodh, son of Seaán Buidhe Mac Mathghamhna of Dartraighe

Franciscan priory of Cavan becomes Observant

Tadhg, son of Tomaltach Mac Diarmada, *tánaiste* of Magh Luirg, killed by Clann Ruaidhrí; Sliocht Conchobhair finally excluded from succession

1503

Mar. 5 Theobald Burke (Mac William) dies; succ. by his brother Ricard

Mar. 26 Seaán Mág Uidhir, kg of Fir Manach, dies; succ. by his cousin Conchobhar Mór

c. **May 1**–*c.* **Aug. 7** Kildare leaves for England; Walter FitzSimons, abp of Dublin, app. his deputy (Apr.)

Gerald, son of earl of Kildare, marries Elizabeth, daughter of Sir John Zouche; Kildare returns to Ire. (Aug.)

Sept. 26   Kildare campaigns in Ulster; burns Belfast castle

Uilleag Fionn Burke (Clanricard) defeats Ó Ceallaigh and Mac William at Béal Átha na Garbhan (? in Uí Mhaine)

Donnchadh na nOrdóg, son of Aodh Ruadh Ó Domhnaill, mutilated and killed by his father

Compilation of Book of Kildare begins

Clann Mhathghamhna Uí Bhriain intervene in Iar-Chonnacht in support of Eóghan Ó Flaithbheartaigh

Toirdhealbhach Óg Ó Conchobhair Donn (O'Connor Don) dies; succ. by Conchobhar Ó Conchobhair Donn

Tadhg Liath Mac Carthaigh, kg of Desmond, dies; succ. by his son Domhnall

1504

Aug. 19   Battle of Knockdoe, near Galway: earl of Kildare with Ó Domhnaill and English of Pale defeat Clanricard and Ó Briain

1504-5

Plague ravages Ire., especially Ulster

1505

July 11   Aodh Ruadh Ó Domhnaill, kg of Tír Conaill, dies; succ. by his son Aodh Dubh (inaugurated, 2 Aug.)

July   Ó Domhnaill invades Tír Eóghain, burns Dungannon and recovers Castlederg from O'Neills

Domhnall Clarach Ó Néill raids Dartraighe; Aodh, son of Seaán Buidhe Mac Mathghamhna, killed

Finghín Mac Carthaigh Riabhach (MacCarthy Reagh) dies; succ. by his brother Diarmaid (d. 1506; succ. by Domhnall, son of Finghín)

a. 1506

Catherine, daughter of 8th earl of Desmond, wife of Mac Carthaigh Riabhach, builds castles at Benduff (Castle Salem, Co. Cork) and Dunmany (Co. Cork)

1506

June 26   Maurice O'Fihely, O.F.M. Conv., provided to see of Tuam

July 31   Walter, son of Cormac Mac Uidhilín, killed by Tomás, son of Aibhne Ó Catháin

Toirdhealbhach Donn Ó Briain builds bridge across Shannon at Portcrush

Trim severely damaged by lightning

Henry VII plans expedition to Ire. with 6,000 men

1507

Niall Mór Mac Uí Néill Buidhe captures Carrickfergus

Séamus, son of Séamus Barry (Barry Roe) drowned while returning from pilgrimage to Spain

Aodh Dubh Ó Domhnaill visits earl of Kildare

Mar.   Monastery of Clogher damaged by fire

Church of Achadh Beithe (Aghavea, Co. Fermanagh) damaged by fire

Clann Aodha Buidhe and Clann Airt Uí Néill at war with Domhnall Clárach Ó
   Néill (war continues, 1508)

1507/8

St Mary's priory (O.P.), Ballindoon, Co. Sligo, founded by Tomás Ó Fearghail

1508

July 6   Gerald, son of earl of Kildare, app. treasurer

Oct. 6   Parliament at Dublin: subsidy renewed for 10 years

Domhnall Mac Carthaigh, kg of Desmond, dies; succession contested between
   his son Tadhg na Leamhna, and his brother Cormac Ladhrach

O.F.M. Observant friary at Dromahair (Co. Leitrim) founded by Margaret, wife of
   Eóghan Ó Ruairc

1509

Ó Néill's castle of Dungannon captured by sons of Conn Ó Néill; earl of Kildare
   invades Tír Eóghain on their behalf and destroys Omagh

Apr. 21   Henry VII, kg of England, dies; succ. by his son Henry VIII

July 7   Ricard Burke (Mac William) dies; succ. by Edmund, son of Ricard Ó
   Cuairsge Burke

July 28   Earl of Kildare summoned to English court

Aug. 6   Domhnall Clárach Ó Néill, kg of Tír Eóghain, dies; succ. by his cousin
   Art

Irish Dominican Observant congregation formed

Uilleag Fionn Burke (Clanricard) dies; succ. by his brother Ricard Óg

1510

Aodh Dubh Ó Domhnaill makes pilgrimage to Rome

Earl of Kildare campaigns with O'Donnells in Munster; establishes castle at
   Carrigkettle, Co. Limerick; checked by Toirdhealbhach Donn Ó Briain
   and earl of Desmond at bridge of Portcrush (O'Brien's bridge), which
   Kildare breaks down

Nov. 8   Earl of Kildare confirmed as deputy

Seaán, son of Cathal Ó Raghallaigh, kg of Muintir Maoilmhórdha, dies; succ. by
   his brother Aodh

1511

Aodh Dubh Ó Domhnaill knighted by Henry VIII

Cathaoir Ó Conchobhair Failghe (O'Connor Faly) killed by Clann Taidhg and
   Clann Seaáin Bhallaigh (septs of O'Connors); succ. by his cousin Brian

Early sections of church at Armagh severely damaged by fire

Oct. 6 Formation of Holy League, comprising papacy, Venice and Aragon

1512

Apr. 11 Niall Mór Mac Uí Néill Buidhe (O'Neill of Clandeboye), dies; succ. by his son Aodh Buidhe; earl of Kildare campaigns in Trian Conghail; captures Aodh Buidhe and destroys Belfast and Glenarm castles

Aodh Dubh Ó Domhnaill campaigns against Edmund Burke (Mac William) in Gallen and Tireragh; captures Enniscrone and Ballinclare castles

Art Ó Néill concedes jurisdiction over Fir Manach, Cenél Moen, and Inishowen to Ó Domhnaill, who rebuilds and garrisons Omagh castle

Kildare captures Roscommon and Cavetown castles

Fifth Lateran council: Abp Maurice O'Fihely of Tuam and Bp Thomas Halsey of Leighlin attend

1513

Art Ó Néill, kg of Tír Eóghain, dies; succ. by Art Óg, son of Conn Ó Néill

Ó Néill campaigns against Mac Uidhilín and Scots in Antrim

Piers Ruadh Butler, Ó Cearbhaill, and MacMurroughs raid Imokilly and Connelloe

June Octavianus de Palatio, abp of Armagh, dies

June 30–Oct. 22 Henry VIII in France

Sept. 3 Gerald, 8th earl of Kildare (Gearóid Mór) dies at Athy, from gunshot wounds received in campaign against O'Mores; succ. by his son Gerald (Gearóid Óg)

Sept. 9 Battle of Flodden: James IV, kg of Scotland, defeated and killed by earl of Surrey

Oct. 24 John Kyte provided to see of Armagh

Nov. 26 Gerald, 9th earl of Kildare, app. deputy

Aodh Dubh Ó Domhnaill at Scottish court for 3 months

Rise to prominence of Cú Chonnacht Óg Mág Uidhir ('An Comharba')

Ó Néill recovers Dungannon, with assistance of earl of Kildare, from Clann Airt Uí Néill

Rossa Mac Mathghamhna, kg of Oirghialla, dies; succ. by Réamonn, son of Glaisne, son of Réamonn Mac Mathghamhna

1514

Earl of Kildare campaigns against Ó Mórdha of Laoighis; destroys Abbeyleix castle

Feb. 23 Edmund Burke (Mac William) killed by sons of his brother Walter; succ. by Meiler, son of Theobald Burke

July Kildare campaigns against Aodh Ó Raghallaigh; destroys Cavan; kills Ó Raghallaigh; succession of his brother Eóghan Ruadh

Aug. 7   Truce between Henry VIII and Louis XII announced

James, son of earl of Desmond, and Ó Cearbhaill attack Piers Ruadh Butler in Middlethird (Co. Tipperary)

Kildare campaigns against James FitzGerald in Connelloe; checked by Toirdhealbhach Donn Ó Briain

Tadhg na Leamhna Mac Carthaigh, kg of Desmond in opposition to his uncle, Cormac Ladhrach, dies

Aodh Dubh Ó Domhnaill intervenes in dispute between sons of Brian, son of Éamonn Mág Uidhir

1515

Aodh Buidhe Mac Uí Néill Buidhe submits to Art Óg Ó Néill

James FitzGerald attempts to expropriate his uncle John; checked by O'Briens, O'Carrolls, and MacNamaras

Clandeboye jurisdiction over Killultagh (south-west of Co. Antrim) restored

Apr. 13   William Preston, Viscount Gormanston, app. jcr

May-c. Sept.   Earl of Kildare at English court

June 24   Sir William Darcy indicts Kildare's government before king and council at Greenwich

July 8   Commission of inquiry into inheritance of earl of Ormond

July   Duke of Albany app. protector of Scotland

Aug. 3   Thomas, 7th earl of Ormond, dies without male heir

Sept. 10   Thomas Wolsey created cardinal (receives cardinal's hat at Westminster abbey, 18 Nov.)

a. **Sept. 20**   Kildare confirmed as deputy

Oct. 7   Kildare granted privileges in respect of towns of Kildare, Athy, Maynooth, and Ardmullan

Nov. 25   Domhnall, son of Aodh Ruadh Ó Domhnaill, *tánaiste* of Tír Conaill, murdered by his nephew Aodh Buidhe

Anonymous treatise, 'State of Ireland, and plan for its reformation'

1516

Book of Fenagh compiled by Muirgheas, son of Páidín Ó Maoil Chonaire (d. 1543) for Tadhg Ó Rodacháin

Jan. 23   Ferdinand, kg of Spain, dies; succ. by his nephew Charles I (elected emperor as Charles V, 28 June 1519)

Mar. 24   Earl of Kildare confirmed as deputy with power to appoint all officials

Seaán, son of Conn Ó Néill, *tánaiste* of Tír Eóghain, supports Aodh Dubh Ó Domhnaill in raids on Tír Eóghain

Duke of Albany sends guns to Ó Domhnaill

Aodh Dubh Ó Domhnaill captures castles of Sligo, Collooney, Lough Dargan, and Dún na Móna; expels Clann Feidhlimidh meic Toirdhealbhaigh Uí Chonchobhair

Kildare campaigns against Ó Cearbhaill; destroys Leap castle

Piers Ruadh Butler recognised as earl of Ormond; defeated by Edmund, son of Thomas Butler

Ó Domhnaill attends council at Dublin

Cormac Ladhrach Mac Carthaigh, kg of Desmond, dies; succ. by his son Domhnall

1517

Earl of Kildare campaigns with Ormond against Ó Cearbhaill; destroys Garry-castle

Aodh Dubh Ó Domhnaill campaigns in Tír Eóghain in support of Aodh Buidhe Mac Uí Néill Buidhe; burns Dungannon

Kildare campaigns against Feidhlimidh Mág Aonghusa; destroys Dundrum castle (Co. Down)

Seaán Ó Néill, *tánaiste* of Tír Eóghain, dies

Brian Ó Conchobhair Failghe (O'Connor Faly) dies; succ. by his brother An Calbhach

Clann Chormaic Ladhraigh Meic Carthaigh expelled from Loch Leane (Killarney) into territory of Mac Muiris Ciarraighe

Christopher Fleming, baron of Slane, dies

Oct. 31   Ninety-five theses exhibited by Luther at Wittenberg

Nov. 25   Art Buidhe Mac Murchadha, kg of Leinster, dies; succ. by his brother Gearalt

1518

Murchadh Ó Maoilsheachlainn, kg of Midhe, killed by his brother Toirdheal-bhach, who succeeds to kingship

May 17   Cardinal Wolsey app. legate *a latere* in England

Armagh O.F.M. friary becomes Observant

1519

Jan. 12   Earl of Kildare summoned to English court

Art Óg Ó Néill, kg of Tír Eóghain, dies; succ. by his half-brother Conn Bacach

Sir Roland (Raibhilin) Savage, seneschal of Ulster (1482-   ), dies in exile

Feidhlimidh, son of Maghnus Ó Conchobhair Sligigh (O'Connor Sligo, 1495-   ) dies

Aug. 31   Ricard Óg Burke (Clanricard) dies, succ. by his nephew Uilleag Óg, son of Uilleag Fionn

Eóghan, son of Feidlimidh Ó Conchobhair Ruadh (O'Connor Roe) dies; succ. by his cousin Tadhg Buidhe

Friction between Waterford and New Ross

Nov. 5   Wardship of Thomas FitzGerald, son of earl of Kildare ('Silken Thomas'), granted to Edward, duke of Buckingham

Recurrence of plague (continues, 1520)

1520

Mar. 10   Thomas Howard, earl of Surrey, app. L.L. (arrives in Ire. with 500 men, 23 May)

Apr. 24   Uilleag Óg Burke (Clanricard) dies; succ. by his brother Ricard Mór

Apr. 28   Meiler Burke (Mac William) murdered; succ. by Edmund, son of Uilleag Burke

May 4   Earl of Kildare bound to remain in London area

June 11   Kildare with Henry VIII at Field of Cloth of Gold

July   Surrey campaigns in Leinster; Ó Cearbhaill submits

Aug.   Surrey campaigns against Ó Néill: obtains his submission and that of Ó Domhnaill

Sept. 21   Cormac Óg Mac Carthaigh Múscraighe defeats earl of Desmond

Sept. 23   Aodh Dubh Ó Domhnaill marries Margery, daughter of Sir William Darcy

Sept. [?]   Henry VIII directs Surrey to subdue Irish lords 'rather . . . by sober ways . . . and amiable persuasions, founded in law and reason, than by . . . strength or violence'

c. **Oct. 1**   Surrey campaigns in Munster; obtains submissions of Mac Carthaigh Mór and Mac Carthaigh Riabhach

c. **Nov.**   Kildare released on sureties

Maurice, 10th earl of Desmond, dies; succ. by his son James

Plague in Dublin

1521

c. **Apr. 1**   Réamonn Mac Mathghamhna, kg of Oirghialla, dies; succ. by his son Glaisne Óg

June 4   Parliament at Dublin: bill of resumption affecting all customs; bill for endorsement of all Irish statutes since 1480; act forbidding export of wool; act defining burning of corn, ricks, and houses as treason (13 Hen. VIII, cc. 1, 2)

June 30   Surrey submits outline of plan for reconquest to Henry VIII

July 9-23   Ó Conchobhair Failghe, Ó Mórdha, and Ó Cearbhaill attack Pale; Surrey campaigns against them: captures Edenderry; earl of Ormond defeats Ó Cearbhaill

Sept. 16   Surrey requests his own recall

Oct. 2   George Cromer provided to see of Armagh

Tadhg Buidhe Ó Conchobhair Ruadh and Maelsheachlainn Ó Ceallaigh defeated by Sliocht Donnchadha Uí Cheallaigh; Ó Ceallaigh and his son Tadhg killed; Ó Conchobhair Ruadh captured

Dealbhna Meic Cochláin (bar. Garrycastle, Co. Offaly) divided between Feardorcha, son of Toirdealbhach, Cormac, son of Maolsheachlainn Mac Cochláin, and Finghín Ruadh Mac Cochláin

Henry VIII sends livery of knighthood to Conn Bacach Ó Néill

Dec. 21   Surrey leaves for consultations in England

1522

Cú Chonnacht Óg Mág Uidhir ('An Comharba') submits to Conn Bacach Ó Néill

Mar. 6   Piers Ruadh Butler, earl of Ormond, deputy (sworn in, 26 Mar.)

June 11   Ó Néill captures Ballyshannon from Ó Domhnaill's garrison

June 19   Treaty of Windsor between Henry VIII and Emperor Charles V

Aug. 8   Sligo castle besieged by lords of Connacht and Munster, led by Clanricard

c. **Aug. 15**   Aodh Dubh Ó Domhnaill defeats Ó Néill's confederation of Irish kings and lords at Knockavoe (near Strabane, Co. Tyrone); relieves Sligo

Sept.   Four English ships sent to patrol Irish Sea to hinder communication between Scotland, Ire., and France

Dec. 28   Rhodes surrendered to Suleiman I

Earl of Desmond communicates with Francis I, kg of France; convention made (20 June 1523)

1523

Jan. 1   Earl of Kildare returns to Ire.

Gearalt Mac Murchadha, kg of Leinster, dies; succ. by his brother Muiris

Conn Bacach Ó Néill accompanies earl of Kildare on campaign against Ó Conchobhair Failghe, Ó Mórdha, and other Leinster lords and negotiates peace between them

May   Kildare campaigns against Aodh Buidhe Mac Uí Néill Buidhe; captures Belfast castle and Carrickfergus

Oct.   Truce between Ó Néill and Ó Domhnaill

Ó Domhnaill overruns Bréifne

Tadhg, son of Toirdhealbhach Ó Briain, killed at parley with earl of Ormond

Dec.   Robert Talbot of Belgard murdered by James, brother of earl of Kildare, while going to visit earl of Ormond at Kilkenny

Maghnus, son of Aodh Dubh Ó Domhnaill, at Scottish court

1524

Eóghan and Niall, sons of Aodh Dubh Ó Domhnaill, killed in battle against each other

May 13   Earl of Kildare reapp. deputy; Piers Ruadh Butler, earl of Ormond, app. treasurer

June 20   Commissioners (Sir Ralph Egerton, Sir Anthony Fitzherbert, and James Denton, dean of Lichfield) arrive at Howth, to compose differences between Kildare and Ormond

July 28   Indenture between earls of Ormond and Kildare on levying of coyne and livery

Sept.   Kildare and Conn Bacach Ó Néill campaign in Tír Conaill and Trian Conghail; Aodh Buidhe Mac Uí Néill Buidhe (O'Neill of Clandeboye) killed; succ. by his brother Brian Ballach

Oct. 21   Edmund, son of Piers Ruadh Butler, provided to see of Cashel

Ó Conchobhair Ciarraighe captured by Cormac Óg Mac Carthaigh Múscraighe while plundering Duhallow; Domhnall Mac Carthaigh Riabhach captured while plundering Glenflesk

1525

Feb. 24   Battle of Pavia: Emperor Charles V defeats and captures Francis I, kg of France

early   Deputy (earl of Kildare), council, and commrs at Dublin fail to reconcile Conn Bacach Ó Néill and Aodh Dubh Ó Domhnaill

Aug. 18   Maurice Mac Murchadha, kg of Leinster, surrenders Arklow to earl of Ormond

1526

Jan. 14   Treaty of Madrid between Charles V and Francis I

Earl of Ormond in England

spring   Earl of Kildare again fails to reconcile Conn Bacach Ó Néill and Aodh Dubh Ó Domhnaill

Eóghan Ruadh, son of Cathal Ó Raghallaigh, kg of east Bréifne, dies; succ. by his nephew Fearghal, supported by earl of Kildare

Ó Domhnaill campaigns against Brian and Tadhg Ó Conchobhair Sligigh and sons of Cormac Mac Donnchadha; destroys Castlehill, Crossmolina, and Grange

Kildare campaigns in Connacht; captures Castlereagh and Ballintober; delivers them to Ó Conchobhair Ruadh

Ormond campaigns against Clann Éamainn meic Tomáis Butler; captures Sir Éamann Butler

Glaisne Mág Aonghusa, prior of Down and abbot of Newry, murdered by Domhnall Óg Mág Aonghusa

Aug. 29   Battle of Mohacs: Louis II, kg of Hungary, defeated and killed by Suleiman I

Nov. 5   Kildare appoints his brother, Sir Thomas FitzGerald of Leixlip, his deputy and departs for England (a. 31 Dec.)

1527

Peace arbitrated at Dublin between Conn Bacach Ó Néill and Aodh Dubh Ó Domhnaill; Ó Néill retains jurisdiction over Cois Deirge (west Co. Tyrone), Lurg (Co. Fermanagh bar.) and Fir Manach east of Lough Erne

Conchobhar Mór Mag Uidhir, kg of Fir Manach, dies; succ. by Cú Chonnacht Óg ('An Comharba') of Clann Briain Még Uidhir

Ó Domhnaill campaigns in Magh Luirg; captures castles of Castlemor Costello, Banada, Callow, Baile na hUamha (Caultown), and Castlereagh

Earl of Kildare examined before king's council; charges not pressed

Apr. 30   Alliance between France and England

May 5   Rome sacked by army of Charles V

summer   Maghnus Ó Domhnaill builds castle at Lifford

p. **Sept. 14**   Richard Nugent, Lord Delvin, app. deputy to Kildare

Sept. 29   Edmund Burke (MacWilliam) dies; succ. by Seaán an Tearmainn, son of Ricard Burke

Ó Domhnaill's wardens surrender Castlereagh to Clann Ruaidhrí Meic Diarmada and Tadhg Buidhe Ó Conchobhair Ruadh

Dec. 4   Earl of Desmond campaigns in earl of Ormond's territory; besieged by James Butler in Dungarvan; escapes to Youghal

c. **1528**

Migrations of Munster Irish into Pembrokeshire

1528

early   Alliance of Sir John FitzGerald of Dromana, his son Gerald, and Sir Thomas FitzGerald of Desmond with Sir James Butler against earl of Desmond

Feb. 18   Indenture between Henry VIII, Piers Ruadh Butler (8th earl of Ormond) and heirs general of Thomas, 7th earl of Ormond: Butler created earl of Ossory (23 Feb.); Sir Thomas Boleyn, earl of Wiltshire, son-in-law of 7th earl, created earl of Ormond

Mar. 24   Conn Bacach Ó Néill asks Wolsey to allow his subjects free passage throughout the Pale

May 12   Lord Delvin captured by Ó Conchobhair Failghe; Thomas FitzGerald of Leixlip reapp. 'captain' by council (15 May)

Aug. 4   Earl of Ossory app. deputy

Sept. 19   John Alen, abp-elect of Dublin, app. chancellor; John Rawson app. treasurer

Attainder of earl of Desmond (to take effect from 10 Nov. 1522)

Toirdhealbhach Donn Ó Briain, kg of Thomond, dies; succ. by his son Conchobhar, brother-in-law of earl of Desmond

Oct.   Earl of Ossory installed as deputy in presence of Ó Cearbhaill, Ó Mórdha, and other Irish lords

Butlers support Cathaoir Ruadh Ó Conchobhair Failghe's attempt to oust his brother Brian from lordship

Nov. 11   Earl of Desmond's envoy, Galfridius, at Toledo to negotiate defensive alliance with emperor and procure munitions

Thomas Bathe, merchant of Drogheda, prepares memorandum on reform of Ire.

1529

Maghnus Ó Domhnaill captures Castleforward

Brian Ballach Mac Uí Néill Buidhe (O'Neill of Clandeboye) killed by Cormac Mac Uidhilín; succ. by his brother Feidhlimidh Bacach

Feb. 24   Gonzalo Fernandez, chaplain of Charles V, arrives in Ire. to treat with earl of Desmond

June 1   John Alen, abp of Dublin, app. by Wolsey as vice-legate for Ire.

June 18   James, 11th earl of Desmond, dies

June 22   Henry fitz Roy (b. 1519), duke of Richmond and Somerset, app. lieutenant

July   William Skeffington app. king's special commr in Ire. (arrives in Ire., 24 Aug.)

Aug. 4   Earl of Ossory displaced from deputyship by 'secret council' composed of Abp Alen, Patrick Bermingham, and John Rawson

Sept. 3   Edward Staples provided to see of Meath

Oct. 18   Wolsey removed from chancellorship of England

Nov. 3   First session of 'reformation parliament' at Westminster

Nov. 4   Ossory app. justice of peace in Counties Kilkenny and Tipperary, and in Ormond

1530

Apr.   Richard Mór Burke (Clanricard) dies; succ. by John Burke

June 22   William Skeffington app. deputy; Kildare returns to Ire.

Skeffington and Kildare attack Ó Mórdha

July   Tadhg Buidhe Ó Conchobhair Ruadh submits to Ó Domhnaill

Ó Domhnaill burns Mac Consnámha's crannog on Lough Allen and ravages west Bréifne

1531

Muiris Mac Murchadha, kg of Leinster, dies; succ. by Cathaoir ('Mac na hInghine Crosda'), son of Murchadh Ballach Mac Murchadha (1532)

Domhnall Mac Carthaigh Riabhach (MacCarthy Reagh) dies; succ. by his son Cormac

Aodh Buidhe, son of Aodh Dubh Ó Domhnaill, captures Belleek castle

Maghnus Ó Domhnaill defeated by Aodh Dubh Ó Domhnaill and Cú Chonnacht Óg Mág Uidhir at Castlefin

Feb. 11   Henry VIII recognised as 'supreme head of the Church of England' by convocation of Canterbury (by convocation of York, c. May)

Skeffington invades Tír Eóghain; destroys castles at Portnelligan and Caledon; Ó Néill submits

May 6   Indenture of submission by Ó Domhnaill presented to Skeffington at Drogheda

Sept. 15 Parliament at Dublin: subsidy renewed for 10 years; pension granted to Elizabeth, countess of Kildare; Kildare's rights to waste lands in Counties Carlow and Kildare curtailed

Earl of Desmond reconciled to government

c. **Dec.** Skeffington campaigns in Ulster against Feidhlimidh Bacach Mac Uí Néill Buidhe

1532

Maghnus Ó Domhnaill writes 'Beatha Choluim Chille' at Lifford

Jan. 15 Third session of 'reformation parliament' at Westminster: conditional act (23 Hen. VIII, c. 20) restraining payment of annates to papacy (19 Mar.; confirmed and extended by 25 Hen. VIII, c. 20, 9 July 1534)

Earl of Kildare in England

Aodh Dubh Ó Domhnaill and Cú Chonnacht Óg Mág Uidhir meet Skeffington in Drogheda

Skeffington, accompanied by Mág Uidhir, Mac Mathghamhna, Ó Raghallaigh, and Niall Óg Ó Néill, campaigns in Tír Eóghain against Conn Bacach Ó Néill; sacks Dungannon

May 14 Depositions of Sir John Rawson before English privy council upon government of Skeffington

July 5 Gerald, 9th earl of Kildare (Gearóid Óg) app. deputy; James Butler, son of earl of Ossory, app. treasurer; George Cromer, abp of Armagh, app. chancellor

Sept. 21 Maolruanaidh Ó Cearbhaill, lord of Éile, dies; succ. by his son Fearganainm, with opposition from his uncle Uaithne Carrach of Clann tSeaáin Uí Chearbhaill

Thomas Butler, son of earl of Ossory, killed by Diarmaid Mac Giolla Phádraig

Marriage of James Butler, son of earl of Ossory, to Joan, daughter of James, 11th earl of Desmond

1532/3

Kildare wounded by gunshot while assisting Fearganainm Ó Cearbhaill to dislodge Clann tSeaáin Uí Chearbhaill from Birr castle

1533

Tadhg Óg Ó Conchobhair of Sliocht Toirdhealbhaigh Charraigh captures Sligo castle from Ó Domhnaill

Jan. 25 Henry VIII marries Anne, daughter of Sir Thomas Boleyn, earl of Wiltshire and Ormond

Feb. 4 Fifth session of 'reformation parliament' at Westminster: act (24 Hen. VIII, c. 12) restraining appeals to Rome

Feb. 21 Thomas Cranmer provided by pope (Clement VII) to see of Canterbury

May 19 Parliament at Dublin: subsidy granted for 3 years

June-July Mission of Eric Godscalco to treat with earl of Desmond on behalf of Charles V

July   John Alen sent by Irish council to English court with report on Kildare's government; app. master of the rolls (5 July)

July 11   Clement VII excommunicates Henry VIII

c. **Sept.**   Earl of Kildare summoned to English court

Éamann Óg Ó Broin attacks Dublin; enters Dublin castle and releases prisoners

Feidhlimidh Bacach Mac Uí Neill Buidhe (O'Neill of Clandeboye) dies; succ. by his brother Niall Óg

1534

Jan.-Mar.   Sixth session of 'reformation parliament' at Westminster: breach with Rome completed; act (25 Hen. VIII, c. 22) fixing succession on children of Henry VIII and Anne Boleyn

Feb.   Kildare leaves for England; his son Thomas, Lord Offaly, app. his deputy

EARLY MODERN IRELAND, 1534-1691

INTRODUCTION

THE evidence for precise dating of events increases substantially from the beginning of the sixteenth century with the growth of new types of material, especially the letters and papers and other records of the expanding English administration of Ireland. An immense amount of the archival deposit of this administration, notably the great series organised as 'State papers relating to Ireland' and its successors, is preserved in the English Public Record Office, and this goes far to make up for the destruction in 1922 of the main body of the archives accumulated and preserved in Dublin. The material in the English Public Record Office, much of it available in printed calendars,[1] is supplemented by private collections of dynastic families in Ireland, such as those of Ormond, Inchiquin, and Cork, and of English statesmen such as Salisbury and Strafford. Older types of material such as the Annals continue, and both in Irish and English tend to be fuller and more informative, but after 1603 they are of little importance for chronology. Contemporary histories and descriptions become increasingly plentiful and valuable from the late sixteenth century; in the seventeenth century the first newspapers begin to be published. Moreover Ireland's increasing connections with the Continent have left their traces in the large mass of records and other primary material scattered among the archives and libraries in many countries of western Europe.

A staple element in the chronology of this period down to 1603 continues to be internecine conflict and wars between English and Irish; and to this has to be added religious conflict. At the same time there is increasing evidence of peaceful development and constructive achievement. In the seventeenth century this aspect of Irish life is exemplified with increasing fullness and precision in our chronology, despite the two short periods of extreme violence and the great land-confiscations that have given this century so sombre a character in Irish history. A new type of entry reflects the peaceful revolution in European life caused by the invention of the printing press: for the first time the titles of printed books and pamphlets appear, both those printed in Ireland and works of the Irish diaspora on the Continent.

During this period the reform of the calendar introduced by Pope Gregory XIII in 1582 affects the dating of continental events in the

---

[1] *Calendar of state papers relating to Ireland, 1509-73—1669-70* (24 vols, 1860-1911); from 1671 the series is merged in *Calendar of state papers, domestic series, 1671—1703-4* (31 vols, 1895-1925).

chronology from then onwards, as explained in our general introduction (above, pp 2-3), though the New Style dating was not adopted in Ireland till 1752.

We have received helpful cooperation in this section of the chronology from Professor Patrick J. Corish, Mr K. W. Nicholls, and Dr T. C. Barnard, which we acknowledge with thanks.

CHRONOLOGY, 1534-1691

(A) 1534-1603

DARACH MAC FHIONNBHAIRR AND J. G. SIMMS

1534

June 11   Offaly ('Silken Thomas') repudiates allegiance to Henry VIII

June 29   Kildare imprisoned in Tower of London

July 28   Abp Alen murdered by supporters of Silken Thomas (he and his supporters declared excommunicate by Dublin clergy)

July 30   Sir William Skeffington app. L.D.

Aug. 26   Sir William Brabazon app. vice-treasurer

Sept. 2   Kildare dies in Tower of London (Silken Thomas succeeds as 10th earl)

Sept.   Silken Thomas besieges Dublin (siege abandoned, 4 Oct.)

Oct. 24   Skeffington arrives in Dublin with troops

Nov. 18   English act of supremacy (26 Hen. VIII, c. 1)

Dec. 19   Truce begins between Silken Thomas and Skeffington (ends, 6 Jan. 1535)

c. **Dec.**   Conn Bacach O'Neill raids Louth

Ordinance against Irish minstrels, rhymers, bards, etc.

Coinage for Ire. struck in London ('coin of the harp')

1535

Jan.-Feb.   Earl of Ossory intervenes in internal disputes of Desmond Fitz-Geralds and O'Briens to prevent support for Silken Thomas

Mar. 23   Skeffington takes Maynooth castle

May   Silken Thomas's envoy appeals to pope for absolution for murder of Abp Alen (see 28 July 1534)

June 9   Royal commn for suppression of house of Augustinian canonesses at Graney, Co. Kildare

June 14   Silken Thomas's envoy arrives in Spain with appeal to emperor

July 26   Agreement between Skeffington and Conn O'Neill at Drogheda: O'Neill promises allegiance in return for support from L.D. and annual stipend

July 28 Lord Leonard Grey arrives in Dublin as marshal of the army

c. **July 30** John Travers, chancellor of St Patrick's cathedral, Dublin, executed for treason

Aug. 24 Skeffington informs Henry that Silken Thomas has surrendered to him (taken to England by Grey)

Sept. 20 Dungarvan castle surrenders to Skeffington

Oct. Grey returns to Ire.

Dec. 31 Skeffington dies

1536

Jan. 1 Grey app. L.J. by Irish council

Jan. 11 George Browne nominated abp of Dublin (consecrated 19 Mar. at Lambeth)

Feb. 14 Council inform kg that they are sending 5 brothers of 9th earl of Kildare to England

Feb. 23 Grey app. L.D.

May 1–31 First session of 'reformation parliament', held in Dublin: act (28 Hen. VIII, c. 1) for attainder of 9th earl of Kildare, Silken Thomas, and others; act (28 Hen. VIII, c. 3) resuming to crown the lands of absentee owners; act (28 Hen. VIII, c. 4) suspending Poynings' law; act (28 Hen. VIII, c. 5) recognising Henry as 'supreme head in earth of the whole church of Ireland'; act (28 Hen. VIII, c. 6) forbidding appeals to Rome

May 19 Anne Boleyn executed

June Mutiny in army in protest against failure to pay arrears

July 11 'Ten articles' (statement of doctrine approved by Henry) presented to convocation of English clergy

July 18 Act (28 Hen. VIII, c. 18 [Eng.]) for attainder of Silken Thomas and his 5 uncles

July 25–6 Parliament at Kilkenny (reassembles at Cashel, 28 July; at Limerick, 2–19 Aug.)

Aug. 6 O'Brien's bridge on Shannon demolished by Grey

Sept. 15 Parliament reassembles in Dublin (session ends 28 Sept.)

Oct. 'Pilgrimage of grace'; rising in northern England in protest against Henry's religious and fiscal policies

Dec. 17 Earl of Desmond promises submission to Grey

Richard Nangle app. bp of Clonfert by kg (expelled *a.* 19 July 1538 by papal nominee, Roland Burke, who is recognised by kg, 24 Oct. 1541)

1537

Jan. 20–Feb. 5/6 Parliament in session in Dublin: commons refuse to pass taxation bills and bill for suppression of certain monasteries

Feb. 3 Silken Thomas and his 5 uncles executed at Tyburn, London (his half-brother, Gerald, is only male survivor of house of Kildare)

Feb. 15   Christopher Bodkin, bp of Kilmacduagh, app. abp of Tuam by kg

May 29   Grey sets out on expedition against Brian O'Connor of Offaly (takes Dangan, 5 June)

July 5   Hugh O'Donnell, lord of Tyrconnell, dies (succ. by son Manus)

July 31   Commn under Anthony St Leger (knighted *c*. Jan. 1539) app. to inquire into state of Ire. (arrival, 8 Sept.)

Henry censures Abp Browne for neglect of duty

Sept. 27   Browne defends himself to kg, claiming to have spoken against 'sacramentaries'

Oct. 13–Dec. 20   Parliament in session: act (28 Hen. VIII, c. 12) for suppression of clerical proctors; act (28 Hen. VIII, c. 13) 'against the authority of the bishop of Rome'; act (28 Hen. VIII, c. 15) for 'English order, habit, and language' (section 9 providing for parish schools to teach English); act (28 Hen. VIII, c. 16) for suppression of 13 monasteries

1538

Feb. 22   Piers Butler, earl of Ossory, restored to earldom of Ormond

Mar. 6   Brian O'Connor of Offaly submits to Grey: gives undertakings that contain germ of 'surrender and regrant' policy (see 27 Jan. 1541)

Apr. *c*. 3   St Leger's commn (see 31 July 1537) returns to England

May 5   Dublin clergy refuse to read 'form of the beads' drawn up by Abp Browne

June 17–July 25   Grey campaigns in Offaly, Ely O'Carroll, Munster, and Connacht

c. **June**   Manus O'Donnell married to Lady Eleanor (Fitzgerald), widow of MacCarthy Reagh, and sister of 9th earl of Kildare; Manus undertakes to protect Gerald Fitzgerald, Eleanor's nephew

June 28   Agreement between Grey and Ulick Burke of Clanricard

July 1   James V, kg of Scotland, writes to Pope Paul III about provision to see of Raphoe

July 11   Grey received by mayor and citizens of Galway

Sept.   Grey campaigns against Kavanaghs in Carlow

Oct. 7   Papal provision of Arthur O'Friel to see of Tuam

Oct. 18   Sir John Alen app. L.C.

1539

Feb. 3   Grant to mayor and citizens of Dublin of priory of All Hallows near Dublin, in consideration of their services during Silken Thomas's rebellion (see 3 Mar. 1592)

Apr. 7   Henry appoints Alen L.C., Abp Browne, and others to be commrs to accept surrenders of monasteries and to punish heads of houses who refuse to surrender

May *c.* **1**   Grey advances to Armagh in attempt to induce O'Neill and O'Donnell to surrender Gerald Fitzgerald

May 21   L.D. and council plead, unsuccessfully, for retention of St Mary's abbey, Dublin, and 5 other religious houses

June 23   Agreement between Manus O'Donnell and Tadhg O'Connor concerning Sligo castle

June 28   English act for 'abolishing of diversity of opinions' (31 Hen. VIII, c. 14), giving statutory authorisation to conservative 'six articles'

July 23   Robert Wauchop app. administrator of Armagh by pope (Cromer suspended for contumacy)

Aug. 26   Piers Butler, earl of Ormond and Ossory, dies

Aug.   O'Neill and O'Donnell, returning from raids on Pale, routed by Grey at Bellahoe, or Ballyhoe, on border of Meath and Monaghan

Nov.-Dec.   Grey campaigns in Munster

1540

Jan. 24   Grey advances to Dungannon in campaign against O'Neill

Mar. 21   Gerald Fitzgerald arrives at Saint-Malo from Ire.

May *c.* **1**   Grey leaves for England (Sir William Brereton app. L.J. by council, 1 Apr.)

May 20   Chancellor Alen, Vice-treasurer Brabazon, and Robert Cowley app. to survey rents and revenues of dissolved religious houses

July 28   Thomas Cromwell executed on Tower Hill, London

Aug. *c.* **12**   St Leger sworn in as L.D.

Aug. 16-26   St Leger on campaign against Kavanaghs (submission of Cahir Mac Art MacMurrough)

Sept. 27   Paul III approves establishment of Jesuit order, founded by Ignatius of Loyola

Nov.   St Leger permits Turlough O'Toole to go to England to petition kg for terms of surrender

1541

Jan. 16   Earl of Desmond submits to St Leger at Cahir

Jan. 27   Henry VIII approves 'surrender and regrant' terms for O'Toole

Mar. 12   Ulick Mac William Burke petitions kg for settlement

Mar. 26   Mac Gillapatrick made a lord of parliament (patent as baron of Upper Ossory, 11 June)

June 13-July 20/23   Session of parliament in Dublin

June 18   Act (33 Hen. VIII, c. 1) declaring kg of England to be kg of Ire. (bill presented in Irish as well as English)

June 28   Lord Leonard Grey executed at Tower Hill, London

July 2   Arbitration by L.D. and council in parliament, dividing Ely O'Carroll between Tadhg and Calvagh O'Carroll

Aug. 6   Manus O'Donnell submits to St Leger at Cavan

Sept. 23   Henry issues instructions to L.D. on policy of 'surrender and regrant'

Sept.-Dec.   St Leger campaigns against Conn O'Neill

Dec. 28   O'Neill submits to St Leger at Dundalk

Ruaidhrí Ó Casaide, continuator of Annals of Ulster, dies

1542

Feb. 15-Mar. 7/10   Session of parliament at Limerick: act (33 Hen. VIII, sess. 2, c. 5) for suppression of Kilmainham and other houses, confirming crown's title to houses submitting voluntarily

Act for the kg's style re-enacted for benefit of Munster and Connacht; Murrough O'Brien submits to St Leger (see 1 July 1543)

Feb.-Mar.   First mission of Jesuits to Ire.

Apr. 22   Manus O'Donnell asks kg for earldom of Sligo (request refused)

May 13   Rory O'More of Leix submits to L.D.

June 12-21   Session of parliament at Trim: act (34 Hen. VIII, c. 1) for division of Meath

July   War breaks out between England and Scotland

July 4   Tadhg O'Byrne submits to L.D. (agrees to renounce Irish manners and petitions for his country to be shired as County Wicklow)

Sept. 2   Order for printing Irish statutes

Oct. 1   Conn O'Neill created earl of Tyrone at Greenwich (with succession to illegitimate son, Matthew, created baron of Dungannon)

Nov. 6-18   Session of parliament in Dublin

Nov. 24   Scots army defeated by English at Solway Moss

Dec. 14   James V, kg of Scotland, dies; succ. by Mary, queen of Scots

1543

Apr. 17-May 2   Session of parliament

Apr. 19   George Dowdall nominated abp of Armagh by kg in place of Cromer, deceased (provided by pope, 1 Mar. 1553)

June 22   Henry issues ultimatum to France (leading to war)

July 1   Treaties of Greenwich between England and Scotland: provision for betrothal of Queen Mary to Edward prince of Wales

Ulick Mac William Burke created earl of Clanricard: Murrough O'Brien created earl of Thomond (nephew and tanist, Donough, created baron of Ibracken with right of succession to earldom)

July 14   Agreement between O'Neill and O'Donnell drawn up in Dublin before L.D. and council

Nov. 6-19   Session of parliament

Dec. 11   Scots parliament repudiates treaties of Greenwich (see 1 July) and renews alliance with France

Muirgheas Ó Maoil Chonaire, Irish scribe and historian, dies

1544

Feb. *c*. 10   St Leger leaves for England (Brabazon sworn in as L.J.)

May 4   Earl of Hertford and English army invade Scotland

May 18   St Leger installed as knight of the garter

July 19–Sept. 14   Siege of Boulogne: Irish contingent with Lord Power serves in English army

Aug. 11   St Leger returns to Ire.

Annals of Connacht end

1545

Feb. 27   Scots defeat English force at Ancrum, near Jedburgh (Irish contingent in English army reported to have been all killed)

Mar. *a*. 23   Robert Wauchop (see 23 July 1539) granted pallium of Armagh by pope

Sept. 5   Earl of Ormond app. to command troops for service against Scots

Sept.   English mint issues debased coinage for use in Ire.

Dec. 13   General council of catholic church opens at Trent in Austrian Tyrol (continues till 4 Dec. 1563)

Discovery of silver at Potosí, Peru (later Bolivia)

1546

***c*. Apr. 1**   St Leger and Ormond leave for England, summoned to court as result of dispute between them (Brabazon sworn in as L.J., 1 Apr.)

June 7   Peace concluded between England and France

July   Brabazon campaigns in Offaly and fortifies Dangan (Fort Governor)

Aug. *c*. 27   Alen, L.C., found responsible for bad blood between St Leger and Ormond, deprived of office

Dec. 16   St Leger returns to Ire.

1547

Jan. 28   Henry VIII dies; succ. by Edward VI (earl of Hertford app. protector, 31 Jan.; created duke of Somerset, 16 Feb.)

Apr. 23   Nicholas Bagenal app. marshal of the army

May 31   L.D. informed by English council that Sir Edward Bellingham is being sent with reinforcements to restore order in Ire., and that his advice on military matters should be followed

summer   O'Mores and O'Connors ravage Kildare, but are driven back by Bellingham

Sept. 10 Scots army defeated by English at Pinkie, near Edinburgh

Dec. English act (1 Edw. VI, c. 12) repealing act of 6 articles (see 28 June 1539) and other parts of Henry VIII's religious legislation

c. **Dec.** Brabazon compiles list of complaints against St Leger

Athlone castle reconstructed by Brabazon

1548

Feb. 10 Exchequer order for coining groats issued to under-treasurer of mint in Dublin castle

Mar. 8 Order of communion issued

Apr. 22 Alen reapp. as L.C. (see *c.* 27 Aug. 1546)

May 21 Bellingham sworn in as L.D. (St Leger recalled)

May-June Erection of Fort Protector in Leix

p. **Aug. 19** Cahir, brother of O'Connor of Offaly, captured and executed

c. **Nov.-Dec.** O'Connor and O'More submit, and are sent to England

1549

c. **Jan.** Garrison established at Leighlinbridge, Co. Carlow

Feb. 7 Ordinance, made by kg's commrs at Limerick, prohibiting 'poems or anything which is called *auran* to any person except the king'

Mar. 14 First English act of uniformity (2 & 3 Edw. VI, c. 1), prescribing use of Book of Common Prayer

June 9 First Book of Common Prayer ordered to be used in Ire.

July-Aug. Kett's rebellion in Norfolk (suppressed by earl of Warwick, 26 Aug.)

Aug. 8 Outbreak of war between England and France

Oct. 10 Somerset deprived of his office as protector (imprisoned in Tower of London, 14 Oct.)

Dec. 16 Departure of Bellingham (Sir Francis Bryan elected L.J. by council, 27 Dec.)

1550

Feb. Earl of Warwick (duke of Northumberland, 11 Oct. 1551) becomes president of council of England

Feb. 2 Bryan, L.J., dies; succ. by Sir William Brabazon

Feb. French envoys visit and conclude treaties with O'Neill, O'Donnell, and O'Doherty

Mar. 29 Treaty of Boulogne between England and France

June 27 English council decides to establish mint in Ire.

July 17 Grant to Humphrey Powell to start printing in Ire.

July Instructions to L.D. for resumption, surveying, and leasing of Leix and Offaly

Aug. 5 Sir Thomas Cusack app. L.C. *vice* Alen removed (resigns, 3 July 1555)

Sept. 10   St Leger sworn in after reappointment as L.D.

St Leger issues proclamation against catholic ceremonies

Secret visit of Abp Wauchop to Ire.

1551

Feb. *c.* **24**   Sir James Croft sent to survey and fortify southern ports

May 23   Croft sworn in as L.D. (St Leger recalled)

June–July   Croft campaigns in Munster; submission of MacCarthy Mór

Sept.   Croft campaigns against MacDonnells in Ulster; attacks Rathlin Island; captures O'Neill on return journey

Oct.   Encounter between Matthew, baron of Dungannon (see 1 Oct. 1542) and Shane O'Neill, legitimate son of earl of Tyrone

Nov. 10   Abp Wauchop dies in Paris

The boke of the common praier after the use of the Churche of England (Dublin; first book printed in Ire.; see 1453 × 1455)

1552

Apr. 14   Second act of uniformity (5 & 6 Edw. VI, c. 1 [Eng.]), prescribing revised Book of Common Prayer

June 7   Kg orders currency in Ire. to be reduced to parity with that of England

c. **July**   Croft campaigns in Clandeboye; Belfast castle taken

Oct. 22   John Bale nominated bp of Ossory (consecrated, 2 Feb. 1553)

Oct. 28   Hugh Goodacre nominated abp of Armagh by kg (consecrated, 2 Feb. 1553; Dowdall deemed to have vacated see)

Dec. 4   Croft leaves Ire. (Sir Thomas Cusack and Sir Gerald Aylmer L.J.s.)

1553

Mar. 1   Papal provision of Dowdall to see of Armagh (in succession to Wauchop, d. 10 Nov. 1551)

July 6   Edward VI dies; succ. by Mary I

July 10   Proclamation, claiming throne, by Lady Jane Grey

July 19   Proclamation by Mary of her accession to throne

Aug. 22   Duke of Northumberland executed

Aug.   Catholic demonstrations in Kilkenny (Bp Bale leaves diocese)

Nov. 19   St Leger sworn in on reappointment as L.D. *vice* Croft resigned

1554

Apr. 14   Commn to Primate Dowdall and others to deprive married clergy

May 13   Earldom of Kildare restored in favour of Gerald Fitzgerald, 11th earl

June 29   Edward Staples, bp of Meath, deprived on ground of being married

July 25 Mary I marries Philip son of Emperor Charles V (succeeds as Philip II of Spain, 16 Jan. 1556) in Winchester cathedral

Earl of Kildare and baron of Delvin campaign against Phelim Roe O'Neill of Clandeboye

1555

Feb. 18 Hugh Curwin nominated by queen as abp of Dublin (Browne deprived, 1554)

June 7 Bull of Pope Paul IV making Ire. a kingdom

June 21 Papal provision of Curwin to see of Dublin (consecrated 8 Sept. in St Paul's, London)

Sept. 25 Peace of Augsburg: Lutheranism recognised in Empire

Manus O'Donnell, lord of Tyrconnell, captured by his son Calvagh

Hugh O'Neill, lord of Clandeboye, killed in skirmish with Scots

1556

Mar. 21 Abp Cranmer burned at stake at Oxford

Apr. 13 Sir Henry Sidney app. vice-treasurer

Apr. 28 Instructions to L.D. for plantation of Leix and Offaly

May 26 Thomas Radcliffe, Lord Fitzwalter (succeeds as earl of Sussex 17 Feb. 1557) sworn in as L.D. *vice* St Leger recalled

July Fitzwalter campaigns against Scots in Ulster

1557

June 1–July 2 Parliament in session in Dublin: act (3 & 4 P. & M., c. 1) for disposition of Leix and Offaly; act (3 & 4 P. & M., c. 2) for establishment of Queen's and King's Counties (Forts Protector and Governor renamed Maryborough and Philipstown); act (3 & 4 P. & M., c. 4) for the explanation of Poynings' law, amending it so as to permit additional bills to be transmitted after a parliament had been called, and making explicit kg's right to amend legislative proposals; act (3 & 4 P. & M., c. 8) repealing statutes made against see of Rome; act (3 & 4 P. & M., c. 14) declaring regal power over Ire. to vest in queen

June 7 England declares war on France

July 10–19 Sussex campaigns against O'Connors of Offaly

Oct. 24–8 Sussex campaigns against Shane O'Neill; burns Armagh (27 Oct.)

Dec. 4 Sussex leaves for England (Abp Curwin and Sir Henry Sidney sworn in as L.J.s, 5 Dec.)

Shane O'Neill defeated by O'Donnell at Balleeghan on Lough Swilly, Co. Donegal

1558

Jan. 7   Calais surrenders to French

Mar. 8   Restoration of priory of St John of Jerusalem, Kilmainham (again dissolved, 3 June 1559)

Apr. 24   Mary, queen of Scots, married to dauphin (succeeds as Francis II of France, 10 July 1559; d. 5 Dec. 1560)

Apr. 27   Sussex returns to Ire.

May 18   Attack on Maryborough by O'Mores and O'Connors repelled

June 14   Sussex sets out for campaign in Thomond (returns to Dublin, *c.* 25 July)

Sept. 15   Sussex sails for Scotland on expedition to Kintyre and islands of Arran and Cumbraes; on way back campaigns against Scots in Antrim (returns to Dublin, 8 Nov.)

Nov. 17   Mary I dies; succ. by Elizabeth I

Dec. 13   Sussex leaves for England (Sidney app. L.J. by council, 12 Dec., in vacancy caused by death of Mary)

Matthew, baron of Dungannon, killed by order of Shane O'Neill

1559

Apr. 2   Peace of Cateau Cambrésis between Spain and France

May 8   English acts of supremacy and uniformity (1 Eliz., cc 1, 2)

May 14   Calvagh O'Donnell taken prisoner by Shane O'Neill

July 3   Sussex reapp. L.D. (sworn in, 30 Aug.)

a. **July 17**   Conn Bacach O'Neill, first earl of Tyrone, dies (succ. in O'Neill lordship by Shane O'Neill)

1560

Jan. 11/12–Feb. 1   Parliament in session in Dublin: act of supremacy (2 Eliz., c. 1) repealing 3 & 4 P. & M., c. 8, restoring supremacy of crown in matters ecclesiastical, and imposing oath to be taken by ecclesiastics, officials, and persons suing for livery or taking university degrees; act of uniformity (2 Eliz., c. 2) prescribing use of second prayer book of Edward VI, with some modifications, and ordering attendance at parish churches on pain of fine of 12*d.*

Feb. *c.* **13**   Sussex leaves for England (Sir William Fitzwilliam sworn in as L.J., 15 Feb.)

May 6   Sussex app. L. L. (sworn in, 25 June).

July 6   Treaty of Edinburgh between England and France; withdrawal of French troops from Scotland

Aug. 2   David Wolfe, S.J., app. papal nuncio to Ire. (lands at Cork, *c.* 20 Jan. 1561)

1561

Jan. 30   Sussex leaves for England (Fitzwilliam sworn in as L.J., 2 Feb.)

June 5   Sussex on return sworn in as L.L.

June 8   Proclamation by L.L. and council declaring Shane O'Neill a traitor

June-July   Sussex campaigns against Shane O'Neill

c. **July**   English garrison placed in Armagh cathedral

Sept.   Sussex makes unsuccessful expedition to Lough Foyle

1562

Jan. 6   Shane O'Neill submits to Elizabeth at Whitehall

Jan. 16   Sussex leaves for England (Fitzwilliam sworn in as L.J., 22 Jan.)

a. **Mar. 21**   Palesmen's complaints about administration in Ire. presented to English privy council by Irish students

Apr. 12   Brian O'Neill, second baron of Dungannon, killed by Turlough Luineach O'Neill, tanist to Shane O'Neill (Brian's brother, Hugh, taken by Sidney to England)

Apr.-July   Earls of Ormond and Desmond at English court for settlement of their differences

May 26   Shane O'Neill lands at Dublin on return from England

July 3   Order for establishment of court of castle chamber in Ire.

July 24   Sussex returns to Ire. (sworn in, 29 July)

Sept.   Con, son of Calvagh O'Donnell, makes agreement with Shane O'Neill

Oct. 30   Adam Loftus nominated as abp of Armagh (consecrated, 2 Mar. 1563)

Nov.   Shane O'Neill lays waste Maguire's country

1563

Feb. 9   Manus O'Donnell dies (see 1555)

Apr.   Sussex campaigns against Shane O'Neill

May 18   Commn for administration of oath of supremacy to all ecclesiastics and state servants

Sept. 11   Shane O'Neill submits to Sussex

Oct. 21   Hugh Brady nominated as bp of Meath (consecrated, 19 Dec.)

Dec. 4   Council of Trent ends (see 13 Dec. 1545)

1564

Feb.   Rising of O'Connors and O'Mores in Offaly and Leix

Mar. 22   Papal provision of Richard Creagh to see of Armagh (consecrated in Rome, Apr.)

May 25   Sussex finally leaves Ire. (Sir Nicholas Arnold, L.J.)

July 12   Agreement between Shane O'Neill and Con O'Donnell, latter ceding Castlefinn

Aug. 6   Philip II directs his ambassador in London to break off negotiations with Irish catholics

Sept.   Shane O'Neill campaigns against MacDonnells of Antrim; builds castle at Coleraine

Oct. 6   Order for establishment of court of high commission to enforce religious conformity

1565

c. Feb. 8   Desmond defeated and taken prisoner by Ormond at Affane, Co. Waterford (both earls summoned to England)

Feb. 22   Abp Creagh 'committed to the close prison' of the Tower of London (escapes to Continent, c. 29 Apr.)

May 2   Shane O'Neill defeats MacDonnells at Glenshesk, near Ballycastle, Co. Antrim (Sorley Boy MacDonnell taken prisoner)

June 24   MacCarthy Mór created earl of Clancare

July 13   William Walsh, Marian bp of Meath, imprisoned

July 29   Mary, queen of Scots, married to Lord Darnley

Oct. 12   Papal provision of Miler Magrath to see of Down and Connor

Oct. 13   Sir Henry Sidney app. L.D. (Sussex resigns; Sidney sworn in, 20 Jan. 1566)

1566

Apr. 25   Shane O'Neill asks Charles IX, kg of France, for aid and offers allegiance

c. June   Negotiations between earl of Argyll and Shane O'Neill; release of Sorley Boy MacDonnell

Aug. 2 or 3   Shane O'Neill proclaimed traitor, and reward offered for his capture or death

Aug.   Abp Creagh in Armagh

Shane O'Neill burns Armagh cathedral

Sept. 6   Expeditionary force under Col. Edward Randolph sails from Bristol for Lough Foyle

Sept. 17–Nov. 12   Sidney's campaign in Armagh, Tyrone, and Tyrconnell (reaches Derry, 12 Oct.)

Oct. 26   Calvagh O'Donnell dies; succ. by his brother, Hugh

Nov.   Shane O'Neill attacks Randolph's position at Derry; Randolph killed

1567

Feb. 10   Darnley (see 29 July 1565) murdered in Kirk o' Field, Edinburgh

Mar.   Desmond captured by Sidney at Kilmallock, Co. Limerick

Apr. 21   Powder explosion in ruined cathedral of Derry; English camp destroyed; survivors withdraw to Carrickfergus

Apr. 30   Abp Creagh captured by O'Shaughnessy

Apr.   *Foirm na nvrrnvidheadh . . . ar na dtarraing as Laidin agus as Gaillbherla in Gaoidheilg* (Edinburgh), Gaelic translation of Book of Common Order, by John Carswell, bp of the Isles; first printed book in Gaelic (cf. 1551)

May 8   Shane O'Neill defeated by O'Donnell at Farsetmore, near Letterkenny

May 15   Mary, queen of Scots, married to earl of Bothwell

June 2   Shane O'Neill killed by MacDonnells at Cushendun, Co. Antrim

June 4   Papal provision of Maurice MacGibbon to see of Cashel

June   Turlough Luineach inaugurated as O'Neill

July 24   Mary, queen of Scots, abdicates; accession of James VI (b. 19 June 1566)

Aug. 9   Adam Loftus translated by queen from archbishopric of Armagh to that of Dublin

Oct. 9   Sidney leaves for England (Robert Weston, L.C., and Sir William Fitzwilliam sworn in as L.J.s., 14 Oct.)

Dec.   Earl of Desmond sent as prisoner to London

Robert Lythe, cartographer, at work in Ire.

David Wolfe imprisoned

Bps urged to complete printing of New Testament in Irish, failing which they are required to repay money given by queen for type

1568

Mar. 1   Order for recognition of Hugh O'Neill as baron of Dungannon

Mar. 12   Thomas Lancaster nominated abp of Armagh (consecrated, 13 June)

May 16   Mary Stuart flees to England

July 1   James Fitzmaurice, claiming to be 'captain' of Desmond Fitzgeralds in earl of Desmond's absence, makes unsuccessful attack on Thomas Fitzmaurice, baron of Kerry and Lixnaw

Oct. 28   Sidney returns and is again sworn in as L.D.

Dec. 7   Barony of Idrone, Co. Carlow, adjudged to Sir Peter Carew, claiming as descendant of Robert FitzStephen, Norman grantee (decree confirmed by L.D., 22 Dec.) (see June 1569, 10 June 1573)

Dec.   Elizabeth seizes Spanish treasure, leading to strained relations between England and Spain (continuing till 1574)

1569

Jan. 17   Parliament meets in Dublin

Feb. 21   Act (11 Eliz., sess. 2, c. 1) for suspension of Poynings' law

c. **Feb.**   James Fitzmaurice, earl of Clancare, and others resolve to send envoys to kg of Spain

Mar. 11   Act (11 Eliz., sess. 3, c. 1) for attainder of Shane O'Neill: O'Neill lordship declared abolished

Mar. 20   Licence granted to John Hooker to print Irish statutes

c. **Apr.**   Abp MacGibbon (see 4 June 1567) presents appeal from Irish catholics to Philip II, offering allegiance

June 1   Sir Edward Fitton app. president of Connacht

June 16   James Fitzmaurice devastates lands leased by Sir Warham St Leger in barony of Kerrycurrihy, Co. Cork

June 20   Mayors of Cork and Youghal appeal to L.D. for help against James Fitzmaurice

June   Sir Edmund Butler, brother of Ormond, devastates lands in Idrone, Co. Carlow (see 7 Dec. 1568)

July–Sept.   Sidney campaigns in south Leinster and Munster against Sir Edmund Butler and Fitzgeralds of Desmond

Aug. 14   Arrival of Ormond from England

c. **Sept.**   Turlough Luineach O'Neill marries Lady Agnes Campbell, daughter of 3rd earl of Argyll and widow of James MacDonnell of Dunvegan

c. **Oct.**   Humphrey Gilbert (knighted, 1 Jan. 1570) put in charge of Munster operations

Nov.–Dec.   Abortive rising of northern earls in England

Edmund Campion in Dublin (leaves Ire., *c.* 31 May 1572)

1570

Feb. 25   Pius V issues bull, *Regnans in excelsis*, excommunicating Elizabeth

Feb. 28   Sir Edmund Butler and his brother Piers submit to L.D. and council

Feb.   Earl of Thomond in rebellion; he objects to inclusion of Thomond in jurisdiction of president of Connacht, and forces Fitton to withdraw from Ennis

June 26   Act (12 Eliz., c. 1) for establishment of free school in each diocese; act (12 Eliz., c. 6) for attainder of Munster rebels unless they surrender as required by proclamation

June   Thomond proclaimed traitor; he leaves for France (later submitting to English ambassador in Paris)

Sept. 18   Miler Magrath (see 12 Oct. 1565) app. bp of Clogher by queen

Dec. 13   Sir John Perrot app. president of Munster (lands at Waterford, 27 Feb. 1571)

Dec. 21   Thomond surrenders Clare, Bunratty, and other castles to queen

Dec.   French force occupies Dingle

1571

Feb. 3   Miler Magrath app. by queen abp of Cashel

Mar. 25   Sidney leaves Ire. (Sir William Fitzwilliam sworn in as L.J., 1 Apr.)

Mar.   James Fitzmaurice burns Kilmallock, Co. Limerick

June   John Kearney's *Aibidil Gaoidheilge & Caiticiosma* ('Gaelic alphabet and catechism') (Dublin; first book in Irish printed in Ire.) (cf. Apr. 1567, 1551)

Sept.-Oct.   Discovery of Ridolfi plot to overthrow Elizabeth and put Mary Stuart on throne

Oct. 7   Spanish fleet, commanded by Don John of Austria, defeats Turkish fleet at Lepanto, Gulf of Corinth

Nov. 16   Sir Thomas Smith and his son, Thomas, granted lands in Clandeboye and the Ards

Dec. 11   Fitzwilliam app. L.D. *vice* Sidney (sworn in, 13 Jan. 1572)

Annaly shired as Co. Longford

1572

Jan.   Philip II rejects proposal for invasion of Ire. submitted by Thomas Stukeley, English adventurer

Mar.   Earl of Clanricard captured by Fitton and sent to Dublin

Apr. 1   Dutch 'sea beggars' take Brill from Spaniards

Apr. 29   Treaty of Blois (defensive league between England and France)

May   Fitton campaigns against Clanricard's sons

July   Clanricard's sons raid Westmeath

Aug. 6   Clanricard released and given discretionary powers to issue pardons in Connacht

Aug. 24   Massacre of huguenots in Paris on St Bartholomew's day

Aug. 31   Thomas Smith, jun., lands with *c.* 100 colonists at Strangford Lough

1573

Feb. 23   James Fitzmaurice submits to Perrot at Kilmallock

Mar. 25   Earl of Desmond returns to Ire.; rearrested and imprisoned in Dublin

Apr. 14   Grant of denisation to Sorley Boy MacDonnell and other Scots

June 10   L.D. and council advise against further proceedings on Sir Peter Carew's claims to land titles (see 7 Dec. 1568)

July 9   Agreement between Elizabeth and Walter Devereux, earl of Essex, giving him rights over greater part of Antrim for colonisation

July   Perrot leaves Ireland on grounds of ill health

Aug.   Essex arrives at Carrickfergus

Sept. 29   Commission of 'general captainship in all Ulster' to Essex

Sept.   Brian MacPhelim O'Neill of Clandeboye supported by Turlough Luineach O'Neill in opposition to Essex

Oct. 18   Thomas Smith, jun., killed in the Ards

Oct.   Essex, assisted by Hugh O'Neill, baron of Dungannon, in action against Brian O'Neill of Clandeboye

c. **Oct.**   David Wolfe, papal nuncio, escapes to Spain

Nov. *c.* **11**   Desmond escapes from custody in Dublin

1574

May 8   Brian O'Neill, having submitted to Essex, begs queen for mercy

Aug.   Fitzwilliam campaigns against Desmond: his castle of Derrinlaur, near Clonmel, taken, and defenders executed

Sept. 2   Desmond submits to Fitzwilliam

Sept.   Essex campaigns against Turlough Luineach O'Neill

Nov.   Essex summons Brian O'Neill to conference in Belfast, and attacks his followers; Brian taken prisoner and sent to Dublin, where he is executed

1575

Mar.   James Fitzmaurice leaves for France

May 22   Elizabeth informs Essex that she withdraws support for his project for colonisation in Ulster

June 27   Turlough Luineach submits to Essex

June   Essex builds bridge over Blackwater, north of Armagh, together with fort

July 26   Force sent by Essex takes Rathlin Island and massacres inhabitants

Aug. 5   Sidney reapp. L.D., *vice* Fitzwilliam recalled (sworn in, 18 Sept.)

Aug.-Sept.   Plague in Leinster

1576

Mar. 9   Essex app. earl marshal of Ire.

Apr. 23   William Gerrard (knighted, 11 Oct. 1579) app. L.C.

Apr.   Sidney in Connacht: province shired into 4 counties (Galway, Mayo, Roscommon, Sligo)

May 9   Essex granted bar. Farney, in Monaghan

June 20   Sir William Drury app. president of Munster

June   Clanricard's sons attack Athenry

July 23   Capt. Nicholas Malby (knighted 7 Oct.) app. military governor of Connacht (president, 31 Mar. 1579)

Aug.   Clanricard imprisoned by L.D. for failure to apprehend his sons who have escaped from custody in Dublin

Sept. 22   Essex dies in Dublin

1577

Jan. 11   Renewed complaint of Palesmen at burden of cess (they send agents to England who are imprisoned there) (see *a.* 21 Mar. 1562)

Feb. 25   Brief of Pope Gregory XIII in support of James Fitzmaurice's expedition to Ire.

June   James Fitzmaurice in Spain

Sept. 14   Charter incorporating Dublin barbers and surgeons

Oct. 25   O'Rourke makes agreement with Malby for payment to crown for Bréifne

Dec.   Tadhg Dall Ó hUiginn and other poets entertained by Turlough Luineach O'Neill at Christmas

Nov./Dec.   O'Connors and O'Mores massacred by English soldiers at Mullaghmast, Co. Kildare

Raphael Holinshed's *Chronicles of England, Scotlande and Irelande* (3 vols, London; 2nd ed., 1587)

1578

Feb. 3   Thomas Stukeley leaves Italy to join James Fitzmaurice (puts in to Lisbon, *c*. mid-Apr., where kg persuades him to join his expedition to Morocco)

June 11   Charter for colonising Newfoundland granted to Sir Humphrey Gilbert

June 30   Rory Óg O'More killed in fight with MacGillapatrick

Aug. 4   Battle of Alcazar in Morocco: Sebastian, kg of Portugal, and Stukeley killed

Sept. 12   Sidney finally leaves Ire. (Sir William Drury sworn in as L.J., 14 Sept.)

1579

July 18   James Fitzmaurice, accompanied by Nicholas Sanders, papal legate, lands on Dingle peninsula, Co. Kerry (builds Dún an Óir, or Golden Fort, at Smerwick)

July 24   Commn to Sir Humphrey Gilbert to attack James Fitzmaurice

Aug. 1   Henry Davells murdered by Desmond's brothers, Sir John and Sir James

Aug. 16   Perrot app. admiral of the fleet, with instructions to prevent assistance from abroad reaching rebels in Ire.

Aug. 18   James Fitzmaurice killed in skirmish with Burkes of Castleconnell, Co. Limerick

Aug. 21   O'Reilly's country shired as Co. Cavan

Oct. 3   Malby defeats force led by John and James of Desmond at Monasternenagh, Co. Limerick

Oct. 11   Sir William Pelham elected L.J. by council *vice* Drury (d.3 Oct)

Nov. 2   Desmond proclaimed traitor

Nov.   Desmond burns Youghal

Dec.   Ormond campaigns against rebels in Munster

1580

Jan. 31   Henry, kg of Portugal, dies childless (throne of Portugal successfully claimed by Philip II of Spain)

Mar. 14   Miler Magrath (see 3 Feb. 1571) deprived by Gregory XIII of bishopric of Down and Connor

c. **Mar. 17**   Sir William Winter app. to cruise off Irish coast to intercept Spanish shipping

Mar. 29   Pelham takes Desmond castle of Carrigafoyle

May 13   Papal grant of city of Limerick to Sir John of Desmond

July 15   Lord Grey de Wilton app. L.D. (lands, 12 Aug., sworn in, 7 Sept.; delay caused by Pelham's absence in Munster)

July   Rising in Leinster headed by Viscount Baltinglass and Fiach MacHugh O'Byrne

Aug. 4   Sir James of Desmond captured (executed, 3 Oct.)

Aug. 25   Grey defeated by Fiach MacHugh O'Byrne at Glenmalure, Co. Wicklow

Sept. 12-13   Papal force of Italians and Spaniards commanded by Sebastian San Giuseppe lands at Smerwick

Nov. 7-9   Grey attacks Dún an Óir at Smerwick (garrison massacred, 10 Nov.)

1581

Mar. 22   Edmund Spenser, secretary to L.D., app. clerk of the faculties

c. **Mar.**   Rising of Kavanaghs, O'Connors, and O'Mores

c. **Apr.**   Nicholas Sanders, papal legate, dies

June   Grey on campaign against Kavanaghs

Aug. 16   Abp Loftus app. L.C. (*vice* Gerrard, d. 1 May)

Sept. 11   Papal provision of Dermot O'Hurley to see of Cashel (*vice* MacGibbon, d. 1578)

Nov.   Baltinglass leaves for Spain

John Derricke's *The image of Irelande* (London): verse and woodcuts

1582

Jan. 3   Sir John of Desmond killed near Castle Lyons, Co. Cork

Feb. 24   Bull of Gregory XIII for reformation of calendar: 4 Oct. 1582 to be immediately followed by 15 Oct.; year to begin 1 Jan. (see 22 May 1751)

Apr. 6   Execution of Nicholas Nugent, late justice of court of common pleas, convicted on charge of treason

Aug. 31   Grey leaves for England; Loftus and Sir Henry Wallop sworn in as L.J.s

Proclamation offering general pardon to Munster rebels who submit

1583

Feb.   Desmond takes refuge in Sliabh Luachra (region of west Cork and east Kerry)

Aug. 5   Gilbert takes formal possession of Newfoundland (no colony established; Gilbert drowns at sea, 9 Sept.)

Oct.   Abp O'Hurley arrested; interrogated under torture

Nov. 11   Desmond killed by O'Moriartys near Tralee

1584

Jan. 7   Sir John Perrot app. L.D. *vice* Grey (lands, 9 June; sworn in, 21 June)

Mar.   Richard Bingham app. president of Connacht (*vice* Malby, d. 4 Mar.)

Hugh O'Neill, baron of Dungannon, made tanist of Turlough Luineach O'Neill

Mar. 22/Apr. 1   Easter celebrated according to Gregorian calendar (see 24 Feb. 1582) by O'Neill, O'Donnell, and Maguire

June 19   Commn to Sir Henry Wallop, Sir Valentine Browne, and others for survey of rebels' lands in Munster

June 20   Abp O'Hurley executed in Dublin

June 24   John Norris (knighted, 26 Apr. 1586) app. president of Munster

June 30/July 10   William the Silent, prince of Orange, assassinated

July 6   Sir Nicholas Bagenal app. commr for Ulster

July 8   Commn under Sir Richard Bingham to execute martial law in Connacht and Thomond

Aug. 6   Proclamation for return of Irish fugitives from abroad on pain of forfeiture of goods

Aug. 21   Perrot submits to Sir Francis Walsingham a proposal to convert St Patrick's cathedral, Dublin, into court house and apply its revenues to foundation of two colleges (proposal blocked by Abp Loftus)

Aug.-Sept.   Perrot on campaign against MacDonnells in Antrim (Dunluce castle captured, *c.* 17 Sept.)

Sept.-Nov.   Survey of forfeited lands in Munster

Richard Stanihurst's *De rebus in Hibernia gestis* (Antwerp)

1585

Mar. 29   English act (27 Eliz., c. 2) against Jesuits and seminary priests

Apr. 26-May 25   Parliament in session in Dublin: act (27 Eliz., c. 1) for attainder of Baltinglass; bill for suspension of Poynings' law rejected; Hugh O'Neill takes seat as earl of Tyrone

July 15   Commn to Bingham and others to make agreements with Connacht landowners (composition of Connacht)

July-Aug.   Perrot in Ulster; confirms agreement between O.Neills (10 Aug.)

Aug.   First English colony planted in New World, on Roanoke Island, Virginia (evacuated, 18 June 1586; see 23 July 1587)

Oct. 3   Completion of returns for composition of Connacht

Oct. 14   Abp Creagh dies in Tower of London

Oct.   MacDonnells recapture Dunluce

Dec.   Scheme for plantation in Munster drawn up

1586

Apr. 26–May 14   Parliament in session in Dublin: act (28 Eliz., c. 7) for attainder of Desmond and his supporters

June 18   Agreement between Perrot and Sorley Boy MacDonnell; Route divided between Sorley Boy and MacQuillan

June 27   Elizabeth gives consent to amended scheme for plantation in Munster

July 5   Treaty of Berwick between Elizabeth and James VI of Scotland

Sept. 22   Bingham massacres Scots supporters of Mayo Burkes at Ardnaree, on River Moy

William Camden's *Britannia* (London; trans. Philemon Holland, 1610; later translations)

1587

Feb. 8   Mary Stuart executed

Feb. 28   Elizabeth orders grant to Sir Walter Raleigh of $3\frac{1}{2}$ seignories in Counties Cork and Waterford

May 10   Patent granting Hugh O'Neill title of earl of Tyrone

July 23   Second English colony planted on Roanoke Island, Virginia (disappears, *a*. Aug. 1590; see Aug. 1585)

Sept. *c*. 22   Hugh Roe O'Donnell kidnapped on English ship at Rathmullen, Co. Donegal (imprisoned in Dublin castle)

Latin school founded in Dublin by James Fullerton and James Hamilton

William Farmer's *Almanack for Ireland* (Dublin); earliest known Irish almanac

1588

Jan. 5   Sir Donnell O'Connor Sligo dies

Feb. 17   Sir William Fitzwilliam app. L.D. *vice* Perrot (sworn in, 30 June)

May 20/30   Spanish armada sails from Lisbon

July 29/Aug. 8   Spanish armada defeated by English fleet off Gravelines (between Calais and Dunkirk); remaining ships try to return to Spain by west of Scotland and Ire.

Sept.   About 25 armada ships wrecked off Irish coast; castaways helped in Ulster and north Connacht, but elsewhere put to death

Oct. *c*. 18   *Girona*, making for Scotland from Killybegs, Co. Donegal, wrecked on Antrim coast near Dunluce

Nov. 4–Dec. 23   Fitzwilliam's journey to Sligo and Tyrconnell in search of Spanish castaways

1589

Apr. 5   Commn to deal with disturbances in Connacht

May   Commn to inquire into progress of Munster plantation

June 17   Cú Chonnacht Maguire, lord of Fermanagh, dies; succ. by his son Hugh

Aug.   Rossa MacMahon, lord of Monaghan, dies; succ. by Hugh Roe

Dec. 5   L.D. and council clear Sir Richard Bingham of charges of misgovernment in Connacht

Dec. 12   Commn to Bingham to prosecute Burkes and others in rebellion in Connacht

Dec. 23–Jan. 14 1590   Fitzwilliam in Connacht to restore order

1590

Mar. 14, 15   L.D. orders Bingham to campaign against Brian O'Rourke, lord of Leitrim

Mar.–July   Tyrone at English court

May 9   O'Rourke takes refuge in Tyrconnell (later going to court of James VI, king of Scotland, who hands him over to Elizabeth)

Sept. or Oct.   Hugh Roe MacMahon executed (see Aug. 1589)

Dec. *a.* 26   Hugh Roe O'Donnell escapes from Dublin castle, but is recaptured

Edmund Spenser's *The faerie queene*, pt 1 (London; pt 2, 1596)

1591

Aug. 3   Earl of Tyrone marries Mabel Bagenal, sister of Sir Henry Bagenal, marshal of the army

Nov. 3   Brian O'Rourke executed at Tyburn, London

Nov.   Barnaby Rich submits memorandum for more effective control of recusancy

Dec. 26   Hugh Roe O'Donnell makes second, and successful, escape from Dublin castle

Death of Tadhg Dall Ó hUiginn (see Dec. 1577)

1592

Feb.   Capt. Humphrey Willis, sheriff of Fermanagh, expelled from Donegal priory by Hugh Roe O'Donnell

Mar. 3   Charter incorporating College of the Holy and Undivided Trinity, near Dublin (foundation stone laid, 13 Mar., on site of former priory of All Hallows; see 3 Feb. 1539)

May 3   Hugh Roe O'Donnell inaugurated as lord of Tyrconnell, his father, Hugh, having resigned

July 23/Aug. 2   Philip II gives approval and promise of financial support to newly founded College of St Patrick at Salamanca

Aug. 2   O'Donnell submits to L.D. at Dundalk

c. **Dec.**   Synod of catholic bps in Tyrconnell

1593

Feb. 12 Order for apprehension of catholic bps

Apr. Mission of James O'Hely, catholic abp of Tuam, to treat with Philip II on behalf of O'Donnell

June 23 Edmund Magauran, catholic abp of Armagh, killed in engagement between Maguire and Bingham

Sept. 26-Oct. 7 Enniskillen unsuccessfully invested by Bagenal and Tyrone

Sept.-May 1594 Sir John Norris, president of Munster, on campaign in Brittany against Spanish

1594

Feb. 2 Enniskillen captured by English force under John Dowdall and George Bingham

May 16 Sir William Russell app. L.D. (Fitzwilliam recalled; Russell sworn in, 11 Aug.)

June O'Donnell and Maguire besiege Enniskillen

Aug. 7 English force under George Bingham, coming to relief of Enniskillen garrison, defeated by Maguire at 'Ford of the Biscuits' on Arny river

Aug. 30 Russell, L.D., relieves Enniskillen

College of St Patrick at Douai founded

1595

Feb. 1-24 Russell campaigns against Fiach MacHugh O'Byrne

Feb. 16 Tyrone's brother, Art O'Neill, burns fort and bridge on Blackwater (see June 1575)

Mar. 19 English reinforcements from Brittany arrive at Waterford

May 4 Sir John Norris lands at Waterford with commn as military commander for Ire.

May c. 15 O'Donnell and Maguire take Enniskillen

June 13 Tyrone successfully attacks Sir Henry Bagenal's force at Clontibret, Co. Monaghan

June 23 Tyrone proclaimed traitor

June 26-July 13 Russell and Norris campaign against earl of Tyrone

June c. 29 Tyrone razes his castle at Dungannon

c. July 1 Armagh cathedral converted to garrison post by Russell, L.D.

July 18 Scottish proclamation against assistance to Tyrone and O'Donnell (similar proclamations, 1598, 1601)

Aug. 22 Tyrone makes overtures to Norris for pardon

Aug. 22-Sept. 5 Norris campaigns against earl of Tyrone

Aug. 23 Tyrone and O'Donnell offer kingship of Ire. to Archduke Albert, governor of Spanish Netherlands

Sept. *c.* 10 Turlough Luineach O'Neill dies (succ. in O'Neill lordship by Tyrone)

Sept. 17 Tyrone and O'Donnell write to Philip II, asking for help and promising to secure him a kingdom

Oct. 18 Tyrone and O'Donnell submit (agreement for truce, 27 Oct.)

1596

Apr.-May Mission of Alonso Cobos to Tyrone and O'Donnell

May 12 Pardon granted to Tyrone

June 20/30 Spanish fleet at Cadiz attacked by 2nd earl of Essex, who occupies town (withdraws after sacking it, 5/15 July)

July 5 L.D. and council directed to summon Sir Richard Bingham to answer complaints against his administration

July 6 Tyrone and his associates call on 'gentlemen of Munster' to join them in making war on English

July 7/17 Tyrone and O'Donnell request pope for *ius patronatus* in ecclesiastical appointments

Sept. 17-18 Spanish ships with arms and munitions arrive at Killybegs, Co. Donegal

Sept. Fiach MacHugh O'Byrne rebels in Wicklow (see 25 Aug. 1580; killed, 8 May 1597)

Oct. 18/28 Spanish ships intended for invasion of England and Ire. dispersed by storm off Finisterre

Nov. Tyrone attacks Armagh garrison, establishing blockade (continues till 19 Jan. 1597)

Dec. 2 Sir Conyers Clifford app. chief commr of Connacht (*vice* Bingham, suspended Sept. 1596; Clifford app. president, 4 Sept. 1597)

1597

Feb. 6 Order for prohibition of trade between Ire. and Spain

Mar. 5 Thomas, Lord Burgh, app. L.D. (sworn in, 22 May; Russell recalled)

July Burgh marches against earl of Tyrone via Armagh; Clifford marches against O'Donnell via Ballyshannon

Sept. 20 Sir Thomas Norris app. president of Munster (*vice* Sir John Norris, d. *a.* 9 Sept.)

Oct. 2 Tyrone unsuccessfully assaults fort erected by Burgh on Blackwater (Portmore)

Oct. 13 Burgh dies of typhus at Newry

Oct. 29 Ormond app. military commander

Oct. Spanish armada intended for invasion of England driven back by storm

Nov. 15 Abp Loftus and Richard Gardiner, C.J., app. L.J.s

Dec. 22 Tyrone submits to Ormond; truce agreed to

1598

Apr. 3/13 Henry IV of France issues edict of Nantes safeguarding rights of huguenots

Apr. 22/May 2 Treaty of Vervins between France and Spain

June 25-July 24 Ormond on campaign in Leinster

Aug. 14 Sir Henry Bagenal, marshal of the army, marching to relieve Portmore, attacked by Tyrone, O'Donnell, and Maguire at the Yellow Ford between Armagh and Blackwater; Bagenal killed and his force retire in disorder; Portmore surrendered to Tyrone

Sept. 3/13 Philip II, kg of Spain, dies; succ. by his son Philip III

Oct. 10 James Fitzthomas Fitzgerald, grandson of 14th earl of Desmond, assumes title (nicknamed *súgán*, or straw-rope, earl)

Oct. Munster plantation attacked by '*súgán* earl' and his supporters; Spenser's castle of Kilcolman, Co. Cork, burned

Viscount Mountgarrett (Edmund Butler) and Lord Cahir (Thomas Butler) join Tyrone

Nov.-Dec. Irish raids on Dublin suburbs

1599

Jan. 18 Sir Richard Bingham dies

Mar. 12 Robert Devereux, 2nd earl of Essex, app. L.L. (sworn in, 15 Apr.)

May 9-July 1 Essex on campaign in Leinster and Munster (takes Cahir castle, Co. Tipperary, 28 May)

May *c.* 27 Spanish ships arrive in Lough Foyle with arms and ammunition

May 29 Phelim MacFeagh O'Byrne routs English force at Deputy's Pass near Wicklow

Aug. 5 Sir Conyers Clifford, president of Connacht, killed in engagement with O'Donnell in Curlew mountains, Co. Roscommon

Sept. 7 Meeting of Essex and Tyrone at Aclint on Louth-Monaghan border, followed by truce

Sept. 18/28 Tyrone requests Clement VIII for subsidy

Sept. 24 Essex leaves Ire. without permission; Abp Loftus and Sir George Carey elected L.J.s by council

1600

Jan. 21 Charles Blount, Lord Mountjoy, app. L.D. (sworn in, 28 Feb.)

Feb.-Mar. Tyrone campaigns in Munster (Hugh Maguire killed, 1 Mar.)

Mar. 6 Sir George Carew app. president of Munster

Apr. 8/18 Plenary indulgence granted by Clement VIII to supporters of Tyrone; pope refuses to excommunicate those who support the queen

Apr. 10 Ormond captured by Owney O'More (released, 13 June, through intervention of Tyrone)

Apr. *c.* **17**   Mateo de Oviedo, O.F.M. (app. abp of Dublin, 25 Apr./5 May) arrives in Tyrconnell with consignment of arms

May 15   Expedition to Lough Foyle under Sir Henry Docwra lands at Culmore, near Derry

May   Mountjoy campaigns against earl of Tyrone

May-July   Carew campaigns in Limerick

June-July   O'Donnell campaigns in Connacht and Thomond

July 16-Aug. 5   Mountjoy campaigns in Offaly

July 23-Aug. 16   Carew campaigns in Kerry

Aug. 12-26   Mountjoy campaigns in south Leinster (Owney O'More killed, 17 Aug.)

Sept. 25-Oct. 2   Mountjoy forces passage through Moyry Pass (between Dundalk and Newry) against strong opposition from Tyrone

Oct. 1   Queen issues patent restoring earldom of Desmond to James, son of 15th earl

Oct. 3   Niall Garbh O'Donnell, cousin of Hugh Roe, joins Docwra (takes Hugh Roe's castle of Lifford, 9 Oct.)

Oct. 29   Florence MacCarthy submits to Carew

Dec.   Spanish ships bring arms and munitions to Teelin, Co. Donegal

Peter Lombard completes 'De regne Hiberniae sanctorum insula commentarius' (published 1632)

Richard Bartlett (or Barthelet), cartographer, engaged in making maps in Ulster (continues till 1603)

1601

Feb. 25   Essex executed on Tower Hill, London

May 7/17   Ludovico Mansoni, S.J., app. nuncio in Ire. by Clement VIII

May 20   Proclamation regarding issue of new (debased) coinage for Ire.

May 29   *Súgán* earl of Desmond captured (sent to Tower of London; dies there, Apr. 1607)

June 29/July 9   Papal provision of Peter Lombard to see of Armagh

Aug. 12   Niall Garbh O'Donnell occupies Donegal abbey

Sept. 21   Spanish fleet arrives at Kinsale with army commanded by Don Juan del Águila

Sept. 27   Mountjoy arrives at Cork to take charge of operations against Spanish

Oct. 23   O'Donnell begins his march south

Oct. 26   Mountjoy invests Kinsale

Oct. 30   Tyrone begins his march south

Nov. 1   Rincurran fort on Kinsale Harbour surrendered by Spanish to English

Nov. 7   Carew sets out from Kinsale camp to meet O'Donnell

Nov. 22   O'Donnell eludes Carew by forced march over frozen Slievephelim mountains, Co. Tipperary

Dec. *c.* 1   More Spanish ships arrive at Castlehaven, Co. Cork

Dec. *c.* 5   Tyrone joins O'Donnell at Bandon, Co. Cork

Dec. 24   Battle of Kinsale: Tyrone and O'Donnell routed, with heavy losses, by Mountjoy

Dec. 27   O'Donnell leaves for Spain (Tyrone withdraws to Ulster)

1602

Jan. 2   Águila surrenders Kinsale to Mountjoy

Mar. 16   Águila leaves Ire. for Spain

Mar. 25   Ballyshannon castle taken by English force

June 10–Sept. *c.* 15   Mountjoy in Ulster

June 11–18   Carew besieges and captures Dunboy (O'Sullivan castle near Berehaven, Co. Cork)

June *c.* 20   Tyrone burns Dungannon

July 27   Donal O'Cahan, principal vassal of Tyrone, submits to Docwra

Aug. 31/Sept. 10   Hugh Roe O'Donnell dies at Simancas

Sept. *c.* 1   Mountjoy destroys O'Neill inaugural chair at Tullaghoge, Co. Tyrone

Dec.   Mountjoy in Connacht; Rory O'Donnell, brother of Hugh Roe, submits

Maoilín Óg Mac Bruaideadha, Thomond poet who assisted in translation of New Testament, dies

1603

Feb. 17   Elizabeth authorises Mountjoy to offer Tyrone pardon in return for his surrender

Mar. 24   Elizabeth I dies; succ. by James VI of Scotland as James I of England and Ire.

T. W. MOODY, J. G. SIMMS, AND C. J. WOODS

1603

Mar. 30   Tyrone submits to Mountjoy at Mellifont

Apr. 5   James I proclaimed kg in Dublin

Apr. 12   Mountjoy reapp. L.D. by kg (L.L., 25 Apr.)

Apr.   Catholic clergy, supported by civic authorities, repossess churches and restore catholic worship in Kilkenny, Wexford, and in Munster towns

Apr.–May   Mountjoy asserts royal authority over towns that have restored catholic worship

May 30   Sir George Carey app. L.D. (Mountjoy leaves for England, accompanied by Tyrone, *c*. 31 May)

Sept. 12   Warrant of pardon to Tyrone

Sept. 17   James I authorises striking of new silver coinage for Ire.

Nov. 20   John Davies (knighted, 18 Dec.) arrives in Ire. as solicitor general (app. attorney general, 29 May 1606)

First assizes held in Donegal; first sheriffs appointed for Donegal and Tyrone

Tiomna nuadh (Dublin), Irish translation of New Testament, by William O'Donnell (protestant abp of Tuam, 1609–28 (see 1608)

1604

July 11   Charter incorporating Derry as a city (reincorporated as Londonderry, 29 Mar. 1613)

1605

Feb. 3   Sir Arthur Chichester sworn in as L.D.

Mar. 11   Proclamation declaring all persons in realm to be free, natural, and immediate subjects of kg, and not subjects of any lords or chiefs

Apr. 16   James I grants to James Hamilton lands of Upper Clandeboye and Great Ards, later to be divided between Con O'Neill, Sir Hugh Montgomery and Hamilton himself

June 13   George Montgomery app. bp of Derry, Raphoe, and Clogher

July 4   Proclamation commanding all seminary priests and Jesuits to leave Ire. by 10 Dec. 1605, and directing laity to attend divine service in accordance with law

Nov. 5   Discovery of gunpowder plot at Westminster

Nov. 13   Mandates issued by L.D. requiring selected citizens to attend service of established church

Nov. 22   Dublin citizens fined and imprisoned for failing to obey mandates

Nov.   Petition of Pale landowners claiming right to 'the private use of their religion and conscience'

Dec. 6   Promoters of petition imprisoned

Dec.   Tyrone's son, Henry O'Neill, becomes colonel of Irish regiment to be raised for Spanish service

1606

Jan. or Feb.   Irish custom of gavelkind declared illegal by judges

July 22   Commn for remedying defective land-titles

July–Aug.   Davies accompanies Chichester on tour through Monaghan, Fermanagh, and Cavan

Foundation of St Anthony's Franciscan College, Louvain (confirmed by papal bull, 24 Mar./3 Apr. 1607)

1607

May 14   First settlers reach mainland of Virginia

June   Society of the King's Inns restored as voluntary association of lawyers

July 16   Tyrone and O'Cahan summoned to London

Sept. 4   Tyrone, Tyrconnell, and others sail from Lough Swilly ('flight of the earls')

Sept. 7   Proclamation of L.D. declaring that natives of Donegal and Tyrone will not be disturbed in peaceable possession of their lands so long as they behave as dutiful subjects

Sept. 17   Chichester submits to English privy council proposals for disposal of fugitives' lands

Dec.   Bills of indictment brought in by grand juries of Donegal and Tyrone, charging earls and their associates with high treason and declaring their lands forfeited

1608

Jan. or Feb.   Tanistry declared illegal by court of king's bench

Mar. 10   Chichester's 'notes of remembrance' for an intended plantation in Ulster (revised, c. Oct. 1608)

Apr. 18-19   Sir Cahir O'Doherty, in revolt, seizes Culmore and Derry

Apr. 19/29   Tyrone and Tyrconnell arrive at Rome

July 5   O'Doherty killed at Kilmacrenan, Co. Donegal

July 18/28   Death of Tyrconnell in Rome

July 19   Commn authorising survey of six counties in Ulster—Donegal, Coleraine, Tyrone, Armagh, Fermanagh, and Cavan

July 27-Sept. 6   Survey of 6 counties in Ulster finds almost entire area to be escheated to kg

Leabhar na nVrnaightheadh gComhchoidchiond (Dublin), Irish translation by William O'Donnell of Book of Common Prayer (cf. 1603)

1609

Jan.   Detailed plan for plantation in 6 escheated counties of Ulster completed; conditions to be observed by participants published; land allocated to support free schools at Armagh, Cavan, Derry, Donegal, Limavady, and Mountjoy

July 21   Commn for new survey of escheated lands in Ulster, and for giving effect to plantation scheme

July 31-Sept. 30   New survey, with maps of escheated counties, and their division into plantation precincts

Oct.   Three ships under Sir Robert Stewart sail from Derry carrying Irish swordsmen bound for Sweden

1610

Jan. 28   Agreement between English privy council and city of London for plantation of city of Derry, county of Coleraine, and barony of Loughinsholin

Apr. 7   Revised conditions to be observed by servitors and natives in Ulster plantation

Apr.   Revised conditions to be observed by British undertakers in Ulster plantation published

Apr.-May   Land assigned to British undertakers in Ulster

Aug. 23   Proclamation permitting native Irish to remain on land assigned to British undertakers till following May (removal date subsequently deferred to 1 May 1612; see also 1 Oct. 1618, 5 June 1628)

Nov. 22   Chichester announces kg's intention to hold parliament in 1611

Nov. 28   Third plantation commn, authorising Chichester and others to convey land to grantees

1611

Feb. *c.* **18**   Sir Humphrey Winch, L.C.J., sent to London with drafts of government's proposals for legislation

May 7   'Surrender and regrant' in Wicklow, Wexford, and Carlow authorised

June   Lord Carew appointed to inquire into problems of Irish government

July 11-Oct. 21   Carew in Ire.

July 13   Reissue of proclamation of 4 July 1605 against seminary priests and Jesuits

Aug.   Carew's survey of Ulster plantation

Nov. 25   Nobility and gentry claim right to see bills that government intends to transmit for forthcoming Irish parliament

Bonaventura Ó hEodhasa's [O'Hussey's] *An teagasg criosdaidhe* (Antwerp), first catholic devotional work printed in Irish

1612

Feb. 1   Cornelius O'Devany, O.F.M., catholic bp of Down and Connor, convicted of treason (Jan.), hanged in Dublin

Oct.   First English factory established in India, at Surat, on coast of Gujarat

Nov. 27   Charter incorporating Dungannon, first of 40 new boroughs created between Nov. 1612 and May 1613

Sir John Davies's *Discovery of the true causes why Ireland was never entirely subdued until the beginning of his majesty's happy reign* (London)

1613

Feb. 2-Apr. 25   Sir Josias Bodley's first survey of Ulster plantation

Mar. 6   Commn for calling parliament issued

Mar. 25   Charter incorporating town of Coleraine

Mar. 29   Charter incorporating Derry as city of Londonderry, creating new county of Londonderry, incorporating Irish Society of London, and granting to it greater part of temporal land in Co. Londonderry

Apr. 27   Charter incorporating Belfast

Apr.-May   Elections to Irish parliament

May 17   Petition of recusant lords to Chichester, one of a series of catholic protests against his conduct over summoning of parliament

May 18   Opening of James I's Irish parliament; dispute over election of speaker of H.C. leads to withdrawal of catholic members

May 24   Meeting of convocation of Church of Ireland in St Patrick's cathedral, Dublin

June 5   Parliament prorogued

June 28   Charter incorporating Coleraine and superseding earlier charter of 25 Mar. 1613

Aug. 27   James I appoints commn of inquiry into catholic allegations of illegality in elections to parliament, and into other matters

Nov. 12   Report of commrs of inquiry of 27 Aug.

1614

Apr. 21   James I rebukes deputation from catholic opposition in Irish parliament

June 22   Synod of Kilkenny regulates discipline and practice of catholic church in province of Dublin (similar regulation in other provinces, 1615-31)

Aug. 7   James I's final judgment on complaints of catholic opposition in parliament

Sept.   Sir Josias Bodley's second survey of Ulster plantation

Oct. 11-Nov. 29   Second session of James I's Irish parliament

Nov. 15   Death in Louvain of Bonaventura Ó hEodhasa, O.F.M., Irish poet

1615

Apr. 18 Chichester informs English privy council of plot for massacre of settlers in Ulster and of arrest of many conspirators

Apr. 18-May 16 Third session of James I's Irish parliament

Apr. 25 Convocation of Church of Ireland ends, having adopted 104 articles of religion

June 22 Commn to L.C. and others for general visitation throughout Ire.

Oct. 24 James I's Irish parliament dissolved

Dec. English privy council authorises cttee to investigate possibility of setting up court of wards in Ire.

Act (11, 12 & 13 James I, c. 7) making parishes responsible for maintenance of roads and requiring cottiers and labourers to give 6 days' labour a year for this purpose

1616

Apr. 20 Letters patent confirming kg's order to L.D. to convey lands to abp of Armagh for establishment of schools in Donegal, Derry, Tyrone, Armagh, Fermanagh, and Cavan

July 10/20 Hugh O'Neill, earl of Tyrone, dies in Rome

Aug. 30 Sir Oliver St John sworn in as L.D.

c. **Nov.** Sir Josias Bodley's third survey of Ulster plantation

David Rothe's *Analecta sacra et mira de rebus catholicorum in Hibernia gestis*, pt. 1 (N.P.; pts 2, 3, Cologne 1617, 1619)

Flaithrí Ó Maoil Chonaire's [Florence Conry's] *Desiderius, otherwise called Sgáthán an crábhaidh* (Louvain)

c. **1616**

Lughaidh O'Clery's 'Life of Hugh Roe O'Donnell' written

1617

Apr. 29/May 9 Laying of foundation stone of permanent buildings of Irish College of St Anthony, Louvain

Oct. 17 Proclamation ordering banishment of priests educated abroad

Fynes Moryson's *Itinerary* (London)

1618

Jan. 23 Charter of Waterford revoked after election of recusants (restored 1626)

May 13/23 Rebellion in Bohemia, leading to thirty years war

Oct. 1 Native Irish ordered to leave lands of British undertakers in Ulster by 1 May 1619 or pay fines

Dec. 1 Capt. Nicholas Pynnar's survey of Ulster plantation begins (completed 28 Mar. 1619)

Aodh MacAingil's [Hugh MacCaghwell's] *Scáthán shacramuinte na h-aithridhe* (Louvain)

1619

Oct. 25/Nov. 4   Frederick, elector palatine, crowned kg of Bohemia

Dermot O'Meara's *Pathologia haereditaria generalis* (Dublin), first work in Latin published in Ire.

1620

Oct. 29/Nov. 8   Battle of White Mountain near Prague, resulting in defeat and flight of Frederick, elector palatine

1621

Jan. 20   Letters patent issued in Dublin for grants for plantations in parts of Leitrim, King's County, Queen's County and Westmeath

Sept. 29   Lionel Cranfield app. lord treasurer of England (suspended, 25 Apr. 1624)

Dec. 27/6 Jan. 1622   Gregory XV formally establishes Sacred Congregation de Propaganda Fide (confirmed by bull *Inscrutabili divinae*, 12/22 June 1622)

Philip O'Sullivan Beare's *Historiae catholicae Iberniae compendium* (Lisbon)

1622

Mar. 20   Commn to inquire into ecclesiastical and temporal state of Ire.

Aug.-Oct.   Survey of six escheated counties in Ulster (survey of Co. Londonderry by Sir Thomas Phillips and Richard Hadsor, with maps and illustrations)

c. **Aug.**   *His majesty's directions for the ordering and settling of the courts*

Sept. 8   Viscount Falkland sworn in as L.D.

James Ussher, bp of Meath (see 21 Mar. 1625), preaching before L.D., demands severe measures against catholics

Ussher's *Discourse of the religion anciently professed by the Irish and Scottish . . .* (Dublin)

Dec. 23   Court of wards and liveries established

1623

June 20   Orders issued for tendering oath of supremacy to all officers in cities and corporate towns and for enforcement of excommunication against relapsed aldermen

1624

Jan. 21   Proclamation ordering all catholic ecclesiastics to leave Ire. within 40 days (suspended a month later)

Sept. 24   James I approves revised programme of reform for Londonderry plantation

1625

Mar. 21   Ussher app. abp of Armagh

Mar. 27   James I dies; succ. by Charles I

Sept. 7   Treaty of Southampton between England and Dutch republic, leading to war between England and Spain

Sept. 28   Edward Sherlock and Paul Browne, O.D.C., arrive in Dublin on mission to introduce Order of Discalced Carmelites to Ire. (they open friary and chapel in Cook Street, Oct.)

Oct.–Nov.   Unsuccessful English expedition against Cadiz

Philip O'Sullivan Beare's 'Zoilomastix' written (selections from, published by Irish Manuscripts Commission, 1960)

St. Isidore's Franciscan College, Rome, taken over by Irish Franciscans under Luke Wadding as superior

Luke Wadding's *Annales minorum*, vol. i (Lyons; vols. ii–vii, Lyons, 1628-48; vol. viii, Rome, 1654; several later eds)

1626

Sept. 22   Charles I offers 26 concessions ('graces') to his Irish subjects in return for subsidies to maintain an expanded army of 5,000 foot and 500 horse

Nov. 15   Assembly of notables meets in Dublin to discuss kg's proposals

Nov. 26   Private meeting of protestant bps condemns proposed toleration for catholics

1627

c. **Jan.**   England at war with France

Apr. 19   Delegate meeting in Dublin ('great assembly') rejects Charles I's proposals

Apr. 22   George Downham, bp of Derry, preaching before Falkland, L.D., in Christ Church, Dublin, denounces proposed toleration for catholics

May 2   L.D. dismisses 'great assembly'

June 26   L.D. agrees to initiate elections in each county to choose delegates to provincial conventions which will in turn nominate delegates to meet kg

June–Nov.   Unsuccessful English expedition to La Rochelle in support of huguenots

July–Nov.   Selection by local conventions of delegates to meet kg

Aug. 16   William Bedell admitted provost of Trinity College, Dublin

Dec. 22/1 Jan. 1628   Irish College, Rome, opens to students

Aodh Ó Dochartaigh, under patronage of Capt. Somhairle Mac Domhnaill in Netherlands, transcribes 'Duanaire Finn', collection of Irish poems (second collection, later known as 'Book of O'Conor Don', transcribed 1629-30)

1628

Jan.   Irish delegates (8 Old English, 3 New English) arrive in London

Mar. 20   Delegates, in audience with Charles I, offer financial support in return for concessions

May 24   Charles I issues 51 instructions ('graces') in return for delegates' promise of subsidy of £40,000 a year for 3 years

May–Oct.   Preparations for summoning of parliament to confirm the 'graces' prove abortive, owing to L.D.'s failure to observe Poynings' law procedure

June 5   British undertakers in Ulster, in return for fines and doubled rents, permitted to have native Irish tenants on one-quarter of their estates

July 11   Sir Brian Maguire, Lord Enniskillen, surrenders Fermanagh to kg

Aug. 21   Laying of foundation stone of protestant cathedral at Derry (completed, 1633)

1629

Apr. 1   Proclamation forbidding exercise of ecclesiastical jurisdictions derived from Rome and ordering dissolution of all catholic religious houses

Apr. 14/24   Treaty of Susa ends war between England and France

Sept. 13   William Bedell consecrated bp of Kilmore and Ardagh

Oct. 26   Falkland, L.D., leaves Ire.; Viscount Loftus and earl of Cork, L.J.s

Dec. 26   Abp and mayor of Dublin raid Franciscan chapel in Cook Street, Dublin and suppress 16 religious houses in city; riot follows; decree of L. J.s ordering suppression of religious houses throughout kingdom

Under supervision of Bp Bedell, Murtagh King and James Nangle begin translating Old Testament into Irish (published, 1685)

1630

Apr. 19   Michael O'Clery's 'Félire na naomh nÉrennach' (Calendar of Irish saints, later known as Martyrology of Donegal), completed

Oct. 26/Nov. 5   Treaty of Madrid ends war between England and Spain

1631

June 20   Baltimore, Co. Cork, sacked by Algerine pirates

Foundation of Irish Franciscan house at Prague

Geoffrey Keating (Seáthrún Céitinn) completes 'Eochairsgiath an aifrinn' and 'Trí biorghaoithe an bháis'

1632

Jan. 12   Charles I announces decision to appoint Viscount Wentworth L.D.

Sept. 8   Government order for destruction of buildings of St Patrick's Purgatory on Lough Derg, Co. Donegal

Peter Lombard's *De regno Hiberniae* (Louvain)

Compilation of 'Annála ríoghachta Éireann' ('Annals of the kingdom of Ireland', later known as 'Annals of the Four Masters') begun by Michael O'Clery and others (completed 10 Aug. 1636)

1633

July 25   Viscount Wentworth (created earl of Strafford, 12 Jan. 1640) sworn in as L.D.

Sept. 19   William Laud app. abp of Canterbury

Thomas Stafford's *Pacata Hibernia* (anon., London)

Sir James Ware's edition of works by Spenser, Campion, and Hanmer published as *The history of Ireland* (Dublin)

1634

Jan. 22   Wentworth enunciates his Irish policy to Charles

Feb. 15/25   Albrecht von Wallenstein assassinated in Eger, Bohemia, by Walter Devereux, captain in regiment of Col. Walter Butler

May 23   Proclamation summoning parliament for 14 July

May 26   John Bramhall consecrated bp of Derry

June-July   Elections to Irish parliament

June 29   Commission for remedying defective land-titles

July 14-Aug. 2   First session of Charles I's first Irish parliament

Aug. 26-7   Swedes defeated by Imperial troops at Nördlingen, Bavaria

Nov. 4-Dec. 14   Second session of Charles I's first Irish parliament

Nov. 27   Wentworth makes policy statement on 'graces' thereby precipitating brief parliamentary crisis

Dec. 10   Convocation of Church of Ireland adopts English 39 articles

Dec. 15   Statute of uses (10 Chas I, sess. 2, c. 1), restricting evasion of feudal dues

   Act (10 Chas I, sess. 2, c. 26) empowering royal justices and justices of the peace in quarter sessions, with assent of grand jury, to levy charges on localities for building and repairing of bridges and causeways on kg's highways

c. 1634

Completion of Geoffrey Keating's 'Foras feasa ar Éirinn' ('Basis of knowledge about Ireland')

1635

Jan. 26-Mar. 21   Third session of Charles I's first Irish parliament

Jan. 28   Beginning of trial in court of Star Chamber of city of London and Irish Society for mismanagement and neglect of Londonderry plantation

Feb. 28   End of Star Chamber trial of city of London and Irish Society: defendants sentenced to fine of £70,000 and surrender of Londonderry charter

Mar. 24-Apr. 18   Fourth session of Charles I's first Irish parliament

Apr. 18   Act for erecting houses of correction and for punishment of 'rogues, vagabonds, sturdy beggars and other lewd and idle persons' (10 & 11 Chas I, c. 4)

   Act 'for keepers of alehouses to be bound by recognizances' (10 & 11 Chas I, c. 5); first Irish act requiring sellers of drink to be licensed by magistrates

   Act against 'ploughing by the tail' and pulling the wool off live sheep (10 & 11 Chas I, c. 15)

June 30   Proclamation regulating manufacture of linen cloth

July 9-31   In Wentworth's presence, juries find kg's title to land in counties of Roscommon, Sligo, and Mayo

Aug. 16   Galway jury refuses to find kg's title

1636

May 27-8   Cross-examination of Galway jury on charge of refusing to find kg's title, resulting in heavy fines and imprisonment

May 31   Proclamation regulating production of linen yarn

June 3   Wentworth leaves for England (returning 23 Nov.)

July 17   Charles I orders establishment of admiralty dockyard in Ire. (Kinsale designated, 1638)

Dec.   Galway jury submits and is liberated

1637

May 25   Letters patent authorising 'Laudian statutes' for Trinity College, Dublin

July 23   Riot in St Giles's church, Edinburgh, when Laud's new service-book is first used

July 25   Christopher Wandesford acquires estate in Castlecomer area of Co. Kilkenny on which he afterwards discovers and exploits coal deposits; beginning of discovery and exploitation of Leinster coalfield (see 1814)

Dec. 22   Charter incorporating guild of goldsmiths in Dublin

Opening of St Werburgh Street theatre, first in Dublin (closed, *c.* Oct. 1641)

1638

Jan. 13   Proclamation enforcing Wentworth's tobacco monopoly

Feb. 28   John Ogilby app. master of revels by Wentworth

Mar. 1   National covenant subscribed at Edinburgh in opposition to kg's ecclesiastical innovations in Scotland

Sir Richard Bolton's *A justice of peace for Ireland* (Dublin)

1639

May-June   First 'bishops' war' (ended by treaty of Berwick, 18 June)

May 21   Proclamation requiring Scots in Ulster to take oath of loyalty and obedience to kg ('black oath')

July 23   Wentworth summoned by kg to England (leaves Ire., 12 Sept.)

Catechismus: an teagasc Críostuí (Brussels), by Theobald Stapleton (Teabóid Gállduf), first work in Irish printed in conventional roman type

Duns Scotus's *Opera omnia*, ed. Luke Wadding and collaborators (16 vols, Lyons)

1640

Jan. 12   Wentworth created earl of Strafford (app. L.L., 13 Jan.)

Feb.-Mar.   Elections to Irish parliament

Mar. 16-June 17   First session of Charles I's second Irish parliament

Apr. 1   Christopher Wandesford app. L.D.

Apr. 3   Strafford finally leaves Ire.

Apr. 13–May 5   'Short parliament' in England

May 18   High commission court deprives Bp Adair of Killala and Achonry of his see for seditious words and fines him £2,000 and sentences him to imprisonment during pleasure

June–Aug.   Owen Roe O'Neill in Spanish service defends Arras against French

July   Government's newly formed army assembles at Carrickfergus

Aug. 20   Scottish army crosses Tweed: beginning of second 'bishops' war'

Aug. 28   Scots defeat king's army at Newburn, near Newcastle-upon-Tyne

Oct. 1–Nov. 12   Second session of Charles I's second Irish parliament

Oct. 21   Treaty of Ripon: truce between English and Scots (peace concluded, June 1641)

Nov. 3   Meeting of parliament (the 'long parliament') in England

Nov. 7   Irish H.C. adopts petition of remonstrance, which delegation later conveys to England

Nov. 11   English H.L., after hearing H.C.'s charge delivered by John Pym, authorises proceedings for impeachment of Strafford

Dec. 3   Death of Wandesford

1641

Jan. 26–Mar. 5   Third session of Charles I's second Irish parliament

Jan. 30   Articles of impeachment against Strafford sent by English H.C. to H.L.

Feb. 10   Sir William Parsons and Sir John Borlase sworn in as L.J.s

Mar. 4   H.C. draws up articles of impeachment for high treason against Bolton, L.C., Bp Bramhall, Lowther, L.C.J., and Sir George Radcliffe (proceedings subsequently dropped)

Mar. 22   Beginning of Strafford's trial at Westminster

Apr. 21   Bill for attainder of Strafford passed by English H.C.

May 10   Act for attainder of Strafford (16 *recte* 17 Chas I, c. 38 [Eng.])

May 11–Nov. 17   Fourth session of Charles I's second Irish parliament

May 12   Strafford executed on Tower Hill, London

May 17   Cttees of Irish parliament in England present memorial on Poynings' law to kg

June 9   Patrick Darcy, on behalf of H.C., presents to H.L.'s cttee his argument that Irish parliament is sole legislative authority for Ire.

Aug. 7   Parliament adjourned (see 16 Nov.)

Oct. 22   Outbreak of rebellion in Ulster (many protestants killed by insurgents during ensuing 6 months; see 16 Mar. 1643)

Oct. 23   Attempt to seize Dublin castle thwarted

Nov.   At least 80 protestants killed by rebels at Portadown bridge

Nov. 4   Sir Phelim O'Neill issues proclamation purporting to be from kg

Nov. 11   Earl of Ormond app. lieutenant general of kg's army

Nov. 16   Parliament reassembles (prorogued, 17 Nov.)

Nov. 21   Ulster rebels begin siege of Drogheda

Nov. 29   Government force, sent to relieve Drogheda, defeated at Julianstown, Co. Meath

Dec. *c*. 3   Meeting at Knockcrofty, near Drogheda, leading to alliance between Ulster Irish and Old English

Dec. 23   L.J.s issue commn to record depositions on matters connected with the rebellion

1642

a. **Jan. 8**   About 50 catholics killed by Scots on Islandmagee, Co. Antrim

Jan. 11-9 Feb. 1647   Fifth session of Charles I's second Irish parliament

Mar.   Siege of Drogheda raised

Mar. 19   'Adventurers' act' (16 Chas I, c. 33 [Eng.]), 'for the speedy and effectual reducing of the rebels in his majesty's kingdom of Ireland', offering allotments of forfeited land in proportion to contributions of money

Mar. 22   Catholic bps and vicars of province of Armagh meet at Kells

Apr. 15   Ormond defeats insurgents at Kilrush, Co. Kildare

Robert Monro lands at Carrickfergus with Scottish army

May 10-13   Meetings of catholic clergy and laity at Kilkenny

June 10   First meeting, at Carrickfergus, of presbytery formed by 4 kirk sessions of Scottish army; first regularly constituted presbytery in Ire.

June 22   Forty-one catholics expelled from parliament

June   Oath of association drawn up for confederate catholics at Kilkenny (see Mar. 1647)

July 8 or 9   Owen Roe O'Neill lands at Doe Castle on Sheephaven Bay, Co. Donegal

Aug. 22   Beginning of civil war in England (first battle, at Edgehill, 23 Oct.)

Sept.   Thomas Preston lands at Wexford

Oct. 24-Nov. 21   First general assembly at Kilkenny

Nov. 24/Dec. 4   Cardinal Richelieu dies

1643

Mar. 16   L.J.s and council, reporting to kg on condition of Ire., allege that, by end of Mar. 1642, 154,000 protestants have been killed by rebels, and thousands more since that date

Mar. 17   Meeting at Trim between representatives of Kilkenny and Dublin

Mar. 18   Ormond, after failing to take New Ross, defeats Preston near Old Ross

Apr. 23   Royal commn to Ormond to treat with confederates

May 20-June 19   Second general assembly of confederates at Kilkenny

June 13   Owen Roe O'Neill defeated by Sir Robert Stewart at Clones

June 20   Fort of Galway surrenders to confederates

June 24   Truce negotiations begin between confederates and Ormond

July 14   Ordinance of English parliament offering double allotment of land to adventurers increasing their contributions by one-quarter

July   Arrival at Kilkenny of Pier Francesco Scarampi, papal envoy to confederates

Aug. 6   Galway townspeople join confederates

Sept. 15   One-year truce between Ormond and confederates

Sept. 20   First battle of Newbury, Berks., followed by retreat of royalists

Sept. 25   'Solemn league and covenant' between English parliament and Scots

Nov. *c.* 7-Dec. 1   Third general assembly of confederates at Kilkenny

Nov. 13   Marquis of Ormond app. L.L. by Charles I (sworn in, 21 Jan. 1644)

Nov. 19   Confederates nominate 7 delegates to meet Charles I at Oxford

Micheál Ó Clérigh's *Foclóir no sanasán nua* ('A new vocabulary'; Louvain)

Patrick Darcy's *Argument* (Waterford; see 9 June 1641)

1644

Mar. 24   Confederate agents arrive at Oxford for negotiations with kg

Apr. 1   Charles grants plenary powers to earl of Glamorgan

Apr. 17   Irish protestant delegation arrives at Oxford

May 5-July 7   François de La Boullaye Le Gouz, French traveller, tours Ire.

May 14   Monro seizes Belfast

June 24   Charles I commissions Ormond to continue negotiations with confederates

June 27   Force raised by earl of Antrim and commanded by Alaster McDonnell sails from Waterford to join marquis of Montrose in Scotland

July 2   Battle of Marston Moor, Yorks.: royalists defeated by combined force of parliamentarians and Scots

July 17   Lord Inchiquin abandons royalist cause and declares for parliament

July 20-Aug. 31   Fourth general assembly of confederates at Kilkenny

Sept. 1   McDonnell's force takes part in Montrose's victory over covenanters at Tippermuir, near Perth

Oct. 24   English parliament's no-quarter ordinance: any Irishman taken in arms in England or Wales to be put to death

Dec. 31   Mission of Richard Bellings to seek help for confederates from continental powers begins

1645

Jan. 20   Preston invests Duncannon fort

Mar. 12 Charles I's final commn to Glamorgan

Mar. 19 Duncannon fort taken by Preston

May 9 Montrose, with Irish under McDonnell, defeats covenanters at Auldearn, near Nairn

May 15-*p*. Aug. 31 Fifth general assembly of confederates at Kilkenny

June 14 Battle of Naseby, Northants.: decisive victory of New Model army over royalists

June end Glamorgan arrives in Ire.

July 8 Parliamentary force under Sir Charles Coote takes Sligo from confederates

Aug. 25 Secret treaty between Glamorgan and confederates

Sept. 13 Montrose and McDonnell defeated by covenanters at Philiphaugh, near Selkirk

Oct. 12 Abp Giovanni Rinuccini, papal envoy to confederates, land at Kenmare, with Bellings

Oct. late Malachy O'Queely, catholic abp of Tuam, killed in skirmish near Sligo

Nov. 10/20 Treaty between Innocent X and Sir Kenelm Digby, envoy of Queen Henrietta Maria, signed at Rome

Nov. 12 Rinuccini arrives at Kilkenny

Dec. 20 Second secret treaty between Glamorgan and confederates, Rinuccini dictating its terms

Dec. 26 Arrest of Glamorgan in Dublin by Ormond

Anthony Gearnon's *Parrthas an anma* ('The paradise of the soul'; Louvain)

Cornelius Mahony's *Disputatio apologetica de jure regni Hiberniae* (Lisbon), advocating Gaelic Irish monarchy

John Colgan's *Acta sanctorum Hiberniae* (Louvain)

Compilation of An Dubhaltach Mac Fir Bhisigh's book of genealogies begun (completed 1650)

1646

Jan. 22 Ormond releases Glamorgan

Feb. 3 Chester falls to parliamentary forces

Feb. *c*. 7-Mar. 4 Sixth general assembly of confederates at Kilkenny

Feb. 19 Confederates agree to prolong truce to 1 May

Mar. 28 Peace agreed between confederates and Ormond

May 5 Charles I gives himself up to Scots near Newark

June 5 Monro's forces defeated at Benburb, Co. Tyrone, by Owen Roe O'Neill

July 14 Capture of Bunratty, Co. Clare, by confederates

July 30 Ormond peace proclaimed in Dublin

Aug. 3 Ormond peace proclaimed by supreme council at Kilkenny

Aug. 12 Rinuccini's legatine synod at Waterford declares confederate catholics adhering to Ormond peace to have broken oath of association (see June 1642)

Aug. 17   Waterford synod lays interdict on all places accepting Ormond peace

Sept. 1   Waterford synod excommunicates all who show themselves in favour of Ormond peace

Sept. 18   Rinuccini returns to Kilkenny to dictate terms to supreme council

Sept. 26   New council nominated under presidency of Rinuccini

Nov. 26   Completion by Westminster assembly of confession of faith

Sir John Temple's *The Irish rebellion: or the history of the beginning and first progress of the general rebellion raised within the kingdom of Ireland upon the three and twentieth day of October 1641* (London)

1647

Jan. 10–Apr. 4   Seventh general assembly of confederates at Kilkenny

Jan. 30   Scots evacuate Newcastle-upon-Tyne, leaving Charles I in hands of parliamentary commrs

Feb. 2   Declaration of confederate general assembly against Ormond peace

Mar. 26   Parliament reassembles

Mar.   New oath of association adopted by general assembly of confederates under pressure from clergy

June 4   Charles I seized by parliamentary army at Holmby, Northants

June 7   Parliamentary force of 2,000 under Col. Michael Jones lands near Dublin

June 19   Ormond agrees to surrender Dublin to parliamentary commrs

Parliamentary commrs recommend Dublin clergy to cease using Book of Common Prayer (formal order, 24 June)

July 28   Ormond withdraws to England

Aug. 8   Jones defeats Preston at Dungan's Hill, near Trim

Aug.   Ormond confers with Charles I at Hampton Court

Sept. 14   Inchiquin sacks Cashel

Nov. 12–Dec. 24   Eighth general assembly of confederates at Kilkenny

Nov. 13   Inchiquin defeats confederate army of Munster at Knocknanuss, near Mallow

Dec. 26   'Engagement' between Charles I and Scottish commissioners signed at Carisbrooke, Isle of Wight: germ of second civil war

John Colgan's *Triadis thaumaturgae acta* (Louvain)

John Woodhouse's *Guide for strangers in the kingdom of Ireland* (London)

1648

Feb.   Confederate envoys set out for France and Rome

Mar.   Ormond arrives in Paris

May 20 Truce between Inchiquin and confederates

May 27 Rinuccini excommunicates supporters of truce with Inchiquin

May 31 Supreme council decides to appeal to Rome against Rinuccini's excommunication

May–Aug. Second civil war

June 27 Publication of Westminster confession of faith as authorised by both houses of English parliament

Aug. 17 Oliver Cromwell defeats Scots at Preston, Lancs.

Sept. 4–17 Jan. 1649 Ninth (and last) general assembly of confederates at Kilkenny

Sept. 12 Col. George Monck takes Carrickfergus

Sept. 30 Ormond lands at Cork

Supreme council proclaims Owen Roe O'Neill traitor

Oct. 14/24 Peace of Westphalia ends thirty years war

Nov. 21 Confederate envoys return from Rome

Dec. 28 News reaches Kilkenny of parliamentary army's demand that Charles I be put on trial for his life

Outbreaks of small-pox and dysentery, becoming endemic during next few years (see July 1649)

1649

Jan. 17 Peace treaty between Ormond and confederates

Jan. 30 Charles I executed

Feb. 23 Rinuccini leaves Ire. for Continent, via Galway

Mar. 30 English parliament approves appointment of Cromwell as commander-in-chief in Ire.

Apr. 1–Aug. 8 Parliamentary force under Sir Charles Coote besieged in Derry by Ulster Scots under Lord Montgomery and Sir Robert Stewart; siege raised when Owen Roe O'Neill marches to relieve Coote

June 5 Parliamentary army ordered to set out for Ire.

June 22 Parliament approves commn, limited to 3 years, to Cromwell to be governor general of Ire.: 'civil and military power shall be for the present conjoined in one person'

July 10 Cromwell leaves London for Milford Haven

July Plague reaches Galway from Continent (spreads throughout Ire., causing innumerable deaths, 1649–51)

Aug. 2 Ormond defeated by Jones at Rathmines, near Dublin

Aug. 15 Cromwell lands at Dublin

Aug. 23, 24 Cromwell's declarations of civil liberty for peaceful people

Sept. 11 Drogheda taken by Cromwell; massacre of garrison (about 2,600) and townspeople

Oct. 11 Wexford taken by Cromwell; second massacre (about 2,000)

Oct. 19 New Ross surrenders to Cromwell, who informs governor that 'where the parliament of England have power' mass will not be allowed

Oct. 20 Treaty between Ormond and Owen Roe O'Neill

Nov. 2 Scots defenders of Carrickfergus agree to surrender town to Coote and Robert Venables

Nov. 6 Death of Owen Roe O'Neill at Cloughoughter, Co. Cavan

Nov. 20 Carrick-on-Suir taken by Cromwellian forces (which repel an attack from Inchiquin a few days later)

Nov. 24 Cromwell invests Waterford

Dec. 2 Cromwell raises siege of Waterford

Dec. 4 Synod of catholic bps at Clonmacnoise; declarations issued appealing for unity in cause of catholicism and kg against Cromwell

1650

Jan. Cromwell's reply to Clonmacnoise declarations, *A declaration of the lord lieutenant of Ireland for the undeceiving of deluded and seduced people*; contains his view of 1641 massacres

Feb. 3 Surrender of Fethard, Co. Tipperary, to Cromwell, on specially favourable terms

Feb. 24 Cahir surrenders

Feb. 25 Proclamation rendering 'popish inhabitants' of a barony liable for robberies committed there against protestants by 'tories' and rebels

Mar. 1 Fall of Ballisonan, Co. Kildare

Mar. 8 Ormond meets catholic bps at Limerick

English act applies revenues of archbishopric of Dublin and St Patrick's cathedral to educational purposes

Mar. 18 Heber MacMahon, catholic bp of Clogher, app. commander in Ulster in succession to O'Neill (appointment endorsed by Ormond, 1 Apr.)

Mar. 27 Kilkenny surrenders to Cromwell

Apr. 10 Lord Broghill defeats catholic forces under Lord Roche and Boetius MacEgan, bp of Ross, at Macroom, Co. Cork (MacEgan hanged, 11 May)

May 10 Clonmel surrenders to Cromwell, after tenacious defence by Hugh Duff O'Neill

May 26 Cromwell leaves Ire., Henry Ireton remaining as deputy

June 21 Ulster army under Bp MacMahon defeated by Coote at Scarrifhollis, near Letterkenny, Co. Donegal

July 2 Parliament approves Cromwell's action in appointing Ireton as his deputy, and appoints Edmund Ludlow and John Jones commrs for Ire. (John Weaver and Miles Corbet added later)

July 24 Carlow surrenders to Ireton

Aug. 6   Meeting of catholic bps at Jamestown, Co. Leitrim
   Waterford surrenders to Ireton

Aug. 12   Declaration of bps at Jamestown, repudiating Ormond

Aug. 14   Charlemont fort surrenders

Aug. 16   Charles II's declaration at Dunfermline repudiating 'the bloody Irish rebels'

Aug. 17   Duncannon surrenders

Sept. 15   Catholic bps excommunicate supporters of Ormond

Oct. 4   Parliament approves instructions to commrs for Ire.

Nov. 26   Assembly of catholic laity at Loughrea, Co. Galway

Dec. 6   Ormond appoints marquis of Clanricard his deputy

Dec. 11   Ormond leaves Ire. for France, accompanied by Inchiquin, Bellings, Daniel O'Neill, and others

Vindiciarum catholicorum Hiberniae libri duo, by 'Philopater Irenaeus' (John Callaghan) (Paris)

1651

Jan.   Corbet, Jones, and Weaver, parliamentary commrs, arrive in Ire.

Feb. 26   Stephen de Henin, ambassador of Charles, duke of Lorraine, arrives in Ire. to treat with confederates opposed to Ormond

May 1   Proclamation warning officers and soldiers not to marry catholics (extended to civil officers, 22 July 1653)

June 4   Ireton formally invests Limerick

June 18   Articles for surrender of Athlone castle

Sept. 3   Charles II defeated by Cromwell at Worcester

Oct. 9   Navigation act, providing that goods imported into England, Ire., and other lands belonging to commonwealth of England shall be carried in English ships only

Oct. 27   Limerick surrenders to Ireton (Bp O'Brien of Emly hanged, 31 Oct.)

Nov. 26   Ireton dies in Limerick

Dec. 2   Ludlow app. commander-in-chief by fellow commrs

1652

Apr. 12   Galway surrenders

May 12   Leinster army surrenders at Kilkenny

June 3   Samuel Winter app. provost of Trinity College, Dublin

June 22   Ross Castle, Co. Kerry, surrenders to Ludlow

June 28   Clanricard submits to Coote

June 30   Negotiations between England and Dutch republic broken off, leading to war

July 9   Parliament appoints Lt-general Charles Fleetwood to be commander-in-chief of forces in Ire., and to be a commr for civil affairs in Ire.

Aug. 12 Act for the settling of Ire., classifying opponents of parliament according to degree of guilt imputed to them, and setting out qualifications for treatment of those not excepted from pardon of life and estate

Aug. 24 Parliament approves instructions to commrs for Irish affairs

Sept. *c.* **10** Fleetwood lands at Waterford

Oct. High court established in Dublin

Gerard Boate's *Ireland's natural history* (London)

1653

Jan. 6 Parliamentary commrs' edict expelling from Ire. all catholic priests

Feb. 4 Capture of Sir Phelim O'Neill

Feb. 14 Articles for surrender of Inishbofin, off coast of Connemara

Mar. 2 Long Parliament votes that Ire. shall be represented by 30 members in new assembly of 460

Mar. 10 Sir Phelim O'Neill, convicted of high treason, executed in Dublin (see 4 Nov. 1641)

Apr. 20 Cromwell expels 'rump' of Long Parliament

Apr. 27 Philip MacHugh O'Reilly surrenders at Cloughoughter: last formal capitulation of war

May 23 Order for transplantation of Ulster presbyterians to Kilkenny, Tipperary, and Waterford

June 20 Drawing of lots for adventurers' lands begins in London

June 22 Order authorising 'gross survey', survey by inquisition ('civil survey'), and mapped survey ('down survey')

June 29 Commrs order commanders of districts to appoint days for hunting wolves; rewards: £6 for bitch, £5 for dog wolf

July 1 Overseers of precincts ordered to arrange for transporting vagrants to America

July 2 Council of state in England sends instructions to parliamentary commrs regarding transplantation of Irish (see 30 Nov. 1654): all those entitled to qualifications specified in act for settling of Ire. (1652) to remove to Connacht or Clare by 1 May 1654; commrs to be appointed to allot land to transplanted persons

July 4-Dec. 12 'Little' or 'Barebones' parliament, in which Ire. and Scotland are represented by 6 and 5 members respectively

Sept. 26 'Act of satisfaction', providing for allotment of land to adventurers and settlers, and reserving greater part of Connacht and Clare for transplanted Irish

Official date for end of rebellion in Ire.

Dec. 15 'Instrument of government', defining constitution of protectorate, accepted by Cromwell

Dec. 16 Cromwell becomes lord protector (proclaimed in Dublin, 30 Jan. 1654)

Piaras Feiritéir, poet, hanged at Killarney

John Punch's *D. Richardi Bellingi vindiciae eversae* (Paris)

1654

Jan. 6   Commrs app. to sit at Loughrea, Co. Galway, to allot land to transplanted Irish

Apr. 5   Treaty of London ends war with Dutch republic

Apr. 14   Order directing 'civil survey' to be undertaken

May 1   Date for completion of transplantation to Connacht (extended to 1 Mar. 1655)

May 31   Proclamation against catholic schoolmasters

June 27   Ordinance in favour of Munster protestants who went over to Cromwell in 1649

Aug. 22   Board of commrs for Irish affairs ordered to be dissolved

Aug. 27   Cromwell issues instructions to Fleetwood, styled as deputy, and to his council (Miles Corbet, Robert Goodwin, Robert Hammond, Richard Pepys, William Steele, Matthew Tomlinson)

Sept. 3   Meeting of first protectorate parliament, in which Ire. is represented by 30 members (dissolved, 22 Jan. 1655)

Nov. 30   All 'transplantable persons' (those in categories set out in act for settling of Ireland, 12 Aug. 1652) ordered to move by 1 Mar. 1655 (see 14 July 1655)

Dec. 11   William Petty appointed to map forfeited lands set apart for soldiers in 22 counties ('down survey')

Dec. 25   Henry Cromwell app. to Irish council

Dec. 28   Appointment of commrs to sit at Athlone to decide claims of transplanted Irish

1655

Jan. 3   Vincent Gookin's pamphlet, *The great case of transplantation in Ireland discussed* (London), points out disadvantages of general transplantation of catholic Irish

Jan. 26   Governor of Dublin ordered to ship to Barbados all catholic priests in his custody not found guilty of murder

Mar. 9   Richard Lawrence's *The interest of England in the Irish transplantation stated* (London), in answer to Gookin (see 3 Jan.)

Mar. 19   Courts martial appointed to try cases of failure to transplant, with power to inflict sentence of death

Apr. 3   Deputy and council pass orders on claims submitted under articles for surrender of Kilkenny

Apr. 8-11/18-21   Vaudois protestants massacred in Piedmont

Apr. 13   Proclamation prohibiting keeping of Easter

May 10-17   Jamaica seized from Spain by English force

June 16   Additional instructions to Loughrea commrs, laying down rules for allotment of land by baronies

July 9   Henry Cromwell arrives as major-general of army in Ire.

July 14   Orders defining 'transplantable persons' (see 30 Nov. 1654) as proprietors and soldiers

July 23   Deputy and council pass orders on claims under articles of Galway

Sept. 6   Fleetwood leaves Ire.

1656

Feb. 12   Proposals submitted to council for affairs of Ire. for allotment of specific baronies in Connacht and Clare to persons transplanted from particular counties

Sept. 17   Meeting of second protectorate parliament (dissolved, 4 Feb. 1658)

1657

Apr. 6/16   Edmund O'Reilly nominated catholic abp of Armagh (consecrated, 16/26 May 1658, in Brussels)

May 25   'Humble petition and advice', providing for new constitution for protectorate with increased powers for lord protector

June 9   'Act for the assuring, confirming and settling of lands and estates in Ireland'

June 26   'Act for convicting, discovering and repressing of popish recusants', requiring suspected catholics to take oath of abjuration, abjuring supremacy of pope and denying doctrine of transubstantiation, on pain of sequestration of two-thirds of their property

'Act for the attainder of the rebels in Ireland'

Sept. 23   Henry Cromwell, writing to Thurloe, regrets requirement from Irish catholics of oath of abjuration

Nov. 17   Henry Cromwell app. L.D. (L.L., 6 Oct. 1658)

Augustine Gibbon de Burgo becomes dean of theological faculty, University of Erfurt (see 1663)

1658

Apr. 23   Convention of ministers, summoned by Henry Cromwell, meets in Dublin

Sept. 3   Oliver Cromwell dies; succ. by Richard Cromwell as lord protector

1659

Jan. 27-Apr. 22   Third protectorate parliament

May 6   'Rump' of Long Parliament reassembles

May 24   Richard Cromwell resigns protectorate under pressure from parliament

June 7   Parliament resolves that administration of government of Ire. shall be by commrs nominated and authorised by parliament, and not by any one person; Henry Cromwell to be recalled; Robert Goodwin, John Jones and

William Steele nominated as commrs (Miles Corbet and Matthew Tomlinson added, 7 July)

June 27   Henry Cromwell leaves Ire.

July 7   Act confirming appointment of commrs and stating powers entrusted to them

Oct.   Edmund O'Reilly, catholic abp of Armagh, returns to Ire.

Dec. 14   Declaration by army officers headed by Sir Hardress Waller in support of restored parliament

1660

Jan.   Lord Broghill, Sir Charles Coote and Major William Bury app. commrs for government of Ire.

Feb. 3   General George Monck (later duke of Albemarle) enters London to restore representative parliament

Feb. 7   Opening meeting of convention in Dublin

Feb. 21   Monck orders readmission to parliament of excluded members

Mar. 16   Long Parliament dissolves itself

Apr. 4/14   Charles II makes declaration of Breda, promising pardon to those who opposed royalist cause, and liberty to tender consciences

Apr. 24   Convention issues order for poll tax (lists of taxpayers in *A census of Ireland* c. *1659*, ed. Séamus Pender, Dublin, 1939)

May 14   Charles II proclaimed kg in Dublin

May 29   Charles II makes formal entry into London

July 25   Lord Robartes app. L.D. (duke of Albemarle L.L.; neither assumes office)

Aug. 29   'An act of free and general pardon, indemnity, and oblivion' (12 Chas. II, c. 11 [Eng.]); section 25 states that act does not cover persons concerned in Irish rebellion

Sept. 13   Navigation act (12 Chas II, c. 18 [Eng.]), allowing trading rights to Ire., but not to Scotland

Nov. 30   Charles II makes declaration confirming Cromwellian soldiers and adventurers in ownership of lands in their possession and also providing for 'innocent papists' and those who have supported monarchy

Dec. 31   Sir Maurice Eustace, L.C., Roger Boyle, earl of Orrery (Lord Broghill), and Charles Coote, earl of Mountrath, sworn in as L.J.s

1661

Jan. 1   Peter Walsh, O.F.M., app. agent of catholic primate and other ecclesiastics

Jan. 18   John Bramhall app. abp of Armagh

Jan. 27   Consecration in St Patrick's cathedral, Dublin, of 2 abps and 10 bps (including Jeremy Taylor, bp of Down and Connor)

Feb. 19   Thirty-six commrs app. to give effect to Charles's declaration on land settlement

Apr. 25   Primate O'Reilly leaves Ire., having been recalled to Rome

May 8–July 31   First session of Charles II's Irish parliament

May 8   Patent for appointment of John Ogilby as master of the revels (see 1638)

Sept. 6–22 Mar. 1662   Second session of Charles II's Irish parliament

Nov. 6   H.C. in one-day session; cttee appointed to desire L.J.s to prepare and transmit bill for suppression of catholic hierarchy

Dec.   Group of catholics draw up 'remonstrance', declaring unqualified allegiance to kg, and disclaiming pope's authority to absolve them from such allegiance

Robert Boyle's *Sceptical chymist* (London)

Writing of 'Commentarius Rinuccinianus', by Richard O'Ferrall and Robert O'Connell, capuchins, begun (completed, 1666)

1662

Feb. 21   Duke of Ormond app. L.L.

Apr. 17–16 Apr. 1663   Third session of Charles II's Irish parliament

May 19   English act (14 Chas II, c. 18) making export of Irish wool a felony

July 27   Duke of Ormond sworn in as L.L.

July 31   Act of settlement (14 & 15 Chas II, c. 2), designed to give effect to Charles II's declaration of 30 Nov. 1660 and to resolve conflicting claims of Cromwellians and former proprietors

  Acts (14 & 15 Chas II, cc 8, 9) granting excise and customs to crown in perpetuity, including duties on imported spirits

Sept. 20   Opening of first court of claims (to hear claims under act of settlement)

Sept. 27   'Act for encouraging protestant strangers and others to inhabit and plant in the kingdom of Ireland' (14 & 15 Chas II, c. 13)

c. **mid Oct.**   John Ogilby opens new theatre in Smock Alley, Dublin

Dec. 20   Hearth-tax act (14 & 15 Chas II, c. 17)

  'Act for taking away the court of wards and livery, and tenures in capite and by knight's service' (14 & 15 Chas II, c. 19)

John Lynch's *Cambrensis eversus* (Saint-Malo)

Compilation by Richard Plunkett of 'Vocabularium Latinum et Hibernum' (earliest known Irish-Latin dictionary)

1663

Jan. 1   Franciscan chapel in Cook Street, Dublin, raided by military

May 21   Failure of Col. Thomas Blood's plot to seize Dublin castle in support of claims of Cromwellian soldiers

  Parliament prorogued

May 26   Charles II directs L.L. to enclose Phoenix Park with a stone wall and to stock it with deer

July 27   English 'act for the encouragement of trade' (15 Chas II, c. 7) restricts Irish trade with colonies and importation of Irish cattle into England

Aug. 20   James Margetson, abp of Dublin, app. abp of Armagh

Aug. 21   Closure of first court of claims, after issuing 566 decrees of innocence to catholics, but leaving many claims unheard

Augustin Gibbon de Burgo's ecumenical work, *De Luthero-Calvinismo, schismatico quidem sed reconciliabile* (Erfurt; see 1657)

1664

Aug. 1/11   John Lisle, regicide, shot dead at Lausanne by James Cotter and other Irish agents of crown

John Lynch's *Alithinologia* (Saint-Malo)

Sir James Ware's *Rerum Hibernicarum annales 1485–1558* (Dublin)

1665

Feb. 22   England declares war on Dutch republic

May–Sept.   Plague in London

Oct. 26–7 Aug. 1666   Fourth session of Charles II's Irish parliament

Dec. 23   Act of explanation (17 & 18 Chas II, c. 2), providing that, with specified exceptions, Cromwellians should give up one-third of their holdings to make land available for restoration to catholics

Sir James Ware's *De praesulibus Hiberniae commentarius* (Dublin)

1666

Jan. 4   Opening session of second court of claims

Jan.   France declares war on England

May   Mutiny of Carrickfergus garrison

June 11–25   Meeting of catholic bps and clergy in Dublin to consider acceptance of 'remonstrance' (see Dec. 1661); modified version adopted, pledging allegiance to kg, but not specifically referring to pope's authority; it is rejected by Ormond

June 18   Act of uniformity (17 & 18 Chas II, c. 6) prescribing revised Book of Common Prayer, requiring episcopal ordination of clergy, and prohibiting schoolmasters from teaching without licence from bp of established church

June 25   Proclamation offering £20 for arrest or head of Dudley Costello, Edmund Nangle, and other tories

Aug. 7   Charles II's Irish parliament dissolved

Sept. 3   Start of great fire of London

1667

Jan. 18   English act (18 Chas II, c. 2) prohibiting importation into England of cattle from Ire.

June 12–13   Dutch fleet in River Medway

July 11/21   Treaty of Breda, ending hostilities with French and Dutch

Aug. 8   Charter incorporating College of Physicians in Dublin (see 15 Dec. 1692)

Aug. 30   Earl of Clarendon, L.C. of England, dismissed

1668

The narrative of the sale and settlement of Ireland, attributed to Nicholas French, catholic bp of Ferns, published (Louvain)

1669

Jan. 2   Last sitting of second court of claims

Feb. 14   Charles II declares his intention to remove Ormond from office of L.L. (see 18 Sept.)

Mar. 26   Royal charter empowering Erasmus Smith to erect grammar schools

Apr. 29/May 9   Peter Talbot consecrated catholic abp of Dublin (in Antwerp)

May-Aug.   George Fox tours Ire., organising quaker meetings

Sept. 18   Lord Robartes sworn in as L.L. (see 21 Apr. 1670)

Nov. 21/Dec. 1   Oliver Plunkett consecrated catholic abp of Armagh (in Ghent)

1670

Apr. 21   Lord Berkeley sworn in as L.L.

May 22   Secret treaty of Dover, in which Charles II undertakes to declare himself a catholic in return for French subsidy

June 17   Synod of catholic bps meets in Dublin

Aug. 15   Charter incorporating guild of St Luke the Evangelist (cutlers, painter-stainers, and stationers)

Dec. 26   Galleries in Smock Alley theatre, Dublin, collapse during performance attended by L.L.

1671

Jan. 18   Richard Talbot presents petition to Charles II on behalf of catholic nobility and gentry

Jan.   Murder of An Dubhaltach Mac Fir Bhisigh, historian

Mar. 13   Both houses of English parliament present address to kg against growth of popery, referring to 'insolencies of the papists in Ireland'

Apr. 22   Navigation act (23 Chas II, c. 26 [Eng.]), prohibiting direct imports from colonies to Irish ports

June 10   Charles II grants permission to Sir George Hamilton to raise regiment for service in France

Aug. 1   Commn to examine land settlement, headed by Prince Rupert

Aug. 4   Viscount Ranelagh's 'undertaking' to manage Irish revenues of crown

Aug. 27/Sept. 6   John Brenan consecrated in Rome as catholic bp of Waterford (app. abp of Cashel, 19/29 Jan. 1677)

Dec. 5   Royal charter granted to King's Hospital, Dublin ('Bluecoat school')

1672

Feb. 25/Mar. 6   John O'Molony consecrated catholic bp of Killaloe (in Paris)

Mar. 15   Charles II issues declaration of indulgence, announcing intention to suspend penal laws against nonconformists and recusants

Mar. 17   England declares war on Dutch republic

Aug. 5   Earl of Essex sworn in as L.L.

Sept. 24   New rules for corporations, requiring elected representatives to take oath of supremacy (L.L. empowered to exempt individuals)

c. **Oct.**   First grant of *regium donum* to presbyterian ministers

John Lynch's 'De praesulibus Hiberniae' written (published, Dublin, 1944)

Sir William Petty's 'Political anatomy of Ireland' written (published, Dublin, 1691)

1673

Jan. 17   Second commn to Prince Rupert to examine land settlement

Feb. 10   English H.C. declares declaration of indulgence (see 15 Mar. 1672) illegal (declaration withdrawn by kg, 7 Mar.)

Mar. 25   English H.C. demands recall of Prince Rupert's commn

Mar. 29   Test act (25 Chas II, c. 2 [Eng.]), requiring office-holders to take sacrament according to usage of Church of England (see 4 Mar. 1704)

Sept. 30   James, duke of York (later James II), marries, as second wife, Mary of Modena

Oct. 27   Proclamation for banishment of catholic bps and regular priests, and closure of religious houses and schools

Nov.   Jesuit schools in Drogheda closed

1674

Feb. 9   Peace of Westminster, ending war with Dutch republic

Peter Walsh's *History and vindication of the loyal formulary or Irish remonstrance* (N.P.)

1675

Sept. 22   Charles II orders commn to be set up to determine cases of Connacht transplanters

1676

Feb. 16/26   Charles II concludes secret treaty with Louis XIV promising, in return for subsidy, to enter into no engagement with any other power without consent of France

Francis Molloy's *Lucerna fidelium; Lóchrann na gcreidmheach* (Rome)

1677

Aug. 24   Ormond again sworn in as L.L.

Nov. 4   Marriage in London of William of Orange and Mary, elder daughter of duke of York

Francis Molloy's *Grammatica Latino-Hibernica* (Rome)

1678

July 31/Aug. 10   Treaty of Nijmegen between France and Dutch republic

Sept. 28   Titus Oates appears before English privy council and makes statement on 'popish plot'

Oct. 8   Order for arrest of Abp Peter Talbot

Oct. 16   Further proclamation for banishment of catholic bps and regular priests, and closure of religious houses and schools (see 27 Oct. 1673)

1679

Feb. 27   Michael Boyle, abp of Dublin, app. abp of Armagh

May 15   Exclusion bill introduced into English H.C., barring duke of York, as a catholic, from succession to crown

June 22   Scots covenanters defeated at Bothwell Brig

Dec. 6   Abp Plunkett arrested

1680

Apr. 29   Laying of first stone of Royal Hospital, Kilmainham (for retired soldiers); architect William Robinson (opened, 25 Mar. 1684)

July 23-4   Trial of Abp Plunkett at Dundalk; ends without indictment

Nov. 15   Peter Talbot dies in Dublin castle

Thomas Dineley's tour of Ire.

Edmund Borlase's *History of the execrable Irish rebellion* (Dublin)

1681

Jan. 4   English H.L. finds that there was catholic plot in Ire. to massacre English and subvert protestantism

Jan. 18   English navigation act of 22 Apr. 1671 expires, allowing resumption of shipping direct from colonies to Ire.

Apr. 25   Death of Redmond O'Hanlon, leading tory of Co. Armagh

May 3   Plunkett arraigned for high treason before court of king's bench in London

July 1   Abp Oliver Plunkett executed (see 23 May 1920, 12 Oct. 1975)

July 7/17-Sept. 2/12   Turks besiege Vienna, without success

1682

Apr.   Construction begins of Long Bridge, with 21 arches, over Lagan at Belfast (completed, *c.* 1688; demolished, 1841)

Convent of Irish Benedictine nuns established at Ypres (see 2 Feb. 1688)

1683

June 23-4   Rye House plot to assassinate Charles II

Nov.   Beginning of severe frost throughout Ire. lasting until following March

1684

Jan.   William Molyneux establishes Dublin Philosophical Society

Feb. 18   'Court of grace' appointed to inquire into land-titles

Roderick O'Flaherty's 'Chorographical description of West or h-Iar Connaught' written (published, Dublin, 1846)

1685

Feb. 6   Charles II dies; succ. by James II

Mar. 7   Regiments given to Richard Talbot and Justin MacCarthy (catholics exempt from oath of supremacy)

Mar. 20   Ormond leaves Ire. on termination of viceroyalty; Primate Michael Boyle and earl of Granard L.J.s

May   Roderick O'Flaherty's *Ogygia* (London)

Sir William Petty's *Hiberniae delineatio* (London)

June 20   Richard Talbot created earl of Tyrconnell

July 2   English act (1 Jas II, c. 17) renewing prohibition on direct shipping from colonies to Ire.

July 6   Duke of Monmouth defeated by royal army at Sedgemoor

Aug.   Supposedly first number of Dublin *News-letter* published

Oct. 8/18   Revocation of edict of Nantes

1686

Jan. 9   Second earl of Clarendon sworn in as L.L.

Feb.   *Leabhuir na sein-tiomna*, Irish translation of Old Testament sponsored by Bp Bedell (see 1629), published at expense of Robert Boyle (London)

First known advertisement for music printed in Ire. published in Dublin *News-letter*

Mar. 22   Royal warrant for payments to catholic abps and bps

Apr. 16   Primate Boyle replaced as L.C. by Sir Charles Porter (three catholic judges app., 20-24 Apr.)

June 5   Tyrconnell returns from England to command Irish army

July 7/17   League of Augsburg formed to resist Louis XIV

Aug. 26   Tyrconnell goes back to England with catholic lawyer, Richard Nagle

Oct. 26   'Coventry letter', addressed to Tyrconnell by Nagle, attacks land settlement

1687

Feb. 6   Earl of Tyrconnell returns to Dublin (sworn in as L.D., 12 Feb.)

Feb. 10   Barbers, surgeons, and apothecaries reincorporated by charter

Feb. 12   Porter replaced as L.C. by catholic Sir Alexander Fitton (created Lord Gawsworth by James II, 1 May 1689)

Feb. 24   Warrant to pay Capuchins £30 a year to cover rent for their Dublin house

June 7   Royal warrant to L.D., empowering him to issue new charters to cities and corporate towns

Aug.   Tyrconnell meets kg at Chester to discuss future legislation

Dec.   Serious flooding in Dublin, a coach and horses being swept away when crossing Essex Bridge

'Lillibullero', song satirising Tyrconnell's administration, written by Thomas Wharton

1688

Feb. 2   House of Benedictine nuns from Ypres consecrated in Sheep Street, Dublin (see 1682)

Mar. 17   Two judges set out for London with proposals for altering land settlement

May 7/17   Papal provision of Gregory Fallon to see of Clonmacnoise, on nomination of James II

June 10   Birth to James II's wife, Mary of Modena, of son, James (later known as the Old Pretender)

June 18   Royal warrant that appointments of masters of schools should be given to Jesuits

June 30   Acquittal in London of 'seven bishops'

   Leading whigs and tories invite William of Orange to invade England

July 21   James, 1st duke of Ormond, dies; succ. as 2nd duke by his grandson, James

Oct.   Irish regiments sent to England

Nov. 5   William of Orange lands at Torbay, Devon

Nov. 16/26   Louis XIV declares war on Dutch republic

Dec. 7   Shutting of gates of Derry against earl of Antrim's regiment

Dec. 11   James II flees from London (but is seized and brought back)

Dec. 23   James II leaves England for France

1689

Jan. 4   Protestant association in Sligo declares support for English revolution

Jan. 8   Richard Hamilton, sent by William of Orange to negotiate Tyrconnell's submission, arrives in Dublin and joins Tyrconnell

Jan.   Pointis, French naval officer, arrives in Dublin to report on Jacobite prospects and feasibility of French support

Feb. 13   William of Orange and his wife, Mary, elder daughter of James II by his first marriage, having accepted bill of rights, become joint monarchs of England and Ire.

Feb. 22   William III's declaration calling on Irish Jacobites to submit by 10 Apr.

Feb. 25   Protestants of Bandon, Co. Cork, attack Jacobite garrison (town reduced and fine imposed by Justin MacCarthy, 2 Mar.)

Mar. 12   James II lands at Kinsale, accompanied by French ambassador, Comte d'Avaux, and Jacobite and French officers

Mar. 14   Richard Hamilton routs Ulster protestants under earl of Mountalexander at 'break of Dromore', Co. Down

Mar. 21   Captain James Hamilton arrives at Derry with arms, ammunition, £1,000 and commission for Col. Robert Lundy, commander of garrison

Mar. 25   James II holds council in Dublin, calling parliament for 7 May

Apr. 15   Engagement at Clady on River Finn between Jacobites under Richard Hamilton and protestants based on Derry

Apr. 18   James refused entry to Derry; siege begins

May 1   Engagement in Bantry Bay, Co. Cork, between English and French fleets

May 2/12   Treaty of Vienna between Emperor Leopold and William as stadholder of the United Provinces

May 7   Enniskillen protestants defeat Jacobite forces at Belleek

May 7-July 18   James II's Irish parliament

May 7/17   England declares war on France

May 10   Introduction into H.C. of bill for repeal of restoration land settlement

May 15   Introduction into H.C. of bill for repeal of Poynings' law (dropped on account of James's opposition)

June 13   Williamite force, sent to relieve Derry, arrives in Lough Foyle

June 18   James's proclamation providing for circulation of 'brass money'

June 22   Act for repeal of land settlement

June 30   Proclamation by Conrad von Rosen, French general, threatening to drive rural protestants before walls of Derry

July 25   William King, dean of St Patrick's cathedral, Dublin, imprisoned in Dublin castle

July 27   Jacobite army under Viscount Dundee defeats Williamite army at Killiecrankie (but Dundee's death leads to collapse of Jacobite cause in Scotland)

July 28   Williamite ships break boom on River Foyle and bring relief to Derry

July 31   Jacobite forces under Richard Hamilton and von Rosen lift siege of Derry

Jacobite force under Justin MacCarthy defeated by Enniskilleners at Newtownbutler, Co. Fermanagh

Aug. 13   Williamite force under Marshal Schomberg lands in Bangor Bay, Co. Down

Aug. 28   Carrickfergus surrenders to Schomberg

Sept. 6   Trinity College, Dublin, occupied by Jacobite soldiers (library preserved through efforts of Rev. Michael Moore, catholic priest app. provost by James II on recommendation of catholic bps)

Sept. 21   James advances to Dundalk; his challenge declined by Schomberg

Sept. 27   Christ Church cathedral, Dublin, seized by Jacobite authorities and handed over to catholic church

Sept.-Oct.   Schomberg's army camps near Dundalk, suffering heavy losses from exposure and sickness

Nov.   James returns to Dublin; Schomberg retires to Lisburn

Sir Richard Cox's *Hibernia Anglicana*, pt 1 (London; pt 2, Feb. 1690; 2nd ed. 1692)

George Walker's *True account of the siege of Londonderry* (London)

1690

Mar. 12   French regiments under comte de Lauzun land at Cork

Mar. 13   Danish force, hired by William III, arrives in Belfast Lough

Apr. 18   Irish regiments under Justin MacCarthy, Viscount Mountcashel, leave Cork for France

May 14   Charlemont surrenders to Schomberg

June 14   William III lands near Carrickfergus

June 19   William orders *regium donum* to presbyterian ministers to be increased to £1,200 yearly (see *c*. Oct. 1672)

June 30   French defeat combined English and Dutch fleets off Beachy Head

July 1   William's army defeats James's at River Boyne

July 4   James sails from Kinsale for France

July 6   William enters Dublin

July 7   William issues declaration at Finglas, Co. Dublin, demanding unconditional surrender of Jacobites

July 17-24   Williamite force under Lt-general James Douglas besieges Athlone without success

Aug. 9-30   William lays siege to Limerick without success

Aug. 11   Jacobite force under Patrick Sarsfield destroys Williamite baggage train containing guns and ammunition at Ballyneety, near Limerick

Sept. 5   William leaves Ire. and returns to England

Sept. *c*. 12   Tyrconnell and French army sail from Galway for France

Sept. 15   Viscount Sidney and Thomas Coningsby sworn in as L.J.s (Sir Charles Porter sworn in, 24 Dec.)

Sept. 23   Earl of Marlborough lands at Passage West, near Cork

Sept. 28   Cork surrenders to Marlborough

Oct. 7   Earthquake experienced in Leinster

Oct. 15   Kinsale surrenders to Marlborough

Nov.   Williamite courts established in Dublin; outlawry proceedings against Jacobites begin

John Mackenzie's *Narrative of the siege of Londonderry* (London)

1691

Jan. 5   William III gives pledge to English parliament not to make grants of forfeited estates in Ire. until that parliament has opportunity of settling matter

Jan. 14   Tyrconnell returns to Ire., landing at Limerick

Jan. 25   William King consecrated bp of Derry

Apr. 7   Patent granted to Nicholas Dupin conferring sole right to manufacture white paper in Ire. for 14 years (mill opened, probably at Rathfarnham near Dublin, by early 1693)

May 9   Marquis de Saint-Ruth, French general, lands at Limerick

June 21-30   William III's Dutch general, Baron von Ginkel, besieges and takes Athlone

c. **June**   George Story's *A true and impartial history of the last two years* (London)

July 9   Ginkel issues proclamation (dated 7 July 1691) offering pardon and security of property to Jacobite officers bringing over troops or surrendering garrisons, and to citizens of Galway and Limerick who procure surrender of those towns

July 12   Jacobite army defeated by Ginkel at Aughrim, Co. Galway; thousands killed, including Saint-Ruth, Jacobite commander-in-chief

July 21   Galway surrenders on terms to Ginkel

Aug. 14   Tyrconnell dies in Limerick

Aug. 25   Ginkel begins second siege of Limerick

Sept. 14   Surrender of Sligo to Williamites

Sept. 24   Truce in siege of Limerick (formal treaty negotiations begin, 26 Sept.)

Oct. 3   Treaty of Limerick signed in form of 2 sets of articles: (1) military, allowing Irish army to go to France and continue fighting in James's service; (2) civil, promising catholics of Ire. the religious privileges enjoyed in Charles II's reign, or as are consistent with the laws; offering them hopes of further concessions; and guaranteeing to those holding out to the end security of property and professional rights

EIGHTEENTH-CENTURY IRELAND
1691–1800

INTRODUCTION

THE newer sources for chronology that we characterised in our introduction to the preceding period (above, p. 195) become fully developed in the eighteenth century. Newspapers, directories, and other periodical publications now provide a standard frame of reference, supplementing records, public and private, printed and manuscript. Parliament, in becoming a continuous institution, meeting at regular intervals, becomes a major producer of historical evidence both in its debates and its legislation.

Till the last decade of this century Ireland experienced an unprecedented era of unbroken peace, which is reflected in economic and social growth and in the arts. The chronology exemplifies these developments, as in the numerous references to the founding of social, charitable, and cultural institutions, the erection of public buildings, and the opening of canals.

The century witnessed the adoption in Britain and Ireland of the Gregorian calendar (see above, pp. 2–3), so that from 1752 onwards the distinction between New and Old Style dating disappears from our chronology.

CHRONOLOGY, 1691–1800

T. W. MOODY, J. G. SIMMS, AND C. J. WOODS

1691

Oct. 20   French fleet arrives in Shannon estuary

Dec. 22   Sarsfield sails for France with last contingent of Jacobite soldiers

Dec. 24   English act (3 Will. & Mary, c. 2) substitutes new oath and anti-catholic declaration for oath of supremacy: catholics effectively barred from membership of parliament and other public positions in Ire.

William King's *State of the protestants in Ireland under the late King James's government* (London)

Sir William Petty's *Political anatomy of Ireland* (London)

1692

Feb. 13   Massacre of Glencoe Macdonalds on pretext that they have not taken oath of allegiance to William III

Apr. 6   Privy council begins hearing claims under articles of Limerick

May 19-24/May 29-June 3   French fleet defeated at La Hogue

June c. 14/24   1,400 Irish soldiers under Bryan Magennis, Viscount Iveagh, enter Imperial service

July 24/Aug. 3   Irish Jacobite regiments take part in French defeat of William at Steenkirk

Sept. 4   Viscount Sidney sworn in as L.L.

Oct. 5   Opening of William III's first Irish parliament

Oct. 27-8   H.C. claims 'sole right' to prepare money bills, and rejects government's corn bill

Nov. 3   'Act for encouragement of protestant strangers to settle in this kingdom of Ireland' (4 Will. & Mary, c. 2), allowing them to worship in the form to which they have been accustomed

Sidney rebukes H.C. and prorogues parliament (dissolved, 26 June 1693)

Dec. 15   College of Physicians in Dublin reincorporated by charter as King and Queen's College of Physicians (name changed to Royal College of Physicians of Ireland, 1890)

Anthony Dopping, bp of Meath's *Modus tenendi parliamenta in Hibernia* (Dublin)

1693

Mar. 9   English H.C. presents address to William III, complaining of mismanagement of affairs in Ire.

June 13   Sidney recalled

July 19/29   Sarsfield mortally wounded at battle of Landen (Neerwinden)

July 28   Lord Capel, Sir Cyril Wyche, and William Duncombe sworn in as L.J.s

1694

Jan. 9   Henry Purcell's ode 'Great parent, hail!' and John Blow's anthem 'I beheld, and lo!' performed in Christ Church cathedral, Dublin, in honour of centenary of Trinity College

Dec. 3   English triennial act (6 & 7 Will. & Mary, c. 2) fixes maximum duration of parliament in England at 3 years (see 7 May 1716)

Dec. 28   Mary II dies

1695

Scotland experiences first of series of cold and wet summers followed by early frosts ('seven ill years'), resulting in ruined crops and stunted animals and in massive emigration to Ulster

May 27   Lord Capel sworn in as L.D.

Aug. 27 Opening of William III's second Irish parliament

Sept. 7 Act (7 Will. III, c. 4) forbids catholics to send their children abroad for education or to 'teach school' in Ire.

Act (7 Will. III, c. 5) forbids catholics to keep arms, or horses valued at £5 or more

Sept. 9 H.C. appoints committee to examine accounts and papers relating to revenue

Dec. 7 Act (7 Will. III, c. 21) for suppressing tories, robbers, and rapparees: local catholics to pay collectively for crimes of catholics, protestants for crimes of protestants (amended by 9 Will. III, c. 9)

Dec. 14 Parliament adjourns

1696

Feb. 15 Jacobite plot to assassinate William III foiled

Apr. 27 English act (7 & 8 Will. III, c. 39) 'for encouraging the linen manufacture of Ireland', permits import of plain Irish linen into England free of duty

May 30 Lord Capel, L.D., dies

John Toland's *Christianity not mysterious* (London) (see 11 Sept. 1697)

Dáibhídh Ó Duibhgeanáin, Irish scribe, dies

1697

Apr. 5 First of series of bills introduced in English H.C. for banning export of Irish woollen goods

May 31 Charles Powlett, marquis of Winchester (succeeds as duke of Bolton, 27 Feb. 1699), and Henri de Ruvigny, earl of Galway, sworn in as L.J.s

July 27 Reassembly of William III's second Irish parliament (prorogued, 3 Dec.)

Sept. 10-11/20-21 Treaties of Ryswick between France and England, Holland and Spain

Sept. 11 Toland's *Christianity not mysterious* burned in Dublin by order of H.C.

Sept. 25 Banishment act (9 Will. III, c. 1) requires catholic bps, vicars general, deans and regular clergy to leave Ire. by 1 May 1698

Act (9 Will. III, c. 2), confirming articles of Limerick (7 bps and 7 lay lords having protested (23 Sept.) that act is not in conformity with articles)

Oct. 20/30 Emperor Leopold I concludes treaty with Louis XIV

Oct. 27 Adjudication of claims under articles of Limerick and Galway begins before judges (ends, 1 Sept. 1699)

Nov. 27 H.L. rejects bill 'for security of king's person' on ground that it obliges catholics to take oath contrary to their conscience (three abps and eleven lay lords protest against rejection)

Dec. 3 Act (9 Will. III, c. 17) for erection of street lamps in Dublin

1698

Jan.   Dáibhídh Ó Bruadair, Irish poet, dies

Apr.   William Molyneux's tract, *The case of Ireland's being bound by acts of parliament in England stated* (Dublin)

May 24   English H.L. denies appellate jurisdiction of Irish H.L. in case of bp of Derry *v.* Irish Society of London

June 1-3   General synod of Ulster meeting at Antrim pronounces subscription to Westminster confession of faith to be necessary qualification for entry to ministry

June 9   Daniel Roseingrave appointed organist to St Patrick's cathedral, Dublin (to Christ Church also, 11 Nov.)

June 27   English H.C. resolves that Molyneux's tract 'is of dangerous consequence to the crown and people of England'

July 1   English H.C. presents address to William requesting him to discourage woollen manufacture in Ire. and encourage linen

Dec.   First public performance of George Farquhar's 'Love and a bottle', at Drury Lane theatre, London (first public performance of 'The twin rivals' there, 14 Dec. 1702; of 'The beaux' stratagem', at Queen's theatre, London, 8 Mar. 1707)

1699

Jan. 26   Last meeting of William III's second Irish parliament (dissolved, 14 June 1699)

Act (10 Will. III, c. 5) imposes duties on woollens exported from Ire.

Act (10 Will. III, c. 6), encouraging building of parsonages by providing for proportional contributions from succeeding incumbents

Act (10 Will. III, c. 12) imposes obligation on landowners and leaseholders to plant and preserve trees

'An act to prevent papists being solicitors' (10 Will. III, c. 13)

Feb. 1   English act (10 Will. III, c. 1) directs that foreign troops in Ire. should be disbanded and limits royal army to 12,000

May 4   English act of supply (10 & 11 Will. III, c. 9); sect. 94, 'tacked' to act, provides for appointment of commissioners of inquiry into administration of forfeited estates in Ire.

English act (10 & 11 Will. III, c. 10) prohibits export of Irish woollens to lands other than England

c. **late July-early Aug.**   Edward Lhuyd, Welsh antiquary, begins tour of Ire. (lasting altogether nine months)

1700

Feb. 14   Warrant to L.J.s to pay subsidy to Louis Crommelin 'for establishing a linen manufacture in Ireland'

Apr. 11   English act (11 & 12 Will. III, c. 2) for resumption of William's grants of forfeited estates in Ire.; trustees appointed to sell estates

July 10   Thomas Burgh app. surveyor general

Oct. 21/Nov. 1   Charles II of Spain dies

1701

July 1   Unveiling of Grinling Gibbons's equestrian statue of William III in College Green, Dublin, erected at expense of Dublin corporation

Aug. 27/Sept. 7   'Grand alliance' between England, Dutch republic, and Emperor against France

Sept. 6/17   James II dies at St Germains (Louis XIV recognises his son as James III)

Sept. 18   Earl of Rochester sworn in as L.L.

Building of Abp Marsh's library, Dublin, first public library in Ire.; architect Sir William Robinson

1702

Jan. 20-21/Jan. 31-Feb. 1   Regiments of Dillon and Burke take part in French defence of Cremona against Prince Eugene of Savoy

Mar. 8   William III dies; succ. by Anne

May 4/15   England, Dutch republic, and Emperor declare war on France (war of Spanish succession, 1702-13)

1703

Feb. 18   Abp Marsh translated from Dublin to Armagh

Feb. 27   English act (1 Anne, stat. 2, c. 17) requires office-holders, lawyers, and schoolmasters in Ire. to take oath of abjuration (declaring Anne to be rightful sovereign and disclaiming pretender)

Mar. 11   William King app. abp of Dublin

c. Apr.   Henry Maxwell's *Essay towards an union of Ireland with England* (anon., London)

June 4   Second duke of Ormond sworn in as L.L.

June 24   Last day allowed for trustees' sale of forfeited estates (see 1 Apr. 1700)

Sept. 21-Mar. 4 1704   First session of Anne's first Irish parliament

Oct. 20   H.C. makes representations to queen calling for 'a full enjoyment of our constitution, or . . . a more firm and strict union with your majesty's subjects of England'

William Viner app. master of state music (d. 1716)

1704

Mar. 4   'Act to prevent the further growth of popery' (2 Anne, c. 6) prohibits catholics from buying land or acting as guardians, and imposes other restrictions; sect. 17 imposes a sacramental test for public office, applicable equally to protestant dissenters

Registration act (2 Anne, c. 7) requires catholic clergy to register with clerks of peace at next quarter sessions

Dublin workhouse act (2 Anne, c. 19) provides for erection of workhouse in Dublin for employing and maintaining poor

Aug. 2/13   Duke of Marlborough defeats French at Blenheim

Dec. 9   English act (3 & 4 Anne, c. i) settling dispute between Irish Society of London and bp of Derry over fisheries in Foyle and Bann

1705

Feb. 10-June 16   Second session of Anne's first Irish parliament

Mar. 14   English act (3 & 4 Anne, c. 8) permits export of Irish linen to American colonies

1706

May 12/23   Marlborough defeats French at Ramillies

Tadhg Ó Rodaighe, Irish scholar, dies

John O'Heyn's *Epilogus chronologicus* (Louvain); history of Irish Dominicans

Tailors' Hall, Back Lane, Dublin, built

1707

Apr. 14/25   Duke of Berwick, commanding French and Irish troops, defeats earl of Galway at Almanza, south-east Spain

May 1   Union of English and Scottish parliaments comes into effect

c. **May**   Edward Lhuyd's *Archaeologia Britannica* (Oxford)

June 24   Earl of Pembroke sworn in as L.L.

July 1-Oct. 30   Third session of Anne's first Irish parliament

Oct. 24   Act (6 Anne, c. 2) establishes registry of deeds (opens, 25 Mar. 1708)

Act (6 Anne, c. 20) establishes Dublin ballast office, to control port, harbour, and river

Oct. 30   Act (6 Anne, c. 19) regulates Abp Marsh's library (see 1701)

1708

Mar. 13   Failure of Jacobite attempt to land in Scotland

Apr. 25   Belfast castle destroyed by fire

June 30/July 11   Marlborough defeats French at Oudenarde

1709

Apr. 21   Earl of Wharton sworn in as L.L.

May 5-Aug. 30   Fourth session of Anne's first Irish parliament

May 9   H.L. presents address to L.L. expressing hope that Irish union with England will follow Scottish union

Aug. 30   Amending act (8 Anne, c. 3), strengthens provisions of 2 Anne, c. 6: registered priests required to take oath of abjuration

'Act for the better payment of inland bills of exchange and for making promissory notes more obligatory' (8 Anne, c. 11); first Irish banking act

Aug. 31/Sept. 11   Marlborough's 'pyrrhic victory' over French at Malplaquet

Sept. 4-8   Nearly 800 Palatine families arrive in Dublin to settle in Ire.

c. **Dec.**   Hougher disturbances in Connacht begin

George Berkeley's *An essay towards a new theory of vision* (Dublin)

1710

May 19-Aug. 28   Fifth session of Anne's first Irish parliament

June 14   Board of Trinity College, Dublin, assigns ground for erection of medical school (building completed, 16 Aug. 1711)

Aug. 9   Tory administration in G.B., headed by Robert Harley

Aug. 28   Act (9 Anne, c. 3) establishes board of trustees for linen manufacture

Act to prevent maiming of cattle (9 Anne, c. 11) provides for compensation to be levied collectively on parts of Co. Galway where houghing prevalent

1711

Jan. 22   Sir Constantine Phipps app. L.C.

Feb. 17   Queen Anne's bounty (first fruits and twentieth parts) granted to Church of Ireland

Apr. 15   Fire destroys surveyor-general's office in Essex Street, Dublin, and much of the collection of state papers kept there

July 3   Second duke of Ormond again sworn in as L.L.

July 9-Nov. 9   Sixth session of Anne's first Irish parliament

Aug. 16   Building for Trinity College medical school completed

Oct. 10   First meeting of linen board

Nov. 9   Last meeting of Anne's first Irish parliament (dissolved, 6 May 1713)

Nov. 27   Jonathan Swift's *Conduct of the allies* (London)

1712

Jan. 1   Ormond app. commander-in-chief, replacing Marlborough

May 12   Laying of foundation stone of library of Trinity College, Dublin (library completed 1732; architect Thomas Burgh)

Nov. 4   Riot in Dublin theatre at performance of Nicholas Rowe's 'Tamerlane' on William III's birthday

John Richardson's *A proposal for the conversion of the popish natives of Ireland* (London); advocates use of Irish language

1713

Mar. 31/Apr. 11   Treaty of Utrecht, ending war of Spanish succession

May 23   Edward Tyrrell, 'priest-hunter', executed 'for having several wives'

June 13   Jonathan Swift installed as dean of St Patrick's cathedral, Dublin

Oct.   James Kirkpatrick's *Historical essay upon the loyalty of presbyterians* (anon., N.P.)

Oct. 27   Duke of Shrewsbury sworn in as L.L.

Nov. 25-Dec. 24   Session of Anne's second Irish parliament

1714

Jan. 4   Parliament prorogued (dissolved by death of queen, 1 Aug.)

June 5   Shrewsbury, L.L., leaves Ire.

June 7   Thomas Lindsay, abp of Armagh, Sir Constantine Phipps, L.C., and John Vesey, abp of Tuam, sworn in as L.J.s

July 27   Robert Harley, earl of Oxford, dismissed from office of lord treasurer of England (succ. by Shrewsbury, 30 July)

Aug. 1   Anne dies; succ. by George I

Sept. 9   Abp King and earl of Kildare sworn in as L.J.s, *vice* Lindsay and Phipps, removed

Oct. 11   Alan Brodrick (created Lord Midleton, 13 Apr. 1715) app. L.C., *vice* Phipps removed

1715

Feb. 1   First number of Cork *Idler*, first Irish newspaper published outside Dublin

June 21   British H.C. resolves to impeach Ormond of high treason

July 27/Aug. 7   Ormond arrives in Paris to join James III, the Old Pretender (see 6/17 Sept. 1701)

Aug. 20   British act (1 Geo. I, stat. 2, c. 17) for attainder of Ormond 'unless he shall render himself to justice' (see 20 June 1716)

Aug. 21/Sept. 1   Louis XIV dies; succ. by Louis XV

Sept. 6   Earl of Mar raises Jacobite standard at Braemar, Aberdeenshire; start of 1715 rising

Nov. 12   Opening of George I's Irish parliament (dissolved by death of kg, 11 June 1727)

William Conolly elected speaker of H.C.

Nov. 13   Jacobites checked at Sheriffmuir, near Stirling

Nov. 14   Jacobite force capitulates at Preston, Lancs.

Dec. 22   Pretender lands in Scotland

1716

Feb. 4   Pretender and Mar leave Scotland for France

May 7   Septennial act (1 Geo. I, stat. 2, c. 38 [G.B.]) increases maximum duration of parliament in G.B. from three years to seven (see 18 Aug. 1911)

June 20   Act (2 Geo. I, c. 8) confiscating Ormond estates and abolishing Tipperary palatinate (see 20 Aug. 1715, 24 June 1721)

Drainage and navigation act (2 Geo. I, c. 12) authorises drainage schemes for making Shannon navigable

Nov. 12   Johann Sigismund Kusser (Cousser) app. master of state music (d. 1727)

Nov. 17/28   Dual alliance between G.B. and France (converted into triple alliance by accession of Dutch republic, 24 Dec. 1716/4 Jan. 1717)

1717

Aug. 7   Duke of Bolton sworn in as L.L.

Hugh MacCurtin's *A brief discourse in vindication of the antiquity of Ireland* (Dublin)

1718

c. **June–July**   Beginning of extensive emigration from Ulster to American colonies (see 1729)

Oct. 28   Jewish congregation in Dublin leases land at Ballybough for use as cemetery

Dec. 17   G.B. declares war on Spain

Charitable infirmary established in Cook Street, Dublin (removed to Inns Quay, 1728; to Jervis Street, 1786); first modern charitable hospital in Ire. or G.B.

1719

Mar.   Ormond app. captain general of kg of Spain for projected invasion of England

Apr. 16/27   Chevalier Charles Wogan rescues Maria Clementina Sobieski (bride of Pretender) from captivity at Innsbruck

Aug. 10   H.C. approves heads of anti-popery bill, invalidating reversionary leases by catholics, and providing that unregistered priests found in Ire. after 1 May 1720 shall be branded on cheek

Aug. 25   L.L. transmits anti-popery bill as amended by privy council to change penalty from branding to castration (amendment rejected by English privy council)

Sept. 8   Earl of Abercorn and others submit petition to kg for powers to establish national bank in Ire. (see 9 Dec. 1721)

Oct. 20   Irish H.L. presents address to L.L. for submission to kg protesting against proceedings of British H.L. in case of Annesley *v.* Sherlock (appellate case that leads to declaratory act; see 7 Apr. 1720)

Nov. 2   H.L. rejects anti-popery bill on account of invalidation of leases

Toleration act (6 Geo. I, c. 5) exempts protestant dissenters from obligation to attend services of established church, and exempts protestant dissenting ministers from penalties provided by act of uniformity, 1666

Dec. 9   Rev. John Abernethy preaches sermon before Belfast Society (published as *Religious obedience founded on personal persuasion*, Belfast 1720), thereby initiating non-subscription controversy among presbyterians (see 21–5 June 1726)

1720

Apr. 7   Declaratory act (6 Geo. I, c. 5 [G.B.]) asserts British parliament's right to legislate for Ire., and denies appellate jurisdiction of Irish H.L. (repealed, 21 June 1782)

c. **May**   Swift's *A proposal for the universal use of Irish manufacture* (anon., Dublin)

Sept. 26-8   Height of panic caused by collapse of 'South Sea bubble'

1721

Apr. 4   Robert Walpole becomes first lord of treasury

June 24   British act (7 Geo. I, c. 22) enabling Charles, earl of Arran, to buy forfeited estates of his brother, James, duke of Ormond (see 20 June 1716)

Aug. 28   Duke of Grafton sworn in as L.L.

Dec. 9   H.C. rejects heads of bill to establish national bank (see 8 Sept. 1719)

Basin or reservoir constructed near St James's Street, Dublin, to improve city's water supply; engineer Thomas Burgh

1722

Jan. 18   Act (8 Geo. I, c. 13) reduces legal rate of interest on borrowed money from 8 to 7 per cent

July 12   Letters patent granting William Wood of Wolverhampton exclusive right of coining copper halfpence and farthings for circulation in Ire.

Aug. 7   Commrs of revenue protest to C.S. at manner of granting coinage patent

Building of Castletown, Co. Kildare, residence of Speaker Conolly (later attributed to architects Alessandro Galilei and Edward Lovet Pearce)

1723

Spring unusually hot and dry; summer excessively so; autumn also unusually so

c. **mid Aug.**   James Maculla's *Ireland's consternation* (anon., Dublin); opens campaign against Wood's halfpence

Sept. 9   H.C. resolves 'to take into consideration the state of the nation, particularly in relation to the importing and uttering of copper halfpence and farthings in this kingdom'

Sept. 13   H.C. votes address to L.L. asking for copy of patent relating to copper halfpence

1724

Feb. or Mar.   First of Swift's Drapier letters, *A letter to the shopkeepers and common people of Ireland, concerning the brass half-pence coined by Mr Woods* (anon., Dublin)

Feb. 10 or 21   Death of Edmund Byrne, catholic abp of Dublin, subject of laments in Irish by Aodh Buidh Mac Cruitín, Seán Ó Neachtain and his son Tadhg

Aug. 6   Swift's second Drapier letter

Aug. 31   Hugh Boulter, bp of Bristol, app. abp of Armagh

Sept. 5   Swift's third Drapier letter

Oct. 22   Lord Carteret sworn in as L.L.

Swift's fourth Drapier letter, *A letter to the whole people of Ireland* (anon., Dublin

Oct. 27   Proclamation offering reward for discovery of author of fourth Drapier letter

A collection of the most celebrated Irish tunes, including 20 tunes by Turlough Carolan, published in Dublin by John and William Neale; probably first collection of Irish secular music to be printed

Cornelius Nary's *Case of the Roman Catholics of Ireland* (anon., Dublin)

Bp William Nicholson's *Irish historical library* (Dublin)

1725

Mar. 27   First number of *Faulkner's Dublin Journal*

Aug. 26   Five children receive smallpox inoculation in Dublin; earliest recorded cases in Ire. (see 14 Jan. 1804)

Sept. 21   L.L. informs parliament of surrender of Wood's patent

Oct. 23   Edward Synge, chancellor of St Patrick's (later bp of Clonfert), preaches sermon in defence of religious toleration

1726

Mar. 1   Abraham Shackleton, quaker, opens boarding school at Ballitore, Co. Kildare (continues as headmaster till 1756, his most distinguished pupil being Edmund Burke, 1741-3)

Mar. 8   Act (12 Geo. I, c. 3) to prevent catholic priests or degraded clergy of established church marrying protestants

Apr. 5 or 9   Eoghan Ó Caoimh, Irish poet and scribe, dies

June 21-5   General synod of Ulster at Dungannon, ending in separation of non-subscribers from main presbyterian body to form presbytery of Antrim (see 9 Dec. 1719)

c. **Aug.**   Succession of harvest failures begins (continuing to 1728)

Oct. 28   Swift's *Gulliver's travels* (London; numerous later editions)

Caleb Threlkeld's *Synopsis stirpium Hibernicarum* (Dublin), first published catalogue of Irish flora

1727

c. **Apr.**   Priest executed at Limerick for marrying couple contrary to 12 Geo. I, c. 3 (see 8 Mar. 1726)

June 11   George I dies; succ. by George II

June 14   Mead & Curtis, Dublin bankers, suspend payments

Nov. 28   Opening of George II's Irish parliament (dissolved, 25 Nov. 1760)

1728

Jan. 11   H.C. select cttee app. to consider erection of new parliament house

Mar. 9 or 14   First Irish performance of John Gay's 'The beggar's opera', at Smock Alley, Dublin

May 6   Catholics explicitly deprived of parliamentary franchise (1 Geo. II, c. 9, s. 7)

Corn and husbandry act (1 Geo. II, c. 10) requires occupiers of 100 acres or more to put 5 per cent under plough

Dublin poor relief act (1 Geo. II, c. 27) provides for care of foundlings

Nov. 14   Linen Hall opened on site near North King Street, Dublin

Matthew Dubourg app. master of state music (leaves Ire., 1765)

Charles Brooking's *Map of Dublin*

c. **1728**

Aodhagán Ó Rathaille, Irish poet and scribe, dies

1729

Feb. 3   Foundation stone laid of new parliament building in College Green, Dublin; architect Edward Lovet Pearce

Mar. 9   Seán Ó Neachtain, Irish poet and scholar, dies

Aug. 21   First number of *Waterford Flying Post*

Oct. 13   Sir Ralph Gore elected speaker of H.C. on resignation of Conolly

Oct.   Swift's *Modest proposal* (anon., Dublin)

Thomas Prior's *List of the absentees of Ireland* (anon., Dublin; several later editions)

Dec. 22   Act (3 Geo. II, c. 2) imposes tax of 4*s*. in £ on Irish income of non-resident pensioners, etc., on Irish establishment

Fresh wave of emigration of Ulster Scots to America (see 1718)

Arthur Dobbs's *An essay on the trade and improvement of Ireland*, pt 1 (Dublin; pt 2, 1731)

1730

Apr. 15   Act (3 Geo. II, c. 3) providing for appointment of commrs for inland navigation

Act (3 Geo. II, c. 14) to prevent unlawful combinations of workmen

Acts (3 Geo. II, cc 18, 19) appointing trustees to maintain roads from Dublin to Kilcullen, Co. Kildare, and to Navan, Co. Meath, and for this purpose to levy tolls on vehicles and animals using them; first turnpike acts

Act (3 Geo. II, c. 21) establishing ballast offices in Cork, Galway, Sligo, Drogheda, and Belfast, to control ports

George Rye's *Considerations on agriculture* (Dublin), first Irish manual of its kind

1731

Jan. 16   Edward Lovet Pearce app. surveyor general (knighted, 10 Mar. 1732)

Mar. 5/16   Treaty of Vienna, between G.B. and Austria, marks end of close alliance between G.B. and France (see 17/28 Nov. 1716)

May 7 British act (4 Geo. II, c. 15) permits importation direct from American colonies to Ire. of goods not specifically prohibited by act of parliament

June 25 Dublin Society for Improving Husbandry, Manufacturing, etc., formed (see 26 Mar. 1746, 2 Apr. 1750, 14 Dec. 1814)

Oct. 5 Parliament meets in new Parliament House, College Green, for first time

Oct. 20 Mayor and magistrates of Galway authorise sheriffs to apprehend catholic clergy and suppress religious orders in Galway town (raids carried out, early Nov.)

Dec. 6 H.L. hears report of cttee on 'state of popery' in Mayo and Galway

John Browne (cr. Lord Monteagle, 10 Sept. 1760, earl of Altamont, 4 Dec. 1771) begins construction of Westport House, Co. Mayo; architect Richard Castles or Cassels

1732

Mar. 8 Report of H.L. cttee on 'state of popery'

Mar. 10 Act (5 Geo. II, c. 7) reduces interest on loans to 6 per cent

Conor Begley and Hugh MacCurtin's *English-Irish dictionary* (Paris)

1733

Jan. Outbreak of influenza epidemic

Feb. Séamas Dall Mac Cuarta, Irish poet, dies

June 25 Burton's bank, Dublin, closes

July 2 Opening of Dr Steevens' Hospital, Dublin

Oct. 4 Henry Boyle (later earl of Shannon) elected speaker of H.C.

Oct. 24 Incorporated Society in Dublin for Promoting English Protestant Schools established by charter

1734

Apr. 29 Act (7 Geo. II, c. 6) prohibits converts to established church, who have catholic wives, from educating their children as catholics or from acting as justices of the peace

Act (7 Geo. II, c. 13) for encouraging home consumption of wool by prescribing burying in wool

Act (7 Geo. II, c. 26) for relief of creditors of banks of Benjamin and Samuel Burton, Daniel Falkiner, and Francis Harrison

May 19 George Berkeley consecrated bp of Cloyne

Aug. 17 Mercer's Hospital, Dublin, opened

Nov. George Faulkner, Dublin printer, publishes first three volumes of his edition of collected works, the first, of Swift (vols. iv–xx, 1735–69)

1735

c. **Dec.** Berkeley's *Querist*, pt 1 (anon., Dublin; pt 2, 1736; pt 3, 1737)

1736

Mar. 17   Act (9 Geo. II, c. 25), for rebuilding St Finbar's cathedral and erecting workhouse at Cork

Mar. 18   H.C. passes series of resolutions condemning tithe of agistment on pasturage for dry and barren cattle

Apr. 17   Duke of Dorset, L.L., lays foundation stone of obelisk at Oldbridge, on River Boyne, to commemorate battle (see 1 July 1690, 31 May 1923)

June   *S—t contra omnes: an Irish miscellany* (London), containing first published version of Swift's 'A character, panegyric, and description of the Legion Club', satirising Irish parliament

c. **Aug.**   Thomas Carte's *Life of James, duke of Ormonde* (London)

Oct. 6   First number of James Hamilton's *Dublin Daily Advertiser*

Bp James Gallagher's *Sixteen Irish sermons in an easy and familiar style on useful and necessary subjects* (anon., Dublin; several later editions)

1737

Aug. 29   Proclamation reducing ratio of gold to silver in Ire. in conformity with British standard

Sept. 1   First number of Francis Joy's *Belfast News-letter*

Sept. 7   Duke of Devonshire sworn in as L.L.

1738

Mar. 23   Act (11 Geo. II, c. 7) for preventing enlistment in foreign service without licence

Act (11 Geo. II, c. 10), grants immunity from prosecution to persons contracting presbyterian marriages

Mar. 25   Carolan, poet and musician, dies at home of patroness, Mrs Mary MacDermott Roe of Alderford, Kilronan, Co. Roscommon

Samuel Madden's *Reflections and resolutions proper for the gentlemen of Ireland* (anon., Dublin)

1739

Apr. 20   Brabazon Ponsonby, Viscount Duncannon (created earl of Bessborough, 6 Oct.), app. chief commr of revenue

June 14   British act (12 Geo. II, c. 21) removes duties on Irish woollen and bay yarn entering G.B.

c. **June–Aug.**   Excessively wet summer; grain harvest reduced; cut turf does not dry

Sept. 26   'Address of the Roman Catholics of Ireland' to kg, in favour of longer leases for catholics

Oct. 8/19   G.B. declares war on Spain; 'war of Jenkins's ear' begins

Dec. 27   Severe frost sets in (continuing till mid Feb. 1740); idleness, distress, famine, and mortality ensue

1740

Mar. 31   Act (13 Geo. II, c. 6) reinforces prohibitions on catholics keeping arms

May 20/31   Frederick II ('the great') becomes kg of Prussia

May 31-June 2   Bread riots in Dublin

c. **June-Aug.**   Cold and excessively dry summer; grain and potato crops small

c. **Sept.-Nov.**   Cold and frosty autumn; snow in Belfast, mid-Oct.

Oct. 9/20   Emperor Charles VI dies; succ. by Maria Theresa as ruler of Habsburg dominions

Dec. 5/16   Prussians invade Silesia; war of Austrian succession begins

Dec.   Severe frost

c. **Dec.**   Famine returns, accompanied by fever and dysentery

Steam-engine installed at Doonane colliery, Shrule, Queen's County; first in Ire.

Walter Harris's *Topographical and chorographical survey of the county of Down* (anon., Dublin), first Irish county history (revised and enlarged by author and Charles Smith and published in 2nd ed. as *The antient and present state of the county of Down*, anon., Dublin, 1744)

1741

Bliadhain an áir ('year of the slaughter'); famine at its height (Dec. 1740-Apr. 1741); mortality later estimated at between 200,000 and 400,000 (1740-41)

c. **June-Aug.**   Unusually dry and hot summer; grain crop much improved on that of 1740 but fever and dysentery aggravated

Oct. 2   Opening of Music Hall in Fishamble Street, Dublin

Nov. 18   George Frederick Handel arrives in Dublin (departs, 13 Aug. 1742; see 13 Apr. 1742)

Obelisk and walls erected on Killiney Hill, Co. Dublin, as relief measure, by John Mapas of Rochestown

1742

Feb. 11   Sir Robert Walpole resigns as first lord of treasury

Feb. 15   'Act for the better regulation of partnerships to encourage the trade and manufactures of this kingdom' (15 Geo. II, c. 7)

'Act for the more effectual securing the payment of rents and preventing frauds by tenants' (15 Geo. II, c. 8)

Mar. 28   Arrival in Dublin from Lough Neagh of collier, *Cope*, first vessel to pass through Newry canal

Apr. 13   Handel's 'Messiah' performed for first time, in Music Hall, Fishamble Street, Dublin

July-Sept.   John Kent, agent of Sacred Congregation de Propaganda Fide, visits Ire. to inquire into state of catholic church (report, *a*. 21 Jan./1 Feb. 1743)

Sept.   First visit to Ire., at invitation of certain presbyterians in Templepatrick area, Co. Antrim, of Thomas Ballantyne, preacher belonging to Scottish associate presbytery (seceders); beginning of seceding movement in Ire.

Andrew Donlevy's *An teagasg críosduidhe* (Paris; 2nd ed., Dublin, 1822; 3rd ed., Dublin, 1848); Irish and English text

1743

c. **Apr.**   Charles Lucas's pamphlet, *A remonstrance against certain infringements on the rights and liberties of the commons and citizens of Dublin* (Dublin)

1744

Feb. 26   House in Pill Lane, Dublin, collapses during celebration of mass there; priest and 9 worshippers die

Mar. 4/15   France declares war on G.B.

Apr. 14   Formation in Dublin of Physico-historical Society for preservation of 'manuscripts, rare printed books, and natural curiosities relating to Ireland'

May 23   Hospital for Incurables, Dublin, opened

July 31/Aug. 11   Spanish success against Austrians at Velletri, near Naples; Irish in both armies

Aug. 6   John Ponsonby app. chief commr of revenue

c. **Oct.**   Season unusually wet and cold: oat and potato crops spoiled in north of Ire.—'the rot year'

Dec. 6   First performance of Handel's 'Messiah' in Cork (St Finbar's cathedral)

Drawing school of Dublin Society founded

1745

Mar. 15   Opening of Dr Bartholomew Mosse's lying-in hospital in George's Lane, Dublin, first under the crown (cf. 9 July 1751)

Apr. 30/May 11   Battle of Fontenoy: defeat of British and Dutch by French army, in which Irish brigade in French service distinguishes itself

July 25   Charles Edward, the Young Pretender, lands near Moidart

Aug. 31   Earl of Chesterfield sworn in as L.L.

Sept. 18   Apothecaries reincorporated by charter (separately from guild of barber-surgeons) as guild of St Luke

Sept. 21   Jacobite success over government forces at Prestonpans, near Edinburgh

Oct. 19   Jonathan Swift dies

Dec. 6   Charles Edward retreats from Derby

Building of Kildare House (later Leinster House), Dublin, begins; architect Richard Castles or Cassels

1746

Jan. 17   Jacobite success at Falkirk

Mar. 19   British act (19 Geo. II, c. 12, s. 19) prohibits export of glass from Ire.

Mar. 26   George II grants Dublin Society £500 a year from privy purse

Apr. 11 'Act for licensing hawkers and pedlars and for the encouragement of English protestant schools' (19 Geo. II, c. 5) provides grant for charter schools

Act (19 Geo. II, c. 7) disabling subjects of kingdom of Ire. in French or Spanish service from holding property

Act (19 Geo. II, c. 13) annulling future marriages celebrated by catholic priests between 2 protestants or between protestant and catholic

Apr. 16 Jacobite defeat at Culloden, near Inverness

June Rev. John Cennick arrives in Dublin to propagate in Ire. doctrine and discipline of Moravian church

Aug. 8 Charter for erecting and endowing St Patrick's hospital, Dublin (for the insane, endowed by Swift, opened 1757)

Charles Smith's *The antient and present state of the county and city of Waterford* (Dublin)

1747

Jan. 19 Disturbance at Smock Alley theatre, Dublin, arising from altercation between Thomas Sheridan, proprietor, and gentleman behind the scenes

Mar. 13 George Stone, bp of Derry, app. abp of Armagh

Apr. 21 First meeting of Edmund Burke's club for discussion of historical and philosophical questions

Aug. 9–24 John Wesley's first visit to Ire.

Sept. 9–20 Mar. 1748 Charles Wesley's first visit to Ire.

Sept. 13 Earl of Harrington sworn in as L.L.

1748

Mar. 8 John Wesley arrives in Dublin for his first tour of Irish midlands

Apr. 9 'Newtown act' (21 Geo. II, c. 10) makes residence in parliamentary borough unnecessary for burgesses

Oct. 7/18 Peace of Aix-la-Chapelle ends war of Austrian succession

Walter Harris's *Hibernica, or some antient pieces relating to Ireland*, pt 1 (Dublin; pt 2, 1750; 2nd ed., 1770)

1749

June First number of Charles Lucas's *Censor*

Aug. 13–Oct. 8 Charles Wesley's second visit to Ire.

Oct. 16 H.C. passes resolutions declaring Lucas an enemy to his country, urging his prosecution and committing him to Newgate, resulting in Lucas's flight

James Simon's *An essay towards an historical account of Irish coins* (Dublin)

1750

Apr. 2 Dublin Society for Promoting Husbandry and Other Useful Arts in Ireland incorporated

Nov. 24 First number of *Dublin Directory* (for 1751); publisher Peter Wilson

Charles Smith's *The antient and present state of the county and city of Cork* (Dublin)

Sylvester O'Halloran's *A new treatise on the glaucoma or cataract* (Limerick)

1751

c. **Jan.** Sacred Congregation de Propaganda Fide issues decrees restricting regular clergy and regulating bps and parochial clergy in Ire.

May 22 'An act for regulating the commencement of the year and for correcting the calendar now in use' (24 Geo. II, c. 23 [G.B.]), abolishing Julian calendar and bringing calendar in British dominions into conformity with Gregorian calendar (see 24 Feb. 1582, 2 Sept. 1752)

July 9 Laying of first stone of Dr Bartholomew Mosse's new lying-in hospital (known as Rotunda hospital from 1767); architect Richard Castles or Cassels (opened 8 Dec. 1757)

Sept. 19 Duke of Dorset sworn in as L.L.

Dec. 19 Act (25 Geo. II, c. 2) authorises application of revenue surplus to reduction of national debt

1752

May 1 Incorporation, under 25 Geo. II, c. 10, of commrs for promoting inland navigation (see 15 Apr. 1730)

a. **July** Methodist chapel opened in Whitefriar Street, Dublin (closed, Nov. 1849)

Aug. 28 First meeting of Belfast Charitable Society

Sept. 2 Julian calendar (Old Style) ceases to have effect in British dominions, following day becoming officially 14 Sept. 1752 under Gregorian calendar (New Style) (see 22 May 1751)

Building of west front of Trinity College, Dublin, begun; architects Henry Keene and John Sanderson (completed, 1759)

1753

Apr. St Nicholas's Hospital, Francis Street, Dublin, opened

Dec. 17 H.C. rejects bill to apply revenue surplus to reduction of national debt

Dec. 22 Act (27 Geo. II, c. 3) for making River Lagan navigable and opening a passage by water between Lough Neagh and Belfast (see 7 Sept. 1763, 1 Jan. 1794)

Charles O'Conor's *Dissertations on the ancient history of Ireland* (anon., Dublin)

1754

Mar. 2 Riot occurs at Smock Alley theatre, Dublin, during performance of F. M. A. Voltaire's 'Mahomet' (Thomas Sheridan consequently gives up managership; leaves Ire., 15 Sept.)

Mar. 6 Dillon & Ferrall, bankers, suspend payments; first of series of three bank failures (1754–5)

John Lodge's *The peerage of Ireland* (4 vols, Dublin; 2nd ed., revised, enlarged and continued by Mervyn Archdall, 7 vols, 1789)

1755

Apr. 10   New Essex Bridge over Liffey open for carriages

May 5   Marquis of Hartington (succeeds as duke of Devonshire, 5 Dec.) sworn in as L.L.

June   Charles O'Conor's *The case of the Roman Catholics of Ireland* (anon., Dublin; 3rd ed., 1756)

Nov. 1   Lisbon earthquake felt in Munster

Commrs for inland navigation begin work of making Shannon navigable between Limerick and Lough Allen (completed between Killaloe and Roosky by 1769; wholly completed, 1850)

1756

Jan. 6   Viscount Limerick introduces in H.L. heads of bill for registration and restriction of catholic priests, and exclusion of bps (dropped, 29 Apr.)

Apr. 26   John Ponsonby elected speaker of H.C.

c. **Apr.**   Dearth of corn and potatoes (continues into 1757)

May 8   Act (29 Geo. II, c. 12) to prevent unlawful combinations

May 18   G.B. declares war on France; 'seven years war' begins

Commrs for inland navigation begin construction of Grand Canal to link Dublin with Barrow (completed 1791) and Shannon (completed 1805)

1757

Apr. 21   Edmund Burke's *A philosophical enquiry into the sublime and beautiful* (anon., London; numerous later eds)

Sept. 25   Duke of Bedford sworn in as L.L.

Oct. 12   Earl of Clanbrassil (formerly Viscount Limerick) introduces in H.L. heads of new bill for control of catholic priests and bps (rejected by British privy council, 18 Jan. 1758)

Founding of musical academy in Dublin by Hon. Garret Wesley (succeeds as Lord Mornington, 31 Jan. 1758; see 14 July 1764)

1758

Mar. 3   Act (31 Geo. II, c. 3) granting bounty on grain and flour brought by land to Dublin

Apr. 29   Act (31 Geo. II, c. 19) appointing commrs ('wide street commissioners') to make 'a wide and convenient street from Essex Bridge to the castle of Dublin'

June 20   British act 'to permit the importation of salted beef, pork and butter from Ireland' (31 Geo. II, c. 28)

Viscount Charlemont (created earl, 23 Dec. 1763) begins building Casino in Marino, near Dublin; architect William Chambers (completed, *c.* 1765)

Abbé James MacGeoghegan's *Histoire de l'Irlande*, vol. i (Paris; vols ii and iii, 1762; English trs. by Patrick O'Kelly, Dublin, 1831-2)

1759

Apr. 5 British act (32 Geo. II, c. 11) removes restrictions on import of Irish cattle into G.B.

May 15 First volume of *Annual Register* (for 1758), edited by Edmund Burke (London)

Nov. 20 Battle of Quiberon Bay: heavy loss inflicted on French Atlantic fleet by British navy

Nov. 21 Henry Flood enters parliament

Dec. 3 Rioting in Dublin on rumour of legislative union with G.B.

Dec. 31 Arthur Guinness obtains lease of brewery at St James's Gate, Dublin

1760

Feb. 21 François Thurot lands French force in Belfast Lough, capturing Carrickfergus

c. **Mar. 31** Meeting of catholics at Elephant Tavern in Essex Street, Dublin, giving rise to first 'catholic committee'

Apr. 15 H.C. resolves to sit as cttee of inquiry into recent bank failures

May 17 Act (33 Geo. II, c. 8) regulating use and maintenance of roads and abolishing compulsory road labour

Dublin city corporation act (33 Geo. II, c. 16) increases power of guilds to elect representatives to common council

Public lighting act (33 Geo. II, c. 18), empowering Dublin vestries to levy lighting tax

Oct. 25 George II dies; succ. by his grandson, George III

1761

Mar. 15 Charles Lucas returns to Dublin

Oct. 22 First meeting of George III's first Irish parliament (dissolved, 28 May 1768)

c. **Oct.-Dec.** Beginning of 'whiteboyism' in Munster

Dec. 18 Dublin Society granted £12,000 from public funds (1 Geo. III, c. 1, s. 14)

Dec. 19 First performance of Italian opera in Ire. (Giuseppi Scolari's 'La cascina' at Smock Alley)

Henry Brooke's *The trial of the cause of the Roman Catholics* (Dublin; 4th ed., 1762)

1762

Jan. 4 G.B. declares war on Spain

Feb. *c.* **1** Catholic nobility and gentry sign address offering services to kg

Feb. 23   Secretary of state conveys to L.L. kg's appreciation of catholics' offer and his intention of employing them in service of Portugal

Apr. 12   H.C. rejects (113–63) motion for address to L.L. asking whether there is any intention to send catholics to be employed as soldiers in service of any foreign prince (proposal to send 7 catholic regiments to Portugal not put into effect)

Apr. 30   'Act for the security of protestant purchasers' (1 Geo. III, c. 12), gives them immunity from proceedings under acts to prevent further growth of popery and other penal laws

   'Act for quieting the possessions of protestants deriving under converts from the popish religion' (1 Geo. III, c. 13), gives immunity from penalties for converts' failure to observe requirements of conformity

May 14   First public performance of Charles Macklin's 'The true-born Irishman' in Crow Street theatre, Dublin

June 21   Construction of Poolbeg lighthouse at entrance to Dublin harbour begun (completed, 1768)

July 9   Peter III, tsar of Russia, deposed and succ. by his wife Catherine ('the great')

Sept. 17   Francesco Geminiani, Italian violinist, dies in Dublin

Sept.   Seán Ó Murchadha, Irish poet and scribe, dies

Nov. 20   Francis Andrews app. first professor of history in University of Dublin

1763

Feb. 10   Peace of Paris between Britain and France; 'seven years war' ends

c. **mid–**   Outbreak of 'hearts of oak' or 'oakboy' disturbances in Ulster

Sept. 7   Opening of Lagan navigation, Belfast to Lisburn (see 22 Dec. 1753, 1 Jan. 1794)

Sept. 10   First number of *Freeman's Journal* (see 19 Dec. 1924)

Nov. 11   Lord mayor and aldermen of Dublin present to H.C. petition in support of scheme of city's pipe-water cttee to bring water to Dublin via Grand Canal for inhabitants' use (scheme approved; completed, *c.* 1776) (see 22 July 1861)

Construction begins of 5-storeyed flour-mill on Boyne at Slane, Co. Meath; first major industrial building in Ire. (completed, 1767)

1764

Feb.   Formation of Society of Artists in Ire.

Mar. 9   Paris *parlement* orders Jesuits to leave France

May 12   Act (3 Geo. III, c. 19) to indemnify magistrates and peace officers for action taken in suppressing riots

July 14   Earl of Mornington elected first professor of music at University of Dublin

Building of Rotunda concert hall, Dublin

1765

Feb. 8   Richard Robinson, bp of Kildare (created Baron Rokeby, 26 Feb. 1777), app. abp of Armagh

Mar. 22   Stamp act (5 Geo. III, c. 12 [G.B.]) imposes stamp duties on American colonists

c. **Apr.**   Beginning of severe drought (continues throughout summer, resulting in poor harvests and stunted livestock)

Henry Brooke's *The fool of quality*, vols i–iv (Dublin; vol. v, 1770)

1766

Jan. 1   James III, the Old Pretender, dies

Mar. 15   Rev. Nicholas Sheehy, catholic priest, executed at Clonmel following conviction for instigating whiteboys to commit murder

Mar. 17   St Patrick's day celebrated in Vienna by Count O'Mahony, Spanish ambassador at Imperial court

Mar. 18   Stamp act (see 22 Mar. 1765) repealed by 6 Geo. III, c. 11 [G.B.]

British declaratory act (6 Geo. III, c. 12) asserts right of British parliament to legislate for American colonies 'in all cases whatsoever'

Mar. 27   Oliver Goldsmith's *Vicar of Wakefield* (London)

May 7   First performance of Italian *opera seria* in Ire. (Tommaso Giordani's 'L'eroe cinese' at Smock Alley)

June 7   Tumultuous risings act (5 Geo. III, c. 8), directed against whiteboys

County infirmaries act (5 Geo. III, c. 20)

June–Aug.   Widespread rioting, owing to scarcity and high price of food

c. **Aug.**   Viscount Taaffe's *Observations on affairs in Ireland* (Dublin)

Walter Harris's *History and antiquities of the city of Dublin* (Dublin)

1767

Apr. 2   Jesuits expelled from Spain

July 20   Earl of Donegall grants new leases for nearly all holdings in Belfast, obliging tenants to redevelop (encumbered estates commrs sell off holdings to tenants, 1850)

Oct. 14   Viscount Townshend sworn in as L.L.

1768

Jan. 29   First performance, at Covent Garden, London, of Oliver Goldsmith's 'The good-natured man'

Feb. 16   Octennial act (7 Geo. III, c. 3) limiting life of parliament to 8 years (cf. 7 May 1716)

Feb. 18   Frederick Hervey, bp of Cloyne (succeeds as earl of Bristol, 23 Sept. 1779), app. bp of Derry

Mar.   Royal authorisation for increase in number of packet-boats in service between Dublin and Holyhead from 3 to 6

May 2 L.L.'s request for augmentation of army from 12,000 to 15,235 rejected by H.C. (105 to 101)

May 27 'Act for promoting the trade of Ireland by enabling the merchants thereof to erect an exchange in the city of Dublin' (7 Geo. III, c. 22)

May 28 Parliament dissolved

John O'Brien's *Irish-English dictionary* (anon., Paris)

1769

Apr. 5 Peadar Ó Doirnín, Irish poet, dies

May 2-June *c.* **7** James Boswell visits Ire.

July Outbreak of 'hearts of steel' or 'steelboy' disturbances in Ulster

Aug. 2 Foundation stone laid of Royal Exchange, Dublin; architect Thomas Cooley (opened 1 Jan. 1779)

Oct. 17 First meeting of George III's second Irish parliament (dissolved, 5 Apr. 1776)

Nov. 21 H.C. rejects supply bill 'because it did not take its rise in this house' (94 to 71)

1770

May Oliver Goldsmith's *Deserted village* (London)

Dec. 23 Hearts of steel attack on Belfast barracks

Opening of Armagh public library (regulated by act 13 & 14 Geo. III, c. 40, 2 June 1774)

1771

Feb. 27 Riot outside Parliament House, Dublin; quelled by military

Feb. First number of *Hibernian Magazine* (continues till July 1812)

Mar. 7 Edmund Sexton Pery chosen speaker of H.C.

Aug. 1 Laying of first stone of Poor House and Infirmary, Belfast

Sept. 5-Oct. *c.* **23** Benjamin Franklin visits Ire. (attends meeting of H.C., 10 Oct.)

Nov. 4 Charles Lucas dies

1772

Mar. 28 Act (11 & 12 Geo. III, c. 5) to repress steelboy disturbances in five Ulster counties (repealed by act 13 & 14 Geo. III, c. 4 in 1774)

June 2 Dublin Foundling Hospital and Workhouse act (11 & 12 Geo. III, c. 11)

Poor infants act (11 & 12 Geo. III, c. 15), requires vestries in towns (except for Dublin and Cork) to appoint overseers to care for abandoned children (extended to rural parishes by act 13 & 14 Geo. III, c. 24 in 1774)

'Bogland act' (11 & 12 Geo. III, c. 21), enables catholics to take 61-year reclamation leases of bog

Mendicity act (11 & 12 Geo. III, c. 30), provides for 'badging' beggars and establishment of 'work houses or houses of industry'

Act (11 & 12 Geo. III, c. 31) provides for establishment of Company of Undertakers of the Grand Canal to complete canal to Barrow and Shannon

Nov. 30   Earl of Harcourt sworn in as L.L. (Townshend recalled)

John Lodge's *Desiderata curiosa Hibernica: or a select collection of state papers* (anon., 2 vols, Dublin)

John Rutty's *An essay towards a natural history of the county of Dublin* (2 vols, Dublin)

1773

Jan. 5   Art Mac Cubhthaigh, Irish poet, dies

Mar. 15   First performance at Covent Garden, London, of Oliver Goldsmith's 'She stoops to conquer'

May 4   Art Ó Laoghaire (Arthur Leary) shot dead near Millstreet, Co. Cork (his death subject of lament in Irish by wife, Eibhlín Dubh Ni Chonaill)

Nov. 8   Opening of Dublin city house of industry, established under 11 & 12 Geo. III, c. 30, s. 2

Nov. 26   Resolution, supported by Flood and others, for tax on absentee landowners, rejected by H.C.

Dec. 16   'Boston tea-party': colonial militants protest against tea duty by throwing tea-chests into Boston harbour

Thomas Leland's *History of Ireland* (3 vols, London; several later eds)

1774

Jan. 28   Act (13 & 14 Geo. III, c. 6) imposes stamp duty on newspapers, pamphlets, advertisements and certain legal documents

Mar. 31   British act (14 Geo. III, c. 19) closing port of Boston as punishment for 'tea-party'

June 2   'Act for paving the streets . . . of Dublin' (13 & 14 Geo. III, c. 22), appointing paving board

'Act to enable his majesty's subjects of whatever persuasion to testify their allegiance to him' (13 & 14 Geo. III, c. 35)

June 22   'Quebec act' (14 Geo. III, c. 83 [G.B.]), allows Quebec catholics free exercise of religion and exempts them from oath of supremacy

July 15   John Hely Hutchinson app. provost of Trinity College, Dublin

Sept. 5   First continental congress assembles in Philadelphia

Nov. 3   Burke elected member of parliament for Bristol

1775

Jan. 17   First public performance of Richard Brinsley Sheridan's 'The rivals', at Covent Garden Theatre, London

Mar. 22   Burke's speech on conciliation with America

Apr. 19   Skirmish at Lexington, Massachusetts, between British troops and local militia; war of American independence begins

June 17   Battle of Bunker Hill, near Boston; pyrrhic victory for British

June   Reconstitution of Irish regiments in French service: regiment of Clare amalgamated with Berwick, Bulkeley amalgamated with Dillon

Oct. 12   James Butler, catholic abp of Cashel, instructs his clergy to read denunciation of whiteboyism from altar

Oct. 24   Citizens of Dublin, assembled at tholsel (city hall), urge peace between Britain and American colonists

Oct. 27   Flood appointed vice-treasurer, abandoning parliamentary opposition

Nov. 28   H.C. votes address (103 to 58) approving despatch of 4,000 troops to America

Dec. 15   Henry Grattan's maiden speech in H.C.

Dec. 24   Establishment of Presentation Order of teaching sisters, founded by Nano Nagle in Cork

John Curry's *Historical and critical review of the civil wars in Ireland* (anon., Dublin; 4th ed., 1810)

1776

Feb. 3   Proclamation imposing embargo on export of provisions from Ire. in order to secure supplies for British forces operating against American colonists

Apr. 4   Act (15 & 16 Geo. III, c. 21) to prevent tumultuous risings—major whiteboy act (made perpetual by 40 Geo. III, c. 96, 1 Aug. 1800)

Apr. 5   Parliament dissolved

June 18   First meeting of George III's third Irish parliament (dissolved, 25 July 1783)

June 20   Arthur Young begins tour of Ire. (his account of it published in 1780)

July 4   Declaration of American independence

Oct. 29   George III grants £100 per annum for professor of French and German, and £100 per annum for professor of Spanish and Italian, at Trinity College, Dublin

Robert Brooke begins building of industrial village, Prosperous, on his property in Co. Kildare, for manufacture of cotton (forced by unprofitability to sell out, 1786; mills burned down by rebels, 1798)

1777

Jan. 25   Earl of Buckinghamshire sworn in as L.L.

Apr. 3   Burke's letter to sheriffs of Bristol, explaining his stand on American question (published, London, 5 May 1777)

May 8   First performance, at Drury Lane, London, of Richard Brinsley Sheridan's 'School for scandal'

Oct. 17 British force, commanded by General John Burgoyne, surrenders at Saratoga, New York

Thomas Campbell's *Philosophical survey of the south of Ireland* (anon., London; 2nd ed., Dublin, 1778)

1778

Feb. 6 Treaties of alliance signed between France and American colonists (leading to war between G.B. and France)

Mar. 17 First company of Belfast Volunteers enrolled

Apr. 6 First of series of bank and merchant failures

Apr. John Paul Jones, American privateer, twice raids Belfast Lough

Protests in England against government bills for relaxation of restrictions on Irish trade

June 11 Act (17 & 18 Geo. III, c. 10) for making a circular road round Dublin

Act (17 & 18 Geo. III, c. 12) incorporates Charitable Musical Society, Dublin

July 1 'Act for the further encouragement of the whale fisheries carried on from Ireland' (17 & 18 Geo. III, c. 18)

Aug. 14 Catholic relief act (17 & 18 Geo. III, c. 49—Luke Gardiner's act), enabling catholics to take leases for 999 years and inherit in same way as protestants

Nov. 4 *Hibernian Journal* publishes letter in name of Benjamin Franklin explaining that cause of America is that of Ire.

1779

May 19 Belfast Charitable Society accepts proposal of Robert Joy and Thomas McCabe to set up manufacture of cotton in poorhouse; beginning of cotton industry in Belfast

June 16 Spain declares war on G.B.

June First boat begins operating on Grand Canal, between Dublin and Bally-healy near Celbridge, Co. Kildare, carrying 24 to 27 tons

Oct. 20-21 First Irish burgher (secession) synod meets at Monaghan (see 5-6 Aug. 1788)

Nov. 4 Volunteers parade on College Green, Dublin, demanding relief from commercial restrictions

Nov. 24 Grattan carries in H.C. by 170 to 47 resolution 'that at this time it would be inexpedient to grant new taxes'

John Hely Hutchinson's *Commercial restraints of Ireland* (anon., Dublin)

1780

Feb. 24 British act (20 Geo. III, c. 10) allows Ire. to trade with British colonies in America, West Indies and Africa on equal terms with G.B.

May 2 Protestant dissenter relief act (19 & 20 Geo. III, c. 6) repeals sacramental test imposed by s. 17 of 2 Anne, c. 6 (see 4 Mar. 1704)

June 2-9   Gordon riots in London, directed against catholics

July   Setting of Brian Merriman's 'Cúirt an mheáin oidhche' ('The midnight court') (see Sept. 1926)

Aug. 19   Revenue act (19 & 20 Geo. III, c. 12) prescribes minimum revenue for each still (discourages small distilleries; great increase in illicit distillation) (see 18 July 1823)

Dec. 16   John Beresford app. chief commr of revenue

Dec. 23   Earl of Carlisle sworn in as L.L.

Arthur Young's *A tour in Ireland* (2 vols, London; several later eds)

Spirits legally manufactured in Ire. command greater share of Irish spirit market for first time (1.2 million gallons, against 1 million gallons of imported brandy and rum)

1781

Aug. 8   Laying without formality of first stone of Custom House, Dublin; architect James Gandon (opened, 7 Nov. 1791)

Oct. 19   Earl Cornwallis surrenders at Yorktown; virtual end of war of American independence

1782

Feb. 12   Liberty of the subject act (22 Geo. III, c. 11—Sir Samuel Bradstreet's act) clarifies right of habeas corpus

Feb. 15   Dungannon Volunteer convention adopts resolutions in favour of legislative and judicial independence, relaxation of penal laws, etc.

Feb. 21   Edmund Burke's letter to Viscount Kenmare on catholic relief (published as *A letter from a distinguished English commoner to a peer of Ireland* (London, 1783))

Mar. 1   Hely Hutchinson urges admission of catholics to Trinity College

Mar. 20   Resignation of Lord North's ministry

Mar. 27   Marquis of Rockingham forms ministry, including Burke

Apr. 14   Duke of Portland sworn in as L.L.

Apr. 16   Grattan for third time moves declaration of rights, which both houses carry unanimously

May 4   Catholic relief act (21 & 22 Geo. III, c. 24—Gardiner's act) allows catholics to acquire land (except in parliamentary boroughs)

Protestant dissenter relief act (21 & 22 Geo. III, c. 25—James Stewart's act) declares validity of marriages by presbyterian ministers

Bank of Ireland act (21 & 22 Geo. III, c. 26)

May 17   Leave given in British H.C. to bring in bill to repeal declaratory act (6 Geo. I, c. 5; see 7 Apr. 1720)

May 27   L.L. announces to parliament that British legislature has agreed 'to remove the causes of your discontents and jealousies'

May 31   H.C. unanimously resolves to request kg that £50,000 be laid out 'in the purchase of lands in this kingdom to be settled on Henry Grattan, Esq.'

June 21   British act (22 Geo. III, c. 53) for repeal of declaratory act (see 17 May)

July 27   Poynings' law amended by 21 & 22 Geo. III, c. 47 (Barry Yelverton's act), providing that all bills approved by both houses of parliament (and no other bills) be transmitted unaltered to England

Independency of judges act (21 & 22 Geo. III, c. 50—John Forbes's act)

Protestant dissenter relief act (21 & 22 Geo. III, c. 57—Isaac Corry's act), exempts seceders from kissing bible when taking oaths

Catholic relief act (21 & 22 Geo. III, c. 62—Gardiner's act), permitting catholics 'to teach school' and act as guardians

Sept. 15   Earl Temple sworn in as L.L.

Nov. 7   First number of *Volunteer Journal*, ed. Mathew Carey (continues till 1787)

1783

Jan. 22   Henry Ussher elected first professor of astronomy at Trinity College, Dublin, with responsibility for completing observatory at Dunsink (contract signed, 10 Dec. 1782)

Feb. 10   Dublin Chamber of Commerce founded

Apr. 17   British renunciation act (23 Geo. III, c. 28) acknowledges exclusive right of Irish parliament to legislate for Ire., and exclusive jurisdiction of Irish courts

Apr. 28   Foundation stone of White Linen Hall, Belfast, laid (opened, 13 Sept. 1784; demolished, 1896)

June 1   Newly built presbyterian meeting house in Rosemary Street, Belfast, of first (non-subscribing) congregation, opened for worship; architect Roger Mulholland

June 3   Earl of Northington sworn in as L.L.

June 25   Bank of Ireland opens for business

Sept. 8   Ulster Volunteer reform convention at Dungannon (cf. 15 Feb. 1782), first of 4 provincial conventions

Oct. 14   First meeting of George III's fourth Irish parliament (dissolved, 8 Apr. 1790)

Oct. 28   Parliamentary battle between Grattan and Flood, each attacking character of the other

Nov. 10–Dec. 2   National Volunteer convention at Rotunda, Dublin

Nov. 29   H.C. refuses, 157 to 77, to accept Volunteers' parliamentary reform bill

Dec. 19   William Pitt the younger app. P.M.

Waterford glass-factory established

1784

Jan. 5   First performance of English version of Christoph Willibald Gluck's opera 'Orpheus and Eurydice', at Smock Alley Theatre, Dublin

Feb. 11   Royal College of Surgeons in Ireland incorporated by charter

Feb. 24   Duke of Rutland sworn in as L.L.

Mar. 21   Volunteers' parliamentary reform bill defeated on second reading in H.C., by 159 to 85

May 14   Irish post-office established by statute (23 & 24 Geo. III, c. 17)

Act for regulating corn trade (23 & 24 Geo. III, c. 19—Foster's act) provides for export subsidies when prices low and prohibits export when prices high

May 30   Opening of St Mary's catholic chapel, Belfast, attended by 1st Belfast Volunteer Company as guard of honour

June   Eoghan Ruadh Ó Súilleabháin, Irish poet, dies

July 4   Dispute at Markethill, Co. Armagh, leading to formation of Peep o' Day Boys (protestant) and Defenders (catholic)

Oct. 25-7   First session of radical reform congress in William Street, Dublin

Nov. 19   First of William Drennan's letters on parliamentary reform published anonymously in *Belfast News-letter* (last letter, 4 Jan. 1785; series republished as *Letters of Orellana, an Irish helot, to the seven northern counties* (anon., Belfast, 1785; 2nd ed., Dublin))

Richard Kirwan's *Elements of mineralogy* (London; revised ed., 2 vols, 1794-6; 3rd ed., 1810)

Movement for protection of Irish industries

1785

Jan. 19   Richard Crosbie makes first balloon ascent from Irish soil (at Ranelagh Gardens, near Dublin)

Jan. 20-Feb. 4   Second session of radical reform congress (see 25-7 Oct. 1784)

Feb. 7   Pitt's commercial propositions (for freeing of trade between G.B. and Ire.) laid before Irish H.C. by Thomas Orde, C.S.

Feb. 12   H.C. approves (*nem. con.*) 10 resolutions generally supporting Pitt's propositions

Mar. 24   'Act for granting certain duties upon licences' (25 Geo. III, c. 8) permits licensing of grocers to sell drink for consumption off the premises

Mar.-Apr.   Numerous protests in G.B. against Pitt's propositions

Apr. 20-30   Final session of radical reform congress

May 3   First meeting of Irish Academy (Royal Irish Academy by charter of 28 Jan. 1786) at house of earl of Charlemont in Dublin

May 12   Pitt's speech in British H.C., modifying original propositions

June 30   'Act for establishing a complete school of physic in this kingdom' (25 Geo. III, c. 42)

June   Irish Academy begins collection of Irish MSS with acquisition of Book of Ballymote

Aug. 2   British H.C. gives first reading to bill for regulating trade with Ire. in accordance with revised propositions

Aug. 12 Leave granted by Irish H.C., 127 to 108, to introduce bill based on Pitt's revised propositions (first reading 15 Aug.; not proceeded with on account of opposition)

Sept. 5 John Foster elected speaker of H.C.

Sept. 7 Belfast harbour board act (25 Geo. III, c. 64) establishes ballast board

c. **Sept.** Whiteboys, now known as 'Rightboys', renew disturbances in Munster

1786

Mar. 3 Laying of first stone of Four Courts, Dublin; architect, James Gandon

May 1 Belfast Academy opened (becomes Belfast Royal Academy, 1887)

May 8 Dublin police act (26 Geo. III, c. 24) establishes regular police force controlled by 3 paid commrs of the peace

Prisons act (26 Geo. III, c. 27) provides for appointment of inspectors, physicians, chaplains, etc.

Dec. 3 John Thomas Troy, catholic bp of Ossory, app. abp of Dublin

Joseph Cooper Walker's *Historical memoirs of the Irish bards* (Dublin, London)

Mervyn Archdall's *Monasticon Hibernicum* (Dublin, London)

1787

Jan. Subscription begins for Irish Musical Fund (incorporated 25 Mar. 1794 by act, 34 Geo. III, c. 20)

Mar. 26 Tumultuous risings act (27 Geo. III, c. 15) imposes penalties for rioting (modelled on British riot act, 1 Geo. I, stat. 2, c. 5), and for interference with collection of tithes (made perpetual by 40 Geo. III, c. 96, 1 Aug. 1800)

May 21 Police act (27 Geo. III, c. 40) empowers L.L. to appoint chief constables and grand juries to appoint sub-constables, and empowers L.L. to appoint barristers as assistants to magistrates

June Last performance at Smock Alley theatre, Dublin

Oct. 24 Death of duke of Rutland, L.L., aged 33

Nov. 21 Ambrose O'Higgins app. governor and captain general of Chile (viceroy of Peru, 1795)

Dec. 16 Marquis of Buckingham (formerly Earl Temple, see 15 Sept. 1782) sworn in as L.L.

First bound volume of *Transactions of the Royal Irish Academy*, first Irish scientific serial

1788

Apr. 18 Act (28 Geo. III, c. 15) providing for appointment of commn of inquiry into endowed schools (report submitted, 1791; not published till 1857)

May Lord Belmore (cr. Viscount Belmore, 6 Dec. 1789; earl of Belmore, 20 Nov. 1797) begins construction of Castlecoole, near Enniskillen; architect James Wyatt (completed, 1798)

May 13   Formation of Belfast Reading Society (later known as Belfast Library and Society for Promoting Knowledge or Linen Hall Library)

Aug. 5-6   First Irish anti-burgher (secession) synod meets at Belfast (see 20-21 Oct. 1779)

Nov. 5   George III becomes insane (see 10 Mar. 1789)

Iron-works established at Arigna, Co. Roscommon, to use local coal and ore; first use in Ire. of coal for smelting

1789

Feb. 19   Both houses of parliament present to L.L. their address to prince of Wales

Mar. 10   George III pronounced to have recovered (see 5 Nov. 1788)

Mar. 29   John Wesley, aged 85, begins his twenty-first, and last, visit to Ire. (ends, 12 July)

May 5   Meeting of estates general at Versailles

June 20   John Fitzgibbon (created earl of Clare, 12 June 1795) becomes L.C.

June 26   Whig Club formed in Dublin

July 14   Fall of Bastille, Paris

Oct. 24   Incorporation of Royal Canal Co. to build canal linking Dublin and Shannon by route north of Grand Canal (completed, 1817)

Nov. 6   John Carroll, partly of Irish descent, app. bp of Baltimore; first catholic bp in U.S.A.

Charlotte Brooke's *Reliques of Irish poetry* (Dublin)

Bridge over Foyle at Londonderry begun; engineer Lemuel Cox (completed, 1791)

1790

Jan. 5   Earl of Westmorland sworn in as L.L.

Jan. 19   Catholic Committee resolves to draw up programme to obtain further advantages for catholics

Feb. 28   Northern Whig Club inaugurated in Belfast

Mar. 15   Society for Relief of Sick and Indigent Room-keepers of all Religious Persuasions formed

Apr. 5   Act (30 Geo. III, c. 28) provides £300 to Dublin Society for creation and maintenance of botanic garden (site at Glasnevin near Dublin developed, 1796)

July 2   First meeting of George III's fifth Irish parliament; Theobald Wolfe Tone first makes acquaintance of Thomas Russell, in public gallery of H.C. (probably 2 or 3 July)

July 5   Running of first mail-coaches

July 10   Gervase Parker Bushe reads to Royal Irish Academy 'An essay towards ascertaining the population of Ireland' in which he computes population at

4,040,000 on basis of hearth-money returns made in 1788 (published in *Transactions of the Royal Irish Academy*, iii (1790))

Nov. 1 Edmund Burke's *Reflections on the revolution in France* (London)

Edward Ledwich's *Antiquities of Ireland* (Dublin; 2nd ed., 1803)

1791

Jan. 28 Defenders make violent attacks on family of Alexander Barclay, protestant schoolmaster, at Forkill near Dundalk (Defender violence becomes common, especially in north Leinster and south Ulster, 1792-3)

Mar. 5 Foundation-stone laid of Carlisle bridge, Dublin; architect James Gandon (opened, July 1795; rebuilt, 1880, and renamed O'Connell bridge)

Mar. 10 Pope Pius VI condemns French 'civil constitution of the clergy'

Mar. 13 Thomas Paine's *Rights of man*, pt 1 (London; pt 2, 1792)

Mar. 14 Deputation from Catholic Committee present petition to Robert Hobart, C.S.

May 5 Liquor licences act (31 Geo. III, c. 13) increases licence duties, introduces good-character certificates for publicans, and encourages consumption of beer as against spirits (continued and amended by 32 Geo. III, c. 19)

Act (31 Geo. III, c. 34) establishing Apothecaries' Hall

Act (31 Geo. III, c. 46) establishing observatory in Armagh

May 10 Dublin Library Society founded by Dr Richard Kirwan

July 14 Demonstrations in Dublin, Belfast, and elsewhere, commemorating fall of Bastille

July 21 Irish brigade disbanded by French national assembly

Aug. *c.* 22 Theobald Wolfe Tone's pamphlet, *An argument on behalf of the catholics of Ireland* (anon., Dublin; 2nd ed., ?Belfast, 1791; revised ed., Dublin, 1792)

Oct. 14 Society of United Irishmen founded in Belfast; chairman, Samuel McTier, secretary, Robert Simms

Nov. 9 First meeting of Dublin Society of United Irishmen; chairman, Hon. Simon Butler, secretary, James Napper Tandy

Nov. 26 First convicts from Ire. arrive aboard *Queen* in New South Wales

Dec. 27 Secession from Catholic Committee of Viscount Kenmare and 67 others

Francis Grose's *The antiquities of Ireland* (London)

1792

Jan. 4 First number of *Northern Star*, organ of United Irishmen in Belfast; editor Samuel Neilson

Feb. 14 First public performance by John Field, pianist-composer, at Rotunda, Dublin

Feb. 18 Edmund Burke's *A letter to Sir Hercules Langrishe, bart, M.P., on the subject of the Roman Catholics of Ireland* (Dublin)

Feb. 20 Petition of Catholic Committee for parliamentary franchise and other concessions rejected by H.C. by 208 to 25

Apr. 18 Catholic relief act (32 Geo. III, c. 21—Sir Hercules Langrishe's act), allows catholics to practise as lawyers

May Samuel Burdy's *The life of the late Rev. Philip Skelton* (Dublin)

June 14 Foundation stone laid of courthouse in Green Street, Dublin

July 7 Launching of *Hibernia*, first vessel to be constructed at William Ritchie's shipyard in Belfast

July 11-14 Gathering of Irish harpers in Belfast

July 12 Belfast Volunteers present address to Charlemont in favour of catholic enfranchisement

July 25 Tone formally app. agent and assistant secretary of Catholic Committee

Aug. 10 Earliest recorded cricket match in Ire., between garrison XI and all-Ire. XI on Fifteen Acres, Phoenix Park, Dublin

Oct. 9 Association for Discountenancing Vice and Promoting Religion established

Dec. 3-8 Catholic convention in Tailors' Hall, Back Lane, Dublin; elects 5 members to present petition to kg, 7 Dec. (see *c.* 10 Dec., 2 Jan. 1793)

Dec. *c.* 10-*c.* 18 Catholic delegates, accompanied by Tone, travel from Dublin to London, via Belfast, Donaghadee and Portpatrick, with petition to kg; their coach is drawn through Belfast by sympathisers (12 Dec.)

Dec. 14 Dublin Society of United Irishmen issues declaration to Volunteers: 'Citizen-soldiers, to arms!', favouring revival of volunteering in preference to establishment of militia, and advocating holding of another Volunteer convention on anniversary of that of 1782

Dec. 21 Friends of the Constitution, Liberty and Peace formed in King's Inns Tavern, Dublin; president duke of Leinster, secretary Richard Griffith; whig membership includes Grattan

1793

Jan. 2 Catholic delegates present petition to George III

Jan. 11 Dublin Society of United Irishmen appoints cttee to prepare plan of parliamentary reform (see 15 Feb. 1794)

Jan. 21 Execution of Louis XVI, attended by l'Abbé Henry Edgeworth de Firmont

Feb. 1 France declares war on G.B. and Holland

Feb. 4 Hobart, C.S., introduces catholic relief bill (see 9 Apr.)

Feb. 15-16 Ulster provincial convention of Volunteers at Dungannon

Feb. 25 Act (33 Geo. III, c. 2) to prevent importation of arms and ammunition and their movement without licence

Mar. 11 Proclamation effectively suppressing Volunteers in Ulster

Apr. 9 Catholic relief act (33 Geo. III, c. 21—Hobart's act), extending parliamentary franchise to catholics, enabling them to hold civil and military offices not specifically excepted, and removing statutory bar to university degrees

Militia act (33 Geo. III, c. 22), establishing militia at strength of 14,948 (increased to 21,660 by 35 Geo. III, c. 8 (15 Apr. 1795))

Apr. 20 Construction of bridge over Suir at Waterford begins; engineer Lemuel Cox (opened May 1794)

June 27 Synod of Ulster at Lurgan approves declaration in favour of parliamentary reform

June Col. Eleazer Oswald, agent of French revolutionary government, secretly visits Ire.

Aug. 16 Convention act (33 Geo. III, c. 29) prohibits assemblies purporting to represent the people under pretence of preparing or presenting petitions to the kg or to parliament

Place act (33 Geo. III, c. 41) disqualifies holders of certain government offices and pensions from membership of H.C.

Oct. 1 Opening of St Patrick's College, Carlow, first catholic college for higher studies in Ire.

1794

Jan. 1 Formal opening of extension of Lagan navigation, linking Coalisland, Co. Tyrone, to Belfast (see 22 Dec. 1753, 7 Sept. 1763)

Jan. 29 Archibald Hamilton Rowan, United Irishman, tried on charge of distributing seditious paper (see 14 Dec. 1792) and sentenced to fine of £500 and imprisonment for 2 years (see 2 May)

Feb. 15 United Irishmen's plan of parliamentary reform published in *Dublin Evening Post* (in *Northern Star* 20 Feb.)

Mar. 1 Statutes of Dublin University amended to allow catholics to take degrees

Mar. 4 George Ponsonby's parliamentary reform bill introduced in H.C. and defeated by 142 to 44

Apr. 14 General Arthur Dillon guillotined in France

Apr. 28 Rev. William Jackson, agent of French revolutionary government, arrested in Dublin on charge of high treason (suicide, 30 Apr. 1795)

May 2 Rowan escapes from custody, eventually making his way to France and then America

May 23 Dublin Society of United Irishmen suppressed by police raid on meeting

June 25 William Drennan tried for seditious libel and acquitted

July 11 Duke of Portland joins Pitt's administration; Charles James Fox remains in opposition

July 27-8 Fall and death of Maximilien de Robespierre; Thermidorian reaction in France

Dec. 23 Catholic meeting in Dublin appoints committee of 9 to prepare petitions to parliament for repeal of remaining penal laws

Dec. 27   French invade Holland

1795

Jan. 4   Earl Fitzwilliam sworn in as L.L.

Jan. 9   Fitzwilliam dismisses John Beresford as chief revenue commissioner and Arthur Wolfe as attorney general (more dismissals follow)

Jan. 24   Protestants of Belfast petition parliament for repeal of all penal and restrictive statutes against catholics (petition presented, 2 Feb.)

Feb. 12   Grattan introduces catholic relief bill in H.C.

Feb. 23   Fitzwilliam dismissed (leaves Ire., 25 Mar.)

Feb. 27   Committee of synod of Ulster, sitting at Dungannon, approves address to L.L. in support of Fitzwilliam's policy

Mar. 31   Earl Camden sworn in as L.L.

Apr. 22   Tadhg Gaedhealach Ó Súilleabháin, Irish poet, dies

May 5   H.C. rejects Grattan's catholic relief bill, by 155 to 84

May 10   United Irishmen of Ulster secretly meet in Belfast and adopt new constitution

June 5   'Act for the better education of persons professing the popish or Roman Catholic religion' (35 Geo. III, c. 21), providing for establishment of catholic seminary (see c. 1 Oct. 1795, 20 Apr. 1796)

June 13   Tone embarks at Belfast for U.S.A.

Sept. 1   First and only number of *Bolg an Tsolair or Gaelic Magazine* (Belfast)

Sept. 7   Lawrence O'Connor, schoolmaster and Defender leader, hanged at Naas, Co. Kildare

Sept. 21   'Battle of the Diamond' near Loughgall, Co. Armagh, between Peep o' Day Boys and Defenders (see 4 July 1784), leading to foundation of Orange Order

Oct. c. 1   Catholic seminary, Royal College of St Patrick, opened at Maynooth, Co. Kildare

1796

Feb. 1   Tone arrives in France from U.S.A.

Mar. 24   Act (36 Geo. III, c. 2) removes tax on beer and increases tax on malt (stimulates Irish brewing industry)

Insurrection act (36 Geo. III, c. 20) provides death penalty for administering illegal oath, and imposes curfew and arms searches on districts proclaimed by government as disturbed

Apr. 20   First stone of new buildings of St Patrick's College, Maynooth, laid by Camden, L.L.

Apr. 23   Docks at Ringsend, Dublin, and circular line linking Grand Canal near Dolphin's Barn with Liffey at Ringsend, opened by Camden, L.L.

July 12   Orange parades in Lurgan, Waringstown, and Portadown

Aug. Arthur O'Connor and General Lazare Hoche meet clandestinely in France and discuss possible United Irish support for intended French invasion of Ire.

Sept. 12 Thomas Russell's *A letter to the people of Ireland on the present situation of the country* (Belfast)

Sept. 16 Russell, Samuel Neilson, and several others with French sympathies arrested in Belfast on charges of high treason

Sept. 21 James Louis O'Donel O.F.M.Obs., native of Knocklofty, Co. Tipperary, consecrated bp *in partibus* to serve as vicar apostolic of Newfoundland; first English-speaking catholic bp in British North America

Oct. 17 Grattan's motion in H.C. in favour of admitting catholics to parliament defeated by 143 to 19

Oct. 26 Habeas corpus suspension act (37 Geo. III, c. 1) (continued by 38 Geo. III, c. 14 (24 Mar. 1798), to 1 June 1799)

Nov. 3 Courts sit for first time in new Four Courts building, Dublin

Nov. 9 Act (37 Geo. III, c. 2) for regulating yeomanry corps

Dec. 22–7 French invasion fleet, with troops and Tone on board, in Bantry Bay, Co. Cork; landing prevented by bad weather

1797

Feb. 26 Bank of Ireland suspends gold payments (see 1 June 1821)

Mar. 13 General Gerard Lake's proclamation ordering handing-in of arms in Ulster

May 10 Outbreak of naval mutiny at the Nore, in Thames estuary

May 19 Presses of Belfast *Northern Star* broken up by Monaghan militia

June 4 Orange lodge formed in Dublin

July–Aug. General election of last Irish parliament

Sept. 4 *Coup d'état* of 18 Fructidor; conservative reaction in France

Sept. 28 First number of *The Press*; editor Arthur O'Connor

Oct. 11 Battle of Camperdown: British naval victory, crippling Dutch fleet and removing threat of French invasion of British Isles from Holland

Oct. 14 William Orr, United Irishman, hanged at Carrickfergus

Nov. 10 Sir Ralph Abercromby app. commander-in-chief in Ire. (declares army in Ire. to be 'in a state of licentiousness which must render it formidable to everyone but the enemy', 26 Feb. 1798)

Nov. Edward Bunting's *A general collection of the ancient Irish music*, vol. i (London; vol. ii, London, 1809; vol. iii, Dublin, 1840)

1798

Jan. 9 First meeting of George III's sixth, and last, Irish parliament

Feb. 10 Fall of Rome to French army, leading to expulsion and subsequent arrest of Pope Pius VI

Mar. 12   Police raid meeting of Leinster directory of United Irishmen at Oliver Bond's house at Dublin, arresting 12 leaders; 4 others arrested elsewhere; all but 2 members of supreme executive thus arrested

Mar. 29   Viscount Castlereagh temporarily app. C.S. (permanently, 3 Nov.)

Mar. 30   Privy council proclamation declaring Ire. in state of rebellion and imposing martial law

Apr. 19-21   Earl of Clare's visitation of Trinity College and purge of United Irishmen; 19 expelled

Apr. 25   Lake succeeds Abercromby as commander-in-chief in Ire.

May 17-18   Meetings of new national directory of United Irishmen

May 19   Daniel O'Connell called to Irish bar

Lord Edward Fitzgerald arrested (dies from wound, 4 June)

May 21-2   Trial at Maidstone, Kent, of Arthur O'Connor and Rev. James Quigley, United Irishmen; former acquitted of treason but rearrested, latter convicted and sentenced to death (hanged, 7 June)

May 23-4   United Irish rebellion begins in Leinster

May 26   Insurgents defeated at Tara, Co. Meath

May 27   Battle of Oulart Hill, Co. Wexford; detachment of North Cork militia and local yeomanry almost annihilated

May 29   350 insurgents killed at Curragh, Co. Kildare, by troops under Sir James Duff

May 30-June 21   Wexford town occupied by insurgents

June 5   Insurgents routed at New Ross, Co. Wexford, after heavy fighting; massacre of protestants by insurgents at nearby Scullabogue

June 6   Rebellion breaks out in Ulster: Henry Joy McCracken issues proclamation calling United Irishmen in Ulster to arms

June 7   United Irishmen, led by McCracken, attack Antrim town and are repulsed with heavy loss (McCracken executed in Belfast, 17 July)

June 9   Wexford insurgents, advancing towards Dublin, repulsed at Arklow

June 13   United Irishmen led by Henry Monro defeated at Ballynahinch, Co. Down (Monro executed at Lisburn, 15 June)

June 20   Marquis Cornwallis sworn in as L.L.

June 21   Wexford insurgents defeated at Vinegar Hill, near Enniscorthy

July 14   John and Henry Sheares executed

Aug. 4   Thomas Addis Emmet, Arthur O'Connor, and William James MacNeven deliver to government their 'Memoir, or detailed statement of the origin and progress of the Irish Union' (on United Irish movement)

Aug. 7-14   Examination of MacNeven, O'Connor, Neilson, T. A. Emmet, and Bond by secret committee of H.L.

Aug. 22   French force of about 1,000 under General Jean Humbert lands at Kilcumin, near Killala, Co. Mayo

Aug. 27   Government troops surprised and routed by Humbert at Castlebar, Co. Mayo—'Castlebar races'

Sept. 8   Humbert surrenders to Cornwallis at Ballinamuck, Co. Longford

Sept. 16   Small French force under James Napper Tandy makes brief landing on Rutland Island, Co. Donegal

Oct. 6   Grattan removed from Irish privy council on groundless charge of being sworn member of United Irishmen

Banishment act (38 Geo. III, c. 78) pardons named individuals concerned in rebellion, subject to banishment; return to British dominions or passage to country at war with G.B. prohibited

Fugitives act (38 Geo. III, c. 80) calls on rebels to surrender on pain of being attainted of high treason

Oct. 12-20   French invasion squadron under Admiral J. B. F. Bompart engaged outside Lough Swilly by British squadron under Sir John Borlase Warren; 7 of 10 French ships captured (Tone arrested on landing at Buncrana, Co. Donegal, 3 Nov.)

Nov. 10   Tone tried and convicted by court martial in Dublin; sentenced to be hanged

Nov. 19   Tone dies from self-inflicted wound in provost-marshal's prison, Dublin barracks

Dec. 1   Edward Cooke's *Arguments for and against an union between Great Britain and Ireland considered* (anon., Dublin)

c. **Dec.**   Alexander Knox's *Essays on the political circumstances of Ireland* (anon., Dublin)

1799

Jan. 17-19   Catholic bps meeting in Dublin secretly adopt resolutions in favour of state remuneration of clergy and government veto on nomination of bps (see 25 May, 14-15 Sept., 1808)

Jan. 23   H.C. rejects, by 106 votes to 105, George Ponsonby's motion in favour of continued legislative independence

Jan. 31   Pitt's speech in British H.C. in favour of union (subsequently published and distributed in Ire.)

Mar. 25   Suppression of rebellion act (39 Geo. III, c. 11), empowering L.L. to authorise trial by court martial (continued by successive acts until 1805)

Apr. 9   Arrival of William Steel Dickson, Thomas Addis Emmet, William James Macneven, Samuel Neilson, Arthur O'Connor, Thomas Russell, Robert Simms, John Sweetman and eleven other leading United Irishmen for internment at Fort George, Inverness-shire (see 30 June 1802)

July 1   Thomas Bray, catholic abp of Cashel, assures Abp Troy that he will cooperate in influencing catholics to support union

Sept. 29   Tandy and other Irish political prisoners in Hamburg handed over to British authorities

Nov. 9-10   *Coup d'état* of 18-19 Brumaire brings Napoleon Bonaparte to power as first consul in France

1800

Jan. 10   Grand Orange Lodge adopts rules, including 10 secret articles (see 10 July 1810)

Jan. 13   Daniel O'Connell makes first public speech, at meeting of catholics at Royal Exchange, Dublin, convened to protest against proposed union of Ire. with G.B.

Jan. 15   Opening of last session of Irish parliament

Jan.   Maria Edgeworth's *Castle Rackrent* (London)

Feb. 5-6   H.C. debates government's proposals for union, ultimately approving them by 158 votes to 115

Feb.-Mar.   Orange lodges pass resolutions against union

Mar. 13   Dublin Society decides to sponsor statistical surveys of Irish counties (23 published, 1801-32)

Mar. 14   Cardinal Chiaramonti elected pope as Pius VII

Apr. 10   Habeas corpus suspension act (40 Geo. III, c. 18) (continued by 41 Geo. III, c. 15 (24 Mar. 1801) to 24 June 1801)

May 21   Castlereagh, C.S., obtains leave from Irish H.C., by 160 to 100, to bring in union bill

June 17   British H.C. gives leave to bring in union bill

July 2   British act of union (39 & 40 Geo. III, c. 67)

Aug. 1   Irish act of union (40 Geo. III, c. 38)

Laying of first stone of King's Inns, Dublin; architects James Gandon and Henry Aaron Baker (completed by Francis Johnston, 1817)

Aug. 2   Last meeting of Irish parliament

IRELAND UNDER THE UNION, 1801-1921

INTRODUCTION

THE emergence of an expanding modern administration in an Ireland within the British political system greatly increased the production of public records, both manuscript and printed, providing documentation for chronology on an unprecedented scale. The principal archives of the Irish administration during the period of the union, those of the chief secretary's office and related departments, were kept in a separate repository, the State Paper Office, in the Record Tower of Dublin Castle. Much of this material down to the late 1830s had been transferred to the Public Record Office by 1922, but the records later in date were not involved in the destruction of 1922 and they remain the largest corpus of archival material for the history of English government in Ireland. Manuscripts in libraries and in private ownership, especially the papers of leading politicians, continue for this period to be an indispensable supplement to public records. But there is also a fuller and more continuous body of source-material available in print than for any previous era, and it is on this that the compilers of the present section of the chronology have largely depended for their primary sources. Newspapers, central and local, magazines and reviews, year-books, and directories proliferate, offering an abundance of detailed and dated information. No less informative are the voluminous materials relating to Ireland embodied in the journals, debates, and statutes of the United Kingdom parliament and in British parliamentary papers, a vast collection that includes both periodic reports from governmental and other public bodies and the reports of *ad hoc* commissions and committees of inquiry into a wide variety of public questions.

The increasing range and intensity of state action both require, and provide the material for, an enlarged scale of chronological treatment, and this inevitably entails increasing problems of selection. Moreover, despite the wealth of recent published scholarship on Ireland during the union period, on which the compilers have drawn heavily, many detailed questions of chronology have remained unexplored; and this has meant that laborious research has often had to be undertaken in order to establish a single event.

Among new types of entry the following are specially significant: results of all general elections (including figures for Great Britain as well as for Ireland), all changes of government (under the name of the prime minister), all censuses from 1821, and reports of all major commissions and committees of inquiry. Cross-references are added much more copiously than in previous sections; for example, each entry relating to a general election is cross-referenced to the preceding and the succeeding general election. The numbers of seats won by the respective parties in Great Britain as well as in Ireland are given from 1832, though between that date and 1868 the classification of M.P.s and the nomenclature of parties present serious difficulties. Party allegiance was ill-defined, party organisation minimal, members described themselves by various labels and could easily shift from one allegiance to another. But the practical advantage of uniformly using the terms conservative and liberal, in succession to tory and whig, from 1832, seems to outweigh the disadvantage of over-simplification. In using these terms to describe British parties and governments, the compilers have followed the nomenclature and statistics of Mr F. W. S. Craig,[1] except that, for the 1847 and 1852 elections, they have treated as a separate party the liberal conservative group known as Peelites.[2] For Irish parliamentary elections they have adopted the figures and the party labels used by Dr Brian Walker.[3]

For help received in this section of the chronology we are grateful to Mr Patrick Callan, Dr R. V. Comerford, Dr Fergus D'Arcy, Professor Aloys Fleischmann, the late E. R. R. Green, Dr H. D. Gribbon, Mr Richard Hawkins, Professor Oliver MacDonagh, Dr David W. Miller, Dr Arthur H. Mitchell, Professor Patrick O'Farrell, and Dr Brian M. Walker. Our thanks are also due to Dr David Doyle for many entries relating to the Irish in the U.S.A. and in Britain.

[1] *British parliamentary election results, 1832-1885* (London, 1977); —— *1885-1918* (London, 1974); —— *1918-1949* (Glasgow, 1969); *British electoral facts, 1885-1975* (London, 1977).

[2] W. D. Jones and A. B. Erickson, *The Peelites, 1846-57* (Columbus, Ohio, 1972).

[3] B. M. Walker, *Parliamentary election results in Ireland, 1801-1922* (Dublin, 1978).

CHRONOLOGY, 1801-1921
(A) 1801-70

T. W. MOODY AND C. J. WOODS

1801

Jan. 1 Union of Ire. and G.B. comes into effect

Feb. 3 Pitt (tory) announces his intention to resign as P.M., owing to disagreement with George III over catholic emancipation (Henry Addington (tory) succeeds, 17 Mar.; see 19 Dec. 1783, 10 May 1804)

July 2 Copyright act (41 Geo. III, c. 107) requires one copy of every book published in U.K. to be deposited in libraries of Trinity College and King's Inns, Dublin (ceases to apply to latter, 1836), and makes illegal the 'pirating' in Ireland of British-published books

Nov. 10 Belfast Society for Promoting Knowledge decides to transfer its library to room in Linen Hall, Belfast

Sir Richard Musgrave's *Memoirs of the different rebellions in Ireland* (Dublin; 2nd ed., 1801; 3rd ed., 1802)

1802

Mar. 27 Peace of Amiens ends war between U.K. and France

June 1 Laying of foundation stone of permanent buildings for school recently opened at Waterford by Edmund Rice (see Aug. 1808)

June 30 United Irish internees at Fort George, Inverness-shire, liberated and embark for Continent (see 9 Apr. 1799)

July General election; Addington, P.M. (tory), retains his majority (see Nov.-Dec. 1806)

Richard Lovell and Maria Edgeworth's *Essay on Irish bulls* (London)

1803

Jan. Influenza epidemic, continuing until June

May 18 U.K. declares war on France

July 1 General synod of Ulster accepts government's scheme for augmentation and redistribution of *regium donum*

July 23 Robert Emmet's rising in Dublin

July 29 Habeas corpus suspension act (43 Geo. III, c. 116) (continued by successive acts to 7 Mar. 1806)

Sept. 19 Emmet tried and convicted of high treason (executed next day)

Oct. 20 Thomas Russell at Downpatrick tried and convicted of high treason (executed next day)

Dec. 7 Commissioning of officers in new Irish legion established by Bonaparte

Dec. 14   Michael Dwyer, in rebellion since 1798, surrenders in Wicklow mountains (leaves Ire. on *Tellicherry* for New South Wales, 28 Aug. 1805)

Francis Plowden's *An historical review of the state of Ireland from the invasion of that country under Henry II to its union with Great Britain* (2 vols, London)

1804

Jan. 14   Opening of Cow-pock Institution at 1 North Cope Street, Dublin, for vaccination on Edward Jenner's principle against smallpox (later removed to Sackville Street)

Mar. 4-5   Insurrection at Castle Hill, near Parramatta, New South Wales; many Irish involved

May 10   Pitt returns to office as P.M. (see 3 Feb. 1801, 23 Jan. 1806)

May 18   Napoleon Bonaparte proclaimed emperor of the French by senate and tribunate (consecrated by Pope Pius VII, 2 Dec.)

Sept. 4   Abraham Colles elected professor of anatomy, physiology and surgery at Royal College of Surgeons in Ireland

1805

Mar. 25   Presentation to parliament of Irish catholic petition

Apr. 9   Pius VII grants final approval to Presentation order founded at Cork by Nano Nagle (see 24 Dec. 1775)

May 13-14   H.C. debates Irish catholic petition; Grattan makes his maiden speech at Westminster in its support

July 10   Act permitting grand juries to provide funds for maintenance of dispensaries 'for furnishing medicine and giving medical aid and relief to the poor' (45 Geo. III, c. 111)

William Parnell's *An enquiry into the causes of popular discontents in Ireland, by an Irish country gentleman* (anon., Dublin)

1806

Jan. 23   Pitt, P.M., dies (see 10 May 1804)

Feb. 11   'Ministry of all the talents' formed under Lord Grenville as P.M., with Charles James Fox as foreign secretary (see 31 Mar. 1807)

Mar. 8   William Henry Hamilton and seven other United Irish prisoners released from Kilmainham jail following expiry of habeas corpus suspension act (see 29 July 1803)

Mar. 17   Laying of foundation-stone of Royal College of Surgeons, Dublin; architect, Edward Parke

July 21   Act (46 Geo. III, c. 122) empowering L.L. to appoint commrs to inquire into state of education in Ire. (14 reports, 1809-13)

c. **Sept.**   Thresher disturbances begin in north-west of Ire.

Oct.   *Pharmacopoeia Collegii Medicorum Regis et Reginae in Hibernia* (Dublin; 2nd ed., 1826; English translation, 1828 and 1830)

Nov. 10   Hibernian Bible Society formed

Nov. 21   Napoleon issues Berlin decree: intensification of economic war

Nov.-Dec.   General election; Grenville, P.M., gains supporters (see July 1802, May-June 1807)

Sydney Owenson's *The wild Irish girl: a national tale* (London)

1807

Jan. 19   First meeting of Gaelic Society of Dublin

Feb. 1   Order of Sisters of St Brigid founded at Tullow, Co. Carlow

Feb. 15   Foundation-stone laid of chapel (later called Chapel Royal) at Dublin Castle; architect Francis Johnston; sculptured figures and heads by Edward Smyth (opened, 25 Dec. 1814)

Mar. 20   Charter incorporating Cork Institution for promoting science and agriculture (founded 1803; later renamed Royal Cork Institution)

Mar. 24   Fall of 'ministry of all the talents', owing to disagreement over bill extending right of catholics to hold commns in army

Mar. 31   Duke of Portland (whig) app. P.M. (see 11 Feb. 1806, 4 Oct. 1809)

May-June   'No popery' general election confirms Portland in office (see Nov.-Dec. 1806, Oct.-Nov. 1812)

May 21   William Saurin appointed attorney general (dismissed, 1822)

Aug. 1   Insurrection act (47 Geo. III, sess. 2, c. 13) consolidates provisions of 1796 insurrection act and subsequent amendments (never applied)

Aug. 13   L.L. empowered to appoint up to 3 commrs to carry out paving, cleansing, and lighting of streets of Dublin (47 Geo. III, sess. 2, c. cix)

Possession of arms act (47 Geo. III, sess. 2, c. 54)

Nov.   First number of Watty Cox's *Irish Magazine* (continues till 1815)

Sydney Owenson's *Patriotic sketches of Ireland* (London)

William Parnell's *An historical apology for the Irish catholics* (Dublin)

William James MacNeven's *Pieces of Irish history* (New York)

1808

Jan. 5   Progressive reduction, under article 6 of act of union, of duties on calicoes, muslins, cotton yarn, and cotton twist imported into Ire. from G.B. begins

Jan. 30   Excavation of site on Sackville Street, Dublin, for monument to Viscount Nelson begins (see 8 Mar. 1966)

Apr.   First number of Thomas Moore's *Irish melodies* (?London)

May 25   George Ponsonby, in H.C. debate on catholic petitions presented by Grattan, outlines scheme for royal veto on appointments to Irish bishoprics which he asserts has approval of Irish bps; petitions rejected, by 281 to 128; beginning of 'veto' controversy

June 30   Dublin Police Magistrates Act, 1808 (48 Geo. III, c. 140) places Dublin police force under control of 18 magistrates, of whom 6 are to be elected by corporation and 12 by L.L.

Aug.   Christian Brothers, lay teaching order, founded by Edmund Rice

Sept. 14-15   Catholic bps meet in Dublin and formally repudiate 'veto' proposals

Henry Brooke Parnell's *A history of the penal laws against the Irish catholics* (Dublin; 4th ed., London 1825)

Rev. William Neilson's *An introduction to the Irish language* (Dublin; 2nd ed., Achill, 1843)

1809

Mar. 7   Belfast Harp Society formed, primarily to teach blind children the harp, but also to promote study of Irish language, history, and antiquities

May 24   Formal re-establishment, at meeting of catholics at Exhibition Room, William Street, Dublin, of General Committee of the Catholics of Ireland

June 15   Drainage of Bogs (Ireland) Act, 1809 (49 Geo. III, c. 102) empowers L.L. to appoint commrs to inquire into state of bogs (reports, 10 June 1810, 8 Mar. 1811, Apr. 1814)

July 6   Arrest of Pope Pius VII, leading to deportation to Savona, near Genoa, and later to France

Oct. 4   Spencer Perceval (tory) app. P.M. (see 31 Mar. 1807, 11 May 1812)

Nov.   Sunday School Society for Ire. founded

Thomas Newenham's *A view of the natural, political and commercial circumstances of Ireland* (London)

1810

Mar.   Opening in Dublin of Richmond National Institution for the Instruction of the Industrious Blind

June 10   First report of commrs to inquire into state of bogs; major contribution by Richard Griffith (final report, Apr. 1814)

June 15   Act (50 Geo. III, c. cxciii) incorporating Belfast Academical Institution (foundation stone laid, 3 July; see 1 Feb. 1814)

June 20   Unlawful Oaths (Ireland) Act, 1810 (50 Geo. III, c. 102), replaces and extends insurrection-act powers against secret societies bound by oaths (see 1 Aug. 1807)

July 10   Grand Orange Lodge prepares new rules, omitting secret articles, to forestall any attempt to use convention act against it (see 10 Jan. 1800)

Sept. 1   Commn to inquire into state of Irish records (reports 1-15, 3 vols, 1815-25; reports 16-17 in H.C. 1828 (50), xii; reports 18-19 in H.C. 1830 (74), xvi)

Sept. 18   Aggregate meeting of freemen and freeholders at Royal Exchange, Dublin, resolves to prepare petition for repeal of union

Francis Hardy's *Memoirs of the political and private life of James Caulfield, earl of Charlemont* (London)

1811

Financial and commercial crises in U.K., owing to economic war

Feb. 4-13 Trials at Clonmel, Waterford, and Kilkenny of Caravats and Shanavests

Feb. 5 George Augustus Frederick, prince of Wales, becomes regent owing to insanity of George III

Feb. 12 William Wellesley-Pole, C.S., issues circular to sheriffs and magistrates instructing them to proceed under convention act (see 16 Aug. 1793) against catholics involved in appointment of representatives to Catholic Committee

July 9 Meeting of catholics in Fishamble Street, Dublin, resolves to establish cttee to manage petitions for repeal of remaining penal laws, some members of which are to be app. by catholics of each county or of each Dublin parish

July 30 Proclamation under convention act declaring illegal the appointment of county and parish representatives to catholic petition cttee

Aug. 12 Arrest of Dr Edward Sheridan on charges under convention act (trial and acquittal, 21-2 Nov.)

Dec. 2 Kildare Place Society formed to maintain non-denominational schools

1812

Feb. 3 Thomas Kirwan found guilty of offences under convention act (fined nominal sum, 6 Feb.)

May 11 Spencer Perceval, P.M., assassinated (see 4 Oct. 1809)

June 8 Earl of Liverpool (tory) app. P.M. (see 10 Apr. 1827)

June 28 Trustees of Maynooth College agree to apply Dunboyne legacy to further education of 20 of college's more distinguished students

Aug. 4 Robert Peel app. C.S.

Oct.-Nov. General election: Liverpool remains P.M. (see May-June 1807, 8 June 1812, June-July 1818)

Edward Wakefield's *An account of Ireland, statistical and political* (2 vols, London)

1813

Apr. 30 Grattan introduces catholic relief bill (in effect defeated in H.C. by 251 to 247, 24 May)

July 3 General synod of Ulster at Cookstown declares in favour of 'the abolition of political distinctions on account of religious profession so far as may be consistent with the principles of the constitution'

July 10 Irish endowed schools act, 1813 (53 Geo. III, c. 107), provides for permanent commrs to direct royal schools and supervise others

July 12 Disturbances in Belfast as a result of tension between protestants and catholics (the first of a long succession)

July 26-7 Trial of John Magee, proprietor of *Dublin Evening Post*, on charge of libelling L.L. (sentenced to fine of £500 and 2 years' imprisonment, 29 Nov.)

Dec. 2 Charles Lewis Metzler von Giesecke elected to professorship of mineralogy of Dublin Society (which he holds until his death, 5 Mar. 1833)

1814

Feb. 1 Belfast Academical Institution opened (assumes prefix 'Royal', 1831)

Mar. 1 William Brown, native of Foxford, Co. Mayo, app. commander of navy of revolutionary government of Buenos Aires (River Plate)

Apr. 11 Abdication of Napoleon

May 5 Publication in Dublin of Mgr Quarantotti's letter (dated 16 Feb. 1814) favourable to 'veto'

May 24 Pius VII reenters Rome

May 27 Infirmaries act (54 Geo. III, c. 62) provides for appointment of apothecaries (see 10 July 1805)

May 30 First peace of Paris between France and allied powers

June 3 Catholic Board suppressed by viceregal proclamation

June 22 First public meeting of Hibernian Auxiliary Church Missionary Society, formed to assist Church Missionary Society for Missions to Africa and the East

July 14 Clongowes Wood College (Jesuit) opened

July 25 Peel's peace preservation act (54 Geo. III, c. 131) empowers L.L. to appoint in disturbed areas 'a chief magistrate of police', a clerk, a chief constable and a force of sub-constables, responsible to central government but paid from local rates

July 30 Revised insurrection act (54 Geo. III, c. 180)

Aug. 12 Laying of first stone of Post Office, Sackville Street, Dublin; architect Francis Johnston (opened, 6 Jan. 1818)

Nov. 1 Congress of Vienna opened

Nov. 28 Bp William Poynter sets off for Rome to put case of English catholics in favour of 'veto'

Dec. 14 Dublin Society purchases Leinster House (assumes title Royal Dublin Society, 29 June 1820)

Apprentice Boys of Derry Club formed

William Shaw Mason's *Statistical account or parochial survey of Ireland*, vol. i (Dublin; vol. ii, 1816; vol. iii, 1819)

John Field's first 3 nocturnes published in Germany (15 more follow)

Richard Griffith's *Geological and mining report on the Leinster coal district* (Dublin), first of his 3 reports to Dublin Society on Irish coalfields (1814-29)

1815

Jan. 19 O'Connell at catholic meeting in Dublin warns pope and Irish hierarchy that lower clergy and catholic masses would revolt against any 'veto' arrangement

Feb. 1 O'Connell fatally wounds John Norcot D'Esterre in duel

Mar. 28 Paddle steamer, *Thames*, leaves Dublin for London, the first steamship to make crossing with passengers and cargo

Mar. 28 Laying of foundation-stone of Roman Catholic Metropolitan Chapel (later known as Catholic Pro-Cathedral), Marlborough Street, Dublin (opened, 14 Nov. 1825)

Mar. William Drennan's *Fugitive pieces in verse and prose* (Belfast)

Apr. 26 Cardinal Litta's 'Genoese letter' defends 'veto'

May 25 Grattan speaks in favour of immediate resumption of war following Napoleon's escape from Elba

June 9 Congress of Vienna concludes with 'final act'

June 18 Napoleon finally defeated at battle of Waterloo (see 11 Apr. 1814; again abdicates, 22 June)

June 22 Richmond lunatic asylum act, 1815 (55 Geo. III, c. 107), provides for regulation of recently erected Dublin asylum

July 6 Charles Bianconi runs his first car for conveyance of passengers, from Clonmel to Cahir

Aug. 24 Catholic bps adopt series of anti-vetoist resolutions for presentation to holy see

Sept. 1 Mary Augustine Aikenhead app. by Bp Daniel Murray superior general of new order, Irish Sisters of Charity; first convent, in North William Street, Dublin, occupied

Nov. 20 Second peace of Paris between France and allied powers

1816

Feb. 1 Pope Pius VII's reply to Irish catholic bps confirms contents of 'Genoese letter' (see 26 Apr. 1815)

Feb. 13 Meeting of catholics in Lord Trimleston's house adopts petition to parliament declaring catholics ready to accept 'qualified' emancipation

May 18 National Institution for the Education of Deaf and Dumb Children of the Poor in Ireland founded

June 26 Act (56 Geo. III, c. 88) to facilitate recovery of possession of land by landlords in Ire.

July 1 Consolidated Fund Act, 1816 (56 Geo. III, c. 98) amalgamates exchequers of G.B. and Ire. as from 5 Jan. 1817

July 5 Opening of methodist conference at which sanction is given to administration of eucharist by unordained preachers and so to break with established church

c. **Aug.** Potato crop fails owing to late seasons and excessive rain; beginning of first major famine since 1742

Sept. 30 Horticultural Society of Ireland founded (assumes title Royal, 1838)

c. **Sept.–Oct.** Typhus epidemic begins (becoming widespread, early 1817, continuing till Dec. 1819, and causing some 50,000 deaths)

Nov. *c.* 1 Arthur O'Neill, harper, dies aged 90

1817

Apr. 19   Charles Wolfe's 'The burial of Sir John Moore' in *Newry Telegraph*

May 27   Thomas Moore's *Lalla Rookh* (London)

May 31   First stone laid of pier to form artificial harbour at Dunleary, Co. Dublin

June 16   Poor employment act, 1817 (57 Geo. III, c. 34) empowers L.L. to appoint commrs to direct public works financed by mortgages of rates

June 17   Foundation stone laid of Wellington Testimonial in Phoenix Park, Dublin; architect Robert Smirke (granite obelisk completed, 1820; bronze panels added, 1861)

June   Maria Edgeworth's *Ormond* (London)

July 11   'Act to provide for the establishment of asylums for the lunatic poor in Ireland' (57 Geo. III, c. 106)

   Irish grand jury presentments act, 1817 (57 Geo. III, c. 107), regulates expenditure on public works

July 16   Richard Hayes, O.F.M., delegate of anti-vetoists, forcibly expelled from Rome

c. **July**   Jeffery Sedwards forms total abstinence society in Skibbereen, Co. Cork; first such body in Europe (cf. June 1835)

Sept. 30   National fever cttee app. to disburse government aid for victims of epidemic (£18,629 spent in 2 years)

1818

Jan. 28   Iberno-Celtic Society formed

Apr. 22   Select cttee app. by H.C. to inquire into fever in Ire. (reports, 8, 26 May)

May 30   Fever hospitals act (58 Geo. III, c. 47) provides for establishment of fever hospitals and extension of dispensary system

June 13-14   *Rob Roy* makes first steam crossing between the Clyde and Belfast

June-July   General election; Liverpool (tory) remains P.M.; in several Irish constituencies 40s. freeholders are mobilised by catholic priests in support of pro-emancipation candidates (see Oct.–Nov. 1812, Mar. 1820)

July 9   Burgher and anti-burgher synods (seceders), meeting at Cookstown, Co. Tyrone, unite to form secession synod

John Warburton, James Whitelaw, and Robert Walsh's *History of the city of Dublin* (2 vols, London)

Irish Society for Promoting the Education of the Native Irish through the Medium of their own Language founded; protestant missionary body.

1819

Apr. 6   Select cttee app. by H.C. to inquire into state of disease, and condition of poor, in Ire. (first report, 17 May; second report, 7 June)

Apr. 16   Irish Harp Society founded at Belfast (in succession to Belfast Harp Society)

May 3   Grattan presents several petitions in favour of catholic emancipation and again moves unsuccessfully for cttee to inquire into laws affecting catholics

June 26   First detachment of John Devereux's Irish legion sails from Liverpool in *Charlotte Gambier* to serve in Simón Bolívar's army in South American wars of independence

July 12   Irish fisheries act, 1819 (59 Geo. III, c. 109) provides for appointment of commissioners of fisheries to regulate sea fishing

July 13-14   Murder of Ellen Hanly (alias Scanlan)—the 'colleen bawn'—by drowning in River Shannon (see 1829; 27 Mar. 1860)

c. **Oct.**   Ribbon disturbances proliferate in counties between Dublin, Galway, and Limerick

William Monck Mason's *History and antiquities of the cathedral church of St Patrick, Dublin* (Dublin; 2nd ed., 1820)

William Parnell's *Maurice and Berghetta, or the priest of Rahery: a tale* (anon., London)

1820

Jan. 19   Grand Orange Lodge issues circular against unauthorised orange 'orders'

Jan. 29   First of Rev. John MacHale's letters under pen-name 'Hierophilos' arguing against education of catholics and protestants together

George III dies; succ. by George IV

Feb. 12   *East Indian* and *Fanny*, with about 350 Irish emigrants aboard, leave Cork harbour for Cape Colony (arrive, 30 Apr. and 1 May); Irish contribution to '1820 settlers'

Feb. 24   Kildare Place Society rejects O'Connell's proposal for cttee to investigate religious impartiality of its previous policy

Mar.   General election; Liverpool remains P.M. (see June-July 1818, June-July 1826)

May 13   Catholic deputation received in Dublin by Grattan, who promises to go to London to press for emancipation

May 25   Failure of Roche's Bank and stoppage of Leslie's Bank at Cork; beginning of banking crisis which spreads throughout Munster and then to Dublin

June 4   Grattan dies in London

July 8   'Act for lighting the city and suburbs of Dublin with gas' (1 Geo. IV, c. lv)

Dec. 1   Rev. Patrick Scully arrives at Cape Town to serve catholics in Cape of Good Hope; beginning of Irish catholic missionary effort in Africa

Rev. Charles Robert Maturin's *Melmoth the wanderer* (Edinburgh)

James Hardiman's *History of the town and county of the town of Galway* (Dublin)

1821

Jan. 18 Opening of Theatre Royal, Hawkins Street, Dublin

Apr. 17 William Conyngham Plunket's bill to grant catholic emancipation, subject to government right of veto on appointments of bishops and deans, defeated in H.L. by 159 to 120

May 28 Census taken throughout Ire.: population 6,801,827

First public performance of John Banim's 'Damon and Pythias' at Covent Garden Theatre, London

June 1 Bank of Ireland resumes gold payments (see 26 Feb. 1797)

June 5 Belfast Natural History Society formed (renamed Belfast Natural History and Philosophical Society, 23 Aug. 1842)

July 2 Act (1 & 2 Geo. IV, c. 72) removing monopoly of Bank of Ireland by permitting joint-stock banks outside radius of 50 miles from Dublin

July 10 Catholic meeting at D'Arcy's Tavern, Dublin, accepts invitation to combine with corporation in celebrating kg's coronation

Aug. 12–Sept. 3 George IV visits Ireland; his departure from Dunleary Harbour and completion of its east pier commemorated by renaming place Kingstown

Sept.-Nov. Potato crop fails

Oct. 25 Rev. William Bruce, jr, minister of presbytery of Antrim and holder of mild Arian opinions, elected to chair of Greek, Latin, and Hebrew at Belfast Academical Institution in preference to Rev. R. J. Bryce, minister of reformed presbyterian or covenanting synod and candidate of Rev. Henry Coope; beginning of second non-subscription controversy in synod of Ulster (see 18–20 Aug. 1829)

Dec. 29 Marquis Wellesley sworn in as L.L.

1822

Jan. 15 William Conyngham Plunket app. attorney general *vice* Saurin

Feb. 11 Insurrection act, 1822 (3 Geo. IV, c. 1), essentially similar to those of 1807 and 1814

Habeas corpus suspension act (3 Geo. IV, c. 2), in force until 1 Aug.; first use of this power against agrarian disturbances (no arrests made)

May 24 Poor employment act, 1822 (3 Geo. IV, c. 34), provides £50,000 for building of roads in response to widespread failure of potato crop

June 22 George Canning's bill to admit catholic peers to H.L. defeated in H.L. by 171 to 129

June Fever follows famine in west of Ire. (continuing till Dec.)

July 5 Act (3 Geo. IV, c. 54) abolishes Irish window and hearth taxes (see 20 Dec. 1662)

July 22 Richard ('Humanity') Martin's 'act to prevent the cruel and improper treatment of cattle' (3 Geo. IV, c. 71)

Aug. 1 Irish constabulary act, 1822 (3 Geo. IV, c. 103), establishing police force in each county, app. and directed by local magistrates but regulated by central government, which pays half of cost: further extension of use of salaried magistracy

Aug. 12 Suicide of marquis of Londonderry (formerly Viscount Castlereagh)

Aug. 27 *Duke of Lancaster*, steamship, begins passenger and cargo service between Cork and Bristol

Nov. 5 Frances Ball, member of Institute of the Blessed Virgin Mary, takes possession of house at Rathfarnham, near Dublin (renamed Loreto Abbey); Loreto nuns begin educational work in Ire.

Dec. 14 'Bottle riot' at New Theatre Royal, Dublin, during attendance of Marquis Wellesley, L.L., at performance of 'She stoops to conquer' (see 2 May 1823)

John Lanigan's *An ecclesiastical history of Ireland* (4 vols, Dublin)

1823

Feb. 11 County Dublin by-election: Henry White, pro-emancipation candidate, defeats Sir Compton Domville by 994 votes to 849

Mar. 18 Robert Owen addresses first of series of meetings in Dublin on social reform (Hibernian Philanthropic Society inaugurated at final meeting, 3 May)

May 2 Beginning of H.C.'s inquiry into conduct of sheriff of Dublin following 'bottle riot' (see 14 Dec. 1822)

Customs and excise act, 1823 (4 Geo. IV, c. 23), consolidates boards of customs and of excise of G.B. and Ire.

May 11 Daniel Murray becomes catholic abp of Dublin on death of Troy

May 12 Formation of Catholic Association in Dempsey's Tavern, Dublin

May 23 'Act for lighting with gas the town of Belfast and the suburbs thereof' (4 Geo. IV, c. xxxvii)

July 18 Unlawful oaths act (4 Geo. IV, c. 87), strengthening powers against associations bound by oaths

Excise duties act (4 Geo. IV, c. 94) abolishes minimum charge on stills, encouraging legal distilling industry (see 19 Aug. 1780)

July 19 Irish tithe composition act, 1823 (4 Geo. IV, c. 99), enables incumbents and their parishioners to substitute fixed money payment, settled by arbitrators, in lieu of tithes

Aug. 5 Charter to Royal Hibernian Academy

Sept. 9 Sexton of St Kevin's Church, Dublin, refuses to permit catholic priest to proceed with burial service in churchyard

Nov. 17 Cttee of Catholic Association recommends formation of burial cttee to purchase land for burial grounds (Golden Bridge (Dublin) cemetery opened, 15 Oct. 1829; 9 acres at Glasnevin bought, 29 Sept. 1831; see 22 Feb. 1832)

Bp James Warren Doyle's *A vindication of the religious and civil principles of the Irish catholics* (Dublin)

George Benn's *History of the town of Belfast* (anon., Belfast; enlarged ed., 2 vols, London, 1877-80)

1824

Jan. 1 First number of *Northern Whig*

Jan. 24 O'Connell tells Catholic Association: 'every catholic in Ireland should be called upon to contribute a monthly sum from one penny up to two shillings', thereby initiating 'catholic rent'

Apr. 9 Thomas Moore's *Memoirs of Captain Rock* (anon., London)

Apr. 12 'Act to repeal the duties on all articles the manufacture of Great Britain and Ireland respectively on their importation into either country from the other' (5 Geo. IV, c. 22)

June 14 Commn to inquire into education in Ire. (see 30 May 1825, 27 Jan., 2 June 1827)

June 21 Report of select cttee of H.C. on survey and valuation of Ire.

June 22 Secretary of board of ordnance directs Thomas Colby to make cartographic survey of Ire. (cf. May 1833)

Aug. 1 Deed of copartnership to establish Northern Bank on joint-stock basis

Oct. 29 First number of Dublin *Morning Register*

Dec. 25 Day believed by many protestants to be fixed for their massacre by catholics in accordance with 'Pastorini's prophecies'

Rowley Lascelles's *Liber munerum publicorum Hiberniae*, vol. i (London; vol. ii, 1830; 2nd ed., 1852)

William Thompson's *An inquiry into the principles of the distribution of wealth most conducive to human happiness* (London; 2nd ed., 1850)

1825

Feb. 4 Henry Goulburn, C.S., gives notice of bill prohibiting political societies in Ire. of longer duration than 14 days

Feb. 18 O'Connell arrives in London to lobby against Goulburn's bill

Mar. 9 Unlawful Societies (Ireland) Act, 1825 (6 Geo. IV, c. 4), curtails activities of catholics and orangemen alike; directed against large organisations for petitioning, promoting changes in law, or acting as representative assemblies

Mar. 18 Grand Orange Lodge draws up circular advising 'that any lodge meeting after this day commits a breach of the law'

Catholic Association formally dissolves

Mar. 25 Sir Francis Burdett brings in catholic emancipation bill, subsequently accompanied by measures (known as 'wings') to disfranchise 40s. freeholders in Ire. and to remunerate Irish catholic clergy

c. **Apr.** Thomas Crofton Croker's *The fairy legends and traditions of the south of Ireland* (anon., London; 2 further vols, 1828)

May 18 H.L. rejects Burdett's emancipation bill, with its freehold and clerical 'wings', by 178 to 130

May 30 First report of commrs on Irish education (see 14 June 1824)

June 27 Currency act, 1825 (6 Geo. IV, c. 79), assimilating Irish currency to British as from 5 Jan. 1826

　Excise Licences Act, 1825 (6 Geo. IV, c. 81) reforms Irish licence duties, raising them to level in G.B.

June 30 Final report of parliamentary select cttee on state of Ire.

July 13 Launching of new Catholic Association

July First number of *Christian Examiner*, organ of evangelical party in established church

Oct. 25 First stone laid of Carmelite church, Whitefriar Street, Dublin; architect George Papworth (consecrated, 11 Nov. 1827)

Dec. Over 60 English banks suspend payments, causing severe recession in English and Irish manufacturing industry

1826

Jan. 30 Road bridge over Menai Strait (N. Wales) opened to traffic; engineer Thomas Telford

Apr. 25 First meeting of relief cttee under lord mayor of Dublin (see Dec. 1825, 9 July 1826)

May 5 Act (7 Geo. IV, c. 29) restricting sub-letting of lands and tenements

May 26 Act (7 Geo. IV, c. 62) providing for uniform valuation of lands and tenements in Ire. for purpose of local taxation (Richard Griffith afterwards app. commr of valuation)

c. **May** *Life of Theobald Wolfe Tone edited by his son* (2 vols, Washington)

June-July General election: Liverpool remains P.M.; O'Connell personally joins campaign of Henry Villiers Stuart in Co. Waterford and by mobilising catholic electors helps him to oust Lord George Beresford (see Mar. 1820, Aug. 1830)

July 7 O'Connell announces plan to reinstitute 'catholic rent'

July 9 Some 200 weavers from Liberties area of Dublin march from Wellington Testimonial (i.e. Monument) to Royal Exchange in protest against severe unemployment in textile industry

c. **July** Fever epidemic follows collapse of textile industry in Dublin, Belfast, Cork and other towns

Aug. 30 At Waterford O'Connell instals first members of his 'order of liberators'

John and Michael Banim's *The Boyne Water* (anon., London)

1827

Jan. 27 Fourth report of commrs on Irish education (on Belfast Academical Institution)

Jan.   Amhlaoibh Ó Súilleabháin (Humphrey O'Sullivan), schoolmaster of Callan, Co. Kilkenny, begins writing journal in Irish (runs to 31 July 1835)

Apr. 10   George Canning (lib. tory) app. P.M. (see 8 June 1812, 31 Aug. 1827)

Apr. 19-25   Public debate in Dublin on matters of theological controversy between Rev. R. T. P. Pope (protestant) and Rev. Thomas Maguire (catholic)

June 2   Ninth and final report of commrs on Irish education (see 14 June 1824)

Aug. 31   Viscount Goderich (lib. tory) app. P.M. (see 10 Apr. 1827, 22 Jan. 1828)

Sept. 24   Catherine McAuley opens house in Lower Baggot Street, Dublin, as school and asylum for poor (dedicated to Our Lady of Mercy, 24 Sept. 1828; see 12 Dec. 1831)

Lady Morgan's (alias Sydney Owenson's) *The O'Briens and the O'Flahertys* (London)

Sir Jonah Barrington's *Personal sketches of his own time*, vols i and ii (London; 2nd ed., 1830; vol. iii, 1832)

1828

Jan. 13   'Simultaneous meetings' organised by Catholic Association take place in about 1,600 of 2,500 parishes as challenge to government

Jan. 22   Duke of Wellington (tory) app. P.M. (see 31 Aug. 1827, 22 Nov. 1830)

Mar. 11   H.C. select cttee on Irish education app.

May 9   English test and corporation acts repealed (9 Geo. IV, c. 17)

May 19   Report of select cttee of H.C. on Irish education recommends establishment of government body to control elementary schools

June 9   O'Connell lays foundation-stone of Catholic Model School, Richmond Street, Dublin (later known as O'Connell School)

June 24   O'Connell announces intention of contesting by-election in Clare

June 28   General synod of Ulster at Cookstown adopts resolution for appointment of cttee for theological examination of candidates for ministry, aimed at preventing entry of Arians

July 5   O'Connell elected M.P. for Clare by 2,057 to 982

July 15   Linen and hempen manufactures act, 1828 (9 Geo. IV, c. 62), abolishes linen board (see 10 Oct. 1711)

July 25   Act (9 Geo. IV, c. 82) providing for 'lighting, cleansing and watching' of Irish cities and towns, and election of town commrs for these purposes

Aug. 12   George Dawson, M.P., makes speech at Derry in favour of catholic emancipation, on occasion of unveiling of Walker memorial (see 28 Aug. 1973)

Aug. 14   Founding banquet of Brunswick clubs

Sept. 15   Eustace Chetwoode, British grand secretary, formally revives orange movement in Ireland following lapse of unlawful societies act, 1825 (see 9 Mar. 1825)

Sept. 23   John Lawless's political tour of north halted at Ballybay, Co. Monaghan, by hostility of local orangemen

Oct. 16   Rev. Henry Montgomery, minister of Dunmurry presbyterian church, and Arians in general synod of Ulster adopt remonstrance leading to their separation from synod (first meeting of remonstrant synod, 25 May 1830)

Nov. 24   First number of *Pilot*, thrice-weekly organ of O'Connell

Dec. 11   Wellington's letter to Patrick Curtis, catholic abp of Armagh, stating his anxiety 'to witness the settlement of the Roman Catholic question' (published, 23 Dec.)

1829

Jan. 27   Catholic meeting in St Patrick's chapel, Donegall Street, Belfast, presided over by William Crolly, catholic bp of Down and Connor, and addressed by Rev. Henry Montgomery (see 16 Oct. 1828)

Mar. 4   Andrew Jackson, son of immigrants from Ulster, inaugurated as president of U.S.A.

Mar. 5   'Act for the suppression of dangerous associations or assemblies in Ireland' (10 Geo. IV, c. 1)

Apr. 13   Roman Catholic Relief Act, 1829 (10 Geo. IV, c. 7), provides new oath of allegiance, enabling catholics to enter parliament, belong to any corporation, and hold higher civil and military offices—'catholic emancipation'

Irish parliamentary elections act, 1829 (10 Geo. IV, c. 8), raises county freehold franchise from 40s. to £10

May 15   O'Connell presents himself at bar of H.C. but, declining to take oath of supremacy, is ordered by speaker to withdraw

July 2   First stone laid of church of St Francis Xavier, Upper Gardiner Street, Dublin (opened, 3 May 1832)

July 30   O'Connell again returned as M.P. for County Clare, this time unopposed

Aug. 18-20   General synod of Ulster, at special adjourned meeting at Cookstown, rejects Arian remonstrance and takes measures to effect separation

Aug.-Sept.   Anti-spirits movement begins: Rev. George W. Cart, independent clergyman, forms society against spirit-drinking in New Ross, Co. Wexford (20 Aug.); Dr Joshua Harvey and Dr John Cheyne form Dublin Temperance Society (Sept.; reconstituted as Hibernian Temperance Society, 7 Apr. 1830); Dr John Edgar, presbyterian minister, and others form Ulster Temperance Society in Belfast (24 Sept.)

Gerald Griffin's *The collegians* (anon., 3 vols, London); based on story of 'colleen bawn' (see 13-14 July 1819; 27 Mar. 1860)

1830

Jan. 3   O'Connell announces establishment of Parliamentary Intelligence Office at 26 Stephen Street, Dublin

Feb. 4   O'Connell takes seat in H.C. on first day of session

Feb. 9   Catholic bps issue statement expressing gratitude for emancipation and counselling priests in future to avoid political controversy

Apr. 6   Formation of Friends of Ireland of all Religious Denominations (proclaimed illegal, 24 Apr.)

c. **Apr.**   William Carleton's *Traits and stories of the Irish peasantry* (1st series, 2 vols, Dublin)

May 10   Zoological Society of Dublin formed (later Royal Zoological Society of Ireland) (see 1 Sept. 1831)

May 25-7   First meeting of Remonstrant Synod at Belfast

June 26   George IV dies; succ. by William IV

July 27-9   Revolution in Paris: Charles X abdicates, to be succeeded by Louis-Philippe (proclaimed king of the French, 7 Aug.)

Aug.   General election: swing against Wellington (see June-July 1826, 22 Jan. 1828, May 1831)

Oct. 4   Belgian independence proclaimed in Brussels (dissolution of union of Belgium with Holland recognised by great powers, 20 Dec. 1830, 20 Jan. 1831)

Nov. 22   Earl Grey (whig) app. P.M. (see 22 Jan. 1828, 16 July 1834)

Nov. 29   Nationalist revolt in Poland begins

Thomas and Andrew Mulholland start mill in York Street, Belfast, for wet-spinning of flax by steam power—origin of York Street Flax-spinning Co.

1831

Jan. 18   O'Connell arrested on warrant charging him with conspiracy to violate and evade L.L.'s proclamations under 10 Geo. IV, c. 1

c. **Jan.**   Terry Alt disturbances begin in Clare and Limerick

Mar. 1   First parliamentary reform bill introduced in H.C.

Mar. 3   Force of 120 police moves into Graiguenamanagh, on borders of Carlow and Kilkenny, to seize cattle in payment of tithe

Mar. 11   Postmaster General Act, 1831 (1 Will. IV, c. 8) provides for appointment of one postmaster general for G.B. and Ire.

Mar.-June   Distress in Mayo and Galway as result of potato crop failure in previous year

May 1   First number of *Comet* (Dublin), O'Connellite weekly

May   General election: Earl Grey's government strengthened (see Aug., 22 Nov., 1830, Dec. 1832)

June 13   Charles Forbes René de Montalembert, French liberal catholic, appeals in *L'Avenir* for relief of Irish distress

June 18   'Tithe massacre' at Newtownbarry, Co. Wexford

c. **July-Aug.**   Thomas Moore's *Life and death of Lord Edward Fitzgerald* (2 vols, London)

Aug. 30   Opening concert of Dublin Musical Festival with Niccolò Paganini as chief attraction

Sept. 1   Zoological gardens in Phoenix Park, belonging to Zoological Society of Dublin, opened to public (see 10 May 1830)

Sept. 6 Act authorising construction of Dublin-Kingstown railway (1 & 2 Will. IV, c. lxix)

Sept. 9 Edward Stanley, C.S., moves vote of £30,000 to be placed at disposal of L.L. for educational purposes, thereby providing for 'national system' of education

Oct. 15 Public Works (Ireland) Act, 1831 (1 & 2 Will. IV, c. 33), provides for general reorganisation of board of works

Tumultuous Risings (Ireland) Act, 1831 (1 & 2 Will. IV, c. 44), amends whiteboy acts, replacing capital punishment by transportation

Oct. 20 Richard Whately nominated protestant abp of Dublin

Nov. 1 Belfast museum, maintained by Belfast Natural History Society, formally opened (taken over by Belfast city corporation, 1910)

Nov. Stanley completes final draft of letter (dated Oct. 1831) to duke of Leinster containing guidelines for scheme of national education

Inauguration of Ralahine Agricultural and Manufacturing Cooperative Association in County Clare

Nov. 29 Geological Society of Dublin founded (renamed Royal Geological Society of Ireland, 1864; defunct, 1890)

Dec. 12 Institute of Religious Sisters of Mercy established with Catherine McAuley as superior (see 24 Sept. 1827; approved by pope, 1835)

Dec. 14 Twelve policemen killed in affray during serving of tithe processes at Carrickshock, near Knocktopher, Co. Kilkenny

Dec. 15 Cttees app. by both houses of parliament to inquire into Irish tithes

Census taken throughout Ire.: population 7,767,401 (14·19% increase; see 28 May 1821)

1832

Jan. 19 Irish parliamentary reform bill introduced in H.C.

Feb. 22 First interment in Glasnevin cemetery (see 17 Nov. 1823)

c. **Feb.** Whitefeet disturbances become common in Queen's, Kilkenny and other midland counties

Mar. 1 First number of *Dublin Journal of Medical and Chemical Science* (later *Irish Journal of Medical Science*); editors Robert John Kane, Robert James Graves, and William Stokes

Mar. 15 Asiatic cholera reaches Belfast (reaches Dublin a few days later; epidemic slowly spreads throughout Ire. and persists till 1833)

Mar. 27 First meeting of Central Board of Health for Ireland, app. to contain cholera epidemic

May 31 Select cttee app. by H.C. to inquire into disturbances in Ire. (report, 2 Aug.)

June 1 'Act to facilitate the recovery of tithes in certain cases in Ireland and for relief of the clergy of the established church' (2 & 3 Will. IV, c. 41)

June 30   First number of *Dublin Penny Journal*; editors Caesar Otway and George Petrie

Aug. 7   Representation of the People (Ireland) Act, 1832 (2 & 3 Will. IV, c. 88); Irish seats increased from 100 to 105 and £10 franchise introduced in boroughs (cf. 13 Apr. 1829); electorate increased to 92,141 (1·2% of population)

Aug. 16   First party processions act (2 & 3 Will. IV, c. 118) to curb sectarian conflict (renewed 1838 and 1844)

Irish tithe composition act (2 Will. IV, c. 119) begins process of commutation

Dec.   General election: in G.B.—lib. 408, con. 145; in Ire.—lib. 33, con. 30, repealers 42 (see May 1831, Jan. 1835)

The speech of William Connor, Esq., against rack-rents, &c. (Dublin; reedited and reissued as *The true political economy of Ireland; or rack-rent the one great cause of all her evils with its remedy*, 1835)

William Hamilton Maxwell's *Wild sports of the west* (anon., 2 vols, London; several later eds.)

1833

Jan. 5   First number of *Dublin University Magazine*, founded by Isaac Butt and others

Jan. 18   First meeting of O'Connell's 'national council'

Feb. 12   Viscount Althorp in H.C. seeks leave to bring in Irish church reform bill (presented, 11 Mar; withdrawn, 20 Mar.)

Apr. 2   Suppression of Disturbances (Ireland) Act, 1833 (3 Will. IV, c. 4), empowers L.L. to suppress public meetings and set up courts composed of military officers for specified offences in proclaimed districts

Apr. 23   Althorp brings in new Irish church reform bill

May 27   George Petrie reads paper, 'An inquiry into the origin and uses of the round towers of Ireland', to Royal Irish Academy (published in *Transactions*, vol. xx, 1845, and in other eds)

May   Ordnance-survey map of Co. Londonderry published, first of six-inch series resulting from Colby's survey (see 22 June 1824, completed with map of Co. Kerry, Nov. 1846)

July 20   Commn of inquiry into Irish municipal corporations app. (report, 1835-6)

Aug. 14   Church Temporalities (Ireland) Act, 1833 (3 & 4 Will. IV, c. 37), abolishes 10 bishoprics and provides for appointment of ecclesiastical commrs with powers to divide livings, suspend appointments, and use revenues of suppressed bishoprics and produce of a graduated income tax on livings over £200 to build and repair churches and augment poor livings

Aug. 29   Irish tithe arrears act (3 & 4 Will. IV, c. 100) advances £1m. for relief of tithe-owners on security of arrears

Sept. 25   Royal commn under Abp Whately app. to inquire into condition of poor in Ire. app. (reports, 1835-6)

Sir Jonah Barrington's *Rise and fall of the Irish nation* (Paris)

Illicit distillation at highest recorded level of nineteenth century; 1,349 stills seized by revenue police

Steam-powered printing-machine installed by Philip Dixon Hardy, Dublin printer; claimed to be first in Ire.

1834

Jan. James Clarence Mangan's 'The literary lady', translated from Friedrich Schiller, in *Dublin University Magazine*, first of numerous contributions (last, May 1849)

Jan. 23 St Vincent's Hospital, Dublin, opened by Sisters of Charity; first hospital in U.K. to be run by women

Jan. 28 Catholic bps secretly resolve that chapels shall not be used, as in past, for political meetings and that clergy shall stand aloof from politics

Feb. 20 Edward Littleton, C.S., moves resolution in H.C. proposing commutation of tithes into land tax

Apr. 22-30 Repeal of union debated in H.C. on motion by O'Connell

May Royal Dublin Society's first industrial exhibition

June 3 Select cttee of H.C. app. to inquire into drunkenness in U.K. (reports, 3 Aug.; foundation of subsequent legislation on drink question)

June 4 Commn app. to inquire into religious and other public instruction in Ire. (reports, 1835)

July 16 Viscount Melbourne (lib.) app. P.M. (see 22 Nov. 1830, 17 Nov. 1834)

July 21 John MacHale, bp of Killala, translated to Tuam (abp of Tuam till his death, 7 Nov. 1881)

Oct. 30 At meeting of conservatives at Hillsborough, Co. Down, Dr Henry Cooke 'publishes the banns of a sacred marriage' between presbyterians and anglicans

Nov. Samuel Ferguson's 'O'Byrne's bard to the clans of Wicklow', 'Timoleague', and 'The fair hills of Ireland' in *Dublin University Magazine*

Nov. 17 Duke of Wellington (con.) app. P.M. (see 16 July, 10 Dec.)

Dec. 10 Sir Robert Peel (con.) app. P.M. (see 17 Nov. 1834, 18 Apr. 1835)

Dec. 17 Opening of Dublin-Kingstown railway, the first in Ire.

Dec. 18 Affray at Rathcormac, near Gortroe, Co. Cork, during collection of tithes

1835

Jan. 1 First number of Philip Barron's periodical, *Ancient Ireland*, 'established for the purpose of reviving the cultivation of the Irish language'

Jan. General election: in G.B.—lib. 317, con. 236; in Ire.—con. 37, lib. 34, lib. (repeal) 34 (see Dec. 1832, July-Aug. 1837)

Feb. 18 First meeting of whigs, radicals, and O'Connellites at Lichfield House

Mar. 23 H.C. select cttee on orangeism app. (see 20 July)

Apr. 12   William Crolly translated from bishopric of Down and Connor to archbishopric of Armagh

Apr. 18   Viscount Melbourne (lib.) again app. P.M. (see 10 Dec. 1834, 30 Aug. 1841)

Apr. 29   Michael O'Loghlen app. solicitor general for Ire. (app. attorney general, 31 Aug. 1835; app. a baron of court of exchequer, 10 Nov. 1836); first catholic since reign of James II to become law officer or judge

c. **Apr.**   Thomas Moore's *History of Ireland*, vol. i (London; vol. ii, 1837; vol. iii, 1840; vol. iv, 1845)

June   John Finch, English teetotaller, forms total abstinence society at Strabane, Co. Tyrone; beginning of organised teetotal movement in Ire. (cf. *c.* July 1817)

July 2   William Sharman Crawford opens tenant-right campaign in H.C. by bringing in bill to compensate evicted tenants for improvements

July 20   First report of select cttee on orangeism presented to H.C.

July 25   Thomas Drummond becomes under-secretary (his administration distinguished by liberal and reforming spirit; dies in office, 15 Apr. 1840)

July 31   Government introduces first of 6 Irish municipal reform bills

Aug. 10   Viscount Morpeth, C.S., introduces Irish constabulary bill in H.C. (rejected by 51 to 39 in H.L. 26 Aug.)

Aug. 10-15   British Association for the Advancement of Science meets at Dublin; numerous scientific papers read, many of them relating to Ire.

Aug.   Sir Thomas Larcom's *Ordnance survey of the county of Londonderry* (Dublin; revised edition, 1837)

Aug. 31   Act 'for the better prevention and more speedy punishment of offences endangering the public peace in Ireland' (5 & 6 Will. IV, c. 48); last insurrection act, passed with O'Connell's acquiescence (never applied; expires 1840)

Oct. 8   Adoption of new rules for Apprentice Boys of Derry Club (see 1814)

Oct. 29   First performance of Michael William Balfe's opera 'Siege of Rochelle', at Drury Lane theatre, London (first Irish performance at Theatre Royal, Dublin, 4 May 1836)

1836

Feb.   Total abstinence society formed in Belfast (similar society formed in Dublin, Nov.)

Feb. 18   Morpeth again seeks leave to bring in Irish constabulary bill

Feb. 23   Joseph Hume in H.C. moves address to king aimed at closure of orange lodges in army

Apr. 14   Grand Orange Lodge of Ireland decides to dissolve

May 4   H.C. debates reports of royal commn on Irish poor law (see 25 Sept. 1833)

May 17   First meeting of Petition Committee for Corporate Reform and Settlement of the Tithe Question

May 19 'Act for making a railway from the town of Belfast to the city of Armagh' (6 & 7 Will. IV, c. xxxiii)

May 20 Constabulary (Ireland) Act, 1836 (6 Will. IV, c. 13), consolidates centralised executive government, amalgamating county constabulary and peace preservation force under inspector general, and extending stipendiary magistracy (see 12 Sept. 1867, 4 Aug. 1922)

June 27 H.L. refuses to accept government's Irish municipal reform bill unaltered (bill consequently dropped, 30 June)

July 2 Petition Committee constitutes itself National Association for Municipal Reform (soon better known as General Association of Ireland)

July 4 Dublin Police Act, 1836 (6 & 7 Will. IV, c. 29), establishes 2 police magistrates and police force under L.L. for Dublin metropolitan district

Aug. 13 'Act for making a railway from Dublin to Drogheda' (6 & 7 Will. IV, c. cxxii)

Aug. 20 Grand Jury (Ireland) Act (6 & 7 Will. IV, c. 116) consolidates and amends laws relating to presentment of public money by grand juries

Oct. 20 Royal commn on construction of railways in Ire. app. under Thomas Drummond (first report, 11 Mar. 1837; second report, 13 July 1838)

Oct. 31 O'Connell's wife, Mary, dies

Nov. 15 George Nicholls's report on Irish poor law

William Blacker's *The claims of the landed interests to legislative protection considered* (Dublin)

1837

Feb. First instalment of Charles Lever's 'Confessions of Harry Lorrequer' published in *Dublin University Magazine* (anon.; published in book form, anon., Dublin, 1839)

Apr. Dr William Stokes's *A treatise on the diagnosis and treatment of diseases of the chest* (Dublin)

June 20 William IV dies; succ. by Victoria

July-Aug. General election in G.B.—con. 281, lib. 272; in Ire.—con. 32, lib. 43, lib. (repeal) 30; Melbourne remains P.M. (see Jan. 1835, July 1841)

Nov. 18 First number of Feargus O'Connor's radical newspaper, *Northern Star* (Leeds)

Dublin University Choral Society formed

Dec. 1 Russell introduces Irish poor law bill in H.C.

Samuel Lewis's *A topographical dictionary of Ireland* (2 vols and atlas, London; 2nd ed., 1843)

1838

Apr. 4 *Sirius* leaves Cork for New York, the first steamer to cross Atlantic unaided by sail

Apr. 10   Rev. Theobald Mathew, O.F.M. Cap., with support from William Martin, a quaker, founds total abstinence movement in Cork (see Jan. 1842, 11 Nov. 1844, 8 Dec. 1856)

May 22   In reply to appeal from 32 Tipperary magistrates, Drummond (see 25 July 1835) tells earl of Donoughmore: 'property has its duties as well as its rights'

July 5   Board of Trinity College decrees establishment of chair of Irish (first professor appointed, 1840)

July 13   Second and final report of Irish railway commrs (see 20 Oct. 1836)

July 31   Poor Relief (Ireland) Act, 1838 (1 & 2 Vict., c. 56) extends English poor law to Ireland; elected boards of guardians, responsible to a poor law commn, set up to administer a workhouse system

Aug. 15   Tithe Rentcharge (Ireland) Act, 1838 (1 & 2 Vict., c. 109), converts tithe to rent charge and scales down amount payable

Nov. 10   First meeting of Pathological Society of Dublin, first such society in U.K.

1839

Jan. 6-7   The 'big wind'

c. **Feb.**   Church Education Society for Ireland formed in Dublin to provide and maintain schools of established church outside national system

Mar. 1   H.C. debates report of Irish railway commrs (see 20 Oct 1836, 13 July 1838)

Mar. 12   Letter from prefect of Propaganda, Cardinal Fransoni, to catholic primate of all Ireland, Abp Crolly, exhorting bps and priests to eschew politics (see 15 Oct. 1844, 3 Jan. 1848)

Mar. 21   Select cttee of H.L. app. to inquire into crime and outrage in Ire. since 1835—'Roden committee' (report, 19 July)

May 22   Richard Griffith's *A general map of Ireland to accompany the report of the railway commissioners, shewing the principal features and geological structure of the country* (Dublin)

May 29   Irish Medical Association formed

Aug. 12   Belfast-Lisburn section of Ulster Railway opened (see 19 May 1836)

Aug. 19   'Act for the improvement of the navigation of the River Shannon' (2 & 3 Vict., c. 61)

Aug. 24   Unlawful oaths act (2 & 3 Vict., c. 74), directed against societies using signs or passwords, or formed for purpose of obtaining arms

Gustave de Beaumont's *L'Irlande sociale, politique et religieuse* (2 vols, Paris; 6th ed., 1845; 7th ed., 1863); translated by W. C. Taylor as *Ireland: social, political and religious* (London, 1839)

1840

Mar.   First chapters of Charles Lever's 'Charles O'Malley, the Irish dragoon' in *Dublin University Magazine* (anon.; whole work published in book form, anon., Dublin, 1841)

Mar. 17   Laying of foundation-stone of catholic cathedral at Armagh (dedicated, 24 Aug. 1873)

Irish Archaeological Society founded

Mar. 26   Opening of Music Hall, May Street, Belfast, built by Anacreontic Society (renamed Victoria Memorial Hall, 1887)

Apr. 15   Formation of National Association of Ireland (renamed Loyal National Repeal Association, 13 July)

Apr. 24   First union workhouse (South Dublin) opened

May 15   Isaac Butt defends unreformed Dublin Corporation at bar of H.L.

June 23   Preliminary meeting at earl of Charlemont's house in London to form Ulster Constitutional Association on model of radical associations in G.B.

June 26   Thomas Davis's presidential address to Historical Society of Trinity College

July 10   General Synod of Ulster and the Secession Synod combine to form General Assembly of the Presbyterian Church in Ireland

Aug. 10   Irish municipal reform act (3 & 4 Vict., c. 108)

Aug. 14   First public meeting of Ulster Constitutional Association, at Music Hall, Belfast

Aug.   Abp John MacHale joins Loyal National Repeal Association

Dec.   Franz Liszt begins tour of Ire. (ends Jan. 1841)

Lady Morgan's feminist treatise *Woman and her master* (London)

1841

Feb. 27   Rev. William Bruce, sr, last surviving member of Volunteer convention of 1783, dies

c. **Mar.**   Agricultural Improvement Society formed (incorporated by charter as Royal Agricultural Society of Ireland, 28 June 1860; amalgamated with Royal Dublin Society, 22 Mar. 1880)

Apr. 17   Thomas Davis joins Loyal National Repeal Association

June 6   Census taken throughout Ire.: population 8,175,124 (5·25% increase; see 1831)

Census taken throughout G.B.: Irish-born population of England and Wales 289,404 (1·8% of total); of Scotland, 126,321 (4·8% of total)

June 15   First reading of Morpeth's 'bill for the making and maintaining of public railways in Ireland'

June 17   Society of Attorneys and Solicitors of Ireland formed (incorporated by charter, 5 Apr. 1852; name altered by supplemental charter to Incorporated Law Society of Ireland, 14 Dec. 1888)

July   General election: in G.B.—con. 324, lib. 229; in Ire.—con. 43, lib. 42, repealers 20 (see July–Aug. 1837, Aug. 1847)

Aug. 30   First number of *Cork Examiner*

Peel (con.) again app. P.M. (see 18 Apr. 1835, 30 June 1846)

Sept. 15   Anthony Trollope arrives in Ire. as deputy post-office surveyor at Banagher, King's Co. (in Ire., 1841–51, 1853–7)

Oct. 25   Election of reformed Dublin corporation: liberals secure 49 of 60 seats

Nov. 1   O'Connell elected lord mayor of Dublin

Samuel Carter Hall and Anna Maria Hall's *Ireland: its scenery, character, etc.,* vol. i (London; vol. ii, 1842; vol. iii, 1843), the results of 5 tours made between 1825 and 1840

1842

Jan.   Fr Mathew's total abstinence crusade at peak of success (3 million pledged adherents)

Feb. 22–3   First National Repeal Convention of America meets in Philadelphia; splits on issue of abolition of slavery

Mar. 20   James Thomas O'Brien, an avowed evangelical, consecrated bp of Ossory, Ferns, and Leighlin

Mar. 22   Laying of foundation-stone of Methodist Centenary Chapel, St Stephen's Green, Dublin (opened, 18 June 1843; burnt down, 22 Dec. 1968)

Mar. 28   O'Connell takes part in Cork temperance procession

Apr. 11   John England (b. Cork, 1786), bp of Charleston (South Carolina) since 18 June 1820, dies

June 10   First number of James MacKnight's *Banner of Ulster* (Belfast)

June 18   Capital Punishment (Ireland) Act, 1842 (5 & 6 Vict., c. 27), abolishes death penalty for numerous offences

c. **June**   First series (in 2 volumes) of Richard Robert Madden's *The United Irishmen: their lives and times* (London; 2nd series in 2 vols, London, 1843; 3rd series in 3 vols, Dublin, 1846; 2nd ed., 4 series in 4 vols, 1857–60)

July 9   John Benjamin MacNeill elected to new chair of civil engineering at Trinity College, Dublin

Aug. 5   Drainage (Ireland) Act, 1842 (5 & 6 Vict., c. 89) entrusts commrs of public works with responsibility for drainage schemes

Aug. 10   Fisheries (Ireland) Act, 1842 (5 & 6 Vict., c. 106), empowers board of works to appoint 2 inspectors to enforce regulations on river and deep-sea fishing

Aug. 12   Act (5 & 6 Vict., c. 113) confirms validity of marriages celebrated by dissenting ministers

Sept. 12   Lisburn-Portadown section of Ulster Railway opened (see 12 Aug. 1839)

Oct. 15   First number of *Nation*, edited by Charles Gavan Duffy; weekly organ of group later known as Young Ireland

Oct. 18   All Hallows College, Drumcondra, opened, to train secular priests for foreign missions

Dec. 20   John Joseph Hughes (b. Annaloghan, Co. Tyrone, 1797), coadjutor to catholic bp of New York since 24 July 1837 (abp, 19 July 1850; dies 3 Jan. 1864)

1843

Feb. 28–Mar. 2   Dublin corporation debates O'Connell's motion for petition to parliament for repeal of union; Butt makes case for union

Mar. 9   Monster meeting at Trim

Mar. 31   Laying of foundation-stone of Conciliation Hall, Dublin (opened, 23 Oct.)

Apr. 1   John Kells Ingram's poem, 'The memory of the dead', published anonymously in *Nation*

Apr. 27   Lord Eliot, C.S., introduces arms, gunpowder, and ammunition bill (see 22 Aug.)

June 30   Rev. Theobald Mathew leaves Cork for England on total abstinence propaganda tour

Aug. 15   Monster meeting at Hill of Tara

Aug. 16–24   British Association for the Advancement of Science meets at Cork

Aug. 22   Act (6 & 7 Vict., c. 74) amends law 'relative to the registering of arms, and the importation, manufacture and sale of arms, gunpowder and ammunition'

Sept. 20–3   Second National Repeal Convention of America meets in New York; 'physical force' advocates rebel against 'moral force' leadership; split ensues

Oct. 7   Proclamation prohibits meeting announced by O'Connell for next day at Clontarf; O'Connell cancels meeting

Oct. 14   O'Connell and his son John enter into recognisances to appear in court of queen's bench to answer charges of conspiracy (similarly 7 others, 16 Oct.)

Oct. 16   Sir William Rowan Hamilton discovers his formula for multiplication of quaternions, immediately carving it with his pocket-knife on stonework of bridge over Royal Canal at Ballyboggan, Dublin

Oct. 20   William Smith O'Brien applies to join Repeal Association

Nov. *c.* 1   Daniel Owen Maddyn's *Ireland and its rulers since 1829*, pt 1 (anon., London; pts 2 and 3, 1844)

Nov. 20   Royal commn under earl of Devon app. to inquire into state of law and practice relating to occupation of land in Ire. (see 14 Feb. 1845)

Joseph Ellison Portlock's *Report on the geology of the county of Londonderry and of parts of Tyrone and Fermanagh* (Dublin)

1844

Jan. 15   Opening of state trials of O'Connell and others in Dublin

Feb. 10   On twenty-fourth and final day of state trials O'Connell and others are found guilty on several counts

May 3–9   Rioting among Irish immigrants in Kensington, Philadelphia; 16 killed (anti-Irish riots in Southwark, Philadelphia, 5–7 July)

May 24   Earl de Grey, L.L., formally opens Dublin–Drogheda railway, knights engineer-in-chief J. B. MacNeill, and lays foundation-stone of Amiens Street terminus building, Dublin (architect William Deane Butler)

May 30   O'Connell sentenced to 12 months' imprisonment, fine of £2,000 and to find surety to keep peace for 7 years; removed to Richmond bridewell

June 18   First reading of Irish charitable donations and bequests bill

June   Robert John Kane's *The industrial resources of Ireland* (Dublin; 2nd ed., 1845)

July 19   Nonconformists Chapels Act, 1844 (7 & 8 Vict., c. 45) provides that, in cases where the founders' intentions are not clear, the usage of the previous 25 years shall determine what doctrines are to be upheld

Aug. 6   Act (7 & 8 Vict. c. c) authorising construction of railway from Dublin to Cashel and Carlow, known as Great Southern & Western Railway (extension to Cork and Limerick authorised under 8 & 9 Vict., c. cxxiv, 21 July 1845)

Aug. 9   Marriages (Ireland) Act, 1844 (7 & 8 Vict., c. 81), requires registrar general to keep record of all except catholic marriages

Charitable Donations and Bequests (Ireland) Act, 1844 (7 & 8 Vict., c. 97), establishes bequests board of 13, including 5 catholics

Sept. 4   H.L. reverses judgment against O'Connell and others

Oct. 15   Letter from prefect of Propaganda, Cardinal Fransoni, to catholic primate of all Ireland, Abp Crolly, prescribing that bps and priests eschew politics and urging him to reprove those who refuse to do so (see 12 Mar. 1839, 3 Jan. 1848)

Oct. 16   William Petre arrives at Rome as British chargé d'affaires

Nov. 11   Appeal fund opened to help to pay Fr Mathew's debts (£7,000)

Dec.   Society of St Vincent de Paul introduced to Ire. with founding of branch in Dublin (in Cork, Mar. 1846)

1845

Feb. 14   Report of Devon commn (see 20 Nov. 1843) recommending compensation for improvements and various minor reforms

Feb. 15   Earl of Rosse's 72-inch reflecting telescope comes into effective operation at Birr Castle, King's County, the largest in world till dismantled in 1908

Apr. 3   Peel introduces Maynooth College bill in H.C.

May 9   Sir James Graham introduces Irish colleges bill in H.C.

May 12, 26   O'Connell and Davis differ over colleges bill at meetings of Repeal Association

May 23   Catholic bps adopt memorial to government on colleges bill: system proposed would be dangerous to faith and morals of catholic students, but might be made acceptable if amended on certain crucial points

June 1   Party processions act lapses (see 16 Aug. 1832)

June 30   Maynooth College act (8 & 9 Vict., c. 25) provides for capital grant of £30,000 and increases annual grant from £8,928 to £26,360

c. **July 1**   Thomas MacNevin's *History of the Volunteers of 1782* (Dublin), the first of 'Library of Ireland' series sponsored by Young Ireland group

c. **July 19**   John O'Donovan's *A grammar of the Irish language, published for the use of the senior classes in the College of St Columba* (Dublin)

July 21   Midland Great Western Railway of Ireland Act, 1845 (8 & 9 Vict., c. cxix), empowers construction of railway from Dublin to Mullingar and Longford and purchase of Royal Canal by railway company

July 31   Colleges (Ireland) Act, 1845 (8 & 9 Vict., c. 66), provides for foundation of new colleges of higher education

Aug. 8   Central Criminal Lunatic Asylum (Ireland) Act, 1845 (8 & 9 Vict., c. 107), provides for construction of asylum for criminal lunatics

Aug. 12, 27   Meetings at Enniskillen undertake to revive orange institution, by adopting new rules in conformity with law

Sept. 9   Arrival of potato blight in Ire. reported in *Dublin Evening Post*

Sept. 16   Thomas Davis dies in Dublin of scarlatina, aged 30

Constabulary directed to report weekly on local crops and to estimate extent of loss

Sept. 25   Cutting of first sod in construction of Cork–Bandon Railway

Oct. 31   Mansion House cttee formed to examine extent of potato loss and to suggest remedies

Nov. *c.* **9-10**   Peel, on his own responsibility, orders purchase in U.S.A. of £100,000 of Indian corn for shipment to Ireland

Nov. 15   Lyon Playfair and John Lindley issue report on state of Irish potato crop

Nov. 18   Appointment of Peel's relief commn to administer scheme of relief supplementary to that provided under Poor Relief (Ireland) Act, 1838

Dec. 6   Peel tenders resignation to queen (refused, 20 Dec.)

Dec. 12   Visitors of Trinity College, Dublin, dismiss appeal of Denis Caulfield Heron against board of college for its refusal to elect him to foundation scholarship because, as a catholic, he is disqualified from being a member of the body corporate

Celtic Society founded

Anthony Trollope's first novel, *The Macdermots of Ballycloran*, completed at Mallow (published, London, 1847)

Museum of Economic Geology established in Dublin; director, Dr Robert Kane (renamed Museum of Irish Industry, 1847)

John Grubb Richardson, quaker linen bleacher and warehouseman, purchases linen mill and other property at Bessbrook, Co. Armagh, and begins transforming place into model village, lacking public house, pawnshop, and police

1846

Jan. 23   Public Works (Ireland) Bill, the first of a series of measures intended to relieve distress, introduced in H.C.

Mar. 5   Public Works (Ireland) Act, 1846 (9 Vict., c. 1)

Act (9 Vict., c. 2) authorising county relief works

'Act to encourage the sea fisheries of Ireland by promoting and aiding with grants of public money the construction of piers, harbours and other works' (9 Vict., c. 3)

Drainage (Ireland) Act, 1846 (9 Vict., c. 4)

Mar. 13   Eviction of 300 tenants on Gerrard estate at Ballinglass, Co. Galway

Mar. 24   Irish public health act, 1846 (9 & 10 Vict., c. 6) empowers L.L. to appoint central board of health with power to direct poor law guardians to provide fever hospitals, dispensaries, medicines, and nutriments (see 27 Apr. 1847)

Mar. 28   Sales begin, at Cork, Clonmel and Longford, of food being distributed by relief commn

June 26   Peel's importation of corn act, 1846 (9 & 10 Vict., c. 22), virtually abolishes duties on imported corn, grain, meal, and flour—'repeal of the corn laws'

June 30   Lord John Russell (lib.) app. P.M. (see 30 Aug. 1841, 23 Feb. 1852)

July 11   Earl of Bessborough sworn in as L.L.

Thomas Nicholas Redington app. under-secretary; first catholic to hold this office

July 14   Reappearance of potato disease reported by Sir Randolph Routh to Charles Trevelyan (potato crop fails disastrously)

July 28   Split in Repeal Association between O'Connellites and Young Irelanders over principle of physical force

Aug. 1   Trevelyan's memorandum detailing shortcomings of previous relief scheme and outlining a new plan to meet coming crisis

Aug. 4   Opening of line of Great Southern & Western Railway between Dublin (Kingsbridge) and Carlow

Aug. 17   Lord John Russell tells H.C.: 'we do not propose to interfere with the regular mode by which Indian corn and other kinds of grain may be brought into the country'.

Aug. 18   'Act for regulating the gauge of railways' (9 & 10 Vict., c. 57) fixes standard railway gauge in Ire. at 5 feet 3 inches

Aug. 28   Constabulary (Ireland) Act, 1846 (9 & 10 Vict., c. 97), charges 'all necessary and reasonable costs . . . of the constabulary force and reserve force' to consolidated fund

Poor Employment (Ireland) Act, 1846 (9 & 10 Vict., c. 107), empowers board of works to execute relief works by means of treasury loans

Sept.   Thomas Carlyle visits Ireland (see 3 July 1849)

Sept.-Oct.   William Edward Forster visits Ire. to investigate distress (second visit, Jan. 1847)

Sept. 25   Disturbance at Youghal, Co. Cork, arising out of attempt by crowd to hold up ship laden with oats for export

Nov.   Beginning of unusually severe winter: snow, frost, north-easterly gales

Nov. 13 Meeting of Irish quakers in Dublin, resulting in formation of Central Relief Committee of Society of Friends

Dec. 9 Relief department of board of works issues circular, no. 38, enunciating scheme for payment of labour on drainage and sub-soiling (circular suppressed later by treasury)

Dec. 28 Trevelyan writes to Routh: 'the depots in the western district are to be henceforth opened for the sale of food as far as may be prudent and necessary'

1847

Jan. 1 John MacDonnell of Richmond Hospital performs first operation under general anaesthesia in Ire., amputating arm of country girl, Mary Kane, of Drogheda

Formation of British Association for the Relief of the Extreme Distress in the Remote Parishes of Ireland and Scotland

Jan. 11 James Fintan Lalor writes private letter to Charles Gavan Duffy advocating agrarian reform and Irish independence, to be achieved by physical force (see 24 June 1848)

Jan. 13 Irish Confederation formed at Rotunda, Dublin

Jan. 25 Russell presents to H.C. proposals to substitute soup kitchens for public works as means of relieving distress in Ire., and to permit outdoor relief to be paid for out of local rates

Jan. 26 Duties on importation of corn suspended until 1 Sept. under single-section act (10 Vict., c. 1) (see 26 June 1846)

Feb. 8 O'Connell makes last appearance in H.C.

Feb. 17 Lord George Bentinck's bill providing for comprehensive state-aided railway building scheme to provide employment in Ire. defeated by 332 to 118

Feb. 26 Destitute Poor (Ireland) Act, otherwise known as 'soup kitchen act', 1847 (10 Vict., c. 7), permits appointment of relief commrs to administer outdoor relief

Mar. 8 First reading of William Sharman Crawford's bill to give legal effect to Ulster custom (second reading refused by 112 to 25, 16 June)

Apr. 5 Opening of Alexis Soyer's model soup kitchen on Royal Barracks Esplanade, Dublin

Apr. 27 Irish fever act, 1847 (10 Vict., c. 22), amending and continuing 9 & 10 Vict., c. 6 (see 24 Mar. 1846)

May 4 Breakdown of attempts to reunite Loyal National Repeal Association and Irish Confederation

May 15 O'Connell dies at Genoa (see 5 Aug.)

May 26 Earl of Clarendon sworn in as L.L.

Ulster Tenant Right Association formed at meeting at Derry

June 8 Poor Relief (Ireland) Act, 1847 (10 Vict., c. 31), empowers boards of guardians to grant outdoor relief to aged, infirm, and sick poor and to poor widows with 2 or more dependent children; it also empowers poor law commrs to permit boards to give food to able-bodied poor for limited periods; but persons holding more than quarter acre of land are excluded from benefit

c. **June**   First collection of agricultural statistics, undertaken by constabulary

July 12   Granard (Co. Longford) board of guardians requests, unsuccessfully, its own dissolution owing to intolerable burden of relieving destitute from local rates

July 22   Separate poor law commn for Ire. created by Poor Relief (Ireland) Act, 1847 (10 & 11 Vict., c. 90)

July   Potato harvest sound but small

Aug.   General election: in G.B.—con. 177, Peelites 105, lib. 269; in Ire.—con. 31, Peelites 11, lib. 25, repealers 36, Irish Confederates 2 (see July 1841, July 1852)

Aug. 5   Funeral of O'Connell in Dublin (see 15 May)

Aug. 28   Bailiffs enter Ballina workhouse and seize its goods in distraint for debt

Sept. 19   Meeting of tenant farmers at Holycross, Co. Tipperary, convened by Lalor to form a tenant league

Oct. 1   Cessation of distribution from government soup-kitchens

Nov. 2   Murder of Major Denis Mahon, a landlord of Strokestown, Co. Roscommon, the most notorious of a series of murders

Meeting at Rotunda, Dublin, of 33 Irish M.P.s of different parties to consider urgent Irish business, viz landlord-tenant relations, economic distress and proposed income and property taxes (followed by meeting of M.P.s, peers and other dignitaries, 4 Nov.)

Nov. 23   Dublin Statistical Society (forerunner of Statistical and Social Inquiry Society of Ireland) founded

Nov. 29-30   Crime and Outrage (Ireland) Bill introduced in H.C. (see 20 Dec.)

Dec. early   John Mitchel breaks away from *Nation*

Dec. 20   Crime and Outrage (Ireland) Act, 1847 (11 Vict., c. 2), combines powers of appointing extra police, of controlling possession of arms, of search and of compelling assistance from people in proclaimed districts; augments constabulary reserve to 6 officers and 612 other ranks

Isaac Butt's *A voice for Ireland: the famine in the land* (Dublin)

Asenath Nicholson's *Ireland's welcome to the stranger* (New York)

1848

Jan. 3   Papal rescript to Irish bps urging them to forbid political activity by clergy (published in *Dublin Evening Post*, 5 Feb.) (see 12 Mar. 1834, 15 Oct. 1844)

Feb. 12   First number of John Mitchel's *United Irishman*

Feb. 15   Landlord and tenant bill introduced in H.C. by Sir William Somerville, C.S.

Feb. 22-4   Revolution in Paris: Louis-Philippe abdicates *c*. **Feb**.   John O'Donovan's edition of *Annala rioghachta Ereann; Annals of the kingdom of Ireland by the four masters* (3 vols. Dublin, enlarged ed., 7 vols. 1851)

Mar. 1   Portadown-Armagh section of Ulster Railway opened (see 12 Sept. 1842)

Mar. 7   Crawford reintroduces tenant-right bill (second reading refused by 145 to 22, 5 Apr.)

Mar. 15   At meeting of Irish Confederation at Music Hall, Dublin, William Smith O'Brien and Thomas Francis Meagher advocate physical force

Mar. 21   Informations sworn against O'Brien, Mitchel, and Meagher

Apr. 3   In Paris O'Brien, Meagher, and others present fraternal address of Irish Confederation to Alphonse de Lamartine, minister for foreign affairs in provisional government of French republic; Lamartine makes non-committal reply

Apr. 10   Feargus O'Connor presides over chartist meeting on Kennington Common, Surrey, and afterwards presents mammoth petition to H.C.

Apr. 22   Treason felony act, 1848 (11 Vict., c. 12)

Apr. 25   John Stuart Mill's *Principles of political economy* (2 vols. London; numerous later eds); contains views on Irish questions, especially peasant proprietorship (modified in later eds)

May 13   John Mitchel arrested

May 15   Trial of O'Brien on charge of sedition, etc. (results in disagreement of jury)

May 26   Trial and conviction of Mitchel on charges under treason felony act

May 27   Mitchel sentenced to 14 years' transportation; his *United Irishman* appears for last time

June 10   First number of *Irish Tribune* (only 5 appear)

June 12   Agreement between Loyal National Repeal Association and Irish Confederation to unite as Irish League

June 24   First number of John Martin's *Irish Felon* (see 22 July); includes first of 3 articles by Lalor on theme: 'the land question contains, and the legislative question does not contain, the materials from which victory is manufactured'

July–Sept.   General failure of potato crop owing to blight

July 8   Charles Gavan Duffy arrested

July 22   Fifth and final number of *Irish Felon* (types and other materials seized by police, 28 July)

July 25   Habeas corpus act suspended until 1 Mar. 1849 (11 & 12 Vict., c. 35)

July 27   James Fintan Lalor arrested

July 28   Police arrest 10 members of *Nation's* production staff and seize machinery

July 29   William Smith O'Brien, Terence Bellew McManus, James Stephens, and about 100 Confederates engage about 40 police at Boulagh Commons, near Ballingarry, Co. Tipperary—'battle of Widow McCormack's cabbage-patch'

Aug. 1   Inauguration of regular mail service by rail (but by road-bridge across Menai Strait) between London (Euston) and Ire. via Holyhead and Kingstown

Aug. 5   William Smith O'Brien arrested

Aug. 14   Act to facilitate sale of encumbered estates in Ire. (11 & 12 Vict., c. 48) (see 28 July 1849)

Aug. 31   Unlawful oaths act (11 & 12 Vict., c. 89) (continues with amendments till 1880)

Sept. 4   Acts (11 & 12 Vict., cc 105, 107) to prohibit importation of animals to U.K. from places where disease prevails and to prevent spread of animal disease within U.K.

Sept. 28-Oct. 23   Trials at Clonmel of William Smith O'Brien, Thomas Francis Meagher, Terence Bellew McManus and Patrick O'Donohoe on treason charges

Oct. 7   O'Brien found guilty of high treason (sentenced, 9 Oct., to be hanged, drawn and quartered; see 5 June, 26 June, 9 July 1849)

Oct. 23   Meagher, McManus and O'Donohoe receive same sentence as O'Brien (see 5 June, 26 June, 9 July 1849)

Nov.   Cholera returns to Ire.

Nov. 24   Flight of Pope Pius IX to Gaeta in kingdom of Naples following assassination of his chief minister, Pellegrino Rossi (15 Nov.)

Dec. 10   Louis Napoleon, nephew of Emperor Napoleon, elected president of French Republic

1849

Jan. 6   First number of Joseph Brennan's *Irishman*

Feb. 9   Proclamation of republic in Rome and repudiation of temporal power of pope (republic collapses with occupation of city by French army, 3 July)

Feb. 15   Opening of Drogheda-Dundalk railway (see 23 May 1844), and of Dundalk-Castleblayney railway

Feb. 19   Meeting of antiquaries at Kilkenny gives rise to Kilkenny Archaeological Society, predecessor of Royal Society of Antiquaries of Ireland (new name adopted 14 Jan. 1890)

Mar. 29   Formation of Society for Irish Church Missions to Roman Catholics

Apr. 6   Abp Crolly dies of cholera

Apr. 26   Sir John Romilly introduces second encumbered estates bill in H.C. (cf. 14 Aug. 1848)

May   New rules of Loyal Orange Institution of Ireland adopted by Grand Orange Lodge of Ireland meeting at Monaghan

Reappearance of potato blight

June 5   sentences of O'Brien, Meagher, McManus and O'Donohoe commuted to transportation for life (see 28 Sept., 7 Oct., 23 Oct. 1848; 26 June, 9 July 1849)

June 20   James Clarence Mangan dies, aged 46

June 26   Act (12 & 13 Vict., c. 27) to remove doubts about punishment of treason by transportation

July 1   Fr Mathew arrives at Staten Island to begin total abstinence crusade in U.S.A. (leaves U.S.A. for Ire., 8 Nov. 1851)

July 3   Thomas Carlyle revisits Ire. (departs, 6 Aug.)

July 9   O'Brien, Meagher, McManus, and O'Donohoe transported from Ire. on board *Swift* for Van Diemen's Land

July 12   Sectarian affray at Dolly's Brae, near Castlewellan, Co. Down

July 28   Encumbered estates act (12 & 13 Vict., c. 77), superseding act of 14 Aug. 1848, and providing for appointment of 'encumbered estates court' of three commrs (see 2 Aug. 1858)

Aug. 1   Dublin Improvement Act, 1849 (12 & 13 Vict., c. 97), abolishes wide streets commn and paving board (see 29 Apr. 1758), and vests their powers in Dublin corporation

Aug. 3–12   Visit to Ire. of Queen Victoria and Prince Albert

Sept. 1   Revival of *Nation*

Sept. 16   Attack on Cappoquin police barracks, instigated by Lalor

Sept.   Lord Cloncurry's *Personal recollections* (Dublin)

Oct. 14   Formation by 2 catholic curates, Thomas O'Shea and Matthew O'Keefe, of tenant protection society at Callan, Co. Kilkenny, the first to secure a permanent following

Oct. 18   Formal opening of extension from Mallow to Cork of Great Southern and Western Railway (opened to general traffic, 29 Oct.)

Oct. 24   First meeting of encumbered estates commn

Oct.   Queen's Colleges at Belfast, Cork, and Galway opened to students

Dec. 27   James Fintan Lalor dies

William Thompson's *Natural history of Ireland*, vol. i (London) (vol. ii, 1850; vol. iii, 1851; vol. iv, 1856)

13,384 families evicted from agricultural holdings (19·46% of all net evictions recorded by constabulary, 1849–80)

1850

Jan. 5   Frederick Lucas's *Tablet* published in Dublin for first time (first issue, London, 16 May 1840)

Feb. 18   Landlord and Tenant (Ireland) Bill introduced in H.C. by Sir William Somerville, C.S. (see 15 Feb. 1848)

Feb. 24   Paul Cullen consecrated abp of Armagh

Mar. 12   Party Processions (Ireland) Act, 1850 (13 Vict., c. 2), provides for confiscation of emblems and arms (see 28 Aug. 1860, 27 June 1872)

Mar. 18   George Stephenson's Britannia railway-bridge over Menai Strait open open for general traffic

Apr. 12   Pius IX re-enters Rome protected by French army

Apr. 18   Hurricane causes great damage in Dublin

June 1   The *Viceroy* leaves Galway for Halifax (arriving, 11 June) in attempt to establish former as a major port for trans-Atlantic mail and passengers

Census taken throughout U.S.A.; Irish-born population 961,719 (4·15% of total and 42·8% of foreign-born population)

July 3   General assembly of presbyterian church in Ire. adopts petition to parliament in favour of statutory recognition of tenant right

July 4   Temperance cttee of presbyterian ministers formed in Belfast; revival of temperance cause among Ulster protestants

Aug. 6–9   Tenant-right conference in Dublin, concluding in formation of Irish Tenant League (see 8–9 Sept. 1852)

Aug. 14   Representation of the People (Ireland) Act, 1850 (13 & 14 Vict., c. 69) trebles county electorate but reduces borough electorate by one-fourth

Aug. 22–Sept. 10   National synod of bps at Thurles; statute 5 declares that Queen's Colleges are to be avoided by faithful catholics 'because of grave and intrinsic dangers'

Sept. 3   Charter establishing Queen's University in Ireland

Sept. 29   Pope Pius IX's brief re-establishing catholic hierarchy in England and Wales—'papal aggression'

Nov. 4   Russell, P.M., announces papal brief as 'insolent and insidious'

14,546 families evicted from agricultural holdings (21·15% of all net evictions recorded by constabulary, 1849–80)

First number of *Transactions of the Kilkenny Archaeological Society* (retitled *Journal of the Royal Society of Antiquaries of Ireland*, 1892)

1851

Feb. 7   H.C. begins debate on Russell's motion for leave to introduce ecclesiastical titles bill (resumed 10, 12, 14 Feb.; leave granted by 395 to 63, 14 Feb.)

Mar. 1   The *Tablet* coins expression 'Irish brigade' to describe Irish M.P.s opposing ecclesiastical titles bill

Mar. 30   Census taken throughout Ire., the first to take account of Irish language (preliminary report, 4 Aug.): population 6,552,385 (19·85% decrease; see 6 June 1841)

Census taken throughout G.B.: Irish-born population of England and Wales 519,959 (2·9% of total); of Scotland 207,367 (7·18% of total)

Aug. 1   Ecclesiastical Titles Act, 1851 (14 & 15 Vict., c. 60), directed against papal brief of 29 Sept. 1850, prohibits assumption in U.K. of territorial titles by catholic abps, bps, and deans (dead letter; repealed, 1871)

Opening of extension of Midland Great Western Railway from Mullingar to Galway

Aug. 7   Poor Relief (Ireland) Act, 1851 (14 & 15 Vict., c. 68), provides for establishment of dispensaries

Aug. 19   Meeting in Rotunda, Dublin, of catholics from throughout U.K. in opposition to ecclesiastical titles act; formation of Catholic Defence Association of Great Britain and Ireland

Dec. 2 Coup d'état in France: Louis Napoleon assumes greater powers (proclaimed Emperor Napoleon III, 2 Dec. 1852)

8,815 families evicted from agricultural holdings (12·82% of all net evictions recorded by constabulary, 1849-80)

1852

Jan. 1 Decrees of synod of Thurles promulgated in all catholic chapels in Ire.

Jan. 22 Delegation of 250 Irish members of 'Baltimore movement' meet Millard Fillmore, president of U.S.A., on behalf of Irish political prisoners in Van Diemen's Land

Feb. 23 Earl of Derby (con.) app. P.M. (see 30 June 1846, 19 Dec. 1852)

Mar. 1 Lord Naas becomes C.S. for the first time

Newbridge College (Dominican) opened

Mar. 17 St Patrick's Day demonstration in New York City; first fully organised demonstration of its kind

Mar. Royal Irish Academy removes from 114 Grafton Street, Dublin, to 19 Dawson Street

Apr. 25 Arthur O'Connor, former Volunteer and United Irishman, dies in France

May 3 Abp Cullen translated from Armagh to Dublin

May 8 Isaac Butt first enters parliament, as conservative M.P. for Harwich

May 10 Rev. John Henry Newman delivers at Rotunda, Dublin, the first of a series of lectures on university education (lectures published as *Discourses on the scope and nature of university education* (Dublin, 1852); revised and extended as *The idea of a university defined and illustrated* (London, 1873))

June 1 Completion of submarine telegraph cable between Holyhead and Howth, the first to link Britain and Ire.

June 10 Portadown-Dundalk railway opened (see 15 Feb. 1849); Belfast thus connected by railway with Dublin except for crossing of Boyne

National Exhibition opens in Cork

June 28-30 Rioting between protestants and catholics at Stockport, Cheshire

June 30 Valuation of rateable property act (15 & 16 Vict., c. 63) provides for uniform valuation of whole country on basis of tenements — 'Griffith's valuation'

July General election: in G.B. — con. 249, Peelites 38, lib. 261; in Ire. — con. 40, Peelites 2, lib. 15, lib. (ind.) 48 (see Aug. 1847, Mar.-Apr. 1857)

Aug. 28 Eglinton canal, linking Lough Corrib with sea at Galway, opened (regular steamer service from Galway to Maam via Kilbeg and Oughterard begins, 1860)

Sept. 1-8 British Association for the Advancement of Science meets at Belfast

Sept. 8-9 Tenant League (see 6-9 Aug. 1850) conference in Dublin, attended by 41 liberal M.P.s; adoption of policy of independent opposition to any government not taking up tenant-right question

Sept. 10   Formation of Friends of Religious Freedom and Equality (holds conference in Dublin, 28 Oct.)

Nov. 22   Joseph Napier introduces 4 Irish land bills in H.C.

Nov. 25   Serjeant William Shee introduces tenant-right bill in H.C.

Dec. 13   Thirty-six Irish liberal M.P.s meet to consider their future conduct as a party

Dec. 16   Defeat of earl of Derby's government over budget, by 19 votes, owing to combination of whigs, Peelites and independent Irish against it (Derby resigns, 17 Dec.; see 19 Dec.)

Dec. 19   Earl of Aberdeen (Peelite) app. P.M.; begins to form coalition government of liberals and Peelites which includes members of independent Irish party, John Sadleir and William Keogh (see 23 Feb. 1852, 6 Feb. 1855)

Transactions of the central relief committee of the Society of Friends during the famine in Ireland in 1846 and 1847 (London)

6,550 families evicted from agricultural holdings (9·52% of all net evictions recorded by constabulary, 1849-80)

1853

Mar. 17   Formation of Ossianic Society to publish Fenian poems, tales, etc.

May 10   Thomas Chambers obtains leave of H.C. to bring in bill intended to facilitate inspection of nunneries (dropped, 10 Aug.) (see 14 Mar. 1854)

May 12   Irish Industrial Exhibition opens in Dublin

June 22   Completion of temporary wooden viaduct over Boyne at Drogheda opens all-rail link between Belfast and Dublin (completion of permanent iron viaduct, 5 Apr. 1855)

June 28   Act (16 & 17 Vict., c. 34) extends income tax to Ire. (effective retrospectively from 5 Apr. 1853)

July 19   John Mitchel escapes from Van Diemen's Land bound for U.S.A.

Aug. 29–Sept. 4   Queen Victoria and Prince Albert visit Dublin and environs

Nov. 23   Report of Stafford Northcote and Sir Charles Trevelyan on organisation of civil service recommends 'a proper system of examination' of applicants for admission and promotion according to merit

Dec. 5   Opening of Assembly's College, Belfast, for theological training of presbyterian clergy

Robert Hickson opens yard at Queen's Island, Belfast, for building iron ships (see Dec. 1854)

First number of *Ulster Journal of Archaeology* (1st series 1853-62; 2nd series 1895-1911; 3rd series 1938–)

1854

Jan. 7   First number of John Mitchel's *Citizen* (New York)

Jan. 14   First instalment of Mitchel's 'Jail journal' in *Citizen* (last instalment, 19 Aug.; whole work in book form, New York, 1854; 2nd ed., Glasgow, 1856; enlarged ed., with preface by Arthur Griffith, Dublin, 1913)

Mar. 14 James Whiteside obtains leave of H.C. to bring in bill to restrict disposal of personal property by inmates of nunneries (dropped, 12 July)

Mar. 28 U.K. declares war on Russia: outbreak of Crimean war

Apr. 13 Irishmen's Civil and Military Republican Union founded in New York

May 18 Instructions regulating political conduct of clergy approved by national synod of catholic church in Dublin (see 12 Mar. 1839, 3 Jan. 1848)

July 11 Opening at Killarney of first railway hotel in Ire., erected by Killarney Junction Railway Co.

Aug. 10 Statutory provision made for establishment of national gallery of paintings, sculpture, and fine arts in Ire. by 17 & 18 Vict., c. 99

Towns Improvement (Ireland) Act, 1854 (17 & 18 Vict., c. 103), provides for election of town commrs to administer towns with over 1,500 population

Aug. 19 Derry-Enniskillen railway opened

Aug. 21-6 Last fair held at Donnybrook, near Dublin (suppressed, 1855)

Oct. 29 A Tenant League meeting at Callan decides to take to Rome dispute between local curates (Matthew O'Keefe and Thomas O'Shea) and bp of Ossory who has forbidden them to take further part in politics (see 14 Oct. 1849)

Nov. 3 Opening of Catholic University, with John Henry Newman as rector

Nov. 29 Board of Trinity College establishes 16 non-foundation scholarships open to candidates of all religious denominations

Nov. Congressional elections in U.S.A.: 43 American Party members and up to 70 active sympathisers elected; height of anti-Irish 'know-nothing' agitation

Dec. 3 Military and police attack Eureka stockade at Ballarat, Victoria, erected by insurgent diggers led by Peter Lalor (brother of James Fintan Lalor)

Dec. Edward J. Harland, at 23 years of age, arrives in Belfast to take up appointment as manager of Queen's Island shipyard

William Allingham's collection of verse, *Day and night songs* (London; 2nd ed., 1855)

John Thomas Gilbert's *A history of the city of Dublin*, vol. i (Dublin; vol. ii, 1858; vol. iii, 1859; 2nd ed., 1861; 3rd ed., 1972)

1855

c. **Feb.** Emmet Monument Association formed in New York, by Michael Doheny and John O'Mahony, with object of establishing independence of Ire.

Feb. 6 Viscount Palmerston (lib.) app. P.M. (see 19 Dec. 1852, 20 Feb. 1858)

Mar. 1 Report of commrs on Maynooth College

June 26 Public Libraries (Ireland) Act, 1855 (18 & 19 Vict., c. 40) promotes establishment of free libraries by town councils from proceeds of 1*d.* rate

Aug. 22 Catholic cathedral at Killarney consecrated; architect, Augustus Welby Pugin

Oct. 22   Frederick Lucas dies aged 43

Nov. 2   Opening of Cecilia Street School of Medicine as part of Catholic University of Ireland

Nov. 6   Charles Gavan Duffy leaves Ire. for Australia

The ancient music of Ireland (Dublin) published under editorship of George Petrie and sponsorship of Society for the Preservation and Publication of the Melodies of Ireland

1856

Jan.   James Stephens, formerly associate of William Smith O'Brien (see 29 July 1848), returns to Ire. from exile in France (see 17 Mar. 1858)

Irish Academy of Music founded (title Royal granted, 1872)

Jan. 16   Russia accepts Austrian ultimatum for peace: end of Crimean war

Feb. 13   Collapse of Tipperary Bank

Feb. 17   Suicide of John Sadleir

May 1   University Church, St Stephen's Green, Dublin, opened; architect, John Hungerford Pollen

June 20   Peace Preservation (Ireland) Act, 1856 (19 & 20 Vict., c. 36), continues major provisions of 11 Vict., c. 2 but reduces penalties to not more than one year's imprisonment

Dec. 8   Fr Mathew dies

Phoenix National and Literary Society formed at Skibbereen, Co. Cork, by Jeremiah O'Donovan (later called O'Donovan Rossa)

1857

Mar.-Apr.   General election: in G.B.—lib. 329, con. 220; in Ire.—lib. 48, con. 44, ind. opposition 13 (see July 1852, May 1859)

May   Thomas D'Arcy McGee, former Young Irelander, moves from New York to Montreal at invitation of Montreal Irish community

June 29   Abp Patrick Leahy of Cashel and Bp Thomas Furlong of Ferns issue statement favouring Sunday closing of public houses in Ire.

July 13-19   Sectarian rioting in Belfast

Aug. 17   Illicit Distillation (Ireland) Act, 1857 (20 & 21 Vict. c. 40), transfers duties of revenue police to constabulary

Sept. 6   Beginning of renewed rioting at Belfast following open-air sermon preached by Rev. Hugh Hanna (see 13 June 1886)

Sept. 10   Commn app. to inquire into Belfast riots (report, 20 Nov.)

1858

Feb. 26   Derby (con.) app. P.M. for second time (see 6 Feb. 1855, 12 June 1859)

Mar. 17   Secret organisation later known as I.R.B. (variously Irish Revolutionary Brotherhood or Irish Republican Brotherhood) founded in Dublin by James Stephens

'Orange and green' riot in Toronto: 1 killed (Michael Murphy later founds Hibernian Benevolent Society, Irish catholic self-defence organisation)

Apr. 5   Portadown–Dungannon section of Ulster Railway opened

July 17   First number of Denis Holland's *Irishman* (Belfast; Dublin from 23 Apr. 1859)

July 21   Secret conversations at Plombières-les-Bains between Napoleon III and Count Cavour; basis of agreement for French intervention in Italy against Austria (confirmed by treaty of Turin, 26, 28 Jan. 1859 (see 27 Apr. 1859))

Aug. 2   Act to facilitate sale and transfer of land in Ire. (21 & 22 Vict., c. 72); consolidates provisions of act of 28 July 1849 and subsequent acts dealing with encumbered estates, and alters title of court to 'Landed estates court, Ireland'

Medical Act, 1858 (21 & 22 Vict., c. 90), providing for creation of General Medical Council to maintain standards in medical education in U.K. and for registration of medical practitioners

Irish reformatory schools act, 1858 (21 & 22 Vict., c. 103) provides for inspection and maintenance of schools for 'juvenile offenders' run by denominational bodies

Aug. 20   First message received from New World by transatlantic cable recently completed between Trinity Bay, Newfoundland, and Valentia, Co. Kerry (unrepairable fault occurs, 3 Sept.; see 27 July 1866)

Aug. 23–Sept. 17   Cardinal Wiseman tours Ire.

Sept.   Irish Temperance League (prohibitionist) formed in Belfast by businessmen and presbyterian clergy

Sept. 29   Irish auxiliary of United Kingdom Alliance (prohibitionist) set up in Dublin

Dec. 8   Arrest at Skibbereen and Bantry of 15 members of Phoenix Society

Edward Harland (see Dec. 1854) buys Robert Hickson's shipyard at Queen's Island, Belfast, with money supplied by the Liverpool financier, G. C. Schwabe, and takes into partnership Schwabe's nephew, Gustav Wilhelm Wolff (firm assumes name Harland & Wolff in 1862)

1859

Jan. 1   First number of *Dublin Builder* (retitled *Irish Builder*, 1867)

Jan. 29   Foundation stone laid on Leinster Lawn, Dublin, of National Gallery of Painting and Sculpture (formally opened, 30 Jan. 1864); architects, Charles Lanyon and Francis Fowke

Feb. 2   Castleblayney–Enniskillen railway opened

Mar. 29   First number of *Irish Times*

Mar. 31   Independent Irish party splits, 6 to 5, on vote on second reading of English parliamentary reform bill; Derby's government defeated

Apr.   Organisation in U.S.A. of Fenian Brotherhood under John O'Mahony as counterpart to Irish Republican Brotherhood in Ire.

Apr. 27   Outbreak of war between France, in alliance with Piedmont-Sardinia, and Austria

May   General election: in G.B.—lib. 308, con. 241; in Ire.—con. 55, lib. 50 (see Mar.-Apr. 1857, July 1865)

June 12   Viscount Palmerston app. P.M. for second time (see 20 Feb. 1858, 29 Oct. 1865)

June 29   Massive prayer-meeting in Botanic Gardens, Belfast, marking height of religious revival in Ulster

July 12   Peace of Villafranca signed by Emperors Napoleon III and Francis-Joseph: France disengages from Italy and Austria cedes Lombardy, Piedmont-Sardinia being thus able to impose territorial settlement on papacy

July 18   Opening of Tralee & Killarney Railway, final link in line between Tralee and Dublin

Aug. 5   Joint pastoral of catholic bps stating grievances concerning national system of education, provision of chaplains in army and navy, etc.

1860

Jan.   Series of excessively cold and wet seasons begins (lasts till 1862; droughts follow, 1863, 1864); accompanied by severe agricultural depression

Mar. 27   First public performance, at Laura Keene's Theater, New York, of Dion Boucicault's drama 'The colleen bawn' (see 13-14 July 1819; 1829)

May 11   Giuseppe Garibaldi and 'the thousand' disembark at Marsala to invade Sicily-Naples (enter Naples, 7 Sept.)

May 15   Land improvement act (23 Vict., c. 19) authorises loans for erection of dwellings for labourers

May 16   Official notice issued and distributed throughout Ireland drawing attention to act (59 Geo. III, c. 69) prohibiting foreign enlistment

June 1   Census taken throughout U.S.A.: Irish-born population, 1,611,304 (5·12% of total and 38·9% of foreign-born population)

Aug. 28   Refreshment Houses (Ireland) Act, 1860 (23 & 24 Vict., c. 107), facilitates issue of wine licences

Party Processions (Ireland) Act, 1860 (23 & 24 Vict., c. 141), strengthening powers against provocative behaviour by processionists (see 12 Mar. 1850, 27 June 1872)

Landed Property (Ireland) Improvement Act, 1860 (23 & 24 Vict., c. 153)—'Napier's act'

Landlord and Tenant Law Amendment (Ireland) Act, 1860 (23 & 24 Vict., c. 154)—'Deasy's act'

Sept. 5   French College of the Immaculate Heart of Mary (Holy Ghost Fathers), Williamstown, Co. Dublin, opened (renamed Blackrock College, 1890)

Sept. 11   Piedmont-Sardinian troops invade papal states; seize Umbria and Marches

Sept. 17   Unsuccessful defence of Spoleto by part of Irish battalion in papal service

Sept. 18   Papal forces defeated at Castelfidardo by Piedmont-Sardinian army: strong partisan feelings aroused in Ire. and G.B.

1861

Jan. 15 Terence Bellew McManus, Young Irelander, dies in San Francisco

Feb. 22 Select cttee of H.C. app. to examine operation of poor law in Ire. (see 27 May; report, 5 July)

Mar. 3 Proclamation of edict emancipating serfs in Russia

Mar. 17 Victor Emmanuel II of Piedmont-Sardinia assumes title 'king of Italy'

Mar. 18 National Brotherhood of St Patrick formally inaugurated at banquet held in Rotunda, Dublin, chaired by Thomas Neilson Underwood

Apr. 7 Census taken throughout Ire. (preliminary report, 15 July): population 5,798,967 (11·50% decrease; see 30 Mar. 1851)

Census taken throughout G.B.: Irish-born population of England and Wales 601,634 (2·99% of total); of Scotland, 204,083 (6·7% of total)

Apr. 8-10 John George Adair evicts 47 tenants on his estate at Derryveagh, Co. Donegal, and demolishes their houses

Apr. 12 American civil war begins with attack on Fort Sumter, Charleston, by confederates

Apr. William John Fitzpatrick's *The life, times and correspondence of the Right Rev. Dr Doyle, bishop of Kildare and Leighlin* (2 vols, Dublin) (see 1823)

May 27 Abp Cullen gives evidence to select cttee on Irish poor law, putting catholic case against proselytism in workhouses

June 3 Cttee to bring remains of T. B. McManus back to Ire. formed in Dublin under auspices of National Brotherhood of St Patrick

July 22 Act (24 & 25 Vict., c. clxxii) enabling Dublin corporation to carry out engineering scheme to bring water from Vartry Lake, Co. Wicklow (water turned into new course, 30 June 1863)

July William Edward Hartpole Lecky's *Leaders of public opinion in Ireland* (anon., London; 2nd ed., 1871; 3rd ed., 1903)

Aug. 21-30 Queen Victoria and Prince Albert visit Ire.

Sept. 2 Opening of Dungannon–Omagh section of Ulster Railway (see 5 Apr. 1858), which is thus connected with Derry-Enniskillen railway (see 19 Aug. 1854)

Sept. 24 Mater Misericordiae Hospital, Dublin, opened by Sisters of Mercy; architect John Bourke

Sept.-Dec. Irish brigade of U.S. army formed under T. F. Meagher

Nov. 10 Funeral of T. B. McManus in Dublin, after lying in state in Mechanics' Institute (4-10 Nov.)

1862

Jan. 1 Belfast shipbuilding firm of Harland & Wolff formed through partnership of E. J. Harland with G. W. Wolff (see 1858)

Feb. 11 Rev. Patrick Lavelle, vice-president of Brotherhood of St Patrick, lectures at Rotunda on 'The catholic doctrine of the right of revolution'

May 31-July 2   First major engagements of Meagher's Irish brigade, in James Peninsula campaign (brigade later suffers heavy losses at Antietam (17 Sept.) and Fredericksburg (13 Dec.); never subsequently regains full strength)

July 5   Deputation from Catholic University calls on Palmerston in London to request charter

Aug. 7   Poor Relief (Ireland) Act, 1862 (25 & 26 Vict., c. 83) extends provision for outdoor relief, abolishing 'quarter acre' restriction of 10 Vict., c. 31 (see 8 June 1847)

Sept. 3   Opening of extension of Midland Great Western Railway from Longford to Sligo

Sept. 22   President Abraham Lincoln proclaims all slaves in Confederate-held districts of U.S.A. to be free as from 1 Jan. 1863

Oct. 22   Dublin United Trades' Association provisionally formed at meeting representative of nine trades (rules adopted, 29 Nov.)

1863

Jan. 22   Nationalist revolt in Poland begins

Feb.   First number of *Irish Temperance League Journal* (Belfast)

Apr. 8   Dr Jasper Joly presents to library of Royal Dublin Society a collection of some 23,000 volumes, many on Irish history and topography

Apr. 20   Registration of Births and Deaths (Ireland) Act, 1863 (26 Vict., c. 11)

Apr. 28   Foundation laid of Christian Brothers' schools in Synge Street, Dublin (opened, 11 Apr. 1864)

May 8   Meagher resigns commission in U.S. army on grounds of discrimination against Irish brigade

June 24   Revenue Act, 1863 (26 & 27 Vict., c. 33), encourages consumption of beer, as opposed to spirits, in U.K.

July 13-17   Anti-draft and anti-negro riots in New York City by predominantly Irish mobs; over 1,500 killed

July 28   Registration of Marriages (Ireland) Act, 1863 (26 & 27 Vict., c. 90)

Salmon Fishery (Ireland) Act, 1863 (26 & 27 Vict., c. 114)

Aug.   Brotherhood of St Patrick condemned by catholic bps

Nov. 28   First number of *Irish People*; proprietor Thomas Clarke Luby, manager and publisher Jeremiah O'Donovan Rossa, editor John O'Mahony

1864

Jan. 2   Rev. Patrick Lavelle arrives in Rome to plead his case with pope (but yields on essentials, 25 Jan.)

Jan. 21   Irish National League founded by John Martin and The O'Donoghue

Mar. 7   Abp Cullen issues pastoral for St Patrick's day denouncing fenianism

Apr. 11   Select cttee app. by H.C. to inquire into scientific institutions of Dublin (report, 15 July)

Apr.   Cullen appeals to Rome for definitive ruling on fenianism

June 18   William Smith O'Brien dies

June 30   Beerhouses (Ireland) Act, 1864 (27 & 28 Vict., c. 35), facilitates establishment of beerhouses

July 29   Contagious Diseases Prevention Act, 1864 (27 & 28 Vict., c. 85), provides for medical inspection and control of prostitutes in certain naval and military towns in U.K., including Cork, the Curragh and Queenstown

July   First instalment of Joseph Sheridan Le Fanu's 'Maud Ruthyn' in *Dublin University Magazine* (work republished in book form as *Uncle Silas* later in year)

Aug. 8   Laying of foundation-stone of O'Connell monument in Dublin; leads to 2 weeks of sectarian rioting in Belfast (8–19 Aug.)

c. **Aug.**   James Stephens first declares 1865 to be year for fenian insurrection

Sept.   Association formed in Belfast to agitate for legislation closing public houses on Sunday (see 20 Dec. 1866)

Oct. 28   Abp Martin John Spalding of Baltimore issues circular on fenianism (hierarchy in U.S.A. defers decision on issue)

Nov. 7   First public performance of Dion Boucicault's 'Arrah-na-pogue', at Theatre Royal, Dublin

Dec. 8   The 'syllabus of errors' issued by Pope Pius IX

Dec. 29   Peter Paul MacSwiney, lord mayor of Dublin, presides over aggregate meeting at Rotunda at which National Association of Ireland is inaugurated, with programme of agrarian reform, church disestablishment, and catholic education

1865

Jan. 23   Abp Cullen issues pastoral to his clergy, calling for their co-operation in National Association

Jan.   W. E. H. Lecky's *History of the rise and influence of the spirit of rationalism in Europe* (London)

Feb. 20   First monthly meeting of National Association

Feb. 24   St Patrick's cathedral, Dublin, reopened, after restoration at expense of Sir Benjamin Lee Guinness

c. **Mar.**   *Ancient laws of Ireland*, vol. i (Dublin; vols ii–vi, 1869–1901); sponsored by Brehon Law Commissioners

Apr. 26   End of American civil war

Apr. 30   Henry Edward Manning app. abp of Westminster

May 9   Dublin International Exhibition opened at Dublin Exhibition Palace and Winter Garden in Earlsfort Terrace

May   John Patrick Prendergast's *The Cromwellian settlement of Ireland* (London; 2nd ed., 1870; 3rd ed., 1922)

June   Richard Pigott, manager of *Irishman*, acquires the paper from proprietor, Patrick James Smyth

June 29   Act (28 & 29 Vict., c. 70) abolishes town police force of Belfast and transfers policing of town to Constabulary of Ireland (cf. 9 Aug. 1870)

July   General election: in G.B.—lib. 312, con. 241; in Ire.—lib. 58, con. 47 (see May 1859, Nov. 1868)

Aug. 24   Foundation-stone laid of Methodist College, Belfast (opened to males, 18 Aug. 1868; opened to females, 1869)

Sept. 15   Police raid offices of *Irish People*, arresting O'Donovan Rossa and several others on treason-felony charges (Thomas Clarke Luby and John O'Leary arrested elsewhere after midnight)

Sept. 16   Last number of *Irish People*

Oct. 10   Magee College, Londonderry, formally opened

Cullen, referring to *Irish People*: 'for suppressing that paper the public authorities deserve the thanks and gratitude of all those who love Ireland'

Oct. 29   Earl Russell (lib.) app. P.M. for second time (see 12 June 1859, 28 June 1866)

Nov. 5   Thomas Nulty, bp of Meath, and his clergy withdraw from National Association to form Meath Tenant Right Society

Nov. 11   James Stephens arrested (escapes from Richmond jail, Dublin, 24 Nov.; flees to France, Mar. 1866)

1866

Jan. 24   Opening of extension of Great Northern & Western Railway (backed by Midland Great Western) from Castlebar to Westport

Feb. 17   Bill suspending habeas corpus act in Ireland passes all stages in both houses (receives royal assent as 29 Vict., c. 4, 18 Feb.; suspension continued by four subsequent acts to 1869)

Feb. 20-21   Fenian council of war: majority decides against immediate rising

Feb. 23   John Devoy arrested

Mar. 6   Cattle Disease (Ireland) Act, 1866 (29 Vict., c. 4)

Apr.   First fenian attempt on Canada: scheme to seize Campo Bello, New Brunswick, foiled by U.S. forces without fighting (19 Apr.)

Apr. 30   Parliamentary Oaths Act, 1866 (29 Vict. c. 19)

May 31   Second fenian attempt on Canada: fenian army under Col. John O'Neill crosses Niagara from Buffalo and occupies Fort Erie (success at Ridgeway, 2 June; withdrawal, 3 June)

June 11   Contagious Diseases Act (29 Vict., c. 35) (see 29 July 1864)

June 22   Abp Cullen created cardinal; first Irishman ever to achieve this rank

June 25   Supplemental charter granted to Queen's University in Ireland enabling persons to graduate in university without having attended a Queen's College (see 1 Feb. 1868)

June 28   Derby (con.) app. P.M. for third time (see 29 Oct. 1865, 27 Feb. 1868)

July early   Isaac Butt's *Land tenure in Ireland: a plea for the Celtic race* (Dublin)

July 27   Completion of new submarine cable between Valentia, Co. Kerry, and Trinity Bay, Newfoundland

Sept. 15   John Blake Dillon dies

Oct. 11   Alexandra College, Dublin, for education of young ladies, opened

Dec. 17   Stephens deposed as head centre of Fenian Brotherhood in U.S.A.

Dec. 20   Irish Association for the Closing of Public Houses on Sunday founded in Dublin (similar organisation founded in Manchester, Nov. 1866)

1867

Feb. 11   Attempted fenian raid on Chester castle

Feb. 12   Sixty-seven men arrested on their arrival at North Wall, Dublin, on board Holyhead and Liverpool steamers

Outbreak of fenian rebellion near Kells, Co. Kerry

Feb. 17   In sermon in Killarney cathedral, David Moriarty, bp of Kerry, declares: 'when we look down into the fathomless depths of this infamy of the heads of the fenian conspiracy we must acknowledge that eternity is not long enough nor hell hot enough to punish such miscreants'

Feb. 20   Lord Naas, C.S., introduces bill to suspend habeas corpus act for further period (enacted as 30 Vict., c. 1, 26 Feb.); those arrested to be treated as untried prisoners

Mar. 5-6   Outbreak of fenian rebellion around Dublin and in Munster

Mar. 17   David Moriarty, bp of Kerry, in *Letter on the disendowment of the established church* (Dublin), argues in favour of concurrent endowment

Mar. 27   Major Myles William O'Reilly, M.P. for Longford, introduces first Irish Sunday-closing bill (referred to select cttee, 2 July; end of session on 21 Aug. prevents progress)

Mar. 29   British North America Act, 1867 (30 Vict., c. 3); establishes federal constitution in Canada

Apr. 5   School of Physic (Ireland) Amendment Act, 1867 (30 Vict., c. 9), abolishes religious tests for professorships of anatomy and chirurgery, chemistry and botany in Dublin University

Apr. 12   The *Jackmel* (renamed *Erin's Hope*, 29 Apr.) leaves New York with arms for fenians in Ireland (reaches Sligo Bay, 20 May)

May 31   Naas's act (30 Vict., c. 25) continuing suspension of habeas corpus to 1 Mar. 1868

June 8   Coronation of Francis-Joseph of Austria as king of Hungary in accordance with *Ausgleich* ('compromise') by which Hungary is re-established as monarchy separate from Austria but associated with her for purposes of crown, foreign relations, and defence

June 17   Dublin Port Act, 1867 (30 Vict., c. lxxxi) sets up Dublin port and dock board and commissioners of Irish lights

June 20   United Brotherhood or Clan na Gael founded at New York by Jerome J. Collins

July 12 William Johnston of Ballykilbeg leads vast orange procession from Newtownards to Bangor in protest against party processions act

Aug. 12 Public Records (Ireland) Act, 1867 (30 & 31 Vict., c. 70), provides for establishment and regulation of public record office at Four Courts, Dublin, and regulation of state paper office at Dublin castle

Aug. 17 I.R.B. convention at Manchester appoints Col. Thomas J. Kelly to succeed Stephens as head

Sept. 12 Constabulary of Ireland renamed Royal Irish Constabulary

Sept. 18 Police sergeant, Charles Brett, killed during rescue of 2 fenian prisoners, Colonel Thomas J. Kelly and Captain Timothy Deasy, from police-van in Manchester by body of armed fenians

Oct. 1–3 Catholic bps meet in Dublin and reject principle of endowment of catholic church by state

Oct. 10 Convict-ship *Hougoumont*, with 62 fenians aboard, leaves Portland for Fremantle, Western Australia, the last to sail for Australia (arrives, 10 Jan. 1868)

Oct. Classes begin at Royal College of Science, Dublin, successor to Museum of Irish Industry (see 1845)

Oct. 30 Dr Henry Cooke, formerly moderator of general assembly of presbyterian church, in speech at Hillsborough, Co. Down, defends establishment of Church of Ireland 'because I recognise in her a noble branch of the great protestant tree planted in Europe by the hands of the reformers'

Nov. 23 William Philip Allen, Michael Larkin, and Michael O'Brien executed at Salford jail for murder of Sergeant Brett (see 18 Sept.)

Dec. 12 Viceregal proclamation declaring 'Manchester martyrs' funeral processions illegal

Dec. 13 Explosion beside Clerkenwell jail, London, intended to effect escape of 2 fenian prisoners, causes several deaths and numerous injuries

Dec. 23 Group of Limerick priests, headed by Dean Richard O'Brien, issues declaration in favour of repeal of union

Thomas Gallaher transfers his tobacco-manufacturing business from Londonderry to Belfast (large factory opened, 1896)

Isaac Butt's *The Irish people and the Irish land: a letter to Lord Lifford* (Dublin)

Jacob Poole's *A glossary . . . of the old dialect of the English colony in the baronies of Forth and Bargy*, edited by William Barnes (London; new ed. by T. P. Dolan and Diarmaid O Muirithe, Wexford, 1979)

1868

Jan. 14 Royal commn under earl of Powis app. to inquire into primary education in Ire. (see 21 May 1870)

Jan. John Francis Maguire's *The Irish in America* (London) (reviewed by John Morley in *Fortnightly Review*, 1 Feb.)

Feb. 1 Rolls court grants perpetual injunction against enforcement of supplemental charter of Queen's University (see 25 June 1866)

Feb. 27 Benjamin Disraeli (con.) app. P.M. (see 28 June 1866, 3 Dec. 1868)

Feb. John Stuart Mill's pamphlet, *England and Ireland* (London)

Feb. 29 William Johnston of Ballykilbeg sentenced to 1 month's imprisonment after conviction for offences under party processions act (see 12 July 1867)

Mar. 5 Select cttee of H.C. on Irish Sunday-closing bill ordered; chairman Myles O'Reilly (reports 26 May; revised bill withdrawn, 9 June 1869)

Mar. 12 Supposed fenian, Henry James O'Farrell, attempts to assassinate duke of Edinburgh near Port Jackson, New South Wales (executed at Darlinghurst, 21 Apr.)

Mar. 19 Earl of Mayo, C.S., introduces Irish reform bill in H.C.

Mar. 21 Fenian, Captain William Mackey (alias Lomasney), sentenced to 12 years penal servitude for treason felony

Mar. 23 William Ewart Gladstone proposes motion in H.C. for disestablishment of Church of Ireland

Mar. Unrest at Hokitika, New Zealand, owing to fenian sympathies of many catholic Irish

Apr. 7 Former Young Irelander, Thomas D'Arcy McGee, assassinated in Ottawa, Ontario

May 10-11 'Murphy riots' at Ashton-under-Lyne, Lancashire

May 26 Michael Barrett executed at Newgate for his part in Clerkenwell explosion (see 13 Dec. 1867), the last public execution in England (Capital Punishment Amendment Act, 1868 (29 May) abolishes public executions in G.B. and Ire.)

July 13 Representation of the People (Ireland) Act, 1868 (31 & 32 Vict., c. 49), affecting parliamentary boroughs only: reduction of rated occupier franchise from £8 to £4; introduction of lodger franchise

Aug. 3 Campaign for amnesty of political prisoners begins with introduction of amnesty resolutions in Cork city council

Aug. 15 Conference of teachers at Dublin, giving rise to Irish National Teachers' Organisation

Oct. 20 President of Royal College of St Patrick, Maynooth, Dr C. W. Russell, argues in letter to Gladstone that college is educational, not ecclesiastical, and so has claim to be excluded from church bill

Nov. 12 Butt presides over amnesty meeting at Mechanics' Institute, Dublin

Nov. General election: in G.B.—lib. 321, con. 232; in Ire.—lib. 66, con. 39 (see July 1865, Feb. 1874)

Dec. 3 William Ewart Gladstone (lib.) app. P.M. (see 27 Feb. 1868, 20 Feb. 1874)

Dec. 18 John O'Hagan app. L.C. of Ire. (created Lord O'Hagan, 14 June 1870); first catholic to hold this office since reign of James II

1869

Jan. 26 Aggregate meeting in Dublin for release of fenian prisoners

Irish Permissive Bill Association founded in Dublin to support Sir Wilfrid Lawson's local option bill for restricting drink trade

Feb. 22   Chichester Fortescue, C.S., announces amnesty for 49 of the 81 non-military fenian convicts

Feb. 22, 24, 25   Cardinal Cullen gives evidence before Powis commn on primary education

Mar. 1   Gladstone introduces Irish church disestablishment bill

Mar.   Release of 49 amnestied fenian prisoners, including C. J. Kickham, J. F. X. O'Brien, and James O'Connor (see Jan. 1871)

Apr. 27   At dinner given to 2 released fenian convicts at Cork, the mayor, Daniel O'Sullivan, attributes 'noble and patriotic feelings' to O'Farrell, executed in 1868 for attack on duke of Edinburgh (see 12 Mar. 1868)

Apr. 28   Sectarian rioting at Derry during visit there of Prince Arthur

May 11   H.C., when about to proceed with second stage of bill to degrade and disqualify O'Sullivan as mayor of Cork, hears of his intended resignation (bill withdrawn, 8 June)

May 14   O'Connell's remains moved from temporary to permanent grave in Glasnevin cemetery

May 31   Irish church disestablishment bill read in H.C. for third time

July 26   Irish Church Act, 1869 (32 & 33 Vict., c. 42), disestablishes and partly disendows protestant episcopal church (effective, 1 Jan. 1871); provides for representative body (synod) for government of church, and body (Representative Church Body) to administer finances of church (see 15 Oct. 1870); provides for capital sums to presbyterian churches and catholic church in lieu of *regium donum* and Maynooth College grant; provides for purchase of church land by tenants; provides for vesting of ruinous churches in commrs of public works for preservation as national monuments

Aug. 9   Trades Unions Funds Protection Act, 1869 (32 & 33 Vict., c. 61), protects union funds from embezzlement and misappropriation

Aug. 11   Contagious Diseases Act (32 & 33 Vict., c. 96) (see 11 June 1866)

Aug. 17   Irish Catholic Benevolent Union of America founded at Dayton, Ohio; president Judge Dennis Dwyer (peak of *c.* 30,000 members by 1876; leading Irish-American organisation until overtaken by A.O.H. in early 1890s)

Aug. 18   Supreme council of I.R.B. adopts 'constitution of the Irish Republic'

Aug. 29   Murder of James Hunter near his farm at Tiernaur, near Newport, Co. Mayo

Sept.   Friedrich Engels visits Ire., collecting material for history of Ire. (uncompleted work, not published in English until Aug. 1965)

Oct. 10   Public funeral in London of fenian, Edward Martin (supposedly Col. Thomas J. Kelly), attracts cortège of many thousands

Nov. 19   Route Tenants' Defence Association formed at Ballymoney, Co. Antrim, the first of several such associations in Ulster

Nov. 22   Jeremiah O'Donovan Rossa nominated for Tipperary vacancy (returned by 1,131 votes to 1,028 for Denis Caulfield Heron, 27 Nov.; declared by H.C. to be ineligible as felon serving sentence, 10 Feb. 1870)

Dec. 8   Opening of ecumenical council of Vatican

Dec. 10   Treasury approves Irish government's proposal to appoint detective director of R.I.C.

1870

Jan. 12   Pius IX authorises Holy Office decree explicitly condemning fenians

Jan.   Publication of J. S. Mill's *Chapters and speeches on the Irish land question* (London), reprinted from his *Principles of political economy* and from *Hansard's parliamentary debates*

Feb. 15   Gladstone introduces Irish land bill in H.C.

Mar. 12   First chapter of Charles Joseph Kickham's 'Knocknagow, or the homes of Tipperary' published serially in New York *Emerald* (in Dublin *Shamrock*, 19 Mar. 1870) (whole work in book form published in Dublin, June 1873)

(B) 1870−1921

T. W. MOODY AND C. J. WOODS

1870

Apr. 4   Peace Preservation (Ireland) Act, 1870 (33 Vict., c. 9)

Apr. 19   George Henry Moore dies

May 19   Home rule movement launched by Isaac Butt at private meeting in Bilton's Hotel, Dublin

May 21   Report of Powis commn on primary education (see 14 Jan. 1868)

May 25   Attempted fenian invasion of Canada from Vermont

June 1   Census taken throughout U.S.A.: Irish-born population 1,855,827 (4·81% of total and 33·3% of foreign-born population)

July 12   'Orange and ribbon' riots in New York City; several killed (further riots, 12 July 1871)

July 18   Dogma of papal infallibility promulgated

Michael Davitt sentenced at Old Bailey to 15 years' penal servitude, under treason-felony act, 1848, for fenian activities (see 19 Dec. 1877)

July 19   France declares war on Prussia

July   John Boyle O'Reilly becomes editor of Boston *Pilot* (remains editor until death, 9 Aug. 1890) and resigns from Fenian Brotherhood and Clan na Gael

Aug. 1   Landlord and Tenant (Ireland) Act, 1870 (33 & 34 Vict., c. 46)—first Gladstone land act

Aug. 9   Act (33 & 34 Vict., c. 83) abolishing city police force of Derry and transferring policing of city to R.I.C. (cf. 29 June 1865)

Aug. 27   Launching of *Oceanic*, first of White Star liners built by Harland & Wolff

Sept. 1   At Rotunda, Dublin, Butt's Home Government Association holds its first public meeting

French decisively defeated by Prussians at Sedan (Napoleon III capitulates on field, 2 Sept.; republic declared in Paris, 4 Sept.)

Sept. 20   Fall of Rome to Italian troops; end of temporal power of papacy

Sept.   *Irish World* launched in New York by Patrick Ford (manager and editor until death, 23 Sept. 1913)

Oct. 8   Irish ambulance corps of 300 men leaves Dublin on *La Fontaine* for service in France (arrives at Le Havre, 11 Oct.)

Oct. 15   Charter incorporating Representative Church Body (see 26 July 1869)

William O'Connor Morris's *Letters on the land question of Ireland* (London)

1871

Jan. 1   Gladstone's Irish church act (see 26 July 1869) comes into effect

Jan.   Release of 33 amnestied fenian prisoners, including John Devoy, Jeremiah O'Donovan Rossa, John O'Leary, Thomas Clarke Luby, Denis Downing Mulcahy, and William Mackey Lomasney (cf. Mar. 1869)

Jan. 16-18   Irish company of French foreign legion in action at front near Montbéliard

Jan. 17   John Martin defeats Hon. George Plunkett (liberal) in Meath by-election by 1,140 votes to 684; first electoral victory of Home Government Association

Jan. 18   William I, king of Prussia, proclaimed emperor of Germany in palace of Versailles

Jan. 28   Armistice signed between France and Germany

Apr. 2   Census taken throughout Ire. (preliminary report, 14 June): population 5,412,377 (6·67% decline; see 7 Apr. 1861)

Census taken throughout G.B.: Irish-born population of England and Wales 566,540 (2·49% of total); of Scotland, 207,770 (6·2% of total)

June 16   Protection of Life and Property in Certain Parts of Ireland Act (34 & 35 Vict., c. 25)—'Westmeath act', allowing detention without trial for agrarian offences

July 18   W. J. O'Neill Daunt, Rev. Prof. Joseph Galbraith, and John Martin, delegates of Home Government Association, present home rule case to Dublin corporation, which pledges itself to home rule movement

Sept. 20   Butt returned M.P. for Limerick city in by-election after 6 years' absence from parliament

Sept. 26   Gladstone's speech at Aberdeen on home rule

Oct. 5   Fenian invasion of Canada from Georgetown, Minnesota; custom house at Pembina, Manitoba, briefly held by John O'Neill

Oct. 26   Civil action against William Marcy 'Boss' Tweed (arrested 16 Dec.); control of Democratic party organisation in New York city ('Tammany Hall') passes to 'Honest John' Kelly

Nov. 30   Consecration of St Finbarre's cathedral, Cork; architect, William Burges

George Sigerson's *History of the land tenures and land classes of Ireland* (London)

The Annals of Loch Cé: a chronicle of Irish affairs, 1014-1590, ed. William Maunsell Hennessy (2 vols, London)

1872

Feb. 1   First tramcars (horse-drawn) run in Dublin, from College Green to Rathmines

Feb. 8   Capt. John Philip Nolan, supporter of home rule and tenant right, defeats William Le Poer Trench (conservative) in Galway county by-election by 2,823 votes to 658

Feb. 12   Rowland Ponsonby Blennerhasset, protestant home-ruler, defeats his catholic liberal opponent in Kerry by-election by 2,237 votes to 1,398

Feb. 28   Bill for total Sunday closing of public houses in Ire. introduced in H.C. (talked out in debate on second reading, 26 June)

Apr. 1–May 21   Trial of Galway county election petition

Apr. 23   Commrs of national education decide to dismiss Rev. Robert O'Keefe as manager of Callan national schools

May 2   Gladstone's first speech in H.C. on home-rule demand

May 27   Judge William Keogh declares Capt. Nolan unseated on ground of improper clerical influence at Galway county by-election (cf. 8 Feb. 1872), and delivers heated attack on catholic clergy in general

June 3   Select cttee under Lord Chelmsford appointed by H.L. to inquire into working of land act of 1870 (report, 17 July)

June 27   Act (35 & 36 Vict., c. 22) repeals party processions acts of 1850 and 1860

July 18   Ballot Act, 1872 (35 & 36 Vict., c. 33), institutes secret voting

Aug. 10   Local Government Board (Ireland) Act, 1872 (35 & 36 Vict., c. 69) establishes local government board for Ire., which takes over functions of poor law commission (see 31 July 1838)

Licensing Act, 1872 (35 & 36 Vict., c. 94), introduces new liquor-licences, increases penalties and shortens hours of Sunday trading (cf. 7 Aug. 1874)

Aug. 15-20   Sectarian rioting in Belfast, occasioned by catholic procession on feast of assumption

Aug. 28   First tramcars (horse-drawn) run in Belfast

Oct.   League of the Cross (catholic total abstinence society) founded in England by Cardinal Manning, assisted by Rev. James Nugent of Liverpool

Nov. 7   James Anthony Froude's *The English in Ireland in the eighteenth century*, vol. i (London; vols ii and iii, 1874)

Nov. 26   Catholic Union of Ireland formally launched at meeting in Pro-cathedral, Dublin, to protect catholic interests in Italy, Germany, and Switzerland

1873

Jan. 8   Butt addresses meeting in Free Trade Hall, Manchester, from which Home Rule Confederation of Great Britain develops

Jan.   Patrick Weston Joyce's *Ancient Irish music* (Dublin)

Feb. 8   Catholic bps express disapproval of Gladstone's university bill

Feb. 15, 17-19   Patrick Duggan, bp of Clonfert, tried on charge of undue influence at Galway county by-election; acquitted (cf. 27 May 1872)

Mar. 12   Gladstone's university bill defeated in H.C. by 287 to 284

Mar. 13   Gladstone resigns as P.M. (returns to office, 19 Mar.)

Mar. 17   Convention of I.R.B. in Dublin adopts new constitution, replacing that of 18 Aug. 1869

May 26   University of Dublin Tests Act, 1873 (36 & 37 Vict., c. 21) abolishes religious tests in Trinity College—'Fawcett's act'

July   First number of *Irish Monthly*; editor Rev. Matthew Russell, S.J.

Nov. 18-21   Home-rule conference at Rotunda, Dublin; foundation of Home Rule League

Eugene O'Curry's *On the manners and customs of the ancient Irish* (posthumous, 3 vols, London)

1874

Feb.   General election: in G.B.—con. 317, lib. 232; in Ire.—home-rulers 60, con. 33, lib. 10 (see Nov. 1868, Mar.-Apr. 1880)

Feb. 20   Benjamin Disraeli (con.) app. P.M. for second time (created earl of Beaconsfield, 21 Aug. 1876) (see 3 Dec. 1868, 23 Apr. 1880)

Mar. 3   Home rule M.P.s resolve to constitute themselves separate and distinct party

June 30-July 2   Home rule motion by Butt debated in H.C. and defeated by 458 to 61

July 1   William James Pirrie and Walter H. Wilson taken into partnership by Harland and Wolff (cf. 1 Jan. 1862)

July 30   Joseph Gillis Biggar and other Irish home-rulers use 'obstruction' tactics in H.C. in order to delay progress of government's expiring laws continuance bill; disavowed by Butt

Aug. 7   Licensing Act (Ireland), 1874 (37 & 38 Vict., c. 69), favours interests of drink trade (cf. 10 Aug. 1872)

Nov. 7   Gladstone's pamphlet, *The Vatican decrees in their bearing on civil allegiance* (London)

Dec. 1 Plan of Patrick Keenan, resident commr of national education, for denominational teacher-training colleges adopted by board of commrs (St Patrick's College, Drumcondra, and Our Lady of Mercy College received into connection by board, 14 Aug. 1883; Church of Ireland College, 1884)

Dec. 14 Formation at Dublin of Irish Football Union (developed into Irish Rugby Football Union, 5 Feb. 1880)

1875

Jan. John O'Rourke's *The history of the great Irish famine* (Dublin)

Jan. 13 Gladstone announces his retirement from leadership of liberal party; succeeded by Lord Hartington (3 Feb.)

Jan. 16 First number of *Southern Cross* (Buenos Aires), organ of Irish in Argentina; editor Mgr Patricio José Dillon

Jan. 20-21 Tenant-right conference at Rotunda, Dublin

Feb. 16 John Mitchel returned unopposed at Tipperary by-election (but, as convicted felon, unseated by H.C., 18 Feb.)

Mar. 12 Mitchel again returned as M.P. for Tipperary (but dies, at Dromalane, Newry, 20 Mar.)

Apr. 19 Charles Stewart Parnell returned at Meath by-election (takes seat in H.C., 22 Apr.; makes maiden speech, 26 Apr.)

Apr. 22 Biggar makes $3\frac{1}{2}$-hour speech in H.C. on coercion bill (becomes law, 28 May, as Peace Preservation (Ireland) Act, 1875 (38 Vict., c. 4))

Aug. 5-7 O'Connell centenary celebrations

Aug. 11 Irish pharmacy act (38 & 39 Vict., c. 57) institutes and incorporates Pharmaceutical Society of Ireland

Aug. 30-Sept. 20 National synod of bps at Maynooth: condemnation of Queen's Colleges by synod of Thurles (see 22 Aug. 1850) repeated and applied to Trinity College (see 25 June 1970)

Sept. 1-3 Miner and two mine officials murdered by 'Molly Maguires' at Raven Run and Lansford, Schuylkill county, Pennsylvania (Bp James Frederick Wood of Philadelphia proscribes Molly Maguires, 'otherwise known as the Ancient Order of Hibernians', 15 Dec.)

Dec. 21 John Ireland, native of Co. Kilkenny, consecrated coadjutor bp of St. Paul, Minnesota (bp, 31 July 1884; abp, 15 May 1888; dies, 25 Sept. 1918)

1876

Mar. 'Skirmishing fund' instituted by Rossa at New York

Apr. 1 Great Northern Railway (Ireland) comes into existence with amalgamation of Dublin & Drogheda, Dublin & Belfast Junction, Irish North-Western and Ulster railways

Apr. 17-18 Six fenian convicts, having escaped from near Fremantle prison, Western Australia, are conveyed by fenian rescuers to waiting barque *Catalpa*, sent from Boston by Clan na Gael (reach New York, 19 Aug.)

Apr. 24   Church of Ireland general synod recommends establishment of temperance societies

May 12   H.C. passes resolution in favour of Sunday closing of public houses in Ire. (bill introduced, 14 June; withdrawn after making no progress in cttee, 3 Aug.)

June 30-July 1   Home rule motion by Butt debated in H.C.; defeated by 291 to 61 (1 July)

Aug. 8-15   Decision to form joint revolutionary directory of Clan na Gael and I.R.B. taken at seventh annual convention of Clan na Gael at Philadelphia

Aug. 15   Disturbances in Belfast

Aug. 20   Supreme council of I.R.B., by four votes to three, adopts resolution withdrawing support hitherto given to home rule movement and requesting all members of brotherhood within 6 months to cease active cooperation with that movement

Nov. 1   Clan na Gael delegation meets Russian ambassador at Washington

Dec. 29   Formation in Dublin of Society for the Preservation of the Irish Language

1877

Jan. 28   John O'Mahony, dying, resigns as head centre of Fenian Brotherhood (Rossa elected in succession, 2 Feb.; O'Mahony dies, 6 Feb.)

Feb. 12   Select cttee of H.C. ordered on Irish Sunday-closing bill (reports, 9 May, favouring total Sunday closing)

Feb. 26   Remains of John O'Mahony arrive at Mechanics' Institute, Dublin (address by Kickham and interment at Glasnevin, 4 Mar.)

Mar. 5   Supreme council of I.R.B. enforces decision of 20 Aug. 1876 by calling for resignations of John Barry, Patrick Egan, Joseph Gillis Biggar, and John O'Connor Power; Barry and Egan resign; Biggar and Power refuse to do so (expelled at next meeting of council, Aug. 1877)

Mar. 23   Beer Licences Regulation (Ireland) Act, 1877 (40 & 41 Vict., c. 4)

Mar.   Clan na Gael gains control of 'skirmishing fund' (renamed 'national fund')

May 1   Select cttee under George John Shaw-Lefevre app. by H.C. to inquire into working of land act of 1870 (report, 27 June 1878)

June 21   Ten Molly Maguires hanged at Pottsville and Mauch Chunk, Pennsylvania (10 others executed between 25 Mar. 1878 and 9 Oct. 1879)

July 31-Aug. 1   Biggar, Parnell, Frank Hugh O'Donnell and other Irish 'obstructives' prolong sitting of H.C. over 24 hours

Aug. 14   General Prisons (Ireland) Act, 1877 (40 & 41 Vict., c. 49), establishes prisons board with responsibility for all Irish prisons

Supreme Court of Judicature (Ireland) Act, 1877 (40 & 41 Vict., c. 57) (effective, 1 Jan. 1878)

Dublin Science and Art Museum Act, 1877 (40 & 41 Vict., c. ccxxxiv) provides for purchase of land and collections from Royal Dublin Society to establish national museum and library (see 10 Apr. 1885, 29 Aug. 1890)

Aug. 28 Parnell elected president of Home Rule Confederation of Great Britain, in place of Butt, at Liverpool conference

Oct. 3 James Gibbons succeeds James Roosevelt Bayley as abp of Baltimore, Maryland (cardinal, 7 June 1886; dies, 24 Mar. 1921)

Oct. 17-Nov. 12 Gladstone visits Ire. (presented with freedom of Dublin, 7 Nov.)

Nov. Alexander Martin Sullivan's *New Ireland* (2 vols, London; many later eds)

Dr William Carroll goes to Europe as confidential envoy of Clan na Gael to I.R.B. (returns to U.S.A. in following summer)

Dec. 19 Michael Davitt (see 18 July 1870) released from Dartmoor on ticket-of-leave (arrives in Dublin with 3 other released fenians, 13 Jan. 1878)

Dec. 27 First instalment of William O'Brien's 'Christmas on the Galtees' published in *Freeman's Journal* (last instalment, 5 Jan. 1878

First of 3 years of bad harvests and agricultural depression (culminating in major economic crisis in 1879)

1878

Jan. Lecky's *History of England in the eighteenth century*, vols i and ii (London)

Feb. 7 Pope Pius IX dies

Apr. 2 Earl of Leitrim murdered at Cratlaghwood, near Milford, Co. Donegal

May 12 On train from London to St Helens, Lancashire, Parnell declines Davitt's invitation to join I.R.B.

June Alfred Webb's *A compendium of Irish biography* (Dublin)

Aug. 4 Davitt arrives in New York on first visit to America; makes acquaintance of John Devoy

Aug. 8 Public Health (Ireland) Act, 1878 (41 & 42 Vict., c. 52)

Aug. 16 Intermediate Education (Ireland) Act, 1878 (41 & 42 Vict., c. 66)

Sale of Liquors on Sunday (Ireland) Act, 1878 (41 & 42 Vict., c. 72); cities of Dublin, Cork, Limerick and Waterford and town of Belfast exempted from this prohibition (see 2 May 1882, 22 Feb. 1906)

Sept. 16 Davitt at Philadelphia delivers first lecture of American tour

Oct. 13 Davitt and Devoy, at public meeting at Brooklyn, call for new policy for fenian movement

Oct. 21-2 Convention in Dublin of Home Rule Confederation of Great Britain; Parnell re-elected president

Oct. 24 Cardinal Cullen, abp of Dublin from 3 May 1852, dies

Devoy sends telegram to James O'Connor, offering conditional support of fenians to Parnell (published in New York *Herald*, 25 Oct.)

Oct. 27 New York *Herald* publishes 'interviews' with prominent members of Clan na Gael who express approval of Davitt-Devoy proposals, now first described as 'an Irish new departure'

Nov. 3 Tenant-right meeting at Ballinasloe, Co. Galway, attended by Parnell, John O'Connor Power, Matthew Harris, and James Daly; letters of support read out from Abp MacHale and Bp Duggan

Nov. 5 Irish Association for the Prevention of Intemperance formed in Dublin by amalgamation of Sunday-closing and permissive bill associations

Dec. 8 Davitt's final American lecture, at Boston, expounds 'new departure' programme at length

Dec. 11 Devoy writes letter to *Freeman's Journal* on 'new departure' (published, 27 Dec.); leaves New York for Le Havre on visit to Europe

Dec. 12 Davitt leaves New York for Queenstown

Standish James O'Grady's *History of Ireland*, vol. i (London; vol. ii, 1880; vol. iii, 1881)

1879

Jan. Agricultural depression subject of widespread comment in British press; public apprehension in Ire. that 1879 may prove disaster year for farmers (prediction justified by crop failures later in year)

Jan. 4 Abp MacHale writes letter to editor of *Freeman's Journal* urging unity among Irish home-rule M.P.s (published 6 Jan.)

Jan. 19-26 Supreme council of I.R.B., meeting in Paris, rejects proposals for 'new departure' presented by Davitt and Devoy

Feb. 28 Outbreak of disturbances in Connemara, lasting through spring and summer, arising from animosity between catholic clergy and teachers of Society for Irish Church Missions to Roman Catholics (similar outbreak in Ardrahan (Co. Galway), Aug.)

Mar. 7 Parnell meets Devoy at Boulogne

Mar. 17 Irish Catholic Colonization Association founded at Chicago by Bp John Ireland and William Onahan

Mar. 25 Rev. William Rhatigan, C.C. of Clifden, Co. Galway, advises parishioners to ostracise Irish Church Mission workers (advises complete ostracism of converts, 25 May)

Apr. 6 First meeting of Davitt and Devoy with Parnell in Dublin (second meeting, 1 June)

Apr. 20 Land agitation launched at mass meeting at Irishtown, Co. Mayo, organised by Davitt in cooperation with James Daly and other local leaders

May 5 Isaac Butt dies

May 16 O'Conor Don introduces his Irish university bill (withdrawn, 23 July)

May 29 St Patrick's cathedral, New York City, consecrated

June 7 *Freeman's Journal* publishes letter over name of Abp MacHale condemning meeting announced for following day at Westport, Co. Mayo

June 8 Land meeting at Westport; Parnell advises tenant farmers 'you must show the landlords that you intend to hold a firm grip of your homesteads and lands'

June 30 Earl Cairns introduces University Education (Ireland) Bill

July 21   Irish convention act of 1793 (see 16 Aug. 1793) repealed (42 & 43 Vict., c. 28)

July 26   Parnell's candidate, James Lysaght Finigan, wins Ennis by-election against William O'Brien, Q.C., candidate of council of Home Rule League and local catholic clergy

Aug. 8-11   Ninth convention of Clan na Gael at Wilkes Barre, Pennsylvania; Devoy reports on his mission to Europe (11 Aug.)

Aug. 14   Royal commn under duke of Richmond app. to inquire into causes of agricultural depression in U.K. (cf. 14 Jan. 1881)

Aug. 15   University Education (Ireland) Act, 1879 (42 & 43 Vict., c. 65), provides for dissolution of Queen's University and its replacement by a new, examining university (cf. 27 Apr. 1880)

Aug. 16   National Land League of Mayo founded at Daly's Hotel, Castlebar

Aug. 21   First reported apparition of Blessed Virgin Mary, St Joseph, and St John at Knock, Co. Mayo

Sept.   Terence Powderly, son of emigrants from Co. Meath, succeeds Uriah Stephens as Grand Master Workman of Knights of Labor, leading workers' association in U.S.A. (holds office until 1893)

Oct. 5   John Dillon in speech at Maryborough advocates ostracism of anyone taking up land from which previous tenant has been evicted for non-payment of excessive rent—in essence policy of 'boycott' (cf. 24 Sept. 1880)

Oct. 21   Irish National Land League founded at Imperial Hotel, Dublin; president Parnell, secretaries Davitt, Thomas Brennan, and Andrew Joseph Kettle, treasurers Patrick Egan, Joseph Gillis Biggar, and William Henry O'Sullivan

Nov.   Irish Land Committee formed by landlords to supply information to Richmond commn (see 14 Aug.)

Nov. 19   Arrest of Davitt, James Daly, and James Bryce Killen on charge of sedition

Dec. 18   Duchess of Marlborough, wife of L.L., appeals in *The Times* for funds to relieve distress in Ire. (resulting relief fund totals £135,245 by early Oct. 1880)

1880

Jan. 2   Mansion House relief fund instituted at representative meeting in Mansion House, Dublin, presided over by lord mayor, Edmund Dwyer Gray (resulting relief fund totals £181,665 by 2 Dec. 1880)

Parnell and Dillon land at New York to begin North American tour

Feb. 2   Parnell addresses United States house of representatives (visits President Rutherford Birchard Hayes, 4 Feb.)

Feb. 20   Parnell's 'last link' speech at Cincinnati

Feb. 21   Unveiling of John Foley's equestrian statue of Field-Marshal Viscount Gough in Phoenix Park, Dublin (cf. 23 July 1957)

Mar. 1   Seed Supply (Ireland) Act, 1880 (43 Vict., c. 1) empowers boards of guardians to supply seed potatoes to impoverished tenants

Mar. 8   Beaconsfield announces dissolution of parliament (effected, 24 Mar.) in public letter to L.L. declaring that a portion of Ireland's population 'is attempting to sever the constitutional tie which unites it to Great Britain'

Mar. 11   In New York Parnell launches Irish National Land League of the United States and embarks for Ire. (see 18 May)

Mar. 12   Land League adopts election manifesto 'to the farmers of Ireland'

Mar. 15   Relief of Distress (Ireland) Act, 1880 (43 Vict., c. 4), extends power of Irish local government board to grant outdoor relief

Mar. 30-Apr. 13   General election: in G.B.—lib. 338, con. 211; in Ire.— home-rulers 63 (including 27 Parnellites), con. 25, lib. 15 (see Feb. 1874, Nov.-Dec. 1875)

c. **Mar.**   Gaelic Union for the Preservation and Cultivation of the Irish Language established

Mar.   First bulk order of buckshot cartridges for R.I.C.

Apr. 18   Meath diocesan chapel-door collection, at Bp Nulty's order, to defray Parnell's election expenses

Apr. 23   Gladstone app. P.M. for second time (see 20 Feb. 1874, 23 June 1885)

Apr. 27   Royal University of Ireland incorporated by charter

Apr. 29   National convention on land reform held at Rotunda, Dublin

Apr.   Registration of Belfast shipyard of Workman Clark; first keel laid, on north bank of Lagan

May 4   Salvation Army introduced to Ire., with arrival of 5 women 'soldiers' in Sandy Row, Belfast

May 9   Davitt leaves Queenstown for New York to join Dillon in campaign for funds (returns, 20 Nov.)

May 10   William Edward Forster, C.S., advises cabinet against taking additional repressive powers on expiry of peace preservation act (1 June)

May 17   Parnell elected chairman of Irish parliamentary party by 23 votes to 18 for William Shaw

May 18   First regular convention, at New York, of American Land League

June 1   Census taken throughout U.S.A.: Irish-born population 1,854,571 (3·7% of total and 27·8% of foreign-born population); children of Irish-born parents estimated at 2,756,054

June 19   Forster introduces Compensation for Disturbance (Ireland) Bill (passes third reading, 26 July; see 4 Aug.)

July   Parnell first makes acquaintance of Mrs Katharine O'Shea

July 27   St Stephen's Green, Dublin, opened to public

July 29   Royal commn under earl of Bessborough app. to inquire into working of land act of 1870 (see 4 Jan. 1881)

Aug. 2   Relief of Distress (Ireland) Amendment Act, 1880 (43 & 44 Vict., c. 14) (cf. 15 Mar.)

Aug. 4   Compensation for Disturbance (Ireland) Bill defeated in H.L. by 282 to 51

Sept. 13-18   Trades Union Congress meets in Dublin, for first time in Ire.

Sept. 19   Parnell's 'moral coventry' speech at Ennis

Sept. 24   Beginning of ostracism of Capt. Charles Cunningham Boycott, land agent and farmer, of Lough Mask House, Co. Mayo (see 12-26 Nov.)

Sept. 25   Murder of Viscount Mountmorres near Clonbur, Co. Galway

Sept. 27   Republican convention at Saratoga of New York Irish; John Devoy and others plan to detach Irish vote from Democrats

Oct. 24   Ladies' Land League founded in New York by Fanny Parnell

Oct. 29   In Melbourne, Victoria, Ned Kelly, bush-ranger, sentenced to death for murder (executed, 11 Nov.)

Nov. 2   Proceedings begin against Parnell and others for conspiracy

William R. Grace elected mayor of New York; first Irish-born mayor of a major U.S. city (cf. Jan. 1885)

Nov. 3   Special meeting of Grand Orange Lodge of Ire. at Orange Hall, Dublin, passes resolutions hostile to Land League (half-yearly meeting likewise, 1-2 Dec.)

Nov. 12-26   Relief expedition of orange labourers, mostly from Monaghan and Cavan, saves Boycott's crops

Nov.   Sir Charles Gavan Duffy's *Young Ireland: a fragment of Irish history* (London) (revised ed., 2 vols, 1896)

Dec. 27   Annual meeting of Irish parliamentary party resolves that members shall always sit as opposition

Dec. 28   Opening of trial of Parnell and others (see 25 Jan. 1881)

Dec.   Orange Emergency Committee, to resist Land League, formed by Grand Orange Lodge

Property Defence Association 'to uphold the rights of property' against Land League, formed by group of leading Irish landlords

William Bence Jones's *The life's work in Ireland of a landlord who tried to do his duty* (London)

1881

Jan. 4   Report of Bessborough commn (see 29 July 1880)

Jan. 14   Preliminary report of Richmond commn (see 14 Aug. 1879, 11 July 1882)

Jan. 24   Protection of Person and Property Bill introduced in H.C. by Forster

Jan. 25   Trial of Parnell and others ends in disagreement of jury (see 28 Dec. 1880)

Jan. 26   Ladies' committee under Anna Parnell set up by Land League (origin of Ladies' Land League in Ireland; cf. 24 Oct. 1880; publicly launched, 31 Jan.)

Jan. 27-8   At meeting in H.C. and afterwards in Westminster Palace Hotel, Parnell, Davitt, and other Land League leaders consider but reject plan to withdraw parliamentary party from H.C., set up national convention in Dublin, and launch no-rent campaign

Feb. 2   First reading of coercion bill carried after Speaker has assumed power of closing debate; Irish parliamentary party considers and rejects proposals to withdraw from parliament

Feb. 3   Davitt rearrested in Dublin and taken to London where his ticket-of-leave is withdrawn (4 Feb.)

Feb. 13-18   Parnell visits France

Mar. 2   Protection of Person and Property Act, 1881 (44 & 45 Vict., c. 4)

Mar. 12   Pastoral letter from Edward McCabe, catholic abp of Dublin, denouncing Ladies' Land League published in *Freeman's Journal* (letter from T. W. Croke, catholic abp of Cashel, defending ladies published, 17 Mar.)

Mar. 21   Peace Preservation (Ireland) Act, 1881 (44 & 45 Vict., c. 5) (see 31 Dec. 1906)

Apr. 3   Census taken throughout Ire. (preliminary report, 15 June): population 5,174,836 (4·39% decline; see 2 Apr. 1871)

Census taken throughout G.B.: Irish-born population of England and Wales 562,374 (2·2% of total); of Scotland, 218,745 (5·9% of total)

Apr. 7   Land bill introduced in H.C.

Apr. 21-2   Land League convention at Rotunda, Dublin, considers land bill

May 2   John Dillon arrested (released 8 Aug.)

May 20   Arrest under 44 & 45 Vict., c. 4, of cttee of Kilmallock, Co. Limerick, branch of Land League; its president, Rev. Eugene Sheehy, C.C., first priest arrested during 'land war' (cttee of Kilfinane branch arrested, 24 May)

June 4   Outbreak of serious disorder in Ballydehob, west Cork, extending to adjoining districts of Skull and Skibbereen

Aug. 2   Contract of sale by Richard Pigott of his papers, *Irishman*, *Flag of Ireland*, and *Shamrock* to Parnell's Irish National Publishing Co.

Aug. 13   First number of *United Ireland*, weekly organ of Parnellites; editor William O'Brien

Aug. 22   Land Law (Ireland) Act, 1881 (44 & 45 Vict., c. 49)—second Gladstone land act

Royal University of Ireland Act, 1881 (44 & 45 Vict., c. 52) endows new university with £20,000 per annum from church surplus fund

Aug. 29   Dillon announces his intention to retire from political life

Sept. 15-17   Land League convention in Dublin: 'test the act'

Oct. 3   Earl Granville, foreign secretary, writes letter of recommendation for George Errington, M.P., to take with him to Holy See; quasi-official recognition of 'Errington mission'

Oct. 7   Gladstone's 'resources of civilisation' speech at Leeds (Parnell's retort at Wexford, 9 Oct.)

Oct. 13   Arrest of Parnell under 44 & 45 Vict., c. 4, s. 1 (arrests of Thomas Sexton, J. P. Quinn, William O'Brien, J. J. O'Kelly, John Dillon, and other Land League leaders follow, 14-16 Oct.)

Oct. 18 'No-rent manifesto', written by William O'Brien, issued from Kilmainham jail over names of Parnell, Kettle, Davitt, Brennan, Dillon, Sexton, and Egan

Oct. 19 No-rent manifesto denounced by Abp Croke

Oct. 20 Forster, C.S., proclaims Land League 'an unlawful and criminal association'

Opening of court of land commn established under 44 & 45 Vict., c. 49, at 24 Upper Merrion Street, Dublin; followed by establishment of peripatetic sub-commns (autumn and winter)

Oct. 29 Belfast United Trades' Council formed

Nov. 7 Death of Abp MacHale, aged 90

Dec. 15 Seizure at offices on Abbey Street, Dublin, of issue of *United Ireland* for 17 Dec.

Dec. 16 First 'special resident magistrates' app., each directing police, R.M.s and military in 'division' of several counties

The Irish crisis of 1879–80: proceedings of the Dublin Mansion House relief committee, 1880 (Dublin)

1882

Feb. 3 Queen's University in Ire. dissolved by order in council

Apr. 10-24 Parnell on parole from Kilmainham to visit his sister, Delia, in Paris; discusses with Justin McCarthy (10, 23 Apr.) and Capt. William Henry O'Shea (11, c. 20 Apr.) conditions of an agreement with government

Apr. 25 Parnell, in Kilmainham, sends letter to McCarthy setting out conditions of 'treaty' with government—settlement of arrears question etc., withdrawal of no-rent manifesto, and effective efforts by Parnellites to stop outrages (gist of letter conveyed to Chamberlain)

Apr. 28 Cowper resigns as L.L.; Earl Spencer designated successor (sworn in, 6 May)

Apr. 29 Parnell in letter to O'Shea (predated 28 Apr.) repeats conditions as above (copy of letter given by O'Shea to Forster (30 Apr.), who passes it on to Gladstone)

May 2 Cabinet accepts 'Kilmainham treaty'; Forster resigns; Parnell, Dillon and J. J. O'Kelly released from Kilmainham jail (Davitt released from Portland prison, 6 May)

Bill introduced in H.C. to make Irish Sunday-closing act permanent and remove exemptions (withdrawn, 9 Aug., after strong opposition from home rule M.P.s; see 16 Aug. 1878, 22 Feb. 1906)

May 6 Lord Frederick Cavendish, newly arrived C.S., and Thomas Henry Burke, under-secretary, assassinated in Phoenix Park, Dublin (see 4 Dec.)

May 11 Crimes bill introduced in H.C. (see 12 July)

May 15-16 Arrears bill introduced in H.C. (see 18 Aug.)

May 15-June 14   Anthony Trollope revisits Ire. (final visit, Aug.; leaves Irish novel, *The Landleaguers*, unfinished at his death, 6 Dec.; published, 3 vols, London, 1883) (see 15 Sept. 1841, 1845)

May 23   Col. Henry Brackenbury app. assistant under-secretary for police and crime, with special concern for coordinating detective work (succ. by Edward George Jenkinson, 3 Aug.)

June 6   Davitt's speech at Liverpool advocating land nationalisation in preference to peasant proprietorship

July 11   Final report of Richmond commn (see 14 Aug. 1879)

July 12   Prevention of Crime (Ireland) Act, 1882 (45 & 46 Vict., c. 25)

July   Land Corporation, to counteract intimidation of persons occupying holdings from which tenants have been evicted, formed on initiative of Arthur MacMurrough Kavanagh, M.P.

Aug. early   Agitation in R.I.C. over pay and conditions; strike among Limerick city force; L.L. appoints cttee to investigate grievances (17 Aug.)

Aug. 15   Exhibition of Irish Arts and Manufactures opened in Rotunda hospital gardens, Dublin

Aug. 17   Murder of 5 members of family of Joyce at Maamtrasna, Co. Galway

Aug. 18   Arrears of Rent (Ireland) Act, 1882 (45 & 46 Vict., c. 47)

Labourers' Cottages and Allotments (Ireland) Act, 1882 (45 & 46 Vict., c. 60)

Ancient Monuments Protection Act, 1882 (45 & 46 Vict., c. 73), provides for commrs of works to undertake maintenance of ancient monuments in U.K. (scheduled monuments include 18 in Ire.) (see 27 June 1892)

Aug. 19   British troops under Sir Garnet Wolseley land at Port Said to resist forces of Arabi Pasha (latter destroyed at Tel el Kebir, 13 Sept.); beginning of British occupation of Egypt

Aug. 26-Sept. 8   Discontent among Dublin Metropolitan Police: about 500 constables meet (26 Aug.) to demand grant similar to that given to R.I.C.; 225 dismissed after attending further meeting (31 Aug.) prohibited by commissioner; 700-800 special constables sworn in for temporary duty; 208 of dismissed men reinstated (8 Sept.)

Oct. 3   Catholic University renamed University College (transferred to Jesuits, 26 Oct. 1883)

Oct. 17   Formation of Irish National League at national conference in Antient Concert Rooms, Dublin

Nov.   First number of *Irisleabhar na Gaedhilge: the Gaelic Journal*, organ of Gaelic Union

Dec. 4   John Adye Curran, Dublin magistrate, opens special inquiry under 45 & 46 Vict., c. 25, into Phoenix Park murders (see 9 Apr. 1883)

1883

Jan. 13   Arrests of 17 'Irish invincibles' in connection with Phoenix Park murders (more arrests follow)

Jan. 26   Ulster Land Committee formed at Belfast as central organisation representing tenant-right associations of Ulster

Mar. 17   Abp Croke subscribes £50 to Parnell testimonial fund

Mar. 19   Royal commn under Lord Napier app. to inquire into condition of crofters and cottars in highlands and islands of Scotland (report, 28 Apr. 1884)

Apr. 5   Dynamite conspirators arrested in London and Birmingham, leading to trial, conviction, and sentencing to life imprisonment of Henry Wilson (*alias* Thomas James Clarke) and 3 others, 11-14 June (see 29 Sept. 1898)

Apr. 9   Opening of trials of Invincibles on charges connected with Phoenix Park murders (executions of Joseph Brady, Daniel Curley, Timothy Kelly, Michael Fagan, and Thomas Caffrey, 14 May-9 June)

Apr. 25-7   Third annual convention of American Land League (see 18 May 1880) and first annual convention of Irish National League of America held at Philadelphia

May 11   Letter of Sacred Congregation of Propaganda, 'De Parnellio', forbidding Irish bps and clergy to participate in collection of Parnell testimonial fund (published in *The Times*, 15 May)

June   Sir C. G. Duffy's *Four years of Irish history* (London)

Aug. 25   Labourers (Ireland) Act, 1883 (46 & 47 Vict., c. 60) enables local authorities to borrow on security of rates to erect dwellings for agricultural labourers

United Ireland publishes first allegations against character of County Inspector James Ellis French, detective director of R.I.C.; beginning of 'Dublin Castle scandals'

Sept. 26   Meeting of Tyrone National Registration Association at Aughnacloy, Co. Tyrone, and Orange counter-demonstration; beginning of 'invasion of Ulster' by National League

Sept. 28   Formal opening of Portrush-Bushmills electric railway, second electric line in world

Oct. 2-17   Sir Stafford Northcote visits Ulster

Oct. 16   Rival meetings at Rosslea, Co. Fermanagh; narrow avoidance of collision between nationalists and orange party led by Lord Rossmore, J.P. and grand master for Co. Monaghan (suspended from magistracy, 24 Nov.)

c. **Oct.**   R. Barry O'Brien's *Fifty years of concessions to Ireland, 1831-1881*, vol. i (London; vol. ii, 1885)

Nov. 10-Dec. 7   Third plenary council at Baltimore: hierarchy in U.S.A. agrees on creation of full, separate, and virtually mandatory system of parochial schools (by 1910, 1,237,251 children attending 4,845 schools)

Dec. 11   Parnell receives cheque for over £37,000 as testimonial at public meeting in Rotunda

1884

Jan. 18   General Charles Gordon app. to evacuate Egyptian garrison from Sudan (arrives in Khartoum, 18 Feb.; besieged by Mahdi's forces, 12 Mar.; see 26 Jan. 1885)

Feb. 28   Gladstone seeks leave to introduce bill to extend franchise (see 6 Dec.)

Mar. 8   Sir William Vernon Harcourt, home secretary, gives E. G. Jenkinson (see 23 May 1882) informal powers of directing anti-fenian measures throughout Britain

Aug. 1   John Daly (of Limerick) convicted of treason-felony at Warwick assizes and sentenced to penal servitude for life (see 20 Aug. 1896)

Oct. 1   Catholic bps formally entrust Irish parliamentary party with responsibility for pressing catholic claims in education

Oct. 18   Sir Charles Gavan Duffy discusses an Irish settlement with earl of Carnarvon (latter app. L.L. under Salisbury, 27 June 1885)

Oct. 22   Nine women receive degrees of Royal University of Ireland; first women to graduate in Ire.

Nov. 1   Gaelic Athletic Association formed at meeting in Hayes's Hotel, Thurles

Nov. 27   William Henry O'Shea, claiming to be spokesman for Parnell, gives Chamberlain note of Parnell's views on renewal of crimes act (see 12 July 1882) and on Irish local government (see 5 Jan. 1885)

Dec. 1   Gladstone introduces bill to redistribute parliamentary seats (see 25 June 1885)

Dec. 6   Representation of the People Act, 1884 (48 Vict., c. 3)

Dec. 13   Explosion under London Bridge destroys William Mackey Lomasney and 2 other fenians

Dec.   Michael Davitt's *Leaves from a prison diary* (2 vols, London, dated 1885)

1885

Jan. 5   In a letter to W. H. Duignan, Chamberlain sketches scheme for representative county government and a central board in Ire. (see 14 Jan.)

Hugh O'Brien inaugurated as mayor of Boston, Massachusetts, U.S.A.; first Irish-born mayor of the city (cf. 2 Nov. 1880)

Jan. 14   Memorandum by O'Shea, 'Local self-government in Ireland' (given to Chamberlain, 15 Jan.) (see 25 Apr.)

Jan. 21   Parnell's *'ne plus ultra'* speech at Cork: 'no man has the right to fix the boundary to the march of a nation'

Jan. 24   Dynamite explosions in Westminster Hall, the House of Commons and the Tower of London

Jan. 26   Khartoum taken by Mahdi's forces after siege of 317 days; Gordon killed

Jan.   Split in cabinet over situation in Egypt and Sudan

Feb. 11   Death of Cardinal McCabe, abp of Dublin from 1879

Feb. 21   Irish Amateur Athletic Association formed at Wicklow Hotel, Dublin, in opposition to Gaelic Athletic Association

Mar. 23   Cabinet memorandum by Earl Spencer urges replacement of crimes act by strengthening ordinary law of U.K., and by remedial measures for Ire.: local government, land purchase, and abolition of viceroyalty

Apr. 10 Prince and princess of Wales lay foundation-stone of Science and Art Museum and National Library of Ireland, Dublin; architect Thomas Newenham Deane (see 29 Aug. 1890)

Apr. 25 Memorandum by Chamberlain, 'Local government in Ireland', sent to Cardinal Manning (see 9 May)

May 1 Irish Loyal and Patriotic Union founded to defend union against home rule movement

May 9 Chamberlain's 'central board' scheme (see 25 Apr.) rejected by cabinet

May 20 Lord Randolph Churchill, in speech at St Stephen's Club, Dublin, argues that a conservative government should not think it necessary to renew coercion act

June 16 Inaugural meeting at Trinity College, with William Butler Yeats in chair, of Dublin Hermetic Society (forerunner of Dublin Theosophical Society)

June 23 Marquis of Salisbury (con.) app. P.M., heading 'caretaker' government (see 23 Apr. 1880, 1 Feb. 1886)

William Joseph Walsh app. catholic abp of Dublin

June 25 Redistribution of Seats Act, 1885 (48 & 49 Vict., c. 23) (see 1 Dec. 1884)

July 14 Munster Bank, established in 1879, suspends payment

July 17 Lord Ashbourne introduces Irish land purchase bill in H.L. (see 14 Aug.)

July 24 Submission of evidence collected by select cttee of H.C. on Irish industries

Aug. 1 Secret meeting in London between Parnell and earl of Carnarvon, L.L.

Aug. 14 Purchase of Land (Ireland) Act, 1885 (48 & 49 Vict., c. 73)—'Ashbourne act'—provides for advance of entire purchase money and for annuity payments lower than rents

Labourers (Ireland) Act, 1885 (48 & 49 Vict., c. 77)

Educational Endowments (Ireland) Act, 1885 (48 & 49 Vict., c. 78), sets up commn to draw up schemes for management of educational endowments

Oct. 30 Katharine O'Shea sends Gladstone draft by Parnell of home rule constitution for Ire.

Nov. 17 Gladstone declines to make any explicit declaration on home rule

Nov. 21 Parnell issues manifesto calling on Irish of Great Britain to vote against liberal party in forthcoming general election

Nov. 23-Dec. 19 General election: in G.B.—lib. 335, con. 231, nat. 1; in Ire.—nat. 85, con. 18; nationalist strength equal to liberal majority over conservatives in H.C. (see Mar.-Apr. 1880, July 1886)

Dec. 17 Gladstone's conversion to home rule, disclosed prematurely by his son Herbert, published in London *Standard* and *Leeds Mercury*—'Hawarden kite'

Dec. 28 First meeting of Indian National Congress in Bombay

Irish Defence Union, for protection of landlords, founded under direction of Lord Bandon

Richard Bagwell's *Ireland under the Tudors*, vols i and ii (London; vol. iii, 1890)

1886

Jan. 1 Salisbury's cabinet considers and rejects Gladstone's proposal for bi-partisan settlement of Irish question

Jan. 2 First instalment of Charles Joseph Kickham's 'For the old land: a tale of twenty years ago' published serially in *Irish Fireside* (work republished in book form, Dublin, 1886)

Jan. 8 Conservative meeting at Constitutional Club, Belfast, giving rise to Ulster Loyalist Anti-Repeal Committee (later Union), series of conservative demonstrations against home rule, and numerous local conservative cttees

Jan. 27 Salisbury's government defeated in H.C. by 329 to 250 in vote on queen's speech (resigns 28 Jan.)

Feb. 1 Gladstone becomes P.M. for third time (John Morley C.S., 6 Feb.) (see 23 June 1885, 25 July 1886)

Feb. 1-10 Galway by-election: Parnell overpowers opposition within home rule party to candidature of W. H. O'Shea

Feb. 16 Well-attended meeting of catholic bps expresses approval of home rule: 'it alone can satisfy the wants, the wishes, as well as the legitimate aspirations, of the Irish people' (Walsh to Gladstone, 17 Feb., published in *Freeman's Journal*, 22 Feb.)

Lord Randolph Churchill writes to his friend Gerald FitzGibbon: 'I decided some time ago that if the G.O.M. went for home rule, the orange card would be the one to play.'

Feb. 22 Last of series of Ulster conservative demonstrations against home rule, at Ulster Hall, Belfast; Churchill makes militant speech

Feb. 28 Dublin United Trades' Council formed

Feb. Hon. Emily Lawless's *Hurrish: a study* (2 vols, Edinburgh)

Mar. 15 Joseph Chamberlain and George Otto Trevelyan declare intention to resign from government (resign, 26 Mar.)

Mar. 19 Liberal convention at St George's Hall, Belfast; split develops on home rule question

Apr. 8 Gladstone introduces home rule bill in H.C. (first reading, 14 Apr.)

Apr. 13 Joint meeting of Ulster conservatives and dissident liberals at Ulster Hall, Belfast, agrees to resolutions against home rule

Apr. 16 Contagious diseases acts, 1866 to 1869, repealed (49 Vict., c. 10) (see 11 Aug. 1869)

Apr. 17 John Morley, C.S., introduces land purchase bill (effectively abandoned, 29 May; formally withdrawn, 11 June)

May 24 *Pall Mall Gazette* publishes paragraph entitled 'Mr Parnell's suburban retreat'; first public reference to his residing at Mrs O'Shea's house at Eltham, Kent (see 30 Dec. 1889)

June 4   Ulster Liberal Unionist Committee formally established

June 4-10   Rioting in Belfast, largely by protestant mobs against R.I.C. (especially after 8 June)

June 8   Home rule bill defeated in H.C. by 341 to 311, some 93 liberals voting with majority

June 13   Rev. Hugh Hanna, preaching at St Enoch's, Belfast, denounces government and hints at forcible resistance (cf. 6 Sept. 1857)

July   General election: in G.B.—con. 300, lib. 191, lib. un. 75, nat. 1; in Ire.—nat. 84, un. 17, lib. un. 2 (see 23 Nov.-19 Dec. 1885, July 1892)

July 7   Renewal of rioting in Belfast (intermittent until 19 Sept.; R.I.C. withdrawn from protestant Shankill Road district, 5 Aug.-1 Sept.)

July 25   Marquis of Salisbury app. P.M. for second time (see 1 Feb. 1886, 15 Aug. 1892)

c. **July**   William Joseph O'Neill Daunt's *Eighty-five years of Irish history, 1800-1885* (2 vols, London)

Aug. 18   General Sir Redvers Buller accepts position as temporary special commr for Kerry and Clare (app. under-secretary, 10 Dec.)

Aug. 25   Commn to inquire into Belfast riots app. (report, Jan. 1887)

Sept. 4   Buller informs Sir Michael Hicks-Beach, C.S., that 'both sides [i.e. landlords and tenants] require coercion and protection'

Sept. 29   Royal commn under Earl Cowper app. to inquire into operation of Irish land acts of 1881 and 1885 (see 21 Feb. 1887)

c. **Sept.**   Sir Charles Gavan Duffy's *The league of north and south* (London)

Oct. 16   Royal commn under James Abernethy, civil engineer, app. to inquire into Irish public works, especially harbour, inland navigation, and railway facilities (first report, 9 Apr. 1887; final report, 4 Jan. 1888)

Oct. 23   Plan of Campaign published in *United Ireland* (anonymously, but written by Timothy Harrington)

Oct. 25   Guinness's brewery becomes public limited liability company: £6 million of stocks and shares offered for subscription; rush on London stock exchange (amount subscribed many times over in advance)

Dec. *c*. 9-10   Meeting between Parnell and William O'Brien at Greenwich to discuss Plan of Campaign

Dec. 16   John Dillon, William O'Brien, Matthew Harris, and David Sheehy arrested at Loughrea, Co. Galway, when receiving rents from tenants of marquis of Clanricard in pursuance of Plan of Campaign

Dec. 18   Plan of Campaign proclaimed 'an unlawful and criminal conspiracy'

1887

Jan. 4   Trial, on charge of criminal conspiracy, of Dillon, O'Brien, and others involved in Plan of Campaign begins (ends in disagreement of jury, 24 Feb.)

Jan. 5   Christopher Palles, lord chief baron of exchequer, presiding at Sligo winter assizes, rebukes executive government for illegally withholding support from sheriffs executing writs

Feb. 20   Cardinal James Gibbons of Baltimore defends Knights of Labor and trades unions in brief to Sacred Congregation de Propaganda Fide

Feb. 21   Report of Cowper commn (see 29 Sept. 1886)

Mar. 7   Arthur James Balfour app. C.S.

Mar. 7, 10, 14   *The Times* publishes 3 special articles, 'Parnellism and crime', charging home-rulers with complicity in outrage and murder (reprinted in pamphlet form)

Mar. 10   Capt. Thomas Owen Plunkett, divisional magistrate at Cork, wires to Youghal R.I.C. (in danger of attack) 'if necessary, do not hesitate to shoot'

Mar. 28   Balfour introduces coercion bill in H.C. (see 19 July)

Mar. 31   Earl Cadogan introduces Irish land bill in H.L. (see 23 Aug.)

Apr. 18   *The Times* publishes article 'Parnellism and crime: Mr Parnell and the Phoenix Park murders', including facsimile alleged of letter from Parnell dated 15 May 1882 explaining away his denunciation of the murders; H.C. resumes debate on second reading of coercion bill

May 13   *The Times* resumes publication of 'Parnellism and crime' series (ends, 1 Dec.)

July 7   Abp Ignatius Persico begins fact-finding mission in Ire. as commissary apostolic (ends, 24 Oct.)

July 19   Criminal Law & Procedure (Ireland) Act, 1887 (50 & 51 Vict., c. 20)

Aug. 19   National League proclaimed a 'dangerous' association under 50 & 51 Vict., c. 20, s. 6

Aug. 23   Land Law (Ireland) Act, 1887 (50 & 51 Vict., c. 33), gives land courts power to fix rents of leaseholders and to revise rents determined judicially between 1881 and 1885

Sept. 9   In affray at Mitchelstown, Co. Cork, police open fire from barrack causing 3 fatalities—'Mitchelstown massacre'

Oct. 29   Patrick Ford's *Irish World* breaks with Henry George; maintains 'wise conservatism . . . entirely consistent with wise radicalism'

Nov. 9   Annual convention of G.A.A. at Thurles ends in split between 'fenians' and 'priests'

Nov. 13   Open-air meeting in Trafalgar Square, London, of radicals and Irish nationalists in sympathy with William O'Brien, imprisoned in connection with agrarian agitation, ends in clash with police and troops; over 100 casualties—'Bloody Sunday'

Dec. 17   Duke of Norfolk, accompanied by Capt. John Ross-of-Bladensburg, presents credentials to Pope Leo XIII at Vatican; mission officially to thank pope for his congratulations to Queen Victoria on her jubilee, but really to influence papal policy on Ire.

James Francis Hogan's *The Irish in Australia* (London)

Annala Uladh, Annals of Ulster, otherwise Annala Senait, Annals of Senat: a chronicle of Irish affairs, 431-1131, 1155-1541, vol. i, ed. William Maunsell Hennessy (Dublin; vols ii-iv, ed. Bartholomew MacCarthy, 1893-1901)

1888

Feb. 10   Bills for Sunday and early Saturday closing of public houses in Ire. introduced in H.C. (ordered to be referred to select cttee, 27 Feb.; cttee reports, 2 July, favouring both bills; no further progress)

Apr. 20   Holy Office circular condemning Plan of Campaign and boycotting (summary published in *Freeman's Journal*, 27 Apr.; text, 30 Apr.)

May *c.* 1   *Poems and ballads of Young Ireland* (Dublin), by John O'Leary, T. W. Rolleston, W. B. Yeats, and others

May 5   First number of *Irish Catholic*

May 8   Parnell addresses Eighty Club in London on Plan of Campaign and Holy Office circular

May 14   Royal charter founding Institute of Chartered Accountants in Ireland

July 2-5   O'Donnell *v.* Walter: trial of Frank Hugh O'Donnell's libel action against *The Times* arising from 'Parnellism and crime' series; more letters intended to incriminate Parnell produced

July 17   Salisbury's government introduces bill to establish special commn to inquire into all charges made against M.P.s and others

Aug. 6   Letter in *The Times* by Parnell on negotiations between him and Chamberlain in 1884-5

Aug. 13   Special Commission Act (51 & 52 Vict., c. 35) establishes commn of 3 judges to inquire into charges made by *The Times* against Parnell

Oct. 13   Public library in Royal Avenue, Belfast, opened

Oct. 22-6   Speech of Sir Richard Webster, attorney general and counsel for *The Times*, before Special Commn

Nov. 5   Charter creating borough of Belfast a city (mayor created lord mayor by charter, 20 May 1892)

c. Nov.   William John Fitzpatrick's *Correspondence of Daniel O'Connell* (2 vols, London)

   Two centuries of Irish history, 1691-1870, ed. R. Barry O'Brien, with contributions by James Bryce and others (London; 2nd ed., 1907)

1889

Jan. 9   Balfour issues directive on procedure and equipment (including battering-ram) to be employed by crown forces attending evictions

Jan.   William Butler Yeats's *The wanderings of Oisin and other poems* (London)

Feb. 3   District Inspector William Martin murdered when attempting to arrest Rev. James McFadden at Gweedore, Co. Donegal

Feb. 5   Major Henri Le Caron (alias Thomas Bealis Beach) gives evidence before Special Commn

Feb. 20-22   Richard Pigott gives evidence before Special Commn; exposed as forger (suicide at Madrid, 1 Mar.)

Feb.   The 'Syndicate' formed secretly by Balfour, C.S., to protect Ponsonby estate at Youghal against Plan of Campaign

Apr. 2-12   Speech of Sir Charles Russell, counsel for Parnell and others, before Special Commn

Apr. 30-May 8   Parnell gives evidence before Special Commn

May 4   First conference of Irish Federated Trade and Labour Union, an association of trades councils, held in Dublin

Disappearance of Dr Patrick Henry Cronin of Chicago, active member of Clan na Gael (body found, 22 May); his murder a result of feud within Clan na Gael (subsequent disintegration of Clan until 1899, decline of Irish National League of America, and split in Ancient Order of Hibernians in U.S.A.)

May 19   Death of Mrs Benjamin Wood, aged 96, leaving nearly all her great wealth to her niece, Mrs Katharine O'Shea

June   Rev. James Cullen founds Total Abstinence League of the Sacred Heart (see Feb. 1876, 27 Dec. 1898, 6 Oct. 1901)

Aug. 30   Light Railways (Ireland) Act, 1889 (52 & 53 Vict., c. 66)

Technical Instruction Act, 1889 (52 & 53 Vict., c. 76)

Aug.   Edith Œnone Somerville and Martin Ross's *An Irish cousin* (2 vols, London)

Oct. 24-31   Speech of Davitt for the defence before Special Commn

Oct. 31-Nov. 22   Speech of Sir Henry James, counsel for *The Times*, before Special Commn

Nov. 22   Special Commn meets for 128th and last time

Dec. 18-19   Parnell stays with Gladstone at Hawarden; discussions on home rule

Dec. 24   O'Shea files petition for divorce on grounds of his wife Katharine's adultery with Parnell (see 15, 17 Nov. 1890)

Dec. 30   *Freeman's Journal* reports interview with Parnell in which he asserts: that divorce proceedings have been brought in interest of *The Times*; that O'Shea has always known that Parnell was constantly at Mrs O'Shea's house at Eltham in his absence from 1880 to 1886, and that since 1886 O'Shea has known that Parnell constantly resided there during same period (see 24 May 1886)

Sir John Gilbert's *Calendar of ancient records of Dublin*, vol. i (Dublin; vols ii-vii, 1891-8; vols viii-xiv, by Rosa Mulholland, Lady Gilbert, 1901-44)

1890

Jan.   Resolutions of numerous Irish public bodies expressing confidence in Parnell's leadership

Jan. 21   Irish Democratic Trade and Labour Federation formed at Cork at convention presided over by Davitt; organisation mainly of agricultural labourers and workers in country towns

Feb. 13   Report of Special Commn: Parnell and followers exonerated from most serious charges including complicity in Phoenix Park murders

Apr. 25-May 4   Strike of porters, guards, and signalmen on Great Southern & Western Railway, leading to intervention of Davitt and Abp Walsh

June 1 Census taken throughout U.S.A.: Irish-born population 1,871,509 (2·8 % of total and 20·2 % of foreign-born population); 4,142,199 children with both parents Irish-born

June Sir Charles Gavan Duffy's *Thomas Davis: the memoirs of an Irish patriot* (London)

Aug. 29 Opening of Science and Art Museum and National Library of Ireland

Sept. 18 Dillon and O'Brien arrested on charge of criminal conspiracy in connection with Smith-Barry estates (break bail and abscond to France en route for U.S.A., 9 Oct.)

Sept. 21 First number of Davitt's weekly newspaper, *Labour World* (London)

Oct. 10 Centenary of Fr Mathew's birth (see 10 Apr. 1838, 8 Dec. 1856); Abp Walsh of Dublin and bps of his province order temperance societies to be formed in every parish

Oct. Lecky's *History of England in the eighteenth century* (8 vols, London, 1878–90), vols vii–viii (Irish material revised and extracted for publication as *History of Ireland in the eighteenth century*, 5 vols, London, 1892)

Nov. 4 Congressional elections in U.S.A.: 7 representatives born in Ire. and 9 of Irish parentage elected, all catholics and home-rule sympathisers

Nov. 15, 17 Trial of O'Shea divorce petition in high court, London; no evidence offered by defence; W. H. O'Shea awarded decree nisi (see 24 Dec. 1889, June 1891)

Nov. 18 *Pall Mall Gazette* demands Parnell's retirement; central branch of National League, at meeting chaired by John Redmond, reaffirms confidence in Parnell's leadership

Nov. 19 Dillon and O'Brien sentenced *in absentia* to 6 months' imprisonment for conspiracy to promote non-payment of rent (see 18 Sept.)

Nov. 20 Davitt in *Labour World* calls for Parnell's temporary retirement; nationalist meeting at Leinster Hall, Dublin, originally convened to support evicted tenants, unanimously carries resolution, proposed by Justin McCarthy and seconded by T. M. Healy, expressing unabated confidence in Parnell's leadership

Nov. 20-21 Meeting of National Liberal Federation at Sheffield; strong feeling against Parnell expressed privately to Sir William Harcourt and John Morley

Nov. 25 Parnell unanimously reelected chairman of Irish parliamentary party (afternoon); Gladstone releases to press text of letter to Morley stating that Parnell's continued leadership of Irish party would render his own retention of leadership of liberal party 'almost a nullity' (evening)

Nov. 28 Parnell issues manifesto 'to the people of Ireland' denouncing Gladstone and liberals for seeking to undermine independence of Irish party (published in morning newspapers, 29 Nov.)

Dec. 1-6 Committee-room Fifteen debates, presided over by Parnell; Justin McCarthy and 44 others withdraw, leaving Parnell with 28 followers (6 Dec.) —'split' in Irish party

Dec. 3   Catholic episcopal standing committee publicly denounces Parnell

Dec. 8-22   North Kilkenny by-election: acrimonious and at times violent contest between Parnellites and anti-Parnellites (see 12, 22 Dec.)

Dec. 10   Upon arriving in Dublin, Parnell replaces Matthew Bodkin by Edmund Leamy as editor of *United Ireland*; later makes defiant speech at Rotunda

Dec. 11   Anti-Parnellite manifesto by McCarthy published in *Freeman's Journal*; Parnell at Cork

Dec. 12   Parnell arrives in Kilkenny to campaign for Vincent Scully

Dec. 22   Sir John Pope Hennessy (anti-Parnellite), defeats Vincent Scully (Parnellite) in North Kilkenny by-election by 2,527 votes to 1,362

Dec. 30-31   Negotiations between Parnell and O'Brien opened at Boulogne-sur-Mer (second meeting, 6-7 Jan. 1891)

Douglas Hyde's *Beside the fire: a collection of Irish Gaelic folk stories* (London)

Alphons Bellesheim's *Geschichte der katholischen Kirche in Irland*, vols i and ii (Mainz; vol. iii, 1891)

1891

Feb. 3   Parnell meets O'Brien and Dillon at Calais (negotiations finally break down on question of 'liberal guarantees', 11 Feb.)

Feb. 12   Dillon and O'Brien arrested on arrival at Folkestone from Boulogne and taken to Galway jail (cf. 19 Nov. 1890)

Mar. 7   First number of *National Press*, organ of anti-Parnellites, especially of Healy faction

Mar. 10   Inauguration in Dublin of Irish National Federation, organisation of anti-Parnellites

Mar. 14   Conference in Dublin, composed largely of general labourers, decides to form Irish Labour League and hears speech by Parnell

Mar. 26   Survey by *Pittsburgh Commercial* reveals that only 3 of 63 Irish-American newspapers support Parnell

Apr. 2   North Sligo by-election: Bernard Collery (anti-Parnellite) defeats Valentine Dillon (Parnellite) by 3,261 votes to 2,493

Apr. 5   Census taken throughout Ire. (preliminary report, 26 May): population 4,704,750 (9·08% decline; see 3 Apr. 1881)

Census taken throughout G.B.: Irish-born population of England and Wales 458,315 (1·58% of total); of Scotland, 194,807 (4·84% of total)

May 1   Opening of 'loop line' connecting Dublin railway termini

May 3   Rally of over 10,000 trade unionists in Phoenix Park, Dublin: first massive response in Ire. to call by Second International (1890) for international labour day

June 1   'Stop, thief!', anonymous article (very probably by Healy), published in *National Press*: accuses Parnell of embezzling party funds

June   W. H. O'Shea's divorce decree made absolute (see 15, 17 Nov. 1890)

June 25 Parnell marries Katharine O'Shea before registrar at Steyning, Sussex

July 8 John Hammond (anti-Parnellite) returned in Carlow by-election (polling 7 July) by 3,755 to 1,539

July 18 Conference in Dublin of trade union and trades council representatives in abortive attempt to institute annual congress for Ire.

July 30 Dillon and O'Brien, on release from Galway jail, announce that they will not accept Parnell's leadership

July 31 Edmund Dwyer Gray, major shareholder in *Freeman's Journal*, hitherto organ of Parnellites, announces his support for anti-Parnellites, especially for views of Dillon and O'Brien (newspaper finally abandons Parnell, 21 Sept.)

Aug. 5 Purchase of Land (Ireland) Act, 1891 (54 & 55 Vict., c. 48), extends facilities for land purchase and establishes Congested Districts Board—'Balfour act'

Sept. 27 Parnell speaks in public for last time, at Creggs, Co. Galway

Oct. 6 Parnell dies at Brighton (funeral at Dublin, 11 Oct.)

Nov. 1 Healy in speech at Longford refers to Mrs C. S. Parnell as 'this abandoned woman', which results in his being publicly horsewhipped by Tudor MacDermott, nephew of Parnell (3 Nov.)

Dec. 18 First number of *Irish Daily Independent*, organ of Parnellites

Dec. 24 John Redmond retains Waterford city seat for Parnellites by 1,775 votes to 1,229 (polling, 23 Dec.)

Dec. 28 Irish Literary Society of London established at meeting in London home of William Butler Yeats

Workman Clark, Belfast shipbuilders, start their own engine-works at Queen's Island

1892

Jan. First number of *Journal of the Cork Historical and Archaeological Society*

Feb. 22 William Lawies Jackson, C.S., seeks leave in H.C. to introduce Irish education bill (see 27 June)

Feb. 28 Abp Walsh criticises compulsory attendance clauses of Irish education bill

Feb. Rev. James Cullen's *Temperance catechism* (Dublin)

Mar. 28 Beginning of publication of *Freeman's Journal* and *National Press* as single newspaper

Apr. First number of *Irish Naturalist*, edited by George H. Carpenter and Robert Lloyd Praeger, official organ of several Irish natural history societies

June 17 Ulster Convention, presided over by duke of Abercorn, meets in specially built pavilion in Botanic Gardens, Belfast; 12,000 unionist and liberal unionist delegates resolve 'to have nothing to do with' any home-rule parliament

June 27   Irish Education Act, 1892 (55 & 56 Vict., c. 42) abolishes fees in national schools and makes school attendance compulsory for children aged between 6 and 14

Ancient Monuments Protection (Ireland) Act, 1892 (55 & 56 Vict., c. 46), facilitates application of 1882 act in Ire. (see 18 Aug. 1882)

July   General election: in G.B.—lib. 272, con. 249, lib. un. 42, nat. 1, others 3; in Ire.—nat. 80 (including 71 anti-Parnellites and 9 Parnellites), un. 19, lib. un. 4 (see July 1886, July 1895)

Aug. 15   Gladstone app. P.M. for fourth time (Morley again C.S. 22 Aug.) (see 25 July 1886, 5 Mar. 1894)

Aug. 16   National Literary Society formally inaugurated in Dublin

Sept. 23   Electricity station, owned by Dublin corporation, begins to operate

Sept. 29   Formation of Belfast Labour Party, subsequently to become branch of Independent Labour Party; first labour party in Ire.

Oct. 14   Commn under Sir James Charles Mathew app. to inquire into estates where tenants have been evicted (see 25 Feb. 1893)

Nov. 16-30   Trial of South Meath election petition: Patrick Fulham (anti-Parnellite) unseated on ground of 'undue influence by spiritual intimidation' by Bp Nulty and priests

Nov.   Edith Œnone Somerville and Martin Ross's *Through Connemara in a governess' cart* (anon., London, dated 1893; previously published serially in *Ladies' Pictorial*)

Nov. 25   Douglas Hyde delivers his presidential address to National Literary Society in Dublin 'On the necessity for de-anglicising the Irish people'

Dec. 15-23   Trial of North Meath election petition: Davitt (anti-Parnellite) unseated (see 16-30 Nov. 1892)

1893

Jan. 19   Michael Logue, abp of Armagh, created cardinal

Feb. 13   Gladstone introduces second home-rule bill in H.C.

Feb. 25   Report of evicted tenants commn (see 14 Oct. 1892)

Mar. 2   Orange demonstration in Ulster Hall, Belfast; William Johnston, M.P. (of Ballykilbeg), carries resolution in favour of passive resistance to home rule

Apr. 11   Davitt makes maiden speech in H.C. in support of home rule bill

Apr. 21-2   Disturbances in Belfast as result of news of second reading of home rule bill

Apr. 29   National council of Knights of Columbus founded in U.S.A. (original society founded at New Haven, N.J., 2 Feb. 1882; by Mar. 1910, total membership 235,612)

May 16   Electric tramways begin operating in Dublin suburbs, from Haddington Road to Dalkey (in centre, from Nelson Pillar to North Bull, 19 Mar. 1898)

May 23-30   Salisbury visits Ulster; addresses meeting in Ulster Hall, Belfast, 24 May

July 27   Act (56 & 57 Vict., c. clxxviii) enabling Belfast water commrs to build reservoirs, etc., in Mourne Mountains (Silent Valley scheme begins to operate, 2 Oct. 1901; extended, 1923-33)

July 31   Inaugural meeting of Gaelic League; convened by Eoin MacNeill

c. **Aug.**   Douglas Hyde's *Abhráin grádh chúige Connacht or love songs of Connacht* (Dublin)

Sept. 2   Home rule bill passes third reading in H.C. by 301 to 267

Sept. 5-9   Trade Union Congress meets at Belfast

Sept. 9   Home rule bill defeated in H.L. by 419 to 41

Sept. 17   Meeting at Limerick in support of amnesty for political prisoners

Dec.   W. B. Yeats's *The Celtic twilight* (London)

1894

Feb.   First instalment of Rev. Eugene O'Growney's 'Easy lessons in Irish' in *Irisleabhar na Gaedhilge* (series published in book form as *Simple lessons in Irish*, pt. 1, Dublin, 1894; numerous later eds)

Mar. 1   Gladstone makes his last speech in H.C. (resigns, 3 Mar.)

Mar. 5   Earl of Rosebery (lib.) app. P.M. (see 15 Aug. 1892, 25 June 1895)

Mar. 12   In speaking for first time as P.M., Rosebery declares 'that before Irish home rule is conceded by the imperial parliament, England, as the predominant member of the partnership of the 3 kingdoms, will have to be convinced of its justice'

Apr. 8   Both sections of nationalist party represented at large meeting at Nenagh, Co. Tipperary, convened in attempt to bring reunification

Apr. 18   Irish Agricultural Organisation Society established by Hon. Horace Plunkett

Apr. 19   Morley, C.S., introduces evicted tenants bill in H.C.

Apr. 27-8   First Irish Trade Union Congress

May 8   Somerville and Ross's *The real Charlotte* (London)

May 12   Healy tells anti-Parnellites at Liverpool that they should 'no more . . . have a treaty with the Parnellites than . . . with the orangemen'

May 26   Royal commn under H. C. E. Childers (later under the O'Conor Don), app. to inquire into financial relations between G.B. and Ire. (see 28 Mar. 1895, 5 Sept. 1896)

July 12   Limerick city council pledges itself to support 'the suffering felon John Daly' as parliamentary candidate (see 1 Aug. 1884)

Aug. 14   Motion for second reading in H.C. of evicted tenants bill negatived by 249 to 30

Aug. 22   Dillon and others send circular letter to prominent liberals appealing for funds

Sept. 23   Protestant abp of Dublin, Lord Plunket, assisted by bps of Clogher and Down, consecrates protestant church at Madrid and afterwards consecrates first protestant bp of that city

Oct. 23   Disputed 'Paris fund' released and handed over to Justin McCarthy

Dec. 26   Alfred Webb, M.P. for West Waterford, elected president of Indian National Congress (see 28 Dec. 1885)

1895

Jan. 23   Electricity station owned by Belfast corporation begins operating

Feb. 11   Abp Croke writes to *Freeman's Journal* that 'the hope of attaining a legislature for our country within measurable time is no longer entertained by reasoning men'

Feb. 14   First public performance of Oscar Wilde's 'The importance of being Earnest', at Haymarket Theatre, London

Feb. 18-20   John D. Crimmins forms Irish National Federation (anti-Parnellite) in New York

Mar. 9   First number of *Irish Homestead*, weekly organ of Irish Agricultural Organisation Society

Mar. 28   First report of Childers commn (see 26 May 1894)

Apr. 26   East Wicklow by-election, caused by resignation of John Sweetman, in order to stand as Parnellite: E. P. O'Kelly (anti-Parnellite) receives 1,253 votes, Sweetman 1,191, and Col. C. G. Tottenham (unionist) 1,165

May 8   Jeremiah O'Donovan Rossa in public gallery interrupts H.C. debate on Irish crimes bill

May 25   Oscar Wilde found guilty at Old Bailey, London, of homosexual offences; sentenced to 2 years' hard labour

June 25   Salisbury (con.) app. P.M. for third time (see 5 Mar. 1894, 12 July 1902)

July   General election: in G.B.—con. 323, lib. un. 67, lib. 176, nat. 1; in Ire.— nat. 81 (including 69 anti-Parnellites and 12 Parnellites), un. 17, lib. un. 4, lib. 1 (see July 1892, Oct. 1900)

Aug. 13   Arthur O'Connor's motion at anti-Parnellite parliamentary party meeting for abolition of 'consultative committee' with Justin McCarthy as its president defeated by 34 (Dillonites) to 26 (Healyites), 7 members being absent

Aug. 20   H.C. carries motion by 256 to 74 declaring John Daly, as convict undergoing imprisonment, incapable of sitting as M.P. for Limerick city

Aug. 27   Horace Plunkett writes to press proposing 'recess committee' of representatives of different political parties

Sept. 5   Thomas Joseph Farrell (McCarthyite) defeats William Martin Murphy (Healyite) in South Kerry by-election by 1,209 votes to 474

Sept. 25-7   John Finerty and others form Irish National Alliance in Chicago

Oct. 11   Beginning of strike of engineers at Harland & Wolff shipyard and elsewhere in Belfast (yards reopen, 27 Jan. 1896)

Nov. 7   Executive of Irish National League of Great Britain expels Healy and replaces him with Davitt

Nov. 13   Irish National Federation council meeting at Dublin decides, by 47 to 40, to expel Healy, O'Connor, Murphy, and 2 others from federation's executive

Dec. 29   Dr Leander Starr Jameson leads raid on Transvaal: international crisis and isolation of U.K. follows

1896

Feb. 2   Announcement of McCarthy's resignation as chairman of anti-Parnellite parliamentary party

Feb. 17   In H.C. Horace Plunkett and W. E. H. Lecky, Irish unionists, support Redmond's plea for clemency for Irish political prisoners

Feb. 18   Anti-Parnellite parliamentary party elects Dillon chairman by 38 to 21

Mar. 13   Pope Leo XIII empowers Maynooth College to grant degrees of pontifical university

Mar. 16   R. Bolton McCausland, surgeon at Steevens' hospital, Dublin, uses X-rays to locate needle embedded in palm of woman's hand; first recorded use of X-rays in Ire.

Mar. 31   Women become qualified for election as poor law guardians under Poor Law Guardians (Ireland) (Women) Act, 1896 (59 Vict., c. 5)

Apr. 20   First recorded cinematographic show in Dublin, at Olympia theatre

Apr. 24   Royal commn under Viscount Peel app. to inquire into licensing laws (final report, 4 July 1898, recommends reform of legislation in Ire.)

May 12   Many nationalists, including Dillon, Redmond, and Davitt, support government in H.C. on second reading of English education bill, which is carried by 423 to 156

May 29   Formation in public-house in Thomas Street, Dublin, of Irish Socialist Republican Party; secretary, James Connolly

July 26-7   Some £200,000 of damage caused and several thousand workers made idle by fire at Harland & Wolff and Workman Clark shipyards in Belfast

Aug. 1   Irish 'recess committee' submits to C.S. reports on state promotion of agriculture and industry

Aug. 14   Locomotives on Highways Act, 1896 (59 & 60 Vict., c. 26), removes severe restrictions on power-driven vehicles on public roads, thus permitting practical use of motorcars

Land Law (Ireland), Act, 1896 (59 & 60 Vict., c. 47)

Aug. 18   Dillon's proposed 'Irish race convention' attacked at Healyite meeting in Dublin

Aug. 20   John Daly released from Portland prison (see 1 Aug. 1884)

Sept. 1-3   'Irish race convention' at Leinster Hall, Dublin, under presidency of Patrick O'Donnell, bp of Raphoe

Sept. 5   Publication of final report of Childers commn (see 26 May 1894)

Oct. 6   Rosebery resigns liberal party leadership

Dec. 12 Meeting at Cork, called by conservative lord-lieutenant of county, chaired by nationalist mayor and attended by representatives of all shades of opinion, agrees on deploring 'over-taxation' of Ire.

John O'Leary's *Recollections of fenians and fenianism* (2 vols, London)

1897

Jan. 12 People's Rights Association established at meeting in Dublin of supporters of Healy; dedicated to upholding power of constituencies against that of national leadership

May 17 First Oireachtas (Irish Literary Festival) held in Dublin

May 18-22 First Feis Ceoil (Irish Music Festival)

May Bram Stoker's *Dracula* (Irish translation by Seán Ó Cuirrín, Dublin, 1933)

c. **July** George Sigerson's *Bards of the Gael and Gall* (London; revised ed., 1907)

Oct. 30 Summary dismissal by clerical manager of school-mistress of Leixlip, Co. Kildare, leading to dispute between catholic hierarchy and Irish National Teachers' Organisation that ends in latter submitting and splitting on sectarian lines (autumn 1899)

Nov. 25 Belfast municipal elections: 8 of 60 seats won by candidates of Catholic Association, 6 by labour

1898

Jan. 23 William O'Brien launches United Irish League at meeting at Westport to organise agitation aimed at dividing up grazing lands among small farmers

Feb. 15 Destruction of U.S. battleship *Maine* in Havana harbour, leading to outbreak of war between U.S.A. and Spain (21 Apr.; armistice, 12 Aug.)

Feb. 21 Irish local government bill introduced in H.C.

Mar. 29 Registration (Ireland) Act, 1898 (61 Vict., c. 2), confers local government franchise on women and peers

May 30 Viceregal commn under Christopher Palles app. to inquire into intermediate education (see 22 Dec. 1898, 11 Aug. 1899)

May First instalment of Rev. Patrick Augustine (later Canon) Sheehan's 'My new curate' in *American Ecclesiastical Review* (anon.; complete work in book form, London, 1899)

June 27-July 1 Ancient Order of Hibernians (Board of Erin) unites with A.O.H. of America at Trenton, N.J. (subsequent rapid growth: 127,254 members by 1908)

Aug. 12 Local Government (Ireland) Act, 1898 (61 & 62 Vict., c. 37) provides for creation of elected county and district councils (women qualified to sit on district councils and town commns, but not on county or borough councils, by order of L.L. under act, 22 Dec.)

Aug. 13 First number of James Connolly's *Workers' Republic* (continued intermittently till May 1903; see 29 May 1915)

Sept. 29 Release of Thomas James Clarke from Portland prison (see 5 Apr. 1883, Dec. 1907)

Dec. 22   First report of Palles commn (see 30 May)

Dec. 27   Rev. James Cullen founds total abstinence League of the Sacred Heart for women only (opened to men, Feb. 1901; see June 1889, 6 Oct. 1901)

R. Barry O'Brien's *The life of Charles Stewart Parnell, 1846–1891* (2 vols, London; 2nd ed., 1899; abridged ed., 1910)

1899

Feb. 7   John Dillon resigns chairmanship of anti-Parnellite parliamentary party (remains vacant for 1 year)

Feb. 21   William Joseph Myles Starkie app. resident commr of national education

Mar. 4   First number of Arthur Griffith's *United Irishman*

Mar. 18   First number of *An Claidheamh Soluis*, organ of Gaelic League; editor Eoin MacNeill

Apr. 29   In article in *United Irishman* Griffith refers to constitutional position of Hungary (see 8 June 1867)

May 8   Irish Literary Theatre stages in Antient Concert Rooms, Dublin, Yeats's 'Countess Cathleen' (followed next evening by Edward Martyn's 'The heather field')

June 20   Catholic Truth Society of Ireland formed

Aug. 9   Agricultural and Technical Instruction (Ireland) Act, 1899 (62 & 63 Vict., c. 50) establishes department of agriculture and technical instruction, and consultative council of agriculture including representatives of county councils (see 1 Apr. 1900)

Aug. 11   Final report of Palles commn (see 30 May 1898)

Oct. 11   Outbreak of war in South Africa between U.K. and 2 Boer republics

Oct. 25   Davitt withdraws from parliament in protest against Boer war

Oct. 30   Battle of Modderspruit (Lombard's Kop) in which John MacBride's Irish brigade suffers casualties

Oct.   Somerville and Ross's *Some experiences of an Irish R.M.* (London)

1900

Jan.   First instalment of Sheehan's 'Luke Delmege' in *American Ecclesiastical Review* (complete work in book form, London, 1901)

Jan. 30   Nationalist M.P.s ratify reunion of 2 sections of Irish parliamentary party (John Redmond elected leader, 6 Feb.)

Apr. 1   Beginning of first 3-year term of council of agriculture (see 9 Aug. 1899)

Apr. 3–26   Queen Victoria visits Ire.

May 22   Commrs of national education approve new regulations for national schools: results system ended; history introduced into syllabus

June 1   Census taken throughout U.S.A.: Irish-born population 1,615,419 (2·13 % of total and 15·6 % of foreign-born population); 3,211,445 children of Irish-born parents

June 19-20   Convention in Dublin of reunited nationalists recognises United Irish League (cf. 23 Jan. 1898) as nationalist electoral organisation and endorses election of Redmond as chairman of Irish parliamentary party

July 20   H.C. debates Irish language

Aug. 6   Intermediate Education (Ireland) Act, 1900 (63 & 64 Vict., c. 43), increases membership of intermediate education board from 7 to 12, substitutes capitation grants for 'payment by results' and empowers board to appoint inspectors

Aug. 30   Patrick Egan, Patrick Ford and John Devoy form Irish-American Union to oppose policies of William McKinley (imperialism and Anglo-American understanding) and support William Jennings Bryan

Sept. 1   First number of D.P. Moran's *Leader*

Sept. 30   Formation of Griffith's Cumann na nGaedheal

Oct.   General election ('khaki election'): in G.B.—con. 317, lib. un. 64, lib. 183, lab. 2, nat. 1; in Ire.—nat. 76, ind. nat. 5, un. 17, lib. un. 4, lib. 1 (see July 1895, Jan. 1906)

Nov. 9   George Wyndham app. C.S.

Dec. 11   Healy expelled from Irish parliamentary party

1901

Jan. 22   Victoria dies; succ. by Edward VII

Jan.   Augusta Lady Gregory's *Ideals in Ireland* (London), with preface by herself and contributions by 'AE' (George Russell), D. P. Moran, George Moore, Douglas Hyde, Standish O'Grady, and W. B. Yeats

Mar. 14   Society of Incorporated Accountants in Ireland formed

Mar. 31   Census taken throughout Ire. (preliminary report, 16 May): population 4,458,775 (5·23% decline; see 5 Apr. 1891)

Census taken throughout G.B.: Irish-born population of England and Wales 426,565 (1·3 % of total); of Scotland, 205,064 (4·6 % of total)

July 1   Royal commn on university education in Ire., under Lord Robertson, app. (see 28 Feb. 1903)

Sept. 30   Classes begin at Municipal Technical Institute, Belfast, formed by amalgamation of 5 local colleges of science, art and technology (new building in College Square East formally opened, 30 Oct. 1907)

Oct. 6   First annual meeting of Pioneer Total Abstinence League of the Sacred Heart (papal approval, Nov. 1905; see June 1889, 27 Dec. 1898)

Oct. 21   Irish Literary Theatre stages Douglas Hyde's 'Casadh an tSúgán' at Gaiety Theatre, Dublin, with author in principal role

Nov.   James Joyce's 'The day of the rabblement' and F. J. C. (later known as Francis Sheehy-) Skeffington's 'A forgotten aspect of the university question' published privately in Dublin as a pamphlet, having been refused publication in *St Stephen's*, University College student magazine

Dec. 4   United Irish League of America formed in New York

Dec. 10   United States Federation of Catholic Societies formed at Cincinnati, despite boycott by A.O.H. and Knights of Columbus, foremost Irish catholic organisations

Anti-Treating League formed by catholic clergy in Enniscorthy, Co. Wexford (30,000 anti-treating pledges given by July 1922)

1902

Jan. 20   Dillon in H.C. proposes motion condemning British policy of concentration camps in South Africa; motion defeated by 283 to 64

Mar. 4   Ancient Order of Hibernians achieves unity in Ire. under Board of Erin

Apr. 2   First performance of Yeats's 'Cathleen ni Houlihan'

May 31   Boer war ends with treaty of Vereeniging

July 12   Arthur James Balfour (con.) app. P.M. (see 25 June 1895, 5 Dec. 1905)

July 31   Sale of Intoxicating Liquors (Licences) (Ireland) Act, 1902 (2 Edw. VII, c. 18), to reduce numbers of drink licences

Aug. 18   Thomas Sloan, shipyard worker and candidate of Belfast Protestant Association, defeats Charles W. Dunbar-Buller (unionist) in South Belfast by-election by 3,795 votes to 2,969

Sept. 3   Capt. John Shawe-Taylor's letter inviting landlord and Irish party representatives to a conference to settle land question published (see 20 Dec.)

Sept. 12   Speech before British Association at Belfast by William Joseph Myles Starkie, resident commr of national education, afterwards widely construed as attack on position of clergy in education

Oct.   Michael Davitt's *Some suggestions for a final settlement of the land question* (Dublin)

Nov. 8   Sir Antony MacDonnell app. under-secretary

Nov. 29   First instalment of William Bulfin's 'Rambles in Erinn' in *United Irishman* (whole work in book form, Dublin, 1907); memoir of cycling tour

Nov.   Emergence of Ulster branch of Irish Literary Theatre (renamed Ulster Literary Theatre, 1904) with production of W. B. Yeats's 'Cathleen ni Houlihan' and James Henry Cousins's 'The racing lug' at St Mary's Minor Hall, Belfast

Dec. 20   Conference of representatives of Irish landlords (earls of Dunraven and Mayo, Cols Hutcheson-Poë and Nugent Everard), and tenants (Redmond, O'Brien, Timothy Harrington, T. W. Russell) begins in Mansion House, Dublin; chairman Dunraven, secretary Shawe-Taylor (see 3 Sept.)

1903

Jan. 3   Report of Irish land conference recommends that tenants be enabled to buy out landlords with loans from treasury

Feb. 28   Fourth and final report of Robertson commn (see 1 July 1901); recommends reconstruction of Royal University of Ireland

Mar. 25   Wyndham, C.S., introduces land purchase bill in H.C.

Mar. 27 Seventeenth of March (St. Patrick's Day) becomes bank holiday under Bank Holiday (Ireland) Act, 1903 (3 Edw. VII, c. 1)

Apr. 20 George Moore's *The untilled field* (London)

Apr. 24 Walter Frederick Osborne, painter, dies

Apr. Pogrom of Jews at Kishineff, Bessarabia (reported on by Michael Davitt as special correspondent of Hearst newspapers, May)

May 12 Vice-regal commission on poor law reform in Ire. app. (see 10 Oct. 1906)

June 6 First meeting of National Council, established by Griffith initially to protest against royal visit

June 11 Independent Orange Order formed in Belfast

July 21–Aug. 1 Edward VII visits Ire.

Aug. 14 Irish Land Act, 1903 (3 Edw. VII, c. 37)—'Wyndham act'

Aug. 25 Dillon's speech at Swinford, Co. Mayo, expressing 'no faith in the doctrine of conciliation'

Oct. 8 First performance of John Millington Synge's 'In the shadow of the glen', in Molesworth Hall, Dublin

Nov. 4 William O'Brien announces his withdrawal from public life

1904

Jan. 2 First instalment of Griffith's series 'The resurrection of Hungary' in *United Irishman* (whole work republished as pamphlet later in year)

Jan. 4 Letter signed by Dunraven, but probably drafted by MacDonnell, proposing enlargement of Dublin University by establishment of 2 new colleges, published

Jan. Outbreak of attacks on Jews at Limerick, incited by Redemptorist priest, John Creagh; protest by Michael Davitt 'as an Irishman and a catholic against this spirit of barbarous malignity being introduced into Ireland' (16 Jan.)

Feb. 25 First public performance of J. M. Synge's 'Riders to the sea', in Molesworth Hall, Dublin

Feb. Sir Horace Plunkett's *Ireland in the new century* (London)

Mar. 7 Report of F. H. Dale, inspector of schools, on primary education in Ire.

Apr. 8 Anglo-French treaty settles outstanding colonial disputes; confirmation of 'entente cordiale'

Apr. 26–May 5 Edward VII revisits Ire.

Apr. 28 Foundation-stone laid by kg of new buildings of Royal College of Science in Upper Merrion Street, Dublin; architects Sir Aston Webb and Thomas Manley Deane (opened by George V, 8 July 1911)

May Michael Davitt's *The fall of feudalism in Ireland or the story of the Land League revolution* (London and New York)

June 16 'Bloomsday' of James Joyce's *Ulysses* (see 2 Feb. 1922)

July 4 Coláiste na Mumhan opens at Ballingeary, west Cork; first summer college for training teachers of Irish

Aug. 26 Formation of Dunraven's Irish Reform Association and release of manifesto in favour of 'devolution'

Nov. First number of *Uladh*, review of Ulster Literary Theatre (final number, Sept. 1905)

Nov. 1 First public performance of G. B. Shaw's 'John Bull's other island', at Royal Court Theatre, London

Dec. 2 Conference of Ulster unionist M.P.s at Belfast, leading to formation of Ulster Unionist Council (name adopted, Mar. 1905)

Dec. 27 Opening of Abbey Theatre, Dublin, with Yeats's 'On Baile's strand' and Lady Gregory's 'Spreading the news', in building in Abbey Street, formerly Mechanics' Institute, bought and adapted by Miss A. E. F. Horniman and given to the National Theatre Society (see 17 July 1951)

Eoin MacNeill's first lectures on early Irish history, at University College, Dublin

First number of *Ériu: the Journal of the School of Irish Learning*; editors Kuno Meyer and John Strachan

Rev. Patrick S. Dineen's *Foclóir Gaedhilge agus Béarla* (Dublin)

1905

Feb. 4 First public performance of J. M. Synge's 'The well of the saints' in Abbey Theatre, Dublin

Mar. 6 Wyndham's resignation as C.S. announced by P.M.

Mar. 8 Bulmer Hobson in Belfast inaugurates first Dungannon Club

June 9 First public performance of Padraic Colum's 'The land' at Abbey Theatre, Dublin

July 13 Independent Orange Order manifesto to 'all Irishmen whose country stands first in their affections' issued at demonstration at Magheramorne, Co. Antrim; author Robert Lindsay Crawford, grand master

Sept. 12 Carnegie Free Library, Cork, opened (see 11-12 Dec. 1920)

Sept. 14 William Walker, candidate of Labour Representation Committee, almost defeats Sir Daniel Dixon (unionist) in North Belfast by-election: Dixon 4,440, Walker 3,966 (further unsuccessful attempt, 18 Jan. 1906)

Oct. 10 Joint cttee of presbyterian and methodist churches in Ire. on matters of common interest meets for first time (see 11 June 1910)

Oct. 15 Capuchin order, at invitation of Irish bps, inaugurate temperance crusade (see 7 May 1912)

Nov. 11 Douglas Hyde leaves Ire. for U.S.A. in quest of funds for Gaelic League (returns to Ire., 25 June 1906, having collected $64,000)

Nov. 14 John Redmond and T. P. O'Connor secure promise of home rule from Sir Henry Campbell-Bannerman

Nov. 28 At annual convention of National Council (see 6 June 1903) Griffith proposes policy named Sinn Féin by one of his supporters (Máire Butler)

Dec. 4 Royal commn under Lord George Hamilton app. to inquire into poor law in U.K. (see 14 Apr. 1909)

Dec. 5   Electric tramways begin operating in Belfast

Sir Henry Campbell-Bannerman (lib.) app. P.M. (see 12 July 1902, 8 Apr. 1908)

Dec. 14   James Bryce app. C.S.

John Bagnell Bury's *Life of St Patrick and his place in history* (London)

1906

Jan.   General election: in G.B.—lib. 397, lab. 29, nat. 1, con. 116, lib. un. 23, others 1; in Ire.—nat. 81, ind. nat. 1, lib. 1, un. 16, ind. un. 3, lib. un. 1;— 'liberal landslide' (see Oct. 1900, Jan.-Feb. 1910)

Feb. 22   Bill introduced in H.C. to make Irish Sunday-closing act permanent (becomes law, 29 Nov., as Intoxicating Liquors (Ireland) Act, 1906 (6 Edw. VII, c. 39) (see 16 Aug. 1878)

Apr. 9   Education (England and Wales) Bill introduced by government in H.C. in attempt to remove grievances of nonconformists

Apr.   Ulster Liberal Association established, with backing from William James Pirrie (created Lord Pirrie, 7 July), controlling partner of Harland & Wolff

May 1   Irish catholic episcopal standing cttee urges Irish parliamentary party to oppose English and Welsh education bill (party unanimously agrees to do so, 2 May)

May 5   First number of *Sinn Féin*, editor Arthur Griffith

May 31   Davitt dies in Dublin

June 2   Royal commn under Sir Edward Fry app. to inquire into state of Trinity College and University of Dublin (see 31 Aug. 1906, 12 Jan. 1907)

July 18   Viceregal commn under Sir Charles Scotter app. to inquire into Irish railways (first report, 9 July 1907; final report, 4 July 1910)

July 20   Royal commn on congestion in Ire., under earl of Dudley, app. (see 14 Nov. 1906, 5 May 1908)

Aug. 1   Belfast City Hall opened; architect Alfred Brumwell-Thomas

Aug. 4   Labourers (Ireland) Act, 1906 (6 Edw. VII, c. 37) remedies defects in existing legislation and provides additional finance for labourers' cottages

Aug. 30   Opening of Waterford-Rosslare-Fishguard route to England, the last major Irish railway extension

Aug. 31   First report of Fry commn (see 2 June)

Oct. 10   Report of vice-regal commn on poor-law reform in Ire. (see 12 May 1903)

Oct. 20   First public performance of Lady Gregory's 'The gaol gate', at Abbey Theatre, Dublin

Nov. 1   Walter Hume Long elected leader of Irish unionists in H.C.

Nov. 14   First report of Dudley commn (see 20 July)

Dec. 19   H.L., by insisting on amendments unacceptable to H.C., effectively rejects government's English and Welsh education bill

Dec. 20   Francis Bourne, catholic abp of Westminster, thanks Redmond and Irish party for part in defeat of education bill

Dec. 21   Trade Disputes Act, 1906 (6 Edw. VII, c. 47)

Census of Production Act, 1906 (6 Edw. VII, c. 49), provides for statistical surveys of production in U.K. (preliminary report of first census, relating to 1907, published Sept. 1909)

Dec. 31   Peace Preservation (Ireland) Act, 1881, expires; controls on possession and importation of arms relaxed

Dec.   First number of *The Republic*, editor Bulmer Hobson (weekly, Belfast; continues till May 1907)

Douglas Hyde's *Abhráin diadha chúige Connacht or the religious songs of Connacht* (2 vols, London and Dublin); bilingual text

1907

Jan. 12   Fry commn (see 2 June 1906) reports in favour of establishment of new college acceptable to catholics

Jan. 24-6   Labour party (formerly Labour Representation Committee) holds eighth annual conference at Wellington Hall, Belfast; attendance includes Keir Hardie, James Ramsay MacDonald, Arthur Henderson, and nearly 20 other labour M.P.s

Jan. 25   Bryce, C.S., announces scheme to enlarge Dublin University to include Queen's Colleges of Belfast and Cork and new college for catholics in Dublin

Jan. 28-30   Rioting by audiences accompanies first public performances of J. M. Synge's 'The playboy of the western world', at Abbey Theatre, Dublin

Jan. 29   Augustine Birrell app. C.S.

Mar. 9   First public performance of Lady Gregory's 'The rising of the moon', at Abbey Theatre, Dublin

Apr. 21   Sinn Féin League inaugurated through amalgamation of Dungannon Clubs and Cumann na nGaedheal at convention at Dundalk

May 4   Irish International Exhibition at Ballsbridge, Dublin, opened (ends, 9 Nov.)

May 6   Strike of dockers at York dock of Belfast Steamship Company; beginning of series of strikes organised by James Larkin, official of National Union of Dock Labourers

May 7   Birrell introduces Irish Council bill in H.C.

May 21   Nationalist convention rejects Irish Council bill

May   J. M. Synge's *The Aran Islands* (Dublin), his major prose work; illustrated by Jack B. Yeats

June 3   P.M. announces dropping of Irish Council bill

June 27   Birrell introduces Irish evicted tenants bill in H.C.

July 4   Irish Tobacco Act, 1907 (7 Edw. VII, c. 3), permits growing of tobacco in Ire., previously prohibited under 1 & 2 Will. IV, c. 13

July 6   Discovery of theft of Irish state jewels from Dublin castle

July 24   Police mutiny in Belfast (police replaced by troops, to deal with disorder occasioned by strikes and lock-outs)

Aug. 2 Pius X issues decree, *Ne temere*, affecting marriages between catholics and non-catholics

Aug. 11 James Larkin launches Dublin branch of National Union of Dock Labourers

Aug. 12 Rioting in Falls Road district of Belfast; suppressed by troops

Aug. 28 Evicted Tenants (Ireland) Act, 1907 (7 Edw. VII, c. 56), empowers estates commrs to purchase land compulsorily for evicted tenants and allows Congested Districts Board to make grants to enable reinstated tenants to repair or reconstruct buildings

Sept. 5 National Council (Griffith, Edward Martyn, John Sweetman) and Sinn Féin League (Denis McCullough, P.S. O'Hegarty, P.T. Daly, Bulmer Hobson) amalgamate under name of former (name Sinn Féin adopted, Sept. 1908)

Oct. First number of *Irish Educational Review*; editor Rev. Andrew Murphy, formerly secretary of Catholic Headmasters' Association

Oct. 17 Opening of Marconi transatlantic wireless telegraphy service between Clifden, Co. Galway, and Cape Breton, Canada

Dec. Thomas James Clarke returns to Ire. (see 29 Sept. 1898)

Dec. 13 Formal discussions between John Redmond and William O'Brien for purpose of restoring nationalist unity

Dec. 19 Joint Committee of the Unionist Associations of Ireland formed

Dec. 21 First part of Pádraic Mac Piarais's (Patrick Pearse's) 'In first-century Ireland' in *An Claidheamh Soluis* (three more pts follow)

Louis Paul-Dubois' *L'Irlande contemporaine et la question irlandaise* (Paris; English trs., with introduction by Thomas M. Kettle, as *Contemporary Ireland*, Dublin, 1908)

1908

Feb. 21 North Leitrim by-election: Charles J. Dolan, having resigned seat won as nationalist in order to stand for re-election as Sinn Féin candidate, defeated by nationalist, Francis Meehan, by 3,103 votes to 1,157

Apr. 8 Herbert Henry Asquith (lib.) app. P.M. (see 5 Dec. 1905, 7 Dec. 1916)

May 5 Final report of Dudley commn (see 20 July 1906)

May 19-20 Lindsay Crawford expelled from Independent Orange Order

June 29 Pius X issues decree, *Sapienti consilio*, withdrawing England, Scotland, Ireland, and other lands from jurisdiction of Sacred Congregation de Propaganda Fide (effective, 3 Nov.)

Aug. 1 Irish Universities Act, 1908 (8 Edw. VII, c. 38), provides for replacement of Royal University of Ireland by 2 new universities, one with its seat in Dublin, the other in Belfast (leading to establishment of National University of Ireland and Queen's University of Belfast)

Old Age Pensions Act, 1908 (8 Edw. VII, c. 40)

Aug. George A. Birmingham's (James Owen Hannay's) *Spanish gold* (London)

Sept. 8   Patrick Pearse opens Scoil Eanna (St Enda's school for boys) in Cullens-wood House, Rathmines, Dublin (moves it to the Hermitage, Rathfarnham, 1910; see 23 Apr. 1970)

Nov. 9-12   Strike of dockers and carters at Cork, organised by James Larkin and James Fearon of National Union of Dock Labourers

Nov. 11   Irish Women's Franchise League formed; secretary, Hanna Sheehy Skeffington

Nov. 23   Birrell, C.S., introduces land purchase bill in H.C. (withdrawn owing to lack of time, 10 Dec.; reintroduced next session, 15 Mar. 1909)

Dec. 21   Housing of the Working Classes (Ireland) Act, 1908 (8 Edw. VII, c. 61), increases powers of local authorities to build houses, and sets up Irish housing fund to support house construction

Children's Act, 1908 (8 Edw. VII, c. 67), reforms law affecting children and adolescents

Dec. 29   James Larkin forms Irish Transport Workers' Union with himself as general secretary; renamed 'Irish Transport & General Workers' Union', it soon displaces National Union of Dock Labourers

William Butler Yeats's *Collected works in verse and prose* (8 vols, Stratford-on-Avon)

1909

Jan. 19   Catholic episcopal standing cttee, while welcoming prospect of restoration of Irish language, objects to Irish being made compulsory for matriculation in N.U.I., fearing that catholics ignorant of, or antipathetic to, Irish, may go to Trinity College, Dublin (objection not effective)

Feb. 9-10   United Irish League convention in Dublin, primarily to consider Birrell's land bill; O'Brien shouted down while opposing resolution favourable to bill (carried overwhelmingly, 9 Feb.); Dillon shouted down while opposing resolution favourable to Irish language requirement for matriculation to N.U.I. (carried by ¾ majority, 10 Feb.)

c. **Feb.**   Richard Bagwell's *Ireland under the Stuarts*, vols i and ii (London; vol. iii, 1916)

Mar. 24   John Millington Synge dies, aged 37

Apr. 1   Carnegie Library in Great Brunswick (later Pearse) Street, Dublin, opened

Apr. 14   Report on Ire. of royal commn to inquire into poor law in U.K. (see 4 Dec. 1905)

Apr. 29   David Lloyd George introduces 'people's budget': extra taxes on spirits, tobacco, and liquor licences, and new taxes on land, all especially unwelcome to vested interests in Irish nationalist party (see 29 Apr. 1910)

July 13   Rev. R. J. Patterson of Armagh inaugurates 'Catch my pal' Total Abstinence Association

Aug.   First number of *Irish Book Lover*; editor John S. Crone

Aug. 16   Formation of Fianna Éireann, headed by Constance Countess Markievicz, organised by Bulmer Hobson

Aug. 25   G. B. Shaw's 'The shewing-up of Blanco Posnet' performed at Abbey Theatre, Dublin, after being banned in England by lord chamberlain

Sept. 20   Labour Exchanges Act, 1909 (9 Edw. VII, c. 7), empowers board of trade to establish labour exchanges

Nov. 25   Health Resorts and Watering-Places (Ireland) Act, 1909 (9 Edw. VII, c. 32), empowers local authorities to strike rate for advertising their localities as health resorts; first act relating to tourism

Nov. 30   H.L. rejects Lloyd George's budget

Dec. 3   Irish Land Act, 1909 (9 Edw. VII, c. 42), increases facilities for purchase of land by tenants, and gives powers of compulsory purchase to Congested Districts Board—'Birrell act'

Dec. 10   Asquith makes speech at Albert Hall promising 'self-government' for Ire.

Dec. 20   Volta Cinema, Mary Street, Dublin, opened; first cinematographic theatre in Ire.

Dec. 31   Harry Ferguson makes first aeroplane flight from Irish soil, at Old Park, Hillsborough, Co. Down

1910

Jan.-Feb.   General election: in G.B.—lib. 274, lab. 40, nat. 1, con. 223, lib. un. 29; in Ire.—nat. 70, ind. nat. 11, lib. 1, un. 21; nationalists hold balance in H.C. (see Jan. 1906, Dec. 1910)

Feb. 21   Sir Edward Carson elected leader of Irish unionists in H.C. (see 1 Nov. 1906, 24 Sept. 1913, 4 Feb. 1921)

Mar. 31   William O'Brien establishes All-for-Ireland League at meeting in City Hall, Cork

Apr. 29   Finance (1909-10) Act, 1910 (10 Edw. VII, c. 8), pt II, establishes more stringent system of liquor licences

May 5   First public performance of Padraic Colum's 'Thomas Muskerry', at Abbey Theatre, Dublin

May 6   Edward VII dies; succ. by George V

May 7   Abbey Theatre does not close in mourning for king, thus causing withdrawal of financial support of Miss A. E. F. Horniman

June 11   General assembly of presbyterian church in Ire. decides to cooperate with Church of Ireland and other evangelical churches, on model of its joint cttee with methodist church (see 10 Oct. 1905, 15 Oct. 1911)

June 23   Senate of National University of Ireland decides that from 1913 Irish shall be essential for matriculation (cf. 19 Jan. 1909)

July 4   Publication of fifth and final report of vice-regal commn on Irish railways

July 26   James Connolly returns to Ire. from U.S.A.

Nov.   Connolly's *Labour in Irish history* first published in Ire. (Dublin); previously published serially in Edinburgh *Socialist* and New York *Harp*

First number of *Irish Freedom*; I.R.B. monthly, editor Patrick McCartan (suppressed, Dec. 1914)

Nov. 19   Publication in *Northern Whig* of letter from Rev. William Corkey, presbyterian minister, drawing attention to case of presbyterian wife (Mrs Agnes Jane McCann) deprived of her young children and deserted by her catholic husband, owing to her refusal to be married by a catholic priest in accordance with *Ne temere* decree (see 2 Aug. 1907, 8 June 1911)

Dec.   General election: in G.B.—lib. 270, lab. 42, nat. 1, con. 221, lib. un. 33; in Ire.—nat. 73, ind. nat. 10, lib. 1, un. 19; nationalists again hold balance in H.C. (see Jan.-Feb. 1910, 14 Dec. 1918)

1911

Jan. 23   Ulster Women's Unionist Council formed

Mar.   First number of *Irish Review* (continues till Nov. 1914), monthly magazine of literature, art and science, edited successively by D. G. Houston, Padraic Colum, and Joseph Mary Plunkett; assistant editor Thomas MacDonagh

Mar. 30   First public performance of St John G. Ervine's 'Mixed marriage', at Abbey Theatre, Dublin

Apr.   First instalment of James Stephens's 'Mary: a story' in *New Ireland Review* (last instalment, Feb. 1912; whole work published in book form as *The charwoman's daughter*, London, 1912)

Apr. 2   Census taken throughout Ire. (preliminary report, 18 May): population down to 4,381,951 (1·54% decline; see 31 Mar. 1901)

Census taken throughout G.B.: Irish-born population of England and Wales 375,325 (1·0% of total); of Scotland, 174,715 (3·7% of total)

May 27   First number of *Irish Worker*, organ of Irish Transport & General Workers' Union

June 8   General assembly of presbyterian church in Ire. debates McCann case, and calls unanimously for withdrawal of *Ne temere* decree (see 2 Aug. 1907, 19 Nov. 1910)

June 30   Dublin Employers' Federation formed

July 7-12   George V visits Dublin and neighbourhood

Aug. 18   Parliament Act, 1911 (1 & 2 Geo. V, c. 13) deprives H.L. of all power over money bills, restricts its power over other bills to a suspensive veto of 2 years (see 16, 30 Jan., 7 July, 1913, 25 May 1914), and reduces maximum duration of parliament from 7 years (see 7 May 1716) to 5

Aug. 21   Irish Women's Suffrage Federation formed, comprising Belfast Women's Suffrage Society, Irishwomen's Reform League and Munster Women's Franchise Association

Aug. 26   Lock-out of foundrymen at Wexford owing to their determination to join Irish Transport & General Workers' Union (return to work, 12 Feb. 1912)

Sept. 23	Fifty thousand orangemen and unionists march from Belfast to Craigavon House to demonstration addressed by Sir Edward Carson

First American tour of Abbey Theatre company opens at New Plymouth Theatre, Boston, Mass. (ends at same theatre, 4 Mar. 1912) (see 18 Jan. 1912)

Oct. 1	Parnell monument by Augustus Saint-Gaudens in Upper Sackville Street, Dublin, unveiled by Redmond

Oct. 15	Joint cttee of presbyterian church and Church of Ireland meets for first time (see 11 June 1910, 23 Jan. 1923)

Oct. 17	Report of cttee under Sir Henry William Primrose on Irish finance recommends fiscal autonomy for Ire.

Oct. 19	George Moore's *Hail and farewell!*, vol. i (London; vol. ii, 1912; vol. iii, 1914)

Nov. 8	Balfour resigns leadership of conservative party (succeeded by Andrew Bonar Law, 13 Nov.)

Dec. 16	Local Authorities (Ireland) (Qualification of Women) Act, 1911 (1 & 2 Geo. V, c. 35), enables women to become members of county and borough councils

National Insurance Act, 1911 (1 & 2 Geo. V, c. 55), establishes state scheme of health and employment insurance throughout U.K.; modifications for Ire.

Goddard Henry Orpen's *Ireland under the Normans*, vols i and ii (Oxford; vols iii and iv, 1920)

1912

Jan. 5	Col. R. H. Wallace, secretary of Grand Orange Lodge of Ulster, applies to 2 Belfast magistrates for authorisation of drilling

Jan. 18	Abbey Players technically arrested at Philadelphia on complaint of certain Irish-Americans for performing J. M. Synge's 'Playboy of the western world'

Feb. 3	Rev. James Cullen begins regular Pioneer column in *Irish Catholic* (last column, 29 Oct. 1921; Cullen dies, 6 Dec. 1921)

Feb. 8	Winston Churchill visits Belfast; with Redmond addresses crowd of over 7,000 at Celtic Park

Mar.	First number of *Studies: an Irish quarterly review*

Apr. 9	Andrew Bonar Law at demonstration at Balmoral, near Belfast, pledges support of British unionists for Ulster unionist resistance to home rule

Apr. 11	Asquith introduces home rule bill in H.C.

Apr. 14-15	Sinking of White Star liner *Titanic* (built in Belfast by Harland & Wolff) on her maiden voyage to New York

May 7	Report of Capuchin temperance crusade in Ire. to superior-general in Rome: 2,038 missions and 1,141,191 pledges administered since 1905 (see 15 Oct. 1905)

June 11   T. C. R. Agar-Robartes (liberal) in H.C. moves amendment to home rule bill to exclude Counties Antrim, Armagh, Down, and Londonderry from its provision, declaring: 'I have never heard that orange bitters will mix with Irish whisky' (amendment defeated by 320 to 251, 18 June)

June 28   Irish Trade Union Congress, meeting at Clonmel, constitutes itself into Irish Trade Union Congress and Labour Party

June 29   Protestant Sunday-school excursion party at Castledawson, Co. Londonderry, assaulted by Ancient Order of Hibernians procession

July 1   Daniel Mannix, president of Maynooth College, app. coadjutor bp of Melbourne (succeeds as abp, 6 May 1917; retains office till his death, 6 Nov. 1963)

July 2   Protestant shipyard workers in Belfast expel catholics from yards in reprisal for Castledawson affair

July 10   William Ferguson Massey, native of Limavady, Co. Londonderry, app. P.M. of New Zealand (retains office till his death, 10 May 1925)

July 18-20   Asquith, P.M., visits Dublin; suffragettes from England make violent demonstration

c. **Aug.**   George A. Birmingham's *The red hand of Ulster* (London)

Sept. 14   Scuffle develops into riot at football match at Celtic Park, Belfast, between Celtic (catholic) and Linfield (protestant) supporters

Sept. 28   Solemn League and Covenant to resist home rule signed by unionists throughout Ulster—'Ulster day'

Oct.   James Stephens's *The crock of gold* (London)

Dec. 30   Second American tour of Abbey Theatre company opens at Fine Arts Theater, Chicago (ends at Boston, Mass., 8 Apr. 1913; see 2 Oct. 1937)

1913

Jan. 16   Third reading of home rule bill in H.C. carried by 367 to 257

Jan. 30   Home rule bill defeated in H.L. by 326 to 69

Jan. 31   Formation of Ulster Volunteer Force

Mar. 7   Trade Union Act, 1913 (2 & 3 Geo. V, c. 30), regulates political activities of unions

c. **June**   Robert Dunlop's *Ireland under the commonwealth* (2 vols, Manchester)

July   'Ireland, Germany and the next war' by Shan Van Vocht (Sir Roger Casement), in *Irish Review*

July 7   Home rule bill again passes H.C., by 352 to 243 (again rejected by H.L., by 302 to 64, 15 July)

Aug. 14   Publication of first fasciculus of Royal Irish Academy's *Dictionary of the Irish language* (Dublin) (last fasciculus, 1976)

Aug. 26   Beginning of strike in Dublin of tramway-men belonging to Larkin's Irish Transport & General Workers' Union (developing into general lock-out of members)

Aug. 30–Sept. 1 Disturbances in Dublin arising out of labour unrest; police make series of baton-charges

Sept. 2 Collapse of 2 tenement houses in Church Street, Dublin, killing 7 people

Sept. 3 Dublin Employers' Federation meeting: most members decide to impose on employees pledge not to belong to Irish Transport & General Workers' Union

Sept. 8 W. B. Yeats's poem, 'September 1913', in *Irish Times*

Dublin city council finally rejects, by 23 to 21 votes, plan to build municipal gallery over River Liffey to house Sir Hugh Lane's pictures, despite campaign led by Yeats and Lady Gregory

Sept. 17 Sir Edward Carson in speech at Newry announces that provisional Ulster government will be set up in event of home rule coming into effect

Sept. 24 Standing cttee of Ulster Unionist Council constitutes itself 'central authority for the provisional government', with Carson as chairman, to function in event of home rule bill becoming law

Oct. 6 Irish Women's Suffrage Federation (see 21 Aug. 1911) welcomes Carson's promise that women will be granted vote under provisional Ulster government

Oct. 7 AE's (George William Russell's) open letter 'To the masters of Dublin' published in *Irish Times*

Oct. 21 Abp Walsh's letter, denouncing evacuation of children of striking or locked-out workers to homes of comrades in Britain, published in *Freeman's Journal*

Oct. 24 Meeting of protestants at Ballymoney, Co. Antrim, resolves to counter-act unionist resistance to home rule

Oct. 27 James Larkin sentenced to 7 months' imprisonment for uttering seditious language (see 26 Aug.)

Nov. 1 Eoin MacNeill's article 'The north began', in *An Claidheamh Soluis*, advocates formation of national volunteer force (cf. 31 Jan.)

Nov. 11 First meeting of steering cttee to form Irish Volunteers; 12 members include MacNeill, Hobson, The O'Rahilly, Patrick Henry Pearse, and D. P. Moran

Nov. 19 Citizen Army launched at meeting of Dublin Civic League in Antient Concert Rooms, Dublin

Nov. 25 Irish Volunteers formed at meeting in Rotunda Rink presided over by Eoin MacNeill

Dec. 4 Royal proclamation prohibiting importation into Ire. of military arms and ammunition

1914

Jan. 18 At closed meeting of Irish Transport & General Workers' Union, members are advised to return to work if not obliged to take 'pledge' (see 3 Sept. 1913); consequently work resumed over next few days

Jan. 31 Agreement between Builders' Association and Builders' Labourers' Union to exclude Irish Transport & General Workers' Union members and to resume normal working

Feb. 7 Report on working-class housing in Dublin of departmental cttee of local government board for Ireland

First number of *Irish Volunteer*

Mar. 20 General Hubert Gough, commanding 3rd Cavalry Brigade stationed at Curragh Camp, Co. Kildare, and 57 of his officers (out of 70) announce that they would prefer dismissal from army to being ordered north to enforce home rule—'Curragh incident'

Apr. 2 Cumann na mBan founded as women's counterpart to Irish Volunteers

Apr. 24-5 Ulster gun-running: *Clydevalley* discharges cargo of rifles at Larne, Donaghadee, and Bangor for U.V.F.

May 12 Asquith announces amending bill to modify home rule bill (see 23 June)

May 25 Home rule bill passes H.C. for third time (see 7 July 1913)

June 10 Publication in *Freeman's Journal* of Redmond's letter suggesting addition to provisional cttee of Irish Volunteers of 25 nominees of Irish party

June 15 James Joyce's *Dubliners* (London)

June 16 Majority of provisional cttee of Irish Volunteers accepts Redmond's demand

June 23 Government of Ireland (Amendment) Bill introduced by government in H.L. provides for temporary exclusion of parts of Ulster from home rule scheme by county option

June 28 Archduke Franz Ferdinand and his wife assassinated at Sarajevo, Bosnia, by Slav nationalist

July 8 Government of Ireland (Amendment) Bill amended in H.L. to provide for permanent exclusion of all Ulster (1st reading in H.C., 15 July; 2nd reading in H.C. postponed indefinitely, 30 July)

July 10 Ulster provisional government meets in Belfast

July 21-4 Buckingham Palace conference: unsuccessful attempt by government, opposition, Irish nationalists and Ulster unionists to reach agreement on Ulster question

July 23 Austria-Hungary presents ultimatum to Serbia (declares war, 28 July)

July 26 Rifles landed at Howth, Co. Dublin, and distributed to waiting columns of Irish Volunteers; Dublin Metropolitan Police, supported by troops of King's Own Scottish Borderers, attempt unsuccessfully to disarm column returning to Dublin; troops returning to barracks open fire on hostile crowd in Bachelors Walk, Dublin; 4 killed, 30 wounded

July 27 Birrell, C.S., announces suspension of William Vesey Harrel, assistant commr of Dublin Metropolitan Police, pending inquiry into Howth gun-running and Bachelors Walk incident, and impugns judgement of Harrel and of Sir John Ross-of-Bladensburg, chief commr

Aug. 1-2   Gun-running for Irish Volunteers at Kilcoole, Co. Wicklow

Aug. 3   Germany declares war on France

John Redmond pledges Irish support for England in event of U.K. entering war and proposes that Irish and Ulster Volunteers should be employed in defence of Ire.

Aug. 4   Germany invades Belgium; U.K. declares war on Germany

Aug. 8   Defence of the Realm Act, 1914 (4 & 5 Geo. V, c. 29)

Aug. 10   Education (Provision of Meals) (Ireland) Act, 1914 (4 & 5 Geo. V, c. 35), enables local authorities to provide meals for school-children

Aug. 15   Press censorship comes into operation (continues till 1921)

Aug. 21   Army order authorises raising of six 'new army' divisions, of which 10th (Irish) begins forming shortly afterwards

Aug.   Establishment of 36th (Ulster) Division, based on U.V.F.

Sept. 6-9   French and British counter-offensive on Marne

Sept. 9   Conference in Dublin of revolutionary leaders, mostly members of I.R.B., discusses using opportunity of European war to organise insurrection in Ire.; attendance includes Thomas James Clarke (presiding), Eamonn Ceannt, Sean MacDermott, Joseph Mary Plunkett, Patrick Pearse, Sean T. O'Kelly, John MacBride, Arthur Griffith, Thomas MacDonagh, James Connolly, and William O'Brien (of labour party)

Sept. 11   Army order authorises raising of 6 more divisions, 'second new army', of which 16th (Irish) Division is to be part

Sept. 15   Bill to suspend operation of home rule measure, introduced by government in H.C., passes all 3 readings without division

Sept. 18   Government of Ireland Act, 1914 (4 & 5 Geo. V, c. 90—home rule act); operation suspended by 4 & 5 Geo. V, c. 88

Sept. 20   Redmond in speech at Woodenbridge, Co. Wicklow, appeals to Irish Volunteers to serve 'not only in Ireland itself, but wherever the firing line extends, in defence of right, of freedom, and religion in this war'

Sept. 24   MacNeill and other members of original cttee of Irish Volunteers (see 11 Nov. 1913) issue manifesto repudiating leadership of Redmond

Sept. 25-6   Asquith visits Dublin; with Redmond addresses recruiting meeting in Mansion House

Sept. 28   Irish Neutrality League formed; president, James Connolly

Oct. 1   Report of royal commn of inquiry into landing of arms at Howth

Oct. 5   Sir Roger Casement's letter protesting against Irish involvement in war on British side published in *Irish Independent*

Oct. 12   Sir Matthew Nathan appointed under-secretary

Oct. 17   First number of *National Volunteer*

Oct. 25   Annual convention of Irish Volunteers at Abbey Theatre, Dublin, under chairmanship of MacNeill; while reaffirming allegiance of Volunteers to Ireland only, he seems to suggest that their ultimate object is to save home rule act and avert partition

Oct. Larkin leaves for U.S.A.; Connolly becomes acting secretary of Irish Transport & General Workers' Union and editor of *Irish Worker*

Nov. 6 Capt. Hon. Arthur O'Neill, M.P. for Mid-Antrim, killed on Marne

Dec. 2-4 Police, acting on orders of military, suppress *Sinn Féin, Irish Freedom* and *Irish Worker*

Dec. 27 Casement and Arthur von Zimmerman sign 'treaty' at Berlin providing for establishment of Irish brigade in German service

1915

Jan. 5 William Thomas Cosgrave (Sinn Féin) returned unopposed as member of Dublin corporation

c. **Jan.** Harry Clarke begins work on stained-glass windows for Honan Chapel, Cork (completed, Apr. 1917)

Feb. 7 First number of *Spark*, extreme nationalist organ (continues till 23 Apr. 1916)

Mar. 18 Defence of the Realm Amendment Act, 1915 (5 Geo. V, c. 34), gives non-alien civilians, charged under Defence of the Realm Act, 1914, right to claim trial by jury in civil court

Apr. 25 British troops, including Irish regiments, make landings in Gallipoli (more landings, including 10th (Irish) Division, 6 Aug.)

May 7 Sinking of *Lusitania* off Old Head of Kinsale, with loss of 1,198 lives

May 25 Announcement of Asquith's coalition cabinet; Carson included as attorney general for England, but Redmond excluded at his own wish

May 29 First number of *Workers' Republic* (new series), edited by Connolly and printed at Liberty Hall

c. **late May** Supreme council of I.R.B. sets up military cttee or council consisting of Pearse, Plunkett, and Ceannt

June 11 John D. Nugent, secretary of Ancient Order of Hibernians (Board of Erin) defeats Thomas Farren, president of Dublin Trades & Labour Council, in Dublin College Green by-election by 2,445 votes to 1,816

June 19 First number of *Nationality*, editor Arthur Griffith

July 29 Douglas Hyde, at *árd-fheis* of Gaelic League at Dundalk, declines to continue as league's president; militant nationalists take control

Aug. 1 Funeral in Dublin of Jeremiah O'Donovan Rossa; graveside oration by Pearse

Sept. First meeting of reorganised supreme council of I.R.B.: president Denis McCullough (Ulster), secretary Sean MacDermott (coopted), treasurer T. J. Clarke (coopted); other members Sean Tobin (Leinster), Diarmuid Lynch (Munster), Alex McCabe (Connacht), Dick Connolly (South of England), Joseph Gleeson (North of England), Patrick McCormick (Scotland), Dr Patrick McCartan and P. H. Pearse, coopted

Oct. Pearse's play 'The singer' written (printed in *Collected works: plays, stories, poems*, Dublin, 1917)

mid Dec. Sixteenth (Irish) Division (see 11 Sept. 1914) leaves for France

Dec.   Military council of I.R.B. formed: MacDermott, Clarke, Pearse, Joseph Mary Plunkett, Eamonn Ceannt (Connolly coopted in Jan. 1916, Thomas MacDonagh early in Apr.)

1916

Jan.   Supreme council of I.R.B. decides to launch insurrection at earliest opportunity

Jan. 19-22   Connolly confers with I.R.B. military council at Dolphin's Barn, Dublin

Feb. 10   Redmond and Lord Wimborne, L.L., address recruiting meeting at Mansion House, Dublin

Mar. 26   Sixteenth (Irish) Division takes over Loos and Hulluch sectors of western front, being opposed by Bavarian division

Apr. 3   Pearse, as director of organisation, issues orders to Irish Volunteers for 3-day march and field manoeuvres throughout Ire., to begin on Easter Sunday (23 Apr.)

Apr. 20   Arrival of *Aud* in Tralee Bay with cargo of arms for Irish Volunteers; arrested by British naval patrol vessel (*Aud*'s captain scuttles her off Queenstown, evening of 21 Apr.)

Apr. 21   Sir Roger Casement lands from German submarine at Banna Strand, Co. Kerry, on mission to warn MacNeill that expected German aid, even if received, would be insufficient for insurrection; arrested shortly afterwards

Apr. 22   Eoin MacNeill, chief of staff of Irish Volunteers, issues countermanding order cancelling activities planned for next day (published in *Sunday Independent*, 23 Apr.)

Apr. 23   Military council meets at Liberty Hall, Clarke presiding: unanimous decision to strike next day (Easter Monday) at noon; proclamation, *The provisional government of the Irish Republic to the people of Ireland*, signed by Clarke and six others, printed at Liberty Hall

Apr. 24   General Post Office and several other buildings in Dublin seized by Irish Volunteers and Citizen Army led by Pearse and Connolly; republican proclamation posted—'Easter rising' or 'Sinn Féin rebellion' begins (noon); arrival in Dublin of troops from the Curragh (later)

Apr. 25   Proclamation of martial law in Dublin city and county (elsewhere in Ire., 29 Apr.)

Apr. 26   Francis Sheehy-Skeffington and two others summarily executed at Portobello military barracks on order of Capt. J. C. Bowen-Colthurst (see 6-7 June); General Post Office damaged and Liberty Hall destroyed by gunfire from Trinity College and fishery protection vessel *Helga* in Liffey; proclamation suspending in Ire. operation of sect. 1 of Defence of the Realm Act, 1915 (see 6-7 June, 17 Aug.)

Apr. 27   Birrell, C.S., and General Sir John Maxwell, newly appointed commander-in-chief, arrive in Ire.

Apr. 29   Unconditional surrender of Pearse, Connolly and MacDonagh ends rebellion; some 3,000 casualties, including about 450 dead

May 1   Over 400 insurgents arrive in Britain for internment

May 3   Pearse, Clarke and MacDonagh, having been convicted of treason at courts martial, executed in Dublin by firing squad (morning); Birrell in H.C. announces his resignation as C.S. (afternoon); Redmond in H.C. appeals to government for leniency for rank and file of insurgents

May 4   Joseph Mary Plunkett, Edward Daly, Michael O'Hanrahan and William Pearse executed

May 5   John MacBride executed

May 8   Con Colbert, Eamonn Ceannt, Michael Mallin, and Sean Heuston executed

Redmond in H.C. warns government that executions are alienating many 'who have not the slightest sympathy with the insurrection'

May 9   Thomas Kent executed, in Cork

May 10   Asquith, P.M., announces appointment of commn of inquiry under Lord Hardinge into Irish disturbances

May 11   H.C. debates Irish crisis; Dillon urges cessation of executions

May 12   Connolly and Sean MacDermott executed

May 12-18   Asquith visits Ire.

May 15-17   Preliminary hearing of charge of high treason against Casement

May 18   Opening of inquiry into rebellion

May 23   Asquith entrusts David Lloyd George with negotiation of settlement of Irish question (resulting in scheme to implement home rule act but to exclude 6 Ulster counties from its application for duration of war)

June 6-7   Capt. J. C. Bowen-Colthurst tried by court martial for murder of Francis Sheehy-Skeffington and 2 other civilians (see 26 Apr.); found guilty while insane (detained in Broadmoor asylum; released, 26 Jan. 1918)

June 12   Ulster Unionist Council accepts Lloyd George's proposals for immediate implementation of home rule, 6 Ulster counties being temporarily excluded

June 23   Convention in Belfast, representative of nationalists of Antrim, Down, Armagh, Fermanagh, Tyrone and Londonderry, agrees by 475 to 265 to exclusion of these counties from operation of home rule act

June 26-9   Casement on trial; convicted of high treason and sentenced to death

July   *Catholic Bulletin*, lacking for first time imprimatur of Abp Walsh, begins series entitled 'Events of Easter week', extolling catholic piety of rebels

July 1   Somme offensive begins; 36th (Ulster) Division involved; 60,000 British casualties, including 20,000 killed, the heaviest loss suffered in a single day by any army in first world war (see 13 Nov.)

July 3   Report of royal commn on the rebellion in Ireland

July 20   Public meeting at Derry in opposition to partition, leading to formation of Anti-Partition League (afterwards Irish Nation League)

July 22   George Bernard Shaw's letter, 'Shall Roger Casement hang?', published in *Manchester Guardian* (having been rejected by *The Times*); asks that Casement be treated as prisoner of war

July 24   Asquith in H.C. admits government's unwillingness to allow undiminished Irish representation at Westminster under Lloyd George's home rule scheme, thereby precipitating debate in which failure of home rule negotiations becomes evident; Redmond repudiates Lloyd George's scheme

Aug. 3   Casement hanged in Pentonville jail, London

Henry Edward Duke becomes C.S.

Aug. 17-18   Irish Trade Union Congress and Labour Party convention at Sligo shows neutral attitude to rebellion

Aug. 17   Royal commn app. to inquire into deaths of Francis Sheehy-Skeffington (see 26 Apr.) and 2 others (report published, 16 Oct.)

Aug. 23   Act (6 & 7 Geo. V, c. 45) extending 'Greenwich mean time' to Ire. (in place of 'Dublin mean time', 25 minutes behind (effective, 1 Oct.))

Sept. 9   Thomas M. Kettle, M.P., killed leading charge on Somme

Sept. 25   Yeats's poem 'Easter 1916' (published privately, London, 1916)

Oct. 10   Catholic bps approve project for Irish missionary effort in China (afterwards known as Maynooth Mission to China, or St Columban's Foreign Mission Society; training-college opened at Galway, 7 Feb. 1918)

Nov. 4   Lt-General Sir Bryan Mahon replaces General Sir John Maxwell as commander-in-chief in Ire.

Nov. 13   Somme offensive ends, British having suffered 420,000 casualties, French nearly 200,000, Germans 450,000; little change in western front

Nov.   James Stephens's *Insurrection in Dublin* (Dublin)

Dec. 7   Lloyd George (lib.) app. P.M. of coalition government (see 7 Apr. 1908, 23 Oct. 1922)

Dec. 13   First public performance of Lennox Robinson's 'The white-headed boy', at Abbey Theatre, Dublin

Dec. 22-3   Release from Frongoch and Reading jails of remaining untried Irish political prisoners; convicted insurgents remain in jail

Dec. 29   James Joyce's *A portrait of the artist as a young man* (New York)

1917

Feb. 1   Germany begins unrestricted submarine warfare: all ships, including merchant and neutral, to be sunk at sight and without warning in war zone around British, French, and Italian coasts

Feb. 5   North Roscommon by-election: George Noble Count Plunkett (father of Joseph Mary Plunkett), endorsed as candidate by Irish Nation League and Sinn Féin, is returned with 3,022 votes to 1,708 for Thomas Devine (nationalist) and 687 for Jasper Tully (independent nationalist), but declines to take seat

Feb. 17   Revival of Griffith's *Nationality*

Mar. 7 Lloyd George, P.M., tells H.C.: 'in the north-eastern portion of Ireland you have a population as hostile to Irish rule as the rest of Ireland is to British rule . . . as alien in blood, in religious faith, in traditions, in outlook as alien from the rest of Ireland in this respect as the inhabitants of Fife or Aberdeen'; Redmond and Irish nationalists withdraw

Mar. 8-15 (O.S. Feb. 23-Mar. 2) Revolution in Russia, culminating in establishment of provisional government and abdication of Tzar Nicholas II (15 Mar.)—'February revolution' (see 6-7 Nov./24-5 Oct.)

Apr. 6 U.S.A. declares war on Germany

Apr. 17 Jane Barlow, novelist, dies

Apr. 21 First number of *Young Ireland*, editor Aodh de Blacam

Apr. Ford Motor Co. begins construction at Cork of factory for production of Fordson tractors; proprietor Henry Ford, son of 1847 emigrant from Clonakilty, Co. Cork, to Michigan, U.S.A.

May 8 Declaration against partition signed by 16 catholic and 3 protestant bps, and several prominent laymen, published

May 9 South Longford by-election: Joseph P. McGuinness (Sinn Féin), in Lewes jail, defeats Patrick McKenna (nationalist) by 1,493 to 1,461

May 16 Lloyd George proposes to introduce bill for immediate application of home rule act, with exclusion for 5 years of 6 Ulster counties, or, as alternative, holding of convention of both parties to produce self-government scheme

May 21 Lloyd George announces 'a convention of Irishmen of all parties for the purpose of producing a scheme of Irish self-government'

June 7 Major William H. K. Redmond, M.P., killed in action on western front

June 10 Demonstration in Dublin on behalf of 1916 rebellion prisoners; John Mills, D.M.P. inspector, fatally injured by blow from hurley

June 16 Release from jails in Britain of some 120 remaining Irish prisoners serving sentences for part in rebellion, including MacNeill, Countess Markiewicz, Eamon de Valera, and Joseph P. McGuinness

June 24-5 Disturbances at Cork, as sequel to return of prisoners

July 1 Exchange of shares effects amalgamation of Belfast Bank with London City & Midland Bank (later Midland Bank)

July 10 East Clare by-election: Eamon de Valera (Sinn Féin) 5,010, Patrick Lynch (nationalist) 2,035

July 25 First meeting of Irish Convention, in Trinity College, Dublin; Sir Horace Plunkett elected chairman; Sinn Féin party abstains

July 31 Francis Ledwidge, farm labourer and poet, killed during third battle of Ypres

c. **July** I.R.B. adopts new constitution

Aug. 10 Kilkenny city by-election: William Thomas Cosgrave (Sinn Féin) 772, John Magennis (nationalist) 392

Sept. 25   Thomas Ashe dies in Mountjoy jail after forcible feeding (large funeral, 30 Sept.)

Oct. 3   Agreement for merger of Ulster Bank with London County & Westminster Bank

Oct. 14   Nathaniel Hone, landscape painter, dies

Oct. 25-6   Tenth Sinn Féin *árd-fheis* meets at Mansion House, Dublin; de Valera elected president on first day

Oct. 27   De Valera elected president of Irish Volunteers

Nov. 6-7 (O.S. Oct. 24-5)   Vladimir Lenin and Leon Trotsky achieve power in Russia: 'October revolution'

Dec. 5   Russia signs armistice with Germany and other central powers at Brest-Litovsk (peace, 3 Mar. 1918)

Dec. 11   First public performance of Oliver St John Gogarty's 'Blight', at Abbey Theatre, Dublin

1918

Jan. 8   President Woodrow Wilson propounds 14 points for world peace in address to congress

Jan. 15   In Irish convention Bp O'Donnell, Joseph Devlin, and other nationalists break with Redmond over fiscal autonomy

Feb. 2   South Armagh by-election: Patrick Donnelly (nationalist) 2,324, Patrick McCartan (Sinn Féin) 1,305, T. W. Richardson (independent unionist) 40

Feb. 6   Representation of the People Act, 1918, and Redistribution of Seats (Ireland) Act, 1918 (7 & 8 Geo. V, cc 64, 65); all men over 21 and most women over 30 enfranchised; constituencies made approximately equal in size of electorate

Mar. 6   John Redmond dies

Mar. 12   Dillon elected chairman of Irish parliamentary party in place of Redmond

Apr. 5   Irish convention meets for last time

Apr. 9   Irish catholic episcopal standing cttee protests at government's conscription proposals

Lloyd George, P.M., introduces Military Service Bill in H.C., with provision to empower government to extend conscription to Ire.

Apr. 12   Report of Irish convention published (see 25 July 1917)

Apr. 13   Raid on R.I.C. barracks at Gortatlea, Co. Kerry; two attackers killed

Apr. 18   Military Service (No. 2) Act, 1918 (8 Geo. V, c. 5)

Mansion House conference of representatives of Sinn Féin, Irish parliamentary party, All-for-Ireland League, and Irish Labour Party to concert opposition to conscription; delegation goes to Maynooth to meet catholic bps also in conference

Apr. 23   One-day general strike (except in Ulster) in protest against conscription

May 4   Edward Shortt app. C.S.

May 5   Dillon and de Valera speak from same platform at anti-conscription meeting at Ballaghadereen, Co. Mayo

May 17-18   Sinn Féin leaders, including de Valera, Griffith, Countess Markievicz, Darrell Figgis, W. T. Cosgrave, arrested, simultaneously with publication of vice-regal proclamation alleging Irish collaboration with Germany— 'German plot'; 73 detainees deported to Britain

May   Brinsley Macnamara's *The valley of the squinting windows* (Dublin)

June 20   East Cavan by-election: Griffith (Sinn Féin) 3,795, J. F. O'Hanlon (nationalist) 2,581

June   Ulster Unionist Labour Association formed

Aug. 15   First number of *An tÓglach*, organ of Irish Volunteers

Sept.   George O'Brien's *The economic history of Ireland in the eighteenth century* (Dublin)

Oct. 4   German note to U.S.A. seeks armistice and peace on basis of Wilson's fourteen points

Oct. 10   Irish mail-boat *Leinster* sunk by German submarine, with loss of some 500 lives

Nov. 1   Irish labour party withdraws from expected general election contests

Nov. 3   Austria-Hungary, having largely disintegrated, signs armistice with Italy (Emperor Charles I flees to Switzerland, 11 Nov.)

Nov. 4-9   Revolution in Germany: navy mutiny at Kiel (4 Nov.); Kaiser Wilhelm II flees to Netherlands (9 Nov.); Germany becomes republic

Nov. 11   Armistice between Germany and allied powers effective (11 a.m.); end of first world war

Nov. 21   Parliament (Qualification of Women) Act, 1918 (8 & 9 Geo. V, c. 47), entitles women to sit and vote in H.C.

Dec. 2-3   Dillon, MacNeill, and lord mayor of Dublin confer in attempt to distribute Irish party and Sinn Féin candidates singly among 8 Ulster constituencies where, with a unionist candidate present, seat expected to go to protestants in three-cornered contest but to catholics in straight contest (final allocation made by Cardinal Logue, 4 Dec.)

Dec. 4   Nomination day for general election: 25 Sinn Féin candidates returned unopposed

Dec. 14-28   General election (polling 14 Dec., count and declaration 28 Dec.): in G.B.—con. 357, lib. 163, lab. 61, nat. 1, others 20; in Ire.—Sinn Féin 73, nat 6, un. 25, ind. un. 1; 473 elected as coalition candidates—'coupon election' (see Dec. 1910, 15 Nov. 1922) (Countess Markievicz, Sinn Féin M.P. for St Patrick's Ward, Dublin, first woman to be elected to H.C.)

1919

Jan. 13   James Ian Macpherson app. C.S.

Jan. 15   Proportional representation (single transferable vote) in use for first time, in Sligo municipal elections

Jan. 18   First full meeting of Paris peace conference

Jan. 21   Seumas Robinson, Sean Treacy, Dan Breen, and 6 other Irish Volunteers ambush cart carrying gelignite at Soloheadbeg, Co. Tipperary, killing 2 policemen; afterwards regarded as beginning of war of independence

First meeting of Dáil Éireann: Sinn Féin M.P.s (other than 36 in prison) confer in Mansion House, Dublin, and unanimously adopt provisional constitution of Dáil Éireann ('Irish parliament'), declaration of independence, address to the free nations of the world, and democratic programme

Jan. 22   Cathal Brugha elected acting president (*priomh-aire*) of Dáil Éireann (see 1 Apr.)

Jan. 25   Beginning of strike in Belfast of members of unions belonging to Federation of Engineering and Ship-building Trades for 44-hour working week; shipyards, gas-works, electricity stations, tramways, etc., closed down

Feb. 3   De Valera escapes from Lincoln jail (remaining Sinn Féin detainees released, 6-10 Mar.) (see 17-18 May 1980)

Feb. 7   Thomas Johnson and Cathal O'Shannon admitted to International Labour and Socialist Congress at Berne as Irish delegation separate from British

Feb. 20   End of strike in Belfast with reopening of shipyards; 47-hour working week granted

Apr. 1   De Valera elected president of Dáil Éireann (see 9 Jan. 1922)

Apr. 4   Dáil Éireann authorises issue of 'republican bonds' to value of £250,000

Apr. 14-25   General strike at Limerick; establishment of 'Limerick soviet'

Apr. 28   League of Nations covenant adopted by Paris peace conference (League begins functioning, 10 Jan. 1920)

May 3   Three delegates from Irish-American 'Friends of Irish Freedom', having sought from President Wilson in Paris hearing for Dáil Éireann at peace conference, arrive in Ire. to investigate political situation (submit report, 3 June)

May 29   Public Health (Medical Treatment of Children) (Ireland) Act, 1919 (9 & 10 Geo. V, c. 16), provides for medical care of elementary school children

June 1   De Valera leaves Ire. for New York (arrives, 11 June)

June 3   Local Government (Ireland) Act, 1919 (9 & 10 Geo. V, c. 19), provides for proportional representation at local authority elections

June 15   John William Alcock and Arthur Whitten Brown touch down near Clifden, Co. Galway, completing first non-stop transatlantic flight

June 18   Dáil Éireann decree establishing 'arbitration courts' (some already in existence several months previously)

June 28   Treaty signed at Versailles between Germany and victorious allied powers

July 4   Proclamation suppressing Sinn Féin, Irish Volunteers, Cumann na mBan, and Gaelic League in Co. Tipperary as illegal associations under 50 & 51 Vict., c. 26, sects 3 & 4 (cf. 10 Sept.)

July   P. O Cathasaigh's (Sean O'Casey's) *The story of the Irish Citizen Army* (Dublin)

Aug. 19 Dáil Éireann resolves 'that clergymen be *ex-officio* justices' in its 'arbitration courts'

Aug. 20 Dáil Éireann resolves that Irish Volunteers, as well as its own members and officials, 'must swear allegiance to the Irish Republic and to the Dáil'

Sept. 7 2nd Cork brigade of Irish Volunteers under Liam Lynch fire on soldiers at Fermoy, Co. Cork (soldiers retaliate by looting shops, 8-9 Sept.)

Sept. 10 Proclamation suppressing Sinn Féin, Irish Volunteers, Gaelic League, and kindred bodies in Cork (throughout Ire., 25 Nov.)

Sept. 12 Dáil Éireann declared illegal

Sept. 17 Police and military, acting on warrant, enter *Cork Examiner* premises and dismantle machinery

Sept. George O'Brien's *The economic history of Ireland in the seventeenth century* (Dublin)

Oct. 7 Cabinet committee appointed to consider Irish self-government

Nov. 11 First number of *Irish Bulletin*, organ of Sinn Féin and Dáil Éireann

Clash in Dublin streets between Trinity College and University College students arising out of observance of memory of war dead (11 a.m.)

Nov. 24 Introduction in H.C. of Macpherson's Irish education bill to replace semi-independent boards with education department and establish county education cttees

Dec. 9 Standing cttee of Irish catholic bps objects to Macpherson's education bill, which is consequently withdrawn (22 Dec.)

Dec. 15 Police seize on warrant type and plant for production of *Freeman's Journal* (material returned, 24 Jan. 1920; publication resumed, 28 Jan.)

Dec. 19 Sean Treacy, Dan Breen, Martin Savage, and 8 other members of Irish Republican Army (new name for Irish Volunteers) make unsuccessful attempt on life of Viscount French, L.L., at Ashtown, near Phoenix Park, Dublin; Savage killed

Dec. 21 I.R.A. group led by Peadar Clancy raid *Irish Independent* offices and demolish production plant, owing to resentment at paper's description of Savage as would-be assassin

1920

Jan. 2 R.I.C. enrols first of several thousand British recruits, later dubbed 'Black and Tans'

Jan. 15 Polling in elections to borough and urban district councils: Sinn Féin, with nationalists and labour, obtain control of 172 out of 206 councils

Jan. 30 Mayoral elections: unionist elected at Belfast, nationalist at Derry, labour at Wexford, and Sinn Féiners in 8 other boroughs

Jan. Dáil Éireann floats external loan

Feb. 20 Imposition of curfew, midnight to 5 a.m., in Dublin Metropolitan Police district (effective, 23 Feb.)

Feb. 25 Government of Ireland Bill introduced in H.C. (see 23 Dec.)

Mar. 20   Tomás Mac Curtáin, lord mayor of Cork and commandant of 1st Cork brigade of I.R.A., shot dead, allegedly by R.I.C.

Ulster Unionist Council accepts Government of Ireland Bill

Mar. 26   Alan Bell, magistrate investigating Sinn Féin and Dáil Éireann funds, taken from tramcar in Dublin and shot dead on order of Michael Collins, Dáil Éireann minister for finance and I.R.A. director of organisation and intelligence

Apr. 12   Sir Hamar Greenwood app. C.S.

Apr.   Disturbances at Derry (renewed outbreaks, May and June)

May 16-19   Soviet established at central creamery, Knocklong, Co. Limerick

May 23   Beatification by Pope Benedict XV of Abp Oliver Plunkett (see 1 July 1681, 12 Oct. 1975)

'Munitions strike' by railwaymen at Kingstown, Co. Dublin (spreads soon to most of country; extended later to transporting of armed troops; see 21 Dec.)

June   Elections of county councils, rural district councils and boards of guardians: Sinn Féin successes

June 16   Members of R.I.C. at Listowel, Co. Kerry, reject order to vacate their barracks to military force—'Listowel police mutiny'

June 19   Outbreak of disturbances at Derry, resulting in 18 deaths

June 26   British general and 2 colonels kidnapped while on fishing trip on Blackwater, near Fermoy

June 28   Connaught Rangers mutiny at Jullundur, Punjab (spreading to Solan, 30 June)

July 17   Lt-col. G. B. F. Smyth, divisional commr of R.I.C. in Munster, shot dead by I.R.A. at Cork (funeral at Banbridge, Co. Down, 21 July, occasions expulsion of catholics from town and from nearby Dromore)

July 21-4   Disturbances in Belfast: expulsions of catholics from shipyards, engineering works, etc.; rioting and over a dozen deaths

July 27   Inauguration of para-military force, later called Auxiliary Division, R.I.C., recruited from ex-officers of British army

July 29   Council of Dublin Chamber of Commerce calls for withdrawal of government's home-rule bill and granting of 'a measure of complete self-government'

Aug. 6   Boycott of Belfast protestant firms instituted by Dáil Éireann despite opposition from Ernest Blythe, sole Ulster protestant member, and others

Aug. 9   Restoration of Order in Ireland Act, 1920 (10 & 11 Geo. V, c. 31)

Daniel Mannix, catholic abp of Melbourne, having been prohibited from landing in Ire. owing to his active support for Sinn Féin, disembarks in England (leaves for Rome, Mar. 1921)

Aug. 22   Murder of District Inspector O. R. Swanzy at Lisburn precipitates attacks on persons and property of Sinn Féiners and their expulsion from town

Aug. 23-31   More disturbances in Belfast: stone-throwing, arson, looting, intimidation, and some 30 deaths; curfew imposed (31 Aug.)

Sept. 20   Black and Tan raid on Balbriggan, Co. Dublin

Sept. 28   Disturbances at Mallow, Co. Cork: raid on military barracks followed by sack of town by soldiers

Oct. 25   Terence MacSwiney, lord mayor of Cork and commandant of 1st Cork brigade of I.R.A., dies at Brixton prison on seventy-fourth day of hunger-strike

Nov. 1   Kevin Barry executed in Mountjoy jail for murder of soldier on 20 Sept.; first execution since May 1916

Enrolment of recruits begins in Ulster for Special Constabulary Force in three classes: 'A' (full-time temporary constables; see 10, 15 Dec. 1925), 'B' (part-time, serving locally; see 30 Apr. 1970), and 'C' (emergency reserve; see 4 Feb. 1926)

Nov. 2   Military raid on University College, Dublin

Nov. 9   Lloyd George declares at lord mayor's banquet in London: 'we have murder by the throat!'

Nov. 21   'Bloody Sunday': I.R.A. groups, on order of Collins, systematically shoot dead 14 suspected secret service agents in their Dublin homes; auxiliary police shoot dead Peadar Clancy and Richard McKee, commandant and vice-commandant respectively of Dublin brigade of I.R.A. and organisers of these killings; Black and Tans open fire on crowd at Gaelic football match in Croke Park, Dublin, killing 12

Nov. 27   Arson attacks by I.R.A. in Liverpool

Nov. 28   Patrol of 18 auxiliary police ambushed and entirely wiped out by 3rd Cork brigade of I.R.A. at Kilmichael, between Macroom and Dunmanway, Co. Cork

Dec. 10   Proclamation of martial law in Cork, Kerry, Limerick and Tipperary: unauthorised possession of arms, unauthorised wearing of uniform of crown forces, and aiding, harbouring, or abetting rebels become capital offences

Dec. 11   De Valera leaves U.S.A. for Ire. (arrives, 23 Dec.)

Dec. 11-12   Sack of Cork by auxiliary police and Black and Tans: City Hall, Corn Exchange, and Carnegie Free Library completely destroyed and over £2½ millions of damage caused

Dec. 21   Railwaymen accede to call of labour party to resume normal handling of government traffic as alternative to closure of railways by government

Dec. 23   Government of Ireland Act, 1920 (10 & 11 Geo. V, c. 67), provides for 2 subordinate Irish parliaments and administrations, one in north, other in south, and council of Ire. for consultation on common interests

1921

Jan. 1   Beginning of government-authorised reprisals with destruction of 7 houses at Midleton, Co. Cork, by order of military governor

Feb. 4   Carson announces to Ulster Unionist Council his resignation as leader of Ulster unionists; Sir James Craig elected in his place (see 21 Feb. 1910, 24 Sept. 1913)

Feb. 28 Six republican prisoners executed by firing squad in Cork; 6 British soldiers subsequently killed in incidents in Cork city

Mar. 7 George Clancy, mayor of Limerick, and 2 other leading citizens shot dead in their houses

Mar. 14 Six republican prisoners hanged in Dublin; general stoppage of work till 11 a.m. in Dublin at request of Irish labour party

Mar. 26 Auxiliary police discover clandestine offices of *Irish Bulletin* in Molesworth Street, Dublin

May 2 Viscount Fitzalan sworn in as L.L.; first catholic to hold viceroyalty since reign of James II

May 5 Craig and de Valera meet in Dublin

May 13 Nomination day for general election to two parliaments established by Government of Ireland Act, 1920: all candidates nominated for election to Southern Ireland parliament returned unopposed (124 Sinn Féiners, 4 independents)

May 24 N.I. general election: un. 40, nat. 6, Sinn Féin 6 (see 3 Apr. 1925)

May 25 Custom House, Dublin, destroyed and several lives lost in attack by I.R.A.; records of local government board and other bodies included in destruction; *c.* 100 men of Dublin brigade of I.R.A. captured

June 7 Preliminary meeting of H.C. of N.I.; appointment of cabinet with Sir James Craig as P.M. (created Viscount Craigavon, 20 Jan. 1927; see 24 Nov. 1940)

June 22 George V opens N.I. parliament at Belfast City Hall

June 28 Southern Ireland parliament, attended by only 15 of possible 64 senators and 4 of possible 128 members of H.C., meets in Council Room of Department of Agriculture, Upper Merrion Street, Dublin (see 16 Aug.)

July 9 Truce signed by representatives of British army in Ire. and I.R.A. (effective, 11 July)

July 9-15 Disturbances in Belfast: over 20 deaths

Aug. 16 Sinn Féin M.P.s elected to Southern Ireland parliament assemble in Mansion House, Dublin, as second Dáil Éireann (see 21 Jan. 1919, 9 Sept. 1922)

Sept. 7 Organisation, becoming known as Association of Our Lady of Mercy (renamed Legion of Mary, 15 Nov. 1925), formed by Frank Duff and others

Sept. 14 Dáil Éireann selects 5 delegates to negotiate agreement with Lloyd George's government

Sept. George O'Brien's *The economic history of Ireland from the union to the famine* (London)

Oct. 11 Anglo-Irish conference begins in London

Oct. 18 Roderic Connolly, Liam O'Flaherty, and others expel William O'Brien and Cathal O'Shannon from Socialist Party of Ireland on ground of 're-formism' (party renamed Communist Party of Ireland, early Nov.) (cf. 11 June 1933)

Nov. 22 Operational control of R.I.C. in N.I. passes to Belfast government

Dec. 6 Anglo-Irish treaty signed in London

IRELAND, 1921–76

INTRODUCTION

FOR the final section of this chronology the compilers are very largely dependent on printed sources and secondary works. The coverage of events is much the same as for the preceding period. Both parts of Ireland are treated on the same criteria of selection, but inevitably Northern Ireland receives proportionately greater attention from 1969 onwards. Selection, of course, presents an increasingly difficult problem as we approach the present time, and this is partly the reason for an expansion in the scale of treatment from 1969; for where the past is so close to us it is often impossible to decide which in a series of crowded events are the most significant or the most representative. The difficulty is aggravated by the paucity of scholarly monographs on Irish history from 1921; and this accounts for the omission of certain events as yet imperfectly identified and assessed.

We have received valuable help with this section of the chronology, which we have pleasure in acknowledging, from the late Dr Desmond Clarke, Professor Aloys Fleischmann, Profesor Vivian Mercier, Professor David W. Miller, Dr Arthur H. Mitchell, Dr Leon Ó Broin, Dr Tarlach Ó Raifeartaigh, Mr J. A. Oliver, Dr Brian Reynolds, Dr Brian M. Walker, Dr J. H. Whyte, and from the secretary of the Irish Council of Churches.

CHRONOLOGY 1921–76

T. W. MOODY, J. G. SIMMS, AND C. J. WOODS

1921

Dec. 14 Dáil Éireann begins debate on Anglo-Irish treaty (ends, 7 Jan. 1922)

Dec. 14 Local Government (Emergency Powers) Act (Northern Ireland), 1921 (12 Geo. V, c. 5), permits N.I. government to dissolve unco-operative local councils (Fermanagh county council dissolved, 21 Dec.; 12 more councils dissolved, 14 Mar.–21 Apr. 1922)

1922

Jan. 7 Dáil Éireann approves Anglo-Irish treaty, by 64 to 57

Jan. 9 De Valera resigns as president of Dáil Éireann and stands for reelection; Griffith elected (10 Jan.) (see 1 Apr. 1919, 12 Aug. 1922)

Jan. 14 Provisional government for I.F.S. elected by members of Southern Ireland parliament (see 16 Aug. 1921): Michael Collins chairman (see 22 Aug.)

Jan. 16 Members of provisional government received by L.L. at Dublin castle: formal transfer of power

Jan. 21 Agreement between Collins and Craig, ending Belfast boycott (see 6 Aug. 1920) in return for guarantees to Belfast catholics

Feb. 1 Date fixed for final transfer of duties to 7 government departments in N.I. created by L.L. under Government of Ireland Act, 1920

Minister for education in provisional government assumes powers of commrs of national education and confirms that Irish is to be taught at least 1 hour daily in national schools

Feb. 2 James Joyce's *Ulysses* (Paris)

Feb. 5 Cumann na mBan rejects treaty

Feb. 6 Achille Ratti elected pope as Pius XI

Feb. 12-15 Outbreak of shooting in Belfast, origin attributed to I.R.A.: 27 killed, 68 wounded

Feb. 17 First day of issue of British postage stamps overprinted 'Rialtas Sealadach na hÉireann' ('Provisional Government of Ireland')

Feb. 21 Enlistment begins for police force of provisional government, commonly called civic guard (see 8 Aug. 1923)

Mar. 26-7 Conference of anti-treaty members of I.R.A. establishes executive council headed by Oscar Traynor

Mar. 30 Peace pact concluded at Irish conference in London; signatories include Collins, Craig, and Winston Churchill

Mar. 31 Irish Free State (Agreement) Act, 1922 (12 Geo. V, c. 4 [U.K.]), giving force of law to treaty articles, and providing for transfer of powers to provisional government and for dissolution of parliament of Southern Ire. within 4 months

Apr. 7 Civil Authorities (Special Powers) Act (Northern Ireland), 1922 (12 & 13 Geo. V, c. 5), effective for 1 year only (made permanent by 23 & 24 Geo. V, c. 12 [N.I.], 9 May 1933)

Apr. 14 Anti-treaty force under Rory O'Connor seizes Four Courts, Dublin

Apr. 24 General strike throughout I.F.S. against 'militarism', called by labour party

May 20 Pact between Collins and de Valera providing for panel of Sinn Féin candidates at forthcoming dáil elections, to be drawn from pro- and anti-treaty parties in proportion to their strength in existing dáil

Shane's Castle, Co. Antrim, attacked by armed men (believed to be I.R.A.) and burned: one of several attacks on property in Antrim and Down

May 20-22 Week-end of violence in Belfast: 14 killed, many injured, buildings set on fire; William John Twaddell, member of N.I. parliament, shot dead (22 May)

May 23 N.I. government declares I.R.A., Irish Volunteers, I.R.B., Cumann na mBan, and Fianna illegal organisations

May 31 Constabulary Act (Northern Ireland), 1922 (12 & 13 Geo. V, c. 8), establishes Royal Ulster Constabulary

June 16 I.F.S. general election: pro-treaty Sinn Féin 58, anti-treaty Sinn Féin 36, lab. 17, farmers 7, ind. 10 (see 16 Aug. 1921, 9 Sept. 1922, 27 Aug. 1923)

June 22 Field Marshal Sir Henry Wilson assassinated in London (2 members of London battalion I.R.A. arrested; hanged 10 Aug.)

June 27 Members of anti-treaty force in Four Courts (see 14 Apr.) kidnap pro-treaty General J. J. 'Ginger' O'Connell

June 28 Provisional government forces attack Four Courts; beginning of civil war

June 30 Destruction of Four Courts, including treasury of Public Record Office; Rory O'Connor surrenders

June 30-July 5 Government troops attack anti-treaty headquarters in O'Connell Street, Dublin; buildings destroyed; Cathal Brugha wounded and captured (5 July, dies 7 July)

July 6 Provisional government issues call to arms

July 20 Limerick and Waterford captured by government troops (Cork, 11 Aug.)

Aug. 4 Constabulary (Ireland) Act, 1922 (12 & 13 Geo. V, c. 55 [U.K.]), provides for disbandment of R.I.C. by 31 Aug.

Aug. 12 Arthur Griffith dies, of cerebral haemorrhage (see 9 Jan.)

Aug. 22 Michael Collins killed in ambush at Bealnablath, between Macroom and Bandon, Co. Cork (see 14 Jan., 9 Sept.)

Aug. 25 William Thomas Cosgrave app. chairman of provisional government

Sept. 9 Third dáil (see 16 June) assembles as constituent assembly and elects Cosgrave president, i.e. head of provisional government; anti-treaty deputies absent (see 22 Aug. 1922, 9 Mar. 1932)

Sept. 11 Local Government Act (Northern Ireland), 1922 (12 & 13 Geo. V, c. 15), abolishing proportional representation in local government elections and requiring declaration of allegiance from persons elected to, or employed by, local authorities

Sept. 28 Dáil approves motion to establish military courts with power to impose death penalty

Oct. 10 Catholic bps issue joint pastoral condemning resistance to provisional government; 'the guerilla warfare now being carried out by the Irregulars is without moral sanction, and therefore the killing of national soldiers in the course of it is murder before God'

Oct. 23 Andrew Bonar Law (con.) app. P.M. of U.K. (see 7 Dec. 1916, 20 May 1923)

Oct. 25 Dáil approves Constitution of the Irish Free State (Saorstát Éireann) Bill

Oct. 28 Benito Mussolini marches on Rome (forms fascist government, 30 Oct.)

Nov. 15 U.K. general election: in G.B.—con. 333, lab. 142, lib. 62, national lib. 53, others 12; in N.I.—un. 11, nat. 2 (see 14 Dec. 1918, 6 Dec. 1923)

Nov. 17 First of series of 77 executions of Irregulars by shooting (last, 2 May 1923)

Erskine Childers tried by military court for unlawful possession of revolver (shot 24 Nov.)

Dec. 5 Irish Free State Constitution Act, 1922 (Session 2) (13 Geo. V, c. 1 [U.K.]), ratifying constitution as approved by dáil (see 25 Oct.) and treaty articles (both documents included as schedules to act)

Dec. 6 Dáil approves nominations to executive council of I.F.S.: W. T. Cosgrave president and minister for finance, Kevin O'Higgins vice-president and minister for home affairs, Richard Mulcahy minister for defence, Eoin MacNeill minister for education, Ernest Blythe minister for local government, Joseph McGrath minister for industry and commerce, Desmond Fitzgerald minister for external affairs

T. M. Healy sworn in as first governor general of I.F.S.

First day of issue of 2d. denomination of definitive series of I.F.S. postagestamps (1½d. denomination, 2 Feb. 1923; other denominations follow)

Dec. 7 Both houses of N.I. parliament agree, without division, to opt out of I.F.S.

Dec. 8 Rory O'Connor, Liam Mellows and 2 other Irregulars executed without trial as reprisal for assassination of pro-treaty deputy, Sean Hales

Powers of L.L. lapse in N.I. (duke of Abercorn sworn in as first governor, 12 Dec.)

Dec. 20 Adaptation of Enactments Act (1922/2 [I.F.S.]), adapting British acts in force on 6 Dec. 1922 to circumstances of I.F.S.

1923

Jan. 23 United Council of Christian Churches and Religious Communions in Ireland, a development of joint cttees of presbyterian church with methodist church and Church of Ireland, meets for first time, 8 protestant churches being represented (see 10 Oct. 1905, 11 June 1910, 15 Oct. 1911, 4 Nov. 1966)

Jan. 29 House of Senator Sir Horace Plunkett at Foxrock, Co. Dublin, burned by Irregulars (one of series of attacks on senators and their property)

Feb. 12 Cosgrave signs agreement in London to pay land annuities to British treasury (not made public till 9 Apr. 1932)

Mar. 22 Members of Association of our Lady of Mercy (see 7 Sept. 1921) begin rehabilitation work amongst prostitutes in Bentley Place district of Dublin

Mar. 28 Double Taxation (Relief) Act, 1923 (1923/8 [I.F.S.]), granting relief where there is liability to both I.F.S. and British tax (similar provision in section 5, Irish Free State (Consequential Provisions) Act, 1922, 13 Geo. V, c. 2 [U.K.]))

Local Government (Temporary Provisions) Act, 1923 (1923/9 [I.F.S.]), abolishing workhouse system of poor relief and providing alternatives (continued by Local Government (Temporary Provisions) (Amendment) Act, 1924 (1924/13))

Mar. 31 Customs barriers between I.F.S. and U.K. become effective at midnight

Apr. 10 Liam Lynch, chief of Irregular I.R.A., fatally wounded in engagement with government forces in Comeragh mountains, Co. Waterford

Apr. 12 First performance of Sean O'Casey's 'The shadow of a gunman' in Abbey Theatre, Dublin

Apr. 27 De Valera announces that offensive operations are suspended (similar order by Frank Aiken for Irregular I.R.A. council)

May 20 Bonar Law resigns (dies 30 Oct.; see 23 Oct. 1922, 22 May 1923)

May 23 Stanley Baldwin (con.) app. P.M. of U.K. (see 20 May 1923, 22 Jan. 1924)

May 24 De Valera orders his followers to call off the armed struggle

May 31 Boyne obelisk blown up by unknown persons (see 17 Apr. 1736)

June 3 James Larkin at meeting of No. 1 branch of Irish Transport & General Workers Union delivers speech attacking union executive led by William O'Brien, thereby initiating major split in labour movement

June 11 Sinn Féin reorganisation discussed at meeting of members at Mansion House, Dublin

June 15 Workers' Union of Ireland launched by Larkin

Intoxicating Liquor (Northern Ireland) Act (13 & 14 Geo. V, c. 12) extends Sunday closing to Belfast, abolishes exemption of travellers and reduces number of liquor licences with compensation (amended by 17 & 18 Geo. V, c. 21, 21 Dec. 1927)

June 22 Public Records Act (Northern Ireland), 1923 (13 & 14 Geo. V, c. 20), establishing Public Record Office of Northern Ireland

Education Act (Northern Ireland), 1923 (13 & 14 Geo. V, c. 21), establishing non-denominational schools under local authorities

June 26 Presbyterian general assembly expresses disapproval of education act

July 16 Censorship of Films Act, 1923 (1923/23 [I.F.S.])

July 20 Announcement of appointment of Eoin MacNeill as I.F.S. representative on boundary commn

July 24 Land Law (Commission) Act, 1923 (1923/27 [I.F.S.]), dissolving Congested Districts Board (see 5 Aug. 1891) and transferring its functions to land commn

Aug. 1 Public Safety (Emergency Powers) Act, 1923 (1923/29 [I.F.S.]), enables government to continue to detain without trial

Aug. 8 'An act to establish a police force [see 21 Feb. 1922] to be called the Gárda Siochána (commonly called Civic Guard)' (1923/37 [I.F.S.]) (act made permanent by Gárda Síochana Act, 1924 (1924/25), 17 July 1924)

Aug. 9 Land Act, 1923 (1923/42 [I.F.S.]), vesting in land commn all tenanted lands not already vested, and empowering commn to take over untenanted land—'Hogan act' (cf. 28 May 1925)

Aug. 15 De Valera arrested while addressing public meeting in Ennis, Co. Clare (imprisoned without trial until 16 July 1924)

Aug. 27 I.F.S. general election: Cumann na nGaedheal 63, republican 44, lab. 14, farmers 15, ind. and others 17 (see 15 June 1922, 9 June 1927)

Aug. First number of *Dublin Magazine*; editor Seumas O'Sullivan

Sept. 10 I.F.S. admitted to membership of League of Nations

Oct. 1 Cosgrave addresses opening meeting of Imperial Conference in London

Oct. 14-Nov. 23 Hunger-strike by several hundred detainees in I.F.S. (most released from prison, Dec. 1923-Mar. 1924)

Nov. 14 W. B. Yeats awarded Nobel prize for literature (presented in Stockholm, 10 Dec.)

Dec. 6 U.K. general election: in G.B.—con. 247, lab. 191, lib. 158, others 6; in N.I.—un. 11, nat. 2 (see 15 Nov. 1922, 29 Oct. 1924)

Dec. 28 First performance, in New York, of George Bernard Shaw's 'St Joan' (first London performance, 26 Mar. 1924)

Edmund Curtis's *A history of medieval Ireland* (Dublin; revised ed., London, 1938)

1924

Jan. 21 Lenin dies

Jan. 22 James Ramsay MacDonald app. first labour P.M. of U.K., heading minority government (see 22 May 1923, 4 Nov. 1924)

Feb. 18 Reorganisation of I.F.S. army announced (involving drastic cut in numbers)

Feb. Agreement between I.F.S. government and Siemens-Schuckert of Berlin for hydro-electric scheme on Shannon (see 4 July 1925)

Mar. 3 O'Casey's 'Juno and the paycock' opens at Abbey Theatre, Dublin

Mar. 6 Disaffected I.F.S. army officers issue ultimatum to government, demanding removal of army council, suspension of demobilisation, and discussions on interpretation of treaty (signatories arrested; sporadic outbreaks of mutiny)

Mar. 7 Joseph McGrath, I.F.S. minister for industry and commerce, resigns in protest at handling of army problems

Mar. 10 General Eoin O'Duffy, chief commr of Civic Guard, app. to command I.F.S. defence forces

Mar. 15 Cttee of inquiry into army mutiny appointed; Eoin MacNeill chairman

Mar. 18 Troops, supported by armoured cars, lay siege to public house in Parnell Street, Dublin, occupied by persons implicated in mutiny (10 arrests made on morning of 19 Mar.)

Mar. 19 Executive council expresses disapproval of military action of 18 Mar. (taken without O'Duffy's knowledge), and demands resignation of chief of staff, adjutant general and quartermaster general; Richard Mulcahy, minister for defence, resigns; his portfolio taken over by president

Mar. 21 British soldiers leaving Spike Island in Cork harbour fired on by men in I.F.S. army uniform; 1 killed, 17 wounded

Mar. 29 Sir Charles Villiers Stanford, composer and teacher of music, dies

Apr. 12 Courts of Justice Act, 1924 (1924/10 [I.F.S.]), remodels judiciary

Apr. 21 Ministers and Secretaries Act, 1924 (1924/16 [I.F.S.]) regulating government departments and enabling parliamentary secretaries to be appointed

May 10 N.I. government refuses to make appointment to boundary commn

May 29 Public Libraries Act (Northern Ireland), 1924 (14 & 15 Geo. V, c. 10), empowers county councils to provide public library service (similar provision in I.F.S. under sect. 65 of Local Government Act, 1925 (see 26 Mar. 1925))

May 30 Bill introduced in dáil to reduce hours of drink trading, end mixed trading, and reduce numbers of liquor licences with compensation (becomes law, 19 Dec., as Intoxicating Liquor (General) Act, 1924 (1924/28, 62 [I.F.S.]; amended by 1927/15 [I.F.S.])

June 5 Announcement of appointment of Richard Feetham, judge of supreme court of South Africa, by British government as chairman of boundary commn

Old Age Pensions Act, 1924 (1924/19 [I.F.S.]), reducing pension from 10s. to 9s. a week

June 26 Mulcahy fails to carry motion censuring I.F.S. government for suppressing facts of mutiny

July 11 I.F.S. registers Anglo-Irish treaty with League of Nations

July 23 Railways Act, 1924 (1924/29 [I.F.S.]), provides for amalgamation of 27 railway companies into a single company (Great Southern Railways Co. formed, 1 Jan. 1925)

Aug. 2-17 Tailteann games (named after ancient Irish festival Óenach Tailten; see 716, 772, 811, 888-907, 1007, 1120, 1167/8) in Croke Park, Dublin

Aug. 4 Cosgrave and MacDonald agree to introduce legislation empowering British government to appoint N.I. member of boundary commn in default of N.I. government making appointment

Aug. 5 Military Pensions Act, 1924 (1924/48 [I.F.S.]), providing pensions for those who served in government forces in 1922-3 and in the Irish Volunteers and the I.R.A. in 1916-21 (see 13 Sept. 1934)

Aug. 14 Royal Dublin Society transfers Leinster House, Dublin, to government

Sept. 15 Opening of British Broadcasting Company's station in Belfast (2BE)

Oct. 25 De Valera expelled from N.I. near Newry (re-enters at Derry, 26 Oct.; imprisoned, 1-28 Nov., for defying expulsion order) (see 5 Nov. 1929)

Oct. 29 U.K. general election: in G.B.—con. 399, lab. 151, lib. 40, others 12; in N.I.—un. 13 (see 6 Dec. 1923, 30 May 1929)

Nov. 4   Stanley Baldwin (con.) app. P.M. of U.K. (see 22 Jan. 1924, 5 June 1929)

Nov. 6   First meeting of boundary commn in London

Nov. 8   I.F.S. government declares amnesty for offences committed between 6 Dec. 1921 and 12 May 1923

Nov. 13   First public performance of Hamilton Harty's 'Irish symphony' (third version), at Free Trade Hall, Manchester

Dec. 19   Last number of *Freeman's Journal* (see 10 Sept. 1763)

1925

Jan.   Daniel Corkery's *The hidden Ireland* (Dublin)

Jan. 27   Commn app. to inquire into preservation of Irish-speaking areas in I.F.S. (Coimisiún na Gaeltachta; report, 14 July 1926)

Feb. 11   Cosgrave carries in dáil motion urging senate to consent to standing orders prohibiting introduction of private bills for divorce *a vinculo* (this being only means of securing such divorce)

Mar. 26   Local Government Act (1925/5 [I.F.S.])

Mar.   John Joly's *Surface history of the earth* (Oxford)

Apr. 2   Police Forces Amalgamation Act (1925/7 [I.F.S.]), provides for amalgamation of D.M.P. and Gárda Síochána (see 4 July 1836, 8 Aug. 1923)

Apr. 3   N.I. general election: un. 32, ind. un. 4, nat. 10, lab. 3, republicans 2, ind. 1 (see 24 May 1921, 22 May 1929)

Apr. 24   Final report of Colwyn cttee on financial relations between Belfast and London governments published

Apr. 28   Joseph Devlin and T. S. McAllister take oath and seats in N.I. H.C., first nationalists to do so

May 28   Northern Ireland Land Act, 1925 (15 & 16 Geo. V, c. 34 [U.K.]), vesting all unpurchased tenanted land in land purchase commn, N.I. (cf. 9 Aug. 1923)

June 7   Matt Talbot, 'the saint in overalls', dies in Dublin (declared venerable by Sacra Congregatio pro Causis Sanctorum, 30 Oct. 1975)

June 11   W. B. Yeats speaks in senate against dáil proposal for prohibition of divorce bills (see 11 Feb.); senate approves motion that divorce bills be read a first time in each house before being proceeded with in senate (dáil rejects motion, 25 June)

July 4   Shannon Electricity Act, 1925 (1925/26 [I.F.S.]), authorises Shannon hydro-electric scheme (see Feb. 1924)

Nov. 7   *Morning Post* publishes forecast of findings of Irish boundary commn: no major transfer of territory, part of south Armagh to I.F.S., part of east Donegal to N.I.

Nov. mid   I.R.A. convention adopts new constitution, in effect renouncing loyalty to de Valera

Nov. 20   Eoin MacNeill resigns from boundary commn (resigns as minister for education, 24 Nov.)

Dec. 3 Tripartite agreement between governments of U.K., I.F.S. and N.I. revoking powers of boundary commn and maintaining existing boundary of N.I.; I.F.S. released from liability for part of British public debt, and accepts liability for malicious damage since 21 Jan. 1919; powers of council of Ire. in relation to N.I. transferred to N.I. government

Dec. 10 Craig announces disbandment of 'A' Special Constabulary (see 1 Nov. 1920)

Dec. 15 Members of 'A' Special Constabulary seize barracks and issue ultimatum to N.I. government, insisting on certain conditions for their disbandment (agreement reached; force disbanded by Christmas)

Edith Somerville and Martin Ross's *The big house of Inver* (London)

Liam O'Flaherty's *The informer* (London)

William Lawson Micks's *An account of the . . . Congested Districts Board* (Dublin)

Peacock Theatre constructed in house adjoining Abbey Theatre, to be used for experimental productions and performances by Abbey School of Acting

Discovery of rock phosphates in Co. Clare

1926

Jan. 1 I.F.S. broadcasting station (2RN) opens in Dublin

Feb. 4 Recruitment for 'C' Special Constabulary ends (see 1 Nov. 1920)

Feb. 8 Sean O'Casey's 'The plough and the stars' opens at Abbey Theatre, Dublin (disturbances, 11 Feb.)

Mar. 8 Commn of inquiry into banking in I.F.S. app. (final report, 31 Jan. 1927)

Mar. 9-11 Sinn Féin árd-fheis; de Valera resigns presidency of party, 11 Mar.

Mar. 10 Three more nationalists take seats in H.C. of N.I. (see 28 Apr. 1925)

Mar. 26 Unemployment Insurance (Northern Ireland Agreement) Act, 1926 (16 Geo. V, c. 4 [U.K.]), provides for assimilation of unemployment relief burdens of N.I. and U.K. exchequers

Apr. 13 Coinage Act, 1926 (1926/14 [I.F.S.]), empowers minister for finance to issue silver, nickel, and bronze coins

Apr. 18 Census in I.F.S. and N.I.: population of I.F.S. 2,971,992 (5·34% decline); population of N.I. 1,256,561 (0·5% increase)

May 4-12 General strike in G.B.

May 16 Fianna Fáil party launched by de Valera at La Scala Theatre, Dublin

May 27 School Attendance Act, 1926 (1926/17 [I.F.S.]), to provide more effectively for attendance at elementary school (see 27 June 1892, 3 Mar. 1943)

June 1 Ancient Monuments Act (Northern Ireland), 1926 (16 & 17 Geo. V, c. 12), (see 18 Aug. 1882, 27 June 1892)

July 28 Local Authorities (Officers and Employees) Act, 1926 (1926/39 [I.F.S.]), establishes local appointments commn to fill local government vacancies

Aug. 4 First international horse jumping competition at Royal Dublin Society grounds

Sept. 5   Fire in cinema at Drumcollogher, Co. Limerick: 49 burned to death, 50 injured

Oct. 1   Royal College of Science, Dublin, formally merged with University College, Dublin

Nov. 11   George Bernard Shaw awarded Nobel prize for literature

Nov. 14   Several police barracks in I.F.S. attacked by I.R.A.; 2 gardaí killed (similar attacks, 20, 24 Nov.)

Nov. 19   Imperial conference in London (19 Oct.–23 Nov.) determines that U.K. and dominions are 'autonomous communities within the British empire, equal in status, in no way subordinate one to another'

Public Safety (Emergency Powers) Act, 1926 (1926/42 [I.F.S.]), empowering government to proclaim state of national emergency with consequent powers of arrest and detention on suspicion

Nov.   Sugar-beet factory at Carlow begins operating

Brian Merriman's *The midnight court*, translated by Percy Arland Ussher, with introduction by W. B. Yeats (London) (see July 1780)

1927

Feb. 17   Special cttee of governors of Erasmus Smith endowment (see 26 Mar. 1669) adopts memorandum to seek amendment of charter (ensuing litigation results in expenditure of *c.* £25,000, and alienation to I.F.S. government of half remaining £130,000 by agreement between governors and attorney general, 12 June 1937)

Mar. 10   Conference in Dublin of National League, political party founded by William Redmond (son of John)

Mar. 13   Garrison church at Arbour Hill, Dublin, consecrated for Roman Catholic worship

Apr. 26   Cork broadcasting station opens

May 20   Intoxicating Liquor Act, 1927 (1927/15 [I.F.S.]), restricts opening times of licensed premises and reduces number of licences

May 28   Agricultural Credit Act, 1927 (1927/24 [I.F.S.]), provides for establishment of Agricultural Credit Corporation

Electricity (Supply) Act, 1927 (1927/27 [I.F.S.]), provides for board to control Shannon hydro-electric scheme and to take over all existing electric undertakings (Electricity Supply Board established 11 Aug.)

June 1   John Bagnell Bury, classicist and historian, dies

June 9   I.F.S. general election: Cumann na nGaedheal 47, Fianna Fáil 44, lab. 22, farmers 11, National League 8, Sinn Féin 5, ind. and others 16 (see 27 Aug. 1923, 15 Sept. 1927)

July 10   Kevin O'Higgins, I.F.S. minister for justice, assassinated

July 20   I.F.S. government introduces without notice 3 bills to meet crisis: Public Safety Bill (see 11 Aug.), Electoral (Amendment No. 2) Bill (see 9 Nov.), and Constitution (Amendment) (No. 6) Bill (amending (a) article 47 by restricting to members who have taken their seats power to demand referendum on a bill; (b) article 48 by removing popular initiative for legislation; bill does not proceed beyond second reading)

Aug. 11 Public Safety Act, 1927 (1927/31 [I.F.S.]), providing powers to declare associations unlawful, to suppress periodicals, and to establish special courts with military members (repealed, 28 Dec. 1928)

De Valera and Fianna Fáil deputies take their seats after signing parliamentary oath, 'merely an empty political formula'

Aug. 16 Thomas Johnson's motion in dáil of 'no confidence' in Cosgrave's government defeated by speaker's casting vote (72 to 71); John Jinks (National League) absent

Aug. 20 Currency Act, 1927 (1927/32 [I.F.S.]), establishing separate currency

Sept. 15 I.F.S. general election: Cumann na nGaedheal 62, Fianna Fáil 57, lab. 13, farmers 6, National League 2, ind. and others 13 (see 9 June 1927, 16 Feb. 1932)

Nov. 9 Electoral (Amendment No. 2) Act, 1927 (1927/33 [I.F.S.]), requiring candidates to declare before nomination their intention, if elected, to take prescribed oath

Dec. 15 James MacNeill app. governor general of I.F.S. (sworn in, 1 Feb. 1928)

1928

Jan. 19 R. A. S. Macalister's *The archaeology of Ireland* (London; revised ed., 1949)

Apr. 12-13 Commandant James Christopher Fitzmaurice of Irish Air Corps, Capt. Hermann Köhl, and Baron Günther von Hünefeld make first east-west flight across Atlantic, from Baldonnel near Dublin to Greenly Island in Gulf of St Lawrence

Apr. 20 Yeats writes to Sean O'Casey on behalf of Abbey Theatre, rejecting 'The silver tassie'

May 3 De Valera attempts to present petition, signed by 96,000, urging enactment of legislation, under article 48 of constitution, providing for popular initiation of proposals for laws or constitutional amendments: leave refused for want of notice

July 12 Constitution (Amendment No. 10) Act, 1928 (1928/8 [I.F.S.]), amending constitution by deletion of articles 47 and 48 (referendum and initiative)

July 23 Constitution (Amendment No. 6), Act, 1928 (1928/13 [I.F.S.]), altering senate electorate to members of dáil and senate voting together

Constitution (Amendment No. 13) Act, 1928 (1928/14 [I.F.S.]), inserting additional article 38A, increasing suspensory power of senate from 9 to 18 months (unless dissolution intervenes)

Aug. 27 Galway Gaelic Theatre (afterwards called Taibhdhearc theatre) opens as Irish-medium theatre in Middle Street, Galway, with production of 'Diarmuid agus Gráinne' written and produced by Micheál MacLiammóir

Sept. 29 John Devoy, last survivor of early fenian leaders, dies at Atlantic City, U.S.A.

Oct. 10 Irish Manuscripts Commission app. (Eoin MacNeill chairman 1928-45)

Oct. 14 Dublin Gate Theatre Co. produces its first play, in Peacock Theatre, Lower Abbey Street: Henrik Ibsen's 'Peer Gynt'; directors, Micheál Mac Liammóir, Hilton Edwards and others

Oct. 28 Library Association of Ireland founded

Dec. 26 Public Safety Act, 1928 (1928/38 [I.F.S.]), repealing Public Safety Act, 1927 (see 11 Aug. 1927)

1929

Feb. 5 Arrest of de Valera at Goraghwood, Co. Armagh, leading to month's imprisonment for defiance of exclusion order

Feb. 11 Mussolini and Pius XI sign Lateran treaty: Italy establishes concordat with Vatican, and recognises pope's sovereignty over Vatican city

Feb. 23 Cork City Management Act, 1929 (1929/1 [I.F.S.]), sets precedent for managerial system of local government

Apr. 16 House of Commons (Method of Voting and Redistribution of Seats) Act (Northern Ireland), 1929 (19 Geo. V, c. 5), abolishes proportional representation

May 22 N.I. general election: un. 37, ind. un. 3, National League 11, lab. 1 (see 3 Apr. 1925, 30 Nov. 1933); local option party, formed by temperance movement, fails to win seat

May 30 U.K. general election: in G.B.—lab. 287, con. 249, lib. 59, others 7; in N.I.—un. 11, National League 2 (see 29 Oct. 1924, 27 Oct. 1931)

June 5 Ramsay MacDonald (lab.) app. P.M. of U.K. for second time; second labour minority government (see 4 Nov. 1924, 24 Aug. 1931)

June 22 First day of issue of first commemorative series of I.F.S. postage stamps (marking centenary of 'catholic emancipation')

June 28 Legal Practitioners (Qualification) Act, 1929 (1929/16 [I.F.S.]), requires future law students to pass examination in Irish

July 16 Censorship of Publications Act, 1929 (1929/21 [I.F.S.]), provides for board empowered to censor or ban publications for obscenity or other reasons

July Tomás Ó Criomhthain's *An t-oileánach* (Dublin; translated by Robin Flower as *The islandman*, London, 1934)

Oct. 21 Shannon hydro-electric scheme begins commercial operations

Oct. 29 Collapse of shares on New York stock exchange (leading to international economic crisis)

Dec. 17 University College, Galway, Act, 1929 (1929/35 [I.F.S.]), increases annual grant to college from £12,000 to £28,000 and requires college when making appointments to give preference to Irish speakers

Dec. 20 Housing (Gaeltacht) Act, 1929 (1929/41 [I.F.S.]), authorises grants and loans for housing in Irish-speaking areas

1930

Jan. 15   Papal nuncio, Mgr Paschal Robinson, O.F.M., presents his credentials to governor general of I.F.S.

Feb. 12   First censorship board under Censorship of Publications Act, 1929 (1929/21 [I.F.S.]), appointed

Feb. 26   National Monuments Act, 1930 (1930/2 [I.F.S.]) (see 18 Aug. 1882, 27 June 1892)

Mar.   First issue of *Analecta Hibernica*, organ of Irish Manuscripts Commission

Apr. 1   Irish Trade Union Congress and Labour Party divides into 2 separate organisations (see 28 June 1912)

June 4   Public Charitable Hospitals (Temporary Provisions) Act, 1930 (1930/12 [I.F.S.]), inaugurates hospital sweepstakes (made permanent by Public Hospitals Act, 1933 (1933/18, 27 July 1933))

June 17   Education Act (Northern Ireland), 1930 (20 & 21 Geo. V, c. 14), giving representation on local authority school committees to nominees of former managers; empowering minister to pay half cost of building and equipping new voluntary schools and altering existing voluntary schools; requiring local authority schools to provide undenominational bible instruction if requested by 10 parents (children whose parents disapprove not required to attend) (see 22 June 1923)

July 17   I.F.S. note in reply to Aristide Briand's memorandum on European cooperation declares that Irish interests are less exclusively European than those of continental countries

Local Government (Dublin) Act, 1930 (1930/27 [I.F.S.]), extending city boundaries and establishing borough of Dun Laoghaire

July 21   Vocational Education Act, 1930 (1930/29 [I.F.S.]), setting up local vocational education cttees to maintain vocational schools and technical colleges, and to provide post-primary education in general subjects

Aug. 5   National exhibition of Irish manufactures opened at Royal Dublin Society by governor-general

Sept. 17   I.F.S. elected to council of League of Nations

Dec. 31   I.F.S. minister for local government dissolves Mayo County Council, replacing it by commr, for rejecting recommendation of local appointments commn to appoint as county librarian Miss Letitia Dunbar-Harrison, a protestant

1931

Feb. 11   Sir Charles Algernon Parsons, inventor of steam turbine, dies

Mar. 19   Patrick McGilligan, I.F.S. minister for external affairs, visits king at Buckingham Palace to discuss constitutional matters

Mar. 26   T. M. Healy dies

May 7   An Óige, or Irish Youth Hostel Association, established (hostels opened at Lough Dan, Laragh, and Glencree, Co. Wicklow, May–Sept.)

May 15   Pius XI issues encyclical, *Quadragesimo anno*, on social order

May 7   Muintir na Tire founded by Rev. John Hayes

Aug. 24   Ramsay MacDonald tenders labour government's resignation and forms national coalition government (see 5 June 1929, 7 June 1935)

Sept. 5   First number of *Irish Press*, organ of Fianna Fáil party

Sept. 26-7   First congress of Saor Éire (socialist republican party), at Iona Hall, Dublin

Sept. 29   Sir William Orpen, painter, dies

Oct. 17   Constitution (Amendment No. 17) Act, 1931 (1931/52 [I.F.S.]), ('public safety act'), establishes military tribunal to try cases of sedition, illegal drilling and membership of illegal organisations

Oct. 18   Catholic bps issue joint pastoral condemning implicitly I.R.A. and explicitly Saor Éire

Oct. 20   I.R.A., Saor Éire, Cumann na mBan, and 9 other associations declared unlawful in I.F.S.

Oct. 25   Church of Christ the King, Turner's Cross, Cork, dedicated; architect Barry Byrne

Oct. 27   U.K. general election: in G.B.—con. 459, lib. 32, national lib. 35, national lab. 13, national 4, lab. 42, ind. lib. 4, others 3; in N.I.—un. 11, nat. 2 (see 30 May 1929, 14 Nov. 1935); MacDonald remains P.M.

Dec. 11   Statute of Westminster, 1931 (22 Geo. V, c. 4 [U.K.]), providing that no law of dominion parliament shall be inoperative on ground of repugnancy to British law; any dominion parliament empowered to repeal or amend any act of U.K. parliament in so far as it is part of dominion law

Dec. 22   Landlord and Tenant Act, 1931 (1931/55 [I.F.S.]), giving greater security to tenants in urban areas

Frank O'Connor's *Guests of the nation* (London)

1932

Feb. 9   Formation of Army Comrades Association, organisation of ex-members I.F.S. army (renamed National Guard 20 July 1933; see 22 Aug. 1933)

Feb. 16   I.F.S. general election: Fianna Fáil 72, Cumann na nGaedheal 57, lab. 7, farmers 3, ind. and others 14 (see 15 Sept. 1927, 24 Jan. 1933)

Feb. 22   Sean O'Faolain's *Midsummer night madness* (London), his first collection of short stories

Mar. 9   Éamon de Valera elected president of executive council by 81 to 68 (forms Fianna Fáil administration: Seán T. O'Kelly, vice-president and minister for local government, Seán MacEntee, minister for finance, Frank Aiken, minister for defence, James Geoghegan, minister for justice, Patrick J. Ruttledge, minister for lands and fisheries, Seán F. Lemass, minister for industry and commerce, Thomas Derrig, minister for education, Joseph Connolly, minister for posts and telegraphs; president takes portfolio of external affairs (see 9 Sept. 1922, 18 Feb. 1948)

Mar. 10   Release of 20 political prisoners by new government of I.F.S.

Mar. 16   De Valera outlines to press his government's proposals: suspension of Public Safety Act, withholding of land annuities, abolition of oath, introduction of 'protective' tariffs, merging office of governor general with that of president of executive council

Mar. 17   Society of St Patrick for Foreign Missions (later St Patrick's Missionary Society) formed; house at Kiltegan, Co. Wicklow

Mar. 18   Executive Council passes order suspending Constitution (Amendment No. 17) Act (see 17 Oct. 1931)

Apr. 9   J. H. Thomas, secretary of state for dominions, makes public the agreement entered into by Cosgrave for payment of land annuities (see 12 Feb. 1923)

Apr. 14   As the outcome of prolonged work by E. T. S. Walton, a graduate of Trinity College, Dublin, and J. D. Cockcroft, at Cavendish Laboratory, Cambridge, on development of a particle-accelerator, lithium atoms are first disintegrated by artificially accelerated protons, which opens up a new field of research in nuclear physics (see 15 Nov. 1951)

Apr. 20   De Valera introduces bill to remove oath of allegiance from constitution (see 28 June)

May 11   Nationalist members of N.I. H.C. walk out in protest against not being allowed to discuss, in connection with budget, running of post office, matter reserved for U.K. parliament

May 22   Lady Gregory dies at Coole Park, Co. Galway

June 7   J. H. Thomas meets de Valera in Dublin for discussion of points at issue between Britain and I.F.S.

June 10   De Valera meets P.M. and other members of British government in London; he refuses arbitration by empire tribunal

June 22-6   International Eucharistic Congress in Dublin

June 28   I.F.S. senate returns Constitution (Removal of Oath) Bill to dáil in amended form (see 20 Apr. 1932, 1 Mar. 1933)

June 30   Payment of land annuities to British government withheld (amount lodged in suspense account pending arbitration)

July 9   Foundation-stone laid of new City Hall, Cork (opened, 8 Sept. 1936; see 11-12 Dec. 1920)

July 10   James MacNeill, governor general of I.F.S., releases for publication correspondence with de Valera concerning discourtesies shown to him by some ministers

July 15   De Valera has further meeting in London with MacDonald; no agreement reached

British treasury order under Irish Free State (Special Duties) Act, 1932 (22 & 23 Geo. V, c. 30 [U.K.]), comes into effect, imposing 20% duty on about two-thirds of I.F.S. exports to U.K.

July 17   I.F.S. government issues statement declaring willingness to submit questions at issue to arbitration, provided arbiters not confined to empire

July 21–Aug. 20   Imperial economic conference in Ottawa; I.F.S. delegation headed by Seán T. O'Kelly, vice-president, executive council

July 23   Emergency Imposition of Duties Act, 1932 (1932/16 [I.F.S.]), empowering executive council to vary rates and to limit such variations to goods from particular countries

Aug. 3   Housing (Financial and Miscellaneous Provisions) Act, 1932 (1932/19 [I.F.S.]), providing for government grants to local authority housing schemes

Sept. 9   I.F.S. high commissioner in London presents to George V advice of de Valera to terminate appointment of MacNeill as governor general (appointment terminated, 1 Nov.)

Sept. 18   Announcement of Irish Academy of Letters (founded by Yeats; Shaw first president)

Sept. 26   De Valera makes inaugural speech as chairman of League of Nations assembly at Geneva

Sept. 30   John Beattie, labour member of H.C. of N.I., throws mace on floor in protest at speaker disallowing motion on unemployment

Oct. 4–13   Strikes, marches, and rioting in Belfast in protest against unemployment; police engage crowds (11–13 Oct.)

Oct. 14–15   Meeting in London between members of I.F.S. and British governments: decision that no possibility of reaching agreement exists

Oct. 29   Control of Manufactures Act, 1932 (1932/21 [I.F.S.]), requires majority of shares in any new manufacturing business to be owned by I.F.S. nationals

Nov. 16   Prince of Wales opens N.I. parliament buildings at Stormont, near Belfast; architect Arnold Thornely

Nov. 26   Domhnall Ua Buachalla (Donal Buckley) takes oath as governor general

1933

Jan. 2   Dissolution of dáil

Jan. 4   Agreement between Frank MacDermot, leader of National Farmers' and Ratepayers' League, and James Dillon, independent, to form centre party

Jan. 21   George Moore, writer, dies

Jan. 24   I.F.S. general election: Fianna Fáil 77, Cumann na nGaedheal 48, centre party 11, lab. 8, ind. and others 9 (see 16 Feb. 1932, 1 July 1937)

Jan. 30   Adolf Hitler becomes German chancellor

Jan. 30–Apr. 10   Strike of railwaymen in N.I.

Feb. 22   General Eoin O'Duffy, chief commr of Civic Guard, dismissed

Mar. 1   Dáil returns oath bill (see 28 June 1932) to senate under article 38A of constitution (bill to be deemed to have passed both houses if senate does not pass it in 60 days; see 3 May)

Mar. 24   National executive of Army Comrades Association adopts blue shirt and black beret as distinctive dress of association (first seen in public, 8 Apr.) (see 20 July)

Mar. 27-9 Crowd attack headquarters of Revolutionary Workers Group in Great Strand Street, Dublin

May 3 Constitution (Removal of Oath) Act, 1933 (1933/6 [I.F.S.]) (see 1 Mar.)

May 4 Agricultural Produce (Cereals) Act, 1933 (1933/7 [I.F.S.]), encouraging cultivation of wheat

May 9 Civil Authorities (Special Powers) Act (Northern Ireland), 1933 (23 & 24 Geo. V, c. 12), makes permanent the 1922 act (12 & 13 Geo. V, c. 5 [Northern Ireland])

June 11 Communist party of Ireland formed (cf. 18 Oct. 1921, 10 July 1941)

June 12–July 27 World monetary and economic conference in London (I.F.S. delegate, Senator Joseph Connolly): agreement to differ

July 20 O'Duffy elected leader of Army Comrades Association ('Blueshirts'); he changes its name to National Guard (see 22 Aug.)

July 31 Industrial Credit Act, 1933 (1933/25 [I.F.S.])

Aug. 9 De Valera introduces 3 constitution amendment bills (see 2, 16 Nov.)

Aug. 12 I.F.S. government bans meeting (fixed for 13 Aug.) to commemorate Griffith, Collins, and O'Higgins

Aug. 22 O'Duffy's National Guard ('Blueshirts') proclaimed unlawful association (see 13 Sept.)

Aug. 23 Sugar Manufacture Act, 1933 (1933/31 [I.F.S.]), establishes Comhlucht Siúicre Éireann Teo.

Sept. 2 Launching of United Ireland party (later known as Fine Gael), fusion of Cumann na nGaedheal, Centre Party (see 4 Jan.) and National Guard, under presidency of O'Duffy

Sept. 13 O'Duffy orders National Guard to form youth section of United Ireland party and to take name of Young Ireland Association

Oct. 13 Land Act, 1933 (1933/38 [I.F.S.]), reducing annuities by half and remitting arrears in excess of treble the amount of annuity

Oct. 20 I.F.S. government purchases copyright of 'The soldiers' song' by Peadar Kearney (Irish national anthem)

Nov. 2 Constitution (Amendment No. 20) Act, 1933 (1933/40 [I.F.S.]), transferring from crown representative to executive council power of appropriation under article 37

Constitution (Amendment No. 21) Act, 1933 (1933/41 [I.F.S.]), removing from article 41 crown representative's power of withholding assent to bills and of reserving bills for kg's pleasure

Nov. 16 Constitution (Amendment No. 22) Act, 1933 (1933/45 [I.F.S.]), abolishing right of appeal to privy council

Unemployment Assistance Act, 1933 (1933/46 [I.F.S.])

Nov. 30 N.I. general election: un. 36, ind. un. 3, nat. 9, lab. 2, republican 1, ind. 1 (see 22 May 1929, 9 Feb. 1938)

Dec. 8   John Joly, engineer, geologist, and physicist, dies

Young Ireland Association banned (replaced by League of Youth, 14 Dec.) (see 21 Sept. 1934)

Dec. 17   O'Duffy arrested (high court in Dublin disallows summons on charges of making seditious speech and inciting to murder de Valera, 21 Mar. 1934)

Sean O'Faolain's *A nest of simple folk* (London)

1934

Jan. 17   Opening of 'loop line' at Greenisland, Co. Antrim, constructed as part of government scheme of public works to relieve unemployment

Jan. 22   Seán Lester, I.F.S. representative at League of Nations, becomes high commr, Danzig

Mar. 21   I.F.S. senate rejects Wearing of Uniform (Restrictions) Bill, 30 to 18

Apr. 8   Conference at Athlone of I.R.A. officers and others declares 'that a republic of an united Ireland will never be achieved except through a struggle which uproots capitalism on its way': rise of Republican Congress

Apr. 24   Craigavon declares: 'they still boast of Southern Ireland being a catholic state. All I boast of is that we are a protestant parliament and a protestant state.'

May 29   Town and Regional Planning Act, 1934 (1934/22 [I.F.S.]), provides 'for the orderly and progressive development of cities, towns and other areas'

June 1   I.F.S. senate rejects Constitution (Amendment No. 24) Bill for abolition of senate (see 29 May 1936)

June 5   Representation of the People Act (Northern Ireland), 1934 (24 & 25 Geo. V, c. 7), extending from 3 to 7 years' residence qualification for voting in elections to N.I. H.C., and providing that candidates at nomination must declare intention of taking their seats

July 18   I.F.S. senate rejects Constitution (Amendment No. 23) Bill, for abolition of university seats in dáil (see 24 Apr. 1936)

July 27-Oct. 1   Dublin newspapers suspend publication because of strike by members of I.T.G.W.U.

Sept. 13   Industrial Alcohol Act, 1934 (1934/40 [I.F.S.]), providing for state production and marketing of industrial alcohol

Military Pensions Act, 1934 (1934/43 [I.F.S.]), extending pension rights to anti-treaty forces (see 5 Aug. 1924)

Sept. 21   General O'Duffy resigns from his positions in Fine Gael party and League of Youth

Nov.   Commn app by I.F.S. minister for finance to inquire into banking, currency and credit (report published, Aug. 1938)

Dec. 12   Geographical Society of Ireland established

Dec. 21   Anglo-Irish 'cattle and coal' agreement

Dec.   Robert Lloyd Praeger's *The botanist in Ireland* (Dublin)

1935

Jan. Workman Clark shipyard in Belfast delivers last ship

Feb. 9 Fatal shooting of Richard More O'Ferrall at Edgeworthstown, Co. Longford, by members of I.R.A.

Feb. 19 Public Dance Halls Act (1935/2 [I.F.S.]), making necessary licence from local district court for all public dances

Feb. 28 Sale or importation of contraceptives forbidden under section 17 of Criminal Law Amendment Act, 1935 (1935/6 [I.F.S.]); age of consent raised from 16 to 17 (section 9)

Mar. 3-May 17 Transport strike in Dublin

Apr. 10 Irish Nationality and Citizenship Act, 1935 (1935/13 [I.F.S.]): persons born in N.I. after 6 Dec. 1922 to be citizens of I.F.S. up to age of 21, thereafter ceasing to be so unless they make declaration of retention of citizenship (see 17 July 1956)

Aliens Act, 1935 (1935/14 [I.F.S.]), defining as aliens all persons other than citizens of I.F.S.; executive council empowered to exempt subjects of any country from provisions of act (British subjects exempted)

Apr. 12 First Irish-speaking families from Connemara arrive at Rathcarne, near Athboy, Co. Meath, under Meath Gaeltacht scheme

May 6-9 Disturbances in Belfast, arising out of royal jubilee celebrations

June 6 Judicial committee of privy council rules that I.F.S. parliament has power to abolish right of appeal from courts in I.F.S. to king in council

June 7 Reconstruction of British government; Stanley Baldwin replaces Ramsay MacDonald as P.M. (see 24 Aug. 1931, 28 May 1937)

June 20 Pigs and Bacon Act, 1935 (1935/24 [I.F.S.]), sets up bacon and pigs marketing boards (replaced by Pigs and Bacon Commission, 1 Jan. 1940)

July 12 Renewal of disturbances in Belfast

July 16 Summary Jurisdiction and Criminal Justice Act (Northern Ireland) 1935 (25 & 26 Geo. V, c. 13), transferring to resident magistrates judicial functions of justices of the peace

Road and Railway Transport Act (Northern Ireland), 1935 (25 & 26 Geo. V, c. 15), provides for setting up of N.I. Road Transport Board to run passenger and freight services (see 10 Aug. 1948)

July 17 George Russell (AE), writer and painter, dies

Aug. 2 Widows' and Orphans' Pensions Act, 1935 (1935/29 [I.F.S.])

Sept. 16 At Geneva de Valera affirms to Assembly of League of Nations that I.F.S. will invoke sanctions against Italy

Oct. 22 Lord Carson of Duncairn dies

Nov. 14 U.K. general election: in G.B.—con. 376, national lib. 33, national lab. 8, national 1, lib. 21, lab. 154, ind. lab. 4, others 5; in N.I.—un. 11, nat. abstentionists 2 (see 27 Oct. 1931, 5 July 1945)

Nov. 22 Malcolm MacDonald replaces J. H. Thomas as secretary of state for dominions

1936

Jan. 20   George V dies; succ. by Edward VIII

Feb. 24   Ulster Society for Irish Historical Studies, to promote scientific study of Irish history, founded at Queen's University, Belfast; president R. M. Henry, secretary T. W. Moody (see Nov. 1936; 1, 24 Mar. 1938)

Mar. 24   Vice-admiral Henry Boyle Somerville shot dead at his home in Castletownshend, Co. Cork

Apr. 24   Constitution (Amendment No. 23) Act, 1936 (1936/17 [I.F.S.]), deleting article 27 (university representation in dáil); act passed under article 38A after rejection of bill by senate (see 18 July 1934)

Apr. 26   Census in I.F.S.: population 2,968,420 (0·12% decline; see 18 Apr. 1926)

May 11   Permission given by Holy See to Marie Helena Martin to found a congregation of medical missionaries as proposed by her (receives her vows as Mary of the Incarnation and becomes founder of Medical Missionaries of Mary, 4 Apr. 1937) (see 8 Dec. 1939)

May 19   Final meeting of I.F.S. senate

May 22   Report of commn of inquiry into N.I. Special Powers Act, app. by National Council of Civil Liberties

May 27   Inaugural flight by Aer Lingus, between Dublin and Bristol

May 29   Constitution (Amendment No. 24) Act, 1936 (1936/18 [I.F.S.]), abolishing senate: act passed under article 38A after rejection of bill by senate (see 1 June 1934)

June 18   I.R.A. declared illegal organisation in I.F.S.

June   First number of *Ireland To-day* (continuing till Mar. 1938)

July 17   Garrison at Melilla (Spanish Morocco) revolts: outbreak of Spanish civil war

Aug. 8   Connaught Rangers (Pensions) Act, 1936 (1936/37 [I.F.S.]) (see 28 June 1920)

Aug. 14   Air Navigation and Transport Act, 1936 (1936/40 [I.F.S.]), regulating air transport and providing for formation of Aer Lingus as national airline

Sept. 30   Seán Lester (see 22 Jan. 1934) appointed deputy secretary-general, League of Nations (acting secretary-general, 1940-47)

Nov. 20   General O'Duffy and followers leave Ire. for Spain to fight for nationalists as 'Irish brigade'

Nov. 28   Agricultural Wages Act, 1936 (1936/53 [I.F.S.]), providing minimum rates for farm workers

   Liffey Reservoir Act, 1936 (1936/54 [I.F.S.]), empowering Electricity Supply Board to carry out hydro-electric scheme at Poulaphouca, Co. Wicklow

Nov.   First meeting, at Royal Irish Academy, of Irish Historical Society, formed in Dublin to promote scientific study of Irish history; president Eoin Mac Neill, secretary R. Dudley Edwards (see 24 Feb. 1936, 1, 24 Mar. 1938)

Dec. 11   Edward VIII abdicates; succ. by George VI

De Valera introduces at emergency meeting of dáil: (1) Constitution Amendment (No. 27) Bill (enacted same day as 1936/57), removing from I.F.S. constitution all references to crown and governor general; (2) Executive Authority (External Relations) Bill (enacted following day as 1936/58), giving effect to abdication and recognising crown for purposes of diplomatic representation and international agreements (see 21 Dec. 1948)

Dec. 16   Irish unit led by Frank Ryan, left-wing republican, arrives in Spain to join government forces (cf. 20 Nov.)

1937

Feb. 6-27   Battle of Jarama: Irish volunteers serve on both sides; deaths of Rev. R. M. Hilliard and Charles Donnelly on government side

Feb. 24   Spanish Civil War (Non-intervention) Act, 1937 (1937/1 [I.F.S.])

Feb. 28   Census in N.I.: population 1,279,745 (1·8% increase; see 18 Apr. 1926)

Mar. 15   Dorothy Macardle's *The Irish republic* (London; 4th ed., Dublin, 1951)

Apr. 1   Irish Meteorological Service takes over full operation of meteorological facilities in I.F.S. from British service

May 1   Draft constitution of Éire published

May 28   Arthur Neville Chamberlain app. P.M. of U.K. (see 7 June 1935, 10 May 1940)

June 8   Executive Powers (Consequential Provisions) Act, 1937 (1937/20 [I.F.S.]), transferring to executive council all functions of crown representative

June 14   Dáil approves constitution bill; dáil dissolved

June 22   O'Duffy and Irish brigade return from Spain

July 1   I.F.S. general election: Fianna Fáil 69, Fine Gael 48, lab. 13, ind. and others 8; referendum on new constitution (for 685,105, against 526,945) (see 24 Jan. 1933, 17 June 1938)

July 28-9   George VI visits N.I.

Sept.   Forrest Reid's *Peter Waring* (London)

Oct. 2   American tour of Abbey Theatre company opens at Schubert's Theater, New York (ends at National Theater, Washington, 21 May 1938)

Oct. 10   Michael Browne consecrated bp of Galway

Oct.   Robert Lloyd Praeger's *The way that I went* (Dublin; 2nd ed., 1939; 3rd ed., 1947)

Dec. 29   New constitution of Éire comes into effect

Conrad M. Arensberg's *The Irish countryman: an anthropological study* (London)

1938

Jan. 17-19   Talks in London between de Valera and Chamberlain

Feb. 9   N.I. general election: un. 39, ind. un. 3, nat. 8, lab. 1, ind. lab. 1 (see 30 Nov. 1933, 14 June 1945)

Mar. 1   First number of *Irish Historical Studies: the joint journal of the Irish Historical Society and the Ulster Society for Irish Historical Studies*, edited by R. Dudley Edwards and T. W. Moody (see 24 Feb., Dec. 1936)

Mar. 11-13   German troops occupy Austria—*Anschluss*

Mar. 24   Irish Committee of Historical Sciences, to provide for representation of Irish historical interests on Comité International des Sciences Historiques, founded jointly by Irish Historical Society and Ulster Society for Irish Historical Studies (see 24 Feb., Dec. 1936, 18 May 1938)

Apr. 25   Anglo-Irish agreements on 'treaty ports', finance and trade

Apr. 26   Craigavon announces that U.K. government has agreed to find means to maintain N.I. social services at U.K. level if N.I. revenue proves insufficient

Apr. 27   First meeting of new Seanad Éireann

May 16   Finance (Agreement with U.K.) Act, 1938 (1938/12 [Éire]), giving effect to agreement of 25 Apr.

May 17   Éire (Confirmation of Agreements) Act, 1938 (1 & 2 Geo. VI, c. 25 [U.K.])

May 18   Application for admission of Ire. as a cultural unit to Comité International des Sciences Historiques approved by bureau of Comité, meeting at Brussels (see 24 Mar., 28 Aug.)

May 25   Government defeated in dáil (51 to 52) on issue of compulsory arbitration for civil servants (dáil dissolved, 27 May)

June 17   Éire general election: Fianna Fáil 77, Fine Gael 45, lab. 9, ind. and others 7 (see 1 July 1937, 22 June 1943)

June 25   Douglas Hyde inaugurated as president of Ire. (see 16 June 1945)

July 11   Cork harbour defences transferred to Irish government (last British troops leave, 11 Nov.)

Aug. 15   Clann na Talmhan formed at meeting of small farmers at Athenry, Co. Galway

Aug. 28   Ire. admitted as a cultural unit at eighth quinquennial congress of Comité International des Sciences Historiques, meeting at Zürich (see 18 May)

Sept. 12   De Valera elected president of assembly of League of Nations for session

Sept. 30   Agreement at Munich between Hitler, Mussolini, Chamberlain and Daladier provides for dismemberment of Czechoslovakia

Oct. 17   De Valera offers N.I. retention of its existing status (subject to 'fair' treatment of its minority), with transfer to Dublin of powers reserved to Westminster

Dec. 22   Sir Richard Dawson Bates, N.I. minister of home affairs, invokes special powers act and reintroduces internment; 34 arrests

Dec. 23   Announcement of new movement to promote better understanding between north and south of Ire. (becomes Irish Association for Cultural, Economic and Social Relations)

Short & Harland (becomes Short Brothers & Harland, Nov. 1947) begins production at aircraft factory at Queen's Island, Belfast (first completed plane flies, Mar. 1939)

1939

Jan. 10   Commn on vocational organisation, under Bp. Browne, app. by Éire government (report submitted, Nov. 1943; published, Aug. 1944)

Jan. 12   I.R.A. ultimatum to Viscount Halifax, British foreign secretary, demanding undertaking to withdraw British troops from Irish soil

Jan. 16   First of series of I.R.A. bomb attacks in England (ends, Mar. 1940)

Jan. 28   W. B. Yeats dies at Rocquebrune, near Monaco (see 17 Sept. 1948)

Feb. 10   Pius XI dies (Eugenio Pacelli elected pope as Pius XII, 2 Mar.)

Feb. 19   De Valera states: 'The aim of government policy is to maintain and preserve our neutrality in the event of war.'

Mar. 13   *At Swim-two-birds* by Flann O'Brien (Brian O'Nolan, Myles na Gopaleen) (London)

Mar. 15   German troops occupy Bohemia and Moravia

Mar. 31   End of Spanish civil war

May 4   Chamberlain announces that N.I. will be excluded from British conscription bill

James Joyce's *Finnegans wake* (New York and London)

May 30   Treason Act, 1939 (1939/10 [Ire.]), providing death penalty for treason as defined in article 39 of constitution

June 14   Offences against the State Act, 1939 (1939/13 [Éire])

July 4   Matrimonial Causes Act (Northern Ireland), 1939 (2 & 3 Geo. VI, c. 13), conferring on N.I. supreme court power to grant divorce for adultery, desertion, cruelty, or incurable unsoundness of mind

Aug. 23   Non-aggression pact between Germany and U.S.S.R.

Aug. 25   I.R.A. bomb in Coventry kills 5, wounds 70 (Peter Barnes and James McCormack convicted; hanged 7 Feb. 1940)

Aug.   Steel works of Irish Steel Ltd at Haulbowline in Cork Harbour begins production (closed, owing to financial and operating difficulties, Feb. 1941–Feb. 1943, Nov. 1946–Sept. 1947; firm revived as Irish Steel Holdings Ltd, 23 June 1947)

Sept. 1   Germany invades Poland and annexes Danzig

Sept. 2   De Valera announces government's intention to remain neutral in European war

First Amendment of the Constitution Act, 1939 [Éire], extending term 'time of war' in article 28 to include armed conflict in which state does not participate but in respect of which each house of oireachtas has resolved that national emergency exists

Sept. 3   Britain and France declare war on Germany

Emergency Powers Act, 1939 (1939/28 [Éire])

Sept. 13 Petrol rationing introduced in Éire (in N.I., 23 Sept.)

Sept. 17 U.S.S.R. invades Poland (signs treaty with Germany partitioning Poland, 30 Sept.)

Sept. 22 De Valera informs Chamberlain that he agrees to appointment of Sir John Maffey as U.K. minister in Éire

Dec. 8 Maternity hospital opened at Drogheda by Medical Missionaries of Mary (see 11 May 1936, 8 Sept. 1957)

Dec. 23 I.R.A. raid on Magazine Fort, Phoenix Park, Dublin

1940

Jan. 3 Irish government introduces 2 emergency bills to combat I.R.A.: Emergency Powers (Amendment) Bill (enacted as 1940/1) and Offences against the State (Amendment) Bill (enacted as 1940/2)

Jan. 8 Food rationing (bacon, butter and sugar) introduced in N.I.

Feb. 25 Nine I.R.A. prisoners in Éire begin hunger strike (2 die, 16, 19 Apr.; strike ends)

Mar. 11 First production of Ulster Group Theatre, comprising Ulster Theatre, Northern Irish Players, and Jewish Institute Dramatic Society

Apr. 9 Germany invades Denmark and Norway

May 5 Herman Goertz, member of Abwehr secret service, lands by parachute in Co. Meath (arrested 27 Nov. 1941)

May 10 Germany invades Holland, Belgium, and Luxembourg

Winston Spencer Churchill (con.) app. P.M. of U.K. (see 28 May 1937, 26 July 1945)

May 15 German army pierces French defences near Sedan and sweeps into France, resulting in French collapse

May 29–June 3 British forces evacuated from Dunkirk

June 10 Italy declares war on Britain and France

June 19 Institute for Advanced Studies Act, 1940 (1940/13 [Ire.])

June 22 France concludes armistice with Germany

Aug. 14 Seán Russell, I.R.A. chief of staff, dies in German submarine off Galway coast (Frank Ryan (see 16 Dec. 1936) returns in submarine to Germany)

Aug. 26 Bombs from German aircraft destroy creamery and kill 3 people at Campile, Co. Wexford

5,000-ton prison ship anchors in Strangford Lough for reception of I.R.A. internees

Sept. 6 Execution of Patrick McGrath and Thomas Harte for murder of Detective-officer Richard Hyland (16 Aug.)

Oct. First number of *The Bell*; editor Sean O'Faolain (continues till Dec. 1954)

Nov. 7 De Valera informs dáil of government's unwillingness to lease 'treaty ports' to Britain

Nov. 24 Viscount Craigavon, P.M. of N.I., dies (succ. by J. M. Andrews, 25 Nov.) (see 7 June 1921, 28 Apr. 1943)

Dec. 27 John Charles McQuaid consecrated catholic abp of Dublin

1941

Jan. 1, 2, 3 German bombs dropped in Carlow, Dublin, Kildare, Louth, Meath, Wexford, and Wicklow

Jan. 2 British government decides to restrict volume of shipping to Irish ports

Jan. 10 Severe cut in petrol ration in Éire

Sir John Lavery, painter, dies

Jan. 13 James Joyce dies in Zürich

Jan. 16 Case of foot-and-mouth confirmed near Eglinton, Co. Londonderry

Jan. 28 Emergency Powers Order (No. 67) provides for censorship of press messages to places outside Éire

Feb. 10 Edward John Gwynn, provost of Trinity College, Dublin, dies

Mar. 23 Government announces formation of Irish Shipping Co.

Apr. 7-8 First German air-raids on Belfast and other towns in N.I.

Apr. 15-16 German air-raids on N.I.: main target Belfast—over 700 killed and over 400 seriously wounded; fire-brigades sent from Dublin and other towns in Éire

May 4-5 More German air-raids on Belfast: 150 dead, extensive damage to shipyard and aircraft factory

May 7 Éire government issues order prohibiting wage increases (amending order, 9 Apr. 1942)

May 26 At emergency meeting of dáil de Valera, Cosgrave, and William Norton (leader of labour party) protest against British government's proposal to apply conscription to N.I.

May 31 German bombing of North Strand, Dublin: 34 dead, 90 injured, 300 houses destroyed or damaged

June 19 Irish government announces that German government has expressed regret for bombing of Dublin and promised compensation

June 22 Germany invades Russia

June 30 Kidnapping of Stephen Hayes, formerly chief of staff of I.R.A.

July 10 Dublin branch of Communist Party of Ireland suspends activities owing to question of Éire's neutrality (Belfast branches vigorously support war effort in N.I. henceforth (see 11 June 1933, 15 Mar. 1970))

July W. R. Rodgers's first vol. of verse *Awake! and other poems* (London)

Sept. 18 Seán McCaughey (alias Dunlop) convicted by special military court in Dublin of unlawfully assaulting and detaining Stephen Hayes and sentenced to death (sentence commuted, 25 Sept.)

Sept. 23 Trade Union Act, 1941 (1941/22 [Éire]), setting up tribunal with power to license unions having greatest number of members in given industry as sole negotiators for workers

Dec. 4 Belfast Willowfield by-election: Harry Midgley (lab.) wins traditionally unionist seat in N.I. H.C.

Dec. 7   Japanese attack on Pearl Harbor, Hawaii

Dec. 8   U.S.A. and Britain declare war on Japan

Dec. 11   Germany and Italy declare war on U.S.A.

Dec. 17   Lord Cranborne, secretary of state for dominions, meets de Valera in Dublin for talks on Irish neutrality

An béal bocht, by Myles na Gopaleen (Flann O'Brien, Brian O'Nolan) (Dublin; 2nd ed., 1942; 3rd ed., 1964; translation by Patrick C. Power as *The poor mouth* (London, 1973))

1942

Jan. 26   U.S. troops land in N.I., first to arrive in Europe

Feb. 5   U.S. naval base established in Derry

Feb. 15   Singapore surrenders to Japan

Feb. 17   Éire government demands that German minister cease to use radio transmitter (transmitter deposited in Dublin bank, 21 Dec. 1943)

Feb. 19   James Dillon, deputy leader Fine Gael, resigns from party, following criticism of his advocacy of Irish-American alliance

Mar. 25   Federated Union of Employers (formed from merger of previously existing bodies in Éire) certified as trade union under Trade Union Act, 1941 (see 23 Sept. 1941)

Apr. 3   I.R.A. attack R.U.C. in Dungannon, Co. Tyrone (similar attack in Belfast, 5 Apr.)

Apr.   Patrick Kavanagh's *The great hunger* (Dublin)

May 26   Referendum Act, 1942 (1942/8 [Éire]), laying down procedure for referendums on amendments to constitution or on bills referred by president under article 27 of constitution

July   Eric Cross's *The tailor and Ansty* (London) (banned in Éire, 25 Sept.)

Sept. 2   Thomas Williams, member of Belfast brigade of I.R.A., hanged in Belfast for murder of Constable Patrick Murphy (5 Apr.)

Oct. 23   Battle of El Alamein (in Egyptian desert) begins

Nov. 4   Central Bank Act, 1942 (1942/22 [Éire]), dissolving currency commission and establishing central bank as currency authority (see 28 July 1971)

Emyr Estyn Evans's *Irish heritage: the landscape, the people and their work* (Dundalk)

1943

Feb. 1   Council for the Encouragement of Music and the Arts established in N.I.

Feb. 2   Battle of Stalingrad ends

Feb. 9   West Belfast by-election: Jack Beattie (lab.) wins seat in U.K. H.C.

Mar. 3   Dáil informed that president has referred School Attendance Bill, 1942, to supreme court for ruling whether section 4 (empowering minister to certify standard of private education) is repugnant to constitution

Mar. 17   First number of *Indiu* (spelt *Inniu* from 24 Sept. 1954), weekly newsmagazine in Irish

Mar. 25   Edmund Curtis, Irish historian, dies

Apr. 1   Office of Ulster king of arms, Dublin castle, ceases to exist

Apr. 15   Supreme court, Dublin, rules that section 4 of School Attendance Bill is repugnant to constitution

Apr. 28   J. M. Andrews resigns at P.M. of N.I. (see 24 Nov. 1940; succ. by Sir Basil Brooke (created Viscount Brookeborough, 4 July 1952), minister of commerce, 1 May; see 25 Mar. 1963))

June 22   Éire general election: Fianna Fáil 67, Fine Gael 32, lab. 17, Clann na Talmhan 10, farmers 5, ind. and others 7 (see 17 June 1938, 30 May 1944)

July 10   U.S. and British forces land in Sicily (invade Italian mainland, 3 Sept.)

Sept. 16-Oct. 9   First Irish Exhibition of Living Art

Oct. 26   Comhdháil Náisiúnta na Gaeilge, coordinating body for Irish language organisations, formed

David Allardyce Webb's *An Irish flora* (Dundalk; 2nd ed., 1953; 3rd ed., 1959)

1944

Jan. 7   Irish Transport & General Workers' Union executive serves labour party with notice of disaffiliation

Jan. 14   Disruption in labour party in Éire: 5 deputies, all members of I.T.G.W.U., secede to form National Labour Party (see 6 June 1950)

Jan. 18   W. T. Cosgrave resigns leadership of Fine Gael (Richard Mulcahy elected leader, 26 Jan.)

Feb. 21   David Gray, U.S. minister in Dublin, hands de Valera note requesting Irish government to have German and Japanese representatives recalled (request refused)

Feb. 23   Children's Allowances Act, 1944 (1944/2 [Éire]), provides for grants of 2s. 6d. a week for third and further children under 16

Feb. 25-Apr. 8   Strike at Harland and Wolff shipyard, Belfast

May 9   Éire government defeated (63 to 64) on second reading of transport bill (government announces (10 May) decision to hold general election)

May 30   Éire general election: Fianna Fáil 76, Fine Gael 30, Clann na Talmhan 11, lab. 8, national lab. 4, farmers 2, ind. 7 (see 22 June 1943, 4 Feb. 1948)

June 6   Allied landings in Normandy

June 10   Frank Ryan (see 14 Aug. 1940) dies in Germany

Dec. 8   Transport Act, 1944 (1944/21 [Éire]), establishes Córas Iompair Éireann to take over Great Southern Railways Co. and Dublin United Transport Co. Ltd and generally to control and reorganise transport

1945

Feb. 3   Irish-American agreement at Washington on air traffic; Shannon becomes compulsory port of call

Feb. 4-11   Conference at Yalta, in Crimea: Churchill, Roosevelt, and Stalin discuss plans to secure unconditional surrender of Germany

Feb. 6   Housing Act (Northern Ireland), 1945 (8 & 9 Geo. VI, c. 2), establishes Northern Ireland Housing Trust

Apr. 25   Congress of Irish Unions formed by I.T.G.W.U., 9 other unions also hitherto members of Irish Trade Union Congress, and 5 others; all have head offices in Éire (see 10 Feb. 1959)

Apr. 28   Mussolini killed by partisans

Apr. 30   Hitler kills himself in Berlin

May 2   De Valera, as taoiseach and minister for external affairs, calls upon German minister in Dublin to express official condolences on death of Hitler, German head of state

May 5   Racing Board and Racecourses Act, 1945 (1945/16 [Éire]), providing for improvement of horse breeding and establishing racing board to control racing and betting

May 7-8   Flag incidents at College Green, Dublin, outside Trinity College, and elsewhere in Dublin

May 8   'V.E. day': end of war in Europe

May 13   Winston Churchill, in victory speech, praises N.I. and reproaches de Valera for their respective parts in second world war

May 16   De Valera replies to Churchill

June 14   N.I. general election: un. 33, ind. un. 2, nat. 10, lab. 2, ind. lab. 1, Commonwealth Lab. 1, socialist republican 1, ind. 2 (see 9 Feb. 1938, 10 Feb. 1949)

June 16   Seán T. O'Kelly elected president of Éire on second count, having failed to win absolute majority over opponents Seán Mac Eoin (Fine Gael) and Patrick McCartan (independent republican) (installed 25 June) (see 25 June 1952)

June 19   Seán Lemass tánaiste in succession to Seán T. O'Kelly

June 26   United Nations charter signed at San Francisco

July 5   U.K. general election: in G.B.—lab. 393, con. 188, lib. 12, nat. lib. 11, ind. lab. 3, national 2, others 30; in N.I.—un. 9, ind. un. 1, nat. 2, ind. lab. 1 (see 14 Nov. 1935, 23 Feb. 1950)

July 11   Question from James Dillon in Dáil Éireann elicits from taoiseach assertion that state is republic

July 17-Aug. 2   Potsdam conference: Stalin, Truman, Churchill, and Attlee settle occupation of Germany

July 25   Sir Basil Brooke, replying to de Valera's declaration that Éire is republic, repeats Ulster's determination to remain in U.K.

July 26   Clement Richard Attlee (lab.) app. P.M. of U.K. (heading first labour ministry with overall majority) (see 10 May 1940, 26 Oct. 1951)

Aug. 4   National Stud Act, 1945 (1945/31 [Éire]), vesting stud at Tully, Co. Kildare, in minister for agriculture, with provision for promotion of private company to manage it

Aug. 6   U.S. drops atomic bomb on Hiroshima (second dropped on Nagasaki, 9 Aug.)

Aug. 14   Japan surrenders: end of second world war

Sept. 16   John McCormack, operatic and concert singer, dies

Nov. 14   Irish Anti-Partition League formed at catholic convention at Dungannon

Dec. 13   Family Allowances Act (Northern Ireland), 1945 (1945, c. 19), provides for grants of 5s. per week for second and further children

1946

Jan. 3   William Joyce ('Lord Haw-Haw') hanged in London for treason

Feb. 3   Censorship of Publications Act, 1946 (1946/1 [Éire]), establishes appeal board (see 16 July 1929)

Feb. 19   National Insurance Act (Northern Ireland), 1946 (1946, c. 3), bringing N.I. into line with British welfare legislation

Feb. 28   Public Health (Tuberculosis) Act (Northern Ireland), 1946 (1946, c. 6), providing for setting up of Tuberculosis Authority to coordinate efforts for eradication of tuberculosis (authority dissolved, 31 Mar. 1959, being by then redundant)

Elections and Franchise Act (Northern Ireland), 1946 (1946, c. 8), increasing to 6 number of business votes available in local elections to single occupier

Mar. 4-27   Conference in Dublin, convened on initiative of Provisional International Civil Aviation Organisation, to discuss North Atlantic air navigation

Mar. 20-Oct. 30   Irish National Teachers' Organisation strike in Dublin

May 11   Seán McCaughey dies on hunger strike in Portlaoise prison (see 18 Sept. 1941)

May 12   Census in Éire: population 2,955,107 (0·45 % decline; see 26 Apr. 1936)

June 1   Turf Development Act, 1946 (1946/10 [Éire]), establishing Bord na Móna

July 4   Supreme court, Dublin, rules that main provision of Trade Union Act, 1941 (see 23 Sept. 1941) is repugnant to constitution

July 6   Formation of Clann na Poblachta, republican party with left-wing social policy (leader Seán Mac Bride)

July 24   Dáil Éireann agrees without division to application for membership of United Nations Organisation

July 28   Bread rationing introduced in N.I. (cf. 18 Jan. 1947)

Aug. 13   U.S.S.R. opposes Éire's application for admission to United Nations Organisation on ground that Éire has no diplomatic relations with her

Aug. 27   Industrial Research and Standards Act, 1946 (1946/25 [Éire]), establishes Institute for Industrial Research and Standards

Industrial Relations Act, 1946 (1946/26 [Éire]), providing for establishment of labour court

Oct. 3 Provisional cttee set up for Association for the Preservation of Places of Interest and Beauty in Ireland (articles of association, under title An Taisce: the National Trust for Ireland, approved, 18 Nov. 1947; officers app., 15 July 1948)

Dec. 24 Ministers and Secretaries (Amendment) Act, 1946 (1946/38 [Éire]), creating new departments of health and social services

1947

Jan. 18 Bread rationing introduced in Éire

Jan. 30 James Larkin dies

Feb. Combination of prolonged cold weather and acute shortage of fuel brings industry to virtual standstill

Mar. 27 Education Act (Northern Ireland), 1947 (1947, c. 3), providing for secondary education for all from age of 11 and raising school-leaving age from 14 to 15 (not implemented till 1957); state grant for building and maintaining voluntary schools raised from 50 to 65 per cent of costs

Mar. School of Cosmic Physics established in Dublin Institute for Advanced Studies, following transfer of Dunsink observatory from T.C.D. to D.I.A.S.

Apr. 21 Shannon Airport formally declared customs-free area

June 23-4 Celtic Congress in Dublin, attended by delegates from Brittany, Cornwall, Ire., Isle of Man, Scotland, and Wales.

June 24 De Valera declares: 'As a matter of our external policy, we are associated with the states of the British Commonwealth. We are not at the present time regarded as members of it but we are regarded as associates.'

July 31 Northern Ireland Act, 1947 (10 & 11 Geo. VI, c. 37 [U.K.]) extending legislative power of N.I. parliament to schemes (electricity, water, etc.) operating on both sides of border

Aug. 13 Health Act, 1947 (1947/28 [Éire]), increasing responsibilities of county councils, reducing number of authorities concerned with health, and providing mother-and-child services

Aug. 15 Indian empire becomes independent as two separate states, India and Pakistan

Oct. 7 Catholic hierarchy writes to de Valera expressing disapproval of parts of Health Act, 1947, especially those dealing with mother-and-child services

Oct. 30 Professor Michael Tierney elected president of University College, Dublin

Polling in 3 by-elections, 2 of which are won by Clann na Poblachta; Seán MacBride returned for Co. Dublin

Dec. 23 Safeguarding of Employment Act (Northern Ireland), 1947 (1947, c. 24), restricting employment of persons who are not 'Northern Ireland workers'

1948

Feb. 4 Éire general election: Fianna Fáil 68, Fine Gael 31, lab. 14, national lab. 5, Clann na Poblachta 10, Clann na Talmhan 7, ind. and others 12 (see 30 May 1944, 30 May 1951)

Health Services Act (Northern Ireland), 1948 (1948, c. 3), on lines of British national health service

Feb. 18 John Aloysius Costello elected taoiseach, 75 to 68, becoming head of first coalition government (see 9 Mar. 1932, 13 June 1951)

Mar. 8-Apr. 6 De Valera tours U.S.A. (tours Australia and New Zealand, 27 Apr.-11 June; visits India, 14-16 June)

Mar. 31 U.S. congress passes Marshall aid act to assist European recovery

Mar. Agreement on wages reached between Federated Union of Employers, Irish Trade Union Congress, and Congress of Irish Unions (published, 11 Mar.); first 'national wages agreement'

Apr. 16 Organisation for European Economic Development established; Éire and U.K. members

May 14 Jewish state of Israel established in Palestine

May Waterford Glass Ltd opens training factory (production begins, Sept. 1951)

June 22 R.C. bps issue statement condemning suggestions for abolition of Sunday closing of public houses in rural areas in Éire (see 16 Aug. 1878)

July 14 Martin Corry introduces bill to end rural Sunday closing (defeated in dáil by 106 votes to 23, 17 Nov.)

Aug. 10 Transport Act (Northern Ireland), 1948 (1948, c. 16), establishes Ulster Transport Authority empowered 'to convey goods and passengers by rail, road and inland waterway' (replaced by Northern Ireland Transport Holding Co., 1 Apr. 1968)

Sept. 7 Costello, in Canada, announces government's intention to repeal external relations act of 1936 (see 21 Dec.)

Sept. 14 Body of W. B. Yeats reburied at Drumcliff, Co. Sligo

Oct. 13 Judgment in high court, Dublin, dismissing claim of Foyle and Bann Fisheries Ltd to exclusive fishing rights in link of River Foyle in parish of Clonleigh, Co. Donegal (see 9 July 1950)

Dec. 21 Republic of Ireland Act, 1948 (1948/22 [Éire]), repeals Executive Authority (External Relations) Act, 1936, and provides for declaration of republic (see 11 Dec. 1936, 18 Apr., 2 June 1949)

1949

Jan. 27 Leaders of all political parties in Éire confer at Mansion House, Dublin, and agree on collection of 'anti-partition fund' at all catholic churches on following Sunday (30 Jan.)

Feb. 10 N.I. general election: un. 37, ind. un. 2, Anti-partition League 9, ind. lab. 1, socialist republican 1, ind. 2 (see 5 July 1945, 22 Oct. 1953)

Feb. 23 Seán MacBride, minister for external affairs, announces that continuance of Britain's sovereignty in N.I. makes it impossible for Éire to sign proposed Atlantic pact (see 4 Apr.)

Feb. Elizabeth Bowen's *The heat of the day* (London)

Apr. 3 Formation in Belfast of Irish labour party, anti-partitionist in character and closely connected with labour party in Dublin

Apr. 4 North Atlantic treaty against armed aggression signed in Washington by U.S.A., Canada, Britain, France, and other countries

Apr. 9 N.I. labour party pledges itself to 'maintain unbroken the connection between Great Britain and Northern Ireland as a part of the Commonwealth and to . . . seek the closest possible means of cooperation with the British Labour Party'

Apr. 18 Éire formally becomes republic and leaves Commonwealth

May 5 Ten west European countries including U.K. and R.I. sign convention in London establishing Council of Europe to promote political unity; cttee of ministers and consultative assembly with seat at Strasbourg

June 2 Ireland Act, 1949 (12, 13 & 14 Geo. VI, c. 41 [U.K.]), declaring that Republic is not part of H.M.'s dominions but that it is not to be regarded as a foreign country nor are its citizens to be regarded as aliens in U.K. or colonies; and that in no circumstances will N.I. or any part thereof cease to be part of H.M.'s dominions without consent of N.I. parliament

July 10 Last tramcar runs in Dublin

July 30 Land Reclamation Act, 1949 (1949/25 [R.I.]), providing for state financing of undeveloped land

Sept. 9 Louis MacNeice's *Collected poems* (London)

Sept. 18 Devaluation of £, in U.K. and R.I., from $4.03 to $2.80

Nov. 26 Bread rationing reintroduced in R.I.

Dec. 21 Irish News Agency Act, 1949 (1949/33 [R.I.]), empowering minister for external affairs to promote company for publication of news and information

Máirtín Ó Cadhain's *Cré na cille* (Dublin)

1950

Jan. 1 Holy Year begins (generally celebrated by Irish catholics)

Jan. 19 First peat-fired electricity station, at Portarlington, Co. Leix, comes into operation

Jan. 21 Treaty of friendship, commerce, and navigation between Ire. and U.S.A.

Feb. 23 U.K. general election: in G.B.—lab. 315, con. 272, national lib. and con. 16, lib. 9, others 1; in N.I.—un. 10, Anti-partition League 2 (see 5 July 1945, 25 Oct. 1951)

Apr. 4 Council of education (R.I.) appointed (see 12 Aug. 1954)

June 6 Labour party and National Labour party agree to reunite under leadership of William Norton (see 14 Jan. 1944)

June 8 Thomas Walter Freeman's *Ireland: a general and regional geography* (London; 2nd ed., 1960; 3rd ed., 1965; 4th ed., 1969)

June 13   Erne Drainage and Development Act (1950/15 [R.I.]), to give effect to agreement with government of N.I. for joint scheme of drainage and electricity generation (see 27 June)

June 20   R.C. bps issue statement strongly condemning agitation by publicans for legislation to end Sunday closing in R.I.

June 25   Outbreak of war in Korea (ends 27 July 1953)

June 27   Erne Drainage and Development Act (Northern Ireland), 1950 (1950, c. 15) (see 13 June)

July 9   Belfast and Dublin governments separately announce agreement on control of Lough Foyle fisheries (see 13 Oct. 1948)

Aug. 5   Supreme court in Dublin delivers judgment in Tilson case, ruling (by 4 to 1) that ante-nuptial promises regarding religious upbringing of children are valid, and that under constitution both parents have equal rights in bringing up children

Sept. 6   84 paintings of French Barbizon school presented to National Gallery of Ireland by Alfred Chester Beatty, mining magnate and art collector (see 8 Aug. 1953)

Sept.   Walter Macken's *Rain on the wind* (London)

Oct. 11   R.I. minister for health, Dr Noel Browne, informed, at interview with catholic abp of Dublin and bps of Ferns and Galway, of hierarchy's objections to 'mother-and-child' scheme

Nov. 2   George Bernard Shaw, playwright and critic, dies (see 20 Feb. 1957)

Dec. 1   E. J. Moeran, composer, dies at Kenmare, Co. Kerry

Dec. 20   Industrial Development Authority Act, 1950 (1950/29 [R.I.])

Dec. 23   Bank strike in R.I. (continuing till 16 Feb. 1951)

Dec. 26   James Stephens, writer, dies

1951

Jan. 9   Agreement between governments of R.I. and N.I. on future of Great Northern Railway

Apr. 4   Catholic bps condemn Dr Noel Browne's 'mother-and-child' scheme as 'opposed to catholic social teaching'

Apr. 8   Census in R.I. and N.I.: population of R.I. 2,960,593 (0·19% increase); population of N.I. 1,370,921 (7·1% increase) (see 12 May 1946)

Apr. 11   Dr Noel Browne resigns as minister for health (R.I.) (at request of Seán MacBride, his leader) and from Clann na Poblachta

Apr. 18   France, West Germany, Italy, Belgium, Holland, and Luxembourg ('the six') sign treaty of Paris establishing European Coal and Steel Community (effective, 25 July 1952)

May 8   Arts Act, 1951 (1951/9 [R.I.]), establishing Arts Council

May 30   R.I. general election: Fianna Fáil 69, Fine Gael 40, lab. 16, Clann na Talmhan 6, Clann na Poblachta 2, ind. and others 14 (see 4 Feb. 1948, 18 May 1954)

June 13   De Valera elected taoiseach by 74 to 69 (see 18 Feb. 1948, 2 June 1954)

July 18   Abbey Theatre destroyed by fire

Aug. 23   Public Order Act (Northern Ireland), 1951 (1951, c. 19), requiring written notice of processions (other than customary processions)

Oct. 21-Nov. 4   First Wexford opera festival

Oct. 25   U.K. general election: in G.B.—con. 293, national lib. and con. 19, lab. 295, lib. 6; in N.I.—un. 9, Anti-partition League 2, Irish lab. 1 (see 23 Feb. 1950, 26 May 1955)

Oct. 26   Churchill (con.) app. P.M. of U.K. for second time (see 26 July 1945, 6 Apr. 1955)

Nov. 15   Royal Academy of Sciences, Stockholm, decides to award Nobel prize for physics in equal parts to E. T. S. Walton, professor of natural and experimental philosophy, Trinity College, Dublin, and Sir John Cockcroft, director, Atomic Energy Establishment, Harwell, Berks, 'for their pioneer work in the transmutation of atomic nuclei by artificially accelerated atomic particles' (see 14 Apr. 1932; prize awarded at Stockholm, 10 Dec. 1951)

Dec. 21   Córas Tráchtála incorporated as body for promotion of exports

Dec.   Sam Hanna Bell's *December bride* (London)

1952

Feb. 6   George VI dies; succ. by Elizabeth II

Apr. 8   Foyle fisheries purchase agreement signed in Dublin by R.I. minister for agriculture, N.I. minister of commerce, and 4 members of the Honourable the Irish Society

Apr. 22   Sea Fisheries Act, 1952 (1952/7 [R.I.]), establishing Bord Iascaigh Mhara for improvement and regulation of sea fishing

June 14   Social Welfare Act, 1952 (1952/11 [R.I.]), establishing coordinated system of social insurance

June 25   Seán T. O'Kelly inaugurated as president for second time (see 16 June 1945, 7 June 1959)

July 3   Tourist Traffic Act, 1952 (1952/15 [R.I.]), establishing Bord Fáilte ('welcome board') as organisation for promotion of tourism

July 11-Aug. 29   Suspension of publication of Dublin newspapers, caused by dispute in printing trade

Dec. 9   Inaugural meeting of Irish Management Institute

Dec. 13   Adoption Act, 1952 (1952/25 [R.I.]), providing for legal adoption of children: adopters to be of same 'religion' as child and its parents or, if child illegitimate, as its mother; married couple adopting to be of same 'religion' (certain protestant denominations grouped together for purposes of these provisions; for amendment see 29 July 1974)

1953

Jan. 1 Comhairle Radio Éireann (council of 5 app. by Erskine Childers, minister for posts and telegraphs, to exercise general control, under him, of broadcasting service) takes office, with Maurice Gorham as director of broadcasting (see 12 Apr. 1960)

Jan. 5 First public performance of Samuel Beckett's 'En attendant Godot', at Théâtre de Babylone, Paris (performed in London as 'Waiting for Godot', 3 Aug. 1955)

Jan. 31 Loss of car ferry *Princess Victoria* and about 130 lives, between Stranraer and Larne in storm

Mar. 5 Stalin dies

Apr. 5-26 An tóstal ('pageant'): community festival in Dublin and towns and villages throughout republic

May 1 Official beginning of transmissions from B.B.C.'s temporary television station at Ballygomartin, Belfast

May 3 Gael-Linn, organisation for promotion of Irish, financed by football pool (*linn* = pool), established

May 30 *Irish Independent* begins publication of B.B.C. television schedules, first Dublin newspaper to do so (*Irish Times* following suit, 15 June)

June 2 Coronation of Queen Elizabeth II marked in Dublin by picketing of British embassy by Anti-Partition Association and by absence of Irish government representatives from ambassadorial garden party

June 15 Bomb explodes inside Newry cinema where film on coronation is scheduled

July 1-3 Queen Elizabeth II visits N.I. for first time

Aug. 8 Chester Beatty library opened in Dublin: collection of oriental pictures, manuscripts, etc., assembled by Alfred Chester Beatty (see 6 Sept. 1950)

Sept. 1 Beginning of operation of Great Northern Railway by joint board nominated in equal numbers by governments in Dublin and Belfast

Sept. 27 First Thomas Davis lecture broadcast by Radio Éireann (series treating historical and cultural subjects at scholarly level)

Oct. 3 Sir Arnold Bax, composer, dies in Cork

Oct. 19 Official opening of central bus station (Áras Mhic Dhiarmada, later better known as Busáras), in Store Street, Dublin; architect, Michael Scott

Oct. 22 N.I. general election: un. 38, ind. un. 1, Anti-partition League 7, ind. nat. 2, ind. lab. 1, Irish lab. 1, republican lab. 1, ind. 1 (see 10 Feb. 1949, 20 Mar. 1958)

Oct. 29 Health Act, 1953 (1953/26 [R.I.]), providing free mother-and-child service to dependents of all persons insured under Social Welfare Act, 1952 (see 4 Apr. 1951)

John Kaye Charlesworth's *The geology of Ireland* (Edinburgh)

1954

Feb. 20 Henry Harrison, last surviving member of Parnell's parliamentary party, dies

Apr. 6 Flags and Emblems (Display) Act (Northern Ireland), 1954 (1954, c. 10), making it offence to interfere with flying of union jack, and empowering police to remove other emblems where breach of peace apprehended

Apr. 30 First Cork international choral and folk dance festival opens

May 18 R.I. general election: Fianna Fáil 65, Fine Gael 50, lab. 19, Clann na Talmhan 5, Clann na Poblachta 3, ind. and others 5 (see 30 May 1951, 5 Mar. 1957)

June 2 John Aloysius Costello (Fine Gael) elected taoiseach by 79 to 66, heading second coalition government (see 13 June 1951, 20 Mar. 1957)

June 12 I.R.A. raid on Gough military barracks, Armagh

July 12 Report of commn on emigration and other R.I. population problems (Pr. 2541) published: minority report by Cornelius Lucey, catholic bp of Cork, objecting to disproportionate growth of Dublin as result of state action; family planning recommended by Rev. A. A. Luce of Trinity College, Dublin

July 19 *Irish Times* reports myxomatosis near Bagenalstown, Co. Carlow; first outbreak in Ire.

Aug. 12 *Report of the council of education*, R.I., on the function and curriculum of the primary school (Pr. 2583) published (see 4 Apr. 1950, 25 Apr. 1962)

Oct. 17 I.R.A. attack on Omagh military barracks (see 26 May 1955)

Nov. 19 First public performance of Brendan Behan's 'The quare fellow', at Pike Theatre, Dublin

Dec. 4 Bank officials in R.I. begin working short hours (leading to closure of banks till 23 Mar. 1955)

1955

Jan. 6 National Farmers' Association formed in R.I. (see 1 Jan. 1972)

Apr. 6 Sir Anthony Eden (con.) app. P.M. of U.K. (see 26 Oct. 1951, 10 Jan. 1957)

May 26 U.K. general election: in G.B.—con. 314, national lib. and con. 21, lab. 277, lib. 6; in N.I.—un. 10, Sinn Féin 2 (both Sinn Féin members serving prison sentences for part in attack on Omagh barracks; see 17 Oct. 1954) (see 25 Oct. 1951, 8 Oct. 1959)

July 21 First regular television service in N.I. begins, from Divis transmitter in Co. Antrim

Aug. 3 First public performance of Samuel Beckett's 'Waiting for Godot', at Arts Theatre Club, London (cf. 5 Jan. 1953)

Oct. 14 Abp McQuaid makes known his disapproval of intended football match between R.I. and Yugoslavia (match played as arranged, 19 Oct.)

Nov. 26 Attack on police barracks at Rosslea, south Co. Femanagh, by Saor Uladh—'free Ulster', breakaway from I.R.A. (ban on Saor Uladh announced 29 Nov.)

Dec. 2   R.I. government applies provisions of Offences against the State Act, 1939, prohibiting any form of newspaper publicity for illegal organisations

Dec. 12   Cork opera house burned down (reopened 31 Oct. 1965)

Dec. 14   Admission of R.I. to United Nations Organisation

First number of *Ulster Folklife* (Belfast)

1956

Mar. 13   Gerard Sweetman, R.I. minister for finance, imposes special import levies in attempt to redress balance of payments deficit (imposes further levies; 25 July)

Apr. 8   Census in R.I.: population 2,898,264 (2·11% decline; see 8 Apr. 1951)

May 21-7   First Cork international film festival

May 23   Ivan Neill, N.I. minister of labour and social insurance, introduces family-allowances bill, providing increases for second and third children, but no increase for subsequent children; measure attacked as discriminatory and not included in Family Allowances and National Insurance Act (N.I.), 1956 (1956, c. 9, 24 July 1956)

May 30   Thomas Kenneth Whitaker app. secretary to R.I. department of finance

July 4   Commn of inquiry into liquor licensing laws in R.I. appointed after publicans' representations to department of justice (reports 18 July 1957, recommending abolition of Sunday closing and 'bona fide' traveller exemption) (see 23 June, 21 Oct. 1959)

July 7-10   Jawaharlal Nehru visits Dublin

July 17   Irish Nationality and Citizenship Act, 1956 (1956/26 [R.I.]), permitting persons born in N.I. after 6 Dec. 1922 to be declared Irish citizens (see 10 Apr. 1935)

July 26   Egyptian government nationalises Suez Canal Co.

Oct. 23-Nov. 4   Hungarian uprising; fall of Gerö government (24 Oct.); coalition under Imre Nagy withdraws Hungary from Warsaw Pact (1 Nov.); Russian military intervention establishes government under János Kádár (4 Nov.)

Oct. 29   Israeli army attacks Egyptian positions in Sinai

Oct. 30   Anglo-French ultimatum to Israel and Egypt, followed (31 Oct.) by attack on Egyptian airfields and landing (5 Nov.) in canal zone (operations halted, 6 Nov.)

Nov. 11   Six U.K. border customs posts destroyed or damaged by explosions and fire caused by Saor Uladh

Dec. 12   Ten simultaneous attacks by I.R.A. in N.I.; beginning of I.R.A. campaign lasting till 1962

Dec. 21   Brian Faulkner, N.I. minister of home affairs, makes 10 new security regulations under special powers acts; numerous members of I.R.A. and Saor Uladh arrested and detained

1957

Jan. 4   Funeral at Limerick of Seán South, killed in I.R.A. raid on Brookeborough police barracks, Co. Fermanagh (1 Jan.)

Jan. 10   Harold Macmillan app. P.M. of U.K. (see 6 Apr. 1955, 18 Oct. 1963)

Feb.   First number of *Threshold*, published by Lyric Players, Belfast

Feb. 20   High court, London, finds 'alphabet trusts' created by will of George Bernard Shaw to be invalid, with result that bequest of his estate equally to British Museum, Royal Academy of Dramatic Art, and National Gallery of Ireland becomes immediately effective

Mar. 5   R.I. general election: Fianna Fáil 78, Fine Gael 40, lab. 12, Clann na Talmhan 3, Clann na Poblachta 1, ind. and others 9 (see 18 May 1954, 4 Oct. 1961)

Mar. 20   De Valera again elected taoiseach, by 78 to 53 (see 2 June 1954, 23 June 1959)

Mar. 25   France, West Germany, Italy, Belgium, Holland, and Luxembourg sign treaty in Rome establishing European Economic Community

Mar. 28   Jack B. Yeats, painter, dies

Apr. 3   First public performance of Samuel Beckett's 'Fin de partie', at Royal Court Theatre, London

May 13   Catholics at Fethard-on-Sea, Co. Wexford, begin boycott of protestants, resulting from dispute between protestant husband and catholic wife

May 13-27   First Dublin international theatre festival

May 23   Alan Simpson, director, Pike Theatre, Dublin, arrested for production of 'The rose tattoo' by Tennessee Williams (case discharged, 9 June 1958)

July 5   De Valera's government acts against I.R.A. by bringing into force pt II of Offences against the State Act, 1940 (order published, 8 July)

July 23   Gough monument in Phoenix Park, Dublin, wrecked by explosion (see 21 Feb. 1880)

Sept. 8   First wing of new general hospital at Drogheda, to serve as training centre for Medical Missionaries of Mary (see 8 Dec. 1939), opened; architects D. L. Martin and J. A. White (completed, 1962)

Sept. 22   Oliver Joseph St John Gogarty, surgeon and writer, dies in New York

Sept. 26   Commission on accommodation needs of constituent colleges of N.U.I. app. under Judge Cearbhall Ó Dálaigh (see 2 June 1959)

Dec. 18   Gaeltacht Industries Act, 1957 (1957/29 [R.I.]), establishes Gaeltarra Éireann to run small industries in Irish-speaking districts (effective, 1 Apr. 1958)

An economic survey of Northern Ireland, by K. S. Isles and Norman Cuthbert (Belfast)

Heinrich Böll's *Irisches Tagebuch* (Cologne; translated by Leila Vennewitz as *Irish journal*, 1967); important stimulus to German interest in Ire.

1958

Feb. 19   Agriculture (An Foras Talúntais) Act, 1958 (1958/1 [R.I.]), provides for establishment of An Foras Talúntais (Agricultural Research Institute)

Mar. 20   N.I. general election: un. 37, nat. 7, ind. nat. 1, N.I.L.P. 4, ind. lab. 1, republican lab. 1, ind. 1 (see 22 Oct. 1953, 31 May 1962)

Apr. 28   Inauguration of Aer Lingus service to North America

June 10   Ulster Folk Museum Act (Northern Ireland), 1958 (1958, c. 7) (see 2 July 1964)

June 16   First public performance of Behan's 'An giall' ('the hostage'), at Halla Damer, Dublin

June 27   Departure of 5 Irish defence force officers for service in Lebanon as U.N. observers

July 2   Industrial Development (Encouragement of External Investment) Act, 1958 (1958/16 [R.I.]), amends Control of Manufactures Acts, 1932 and 1934, and removes restrictions on foreign ownership in manufacturing industry (increased inflow of capital follows)

July 16   Appointment of commn to advise on measures to hasten restoration of Irish language (see 10 Jan. 1964)

Aug. 2-9   Social Study Conference (catholic organisation founded in 1952) holds its annual summer school (the 6th) at Garron Tower, Co. Antrim, on theme 'The citizen and the community'—first summer school of conference to be held in N.I.; landmark in public discussion of community relations there

Sept. 4-10   British Association for the Advancement of Science meets in Dublin

Sept. 23   At U.N. general assembly Ire. votes with communist bloc in favour of full debate on admission of China to membership

Oct. 9   Pope Pius XII dies (flag flown half-mast on City Hall, Belfast, arousing protestant objections)

Oct. 28   Cardinal Angelo Giuseppe Roncalli elected to papacy as John XXIII

Nov. 11   *Programme for economic expansion*, R.I. white paper, published (Pr. 4796)

Dec.   *Economic development*, a study of development problems and opportunities in R.I., by secretary of department of finance (T. K. Whittaker) and others (Pr. 4803)

1959

Feb. 10   At separate conferences in Dublin delegates to Congress of Irish Unions and Irish Trade Union Congress vote to combine in new Irish Congress of Trade Unions with separate N.I. cttee (see 25 Apr. 1945)

June 2   Report of commn on accommodation needs of colleges of N.U.I. (Pr. 5089) (see 26 Sept. 1957, 31 Mar. 1960)

June 17   Polling in R.I., resulting in election of Éamon de Valera as president (see 1 June 1966) in succession to Seán T. O'Kelly (see 25 June 1952), but in rejection, by referendum, of proposal to abolish proportional representation

June 23   Seán Lemass, minister for industry and commerce, elected taoiseach, by 75 to 51 (see 20 Mar. 1957, 10 Nov. 1966)

June 23   Catholic bps issue statement rejecting recommendations of commn of inquiry into R.I. licensing laws (see 4 July 1956, 21 Oct. 1959)

Sept. 22-4   Inaugural conference in Dublin of Irish Congress of Trade Unions

Oct. 8 U.K. general election: in G.B.—con. 333, nat. lib. and con. 20, lab. 258, lib. 6, others 1; in N.I.—un. 12 (see 26 May 1955, 15 Oct. 1964)

Oct. 21 James Dillon becomes leader of Fine Gael party in succession to Richard Mulcahy, resigned 20 Oct.

R.I. government introduces bill to abolish rural Sunday closing, despite opposition of catholic bps (becomes law 31 May 1960 as Intoxicating Liquor Act, 1960 (1960/18 [R.I.]))

Oct. 31 Inauguration of Independent Television Authority's service in N.I. (Ulster Television)

Nov. 12 Lemass informs dáil of agreement on pictures bequeathed by Sir Hugh Lane (see Sept. 1913): pictures to be divided into 2 groups, each in turn to be lent by Tate Gallery, London, for display in Dublin during 4 successive 5-year periods

Nov. 24 Funds of Suitors Act, 1959 (1959/32 [R.I.]), authorising payment from suitors' funds of £250,000 towards rebuilding of Abbey Theatre, Dublin (see 18 July 1951, 18 July 1966)

1960

Jan. 26 First public performance of Sam Thompson's 'Over the bridge', at Empire Theatre, Belfast

Feb. 5 First public showing of Gael-Linn film 'Mise Éire'; music by Seán Ó Riada

Feb. 7 Credit Union League of Ireland formed

Mar. 2 Brendan Corish elected leader of R.I. parliamentary labour party in succession to William Norton

Mar. 31 Dáil approves, in vote on universities' estimates, principle of transfer of U.C.D. from Earlsfort Terrace to Belfield, in south Dublin

Apr. 12 Broadcasting Authority Act, 1960 (1960/10 [R.I.]), establishes new Radio Éireann (later Radio Telefís Éireann) authority of 9 members to provide and maintain national radio and television service (see 1 Jan. 1953, 31 Dec. 1961)

June 30 Belgian Congo becomes independent

June Commn under Justice Brian Walsh app. by government of R.I. to inquire into problem of itinerancy (see Aug. 1963)

July 27 Departure of battalion of Irish defence forces for service in Congo

Sept. 20 Frederick H. Boland elected president of U.N. general assembly

Sept. Commn under Chief Justice Cearbhall Ó Dálaigh app. by minister for education to inquire into higher education in R.I. (first meeting 8 Nov.; report signed 24 Feb. 1967; see 22 Mar., 24 Aug. 1967)

Nov. 8 Niemba ambush in Congo; 10 Irish soldiers killed

Nov. 30 Roy Thomson announces acquisition of *Belfast Telegraph*

Dec. 14 Organisation for European Economic Cooperation enlarged to form Organisation for Economic Cooperation and Development

1961

Jan. 16 Dairy Produce Marketing Act, 1961 (1961/1 [R.I.]), provides for setting up of Bord Bainne (Milk Board)

Jan. 20 John Fitzgerald Kennedy inaugurated as president of U.S.A.; first president of Irish descent and catholic religion (see 4 Mar. 1829; 22 Nov. 1963)

Jan. 31 Last train runs on West Clare railway

Feb. 8 Cttee under Lord Robbins app. by P.M. of U.K. to review higher education in G.B. (see Oct. 1963)

Feb. 20 Dublin high court rules parts of Electoral (Amendment) Act, 1959, unconstitutional on ground of substantial inequalities between constituencies (act replaced by Electoral (Amendment) Act, 1961 (1961/19, 14 July 1961))

Apr. 9 Census in R.I.: population 2,818,341 (2·76% decline; lowest figure of any census; see 8 Apr. 1956)

Apr. 17 Arts theatre opened in Botanic Avenue, Belfast

Apr. 23 Census in N.I.: population 1,425,042 (3·9% increase; see 8 Apr. 1951)

Aug. 1 R.I. applies formally for membership of E.E.C. (see 11 May 1967)

Sept. 17 First public performance of Samuel Beckett's 'Happy days', at Cherry Lane Theater, New York

Oct. 3 R.I. enters United Nations Economic, Social and Cultural Organisation

Oct. 4 R.I. general election: Fianna Fáil 70, Fine Gael 47, lab. 16, Clann na Talmhan 2, National Progressive Democratic 2, Clann na Poblachta 1, ind. and others 6 (see 5 Mar. 1957, 7 Apr. 1965)

Nov. 24 Liberal (Sheelagh Murnaghan) wins seat in N.I. H.C. in Queen's University by-election

Dec. 1 Announcement of resignation of Conor Cruise O'Brien (special representative of secretary general of U.N. in Congo since May) from position in U.N. secretariat

Dec. 31 Opening of television services of Radio Éireann

Nítrigin Éireann Teoranta set up by R.I. minister for industry and commerce to establish fertiliser industry at Arklow, Co. Wicklow (production begins Dec. 1965)

1962

Feb. 26 I.R.A. announces calling-off of its border campaign

Mar. 2 Announcement that government has compulsorily acquired mineral rights at Tynagh, Co. Galway, where large deposits of copper, zinc, and lead-silver ore found (deposits exploited till 1980)

Apr. 25 *Report of the council of education* on the curriculum of the secondary school in R.I. (Pr. 5996) published

May 12 Laying of foundation stone of new Liberty Hall, Dublin; architect Desmond Rea O'Kelly (formally opened, 1 May 1965)

May 31   N.I. general election: un. 34, nat. 9, N.I.L.P. 4, ind. lab. 1, republican lab. 1, Irish lab. 1, ind. 1 (see 20 Mar. 1958, 25 Nov. 1965)

July 6   First transmission of Radio Telefís Éireann television series 'The late late show'; compère Gay Byrne

July 10   Motorway (M1) opened from Belfast to Lisburn

Oct. 11   Second Vatican Council opens (concludes 8 Dec. 1965)

Oct. 23   Report of joint working party on economy of N.I. published (Cmd 446 (N.I.), Hall report)

Oct. 25   Denis P. Barritt and Charles F. Carter's *The Northern Ireland problem* (Oxford; 2nd ed., 1972)

Oct.   Survey team, directed by Patrick Lynch, app. in association with O.E.C.D. to forecast future demands on Irish education system and make proposals to meet them (see 23 Dec. 1965)

1963

Feb. 26   Regional plan drawn up by Sir Robert Matthew presented to N.I. parliament (Cmd 45 (N.I.))

Mar. 25   Capt. Terence O'Neill becomes P.M. of N.I. succeeding Viscount Brookeborough, resigned (see 28 Apr. 1943, 28 Apr. 1969)

Apr. 11   John XXIII's encyclical, *Pacem in terris*, urges peaceful settlement of disputes with non-catholics and with communists

Apr. 23   Minister for finance (R.I.) announces in budget statement that new turnover tax of $2\frac{1}{2}\%$ on retail sales and services will be introduced on 1 Nov.

May 20   Dr Patrick Hillery, R.I. minister for education, announces plans for comprehensive secondary schools and regional technological colleges

June 3   Pope John XXIII dies (Rev. Ian Paisley leads march to Belfast City Hall to protest against tributes to him, 4 June)

June 21   Cardinal Giovanni Battista Montini elected pope as Paul VI

June 26-9   John F. Kennedy, president of U.S.A., visits R.I.

July 17   Benson report (Cmd. 458) recommending closure of both railway lines to Derry published

Aug. 22   *Second programme for economic expansion* in R.I. [pt I] (Pr 7239) published (see July 1964)

Aug.   Report of commn on itinerancy (Pr. 7272; see June 1960)

Oct. 9   First meeting of National Industrial Economic Council (R.I.)

Oct. 18   Earl of Home (con.) app. P.M. of U.K. (renounces peerage for life, to become Sir Alexander Douglas-Home, 23 Oct.; see 10 Jan. 1957, 16 Oct. 1964)

Oct.   Robbins cttee (see 8 Feb. 1961) report on higher education in G.B. (23 Sept. 1963; Cmnd 2154) published

Nov. 20   Cttee under Sir John Lockwood app. by minister of finance, N.I., to review facilities for higher education in N.I., having regard to report of Robbins cttee in G.B., and to make recommendations (see 10 Feb. 1965)

Nov.   Survey team, directed by Patrick Lynch, app. in association with O.E.C.D. to estimate technological needs of R.I. in 1960s and 1970s (see 21 Oct. 1966)

Nov. 22   John F. Kennedy assassinated

John Kaye Charlesworth's *Historical geology of Ireland* (Edinburgh)

1964

Jan. 10   Final report of commn on restoration of Irish language published, recommending increased use of Irish in administration, church, and media of culture and entertainment (see 16 July 1958, 16 Jan. 1965): report in Irish (Pr. 7297), summary in English (Pr. 7256)

Mar. 20   Brendan Behan, playwright, dies

Mar. 24   Decision to send Irish troops to Cyprus (see 18 May 1974)

Mar. 26   An Foras Forbartha (National Institute for Physical Planning and Construction Research) incorporated

May 26   Fine Gael parliamentary party approves Declan Costello's 'just society' programme, advocating economic planning to achieve social progress

June 2   Edward McAteer elected leader by nationalist parliamentary party of N.I.

July 2   Ulster Folk Museum, Cultra, Co. Down, opened (see 10 June 1958)

July   *Second programme for economic expansion* in R.I., pt II (Pr. 7670) published (see 22 Aug. 1963, Mar. 1969)

Aug. 24   N.I. cttee of Irish Congress of Trades Unions recognised by N.I. government

Sept. 18   Seán O'Casey, playwright, dies

Sept. 28-Oct. 3   Rioting in Belfast, following removal by police of tricolour flag from Divis Street headquarters of republican candidate in U.K. election

Oct. 15   U.K. general election: in G.B.—lab. 317, con. 286, national lib. and con. 6, lib. 9; in N.I.—un. 12 (see 8 Oct. 1959, 31 Mar. 1966)

Oct. 16   Harold Wilson (lab.) app. P.M. of U.K. (see 18 Oct. 1963, 19 June 1970)

Dec. 18   Submission of Wilson report on economic development in N.I. (Cmd 479)

Sean O'Faolain's *Vive moi! an autobiography* (Boston, Mass.; 2nd ed., London, 1965)

1965

Jan. 14   Seán Lemass, taoiseach, and Terence O'Neill, P.M. of N.I., meet in Belfast

Jan. 16   White paper *Athbheochan na Gaeilge; The restoration of the Irish language* (Pr. 8061; see 10 Jan. 1964), setting out 10-year plan for restoration of Irish as general medium of communication

Feb. 2   Nationalist party decides to accept role of official opposition in N.I. H.C. and senate

Feb. 9   O'Neill and Lemass meet in Dublin

Feb. 10 Lockwood cttee (see 20 Nov. 1963) report on higher education in N.I. (27 Nov. 1964; Cmd 475 (N.I.)) published; principal recommendations: (1) courses of higher education to be made available to all 'who are qualified by ability and attainment to pursue them'; (2) second university to be established at Coleraine, Magee College Londonderry, being discontinued as university institution; (3) an 'Ulster College' combining new regional college of technology in Belfast with colleges of domestic science and art, etc., to be set up; government statement accepting report generally but declaring its intention to investigate further whether Magee College 'can be incorporated in the new university' (see 1 Oct. 1968, 1 Apr. 1971)

Feb. 15 First meeting of N.I. Economic Council

Feb. 23 Arrival in Ire. of presumed remains of Roger Casement (see 3 Aug. 1916)

Mar. Construction of 16-storeyed County Hall, Cork, begun; architect Patrick L. McSweeney (completed, Jan. 1968; formal opening, 16 Apr. 1968; bronze figures by Oisin Kelly formally presented, Jan. 1977)

Apr. 7 R.I. general election: Fianna Fáil 72, Fine Gael 47, lab. 22, Clann na Poblachta 1, others 2 (see 4 Oct. 1961, 18 June 1969)

Apr. 8 Treaty signed at Brussels by 6 E.E.C. countries for merger of executives of E.E.C., European Coal and Steel Community, and European Atomic Energy Community into single European Commission, and of separate councils of ministers into single council

Apr. 21 Liam Cosgrave (son of W. T. Cosgrave, president, executive council, I.F.S. 1922–32) becomes leader of Fine Gael party in succession to James Dillon, resigned

May 6 John McGahern's *The dark* (London)

June 24 New Towns Act (Northern Ireland), 1965 (1965, c. 13) (leading to establishment of Craigavon, new town in Lurgan-Portadown area, Co. Armagh)

July 2 Members of Irish Graphical Society strike, causing closure of 46 Dublin commercial printing houses and non-appearance of Dublin newspapers (work resumed, 12 Sept.)

Aug. 15 Cathedral of Our Lady Assumed into Heaven and St Nicholas, Galway, consecrated

Sept. 16 Dissolution of Clann na Poblachta (see 6 July 1946) announced

Oct. 31 Cork opera house reopened (see 12 Dec. 1955)

Nov. 16 W. T. Cosgrave (see 21 Apr.) dies

Nov. 25 N.I. general election: un. 36, nat. 9, National Democratic 1, N.I.L.P. 2, republican lab. 2, lib. 1, ind. 1 (see 31 May 1962, 24 Feb. 1969)

Dec. 14 Anglo-Irish free-trade agreement (effective, 1 July 1966)

Dec. 22 Succession Act, 1965 (1965/27 [R.I.]), securing to widow third of estate (half, if no children), and empowering court to make provision for children

Dec. 23 *Investment in education: report of the survey team appointed by the* [R.I.] *minister for education in October 1962*, vol. i (Pr. 8311), published (vol. ii (Pr. 8527) published 8 Aug. 1966)

1966

Jan. 24 First of 21 programmes broadcast in Radio Telefís Éireann television series 'The course of Irish history' (last, 13 June; pub., ed. T. W. Moody and F. X. Martin, 26 Jan. 1967)

Mar. 8 Nelson Pillar, Dublin, wrecked by explosion (see 5 Jan. 1808)

Mar. 10 Michael O'Donovan (Frank O'Connor), writer, dies

Mar. 31 U.K. general election: in G.B.—lab. 364, con. 239, national lib. and con. 3, lib. 12; in N.I.—un. 11, republican lab. 1 (see 15 Oct. 1964, 18 June 1970)

Apr. 1 Brian O'Nolan (Flann O'Brien, Myles na Gopaleen), writer, dies

Apr. 10 Beginning of widespread and prolonged commemoration, in both parts of Ire., of 50th anniversary of Easter rising

Apr. 17 Census in R.I.: population 2,884,002 (2·33% increase; see 9 Apr. 1961)

Apr. 27 Twenty-eight members of Irish Creamery Milk Suppliers Association arrested and charged under Offences against the State Act for picketing Dáil Éireann and department of agriculture buildings in Dublin, first of series of such demonstrations

May 6 Closure of commercial banks throughout Ire. caused by strike of junior officials (reopening to public in N.I., 21 June; in R.I., 5 Aug.)

May 19 Seamus Heaney's first volume of poems, *Death of a naturalist* (London)

June 1 Éamon de Valera reelected president of R.I., defeating Thomas F. O'Higgins (Fine Gael) (see 17 June 1959, 30 May 1973)

June 6 Rev. Ian Paisley and supporters demonstrate in Belfast during presbyterian general assembly (see 19 July)

June 21 Catholic bps, as trustees of St Patrick's College, Maynooth, announce proposal to develop seminary as 'an open centre of higher studies' and to admit 'brothers, nuns and laity'

June 26 Catholic barman shot dead, and 2 other catholics wounded, in Malvern St., Belfast (perpetrators later found to be members of U.V.F.; see 14 Oct.)

July 18 First public performance at new Abbey Theatre, Dublin; architect Michael Scott (see 18 July 1951)

July 19 Paisley convicted of unlawful assembly and breach of peace; sentenced to £30 fine and bound over for 2 years, in default 2 months imprisonment; refuses to pay or give bond (committed to prison 20 July; see 6 June)

Aug. 22 Announcement of amalgamation of Munster and Leinster Bank, Provincial Bank of Ireland, and Royal Bank of Ireland as Allied Irish Banks

Sept. 8 Formal opening of phase 3 of restoration of Ballintubber abbey (see 1216; 1st phase of restoration, 1846; 2nd phase, 1889); Abp Walsh of Tuam concelebrant, President de Valera present

Sept. 10 Donogh O'Malley, R.I. minister for education, promises free post-primary education in Sept. 1967

Sept. 21 Disturbances at meeting in Mansion House, Dublin, of Language Freedom Movement (organisation opposed to compulsory Irish)

Sept. 23 N.I. minister of commerce announces £1½ m. loan to Harland and Wolff, conditional on changes in company's board

Oct. 7 Beginning of National Farmers' Association march on Dublin

Oct. 9 Census in N.I.: population 1,484,775 (4·2% increase; see 23 Apr. 1961)

Oct. 14 Augustus ('Gusty') Spence and 2 others sentenced to life imprisonment for murder (see 26 June)

Oct. 21 *Science and Irish economic development: report of the research and technology survey team appointed by the* [R.I.] *minister for industry and commerce in November 1963*, vol. i (Pr. 8975), published (vol. ii (Pr. 9093) published 29 Nov. 1966)

Oct. 24 First section (Shore Road to Glengormley) of Belfast–Ballymena motorway (M2) opened

Nov. 4 United Council of Christian Churches and Religious Communions in Ireland renamed Irish Council of Churches (see 23 Jan. 1923, 3 May 1970)

Nov. 8 Lemass announces his intention to retire as taoiseach (resigns, 10 Nov.)

Nov. 9 Jack Lynch, minister for finance, elected leader of Fianna Fáil party by 52 votes to 19 for George Colley, minister for industry and commerce

Nov. 10 Dáil elects Jack Lynch taoiseach by 71 votes to 64 (see 23 June 1959, 9 Nov. 1966, 14 Mar. 1973)

Nov. 23 Seán T. O'Kelly (president of R.I., 1945–59) dies

1967

Jan. 9 National Farmers' Association blockades roads in R.I. in support of its 'farmers' rights campaign'

Feb. 6 Newly formed Northern Ireland Civil Rights Association states its objectives

Mar. 7 Industrial Training Act, 1967 (1967/5 [R.I.]), provides for establishment of An Chomhairle Oiliúna (AnCO), industrial training organisation

Mar. 22 *Commission on higher education 1960-67, presentation and summary of report* (Pr. 9326) published; principal recommendations: (1) U.C.D., U.C.C., and U.C.G. to become independent universities, replacing N.U.I.; (2) T.C.D. to remain a separate university; (3) majority governing body of each university to be elected by academic staff; (4) universities to be responsible for matching student numbers with resources of staff, accommodation, equipment and facilities, and staff–student ratio to be progressively improved to 1:12 by 1975; (5) Council of Irish Universities to be established by act of oireachtas; (6) part of expanding demand for higher education to be met by institutions of a new type ('New Colleges'), to be established initially at Dublin and Limerick; (7) professional training in agriculture and veterinary medicine to be combined with work of An Foras Talúntais in new National College of Agriculture and Veterinary Sciences; (8) Technological Authority, incorporating Institute of Industrial Research and Standards, to be established to promote technological training and research; (9) national scheme of scholarships, loans, and grants to ensure access to higher education as fully as possible to all qualified students; (10) Commission for Higher Education to be established by act of oireachtas as financial authority for all third-level education (see Sept. 1960, 18 Apr., 24 Aug. 1967, 5 July, 15 Aug. 1968, 7 Apr. 1970, 16 Dec. 1974)

Apr. 3 Announcement of agreement between Erin Foods Ltd and H. J. Heinz Co. to form joint company, Heinz-Erin Ltd, to market products of former

Apr. 18 Donogh O'Malley, R.I. minister for education, announces government's intention to combine Trinity College and University College in one university of Dublin ('the merger'), thus rejecting a major recommendation of commn on higher education (see 22 Mar. 1967, 5 July 1968)

Apr. 26 O'Neill dismisses Harry West, N.I. minister of agriculture, on ground that private land purchase conflicted with his position as minister

May 1 Planetarium opened in grounds of Armagh observatory (see 5 May 1791)

May 11 R.I. and U.K. reapply for membership of E.E.C. and associated organisations (see 1 Aug. 1961)

May 23 Health Services (Amendment) Act (Northern Ireland), 1967 (1967, c. 9), providing acceptable terms for inclusion of Mater Infirmorum hospital, Belfast, in hospitals service

May 30 Lt-col Odumegwu Ojukwu announces secession of eastern region from Federation of Nigeria as Republic of Biafra (large-scale fighting begins, July) (see 27 Jan. 1970)

July 11 Censorship of Publications (Amendment) Act, 1967 (1967/15 [R.I.]), removing ban from books that have been banned for more than 12 years

July 12 Opening of new library building at Trinity College, Dublin, by President de Valera; architect Paul Koralek

Aug. 24 *Commission on higher education, 1960-67, report*, vol. i (Pr. 9389) published (see 22 Mar.; vol. ii (Pr. 9588) published 13 Apr. 1968)

Oct. 5 R.I. minister for transport and power and N.I. minister of commerce sign agreement to link 2 electricity systems, by line from Maynooth to Tandragee

Nov. 4 Cultural agreement between R.I. and France, providing for exchange of teachers and students, reciprocal establishment of cultural centres, etc.

Nov. 18 Statue of Wolfe Tone in St Stephen's Green, Dublin, unveiled; sculptor Edward Delany (see 8 Feb. 1971)

Nov. 30 Patrick Kavanagh, poet, dies

Dec. 11 Jack Lynch, taoiseach, meets Terence O'Neill, P.M. of N.I., at Stormont—beginning of second round of cross-border visits (see 14 Jan., 9 Feb. 1965, 8 Jan. 1968)

1968

Jan. 8 O'Neill and Lynch meet in Dublin

Jan. 20 Sir Alfred Chester Beatty, art collector, philanthropist, and first honorary citizen of Ire., dies

Mar. 10 Donogh O'Malley (see 10 Sept. 1966, 18 Apr. 1967) dies, aged 47

Mar. 26 Education (Amendment) Act (Northern Ireland), 1968 (1968, c. 2), providing for increased grants for capital and recurrent expenditure to voluntary schools which accept on their cttees persons nominated by minister

May 15 Goodyear rubber factory at Craigavon, Co. Armagh, opened

May 29 John F. Kennedy Memorial Park in Co. Wexford opened by President de Valera

June 20 Austin Currie, nationalist M.P., 'squats' in house at Caledon, Co. Tyrone, allocated by unionist local authority to unmarried protestant girl

July 5 Brian Lenihan, R.I. minister for education, announces plans for higher education: N.U.I. to be dissolved; U.C.C. and U.C.G. to become separate universities; T.C.D. and U.C.D. to be combined in one university of Dublin but each to retain identity and to have equal representation on governing body; St Patrick's College, Maynooth, envisaged as associate college of University of Dublin; higher education authority to be established (see 22 Mar., 18 Apr. 1967, 15 Aug. 1968, 7 Apr. 1970)

July 29 Paul VI issues encyclical, *Humanae vitae*, condemning artificial forms of birth-control

Aug. 15 Setting-up of Higher Education Authority (R.I.) announced (see 5 July)

Aug. 24 March from Coalisland to Dungannon, Co. Tyrone, under auspices of N.I.C.R.A.

Sept. 14 Maynooth College admits first lay students to follow degree courses

Sept. Seán O'Connor's 'Post-primary education: now and in the future' in *Studies*

Oct. 1 Opening of The New University of Ulster, Coleraine (see 10 Feb. 1965)

Oct. 5 Clash between civil rights marchers and police in Derry (ban on processions in certain areas of city defied)

Oct. 9 Student demonstration in Belfast; formation of what later becomes People's Democracy; formation of Derry Citizens' Action Committee

Oct. 15 Nationalists cease to be official opposition in N.I. parliament

Oct. 16 Referendum on proposals to amend constitution of R.I. (1) by allowing variation of one-sixth in ratio of dáil deputies to population; (2) by abolishing proportional representation (both heavily defeated)

Oct. 26 New Lyric Theatre opened in Belfast for Lyric Players, founded by Mrs Mary O'Malley in 1951

Nov. 22 O'Neill announces 5-point reform proposals: (1) business vote in local government elections to be abolished and local government system to be reformed within 3 years; (2) fair allocation of local authority housing; (3) ombudsman to investigate grievances arising out of central government administration; (4) special powers act to be reviewed and clauses conflicting with U.K.'s international obligations to be removed; (5) Derry city council to be superseded by development commission

Nov. 28 Electoral Law Act (Northern Ireland), 1968 (1968, c. 20), abolishes university constituency, redistributes seats and provides for permanent boundary commission

Dec. 9 O'Neill makes 'Ulster at the crossroads' broadcast

Dec. 11 William Craig dismissed as N.I. minister of home affairs, allegedly on ground that he challenged O'Neill's statement that U.K. government has power to intervene in N.I. affairs

Dec. 12 O'Neill receives vote of confidence from unionist parliamentary party; 4 abstentions

1969

Jan. 1-4 People's Democracy march from Belfast to Derry; march attacked by militant protestants at Burntollet bridge, near Claudy, Co. Londonderry (4 Jan.)

Jan. 5-10 First Dublin festival of 20th-century music

Jan. 11 Disturbances in Newry, Co. Down, when P.D. march banned from centre of town; 10 members of R.U.C. and 28 others injured

Jan. 24 Resignation of Brian Faulkner from Terence O'Neill's cabinet, accentuating split in unionist party

Jan. 31 Closure of Deerpark colliery, last remaining on Castlecomer coal-field, Co. Kilkenny

Feb. 5 Strike of maintenance craftsmen in R.I. (work resumed, 10 Mar.)

New Ulster Movement, in support of O'Neill's programme, formed

Feb. 24 N.I. general election: un. 36 (24 pro-O'Neill and 12 anti-O'Neill), ind. O'Neill un. 3, nat. 6, N.I.L.P. 2, republican lab. 2, ind. 3 (see 25 Nov. 1965, 28 June 1973)

Mar. 3 Commn under Lord Cameron app. to investigate causes and circumstances of outbreaks of violence in N.I. since 5 Oct. 1968 (see 12 Sept.)

Mar. 30 Explosion causes £½ m. of damage to electricity sub-station at Castlereagh, near Belfast; first in series of explosions

Mar. *Third programme, economic and social development 1969-72*, in R.I. (Pri. 431) published

Apr. 17 Bernadette Devlin returned to H.C. of U.K. as Unity candidate in Mid-Ulster by-election

Apr. 19 Civil-rights supporters in Derry protest at banning of proposed march from Burntollet (see 4 Jan.); rioting develops when they are attacked by protestants; police enter Bogside (accused of brutality, in particular of beating Samuel Devenny (dies 17 July))

Apr. 20 Explosions at Silent Valley reservoir in Mourne mountains, damaging main pipe to Belfast, and at Annaboe, Kilmore, near Armagh, damaging electricity pylon

Apr. 25 Order of minister for local government dissolving Dublin city council for failure to strike sufficient rate comes into effect

Apr. 28 O'Neill resigns as P.M. of N.I. (see 25 Mar. 1963) (succ. by James Chichester-Clark, 1 May) (see 20 Mar. 1971)

1969 continued:

May 6   Amnesty announced for all offences connected with demonstrations in N.I. since 5 Oct. 1968

Official opening by taoiseach, Lynch, of Gulf Oil Company's oil terminal in Bantry Bay, Co. Cork (closed by explosion of French tanker *Betelgeuse*, 8 Jan. 1979, killing 50)

May 19-20   Student 'sit-in' at University College, Dublin

May 29   Opening of car and passenger ferry between Killimer, Co. Clare, and Tarbert, Co. Kerry

June 3   Charles Haughey, minister for finance, defends his sale, for £204,500, of building land owned by him at Raheny, Co. Dublin

June 11   I.R.A. arson attack on 4 farms in Meath and Louth

June 17-19   General and Madame de Gaulle guests of President and Bean de Valera at Árus an Uachtaráin

June 18   R.I. general election: Fianna Fáil 75, Fine Gael 50, lab. 18, ind. 1 (see 7 Apr. 1965, 28 Feb. 1973)

July 1   Sir Edmund Compton, parliamentary commr (ombudsman) for G.B., takes office as parliamentary commr for N.I.

July 12-16   Rioting in Derry between catholics of Bogside and protestants of Fountain Street area; Old Gaol set on fire (15 July)

July 13-14   Rioting in Dungiven, Co. Londonderry: Orange hall attacked by crowd and burned; first death in N.I. disturbances (14 July)

July 21   Neil Armstrong and Edwin Aldrin, American astronauts, make landfall on moon

July 29   Finance Act, 1969 (1961/21 [R.I.]): sect. 2 exempts persons deemed to have written, composed or executed works of cultural or artistic merit from income tax on gains arising from such works

July 30   Agreement on offshore oil prospecting between R.I. minister for industry and commerce and Marathon Petroleum (Ire.) Ltd

Aug. 2-5   Disturbances in Belfast

Aug. 5   U.V.F. bomb explosion at R.T.E. headquarters, Donnybrook, Dublin, first of series of such attacks in R.I.

Aug. 12   Annual parade of Apprentice Boys in Derry stoned by youths, leading to violent clash between Bogside catholics and police, who are followed by protestant crowd

Aug. 13   Derry Bogside in state of siege, in which Bernadette Devlin, M.P., takes active part (see 22 Dec.); disturbances spread to other parts of N.I.

Lynch makes broadcast statement that Irish government, which 'can no longer stand by and see innocent people injured and perhaps worse', is asking British government to request immediate despatch of U.N. peace-keeping force to N.I., and that field hospitals are being prepared in Co. Donegal and other border areas

Aug. 14   Rioting in Derry continues; British troops take over security in city centre; rioting between catholic and protestant crowds in Belfast; houses in some areas burned

Aug. 14-15 Action of trade-union leaders and others prevents shipyard workers at Queen's Island, Belfast, from joining in sectarian conflict

Aug. 15 Rioting continues in Belfast, many houses burned in Bombay Street, in catholic Clonard area; refugees begin moving to republic; in afternoon troops take up duty and succeed in manning 'peace line' between catholic and protestant areas in Belfast

Aug. 19 N.I. ministers meet British ministers in London: joint communiqué that general officer commanding N.I. will have overall responsibility for security, including control of 'B' specials; British government issues 7-point declaration ('Downing Street declaration') affirming that (1) N.I. will not cease to be part of U.K. without consent of its people and parliament; (2) N.I. affairs are matter of domestic jurisdiction; (3) U.K. government has ultimate responsibility for protection of people of N.I.; (4) troops have been temporarily provided to discharge that responsibility; (5) U.K. government welcomes reforms introduced by N.I. government and both governments consider it vital to maintain momentum of reform; (6) both governments are committed to same equality of treatment for all citizens of N.I. as obtains in rest of U.K.; (7) both governments are determined to restore normality in N.I.

Aug. 22 Oliver Wright, foreign office official, app. British government's representative in N.I.

Aug. 26 Advisory cttee under Lord Hunt app. by N.I. government to examine recruitment and organisation of R.U.C. and Ulster Special Constabulary (see 10 Oct.)

Aug. 27 Tribunal of inquiry into recent disturbances, under Sir Leslie George Scarman, app. by governor of N.I.

Aug. 27-9 James Callaghan, British home secretary, visits N.I. (second visit, 8-10 Oct.)

Sept. 12 Cameron commn (see 3 Mar.) report on disturbances in N.I. (16 Aug.; Cmd 532 (N.I.)) published

Sept. 20 In speech at Tralee, Lynch enunciates conciliatory policy towards N.I.

Sept. 24 *Report of Public Services Organisation Review Group, 1966-1969* (Devlin report; Prl. 792)

Oct. 9 First report of Higher Education Authority in R.I.

Oct. 10 Hunt cttee (see 26 Aug.) report published (3 Oct.; Cmd 535 (N.I.)), recommending various reforms including replacement of Ulster Special Constabulary by 2 new forces, one under army control, the other a police reserve (see 18 Dec. 1969, 26 Mar. 1970)

Sir Arthur Young arrives to take up duties as inspector general of R.U.C.

Oct. 11-12 Disturbances in protestant Shankill Road district of Belfast; R.U.C. constable shot dead

Oct. 19 Fatally injured man (later identified as member of U.V.F.) found at foot of pylon near Ballyshannon, Co. Donegal, together with 180 lb gelignite

Oct. 23 Samuel Beckett awarded Nobel prize for literature (declines to go to Stockholm to receive it)

Nov. 24 Car ferry begins operating between Portaferry and Strangford, Co. Down

Nov. 25 Electoral Law Act (Northern Ireland), 1969 (1969, c. 26), lowers qualifying age for franchise to 18, extends local government franchise to all parliamentary electors, and postpones triennial local government elections to 1971

Dec. 1 No. 46 St Stephen's Green, Dublin, Georgian building under immediate threat of demolition, occupied by architectural students and others (see 7 June 1970)

Dec. 17 Review body, under Patrick A. Macrory, app. by N.I. minister for development, to consider reorganisation of local government (see 29 May 1970)

Dec. 18 Ulster Defence Regiment Act, 1969 (1969, c. 65 [U.K.]), establishing part-time security force under army control

Dec. 22 Bernadette Devlin, M.P., sentenced to 6 months' imprisonment (see 13 Aug.)

Dec. 28 Press report that some members of I.R.A. convention have seceded from main body to form provisional army council (see 11 Jan. 1970)

1970

Jan. 1 Director (Edward M. Walsh) app. for National Institute for Higher Education, Limerick (enrolment of students begins, 16 Sept. 1972)

Jan. 6 Judicial inquiry into R.T.E. 'Seven days' programme on illegal money-lending opens (ends, 8 Apr.; report published, 20 Aug.)

Jan. 11 Failing to obtain two-thirds vote in favour of parliamentary abstention, some 80 (supporters of provisional army council) out of 257 delegates at Sinn Féin árd-fheis in Dublin walk out; split between 'Official' (left-wing) and 'Provisional' (right-wing) Sinn Féin (see 28 Dec. 1969)

Jan. 27 As result of fall of Biafra (12 Jan.; see 30 May 1967), 17 Irish catholic missionaries sentenced at Port Harcourt to imprisonment for entering Nigeria illegally

Mar. 2 Banks in R.I. restrict service on account of labour dispute (complete suspension, 30 Apr.; doors reopened to public, 17 Nov.)

Mar. 15 Communist parties in R.I. and N.I. unite to form Communist Party of Ireland (see 10 July 1941)

Mar. 23 First meeting of West Ulster Unionist Council at Omagh

Mar. 26 Police Act (Northern Ireland), 1970 (1970, c. 9), establishing police authority, police association, police advisory board, and R.U.C. reserve

Apr. 3 Garda Richard Fallon murdered during bank robbery in Dublin

Apr. 7 Agreement reached between representatives of T.C.D. and N.U.I. on the following: (1) 4 cooperating universities in R.I.; (2) conference of Irish universities to foster cooperation in attainment of their common aims; (3) model for structure, organisation, and government of 4 independent universities with broadly similar constitutions; (4) allocation of subjects and faculties between 2 independent universities in Dublin—(a) arts to continue in each university, but subjects attracting only a small number of students might be allocated to one or other institution, (b) each university to retain its present range of disciplines, but main centre for physical sciences to be U.C.D., for biological sciences T.C.D., (c) in medicine, there should be 2 independent, cooperating, pre-clinical schools in Dublin and 1 joint university clinical school operating in 3 hospital centres 'in each of which there would be staff and professorial units attached to either one of the universities'; (d) there should be a single faculty of veterinary medicine and of dentistry, located in T.C.D.; (e) there should be 2 university schools of engineering, 1 (in U.C.D.) providing courses in depth in civil, agricultural, mechanical, electrical and chemical engineering, and 1 (in T.C.D.) providing a 4-year non-specialised course in engineering science; (f) there should be a single faculty in commerce, and in social science, located in U.C.D.; (g) T.C.D. to be main centre in legal studies; (h) agriculture and architecture to be only in U.C.D.

Apr. 16   Bannside and South Antrim by-elections, resulting in return of Paisley and a supporter, Rev. William Beattie, to N.I. H.C.

Apr. 21   White paper *Membership of the European communities: implications for Ireland* (Prl. 1110) published

Formation in N.I. of Alliance party (combination of liberal catholics and protestants)

Apr. 23   Scoil Éanna (St Enda's school), Rathfarnham (see 8 Sept. 1908), presented to nation and accepted by President de Valera

Apr. 30   'B' specials disbanded and duties transferred to Ulster Defence Regiment

May 3   Irish Council of Churches and Roman Catholic Church set up joint group on social problems (see 4 Nov. 1966, 26 Sept. 1973)

May 6   Charles Haughey, R.I. minister for finance, and Neil Blaney, minister for agriculture, dismissed by Lynch; Kevin Boland, minister for local government, resigns

May 28   Blaney and Haughey arrested on charges of conspiring to import arms and ammunition (see 2 July, 22 Sept.)

May 29   Macrory report (see 17 Dec. 1969) submitted to N.I. government, recommending that health, social services, education, and other major functions be administered for N.I. as unit through 5 area boards, more local functions being responsibility of 26 new district councils (Cmd 546 (N.I.); see 17 Dec. 1970)

June 7   Demolition workers, accompanied by private security force, strip roofs from 4 Georgian houses in Hume Street area of Dublin; 4 people occupying one of them (no. 46 St Stephen's Green) injured (see 1 Dec. 1969)

June 18   U.K. general election: in G.B.—con. 322, lab. 288, lib. 6, others 2; in N.I.—un. 8, protestant un. 1, republican lab. 1, unity 2 (see 31 Mar. 1966, 28 Feb. 1974)

June 19   Edward Heath (con.) app. P.M. of U.K. (see 16 Oct. 1964, 4 Mar. 1974)

June 25 Catholic bps announce removal of their restrictions on catholics attending Trinity College, Dublin (see 30 Aug.-20 Sept. 1875)

June 26-9 Arrest and imprisonment of Bernadette Devlin, M.P. (26 June), leading to renewed disturbances at Derry and Belfast; Provos in action for first time, in Short Strand district of Belfast (27 June)

July 2 Blaney discharged (see 28 May)

July 3 Catholic bps issue statement discontinuing obligatory Friday abstinence

Army finds Official I.R.A. arms in Balkan Street, Belfast; rioting ensues throughout Falls Road area; G.O.C.N.I. (Sir Ian Freeland) imposes curfew (lifted, 5 July); 6 civilians killed

July 6 Dr Patrick John Hillery, minister for external affairs, pays unnotified visit to Falls Road area of Belfast

July 16 Explosion at Northern Bank, High Street, Belfast; 31 persons injured; one of series of explosions caused by I.R.A.

Aug. 12 Two members of R.U.C. killed by booby-trap near Crossmaglen, Co. Armagh; first policemen to be killed in catholic area in N.I. disturbances

Aug. 21 Formation of Social Democratic and Labour Party in N.I. H.C.: combination of opposition M.P.s—Gerry Fitt, Ivan Cooper, Austin Currie, Paddy Devlin, John Hume, and Paddy O'Hanlon

Sept. 6 Public baths in Belfast opened on Sunday for first time

Sept. 22 Trial of Haughey, Capt. James Kelly, John Kelly, and Albert Luykx on arms charges begins (jury discharged, 29 Sept.; new trial begins, 6 Oct.; acquittals, 23 Oct.) (see 28 May, 2 July)

Sept. 23 Sir Arthur Young (see 10 Oct. 1969) announces resignation as chief constable, R.U.C., with effect from 16 Nov. (succeeded by Graham Shillington)

Oct. 18 Máirtín Ó Cadhain, writer in Irish, dies

Nov. 9 Irish School of Ecumenics (director Rev. Michael Hurley, S.J.) inaugurated at Milltown Park, Dublin, by Rev. Eugene Carson Blake, general secretary, World Council of Churches

Dec. 9 Irish Society for Archives founded (first issue of its journal, *Cumann Cartlannaiochta Eireann*; *Irish Archives Bulletin*, May 1971)

Dec. 17 N.I. government announces general acceptance of Macrory report (see 29 May)

1971

Jan. 11-14 Four consecutive nights of rioting in Ballymurphy, catholic area of Belfast

Jan. 23-4 Rioting in Shankill Road area of Belfast, following clash between police and protestant supporters of Linfield football club

Feb. 3-6 Rioting in catholic areas of Belfast; British soldier shot by Provos (6 Feb.)—first to be killed in N.I. disturbances

Feb. 8 Wolfe Tone statue in St Stephen's Green, Dublin, blown up (see 18 Nov. 1967)

Feb. 12-13 Chichester-Clark in London for talks with Heath

Feb. 15 Decimal currency introduced in U.K. and R.I.

Feb. 25 Housing Executive Act (Northern Ireland), 1971 (1971, c. 5), concentrating public provision of housing in single executive, taking over housing functions of local authorities and Northern Ireland Housing Trust

Mar. 10 Fighting between Provos and Officials in Belfast; some deaths

Three soldiers shot dead in Belfast

Mar. 12 Over 4,000 shipyard workers, claiming to represent all shades of political and religious belief, march to unionist party headquarters, Glengall Street, Belfast, to demand internment of I.R.A. leaders

Mar. 16 Chichester-Clark in London to request British government for new security measures (on return announces that 1,300 more troops are to be flown in)

Mar. 20 Chichester-Clark resigns as P.M. of N.I. (succ. by Brian Faulkner, elected leader of unionist party by 26 votes to 4 for William Craig, 23 Mar.) (see 28 Apr. 1969, 24 Mar. 1972)

Mar. 23 Local Government (Boundaries) Act (Northern Ireland), 1971 (1971, c. 9), providing for division of N.I. into 26 local government districts and appointment of commr to recommend delimitation

Apr. 1 Northern Ireland Polytechnic (Ulster College) at Jordanstown, near Belfast, opened (see 10 Feb. 1965)

Apr. 11 G.A.A., meeting in Belfast, removes ban on 'foreign games'

Apr. 13 Rioting in east Belfast, following firing by Provos on crowd returning from Orange parade

Apr. 18 Census in R.I.: population 2,978,248 (3·3% increase; see 17 Apr. 1966)

Apr. 20 Official I.R.A. blow up British naval launch in Cork harbour (Irish government apologises and promises compensation)

Apr. 25 Census in N.I.: population 1,536,065 (3·45% increase; see 9 Oct. 1966)

May 11 Seán Lemass, taoiseach 1959-66, dies

May 22 Members of Irish Women's Liberation Movement defy law by importing contraceptives at Connolly railway station, Dublin

June 8 Historic Monuments (Northern Ireland) Act, 1971 (1971, c. 17), consolidates law relating to ancient monuments (see 1 June 1926)

June 13 Orange march in Dungiven, Co. Londonderry, broken up by soldiers

July 8 Mrs Mary Robinson's bill in R.I. senate, to liberalise law relating to contraceptives, refused first reading, 14 to 25 (see 16 July 1974)

Two catholics killed in Derry by army

July 10 Offices of British Legion in Dublin destroyed by explosion

July 16 S.D.L.P. announces withdrawal from N.I. parliament as protest at refusal of inquiry into shooting of 2 men by army at Derry on 8 July (see 26 Oct.)

July 28 Central Bank Act, 1971 (1971/24 [R.I.]), increases Central Bank of Ireland's control over banking system (see 4 Nov. 1942)

Aug. 9 Reintroduction of internment without trial in N.I.; 342 arrested; violent reaction resulting in 17 deaths and burning of at least 150 houses in Belfast (army camp for refugees opened in R.I.)

Aug. 18 Two M.P.s, John Hume and Ivan Cooper, arrested in Derry, following demonstrations of passive resistance (convicted, but acquitted on appeal, 23 Feb. 1972)

Aug. 20 N.I. government publishes white paper *A record of constructive change* (Cmd 558 (N.I.)), recording progress made in introduction of measures of reform

Aug. 21 Provos, meeting in Monaghan, announce plans for 9-county Ulster parliament—'dáil Uladh'

Aug. 31 Cttee, under Sir Edmund Compton, ombudsman (see 1 July 1969), app. by U.K. home secretary to investigate allegations of physical brutality committed against persons arrested on 9 Aug. (see 16 Nov.)

Sept. 1 Prohibition of Forcible Entry and Occupation Act, 1971 (1971/25 [R.I.]), providing measures against squatting

Sept. 6-7 Lynch meets Heath at Chequers for talks on N.I.

Sept. 19 Inaugural meeting in Dublin of Aontacht Éireann (Unity of Ireland party) formed by Kevin Boland

Majority of internees moved to new camp at Long Kesh, near Lisburn, Co. Antrim (subsequently named Maze prison)

Sept. 26 David Bleakley, N.I. minister of community relations, resigns in protest against internment policy

Sept. 27-8 Tripartite talks at Chequers between Heath, Lynch, and Faulkner

Oct. 1 Order under sect. 31 of broadcasting act, 1960, restraining R.T.E. from reporting activities associated with illegal organisations

Oct. 3 Seán Ó Riada, composer, dies

Oct. 5 Desmond Boal, Ian Paisley and 2 other M.P.s take seats on opposition benches at Stormont as Democratic Unionist party

Oct. 16 Cargo of arms, allegedly intended for Provos, intercepted at Amsterdam

Oct. 17 *Sunday Times* alleges use of brain-washing techniques in N.I.

Oct. 19 Six suitcases of arms and ammunition found on arrival of liner *Q.E.2* in Cork

Oct. 25 Riot at Long Kesh camp; troops use CS gas, some internees injured

Oct. 26 'Alternative assembly'—'The assembly of the northern people'— convened by S.D.L.P., meets at Dungiven castle, Co. Londonderry, under chairmanship of John Hume, M.P.

Oct. 27 Faulkner appoints Dr Gerard B. Newe (a catholic, not member of either house of parliament) to be minister of state

Oct. 28 Gardaí prevent British troops from blowing up bridge on Fermanagh/ Monaghan border

Nov. 7 Discovery-well in gas-field off Old Head of Kinsale completed (gas later discovered)

Nov. 16   Compton cttee (see 31 Aug.) report (3 Nov.; Cmd 4823) published: finding that there was ill-treatment of detainees, but not brutality or torture

Cttee of 3 privy councillors, headed by Lord Parker, app. by U.K. government to examine methods of interrogating persons suspected of terrorism (see 2 Mar. 1972)

Dec. 4   Explosion at McGurk's bar, Belfast, kills 15, injures 13

Dec. 12   Unionist senator, John Barnhill, shot dead and his house near Strabane, Co. Tyrone, blown up (Officials claim responsibility)

Dec. 22   Rioting in Ballyshannon, Co. Donegal, following arrest of 3 Provos; 7 gardaí injured

Dec. 23   Heath pays 1-day visit to N.I. to inspect troops and meet Faulkner

Dec. 25-6   Provos and Officials observe 48-hour truce in N.I.

1972

Jan. 1   Irish Farmers' Association formed in R.I. by amalgamation of 5 organisations including N.F.A. (see 6 Jan. 1955)

Jan. 17   Seven internees escape from prison ship *Maidstone*, moored in Belfast Lough

Jan. 22   Treaty of accession to E.E.C. signed at Brussels by R.I., U.K., and Denmark

Jan. 23   Clash between British soldiers and civilians at road crater on Fermanagh/Monaghan border

Jan. 30   'Bloody Sunday': 13 civilians shot dead by paratroopers, following banned civil rights march, in Derry (see 14 Feb.)

Jan. 31   Massive protests following killings at Derry: Lynch announces that 2 Feb. will be day of national mourning, and recalls Irish ambassador from London

Feb. 2   Tribunal of inquiry into events of 30 Jan. at Derry, under Lord Widgery, L.C.J., app. by U.K. home secretary (see 14 Feb.)

Further demonstrations against Derry killings; British embassy in Dublin burned by crowd

Feb. 12   First rally of Ulster Vanguard, under leadership of William Craig, held at Lisburn, Co. Antrim

Feb. 14   Opening, at Coleraine, of Widgery inquiry (ends 20 Mar.; see 19 Apr.)

Feb. 22   Bomb explodes at officer's mess of 16th Parachute Brigade H.Q., Aldershot, Hants, killing 6 civilians and army chaplain (Officials claim responsibility)

Feb. 23   Hume and Cooper (see 18 Aug. 1971) acquitted on appeal in Belfast high court on ground that N.I. government is not empowered to give orders to army; Northern Ireland Act, 1972 (1972, c. 10 [U.K.]), passed next day at Westminster conferring retrospective powers on N.I. government

Feb. 25   Attempt to assassinate John Taylor, N.I. minister of state, home affairs; he is seriously wounded

1972 continued

Mar. 2 Parker cttee (see 16 Nov. 1971) report (31 Jan.; Cmnd 4901) published, describing methods of interrogation in N.I.: methods condemned in Lord Gardiner's minority report; Heath announces that hooding, wall-standing, subjection to noise, and deprivation of food and sleep will no longer be used in N.I. interrogations

Mar. 4 Two killed and 136 injured in explosion at Abercorn restaurant, Belfast

Mar. 6 Marcus McCausland, of Drenagh, Co. Londonderry, shot dead near Donegal border (Official I.R.A. claim responsibility)

Mar. 10 Provos announce 72-hour cease-fire and make following demands: (1) immediate withdrawal of British armed forces from N.I. streets and statement by British government of intention of eventual withdrawal of forces; (2) abolition of N.I. parliament; (3) amnesty in U.K. for political prisoners and those on wanted list

Mar. 22 Heath and Faulkner meet in London (Faulkner returns to Belfast and again flies to London for further meetings, 23 Mar.)

Mar. 23 Local Government Act (Northern Ireland), 1972 (1972, c. 9), providing for constitution of district councils (see 23 Mar. 1971)

Mar. 24 On refusal of Faulkner's government to accept transfer of security to Whitehall, British government announces suspension of N.I. parliament and government, and introduction of direct rule from Westminster; William Whitelaw app. secretary of state for N.I. (see 1 Jan. 1974)

Mar. 27-8 Strikes and demonstrations in N.I. in protest against imposition of direct rule

Mar. 28 Last meeting of N.I. parliament (prorogued, 30 Mar.; abolished, 18 July 1973)

Apr. 6 Scarman tribunal (see 22 Sept. 1969) report (4 Feb.; Cmd 566 (N.I.)) published: finds no plot to overthrow N.I. government, no evidence of armed insurrection, but planned acts of violence by extreme groups on both sides; R.U.C. had made some serious mistakes, but were never partisan force

Apr. 7 47 internees and 26 detainees released unconditionally from camps in N.I.

Apr. 15 Joseph McCann, an Official leader, shot dead in Belfast by soldier

Apr. 19 Widgery inquiry (see 2 Feb.) report (10 Apr.; H.L. 101, H.C. 220) published: responsibility for Derry killings placed on N.I.C.R.A., which organised march

Apr. 24 Whitelaw announces £110 m. development plan for Derry

Apr. 27 Whitelaw lifts ban on marches in N.I. and announces amnesty for those who have taken part in illegal processions since 25 Dec. 1971

May 1 Eight bombs explode at Courtauld's chemical fibres factory at Carrickfergus, Co. Antrim; 1 killed, 15 injured

May 10 Referendum on entry of R.I. into E.E.C. (1,041,890 for, 211,891 against)

Incendiary bomb destroys premises of Belfast Cooperative Society in York Street (Provos claim responsibility; further explosions, 15 and 18 Nov.)

May 26   R.I. government issues proclamation, bringing pt V of Offences against the State Act (1939) into operation, establishing special criminal court: court to consist of 3 judges sitting without jury

May 27   Members of Ulster Defence Association (paramilitary organisation of protestant workers), wearing uniforms and dark glasses, march through Belfast to protect rally organised by Loyalist Association of Workers

May 29   Official I.R.A. suspend operations in N.I., reserving right of self-defence and defence of areas attacked by British or sectarian forces

June 13   Whitelaw rejects Provos' invitation to discuss their 3-point programme (see 10 Mar.)

June 20   Republican prisoners in Belfast end hunger-strike for political-prisoner status when Whitelaw announces special category for certain prisoners

June 22   Provos announce suspension of offensive operations provided reciprocal response is forthcoming from British army (cease-fire begins 26 June at midnight)

July 1   School-leaving age raised from 14 to 15 in R.I.

July 7   Whitelaw meets Provo leaders in London

July 9   Provos call off cease-fire following confrontation between British army and catholics attempting to rehouse families in Lenadoon area of Belfast

July 21   'Bloody Friday': 22 explosions in Belfast kill 11 people and injure 130 (Belfast Provos admit responsibility)

July 31   'Operation Motorman': British troops occupy barricaded ('no-go') areas in Belfast and Derry

Three car-bombs explode in Claudy, Co. Londonderry, killing 6 people and injuring 32

Aug. 14   Education and Libraries (Northern Ireland) Order, 1972 (1972, no. 1263 (N.I. no. 12) [U.K.]), sets up 5 area boards to administer education and library services

Sept. 4   Lynch and Heath meet in Munich (at Olympic games) for discussion of N.I. problems

Sept. 20   S.D.L.P. policy document *Towards a new Ireland* published: main proposals that Britain and R.I. should have joint sovereignty over N.I.; that British government should declare itself in favour of eventual unity of Ire.; that there should be a N.I. assembly with increased powers and an all-Ire. senate

Sept. 25   Conference convened by Whitelaw meets at Darlington, Co. Durham (ends inconclusively, 27 Sept.): unionist party, Alliance, and N.I.L.P. attend: nationalist party, S.D.L.P., D.U.P., and republican labour decline

Sept. 29   Commn, under Lord Diplock, English lord of appeal, app. by U.K. secretary of state for N.I. to consider legal procedures for dealing more effectively with terrorist activities in N.I. (see 20 Dec.)

Sept.   Construction begins of Central Bank, Dame Street, Dublin; architects Stephenson Associates (completed, 29 Jan. 1979)

Oct. 2 British soldier, engaged on intelligence operations and posing as laundry man, shot dead on outskirts of Belfast

Oct. 4 Unsuccessful attempt to shoot William Craig, leader of Vanguard

Oct. 12 Armed raiders rob bank in Grafton St, Dublin, taking £67,000 (see 3 Aug. 1973)

Oct. 21 Lynch and Heath meet in Paris

Oct. 30 Whitelaw's green paper, *The future of Northern Ireland: a paper for discussion* published: section on 'Irish dimension' declares that for many years no U.K. government has wished to impede realisation of Irish unity arrived at by genuine consent

Nov. 16-17 Heath visits N.I.: announces that British government will not tolerate any move for N.I. independence

Nov. 24 R.T.E. authority dismissed by government after broadcast of reported interview with Provo leader, Seán Mac Stiofáin; 7 new members app. (replaced, May 1973, by new government; see 14 Mar. 1973)

Lynch and Heath discuss forthcoming white paper on N.I., meeting in London

Nov. 25 Seán Mac Stiofáin sentenced to 6 months' imprisonment for membership of I.R.A. (see 16 Jan. 1973); Kevin O'Kelly, R.T.E. news feature editor, sentenced to 3 months for contempt of court after refusing to identify Mac Stiofáin (sentence on O'Kelly reduced by appeal court to fine of £250, 30 July 1973)

Dec. 1 Two bomb explosions in central Dublin kill 2 persons and injure 127: incident transforms and ends dáil crisis over Offences against the State (Amendment) Bill (third reading carried at 4 a.m. on 2 Dec. by 69 to 22, Fine Gael abstaining)

Dec. 3 Offences against the State (Amendment) Act, 1972 (1972/26 [R.I.]): statement by gárda, not below chief superintendent, that he believes accused is member of unlawful organisation to be admitted as evidence; statements, oral or written, and meetings or demonstrations constituting interference with course of justice declared unlawful

Dec. 6 Whitelaw announces setting up of special task force of military and police to deal with sectarian murders (106 since 1 Jan.)

Dec. 7 Referendum in R.I. to amend constitution: (1) article 16 by reducing minimum age for voting from 21 to 18 (724, 839 in favour, 131,514 against); (2) article 44 by omitting reference to special position of Roman Catholic Church and to recognition of Church of Ireland and other specified denominations (721,003 in favour, 133,430 against); poll 50·7%

Dec. 13 Ownership of Bewley's Cafés Ltd, Dublin, transferred to Bewley Community, in whose control all employees of 3 years' standing are entitled to share

Dec. 20 Diplock commn (see 29 Sept.) report (Cmnd 5185) published, recommending changes in administration of justice in N.I. to deal with terrorist organisations (changing onus of proof in cases of possessing arms or explosives, giving soldiers powers to arrest and detain suspects for 4 hours, trial without jury)

Dec. 22-5 Christmas cease-fire by Provos in N.I.

Dec. 31 R.I., along with U.K. and Denmark, becomes member of E.E.C. at midnight

1973

Jan. 11 Ruairi Ó Brádaigh, president of Provisional Sinn Féin, sentenced to 6 months' imprisonment for membership of I.R.A.

Jan. 16 Seán Mac Stiofáin (see 25 Nov. 1972) ends 58-day hunger-strike at Curragh camp, Co. Kildare

Jan. 20 Car-bomb explodes in Sackville Place, Dublin, killing 1 and injuring 13

Jan. 25 Rioting in Portadown, Co. Armagh, following bomb attack on catholic 'Tunnel' area

Feb. 5 Lynch announces dissolution of nineteenth dáil

Feb. 6 Liam Cosgrave, Fine Gael leader, and Brendan Corish, labour leader, announce substantial agreement on programme for coalition in event of their parties securing overall majority in general election (joint 14-point programme adopted, 7 Feb.)

Feb. 7 Following detention of 2 protestants on 5 Feb. (first loyalists to be detained) Loyalist Association of Workers holds 1-day strike in N.I.; protestants attack homes and property of catholics; 5 killed and several injured in 2-hour gun battle with army

Feb. 9 Seven East Belfast protestants, including militant leader, John Mc-Keague, detained

Feb. 26 Report of R.I. commn on status of women published: recommendations include legislation on equal pay, machinery to prevent sex-discrimination in employment, grant of maternity leave, day-care for children, provision of marriage counselling, and family-planning advice

Feb. 28 R.I. general election: Fianna Fáil 69, Fine Gael 54, lab. 19, ind. 2; majority for Fine Gael-Labour coalition under Cosgrave (see 18 June 1969; Cosgrave app. taoiseach, 14 Mar. 1973)

Mar. 8 Referendum in N.I. on question of remaining within U.K.; S.D.L.P. and republicans discourage voting; 591,820 for, 6,463 against, in 59% poll

Two car-bomb explosions in central London (1 dead, 243 injured); 10 arrested in Heathrow when about to board plane for Belfast

Cosgrave and Corish have talks lasting 4 hours with Heath in London

Mar. 14 Cosgrave app. taoiseach; announces national coalition government including from Fine Gael, Dr Garret FitzGerald, minister for foreign affairs, Richie Ryan, minister for finance, Richard Burke, minister for education; and from Labour, Brendan Corish, tanaiste and minister for health and social welfare, and Dr Conor Cruise O'Brien, minister for posts and telegraphs and spokesman on affairs of N.I. (see 10 Nov. 1966; coalition remains in office till 1977, when Fianna Fáil wins general election)

1973 continued

Mar. 20   British white paper, *Northern Ireland constitutional proposals* (Cmnd 5259) published, proposing unicameral 80-seat assembly to be elected by proportional representation, with nominated executive, including members of catholic community

Mar. 28   Irish naval vessels apprehend Cypriot M.V. *Claudia* off Waterford coast: arms seized and 6 persons arrested, including Joe Cahill, Provo leader (Cahill sentenced to 3 years' penal servitude, 21 May)

Mar. 30   Craig forms Vanguard Unionist Progressive Party to challenge, along with Paisley's D.U.P., official unionists in assembly elections

Apr. 20   Derry brigade of Provos declare cease-fire for week to enable community festival to be held

Apr. 25   Garret FitzGerald, minister for foreign affairs, makes unofficial visit to catholic area of Belfast for discussion with inhabitants

May 3   Northern Ireland Assembly Act, 1973 (1973, c. 17 [U.K.]), establishing assembly of 78 members to be elected by proportional representation from Westminster constituencies

May 30   Presidential election in R.I.: Erskine Childers (Fianna Fáil) elected, defeating Thomas F. O'Higgins (Fine Gael) (Childers inaugurated, 25 June)

Elections in N.I. to newly formed district councils: official unionists 201, S.D.L.P. 76, loyalist coalition of D.U.P. and V.U.P.P. 74, Alliance 59

June 2   Irish Continental Line begins ferry service between Rosslare and Le Havre

June 12   Car-bomb explodes without warning in centre of Coleraine, Co. Londonderry (6 killed, 33 injured)

June 16   Ulster Freedom Fighters (break-away from U.D.A.) admit killing catholics for past year

June 23   Derry city library destroyed by series of bomb blasts

June 28   General election for N.I. Assembly: official un. 23, other ('unpledged') un. 10, S.D.L.P. 19, Alliance 8, D.U.P. 8, V.U.P.P. 7, West Belfast Loyalist Coalition 2, N.I.L.P. 1 (see 24 Feb. 1969, 31 July, 5 Dec. 1973, 29 May 1974, 1 May 1975)

July 2   Cosgrave and Heath meet in London for discussion of N.I. problems

July 18   Northern Ireland Constitution Act, 1973 (1973, c. 36 [U.K.]), abolishing N.I. parliament and office of governor, and providing for executive not exceeding 12, to be appointed by secretary of state when he considers it is likely to be widely accepted; declaration that N.I. shall not cease to be part of U.K. without consent of majority of people expressed in referendum (replacing declaration in Ireland Act, 1949; see 2 June 1949) (maximum number of executive increased to 15 by Northern Ireland Constitution (Amendment) Act, 1973 (1973, c. 69 [U.K.]), 19 Dec. 1973)

July 25   Northern Ireland (Emergency Provisions) Act, 1973 (1973, c. 53 [U.K.]), providing for trial of 'terrorist-type' offences by single judge without jury; Civil Authorities (Special Powers) Act, 1922, repealed; death penalty abolished, amending Criminal Justice Act (Northern Ireland), 1966, c. 20

July 31 First meeting of N.I. assembly ends in disorder after 26 loyalist members refuse to accept presiding officer's ruling that house adjourn

Aug. 3 Kenneth and Keith Littlejohn sentenced in special criminal court to 20 and 15 years' imprisonment respectively for part in Grafton St bank robbery (see 12 Oct. 1972); they allege that they have acted under instructions of British ministry of defence

Aug. 10 Irish government issues statement that it has informed British government of its deep concern over such intelligence activities as Littlejohn affair

Aug. 18 Viscount Brookeborough, former P.M. of N.I., dies, aged 85

Aug. 28 Walker memorial in Derry blown up (see 12 Aug. 1828)

Aug. 28-9 Heath visits N.I. and urges early formation of executive

Sept. 3 Fighting in Belfast between Provos and Officials, following shooting of 2 Provos

Sept. 11 James Flanagan app. chief constable of R.U.C. in succession to Sir Graham Shillington (with effect from 1 Nov.); first catholic head of police in N.I.

Sept. 16 Body of Tommy Herron, former vice-chairman of U.D.A., found near Belfast

Sept. 17 Heath and Cosgrave meet for 9 hours at Baldonnell aerodrome, Co. Dublin, and discuss formation of council of Ire.; first official visit of British P.M. since foundation of state

Sept. 26 First inter-church meeting, at Ballymascanlon Hotel, Co. Louth, convened by catholic bps and presided over jointly by catholic abp of Armagh (William Cardinal Conway), as chairman of Irish Episcopal Conference, and protestant abp of Armagh (G. O. Simms) as chairman of Irish Council of Churches; attended by representatives of all the main churches in Ire. (the first of an annual series of ecumenical conferences at Ballymascanlon)

Oct. 2 Attorney general, Declan Costello, opens Irish case in Strasbourg before European Commission of Human Rights, accusing U.K. of torturing internees (see 9 Aug. 1971; cf 10 Mar. 1976)

Oct. 8 Seamus Twomey, Belfast Provo leader, sentenced to 3 years' imprisonment by special criminal court in Dublin

Oct. 16 Saudi Arabia, Iran and 4 other petroleum-exporting countries on Persian (Arabian) Gulf increase 'posted' price of crude oil from $3 to $5 per barrel (to $11.50, 23 Dec.); world economic recession follows

Oct. 31 Three Provos (Seamus Twomey, J. B. O'Hagan, Kevin Mallon) escape by helicopter from Mountjoy jail, Dublin

Nov. 12 U.F.F. and Red Hand Commandos declared illegal, following series of car-bomb attacks on catholic-owned property in Belfast

Nov. 15 Eight Provos (including Marion and Dolores Price) receive life sentences for part in London car-bombings (see 8 Mar.)

Nov. 18 U.V.F. declare cease-fire till 31 Dec. to give time for political settlement in N.I.

Nov. 22 Official unionists, Alliance, and S.D.L.P. agree to form executive under headship of Faulkner—'power-sharing' (see 6-9 Dec.)

Dec. 2 Francis Pym app. secretary of state for N.I. in place of Whitelaw

Dec. 5 Disorderly scenes in N.I. assembly when members of D.U.P. and V.U.P.P. physically attack unionist supporters of Faulkner

Dec. 6 Delegates from unionist party constituency associations, V.U.P.P., D.U.P., and Orange Order meet in Ulster Hall, Belfast, and resolve to form United Ulster Unionist Council, pledged to oppose power-sharing

Dec. 6-9 Conference at Sunningdale, Berks, between representatives of Irish and British governments and of N.I. executive designate (see 22 Nov.); Irish government declares that there can be no change in status of N.I. until majority of people in N.I. so desires; British government declares support for wishes of majority of people of N.I. (both declarations to be registered at United Nations); agreement to set up council of Ire. confined to representatives of both parts of Ire. with safeguards for British interests; council to consist of council of ministers (7 each from Irish government and N.I. executive) and consultative assembly; agreement that persons committing crimes of violence, however motivated, in any part of Ireland 'should be brought to trial irrespective of the part of Ireland in which they [the criminals] are located'; agreement to set up joint British/Irish commn to examine conference proposals, and, as matter of extreme urgency, most effective method of dealing with violent crimes committed in any part of Ire.

Dec. 18 Car-bomb in Horseferry Road, London, injures 52 (followed by further bomb incidents)

U.N. general assembly approves appointment of Seán MacBride as commissioner for Namibia (South West Africa)

Dec. 19 Supreme court in Dublin, hearing case brought by Mrs Mary McGee, decides by majority of 4 to 1 that ban on import of contraceptives is unconstitutional

Dec. 20 Thirteen letter-bombs discovered in post offices and business houses in Dublin; all detonated by army in controlled explosions

Dec. 28 Thomas Niedermayer, West German businessman, kidnapped from his Belfast home by Provos (body found, 11 Mar. 1980)

1974

Jan. 1 N.I. executive takes office under Faulkner (see 28 May)

Jan. 16 Faulkner meets Cosgrave at Baldonnell aerodrome, Co. Dublin

Suit brought by Kevin Boland, leader of Aontacht Éireann party, for declaration that Sunningdale agreement is repugnant to constitution, dismissed by high court, Dublin (appeal dismissed by supreme court, 22 Feb.)

Jan. 23 Official Unionists, V.U.P.P., and D.U.P. withdraw from assembly in protest against executive

Jan. 24 Three Provo men and 1 woman (Dr Rose Dugdale) hijack commercial helicopter in Co. Donegal and make unsuccessful attempt to bomb police barracks in Strabane, Co. Tyrone (see 26 Apr.)

Feb. 1 Cosgrave and 7 members of his cabinet meet Faulkner and 7 members of his executive at Hillsborough, Co. Down, for discussion on law enforcement and on preparations for proposed council of Ire.

Feb. 4 Bomb in bus carrying service personnel, with members of their families, to Catterick, Yorks, kills 11 persons

Feb. 12 Ten injured in bomb blast at National Defence College, Latimer, Bucks

Feb. 28 U.K. general election: in G.B.—lab. 301, lib. 14, con. 297, others 11; in N.I.—un. 7, D.U.P. 1, V.U.P.P. 3, S.D.L.P. 1 (U.U.U.C. gain 11 out of 12 seats; see 18 June 1970, 10 Oct. 1974)

Mar. 4 Harold Wilson (lab.) app. P.M. of U.K. for second time (see 19 June 1970, 5 Apr. 1976) (Merlyn Rees, secretary of state for N.I., app. 5 Mar.)

Mar. 11 Murder of William Fox, protestant member of R.I. senate, near his Co. Monaghan home (5 sentenced to penal servitude for life, 7 June)

Mar. 13 Cosgrave makes statement in dáil accepting status of N.I. as unalterable except by decision of majority of people of N.I.

Mar. 20 Austin Clarke, poet, dies

Apr. 4 Merlyn Rees announces phased programme of releases of detainees in N.I.

Apr. 5 Catholic abp of Dublin (Dermot Ryan) hands over Merrion Square to corporation for public park

Apr. 18 Harold Wilson visits N.I.

Apr. 26 Paintings valued at £8 m. stolen from Co. Wicklow home of Sir Alfred Beit (recovered, 25 June; Dr Rose Dugdale (see 24 Jan.) sentenced to 9 years' imprisonment, 27 Nov.)

May 2 Irish government opens case against British government for torture of prisoners in N.I. before European Commission of Human Rights at Stavanger, Norway (see 2 Oct. 1973)

May 14 Ulster Workers Council declares general strike following defeat, by 44 to 28, of anti-Sunningdale motion in assembly (strike lasts till 29 May)

H.C. approves removal of ban in N.I. on Sinn Féin and U.V.F. (H.L. does so, 15 May)

May 17 Three car-bomb explosions in Dublin (Parnell Street, Talbot Street, South Leinster Street), killing 25, and one in Monaghan, killing 6; over 100 injured in Dublin

May 18 Government decide to recall Irish army units serving with U.N. in Lebanon, Cyprus, and Sinai, for border security duties

May 19 State of emergency proclaimed in N.I. as result of strike

May 23 Report of Anglo-Irish Law Enforcement Commission published, recommending that additional extra-territorial jurisdiction be conferred on courts in both parts of Ire.

May 25 Wilson makes broadcast speech pledging support for N.I. executive, denouncing Ulster workers' strike, and referring to strikers as 'sponging on Westminster and British democracy'

May 28 Faulkner and 5 other unionist members of N.I. executive resign (see 1 Jan.)

May 29 N.I. assembly prorogued and direct rule from Westminster reimposed; strike called off (assembly dissolved, 28 Mar. 1975)

June 3 Michael Gaughan, I.R.A. hunger-striker, dies in Parkhurst prison, Isle of Wight

June 4 Earl and countess of Donoughmore kidnapped by I.R.A. from home in Co. Tipperary (released, 9 June)

June 7 First meeting of *ad hoc* conference of Irish universities

June 8 Price sisters (see 15 Nov. 1973) call off hunger-strike after 206 days

June 17 I.R.A. bomb in houses of parliament injures 7 and damages Westminster Hall

June Construction begins of Irish Life Centre, Dublin; architect Andrew Devane (phase I completed, Apr. 1977; phase II, Apr. 1978)

July 4 British white paper, *The Northern Ireland constitution* (Cmnd 5675) proposes constitutional convention for N.I., to be elected by proportional representation

July 16 Government bill for regulation of contraception defeated in dáil (taoiseach voting against)

July 17 Northern Ireland Act, 1974 (1974, c. 28 [U.K.]), provides for constitutional convention (see 8 May 1975)

Aug. 18 Nineteen I.R.A. prisoners break out of Portlaoise prison by blasting gate with explosives

Sept. 11–12 Talks in London between Wilson and Cosgrave

Sept. 16 Rory Conaghan, county court judge, and Martin McBirney, magistrate, shot dead at homes in Belfast (responsibility later claimed by Belfast brigade of Provos)

Oct. 5 Five killed and 65 injured in bomb explosions in 2 public houses in Guildford, Surrey

Oct. 8 Seán MacBride (see 18 Dec. 1973) awarded half share of Nobel peace prize (presented in Oslo, 10 Dec.)

Oct. 10 U.K. general election (second within year); in G.B.—lab. 319, lib. 13, con. 277, others 14; in N.I.—un. 6, D.U.P. 1, V.U.P.P. 3, S.D.L.P. 1, ind. 1 (un. leader Harry West defeated by ind.; Enoch Powell returned as un. for South Down) (see 28 Feb.)

Oct. 15 Republican prisoners set fire to buildings at Maze prison (Long Kesh)

Nov. 7 Announcement that Irish will not longer be compulsory for entry into, or promotion within, R.I. civil service

Nov. 17 Erskine Childers, president of R.I. (see 30 May 1973), dies

Nov. 25 Provos declared illegal in G.B.

Nov. 29 Prevention of Terrorism (Temporary Provisions) Act, 1974 (1974, c. 56 [U.K.]), providing for deportation from, and prohibition of entry to, G.B. (as distinct from N.I.)

Dec. 3 Cearbhall Ó Dálaigh elected unopposed as president of R.I. (inaugurated, 19 Dec.)

Dec. 8 Meeting of 80 delegates in Dublin decide to form Irish Republican Socialist party (break-away from Officials) (see 30 Nov. 1975)

Dec. 10 Group of protestant clergy meet Provo leaders at Feakle, Co. Clare, to discuss restoration of peace in N.I.

Dec. 16 Richard Burke, R.I. minister for education, announces plans for higher education: U.C.D. to become independent university, T.C.D. retaining independence with loss of certain faculties; National Institute of Higher Education, Limerick, and new technological college in Dublin to become recognised colleges of one or other of the two Dublin universities

Dec. 22 Provo cease-fire comes into effect at midnight

Dec. 25 Harry Kernoff, oil-painter and woodcut artist, dies

Dec. Government decision to establish a single faculty of veterinary medicine, located in University College, Dublin (see 30 Dec. 1975)

1975

Jan. 1 Ire. assumes presidency of E.E.C. for 6 months

Jan. 6 Split in U.D.A., West Belfast brigade withdrawing from main body (followed, 14 Jan. and 6 Feb., by attempts to assassinate West Belfast commander, Charles Harding-Smith)

Jan. 16 Provo cease-fire (see 22 Dec. 1974) ends at midnight (resumed 10 Feb.)

Jan. 19 Secret talks begin between N.I. officials and Provisional Sinn Féin

Feb. 1 By-pass bridge over Bann at Coleraine opened

Feb. 5 British government issues green paper, discussing system of executive cttees as alternative to ministerial system

Feb. 11 Merlyn Rees announces scheme for 'incident centres' in N.I. to maintain contact with Provos (Provisional Sinn Féin announce decision to set up parallel incident centres, 13 Feb.)

Feb. 27 Loyalist organisations in N.I. announce that they will police loyalist areas

Mar. 3 E.E.C. regional fund allots £35 m. to R.I.

Mar. 10-11 Meeting of heads of E.E.C. governments in Dublin

Mar. 18 Price sisters (see 7 June 1974) transferred from England to Armagh prison

Mar. 25 Wilson visits Belfast and announces date of elections for constitutional convention (see 1 May 1975)

Mar. 26 Announcement that Harland and Wolff's shipyard in Belfast is to be nationalised

Mar. 29   Homes of 10 U.V.F. members in Belfast attacked as result of feud with U.D.A.

Apr. 5-6   Renewed violence in Belfast (10 killed, 75 injured)

Apr. 10   U.K. prevention of terrorism act (see 29 Nov. 1974) renewed for 6 months

Apr. 28   Belfast leader of Officials shot dead in Falls Rd, allegedly by I.R.S.P. (see 8 Dec. 1974)

Apr. 29   Minister for industry and commerce, R.I., Justin Keating, announces licensing terms for oil and gas exploration in Irish waters: 50% to be held by state, royalties 8 to 16%

May 1   General election for N.I. convention: official un. 19, V.U.P.P. 14, D.U.P. 12, ind. loyalist 1 (these 46 endorsed by U.U.U.C.), S.D.L.P. 17, Alliance 8, U.P.N.I. 5, N.I.L.P. 1, ind. 1 (see 28 June 1973, 29 May 1974, 8 May, 8 Sept., 14 Oct., 7 Nov., 3 Mar. 1976)

May 3   High court in Belfast rules that R.I. has no jurisdiction over N.I. coastal waters

May 8   First meeting of N.I. convention: Sir Robert Lowry, chairman

May 10   Federation for Ulster Local Studies inaugurated at conference held at New University of Ulster, Coleraine (see Oct.)

June 3   Three protestants returning from dog-show in Co. Cork ambushed at border and killed

June 5   Referendum in U.K. on remaining in E.E.C.; large majority in favour

July 5   Provos threaten to resume operations unless British government makes declaration of intent to withdraw from N.I.

July 17   Four soldiers killed and 1 seriously injured in ambush near border, Co. Armagh

July 30   Finance (no. 2) Act, 1975 (1975/19 [R.I.]), abolishing death duties

July 31   Three members of Miami showband killed in ambush in Co. Down on way back to R.I.; 2 members of U.V.F. killed in same incident while carrying bomb which explodes prematurely

Aug. 5   Capital Gains Tax Act, 1975 (1975/20 [R.I.]), providing for taxes on gifts and inheritance to replace death duties

Aug. 7   U.K. prevention of terrorism act (see 29 Nov. 1974) applied to N.I.

Aug. 16   Wealth Tax Act, 1975 (1975/25 [R.I.])

Aug. 28   Bomb explosion in Caterham, Surrey, injures 8 (followed by bomb explosions in London, 29, 30 Aug.)

Aug. 29   Éamon de Valera dies, aged 92

Sept. 1   Four Orangemen killed and 12 wounded in attack on lodge meeting in South Armagh (responsibility claimed by South Armagh Republican Action Force)

Sept. 8   U.U.U.C. members of convention vote to reject 'power-sharing' at cabinet level; in protest, William Craig resigns as leader of V.U.P.P. (see 7 Nov.)

Sept. 11 Garda Michael Reynolds shot dead while trying to apprehend armed and masked men who have raided bank in Killester, Co. Dublin (see 9 June 1976)

Sept. 19 State mining-lease granted to Tara lead mines, Navan, Co. Meath

Oct. 2 Seamus Murphy, sculptor, dies

U.V.F. violence in N.I. (11 killed)

Oct. 3 Dr Tiede Herrema, Dutch businessman, abducted in Limerick; abductors demand release of Dr Rose Dugdale (see 26 Apr. 1974) and 2 other republican prisoners (Herrema released unharmed, 7 Nov., after 18-day siege of house in Monasterevan, Co. Kildare) (see 11 Mar. 1976)

Oct. 5 Reopening for worship of Holy Cross Abbey, Co. Tipperary, restored as part of Ireland's contribution to European Architectural Heritage Year

Oct. 12 Blessed Oliver Plunkett canonised by Pope Paul VI (see 1 July 1681, 23 May 1920)

Oct. 14 William Craig and his supporters suspended from U.U.U.C. (expelled, 24 Oct.); Ernest Baird and other Vanguard opponents of Craig admitted to U.U.U.C. as independent loyalists

Oct. 29 Fianna Fáil demand British declaration of commitment to ordered withdrawal from N.I.

Oct. First issue of *Ulster Local Studies*, biannual journal of Federation for Ulster Local Studies (see 10 May)

Nov. 7 N.I. convention votes 42 to 31 to present U.U.U.C. report (rejecting power-sharing at cabinet level) as report of convention, but appending minority's statement (see 3 Mar. 1976)

Nov. 12 Merlyn Rees announces closure of incident centres (see 11 Feb.)

Nov. 22 Three British soldiers killed in Provo attack on isolated post near Crossmaglen, Co. Armagh: one of many such fatal attacks in locality

Nov. 29 One killed and 5 injured in explosions at Dublin airport (responsibility claimed by U.D.A.)

Nov. 30 Eleven former members of I.R.S.P., including Bernadette McAliskey (*née* Devlin), denounce party as 'possibly combining the worst elements' of both wings of republican movement

Dec. 5 Detention without trial in N.I. ends

Dec. 12 Supreme court in Dublin rules that exemption of women from, and property qualification for, jury service are unconstitutional

Dec. 30 R.I. minister for agriculture (Mark Clinton) notifies provost of Trinity College, Dublin (Dr F. S. L. Lyons) that all state funds for veterinary medicine will in future be allocated to University College, Dublin (see Dec. 1974; teaching of veterinary medicine in T.C.D. ceases on 1 Oct. 1977)

1976

Jan. 4 Five catholics shot dead in 2 attacks in Co. Armagh

Jan. 5 Ten protestants shot dead and 1 seriously injured in ambush of minibus in Co. Armagh

John A. Costello, former taoiseach, dies, aged 84

1976 continued

Jan. 7 Report of cttee on attitudes in R.I. to Irish language published, indicating wide support for bilingualism

Jan. 9 116,366 unemployed in R.I., highest figure since 1940

Feb. 6 Bomb derails Belfast–Dublin train in Co. Armagh, near Scarva

Feb. 12 Death of Frank Stagg in Wakefield prison, Yorks, after 60-day hunger-strike (followed by series of shootings, bombings, and hijackings in N.I.)

Feb. 13 Bomb explodes in Shelbourne Hotel, Dublin; fires started by incendiary bombs in several Dublin stores

Feb. 21 Body of Frank Stagg buried, under massive state security, in cemetery near Ballina, Co. Mayo, after being flown from Shannon in army helicopter

Feb. 27 Hijackings and burnings in Belfast by loyalists in protest against phasing out special-category status for prisoners

Mar. 2 Juries Act, 1976 (1976/4 [R.I.]), making electoral roll basis for jury service instead of property qualification (see 12 Dec. 1975)

Mar. 3 N.I. convention breaks up, having failed to reach agreement on 'power-sharing'

E.E.C. rejects Irish government's application for derogation from directive for equal pay to men and women

Mar. 5 Cosgrave meets Wilson in London for discussion on future of N.I.

Mar. 10 President (Ó Dálaigh) refers Criminal Law (Jurisdiction) Bill, empowering courts in R.I. to try certain offences committed in N.I., to supreme court to test its constitutionality (bill found constitutional, signed by president, 6 May (1976/14))

Irish government refers case against U.K., alleging torture of prisoners in N.I., to European Court of Human Rights (see 2 May 1974 and 2 Sept. 1976)

Mar. 11 Eddie Gallagher sentenced to 20 years' imprisonment, and Marion Coyle to 15, for their part in Herrema kidnapping (see 3 Oct. 1975)

Mar. 16 Wilson announces decision to resign as P.M. of U.K. (see 4 Mar. 1974, 5 Apr. 1976)

Mar. 17 Cosgrave in address to both houses of U.S. congress urges halt to donations to Provos by U.S. citizens

Mar. 31 Capital Acquisitions Tax Act, 1976 (1976/8 [R.I.]), imposing duty on gifts and inheritance

Apr. 5 James Callaghan (lab.) succeeds Harold Wilson as P.M. of U.K. (see 16 Mar.)

Apr. 12 Cttee under W. G. H. Quigley app. by secretary of state for N.I. to inquire into economy of N.I. (report, 9 July; see 15 Oct.)

Apr. 25 About 10,000 attend Easter week commemoration rally at G.P.O., Dublin, convened by Provos despite government prohibition

May 5-6 Eight S.A.S. (Special Air Service) men in civilian clothes and carrying guns arrested south of border (charged 6 May in special criminal court; tried 7-8 Mar. 1977; fined £100 each)

May 14-26 R.T.E. television services largely suspended by strike action

June 9 Noel and Marie Murray sentenced to death by special criminal court for capital murder of Garda Michael Reynolds (see 11 Sept. 1975, 9 Dec. 1976)

June 28 Banks in R.I. closed by strike of bank officials (reopen, 6 Sept.)

July 3 Bomb explosions in hotels in Dublin, Killarney, Limerick, and Rosslare (responsibility claimed by U.F.F.)

Special delegate conference of Irish Conference of Trade Unions rejects draft national wage agreement by 211 votes to 202

July 12 G. F. Mitchell's *The Irish landscape* (London)

July 13 Adoption Act, 1976 (1976/29) [R.I.]), allowing adoptions in which adoptive and natural parents are not of same religious denomination

July 15 Bomb explosions in special criminal court, Dublin; 4 prisoners escape, 3 of whom are almost immediately recaptured

July 21 Christopher Ewart-Biggs, U.K. ambassador to R.I., and Judith Cooke, civil servant in N.I. office, killed by land-mine near ambassador's residence at Sandyford, Co. Dublin

July 22 Fair Employment (Northern Ireland) Act, 1976 (1976, c. 25 [U.K.]), establishes agency to promote 'equality of opportunity . . . between people of different religious beliefs'

July 30 Richard Burke, minister for education, announces that University College, Cork, University College, Galway, and St Patrick's College, Maynooth, are to become independent universities

Aug. 5 *A new history of Ireland*, edited by T. W. Moody, F. X. Martin, and F. J. Byrne, vol. iii: *Early modern Ireland, 1534-1691* (Oxford)

Aug. 6 Irish government makes order claiming jurisdiction over area of continental shelf adjacent to Rockall

Aug. 9 Belfast home of Gerry Fitt, leader of S.D.L.P., attacked by supporters of Provos

Aug. 10 Three children killed or fatally injured in Finaghy Road North, Belfast, upon being hit by car driven by Provo being pursued by army; reaction on part of Máiréad Corrigan (aunt of victims) and Betty Williams leads to creation of movement later known as 'Peace People' (see 30 Nov., 5 Dec.)

Aug. 18 Brian Faulkner announces intention to retire from politics (dies in accident, 3 Mar. 1977)

Sept. 1 Dáil and senate declare state of national emergency; second reading of Emergency Powers Bill (see 24 Sept., 15 Oct.)

Sept. 2 Report of European Commission of Human Rights, in which U.K. is found guilty of torture of republican prisoners, officially published (see 2 May 1974)

Sept. 10 Merlyn Rees replaced by Roy Mason as secretary of state for N.I.

Sept. 15 Mrs Anne Letitia Dickson elected leader of U.P.N.I.; first woman to lead political party in Ire.

1976 continued

Sept. 24   President signs criminal law bill (increasing penalties and powers of security forces, 1976/32) but refers emergency powers bill to supreme court to test constitutionality

Oct. 8   Richie Ryan, R.I. minister for finance, appointed chairman of International Monetary Fund and of World Bank

Oct. 15   Quigley report on economy of N.I. published: recommends capital investment programme of £100 m.

Supreme court in Dublin declares emergency powers bill (for securing public safety and preservation of state in time of armed conflict, allowing detention without charge for 7 days) not to be repugnant to constitution; court expresses opinion that bill is not to be read as abnegation of accused persons' rights to communication, legal and medical assistance and access to courts (bill signed by president, 16 Oct. (1976/33))

Oct. 18   Patrick Donegan, R.I. minister for defence, refers to President Ó Dálaigh as 'a thundering disgrace' because of his treatment of emergency powers bill (president resigns 'to protect the dignity of the office', 22 Oct.)

Oct. 26   On London stock exchange £ falls to all-time low of $1.5855

Oct. 28   Mrs Máire Drumm, former vice-president of Provisional Sinn Féin, shot dead while a patient in Mater Hospital, Belfast

Nov. 3   E.E.C. report shows that R.I.'s inflation rate of 18·9% is highest in community

Nov. 9   Dr Patrick Hillery returned unopposed as president of R.I. in succession to Cearbhall Ó Dálaigh (inaugurated 3 Dec.)

Nov. 17   American tour of Abbey Players, the first since 1937-8 (see 2 Oct. 1937), opens with performance of O'Casey's 'Plough and the stars' at Brooklyn Academy of Music

Nov. 26   Richard Burke, minister for education, nominated as R.I.'s E.E.C. commr, in succession to Dr Patrick Hillery

Nov. 29   R.I. becomes member of European Space Agency

Nov. 30   Leaders of Peace People (Betty Williams, Máiréad Corrigan, and Ciarán McKeown) receive 'people's peace prize' of £200,000 in Oslo

Dec. 5   Rally of Peace People from north and south at new bridge over Boyne at Drogheda; 12,000-15,000 present

Dec. 9   Supreme court in Dublin quashes conviction of Noel Murray for capital murder (see 9 June) and alters sentence to life imprisonment (Marie Murray found not guilty of capital murder but guilty of murder, and sentenced to life imprisonment, 3 May 1977)

Dec. 23   R.I. government order, extending fishery limits to 200 miles, in accordance with E.E.C. directive

INDEX

All references in this index are to dates, not pages, months being indicated by numerals; for example: Anacreontic Society, 1840.3; Brí mac Taidg, synod of, 1158.

As far as possible subjects are indexed under precise and concrete headings, such as personal and place names and names of institutions. Very generalised headings are used sparingly: thus we have excluded culture, education, nationalism, religion, because these subjects are so widely diffused through the chronology; and for the same reason entries under catholic and protestant are highly selective.

Among subjects not as a rule indexed, are the following: places incidentally mentioned (for example, as location of events otherwise indexed); persons mentioned as appointed to or holding offices, the holders of which are listed in volume ix; persons incidentally mentioned (for example, as introducing a bill in parliament); the succession of great councils and parliaments, all of which are listed in volume ix; persons, places, and events outside Ireland included in the chronology as part of the wider context of Irish history.

Subjects with not more than five references are entered without captions, unless there is some reason to the contrary.

Acts of parliament are indexed under their subjects, not under 'acts' or 'parliament'.

The indexing of Irish personal names before the twelfth century presents a special problem (see above, pp 4-5). Till the eleventh century surnames were not generally used, and the use of forenames without surnames, but with other identifications, survived till the early twelfth century. Persons so designated are indexed under their forenames, and those with the same forename appear in the following order: (1) according to their office, as 'Áed, bp of Sletty'; (2) according to their relationship, as identified by the compilers of the chronology, with another person, as 'Áed, brother of Congalach'; (3) where the name of father or grandfather is specified in the sources, as 'Áed mac Néill', 'Áed ua Forréid'; (4) where the forename is accompanied by an epithet, as 'Áed Allán mac Fergaile'. Surnames in Mac (sometimes Mág, after 1334) and Ua (Ó from 1216) were coming into general use during the eleventh century and had become the norm by the beginning of the twelfth century, and this is reflected in the index.

Surnames of Irish dynastic families up to the mid-seventeenth century are entered, first in their Middle Irish form, then in their Modern Irish form, and then, in brackets, in their anglicised form; for example, Mac Diarmata, Mac Diarmada (MacDermot).

Surnames in Ua are indexed under Ua if they do not occur after 1216 (see above, p. 4); otherwise they are indexed under Ó. Thus Ua Briain, Ua Conchobair will be found under Ó, but Ua Lothcháin under Ua.

Mc and Mag are treated as identical with Mac.

Besides its use in the formation of patronymics and surnames, the element *mac* also occurs in personal names such as Mac Caírthinn 'son of the rowan', Mac Cuilinn 'son of the holly', Mac Ercae 'son of the red-eared cow'. The feminine equivalent is *der-* or *dar-* (a fossilised survival of the ancient Indo-European word for 'daughter') in such names as Darercae, Derbforgaill.

A name such as 'de Burgh' is entered in that form but under 'B'. Similarly a saint's name such as 'St Patrick' appears in that form but under 'P'.

Members of dynastic families, such as de Burgh, FitzGerald, Mac Carthaig(h), Ó Néill, are entered in chronological, not in alphabetical order. References to the family as a group are indexed first, followed by named individuals in chronological order, and anonymous members of the family are indexed together at the end of the section. The eponymous ancestors of such families, if they are mentioned in the chronology, are indexed under their forenames (for example, Brian Bóruma, ancestor of the Ó Briains) and are listed under their families in volume ix, pts II, III.

We have taken the opportunity afforded by the compilation of this index to correct some errors in the chronology and identify more precisely certain dynasts who are referred to merely by their surnames. A few of the gaps in the chronology that we have noted in the course of indexing are covered by index entries with italicised dates. Corresponding entries are recorded in the addenda to the chronology which it is intended to publish in volume x.

There are a few discrepancies in spelling and the use of capitals as between the chronology and the index. In such cases the form used in the index is to be read as superseding that in the chronology.

Titled persons are entered under the names under which they figure in Irish history at the date cited.

Cross-references are kept to a minimum, but many subjects are indexed under more than one heading without a cross-reference.

This index has been compiled by F. J. Byrne and T. W. Moody, assisted by Richard Hawkins, from cards prepared by Mary Griffiths.

hEochada killed at, 1131; battle near, 1159; Normans in, 1199/1200; jcr's force from, 1312

Ardgar Mac Lochlainn, kg of Ailech, 1061.4, 1064

Ardgar mac Matudáin, kg of Ulster, 970

Ards peninsula (Co. Down), 703, 842, 1571.11, 1573.10

Ardscull, Co. Kildare, 1286, 1316

Ardstraw, Co. Tyrone, 1199, c.1240

Arensberg, Conrad M., *The Irish countryman*, 1937.12

Arianism, 1821.10

Arigna (Co. Roscommon), iron works, 1788

Arklow, 836, 1282.7, 1331.4, 1525.8, 1798.6

Armagh, city of: foundation, 444; disturbances at, 781.2, 788, 819, 893; vikings defeat force from, 831; vikings raid, 832, 840, 852, 869, 921.11; abbot captured, 879; Brian Bóruma and, 1005, 1014; peace between Mac Lochlainn and Ulaid, 1130; grant by Ó Conchobair to school, 1169; de Lacy captures, 1184.3; Philip of Worcester occupies, 1185 c.3; de Courcy raids, 1189; Mac Duinn Sléibe raids, 1199/1200; jcr builds castle near, 1236; Franciscan friars at, 1264; Colton unable to visit, 1390; Mortimer burns, 1396; raided, 1432, 1433; O'Neills defeat Scots at, 1501.3; Sussex burns, 1557.10; garrisoned, 1561 c.7, 1595 c.7; railway, 1848.3

—, buildings: fort, c.290: stone oratory, 788, 1009, 1125; churches, 869, 1126.10, 1511; high-king's house, 870; hospitals, 921.11; royal mausoleum, 935, 1064; guest-house, 1004; castle, 1236; cathedral, 1266, 1566.8, 1595 c.7; public library, 1770; observatory, 1791; catholic cathedral, 1840.3; planetarium, 1967.5

Armagh county: campaign in, 1566.9-11, *1608.1*; survey of, 1608.7; sectarian conflict in, 1784.7, 1791.1, 1795.9; new town in, 1965.6; killings in, 1975.9, 1976.1; train derailed in, 1976.2

Armagh, relics: SS Peter, Paul, and Patrick, 734; Book of, 807-8, 846, 939, 1005; Book of Mac Durnan, 927; Book of Dub dá Leithe, 1049-64; Bell of St Patrick's Testament, 1091 × 1105; Bachall Ísu, 1135; Gospels of Máel Brigte, 1138

Armagh, see of: primacy claimed, 670-c.690; recognised, c.680, 737; relics on circuit, 734; abbatial rule replaces episcopal, 750; abbacy contested, 759, 793, 826-35, 835-52, 965, 1060; primacy contested by Emly, 784, 793, 973; Kells site donated for Columban church, 807; abbacy monopolised by Uí Sínaig, 965; primacy confirmed, 1005, 1106, 1162, 1255.10, 1348.4; Cellach first abp and primate, 1106; proposed union with Clogher, 1240.11; primacy investigated, 1244.2; contested by bp of Meath, 1263; abp to preach crusade, 1291; primacy contested by Dublin, 1313, 1338.1; vicars and bps meet at

Kells, 1642.3; for lists of bps, abbots, and abps of, see vol. ix, pt III

arms, ammunition, and explosives: control of, 1793.2, 1807.8, 1843.4,8, 1847.12, 1850.3, 1881.3, 1906.12, 1913.12; and see penal laws

—, importation: attempted, 1867.4, 1916.4, 1971.10; effected, 1914.4,7,8

—, surrendered to government, 1797.3

Army Comrades Association, 1932.2, 1933.8

Arnold, Sir Nicholas, 1564.5

arrears of rent, act, 1882.5,8

Arthur, Prince, 1869.4

Arthur of Bardsey, bp of Bangor, 1161/2

Artists, Society of, 1764.2

Artrí mac Cathail, kg of Cashel, 793

Artrí mac Conchobair, bp of Armagh, 818, 823, 825, 826-35

Arts Act [R.I.], 1951.5

Arts Council [R.I.], 1951.5

Arts Theatre, Belfast, 1961.4

Ashbourne, Lord, 1885.7; 'Ashbourne act', 1885.8

Ashe, Thomas, 1917.9

Ashton, Robert of, jcr, 1372 c.3

Askulv, kg of Dublin, 1171 c.5

Asquith, Herbert Henry: 1908.4; self-government for Ire., 1909.12; home rule bill, 1912.4; visits Dublin, 1912.7, 1914.9, 1916.5; bill amending home rule bill, 1914.5; coalition cabinet, 1915.5; commn of inquiry into Irish disturbances, 1916.5; negotiation of settlement of Irish question, 1916.5; and home rule, 1916.7

Assembly's College, Belfast, 1853.12

'Assembly of the Northern People', 1971.10

Association for Discountenancing Vice and Promoting Religion, 1792.10

asylums, 1815.6, 1817.7, 1827.9, 1845.8

Athbheochan na Gaeilge; the restoration of the Irish language, 1965.1

Áth in Chip (near Carrick-on-Shannon): castle, 1245; battle, 1270

Athelstan, kg of England, 925-39, 937, 939

Athenry: battle of, 1316.8; de Bermingham of, 1380.12, 1395.5; Clanricard's sons attack, 1576.6

Áth Liac (Athleague, Co. Roscommon), 1200, 1227, 1271, 1499

—, (Ballyleague, Co. Longford), 1153, 1200, 1221

Áth Malais (Ballymalis, Co. Kerry), battle of, 1270

Áth na Caisberna (near Ardee), battle of, 1159

Áth na Dairbrige (near Kells), assembly of, 1161

Athlone: 1120; castle and bridge, 1129; attacked by Ua Briain, 1132; destroyed, 1133; bridge, 1140; fortress destroyed, 1153; parley at, 1195; 2 cantreds near, 1200.11; synod, 1202; bridge and castle, 1210 *p*.8; 'peace of', 1210 *p*.8;

INDEX 483

Boyle, Michael, abp of Dublin, 1679.2, 1685.3, 1686.4
—, Richard, first earl of Cork, L.J., 1629.10
—, Robert; *Sceptical chymist*, 1661; and Irish translation of Old Testament, 1686.2
—, Roger, Lord Broghill, earl of Orrery, 1650.4, 1660.1,12
Boyne: viking fleets on, 837, 842; battle of, 1690.7; obelisk to commemorate, 1736.4, 1923.5
Brabazon, Sir William: vice-treasurer, 1534.8; app. to survey rents and revenues of dissolved religious houses, 1540.5; L.J., 1544.2, 1550.2; campaigns in Offaly, 1546.7; compiles complaints against St Leger, 1547 *c*.12; rebuilds Athlone castle, 1547
Brackenbury, Col. Henry, 1882.5
Bradstreet, Sir Samuel, 1782.2
Brady, Joseph, 1883.4
Bráen mac Máel Mórda, kg of Leinster, 1052
Bramhall, John: bp of Derry, 1634.5, 1641.3; app abp of Armagh, 1661.1
Bran mac Fáeláin, kg of Leinster, 835
Brandub mac Echach, kg of Leinster, 598, 605/8
de Braose, Philip, 1177, 1177.5
—, William: granted lands in Thomond, 1201 *c*.1; flees to Ire., 1203; custody of Limerick, 1203.7; flees to Wales, 1210; captured with his mother, 1210.7; exile in France, 1211
—, Reginald, 1217.6
'brass money', 1689.6
Bray, Thomas, abp of Cashel, 1799.7
bread rationing: in N.I., 1946.7; in R.I., 1947.1
bread riots in Dublin, 1740.5-6
'Break of Dromore', 1689.3
Breen, Dan, 1919.1,12
Brega: Northumbrian invasion, 684; devastated, 721; high-king's victory, 868; forces defeated, 1086
brehon law, see gavelkind, law texts, tanistry
Brehon Law Commissioners, 1865 *c*.3
Bréifne: dynasty established by Uí Briúin, *c*.780; expulsion of Clann Mhuircheartaigh, 1343; campaigns in, 1396; Ó Domhnaill overruns, 1523; west, ravaged, 1530; payment to crown for, 1577.10
St Brendan of Birr, 565
St Brendan of Clonfert, 558, 577/8
Brennan, Joseph, 1849.1
—, Thomas, 1879.10, 1881.10
Brereton, Sir William, 1540.5
Bressal, abbot of Iona, 778
Bressal Bélach, kg of Leinster, 435/6
Brett, Charles, 1867.9,11
Brí mac Taidg, synod of, 1158
Brian Bóruma mac Cennétig: kg of Munster, 978; hostilities with high-king, 982; submission of Leinster, 983; ransom of Airbertach mac Coisse

Dobráin, 990; hostilities with high-king, 990-93; partition of Ire., 997; battle of Glenn Máma, 999; captures Dublin, 1000; acknowledged as high-king, 1002; reign, 1002-14; visits Armagh, 1005; hostages from north, 1006; construction of fortresses, 1013; battle of Clontarf, 1014; dies, 1014
Brictius, bp of Limerick, 1185
St Brigit of Kildare, 524/6
Bristol, 1439
Bristol, earl of, 1768.2
Britain, prehistoric and ancient: Ire. cut off from, 6500 B.C.; invaded by Julius Caesar, 55 B.C.; conquered by Claudius, 43; Agricola in, 78-84; Clodius Albinus in, 196; Septimius Severus in, 208-11; attacked by Picts, 297; by Irish, 297-*c*.450; by Picts, Irish and Saxons, 367-70; legions withdrawn, 383; coasts defended by Stilicho, 395-9; *civitates* to arrange own defences, 410; 'Notitia dignitatum', 428; St Germanus visits, 429, 447; Anglo-Saxon invasion, 449
British Association for the Advancement of Science, 1835.8, 1843.8, 1852.9, 1902.9, 1958.9
British Association for the Relief of the Extreme Distress in the Remote Parishes of Ireland and Scotland, 1847.1
British Broadcasting Company (British Broadcasting Corporation from 1 Jan. 1927), 1924.9, 1953.5, 1955.7
British Isles, earliest reference to, *c*.330-300 B.C.
British Legion offices, Dublin, 1971.7
British North America Act, 1867.3
British undertakers in Ulster plantation: conditions to be observed by, 1609.1; revised conditions, 1610.4; land assigned to, 1610.4-5; and native Irish, 1610.8, 1618.10, 1628.6
Brittany, 1342, 1593.9-1594.5, 1595.3
Broadcasting Authority Act, 1960.4
broadcasting, see British Broadcasting Company, Independent Television Authority, Radio (Telefís) Éireann
Bróen mac Máel Mórda, kg of Leinster, 944
Broghill, Lord, see Boyle, Roger
bronze age: 1800 B.C., 1200 B.C., 800 B.C., *c*.500 B.C., 200 B.C.
Brooke, Sir Basil, see Brookeborough
—, Charlotte, *Reliques of Irish poetry*, 1789
—, Henry: *The trial of the cause of the Roman Catholics*, 1761; *The fool of quality*, 1765
—, Robert, 1776
Brookeborough, Lord, formerly Sir Basil Brooke, 1943.4, 1945.7, 1963.3, 1973.8
Brooking, Charles, *Map of Dublin*, 1728
Brooklyn Academy of Music, and Abbey Players, 1976.11
Brotherhood of St Patrick, 1862.2, 1863.8

communion, order of, issued, 1548.3

Communist Party of Ireland, 1921.10, 1933.6, 1941.7, 1970.3

Compensation for Disturbance (Ireland) Bill, 1880.6,8

comprehensive secondary schools, 1963.5

Compton, Sir Edmund, 1969.7, 1971.8,11

Conaghan, Rory, 1974.9

Conall mac Comgaill, kg of Dál Riatai, 567/8

concentration camps, 1902.1

Conchobar mac Domnaill, *rígdamna* of Ailech, 935

Conchobar mac Donnchada, high-king, 819-33, 827

Conchobar mac Meic Con Chaille, abp of Armagh, 1175

Conchobar mac Nessae, kg of Ulster, 20

Conchobar Machae, kg of Airthir, 698

Conciliation Hall, Dublin, 1843.3

Condálach mac Aiello of Armagh, 781.2

confederate catholics: assembly at Kilkenny, 1642.5; oath of association, 1642.6; first general assembly at Kilkenny, 1642.10-11; royal commn to Ormond to treat with, 1643.4; second general assembly, 1643.5-6; fort of Galway surrenders to, 1643.6; truce negotiations with Ormond, 1643.6; papal envoy to, 1643.7; Galway townspeople join, 1643.8; one-year truce with Ormond, 1643.9; third general assembly, 1643.11-12; 7 delegates to meet Charles I, 1643.11; agents of, at Oxford, 1644.3; Ormond to continue negotiations with, 1644.6; fourth general assembly, 1644.7-8; help sought, 1644.12; fifth general assembly, 1645.5-8; Sligo taken from, 1645.7; secret treaty with Glamorgan, 1645.8; papal envoy to, 1645.10; second secret treaty with Glamorgan, 1645.12; sixth general assembly, 1646.2-3; agree to prolong truce, 1646.2; peace agreed with Ormond, 1646.3; capture Bunratty, 1646.7; declared to have broken oath of association, 1646.8; seventh general assembly, declares against Ormond peace, 1647.2; adopts new oath of association, 1647.3; eighth general assembly, at Kilkenny, 1647.11-12; army of, defeated by Inchiquin, 1647.11; envoys of, to France and Rome, 1648.2; truce with Inchiquin, 1648.5; ninth (and last) general assembly, 1648.9-1649.1; envoys of, return from Rome, 1648.11; peace with Ormond, 1649.1; bps at Jamestown, repudiate Ormond, 1650.8; excommunication, 1650.9; laity at Loughrea, 1650.11; Stephen de Henin to treat with, 1651.2

Confederation of Kilkenny, see confederate catholics

Congal Clóen, kg of Ulster, 637/9

Congalach Cnogba mac Máel Mithig, kg of Brega: plunders Dublin, 944; high-king, 944-56; defeated by Ruaidrí ua Canannáin, 947; defeats Blacair of Dublin, 948; victorious, 949/50; campaigns in Thomond, 950-51; frees Clonard from royal exactions, 951; killed, 956

congested districts board, 1891.8, 1907.8, 1923.7

Congo: Irish battalion in, 1960.7; Niemba ambush, 1960.11; Conor Cruise O'Brien, 1961.12

Congus, bp of Armagh, 750

Coningsby, Thomas, L.J., 1690.9

St Conláed, bp of Kildare, 516/20

Connacht: kgs of, see list in vol. ix, pt III; dynastic strife in, 1136; devastated, 1137; fleet defeats Hebridean fleet, 1154; internal dissension in, 1145-6, 1177; de Courcy campaigns in, 1188; Gilbert de Nangle campaigns in, 1193- ; pope's letter to kg of, 1200 × 1201; invasion of, 1201, 1202; campaigns of William de Burgh, 1203; grant of six cantreds to Hugh de Lacy, 1204; speculative grants in, 1207.11; resumed by crown, 1233.5; restored to Richard de Burgh, 1234.9; jcr campaigns in, 1236; Richard de Burgh campaigns in, 1236; encastellation of, by Anglo-Irish, 1237-8; settlement of waste land in, 1241.6; shired, a.1247; and Stephen Longespée, 1253.7; grant in, 1254.2; campaigns in, 1260, 1288; granted free of rent to William de Burgh, 1309.8; kingship of, 1310; lands of 3rd earl of Ulster, 1334.9; invaded, 1340; Toirdhealbhach Ruadh Ó Conchobhair, 1373; expedition through Lower, 1412.7; Ó Domhnaill marches through, 1433; Neachtan Ó Domhnaill campaigns in, 1446; Lower, divided, 1476; financial dependence on govt., 1493-4; campaigns in, 1499; lords of, besiege Sligo castle, 1522.8; campaigns in, 1526, 1538.6-7; Sir Edward Fitton app. president of, 1569.6; discretionary power to issue pardons in, 1572.8; shired into 4 counties, 1576.4; military governor of, 1576.7; Richard Bingham president of, 1584.3; martial law in, 1584.7; commn to Bingham to make agreements with landowners, 1585.7; composition of, 1585.10; commn to deal with disturbances in, 1589.4; Fitzwilliam to restore order in, 1589.12-1590.1; O'Donnell campaigns in, 1600.6-7; transplantation to, 1654.5; proposals for allotment of baronies in, 1656.2; transplanters, 1675.9; Hougher disturbances in, 1709 *c.12*

Connaught Rangers: 1920.6; Connaught Rangers (Pensions) Act [I.F.S.], 1936.8

Connolly, James: Irish Socialist Republican Party, 1896.5; *Workers' Republic*, 1898.8, 1915.5; returns to Ire., from U.S.A., 1910.7; *Labour in Irish history*, 1910.11; insurrection, 1914.9; Irish Neutrality League, 1914.9; Irish Transport and General Workers' Union, 1914.10;

---

[1] For the method of enumerating successions, as here, see genealogical table 36, and the introduction
to genealogical tables, in volume ix.

1072, 1086, 1100, 1112, 1128, 1169, 1171, 1173, 1274, 1276, 1288, 1294-5, 1308.5-7, 1308.10, 1309, 1369, 1399.6-7, 1400, 1408, 1430, 1520.7, 1523, 1569.7-9, 1598.6-7, 1599.6-7, 1600.8; and Brian Bóruma, 983, 1013; decline of Uí Dúnlainge dynasty, 1014-42; claimed by kg of Osraige, 1033; Uí Chennselaig dominant in, 1042-72; diseases in, 1061; claimed by Ua Conchobair, 1079; seized by Ua Briain, 1089; famine in, 1116; submits to Ua Conchobair, 1118, 1122; to Ua Briain, 1131; divided into 3 'custodies', 1177.5; jcrs on circuit in, 1195; granted to William Marshal, 1208.3; insurgents in, 1377.1; plague in, 1575.8-9; rising in, 1580.7; army surrenders, 1652.5; earthquake in, 1690.10; United Irish rebellion in, 1798.5; and see Laigin, Mac Murchadha, Uí Chennselaig, Uí Dúnlainge

Leinster, Book of, 1152
Leinster, duke of, 1792.12
Leinster House, Dublin, 1745, 1814.12, 1924.8
Leinster, R.M.S., sunk, 1918.10
Leitrim, earl of, 1877.4
Leitrim, plantation in, 1621.1
Leix: castle besieged, 1307 c.7; plantation of, 1550.7, 1556.4; shired, 1557.6-7; rising in, 1564.2; and see Queen's County
Leland, Thomas, *History of Ireland*, 1773
Lemass, Sean Francis: minister for industry and commerce, 1932.3; tánaiste, 1945.6; taoiseach, 1959.6; and Lane collection, 1959.11; meets Terence O'Neill, 1965.1,2; resigns, 1966.11; dies, 1971.5
Lenihan, Brian Joseph, 1968.7
Leo XIII, pope, and Maynooth College, 1896.3
Leslie's Bank, 1820.5
Lester, Seán, 1934.1, 1936.9
Leth Caim (near Armagh), battle of, 827
Lever, Charles: *Harry Lorrequer*, 1837.2; *Charles O'Malley*, 1840.3
Lewis, Samuel, *A topographical dictionary of Ireland*, 1837
lex Patricii, see St Patrick, law of
Lhuyd, Edward: 1699 c.7-8; *Archaeologia Britannica*, 1707 c.5
'Libelle of Englyshe polycye', c.1436
'Liber Anatoli', c.559
'Liber exemplorum', c.1270
Liberty Hall, Dublin, 1916.4, 1962.5
Library Association of Ireland, 1928.10
Licensing Act, 1872.8, 1874.8; and see liquor licences
Liffey Reservoir Act [I.F.S.], 1936.11
Light Railways (Ireland) Act, 1889.8
lighthouse: at Hook Head, Co. Wexford, a.1245; at Poolbeg, 1762.6; commrs for Irish lights, 1867.6

lighting, public, 1697.12, 1760.5, 1807.8, 1820.7, 1823.5, 1828.7
'Lillibullero', 1687
Limerick city: Norse foundation, 922; captured, 1175-6; burned, 1176; abandoned, 1176; Normans fail to capture, 1177; charter, 1197.12; custody of, 1203.7, 1217.6; captured, 1206-7; castle, 1223.6; attacked, 1234; captured, 1237; captured, 1370.7; parliament at, 1483.2, 1543.2-3; financial dependence on govt, 1493-4; papal grant of, 1580.5; Ireton invests, 1651.6,10; William III besieges, 1690.8; Tyrconnell at, 1691.1; Saint Ruth at, 1691.5; second siege of, 1691.8,9; treaty of, 1691.10, 1692.2, 1697.9,10; priest executed at, 1727 c.4; liquor licensing, 1878.8; R.I.C. mutiny at, 1882.8; meeting at, supports amnesty for political prisoners, 1893.9; city council and John Daly, 1894.7; attacks on Jews at, 1904.1; general strike and soviet at, 1919.4; National Institute of Higher Education at, 1970.1, 1974.12
Limerick county: shired, a.1254; financial dependence on govt, 1493-4; Carew campaigns in, 1600.5-7; martial law, 1920.12
—, see of, founded, 1106; and see lists of bps in vol. ix, pt III
—, Viscount, 1756.1, 1757.10
Lincoln, earl of, 1484.8, 1487.5
Lindley, John, 1845.11
linen: regulation of, 1635.6, 1636.5; free importation into England, 1696.4; English H.C. requests kg to encourage manufacture of, 1698.7; Louis Crommelin and, 1700.2; act permits export to American colonies, 1705.3; board of trustees for, 1710.8, 1711.10, 1828.7
Linen Hall: Dublin, 1728.11; Belfast, 1783.4
Linen Hall Library, Belfast, 1788.5, 1801.11
Linn Duachaïll (Annagassan, Co. Louth), and permanent Norse encampment, 841
Lionel, 5th earl of Ulster, 3rd son of Edward III: app. lieutenant, 1361.7; arrives in Ire., 1361.9; cr. duke of Clarence, 1362.11; in England, 1364.4-12; leaves for England, 1366.11; dies, 1368.10; Irish lands of, 1369.8
liquor licences: first act, 1635.4; off-licences, 1785-3; duties increased, 1791.5, 1825.6; wine licences, 1860.8; Revenue Act, 1863.6; Beerhouses (Ireland) Act, 1864.6; Sunday closing, 1864.9, 1866.12, 1867.3, 1868.3, 1872.2, 1876.5, 1877.2, 1888.2; local option, 1869.1, 1929.5; Licensing Acts, 1872.8, 1874.8; Beer Licences Regulation (Ireland) Act, 1877.3; Sale of Liquors on Sunday (Ireland) Act, 1878.8, 1882.5; commn on reform, 1896.4; Sale of Intoxicating Liquors (Licences) (Ireland) Act, 1902.7; Intoxicating Liquors (Ireland) Act, 1906.2; Finance (1909-10) Act, 1910.4;